A HANDBOOK TO EDDIC POETRY

This is the first comprehensive and accessible survey in English of Old Norse eddic poetry: a remarkable body of literature rooted in the Viking Age, which is a critical source for the study of early Scandinavian myths, poetics, culture, and society. Dramatically recreating the voices of the legendary past, eddic poems distil moments of high emotion as human heroes and supernatural beings alike grapple with betrayal, loyalty, mortality, and love. These poems relate the most famous deeds of gods such as Óðinn and Þórr with their adversaries the giants; they bring to life the often fraught interactions between kings, queens, and heroes as well as their encounters with valkyries, elves, dragons, and dwarfs. Written by leading international scholars, the chapters in this volume showcase the poetic riches of the eddic corpus and reveal its relevance to the history of poetics, gender studies, pre-Christian religions, art history, and archaeology.

CAROLYNE LARRINGTON is Official Fellow and Tutor at St John's College, University of Oxford.

JUDY QUINN is Reader in Old Norse Literature in the Department of Anglo-Saxon, Norse and Celtic at the University of Cambridge.

BRITTANY SCHORN is a Research Associate in the Department of Anglo-Saxon, Norse and Celtic at the University of Cambridge.

A HANDBOOK TO EDDIC POETRY

Myths and Legends of Early Scandinavia

CAROLYNE LARRINGTON

University of Oxford

JUDY QUINN

University of Cambridge

BRITTANY SCHORN

University of Cambridge

CAMBRIDGE
UNIVERSITY PRESS

CAMBRIDGE
UNIVERSITY PRESS

University Printing House, Cambridge CB2 8BS, United Kingdom

Cambridge University Press is part of the University of Cambridge.

It furthers the University's mission by disseminating knowledge in the pursuit of
education, learning, and research at the highest international levels of excellence.

www.cambridge.org
Information on this title: www.cambridge.org/9781107135444

© Cambridge University Press 2016

First published 2016

Printed in the United States of America by Sheridan Books, Inc.

A catalogue record for this publication is available from the British Library.

Library of Congress Cataloging-in-Publication Data
Larrington, Carolyne, editor. | Quinn, Judy, editor. | Schorn, Brittany, editor.
A handbook to Eddic poetry : myths and legends of early Scandinavia / [edited by] Carolyne
Larrington, Judy Quinn, Brittany Schorn.
Cambridge : Cambridge University Press, 2016. | Includes bibliographical references.
LCCN 2016016313 | ISBN 9781107135444
LCSH: Old Norse poetry – History and criticism. | Eddas – History and criticism.
LCC PT7235 .L35 2016 | DDC 839/.61009–dc23
LC record available at https://lccn.loc.gov/2016016313

ISBN 978-1-107-13544-4 Hardback

Contents

Illustrations

Contributors

STEFAN BRINK is Professor of Scandinavian Studies at the Centre for Scandinavian Studies at the University of Aberdeen.

DAVID CLARK is Senior Lecturer in Medieval Literatures in the School of English at the University of Leicester.

MARGARET CLUNIES ROSS is Emeritus Professor of English at the University of Sydney, Adjunct Professor at the University of Adelaide, and Honorary Research Associate in the Department of Anglo-Saxon, Norse and Celtic at the University of Cambridge.

R. D. FULK is Class of 1964 Chancellor's Professor in the Department of English at Indiana University.

TERRY GUNNELL is Professor of Folkloristics in the Faculty of Social and Human Sciences at the University of Iceland.

JOSEPH HARRIS is Emeritus Professor of English Literature and of Folklore in the Department of English at Harvard University.

JOHN HINES is Professor of Archaeology in the School of History, Archaeology and Religion at Cardiff University.

LILLA KOPÁR is Associate Professor of English and Director of the Center for Medieval and Byzantine Studies at The Catholic University of America in Washington, DC.

JÓHANNA KATRÍN FRIÐRIKSDÓTTIR is a Marie Curie research fellow at the Árni Magnússon Institute for Icelandic Studies in Reykjavík.

CAROLYNE LARRINGTON is Fellow and Tutor in Medieval English Literature at St John's College, University of Oxford.

JOHN LINDOW is Professor Emeritus in the Department of Scandinavian at the University of California, Berkeley.

HEATHER O'DONOGHUE is Professor of Old Norse and Vigfússon Rausing Reader in Old Icelandic Literature and Antiquities at Linacre College, University of Oxford.

JUDY QUINN is Reader in Old Norse Literature in the Department of Anglo-Saxon, Norse and Celtic at the University of Cambridge.

MARIA ELENA RUGGERINI is Professor of Germanic Philology in the Department of Philology, Literature and Linguistics at the University of Cagliari.

JENS PETER SCHJØDT is Professor of the History of Religions in the Department of Religious Studies at the University of Aarhus.

BRITTANY SCHORN is a Research Associate in the Department of Anglo-Saxon, Norse and Celtic at the University of Cambridge.

BERNT ØYVIND THORVALDSEN is Associate Professor in Norwegian language and literature at University College of Southeast Norway.

Translations and abbreviations of the titles of eddic poems

I: Poems in the Codex Regius

Alvíssmál (All-wise's Sayings)   Alv
Atlakviða (Poem of Atli)   Akv
Atlamál in grænlenzku (Greenlandic Sayings of Atli)   Am
Brot af Sigurðarkviðu   (Fragment of a Poem about Sigurðr) Br
Fáfnismál (Sayings of Fáfnir)   Fm
Grímnismál (Grímnir's Sayings)   Grm
Grípisspá (Grípir's Prophecy)   Grp
Guðrúnarhvǫt (Whetting of Guðrún)   Ghv
Guðrúnarkviða I (First Poem of Guðrún)   Gðr I
Guðrúnarkviða II (Second Poem of Guðrún)   Gðr II
Guðrúnarkviða III (Third Poem of Guðrún)   Gðr III
Hamðismál (Speech of Hamðir)   Hm
Hárbarðsljóð (Hárbarðr's Song)   Hrbl
Hávamál (Sayings of the High One)   Háv
Helgakviða Hjǫrvarðssonar (Poem of Helgi Hjǫrvarðsson)   HHv
Helgakviða Hundingsbana I (First Poem of Helgi Hundingsbani) HH I
Helgakviða Hundingsbana II   (Second Poem of Helgi Hundingsbani) HH II
Helreið Brynhildar (Brynhildr's Ride to Hell)   Hlr
Hymiskviða (Hymir's Poem)   Hym
Lokasenna (Loki's Quarrel)   Ls
Oddrúnargrátr (Oddrún's Lament)   Od
Reginsmál (Sayings of Reginn)   Rm
Sigrdrífumál (Sayings of Sigrdrífa)   Sd
Sigurðarkviða in skamma (Short Poem about Sigurðr)   Sg
Skírnismál (Sayings of Skírnir)   Skm
Vafþrúðnismál (Vafþrúðnir's Sayings)   Vm
Vǫlundarkviða (Poem of Vǫlundr)   Vkv

Vǫluspá (Seeress's Prophecy)   Vsp
Vǫluspá (Hauksbók) (Seeress's Prophecy, Hauksbók)   Vsp(H)
Þrymskviða (Þrymr's Poem)   Þrk

II: Other eddic poems

Baldrs Draumar (Baldr's Dreams)   Bdr
Battle of the Goths and Huns   Hunn
Buslubœn (Busla's Curses)
Darraðarljód (Song of Dörruðr)   Darr
Eiríksmál (Sayings of Eiríkr [blood-axe])   Eirm
Fjölsvinnsmál (Sayings of Fjölsvinnr)   Fjöl
Gestumblinda gátur (Riddles of Gestumblindi)
Grottasǫngr (Song of Grotti)   Grt
Gróugaldr   (Groa's Chant)   Gg
Hákonarmál (Sayings of Hákon)   Hák
Haraldskvæði (Hrafnsmál)
(Poem about Haraldr / The Raven's Sayings)
Hildibrandr's Death-Song
Hjálmarr's Death-Song
Hrókskviða (Poem of Hrókr)
Hugsvinnsmál (Sayings of Hugsvinnr)   Hsv
Hyndluljóð (Song of Hyndla)   Hdl
Krákumál (Sayings of Kráka)
Merlínússpá (Merlin's Prophecy)
Rígspula (List of Rig)   Rþ
Sólarljóð (Song of the Sun)   Sól
Víkarsbálkr (Víkarr's Section)   Vík
The Waking of Angantýr

Introduction

Carolyne Larrington

In the mythological eddic poem *Hymiskviða* the gods order the sea-ruler Ægir to entertain them all at a feast. Ægir responds with the claim that he does not possess a cauldron big enough for the purpose, and Týr and Þórr set off to find a suitable vessel at the home of Týr's mother in *Jǫtunheimar* ('the lands of the giants'). Their success means that *véar hverian vel skulu drekka ǫlðr at Ægis eitt hǫrmeitið* ('the gods will drink well ale at Ægir's every winter', *Hym* 39/4–8). The most capacious of cauldrons is appropriated from Hymir, whose hospitality is distinctly chilly, and brought to a hall where its contents can delight gods and elves alike. The mode of eddic poetry is just such a gigantic kettle, an all-encompassing container for the Old Norse myths and heroic legends which froth, bob, and jostle together within it, whether as substantial whole poems, fragmentary verse sequences, or single *lausavísur* ('free-standing verses'). When in 1955 the English poet Philip Larkin eschewed drawing on the 'common myth-kitty' for the inspiration for his poems (Larkin 1955, 78), he was explicitly rejecting the recent Modernist poetic practice of employing wide-ranging cultural allusions. Yet Larkin's metaphor for all that he refused has found resonance for those who write about traditional story. Thus, this Handbook engages closely with the 'myth-kitty', the shared resources of traditional knowledge that find their form within the accommodating mode of eddic poetry: the myths and legends of the Old Norse–Icelandic tradition. These stories are primarily preserved in the two great anthologies of eddic poetry, the Codex Regius of the Poetic Edda (GKS 2365 4°) and AM 748 I a 4°, but a number of mythological and heroic eddic poems were written down in other manuscripts (see Clunies Ross, Chapter 1 in this Handbook). These poems, or poems very much like them, provided the important Icelandic writer Snorri Sturluson (1179–1241) with the basis for composing his *Edda*, a manual of poetics into which he incorporated a systematic overview of Old Norse myth and offered summarised versions of some of the more important legendary cycles. Had the Codex Regius manuscript not come to light in 1643 and been preserved in Copenhagen for future generations, if we were without our most important eddic manuscript, our understanding of Old Norse myth and legend would be immeasurably the poorer.

The poems transmitted in the anthologies are largely whole, barring the incomplete poems *Sigrdrífumál* and the *Brot af Sigurðarkviðu*, truncated by the missing gathering from the Codex Regius. Only a few of them bear medieval titles, among them *Hávamál* and *Vafþrúðnismál*. The first poem in the manuscript *Vǫluspá* takes its name from Snorri's references to it in his *Edda*, while the poem generally known as *Skírnismál*, titled thus in AM 748 I a 4°, is called *Fǫr Skírnis* (*Skírnir's Journey*) in the Codex Regius. Other titles are the work of later editors and have no medieval equivalents. In her chapter on eddic modes and genres (Chapter 12), Brittany Schorn notes which poem titles originate in the Codex Regius; the varying terms to describe the mode of each poem show how difficult it is to come to solid conclusions about what they might imply about eddic genre. Thus, *-spá* (in *Vǫluspá*) is self-evidently a prophecy, just as *-hvǫt* in *Guðrúnarhvǫt* means 'whetting'; the *-þula* (list) in *Rígsþula* too is self-explanatory – all these titles occur in medieval manuscripts. The distinction between *-mál* and *-kviða* is hard to establish, however; *-mál* seems to imply 'sayings, things uttered', and indeed *Atlamál* contains a sizeable percentage of dialogue, though we might need to construe the title as 'Things said about Atli' rather than 'Things said by Atli', in contradistinction to *Hávamál* (*Sayings of the High One*) where Hávi (Óðinn) seems to be the narrator throughout. Yet *Atlakviða* also switches freely between narrative and dialogue, and the three poems entitled *Guðrúnarkviða* in the Codex Regius contain varying, but often substantial, proportions of direct speech.

The great majority of eddic verses have been transmitted as sequences of stanzas, again usually without title, within prose sagas, in a form known as prosimetrum. Some of these sequences, such as *The Waking of Angantýr* from *Hervarar saga ok Heiðreks* (*The Saga of Hervör and Heiðrekr*), have been assumed to be complete poems and have been assigned titles by their editors, some in Old Norse, some in other languages. Other runs of verses occur across more than one saga, such as the so-called *Hjálmarr's Death-Song*. This sequence is found in two sagas: *Qrvar-Odds saga* (*The Saga of Arrow-Oddr*) and *Hervarar saga*; these two *fornaldarsögur* (legendary sagas) relate the adventures of Hjálmarr's companions and of his opponents respectively. Their versions of the dying viking's lament are constituted by differing verses in differing orders, yet since the two verse sequences manifestly belong both to Hjálmarr and to the 'death-song' subgenre, what, then, *is Hjálmarr's Death-Song?* Editors cannot always agree on whether individual verses do in fact constitute a discrete poem; hence, the work known as *Hlǫðskviða* (*Poem of Hlǫðr*), in English as 'The Battle of the Goths and Huns' and, in Neckel and Kuhn (1962), as *Hunnenschlachtlied*, is treated in the forthcoming volume VIII of *Skaldic Poetry of the Scandinavian Middle Ages* (hereafter *SkP*) as a series of verses delivered by different speakers, and not as a complete poem.

Eddic poetry is anonymous, stanzaic, relatively straightforward in form, and, like its relatives in other Germanic languages, it is capable of mediating all kinds of content: swift-moving narrative, pithy dialogue, grand monologue, and lyric description. It was the medium chosen by those anonymous poets and performers, male or female, who had myths to dramatise, wisdom to impart, and conceptions of the ancient Germanic and heroic past to explore. One of our earliest written sources for eddic verse in Scandinavia is the Rök Stone, probably dating from the first half of the ninth century. In the centuries after the conversion to Christianity the eddic mode retained its usefulness, its formal and thematic authority, and it was employed to educate later generations in Christian wisdom. Its conservatism and its versatility enabled poets to retell culturally important narratives as late as the fourteenth century when new 'neo-eddic' poems such as *Svipdagsmál* were composed. Pastiche poetry in eddic metres continued to be composed into the seventeenth and eighteenth centuries (Hughes 2013): thus, eddic poetry never entirely disappeared from Icelandic tradition.

Most eddic verses, as noted above, are preserved in prosimetric contexts, multiply recopied in paper manuscripts in post-medieval Iceland. These prose narratives usually give some information about the speaker and situation in which the verse is recited. While a series of verses may sometimes be assumed to constitute an entire poem, it is not usually possible to determine the relative age of individual verses. Some stanzas may indeed be ancient and traditional, others might be ad hoc compositions by the prose author, intended to reshape the sequences better to fit the new prose context. The language of eddic poetry is not easily susceptible to dating (see Thorvaldsen, Chapter 4), and criteria for determining the age of stanzas are hard to establish. Yet it is exactly that unageing simplicity, the directness and relative unchangingness of eddic expression which mediates so effectively to us the imagined speeches and the actions of the gods, heroes, and heroines of the past. Eddic poetry does not often depend on riddling kennings, complex syntax, or dense metaphorical reference systems for its effects. Rather, it harnesses rhythm and assonance;

repetition intensifies underlying emotions. *Lengi hvarfaðak, lengi hugir deildusk* ('Long I turned it over, long my thoughts ran on', *Gðr II* 6/1–2), notes Guðrún about the mystery of her husband's death; or, more poignantly, *hnipnaði Grani þá, drap í gras hofði* ('Grani [Sigurðr's horse] hung his head, lowered it to the grass', *Gðr II* 5/5–6); *Hnipnaði Gunnarr, sagði mér Hogni* ('Gunnarr hung his head, Hogni told me', *Gðr II* 7/1–2). Gunnarr regrets the killing of his brother-in-law, which he has been obliged to countenance; just as, earlier, he vacillated in trying to placate his wife's rage and to accommodate his own damaged sexual honour, so he now leaves the communication of Sigurðr's death to the more dispassionate Hogni.

If less riddling than they are in skaldic verse, eddic metaphors are just as vivid: *gnadda niflfarna* ('little beasts, gone to the shades', *Akv* 33/8) is how Guðrún describes her slaughtered sons to their unwitting father. Eddic dialogue allows for dry understatement. The dead Angantýr observes to his fearless daughter: *Kveðkat ek þik, mær ung, mönnum líka, er þú um hauga hvarfar á nóttum* ('I say, young girl, you are not like most men when you hang around burial mounds by night', *SkP*, Angantýr Lv 6^{VIII}/1–4). It can express wistful regret, as in the dying Hjálmarr's meditation on all he has lost: *Hvarf ek frá fögrum fljóða söngvi, alltrauðr gamans, austr við Sóta* ('I turned away from women's lovely songs, all resistant to amusement, eastwards with Sóti', *SkP*, Hjálm Lv9^{VIII}/1–4). Passion, too, finds a voice in eddic verse: when Menglöð learns that at long last her destined lover has come to her hall, she expresses her fierce desire for Svipdagr: *nú er þat satt at vit slíta skulum ævi ok aldri saman* ('now truly we shall together devour life and time', *Fjöl* 40/4–6). Menglöð echoes, whether in a deliberate intertextual reference or by deploying a shared formula associated with female erotic longing, the defiant declaration of the dead Brynhildr, on her way to reunion with her Sigurðr: *við skulum okkrum aldri slíta, Sigurðr, saman!* ('we shall devour our life together, Sigurðr!', *Hlr* 14/5–7). Many of the chapters which follow exemplify and unpack the particular artistry and effectiveness of expression that the eddic mode offers.

There has been an upsurge of interest in eddic poetry during the last decade. The Skaldic Editing Project, in particular *SkP* VIII, containing the poetry preserved in the *fornaldarsögur*, but also *SkP* VI (Runic Poetry) and *SkP* III (Poetry from Treatises on Poetics), will soon make newly edited poems in eddic metres available to a wide readership. The first complete edition of the Codex Regius poems to be published in decades (Jónas Kristjánsson and Vésteinn Ólason 2014) has recently appeared in the Íslenzk fornrit series. This new edition also contains the four poems from other manuscripts usually anthologised as part of the 'Poetic Edda'

(*Baldrs Draumar*, *Rígsþula*, *Hyndluljóð*, and *Grottasǫngr*); the two 'neo-eddic' poems *Gróugaldr* (*Gróa's Chant*) and *Fjölsvinnsmál* (*Sayings of Fjölsvinnr*) are also included. The revised second edition of my translation was published in 2014; this also expanded the 'Poetic Edda' corpus to include the two 'neo-eddic' poems edited by Jónas and Vésteinn, and also *The Waking of Angantýr*.

This Handbook owes its genesis in large part to the impetus of the Eddic Network, a research network founded by the three editors in 2012, in order to consolidate our research interests in eddic poetry and to raise its profile; this was a timely move anticipating the recent renewed focus on eddic poetry noted above. Two workshops were held (2013 and 2014) at St John's College, University of Oxford, in order to bring together the international scholars who have contributed to this volume; other scholars in related fields also gave papers and an enthusiastic group of undergraduate and graduate students – the next generation of eddic scholars – also attended. The Network's aims were, and remain, to develop and encourage new approaches to eddic poetry, to call into question the established categorisation of Old Norse-Icelandic poetry into 'skaldic' and 'eddic', to interrogate the distinction between 'mythological' and 'heroic' (historically, the product of the organisation of the Codex Regius), and, above all, to open up discussion of the whole corpus, beyond the Codex Regius poems. From the substantial poems preserved in *fornaldarsögur* to the quirky eddic stanzas uttered by supernatural figures in the *Íslendingasögur* (sagas of Icelanders), the powerful genealogical and memorial poems composed in mixed eddic metres found in the *konungasögur* (kings' sagas) to the eddic wisdom poems composed most likely in the thirteenth century, eddic poetry encompasses much that has been critically neglected. The later *Sólarljóð* (*Song of the Sun*) and *Hugsvinnsmál* (*Sayings of Hugsvinnr*), often transmitted alongside the mythological and heroic poems in late paper manuscripts, bear witness to the continuing versatility and artistic power of eddic poetry.

This powerful, rhetorically expressive, and flexible mode of verse is thus the subject of this Handbook. The collection of essays is intended primarily to provide tools for understanding eddic poetry for those who are embarking on the study of Old Norse verse, at both undergraduate and graduate level. It also aims to inform scholars working in neighbouring disciplines about the range and depth of this important medieval European verse tradition. Experts in Old Norse-Icelandic literature will, we believe, find much that is new, eye-opening, even provocative, in what follows: fresh critical approaches and new kinds of engagement with familiar issues.

Our contributors – experienced international scholars and newer, younger voices – offer up-to-date accounts of the state of eddic scholarship across the book's eighteen chapters, bringing together the wisdom of a lifetime's eddic study and new theoretically articulated approaches. The consolidated bibliography provides references to enable readers to investigate further poems and topics treated in the individual chapters. The Handbook begins with Margaret Clunies Ross's overview of the contexts in which eddic poetry has been preserved and transmitted (Chapter 1), locating it within wider traditions of Germanic alliterative verse and highlighting the particular problems thrown up by a poetry that is fundamentally oral in origin. Clunies Ross's chapter outlines the scope of the Codex Regius anthology and deals, with an editor's particular expertise, with the preservation and adaptation of stanzas within the prosimetric contexts of the *fornaldarsögur*.

Joseph Harris (Chapter 2) takes up the challenge of describing the history of eddic scholarship, dating the beginning of professional engagement with the poetry from around 1870 (although Jakob Grimm's work was an important precursor of later nineteenth-century scholarly study). This was the period in which eddic editions began to proliferate, the era of the development of comparative scholarship, and of the contextualisation of the poetry within particular historical and philological milieux. Harris also traces the impact of our new conceptualisations of orality – indeed, of the nature of the oral-literary continuum – on our models for transmission, and assesses the findings of old and New Philology. Judy Quinn's chapter on the editing of eddic poetry also takes a historical view, exploring the ways in which the editors of Codex Regius poems have shaped readers' interpretations through particular (often radical) editorial interventions (Chapter 3). To some degree, editors of eddic poetry can be seen to lag behind the recent trend towards more conservative editing, which is premised on greater respect for the manuscript evidence (even when the text is challenging) and heightened awareness of the implications of the oral composition and transmission of much eddic verse. With examples drawn from *Vǫluspá*, *Hávamál*, *Oddrúnargrátr*, and *Hyndluljóð*, Quinn demonstrates how interventionist editing has the potential to falsify not only the poetic record, but also our understanding of the mythology and legends of early Scandinavia.

Bernt Øyvind Thorvaldsen (Chapter 4) addresses the difficult issue of dating eddic poetry, building on the findings of Bjarne Fidjestøl (1999). Thorvaldsen investigates in detail the various criteria for older and more recent dating, demonstrating in many cases their unreliability, and he offers an incisive critique of the dating methods used by, for example, the influential *Edda Kommentar* series (von See et al. 1997–). Thorvaldsen's scepticism anticipates the arguments taken up by Jens Peter Schjødt in his chapter about the relevance of the poetry to the study of the religion of pre-Christian Scandinavia (Chapter 7). Although the information which eddic verse provides is neither reliable nor in most cases securely dateable to an age consistent with a pre-Christian origin, nevertheless, Schjødt argues, eddic poetry provides evidence which, if assessed judiciously, offers strong support for such religious phenomena as kingly initiation and fertility ritual.

Preceding Schjødt's chapter are Terry Gunnell's discussion of performance and audiences in eddic contexts (Chapter 5) and John Lindow's account of eddic mythology (Chapter 6). Gunnell sketches a scale between 'ritual' and 'play' along which performances of eddic poetry must have moved, and suggests a distinction between the performance of material preserved in the *ljóðaháttr* metre, as authoritative mediation of traditional wisdom, and the dramatisation of the narratives and dialogues in swift-moving *fornyrðislag*. The effects of sound in space, the very elements of poetry missing from transmission on the written page, are foregrounded in Gunnell's readings of *Grímnismál* and *Þrymskviða*. John Lindow traces the cultural contexts in which Old Norse mythology is preserved, starting with Snorri's account of it in his manual of poetics, *Snorra Edda*, intended to maintain Iceland's major cultural export: skaldic poetry. The chapter also provides an overview of the organisation and contents of the first part of the Codex Regius where the majority of Old Norse mythological information is preserved. Lindow reminds us too of the lost poems, those which underlie the euhemerised tales in Saxo Grammaticus's *Gesta Danorum*, those very briefly quoted by Snorri, or alluded to in *Vǫlsunga saga* (*The Saga of the Vǫlsungs*). Although the scribe of the Codex Regius marks a clear distinction between the first eleven poems, broadly recounting the adventures of the gods, and those that follow, we should not necessarily adopt one thirteenth-century compiler's view that mythological and heroic are separate spheres, Lindow concludes. Rather (an argument advanced elsewhere in the Handbook), the gods move also in the human and heroic world, and humans (as in *Grímnismál*) interact with gods in mythological contexts. Carolyne Larrington's discussion of heroic legend and eddic poetry extends beyond the anthology manuscripts into the prosimetric texts (Chapter 8). Eddic heroes include the protagonists of legends also known from Middle High German and Old English texts, the Scandinavian ancestors of prominent Icelandic families, and such heroicised Norwegian kings as Haraldr hárfagri ('fairhair'), Eiríkr blóðǫx ('blood-axe'), and Hákon the Good. Verse is primarily employed to mediate dialogue in the *fornaldarsögur*; the genres of death-song and *ævidrápa* (praise-poem about one's life), largely preserved in these contexts, allow the moribund hero to take stock of his past deeds and his imminent entry into Valhǫll.

The next section of the Handbook probes into eddic poetry's relations with real-world contexts: place names, stone sculpture, and archaeology. Stefan Brink and John Lindow (Chapter 9) consider the etymology of place names in three of the longer mythological poems of the Codex Regius. Noting the different frequency of distribution between fictional and actual names in the mythological and heroic poems, they argue that the creativity of eddic poets leads them to coin, or to choose, vivid, metaphorical names for mythic places. Lilla Kopár (Chapter 10) shows how the content of eddic myths and legends was in circulation long before the first texts were written down; scenes from the narratives are carved in stone reliefs surviving across the Viking world. Kopár concentrates on the widespread depictions – from Sweden to North-West England – of Þórr's fishing expedition, during which he catches the *miðgarðsormr* ('world-serpent'), but she also adduces other carvings (Óðinn's fate at *ragnarǫk* and the adventures of Vǫlundr) in support of her discussion of how heroic and mythic motifs interact with words and stone. John Hines (Chapter 11) argues for a fuller mutual engagement between material culture and oral-literary poetic texts; not simply, he urges, in order to flesh out the reader's imaginings of the northern past, but, rather, to investigate the whole range of cultural meanings embedded in both finds and poems. He draws attention to the ways in which artefacts – among them, ring-hilted swords, Icelandic halls, and high-status beds – open up the fruitful possibilities inherent in the writing of a broadly defined cultural history.

A series of chapters on poetics follows, investigating the poems primarily as literary texts. The first of Brittany Schorn's chapters (Chapter 12) sketches the problematic relationship that the eddic mode has with genre, while the second (Chapter 14) uncovers distinctive features of eddic style. Schorn shows how eddic genres are interpenetrative and notes the difficulties (referred to above) of determining how far there was an 'ethnic' genre system in Old Norse poetry. The argument is extended to the (probably) thirteenth-century vision-wisdom poem *Sólarljóð*, composed in *ljóðaháttr* and generically hybrid. Schorn's chapter on style explores eddic lexis, compound words (perhaps newly coined for their poetic contexts), and variation in epithets for frequently occurring concepts, such as the warrior, the beautiful woman, or battle. She analyses the different rhythmic and stylistic effects of the main eddic metres, and discusses the effects of mixed metrical forms within prosimetric sequences. The focus on metre is broadened by Robert Fulk's detailed account of how eddic metres functioned. Explaining stress and alliteration rules across the three most frequent eddic metres – *fornyrðislag*, *ljóðaháttr*, and *málaháttr* – and drawing attention to the scope for variation within poems predominantly composed in one or other of them, Fulk discusses the basis for emendation on the grounds of defective alliteration and metre.

Judy Quinn's chapter on kennings and other forms of figurative language (Chapter 15) explores the variety of ways in which eddic poets engaged with metaphor in their verse. In addition to similes drawn from the natural world, eddic poets often used kennings (poetic circumlocutions comprised of two or more nouns) as substitutes for or embellishments of a noun. Some eddic kennings are unique, while many others draw on the same conventions used to formulate kennings in skaldic praise poetry. An interesting difference, Quinn notes, is the reflexivity of eddic kennings, where valkyries and warriors speak from within figures of speech in the vivid dialogues characteristic of the eddic mode. Maria Elena Ruggerini's chapter (Chapter 16) builds on her comparative work in Old English poetics, demonstrating how alliterative collocations function to create semantic networks in eddic poems. Connections within networks can be strengthened through phonological similarity (in addition to the initial alliterating sound); startling stylistic effects are achieved by substituting an unexpected word for a predicted one. Ruggerini's methodology flags up possibilities for future work in mapping Old Norse semantic fields, enhancing our access to the medieval Scandinavian conceptual universe.

The Handbook concludes with two chapters that trace connections between eddic poetry and modern critical responses. David Clark and Jóhanna Katrín Friðriksdóttir (Chapter 17) engage with issues of gender and queer theory, problematising straightforward gender binaries and arguing for blurred and transgressive gender roles, not just in the mythological poems where Óðinn and Loki experiment with *seiðr*, a kind of magical praxis that involves cross-dressing and other non-normative behaviour, but also in the heroic verse. Maternality and monstrosity are foregrounded as spheres in which eddic poetry unsettles our sense of straightforward gender binaries. Finally, Heather O'Donoghue (Chapter 18) considers the reception of eddic poetry, from Snorri's dependence on it in composing his *Edda* all the way through to *Game of Thrones* and Viking death-metal. O'Donoghue brings into focus the eighteenth-century English rediscovery of the poems, largely through Bishop Percy's *Five Runick Pieces*. Percy's work was widely read; it inspired not only Thomas Gray's version of *Baldrs Draumar*, but also a whole slew of further 'Gothick' verse translations. The nineteenth century saw the beginning of eddic translation into English; thereafter, the heroic poems of the Codex Regius became more influential than the mythological tales. William Morris, Richard Wagner, and J. R. R. Tolkien took inspiration from the Vǫlsung legendary-cycle; Wagner's *Der Ring des Nibelungen* (*The Ring of the Nibelung*) remains perhaps the single most influential response in later centuries to eddic versions of the Northern heroic.

Eddic poetry is ancient, *er fát fornara, fremr var þat hálfu* ('few things are so old that this is not twice as old', *Hm* 2/5–6), and yet ever-new, capable of being remade in a surprisingly modern vein. Thus, almost anticipating modern social media, the thirteenth-century poem *Hugsvinnsmál* st. 28 offers a useful warning:

> Öll tíðindi, þau er upp koma,
>   ræð þú eigi fyrstr með firum;
> betra er at þegja en þat at segja,
>   sem lýðum reyniz at lygi.

> [All the news, that which comes up, don't be first to discuss among men; better to say nothing than to relate that which proves to be a lie among men.]

All the authority of the Old Norse wisdom tradition and the *ljóðaháttr* metre lies behind *Hugsvinnsmál*'s reformulation of the *Distichs of Cato* for a new medieval Icelandic audience (Schorn 2011).

After the contentious events chronicled in *Lokasenna*, Loki prophesies that there will never again be convivial ale-drinking at Ægir's home; Hymir's huge cauldron seems no longer to have a function. The study of eddic poetry, however, and of the myths and heroic legends, the wisdom, rhetoric, and adventure that it mediates to us, remains as vital, fresh, and enthralling as when the compiler of the Codex Regius applied himself to selecting the poems for that anthology, nearly seven hundred and fifty years ago.

Acknowledgements

The editors gratefully acknowledge the important contribution made to this Handbook by St John's College, University of Oxford, through the award of a St John's Research Centre Pump-priming Project Grant for

2013–14 which facilitated the establishment of the Eddic Network. We would like to express our thanks to the many scholars who have contributed to this Handbook, both directly and indirectly. Thanks also go to the editorial team at Cambridge University Press for their role in seeing the volume through to publication. Finally, we warmly acknowledge the generosity of the Corpus of Anglo-Saxon Stone Sculpture in permitting the reproduction of the images in Chapter 10, and the kindness of the National Museum of Denmark in supplying and giving permission for the reproduction of the Tjørnehøj figurine as our cover-image.

Notes about this Handbook

- Primary texts are listed by the title of individual works, rather than author (i.e. under *Gylfaginning* rather than Snorri Sturluson).
- Quotations of poems from the Codex Regius (and the other four poems usually considered as part of the Poetic Edda) are normalised from the fourth edition of Neckel and Kuhn (1962). The editions from which other poems are cited (such as eddic poems edited in *SkP* or the neo-eddic poem *Svipdagsmál*) are noted where they occur.
- Translations are either from Larrington 2014 or are noted as the author's own.
- A list of eddic poems cited, translations of, and abbreviations for their titles is provided at the beginning of the volume.
- The titles of all other Old Norse texts are translated when they first occur within each chapter.
- The alphabetical order in the Consolidated Bibliography and Index is based on English-language conventions with the following adjustments; *d* and *ð* are treated as one letter; *þ* comes after y and is followed by *ä, æ, œ, ö/ø* (treated as the same letter), and *ǫ*; the Icelandic acute accent is disregarded, as are German umlauts. Note that Icelandic names are alphabetised under the first name, followed by the patronymic.

CHAPTER I

The transmission and preservation of eddic poetry

Margaret Clunies Ross

The period of oral composition, performance, and transmission

Prolegomenon

In the period before *c*.1000–1100, when the Scandinavian peoples began to adopt the technology of writing using the Roman alphabet, there is evidence from early runic inscriptions that they, along with other groups speaking Germanic languages, participated in the composition and recitation of alliterative poetry in what has been called the common Germanic verse-form (Lehmann 1956). In Old Norse scholarship, poetry in that common Germanic verse-form is usually referred to as eddic. We only know eddic poetry today from texts that were committed to writing, for the most part, in the thirteenth and fourteenth centuries, so access to Old Norse alliterative poetry from the pre-literate period can never be direct and many questions about its composition, performance, and transmission can never be definitively answered. However, written texts may give us important clues about the nature and significance of eddic poetry in the pre-literate period.

I begin this discussion by considering two passages from West Germanic alliterative poems that have come down to us in writing, but which may reasonably be considered to reflect attitudes to poetry in the common Germanic verse-form. The first of these is from the Old English poem *Beowulf*, whose precise date of original composition is not known, though it must antedate the unique manuscript, BL Cotton Vitellius A XV (*c*.1000), in which it has been recorded, perhaps by some two centuries (Fulk et al. 2008: clxiii–clxxiv). In lines 866b–75a of the poem, the *Beowulf* poet tells how there is great rejoicing after Beowulf has killed the monster Grendel, and one of the king's retainers (*cyninges þegn*) recites a poem about how the legendary hero Sigemund killed a dragon, as an indirect compliment to Beowulf for his killing of Grendel.

                                  Hwīlum cyninges þegn,
guma gilphlæden,   gidda gemyndig,
sē ðe eal fela   ealdgesegena
worn gemunde,   word ōþer fand
sōðe gebunden;   secg eft ongan
sīð Bēowulfes   snyttrum styrian
ond on sped wrecan   spel gerāde,
wordum wrixlan;   wēlhwylc gecwæð,
þæt hē fram Sigemunde[s]   secgan hȳrde
ellendǣdum

[At times a retainer of the king, a man well supplied with words of praise, mindful of songs, who remembered a great number of the whole stock of ancient traditions, devised new (lit. 'other') words, faithfully joined. The man then began to tell with wisdom of Beowulf's journey, and to recite skilfully apt stories, make variations with words; he recited everything that he had heard tell about Sigemund's deeds of valour].[1]

We cannot know at first-hand the place that alliterative poetry occupied in the pre-literate societies of Scandinavia and throughout the Germanic-speaking world, including Anglo-Saxon England. Descriptions such as this one from *Beowulf* can, however, tell us a good deal at second-hand about the role of such poetry in early Germanic-speaking societies. From the passage above we can make a number of deductions: for example, that this poetry was composed and recited to celebrate an important social occasion, and that people were conscious of the exploits of legendary heroes as providing paradigms for heroic conduct in the 'real world', even if, in the case of *Beowulf*, this world was probably long past as far as the Anglo-Saxon audience was concerned. The passage also indicates that poetic recitation was an aristocratic pursuit (the poet is said to be one of the king's retainers) and part of a high-spirited celebration that, according to the poem, was preceded by horse racing.

We can also gain some interesting insights into the status of the poet and the poetic process itself. The poet is not himself distinguished here by any special term (he is a *þegn*) and is presumably one of the warriors celebrating Beowulf's victory, though elsewhere in *Beowulf* a poet reciting in the more formal environment of the Danish king's hall is called a *scop* ('poet, singer', ll. 90, 496, and 1066; see Opland 1980: 196–9). This deduction accords with what we know from later sources about the role of skalds or court poets in Scandinavia: they are not a professional class like the bards of Ireland, but may be ordinary men (or occasionally women) who happen to have the skills and knowledge required for the job, as we learn from many narratives about poets in Old Norse historical sagas of a later period, such as *Morkinskinna* (see Ármann Jakobsson 2014: 113–20, 280–92).

Two necessary qualities of the oral alliterative poet are particularly stressed in this passage. The first is the poet's extensive knowledge of ancient stories (*eal fela worn ealdgesegena*), which he recalls from the storehouse of his memory – he is *gidda gemyndig* ('mindful of songs', l. 867) – for he belongs to a society in which writing has only limited uses, mainly for runic inscriptions, as will be discussed below. The second quality of the oral alliterative poet may be inferred from the *Beowulf* poet's statement that *word ōþer fand sōðe gebunden* ('he devised new [lit. 'other'] words, faithfully joined', ll. 869b–70a) and that, in his recitation, the poet *ongan … wordum wrixlan* ('began to make variations with words', ll. 870b, 873a). These comments both show that the alliterative poet's technique was valued as much as – and perhaps more than – his command of his subject matter. The first observation – that 'he devised new words, faithfully joined' – is usually considered to refer to the structural characteristic of alliteration, which occurs in all poetry in the common Germanic verse-form and binds lines together in pairs, while the second may refer to the alliterative poet's ability to produce numerous poetic phrases for the same referent within a half-line of four metrical positions, a device that *Beowulf* itself amply exemplifies (see Fulk et al. 2008: cxi–cxvii for a discussion). This characteristic of variation is less obvious in Old Norse than in Old English poetry, though it is still present there.

The passage from *Beowulf* represents the oral alliterative poet in action in a social setting. The Old Norse eddic poem *Hávamál* is concerned with the subject of how poetry originated, who controlled it, and its uses in human society (sts 139–42). Here too we can deduce a number of important concepts that must have been associated with the art and practice of poetry in the pre-literate Nordic world. The passage from *Hávamál* is part of a cryptically allusive representation of the god Óðinn's self-sacrifice *vindgameiði á* ('on the windy tree', *Háv* 138/2) that most commentators identify as the World Ash, Yggdrasill. After the speaker of these stanzas, usually identified as Óðinn, had hung on the tree for nine nights, deprived of both food and drink, he says that he gained the runes as his reward, here apparently in the form of wooden rune sticks:

nam ek upp rúnar, œpandi nam . . .

Fimbulljóð níu nam ek af inum frægja syni
   Bǫlþórs, Bestlu fǫður
ok ek drykk of gat ins dýra mjaðar,
   ausinn Óðreri.

Þá nam ek frœvask ok fróðr vera
   ok vaxa ok vel hafask;
orð mér af orði orðs leitaði,
verk mér af verki verks leitaði.

Rúnar munt þú finna ok ráðna stafi (*Háv* 139/4–5, 140–1 and 142/1–1)

[I took up the runes, screaming I took them . . . I learnt nine powerful incantations from the renowned son of Bǫlþórr, father of Bestla, and I obtained a drink of the precious mead, poured from Óðrerir. Then I began to quicken and be wise and to grow and prosper; one word sought for a word from a word for me, one deed sought for a deed from a deed for me. You must discover runes and interpretable letters]

Most scholars of Old Norse mythology understand these stanzas to refer to a kind of initiation whereby the god Óðinn undergoes the pain of hanging and sensory deprivation in order to gain numinous knowledge from otherworldly beings (see Schjødt 2008: 173–206; Clunies Ross 1994: 222–8), here named as the son of Bǫlþórr, who is the father of Bestla, elsewhere identified (*Gylfaginning*: 11) as Óðinn's own mother and a giantess. The myth alluded to here is a variant of another myth, told in *Skáldskaparmál* (3–5), which also details Óðinn's involvement in obtaining the art of poetry in the form of an intoxicating drink, mead, from another giant, Suttungr, and his daughter Gunnlǫð. These myths powerfully endorse the otherworld origin of poetry and Óðinn's role as transmitter of the poetic process to human poets and runic experts.

In the stanzas from *Hávamál* the emphasis lies on the transfer of runic knowledge and practical skills involved in the carving of runes from Óðinn to humans. This transfer is signalled by the change between first-person narrative in stanzas 139–41 and the direct address to a human subject (*rúnar munt þú finna*) in stanza 142 and beyond. This individual is called Loddfáfnir in stanza 137. Even though the stanzas that follow the passage cited here deal quite concretely with the various uses of runes in human life, from healing to the blunting of an enemy's sword, the wording of stanzas 139–42 indicates that the practice of runic writing is inextricably linked in the divine speaker's mind to the ability to create ordered sequences of words and, in the pre-literate period, this probably meant sequences shaped in poetic form:

> orð mér af orði orðs leitaði,
> verk mér af verki verks leitaði. (*Háv* 141/5–8)

[One word sought for a word from a word for me, one deed sought for a deed from a deed for me.]

This passage represents the beginnings of continuous verbal composition as a process in which the speaker (presumed to be Óðinn) is transformed from sacrificial victim to empowered and articulate possessor of structured verbal skills, reified here as possession of the runes. A close link is thus established between words and deeds; words, arranged in particular sequences, can bring about certain effects on those to whom or about whom they are uttered and on the practitioner himself. Such a view of structured language and its illocutionary and perlocutionary effects is pervasive in the eddic poetry preserved in written form, and must, presumably, have been pervasive in earlier times as well.[2] It is also perceptible in much skaldic verse and in the names for the various eddic metres (see Fulk's chapter in this Handbook [Chapter 13]; Quinn 1990a; Clunies Ross 2005: 29–31).

We do not know the precise age of *Hávamál* nor of the myths that underlie it, but they are probably of some antiquity. What can be said is that the ideas it expresses here about the verbal arts and the arts of runic carving are repeated in stereotyped form by many of the kennings for poetry that skaldic poets of the Viking Age and beyond habitually employ to refer to their art and its origin. To give two of many available examples, poetry is *lið Háars* ('the drink of the High One', Eyv *Hál* 1/2[I]) and a poet is *Viðurs skapsmiðr* ('the smith of Viðurr's [Óðinn's] mind', Bragi *Troll* 1/2[III]). While these myths lay stress upon poetry's supernatural origin and the poet as the recipient of a gift from Óðinn, other skaldic kennings emphasise the poet's craft, his role as a workman (*smiðr*). Although there is little evidence from within the texts of the surviving Old Norse eddic poems to back up this view, it is presumed that eddic poets approached their task in a similar spirit, and that their compositional skills were admired like those of the king's retainer in *Beowulf.*

Some key questions about eddic poetry as oral poetry

The literary history of Old Norse eddic poetry poses some major questions for scholarship, principally because of our inability to establish first-hand contact with its pre-literate being and form. Some of the key questions that have engaged researchers in the twentieth and twenty-first centuries include the following:

- How old is eddic poetry as a literary form?
- How old are the individual poems in eddic metres that we now know?
- In what circumstances was eddic poetry performed, and what was its social function?
- Who were the composers and performers of eddic poetry?
- Was eddic poetry composed throughout Scandinavia or only/mainly in the West Norse linguistic area?
- What was the compositional process like among oral performers of eddic poetry?
- How was eddic poetry transmitted from one practitioner or generation to the next, and how was it preserved?
- Is it likely to have changed greatly in the course of its oral history or was it relatively fixed?

A number of these questions demand complex answers, which can only be dealt with in summary fashion here. The question of the ultimate age and origin of eddic poetry cannot be answered precisely. On formal, metrical grounds Old Norse eddic poetry is indubitably a branch of the West Germanic alliterative measure, and is thus likely to be of considerable antiquity (see *SkP*, I, General Introduction, §4.1: li–liv). Its subject matter also suggests antiquity: in the selection of texts that have been preserved in writing, at least, it deals with mythological lore relating to the pre-Christian religion, with narratives about the pre-Christian gods, giants, and dwarfs, and with the deeds attributed to legendary figures, such as Vǫlundr and Sigurðr, who have known counterparts in the alliterative poetry of other West Germanic literatures. The prose *fornaldarsögur* (sagas of ancient times) incorporate legendary poetry that also often has a counterpart in the Danish history of Saxo Grammaticus and in other early sources. An example is the so-called death-song of the hero Hildibrandr, preserved in *Ásmundar saga kappabana* (*The Saga of Ásmundr the Champion-killer*). It is only in Old Norse eddic poetry, however, that we find the subject of the gods and other supernatural beings treated centre-stage. The absence of this topic from the repertoire of Old English, Old Saxon, and Old High German alliterative poetry is presumably to be accounted for as a suppression of pre-Christian lore brought about by those societies' earlier adoption of Christianity, whereas in Old Norse, by the time this poetry came to be written down such topics were no longer regarded as a threat to Christian belief (see Lindow's chapter in this Handbook [Chapter 6]), though Snorri Sturluson's presentation of these poems' content in his *Gylfaginning* is circumspect, to say the least.

Indications from the period of writing in the thirteenth and fourteenth centuries are that poetry in the main eddic verse-form, *fornyrðislag* (old story metre), was considered old by people at that time (hence the verse-form's name). The fact that much eddic poetry is cited in *fornaldarsögur* confirms the medieval view that it belonged largely to a past age, as do certain statements found in the prose links and comments to the major Icelandic compilation of eddic poetry, the Codex Regius of the Poetic Edda (GKS 2365 4°) of *c*.1270. There is also evidence that court poets of the twelfth century and their royal patrons considered *fornyrðislag* inferior to *dróttkvætt*, the main skaldic metre at that time, at least as a medium for poetry composed for important socio-political occasions (see *SkP*, I, General Introduction: lv). On the whole, the legendary and mythological subject matter of much eddic poetry also supports its status as an 'old' art, by contrast with skaldic poetry, which deals largely with living or only recently deceased subjects, while the late medieval genres of *rímur* and ballads revive some of the legendary subjects of eddic poetry in new verse-forms. On the other hand, we cannot draw hard-and-fast boundaries between poetry in eddic verse-forms and skaldic poetry: a good deal of skaldic poetry was composed in *fornyrðislag* at least to the end of the twelfth century (see *Háttatal*: 86–7), and we must also reckon with an antiquarian revaluation of old subjects in later medieval Iceland, such as we find in the reworkings and amplifications of eddic poetry apparent in some of the late manuscripts of certain *fornaldarsögur*, such as *Qrvar-Odds saga* and *Gautreks saga*.

A further question about the age of eddic poetry concerns the relative antiquity of the various poems that have been preserved in writing. This issue has vexed scholars, and a number of arguments have been produced to distinguish individual poems as older or younger than others, but there is little consensus about what the criteria for determining relative age should be: should subject matter, diction, linguistic forms, or metre be paramount here? The most recent and most thorough review of this difficult question has been Bjarne Fidjestøl's posthumous *The Dating of Eddic Poetry* (1999). Questions of relative age are also considered in the individual chapters of *Kommentar zu den Liedern der Edda* (von See et al. 1997–). The difficulty of the dating question is bound up with the possibility that the versions of eddic poems we know from medieval manuscripts may themselves have been adapted to the tastes of later generations and so may be overlaid with neologisms and other 'modern' features (see Thorvaldsen's chapter in this Handbook [Chapter 4]).

The oldest securely datable examples of Old Norse poetry in eddic verse-forms are a small number of runic inscriptions in the Older Futhark (the earliest runic alphabet, *c*.150–700), comprising very short texts, usually of a commemorative nature. The Viking Age produced a greater number of runic inscriptions in verse, mostly in eddic verse-forms, particularly in Sweden where there was a fashion for erecting runestone memorials for dead family members. The most significant example of this period is the long Rök stone inscription from Östergötland (Ög 136, *c*.800), part of which is in *fornyrðislag* verse. The fashion for erecting runestones waned after *c*.1100, when literacy using the Roman alphabet on treated animal skins slowly made headway in Scandinavia. Most of the runic inscriptions of a later period are on wooden sticks, pieces of animal bone, or small artefacts. Some inscriptions are also found on church walls and portals. A considerable number of runic inscriptions from the twelfth century onward, many in verse, were excavated from the merchants' quarter of the Norwegian town of Bergen (cf. Liestøl 1968, 1981), and these have broadened our understanding of the longevity and reach of eddic poetry within Scandinavia. Some of them reveal that both skaldic and eddic poetry known from medieval Icelandic manuscripts were also inscribed on rune sticks by the urban communities of Bergen and Trondheim, and some of this dates from the later fourteenth century, such as the rune stave B257 from Bergen, which bears some similarities to parts of the poem *Skírnismál*. In all probability, if wood had been more commonly preserved, we would have a broader picture of the extent to which eddic and skaldic poetry was recorded on rune sticks and other wooden artefacts in Norway, and perhaps elsewhere.

The performance contexts and social function of poets composing in traditional eddic verse-forms in the pre-literate period in Scandinavia can be deduced in part from comparative evidence, such as the passage from *Beowulf* cited above, and inferred from what we know about the role of poets in Nordic society in the Viking Age. We must bear in mind, however, that the Norwegian courtly environment in which Viking Age skalds flourished was almost certainly rather different from the environment in which traditional eddic poetry was performed. In fact, we know rather little directly about the latter, nor do we know whether traditional poets were men, women, or both.[3] No names of any eddic performers have come down to us, in contrast to the situation with skaldic poetry, where the names of poets have usually been recorded alongside their compositions.

Were eddic poets of high social status, like the *þegn* of *Beowulf*, or could anyone compose and recite eddic poetry (assuming the two functions were performed by the same individual)? Did such poets perform in halls and farmhouses or at open-air religious ceremonies, or on other social occasions, such as at weddings, drinking parties, and funerals? Some *fornaldarsögur*, such as *Qrvar-Odds saga* (*The Saga of Arrow-Oddr*), clearly represent what Lars Lönnroth has called the 'double scene' of poetic performance ([1979] 2011: 243–59), where there are examples of poems comprising insulting dialogue between male rivals – the *mannjafnaðr* ('comparison of men') – presented within a prose narrative describing the performance in a drinking hall. The audience of the saga could then recognise and appreciate a familiar performance context and identify with the participants.

A good number of eddic mythological poems, such as *Vǫluspá* or *Vafþrúðnismál*, purport to be the utterances of supernatural beings in dialogue with one another, or speaking directly to an audience, like parts of *Hávamál*, but it is usually assumed that these poems are literary fictions of a human poetic voice and that a human audience for these fictions completed the locutionary circle. However, some scholars have taken a different view. Writers such as Magnus Olsen (1909) and Bertha Philpotts (1920) have considered eddic poems with mythological subjects as scripts for ritual dramas, in which human actors took the parts of the gods and other supernatural beings whose speech is represented in the poems. This approach has been adopted more recently by Terry Gunnell (1995), who has pointed to features of the Codex Regius manuscript that may resemble stage directions for the various actors. Although there is evidence from post-medieval Scandinavia that dramatic performances, such as Gunnell envisages, existed, there is no contemporary evidence to back up the hypothesis he advances (see Gunnell's chapter in this Handbook [Chapter 5]).

Several key questions that occupied many twentieth-century scholars of eddic poetry were focused on the process of oral composition and on whether Old Norse eddic poetry was the product of a memorial tradition, in which poets memorised poems without great change from one generation to the next, or whether they composed afresh from a repertoire of verbal formulas they stored in their memories, formulas that fitted the metrical requirements of the alliterative line, but could yet express variations on a particular concept, using a selection of different words from a copious fund of poetic diction they had learnt and stored in their memories. These questions were provoked in the middle of the twentieth century by the oral-formulaic theory proposed by the classical scholars Milman Parry and Albert Bates Lord, who set out to investigate how the ancient Greek oral poet Homer could have composed such long and complex epics as the *Iliad* and *Odyssey* in a society without writing (cf. Lord 1960). To answer this question, they conducted field research among non-literate singers in the territory then called Yugoslavia in the period before the Second World War, but their work did not become widely known until the 1950s. Their main hypothesis – that Homer and other pre-literate composers of long poems relied on oral formulas to organise and structure their work – aroused great interest among medievalists, including Old Norse scholars, who studied the oral prehistory of alliterative poetry in the various Germanic languages. Initially, emphasis was laid upon a store of varied phrases (formulas) that could be identified in the corpus of eddic poetry (cf. Kellogg 1988), but later it was generally accepted that eddic poetry probably belonged to a memorial tradition, even though a certain proportion of formulas existed and could be deployed in various ways within eddic poems (Lönnroth 1971 and 1981; Harris 1983). These are particularly evident in the case of *Vǫluspá*, which exists in three separate versions: in the Codex Regius, in Snorri's *Edda*, and in Hauksbók (AM 544 4°), as discussed below. Among the most significant variations we find in this poem is the beginning of stanza 3, referring to the earliest history of the world. Both the Codex Regius and Hauksbók read *Ár var alda | þat er Ymir byggði* ('It was in ancient times when Ymir [a giant] lived', *Vsp* 3/1–2), while Snorri's text replaces the second line with *þat er ekki var* ('when nothing existed'). Both second lines fit the metre, but mean profoundly different things. It has been suggested that Snorri chose his version because it conformed more easily to Christian doctrine (cf. *Gylfaginning*: 58), but it could equally be that it was a variation of some antiquity.

The period of medieval textualisation

As we have seen, textualisation of Old Norse eddic poetry begins with the earliest runic inscriptions, a proportion of which are in poetic form. However, most runic texts are short and purposeful: they commemorate someone who has died, invoke the protection of a god, or warn those who see them not to desecrate a memorial. The advent of writing using the Roman alphabet, together with techniques of preparing animal skins as writing surfaces, was gradual and non-uniform in Scandinavia, extending across the eleventh and twelfth centuries, if not later in some places.

Writing allowed people to record much longer and more diverse texts, both in Latin (the language of learning) and in the Scandinavian vernaculars. As far as we now have evidence, the textualisation of eddic poetry in manuscripts took place only in Iceland, although the Bergen rune sticks show that it was probably written down somewhat more widely in parts of Norway, and perhaps elsewhere in Scandinavia. The late twelfth-century Danish historian Saxo Grammaticus clearly knew some vernacular poetry corresponding to some of the Icelandic eddic poems, both from the Codex Regius compilation and from *fornaldarsögur* (see Friis-Jensen 1987). He records in the Preface to his *Gesta Danorum* that he is indebted to the men of Iceland for some of his material (*Gesta Danorum*: I, 1.4, pp. 6–7), and this may have included eddic poems, although it is also possible that he knew Danish versions of some of these texts.

The Codex Regius of the Poetic Edda

There are several types of textual repository for eddic poetry in the medieval Icelandic manuscript tradition. The first, and best known, is a single manuscript compilation from the latter part of the thirteenth century, GKS (*Den gamle kongelige samling*, The Old Royal Collection) 2365 4°. This small quarto vellum was written in Iceland *c.*1270, although exactly where is unknown, as is its history up until 1643, when it came into the possession of Bishop Brynjólfur Sveinsson of Skálholt. Bishop Brynjólfur was an antiquarian and manuscript collector. He recognised many of the poems in the compilation because he had previously read parts of them in the *Edda* of Snorri Sturluson (see section on 'Snorri Sturluson's *Edda* and its manuscripts'), where they are quoted to support Snorri's exposition of Old Norse mythology. Brynjólfur mistakenly assumed that the poems he found in the new manuscript were composed by an early twelfth-century Icelandic scholar and historian named Sæmundr Sigfússon, and borrowed from there by Snorri, so he named the compilation *Sæmundar-Edda* (*Sæmundr's Edda*), reusing the title *Edda* that had been applied to Snorri's work from medieval times. In 1662 Brynjólfur sent the manuscript as a gift to King Fredrik III of Denmark, and it remained in the Royal Library, Copenhagen, until it was returned to Iceland as a national treasure in 1971. It is sometimes referred to as the Codex Regius ('codex of the king') because of its long stay in the Danish royal collection. It is distinguished from another royal manuscript, the Codex Regius of Snorri's *Edda*, by the phrase Codex Regius of the Poetic (or sometimes Elder) Edda. It is now in the Arnamagnæan Collection of Icelandic manuscripts at the University of Iceland.

It is not known what title the compilation GKS 2365 4° had in the medieval period, or indeed if it bore a title at all. The modern term 'Poetic Edda' is based on Bishop Brynjólfur's false assumption, but cannot now be avoided as it has passed into common parlance and has in fact given its name to Old Norse alliterative poetry generally, as we speak of 'eddic' poetry when we discuss poetry in *fornyrðislag* and other related verse-forms. A number of the poems in this compilation are found nowhere else, and, as an anthology of the repertoire of eddic verse, selected and arranged by one or more anonymous compilers of the thirteenth century, this manuscript is uniquely valuable.

We do not know exactly when Icelanders started to commit their orally transmitted eddic poetry to writing. It has sometimes been suggested that Snorri Sturluson, who is thought to have composed his *Edda* in the 1220s, may have had written texts of some of the eddic poems he cites available to him, possibly in small booklets of a few vellum leaves. This is a plausible hypothesis, but no external proof one way or the other exists.[4] Snorri's texts are not always exactly the same as those in the Codex Regius of the Poetic Edda and other manuscripts in which eddic poetry has been recorded, which may point to competing oral variants circulating in Iceland in the late twelfth and early thirteenth centuries. Certainly the impetus to record and systematise old lore from pre-Christian myth and legend seems to have been common to Snorri and to whoever compiled the Poetic Edda.

The Swedish scholar Gustaf Lindblad, who studied GKS 2365 4° over a period of some years, came to the conclusion that the compilation had a textual history of some complexity, and that more than one compiler was involved in putting it together during the course of the thirteenth century (Lindblad 1954 and 1980). In its present form the manuscript comprises forty-five leaves, but there is a lacuna where a number of leaves have been lost between the poems *Sigrdrífumál* and *Brot af Sigurðarkviðu*, and scholars have speculated about which now-lost poems were in the gap (Schier 1986). To judge by the manuscript's overall arrangement and the witness of *Vǫlsunga saga* (*The Saga of the Vǫlsungs*), they were from the poetic repertoire on the subject of the life and deeds of the hero Sigurðr.[5]

The Codex Regius of the Poetic Edda was shaped by one or more compilers, who should perhaps rather be called editors. They seem to have had the intention of gathering together poetry about the pre-Christian gods and other supernatural beings, on the one hand, and, on the other, poetry about well-known legends and heroes. From a modern perspective all these narratives can be classified as myths, but this seems not to have been the way these medieval scholars saw them. There are thirty-one separate poems in the manuscript, arranged in two groups: the first, mythological group, comprising eleven poems; the second (and larger) group, devoted to heroic subjects. Within the two major groupings, several sub-groups can be identified. The first, third, and fourth mythological poems deal with fundamental lore about the creation of the world, its peopling with various beings, their exploits, and the way in which that world came to an end. These poems – *Vǫluspá*, *Vafþrúðnismál*, and *Grímnismál* (Grímnir is a name for Óðinn) – also formed the basis of Snorri Sturluson's prose account of the same topics in his *Gylfaginning* (*The Deception of Gylfi*) (a legendary Swedish king), and he quotes freely from them in his text. The second poem of the compilation, *Hávamál*, likewise served as a model for Snorri, especially in the frame-narrative to *Gylfaginning*, because it brings the enquiring but naïve human subject into the world of the gods (Lindow 1977). Of the remaining mythological poems, three are dialogic agonistic exchanges (ON *sennur*, sg. *senna*) between supernatural beings, which frame the allusive mention of many myths or myth fragments: *Hárbarðsljóð* (Hárbarðr is a name for Óðinn) is an exchange between the gods Óðinn and Þórr, *Lokasenna* one between the god Loki and numerous gods and goddesses at a banquet, while *Alvíssmál* pits the god Þórr against a dwarf, Alvíss, who intends to abduct Þórr's daughter. The remaining four mythological poems are of a more narrative kind and deal with a single subject (or two subjects, in the case of *Hymiskviða*). They are *Skírnismál*, on the subject of the god Freyr's love for a giantess, Gerðr, and his servant Skírnir's proxy wooing of her; *Hymiskviða*, about the gods Þórr and Týr who visit the giant Hymir in quest of a brewing cauldron for the gods; *Þrymskviða*, the story of how the giant Þrymr stole Þórr's hammer while he was asleep and how the god was forced to impersonate the goddess Freyja in order to recover it; and *Vǫlundarkviða*, about the legendary craftsman Vǫlundr, his capture by a tyrant, Níðuðr, and the vengeance he wreaks on the tyrant's sons and daughter as he escapes his captor by flying away. In some respects *Vǫlundarkviða* belongs more to the heroic than to the mythological poems, and, unlike the latter, has counterparts in other Germanic traditions, especially the Anglo-Saxon and the German, but it also has analogies with the classical myth of Daedalus the master-craftsman.

The heroic poems in the compilation are more numerous than those about the pre-Christian gods and cluster in groups based on their subject matter. Three poems about Norwegian heroes (Helgi Hundingsbani and Helgi Hjǫrvarðsson) begin this section, and they are followed by a large group of poems (which would have been larger if the manuscript did not contain a lacuna) on the legendary clan of the Niflungs, including the hero Sigurðr, slayer of a dragon; his sworn-brother, Gunnarr; and the two women in their lives, Guðrún and Brynhildr. Through Guðrún, her various marriages, and her brothers and sons, the Niflung legend is linked to the story of the deaths of two legendary tyrants, Atli (Attila the Hun) and Jǫrmunrekkr (Ermanaric the Goth), and these latter narratives are told in *Atlakviða, Atlamál,* and *Hamðismál.* Much of the Niflung legend is paralleled in the *fornaldarsaga Vǫlsunga saga,* where a number of the same poems as are found in the Codex Regius are cited within a prose narrative.

The compiler(s) of the Codex Regius of the Poetic Edda attached explanatory prose introductions and colophons to a number of the poems, and sometimes included passages of prose between stanzas of individual poems to explain things they must have thought their audience (or posterity) would find obscure. Sometimes these explanations concern elements of the poem's storyline that are not explicit in the text, while at other times they explain customs or beliefs that were no longer practised. In several of the mythological dialogue poems the speaker is indicated in the manuscript by the extrametrical formula, *kvað X* ('X said'). Gunnell (1995: 282–329) has suggested that these formulas may be indicative of the poems' use by actors in dramatic performances. However, similar extrametrical phrases introducing direct speech are found quite widely in manuscripts recording early Germanic dialogic poetry, including the Old Saxon *Heliand,* the Old High German *Hildebrandslied,* the Old English *Fight at Finnsburh,* and the Old Norse *Eiríksmál* of *c*.954 (see Fulk et al. 2008: 288, n. to *The Fight at Finnsburh,* l. 24; *SkP* I, 2: 1003–13). It is more likely that the device is a method whereby early scribes accounted for the often abrupt transition between indirect and direct speech than an indication that the poem in question was scored for dramatic performance.

The development of prosimetrum in medieval Icelandic writing

Extrametrical interventions in the Codex Regius show how the desire to write down eddic poetry in anthologies necessitated the development of prose links within and between poems. These made narrative progression more explicit than it was in the often allusive or cryptic poems themselves and, indeed, allowed the construction of a narrative that embraced several whole poems. Such prose links could also provide extrametrical connections between one poem and another, and indicate groupings of poems that had common subjects or were linked (as the Niflung group are) by common characters who came, unhistorically, to be regarded as members of extended families. Such impulses towards systematic narrative, particularly clear in the heroic poetry of the compilation, show affinities with two other bodies of Old Icelandic text that combine eddic poetry with prose narrative, Snorri Sturluson's *Edda* and its manuscript tradition on the one hand, and, on the other, the development of the sub-genre of the Icelandic saga called the *fornaldarsaga*. It is likely that these two developments began about the same time, in the late twelfth or early thirteenth century, alongside the development of other saga genres that incorporated skaldic rather than eddic verse in the body of their texts.

The combination of verse and prose in alternating segments of variable proportions is referred to by the term *prosimetrum* (see further Harris and Reichl 1997), and is common in a great deal of Old Icelandic literature composed in the thirteenth and fourteenth centuries, though often extant only in manuscripts of later date. Much of both the eddic and skaldic poetry that has survived in writing has been recorded in prosimetra, and, as the poetry is often presented as having been composed in the period before the advent of writing, its incorporation into more modern prose texts can be understood as allowing what Preben Meulengracht Sørensen (2001) called 'voices of the past' to be heard, and heard authoritatively, in later ages.

Snorri Sturluson's Edda *and its manuscripts*

A group of medieval Icelandic manuscripts record versions of the *Edda* of Snorri Sturluson (1179–1241) and other texts associated with the art of poetry, as well as certain eddic poems, some of which are also in GKS 2365 4°.[6] Together these manuscripts constitute a significant witness to the important place poetry held in early Old Norse, and particularly Icelandic, society. Several manuscript versions of Snorri's *Edda* exist, none earlier than the early fourteenth century. However, it is likely that the work took shape in the 1220s, and it seems to have existed in several versions. Without going into the fine detail of Snorri's work here, it can be stated that in its fullest form his *Edda* comprises four parts: a Prologue that situates the work in the context of medieval discussions of non-Christian religions; *Gylfaginning*, an exposition of Old Norse mythology, carefully framed as the words of a group of euhemerised figures who claim to have knowledge of the old, pre-Christian religion; *Skáldskaparmál* (*The Language of Poetry*), an exposition of the diction of skaldic poetry; and *Háttatal* (*List of Verse-forms*), an exposition of Old Norse metrics exemplified in a poem of 102 stanzas in praise of the Norwegian king Hákon Hákonarson (r. 1217–63) and his uncle jarl Skúli Bárðarson (*c.*1188–1240).

There are two ways in which eddic poetry is preserved in the *Snorra Edda* manuscripts. The first is as citations within Snorri's own text. This happens, as has been mentioned earlier, particularly within the text of the *Gylfaginning* section, where *Vǫluspá* provides a basic framework for Snorri's own account of the creation of the world and its inhabitants, together with their later destruction and the world's partial renewal. A considerable number of stanzas from *Vǫluspá, Vafþrúðnismál,* and *Grímnismál* are cited in *Gylfaginning,* together with some stanzas from other poems in the GKS 2365 4° collection. These stanzas, put into the mouths of ancient gods and giants, function in the prosimetrum as direct witnesses to the deeds and thoughts of these beings in ancient times. Although *Skáldskaparmál* is largely devoted to skaldic poetry, some poems and stanzas in eddic verse-forms appear there, most of which are unknown from any other source. They include a stanza in the verse-form *ljóðaháttr* (song metre), which the god Þórr is said to have addressed to a raging river, Vimur, ordering it to subside so that he could cross it (*Skáldskaparmál*: 25), and the poem *Grottasǫngr* (the name of a magic mill), which is extant in only two *Edda* manuscripts (*Skáldskaparmál*: 52–7; 187–8). *Grottasǫngr* is the complaint of two giantesses, Fenja and Menja, who have been forced by the Danish king Fróði to grind gold, peace, and prosperity for him without a break. They take their revenge by grinding out an army to move against him and kill him (see Tolley 2008; Quinn 2013b).

The second way in which eddic poetry is preserved in manuscripts of Snorri's *Edda* is through addition to the compilations in which it is contained, not by incorporation into Snorri's texts. Two manuscripts, the Codex Wormianus (AM 242 fol of *c.*1350) and AM 748 I a 4° (of *c.*1325), contain eddic poetry that is not presented as part of Snorri's work. An incomplete eddic poem, *Rígsþula,* occurs in the Codex Wormianus immediately after the compilation's presentation of Snorri's *Háttatal.* This poem is found nowhere else; it tells how the god Heimdallr, calling himself Rígr, visits various human families and begets children on them, thereby creating a class-defined society of slaves, free farmers, and aristocrats. There has been considerable debate among scholars about the age and provenance of this poem, with its message of god-given social hierarchy (cf. Hill 1993; Bagge 2000). The manuscript AM 748 I a 4° consists of six leaves and contains a collection of eddic mythological poems, most of which are also found in the Codex Regius collection. This manuscript was formerly bound with AM 748 I b 4°, which contains an incomplete version of the *Skáldskaparmál* section of Snorri's *Edda*. In order of citation, the eddic poems in AM 748 I a are: *Hárbarðsljóð, Baldrs draumar, Skírnismál* (so titled, whereas Regius has *Fǫr Skírnis* 'Skírnir's Journey') to the end of stanza 27, *Vafþrúðnismál* (in part), *Grímnismál, Hymiskviða* (so titled, whereas Regius has the descriptive title *Þórr dró Miðgarðsorm* ('Þórr pulled up Miðgarðsormr')), and the beginning of the prose introduction to *Vǫlundarkviða*. Though the order is different, and there is variation in some lines, all these poems are also in the Codex Regius, with the exception of *Baldrs draumar*, which has not been recorded elsewhere.

Eddic poetry recorded in **fornaldarsögur**

The Icelandic *fornaldarsögur*, a sub-genre of the saga set in the prehistoric past, generally in Scandinavia outside Iceland or even further afield, were composed probably from the late twelfth into the fifteenth centuries. About 70 per cent of them contain poetry, almost all of it in eddic metres. One can deduce that old-style poetry was thought appropriate to stories about the prehistoric age, in contrast to more recent narratives, which were largely authenticated by skaldic verse. The poetic content of individual *fornaldarsögur* varies from a few stanzas to well over a hundred, while the proportion of verse to prose also varies considerably. In some sagas, like *Hervarar saga ok Heiðreks* (*The Saga of Hervǫr and Heiðrekr*) and *Hálfs saga ok Hálfsrekka* (*The Saga of Hálfr and the Hálfr-champions*), it is clear that the prose text, which provides a basic storyline linking several long poems, is quite perfunctory. Each of these sagas exists to provide a narrative frame for eddic poems probably of some antiquity, such as the *Hlǫðskviða* (*Poem of Hlǫðr*) of *Hervarar saga*, which tells of ancient battles between Gothic and Hunnish leaders on the central European plains. *Vǫlsunga saga* is another *fornaldarsaga* in which the main purpose of the prose text is to paraphrase eddic poems, a number of which also appear in the Codex Regius of the Poetic Edda. There are six stanzas or part-stanzas recorded in this saga that are not in the Codex Regius, and these presumably come from poems that were in the lacuna in the Regius manuscript

(Neckel and Kuhn 1962: 321–3). On the other hand, some creators of *fornaldarsögur* did not use much poetry in their narratives, even when it was probably available, as with the famous last battle of the hero Hrólfr kraki in *Hrólfs saga kraka*, which is narrated without any poetic quotation.

All the *fornaldarsögur* mentioned so far were probably based on old stories and incorporated poetry, some of which, at least, was probably old, though some may have been reworked and sometimes augmented or amplified to suit the tastes of later audiences. These sagas were clearly based on legendary material of some antiquity, some of it known in other Germanic literatures and in the Latin writings of Saxo Grammaticus. Other sagas of this genre centre round the exploits of ancestors of families who migrated from Norway to Iceland in the late ninth and early tenth centuries; the group of sagas of the men of Hrafnista (Modern Norwegian Ramsta), an island off the coast of Nord-Trøndelag, falls into this category. The protagonists of these ancestral sagas, like Ketill hœngr (Ketill Salmon) and Ǫrvar-Oddr (Arrow-Oddr), show a number of similarities to their descendants in sagas of Icelanders, such as *Egils saga Skallagrímsson* (*The Saga of Egill, Son of Skallagrímr*). It is hard to know in these cases how old the verses attributed to these half-legendary ancestors may be; their themes, however, and the verse genres to which they belong (see below), are traditional. There are also a number of *fornaldarsögur* that contain eddic poetry that is probably rather young – not earlier than the fourteenth century, maybe sometimes later than that. In some examples of late sagas, as in *Hjálmpés saga ok Ǫlvis* (*The Saga of Hjálmpér and Ǫlvir*) or in *Friðþjófs saga ins frœkna* (*The Saga of Friðþjófr the Bold*), the manuscript preservation of the poetry has been very poor and many lines are unmetrical or garbled. In other cases, younger manuscripts, from the later fourteenth and fifteenth centuries, have greatly amplified the texts of the poetry attributed to the saga protagonists. This is the case with younger manuscripts of *Ǫrvar-Odds saga*, where a comparison with earlier versions of the text reveals the process of amplification over time. It is likely that this process also occurred in other late sagas, such as *Gautreks saga* and *Friðþjófs saga*. Whatever the age of the eddic poetry within individual *fornaldarsögur*, we find poetry using four main traditional modes or compositional units, which can also be found in the poetry of the Codex Regius corpus (see Schorn on genre, Chapter 12 in this Handbook). These are the prophetic or vaticinatory mode, the principal eddic exemplar of which is *Vǫluspá*; the wisdom-contest, found in *Grímnismál*, *Vafþrúðnismál*, and *Alvíssmál*; the gnomic mode, which we encounter in *Hávamál* and *Sigrdrífumál*; and the *senna* and closely related *mannjafnaðr*, which have both mythological and heroic exemplars in the Codex Regius collection, in the form of *Hárbarðsljóð*, *Lokasenna*, and the flytings of the heroes in the three Helgi poems. This maintenance of traditional compositional units, even in young sagas, indicates the persistence of eddic structural conventions into the later medieval period in Iceland, even when metrical conventions had become vague.

Eddic poetry in historical compilations

There are three eddic poems that appear in late Icelandic historical compilations, *Vǫluspá*, *Hyndluljóð*, and *Merlínússpá*, the last of which is an Icelandic translation, done into eddic poetry, of the Latin prose prophecies of Merlin in Geoffrey of Monmouth's *De gestis Britonum* (*c.*1130), formerly known as *Historia regum Britanniae*. While *Merlínússpá* is the work of a known author, the Benedictine monk Gunnlaugr Leifsson (d. 1218 or 1219), the other two poems, like most other eddic poetry, are anonymous. All three of these poems probably owe their place in historical compilations to their literary mode and subject matter, which is vaticinatory; they are poems of prophecy within compilations that deal with the history of the world and encyclopaedic works. *Vǫluspá*, which is also found as the first item in the Codex Regius and is quoted, in part, in Snorri's *Edda*, appears in the compilation Hauksbók, of the early fourteenth century, in the context of Christian theological subjects, clearly as a native theology. *Merlínússpá*, another prophetic poem of native Celtic tradition, also appears in this manuscript as part of the Icelandic prose translation of Geoffrey of Monmouth's work, *Breta sǫgur* (*The Sagas of the British*).

The eddic poem *Hyndluljóð* is preserved only in another large compilation of historical material, Flateyjarbók (GkS 1005 fol.), dated to the late fourteenth century. It falls into two parts. The first part consists of a dialogue between a giantess, Hyndla, and the goddess Freyja, who wishes to discover the ancestry of her protégé, Óttarr, in order that he may understand his heritage and entitlements to ancestral lands. The second part of the poem (stanzas 29–44), which Snorri evidently knew and called *Vǫluspá in skamma* (*The Short Vǫluspá*) (*Gylfaginning*: 10) ranges over topics such as the origin of some of the gods and giants, the coming of a mysterious being *ǫllum meiri* ('greater than all', *Hdl* 43/2), and the events that will lead up to the end of the world.

Conclusion

There was more eddic poetry in Icelandic oral tradition than ever made it into written form. Just how much did not achieve textualisation we do not know, but certainly there are pointers in the direction of lost poems, both from later treatises on medieval poetics, such as the so-called *Laufás Edda* (*c.*1609), which contains texts not known from medieval manuscripts, and from references in Snorri's *Edda* to unknown poems and their subjects. Some of the narratives in Snorri's *Edda*, too, which he cites without any poetic back-up, such as the long narrative of the god Þórr's visit to the Otherworld being Útgarða-Loki, may well have existed in poetic form.

Even though eddic verse-forms were probably considered passé in some circles after the twelfth century, both in Norway and Iceland, their use in Iceland continued into the late medieval period and was favoured for a number of anonymous prophetic and moralising poems, such as *Sólarljóð* and *Hugsvinnsmál*, which are hard to date, but may be from the later thirteenth century or possibly considerably later than that.[7] The influence of *Hávamál* and *Vǫluspá*, in particular, is easily perceptible in these poems: the choice to compose them and *Merlínússpá*, which, like *Hugsvinnsmál*, is a translation from Latin, in eddic metres is clearly based on a recognition that such types of poetry should, by convention, be in eddic rather than skaldic metres. Thus, poets – and presumably their audiences – remained aware of the conventions and inherited subjects of eddic poetry over a long period of time, stretching from the unknown pre-literate beginnings to the early modern period (see Hughes 2013). That a probably seventeenth-century pastiche of eddic mythological poetry, the *Hrafnagaldur Óðins* (*The Chant of Óðinn's Ravens*) (see Lassen 2011), could still be seriously considered medieval by editors and scholars into the twenty-first century speaks both for the continuity of Icelandic knowledge of eddic poetry and for the skill of the composer of this antiquarian work.

Notes

1. The English translations of this and other Old English or Old Norse texts are my own.
2. The terms 'illocution' and 'perlocution' are based on distinctions enunciated by the philosopher J. L. Austin in *How to Do Things with Words* (1962).

An illocution is an act of ordering, warning or undertaking, performed in saying something, whereas a perlocution is an act of speaking or writing that aims to bring about an action but which does not in itself effect or constitute that action. Words of persuasion are perlocutionary acts.

3. In later written texts, women (especially old women) are sometimes associated with the performance of eddic poetry, especially for the purposes of sorcery (e.g. *Buslubœn* in *Bósa saga*) or prophecy, but this may not reflect the situation of eddic poetry in earlier centuries; rather, it may be a symptom of the marginalisation of this type of poetry in the period after the Viking Age.

4. But see the account of the booklet now designated AM 748 I a 4° below; such a collection of poems could well give an idea of what early compilations were like.

5. *Vǫlsunga saga* is preserved in an early fifteenth-century manuscript (NkS 1824 b 4°) but may have been composed as early as the mid-thirteenth century.

6. There have been several explanations of the meaning of the title *Edda*: that it means 'great-grandmother' (and so indicates the poetry it analyses was old-fashioned); that it means 'the book from Oddi' (the farm where Snorri grew up); and that it means 'Poetics'. The last-named is the most likely explanation (see Faulkes 1977a).

7. See the edition of these poems in *SkP* VIII: 287–449. *Hugsvinnsmál* is a free adaptation of the second- or third-century Latin didactic poem *Disticha Catonis* ('The Distichs of Cato').

CHAPTER 2

Traditions of eddic scholarship

Joseph Harris

This chapter characterises some types of eddic scholarship as 'traditions' or 'streams (of tradition)'. It is in no way a full history of scholarship on eddic poetry; but, because traditions everywhere in cultures represent similar phenomena flowing through history, the traditions of eddic scholarship treated here can, it is hoped, suggest the lineaments of such a history. And despite academia's emphasis on originality, tradition is a force in scholarship no less than in literature or culture in general. Possibly scholars are more aware of it even than poets – who famously suffer 'the burden of the past' – precisely because consciousness of our traditions is or should be an integral and conscious part of our practice. The vagueness of this vocabulary – rather than, for example, 'schools' or 'foci' – has the advantage that it obviously seeks to adumbrate rather than to offer sharp differences, and in this way reflects the borderlessness of actual thought. This chapter's contribution is itself part of a tradition – albeit a humble one – of surveys of scholarship, and some of the best of its antecedents (for example, Fidjestøl, cited just below) succeeded in giving their material a historical feeling by allowing underlying binaries to exert structural force. Fully appreciative of that heritage, I nevertheless seek to avoid such structure here. No survey can absorb all its predecessors, so it is still worthwhile reading surveys of various ages and emphases, even the oldest.[1]

At present, the single work best representing the development of eddic scholarship is an unfinished posthumous book, *The Dating of Eddic Poetry* from 1999, written by the Norwegian scholar Bjarne Fidjestøl and saved for us after his premature death by his colleague Odd Einar Haugen. Although Fidjestøl's specific interest is dating, the problem of how to place these poems in time, his reading was so comprehensive and his analyses so fine that the book gives the best available picture of the development of studies in eddic poetry generally, even if only through the prism of dating. Anyone interested in a more comprehensive

historical view of scholarship on eddic poetry would be advised to go
next after this chapter to Fidjestøl's book.[2]

Not every engagement with eddic poetry, even every serious engagement,
is to be counted as scholarship. We reserve the word 'reception' for engage-
ments intended for popular, artistic, and political purposes. Elsewhere in this
Handbook Heather O'Donoghue treats the subject of eddic reception,
especially in the Romantic and pre-Romantic period (mid-eighteenth
century through to the mid-nineteenth) (see Chapter 18). This is the period
of the first wide knowledge of Nordic lore outside Scandinavia and a time
of special interest to students. The study of reception can (as in this
volume) itself be scholarship; a capacious study of eddic reception is
underway in Frankfurt, which should help with research and generally
with information about the broad scope of the ways this material has been
used.[3] Especially pertinent to students of literature after the Romantic
period is the eddic reception of Richard Wagner, William Morris, and
J. R. R. Tolkien in the higher artistic realms, while Thor comic books and
movies occupy a lower level. During the interwar years (and before) there
were considerable cults in the Baltic region and Northern Europe that
fetishised 'the Edda(s)' (O'Donoghue 2007, and Chapter 18 in this
Handbook), and the Nazis made extensive use of eddic material for
propaganda. Difficulties in distinguishing between 'reception' and 'scholarship' arise with earnest would-be scholars of the early periods who are
simply too far below the threshold for scholarship now. As an example:
Jacob Schimmelmann (1712–78) approached 'scholarship' when he
attempted the first German translation of Snorri's *Prose Edda* in 1777,
even though its quality was condemned from the beginning; but he also
believed that 'the Edda' was the oldest book in the world after the Bible,
that it was God's revelation to the people of the North, and that it was
probably written in his very own Prussian province of Pomerania (Fidjestøl
1999: 10, 17–18; Krömmelbein 1998). The dividing line between reception
and scholarship is a gradual one, subject to collective judgements and to
revision over time: what once seemed scholarship eventually slips into the
bucket of reception. Still more difficult are instances of real scholars who
invested labour and learning in producing new contributions, but
who undermined their authority by cultural emotionality or prostituted
their talents to political expediency; this phenomenon too is graded, and
opinions vary about individuals from recent history.[4]

With this distinction established, we can say that the story of *professional
scholarship* on eddic poetry begins, arguably, in the decade around 1870
(although a special word must be said below about Jacob Grimm, who died

in 1863, and about mid-nineteenth-century German scholarship). For a full discussion of this general assertion see Fidjestøl's chapter '"Normal Science" after Grimm' (and cf. Sijmons 1906: cxiv–cxxiv on the period 1860–88). This claim may be easier to make in foreign languages and international English than in traditional English, which does not normally extend 'science and scientific' to the humanities, where, for the impartial pursuit of knowledge, 'scholarship' is employed instead; for example, German *Wissenschaft* and Norwegian *vitenskap* cover both areas, the sciences and the humanities. In any case, a number of scholarly/scientific events around 1870 together strongly support Fidjestøl's idea that, at about this time, eddic scholarship entered a new and more 'scientific' phase (for example, Bugge 1867; Jessen 1863, 1869, and 1871); this scientific phase is most important for Fidjestøl's interest in (scientific) dating, but the era carries similar significance for eddic studies generally. Linguistic, philological, and metrical knowledge made great strides beginning in this period, and more loosely related fields such as archaeology, history, and anthropology seem similarly to have entered new phases in the late nineteenth century.

There are also practical reasons for starting around 1870 and focusing especially on Scandinavian scholarship (following Fidjestøl), but it would be a mistake totally to overlook the foundations laid by nineteenth-century German scholarship. For, in many ways, nineteenth-century Germany boasted the world's intellectual centre and surely the liveliest scene of scholarship in the humanities. Jacob Grimm (1785–1863), in conjunction with his brother Wilhelm (1786–1859), is of course revered as a founder of multiple disciplines in the humanities: folklore and mythology, the historical study of law and language; on his own, Wilhelm was an important initiator of the study of (heroic) legend and aesthetic approaches to early Germanic poetry. The results of the work of the Grimms extensively shaped the milieu in which the eddic 'Great Leap Forward' of about 1870 took place; yet their most important direct contribution was a partial edition, with accurate translation, of the heroic poems in 1815. This had been anticipated in 1812 by a very prolific editor and populariser, Friedrich von der Hagen (1780–1856), who came to hold the most important humanities professorship in Germany. Another excellent German Scandinavianist active in the mid-century period was Theodor Möbius (1821–90), who produced his own edition of almost all the poems in 1860. But probably the most important of these eddic philologists in mid-century Germany was Karl Müllenhoff (1818–84). His most direct effect on eddic scholarship was through the last volume of his ambitious and unfinished series *Deutsche Altertumskunde*; the fifth volume – finally (and partially) printed in 1883, but representing work over a long period of time – consists of an edition of *Vǫluspá* with a defence of its mythology as native and a thorough account of the Codex Regius and its *Liederheftchen* or pre-existing booklets.

Orality, literacy, and scholarship

Writing came to Scandinavia with the Latin of the Church, beginning toward the end of the tenth century and in Iceland more precisely 999/ 1000. But the change from an oral culture such as pre-Christian Scandinavia was in the Viking Age to a high-medieval literate culture would have been a slow process; in fact, neither of these conditions – the oral nor the literate – will have existed in a pure and unified state, and our contemporary literate culture would be a poor conceptual model. The term *Vokalität* has been adapted for the mixed culture of Anglo-Saxon England (Schaefer 1992) and provides a better model for Scandinavia and Iceland, whether or not we adopt the term. The impurity of the oral state is made obvious by the existence of an ancient form of vernacular writing in runes – which may have affected oral poetry (Harris 1996 / 2008 and 2010; Jesch 2001: 10–11 and 2005) – and by the encounters Viking Age travellers must have had with the writing of their southern trading partners (or victims). At least one scholar has recently attempted to assess the overall influence of the newer literate culture upon the traditional oral life that continued side by side with it (Mundal 2010), and others have documented the evidence of the progression and influence of literacy in Iceland (Quinn 2000). Attention to 'oral traditions' in connection with, especially, the prose literatures of Iceland and Norway has a lengthy genealogy (e.g. Gísli Sigurðsson 2004b; Andersson 1964; Liestøl 1930; Heusler 1914), and to a certain extent knowledge that 'oral transmission' must have been involved in the background of the poetry has long been obvious. But since about 1960 this 'knowledge' has evolved, and oral-focused or oral-related studies become an industry. We must investigate briefly some roots and results of this modern consensus.

The origin of modern oral studies can be traced to the 1920s and '30s with a young Harvard classics professor, Milman Parry, who wrestled with one version of the ancient 'Homeric questions' – how did 'the poet' (or poetic tradition) compose the long epics in an epoch before writing? He found the answer in the structures of Homeric language, but confirmation came from the 'living laboratory' of oral epic in Yugoslavia, where illiterate poets still composed in performance – in effect, improvised – thanks to their training in a highly predictable poetic language compounded of formulas, themes, and type-scenes. After Parry's early death in 1935, Albert Lord (1912–91) continued his fieldwork, and it is Lord's *The Singer of Tales* (1960) that earned worldwide recognition for the 'Oral-Formulaic Theory' (later Oral Theory). Lord's work quickly inspired followers in philosophy (e.g. Havelock 1963; Ong 1982) and sociology (e.g. Goody and Watt 1968), as well as philology and literary history (e.g. Magoun 1953). A whole school of folkloristics based on performance was from the beginning influenced by Lord (e.g. Bauman 1977). One exciting thing about Lord's book was its extension beyond its empirical base in Homer and South Slavic, for Lord seemed implicitly to claim that all poetry in pre-literate societies was composed in a manner similar to that of the Serbo-Croatian men's songs or epics and also that formulaic structures in preserved poetry of unknown origin (for example, *Beowulf*) proved it 'oral' in his sense. But these two points also called forth a great deal of controversy. Anthropologists drew attention to a wide variety of poetry in oral cultures (e.g. Finnegan 1977), and philologists showed formulaic structure even in verse translated from Latin. Today, most Anglo-Saxonists would regard *Beowulf* as 'oral-derived' rather than 'oral' in Lord's sense.

In Scandinavia, the effort to extend a strict form of Lord's model, especially to eddic poetry (Gísli Sigurðsson 1990; Mundt 1997), was largely unsuccessful for reasons I have discussed previously (Harris 1979 and 1983). (See Haymes 2000 for a brief but comprehensive sketch of these developments, together with an attractive historical thesis.)[5] But the excitement of Lord's novel vision gave impetus, starting in the 1970s and '80s, to new studies of value (e.g. Lönnroth 1971, 1979, and 1981). A number of different ideas about composition and performance were floated in this period for poetry in Old Icelandic, including eddic poetry, and much of the secondary literature down to about 1984 is listed and discussed in Harris 1985. Since about 1985, several studies have appeared more or less in the vein of the Oral Theory, or tweaking it. Two of the most substantial are Acker 1998, with brilliant refinements of Oral Theory in connection with repetition, and Mellor 2008, a meticulous, text-grounded study directly in the spirit of Lord. A third major work is difficult to classify: Meletinsky 1998, published in Russian in 1968, nods to Parry and Lord but derives from an older and specifically Soviet viewpoint – a complete study of the 'folkloric' bases of eddic poetry and its relationship cross-culturally to the 'archaic epos'.[6] It is no surprise that the oral should figure in studies of the versions of *Vǫluspá* (Quinn 1990b; Mundal 2008). This thought, activating the oral in connection with *Vǫluspá*, goes far back in Old Norse research, and instances of parallel preservation of texts have also been the proving grounds for theories of oral composition/transmission (Lönnroth 1971; Harris 1983), methodologically based, to a large extent, on earlier studies in Old English. Basic studies of the composition and delivery of oral eddic poetry have been attempted (Harris 1983, 2000a, and 2000b; Gunnell 2008), and here one must mention the problematic, probably insoluble, relationship to music (Harris 2003, 2004). The most successful new departure is Terry Gunnell's 1995 (and later) study of dramatic performance, and 'performance' has become a keyword. Beyond the literal level in drama and influence from the Performance School (Harris and Reichl 2012), the ideas of performative social drama (Bauman 1986; Borovsky 1999) and of literature itself as a kind of speech-act performance (Lönnroth 2009) have become familiar in Old Norse studies. The Old English scholar Katherine O'Brien O'Keeffe has made probable the idea that scribes who knew the vernacular verse system sometimes varied their copy poetically in something like composition in (writing) performance (1990). The movement of emphasis in the study of oral eddic verse over time has thus been from composition to transmission, to delivery and performance, and (potentially) back to composition. In the future a more synergetic connection to the literate parallel culture can be expected (see below and see further Gunnell, Chapter 5 in this Handbook). What is quite new in all this is the way – gradually, starting in 1960 or at least since about 1985 – awareness of an oral component has filtered into most studies in the areas of social and literary history and aesthetics.

The Oral Theory was, as I suggested above, made especially appealing by its seemingly universal claim, a sort of evangelical thrust that took the doctrine beyond the homeland of Homer and the Balkans; but exponents of the Theory in Northern Europe may be said to have 'lost the battle but won the war'. Ong's excellent but now inadequate synthesis of 1982 begins to show just how pervasive 'the oral' is in human societies. This is true also of their study: without the concept of 'orality', 'literacy' could not be understood as it is today and would not figure so largely in fields such as history (e.g. Clanchy 1979/1993; Ásdís Egilsdóttir 2006) and sociology (Goody and Watt 1968; and see Goody's later works). In my experience, consciousness of these two interdependent concepts permeates the 'human sciences' as it never did before World War II. The opposition adds subtlety and distinctions to modern (since the '60s, perhaps) thought, whether or not Ong was right that 'writing is a technology that reshapes the mind'.

In fact, anthropologists and sociologists have disagreed for several decades on the 'Great Divide' between an oral and a literate mentality (e.g. Olson and Torrance 1991; Street 1984; Harris 2010: 119–20; Finnegan 1988; Vail and White 1991: 1–39 'The Invention of "Oral Man"'). This has not prevented some Old Norse scholars from accepting this Divide as an important socio-psychological caesura in Nordic cultural history (e.g. concerning gender in cultural history: Mundal 1983; concerning mentality: Bergsveinn Birgisson 2008). It is possible that my brief account here of the 'invention' of orality exaggerates the originary force of the Oral Theory through a sort of Harvardian local patriotism, and I would be happy to be corrected by some less biased future synthesiser, a new Ong. Within Old Norse studies there are still sceptics; but sometimes (like Tolley 2002) their scepticism is directed at outdated models, and in any case their resistance testifies to the importance and ubiquity of the oral topic. This explains why, in our further discussion of the 'traditions' of eddic studies, there will be interventions from the oralist viewpoint.

Age and origin

The prime complex of problems facing the generation of 1870 dated far back into the 'pre-scientific' period: the dating and the provenance of eddic poetry. The two questions are interrelated from the beginning because if the poems are older than the settlement of Iceland (*c*.870–930), as most learned men thought, then they must have originated elsewhere. There was never any doubt that the 'preservation' had been in Icelandic manuscripts.[7] Fidjestøl cites amusing instances of the vast differences of estimated date among the older writers (e.g. 1999: 5, 9) and also shrewd anticipations of later developments (e.g. 1999: 31–2, 40–1), but both date and provenance were given their first *modern* treatment by a Danish philologist, Edwin Jessen (1833–1921), in 1871. However, to appreciate the 'reset' provided by this still radical paper, we need to glance at the scholarly climate of Scandinavian nationalism, particularly in the 1860s. The leader of the 'Norwegian school', Rudolf Keyser (1803–64), believed the eddic poems generally to date from before the Viking Age – in part, long before – and to be of Norwegian origin. This view was countered by the arguments of the Dane Svend Grundtvig (1824–83) for southern Scandinavia as the ultimate home of the poetry and/or more broadly for a 'common Nordic' perspective; he generally agreed with Keyser, however, about the early age of the verse.[8] Keyser was not without critics at home, one of whom, the young Gustav Storm (1845–1903), became a great historian and Old Norse scholar. Jessen's assault on *his* older countryman was sharper. On the provenance question he ridiculed nationalism as old-fashioned and refocused on Iceland as not only the point of preservation, but also that of origin in the most basic sense. This meant that Jessen dated the poems much later than any contemporary (but see Vésteinn Ólason on the Icelandic poet Benedikt Gröndal [2008a]), namely in the eleventh and twelfth centuries, a few even in the thirteenth; the distribution of dates among the poems, however, was not that of more recent scholars. Jessen's evidence was partly linguistic, but to a surprising extent relied on his *feeling* for the material: 'internal criteria'. If, however, a contemporary today should imagine that feeling to be something like 'literary appreciation', he/she would be surprised by Jessen's rather negative assessments of the quality of eddic poetry.

Jessen's 'modern breakthrough' against the Germanic romanticism that held sway from the Grimms up to Grundtvig was joined or anticipated by a few years by the Germans Konrad Maurer (1823–1902) and Theodor Möbius; by an Icelander famously active mainly at Oxford, Guðbrandur Vígfússon (1827–89); and especially by the Norwegian Sophus Bugge (1833–1907). By 1896 Bugge was able to announce a consensus on the age of the poems: all scholars agreed that no poem could be older than the ninth century (Bugge 1896/1899: 2; Fidjestøl 1999: 97). This rare agreement was based mainly on the establishment of the Proto-Nordic/Old Norse boundary (period of syncope) and on metrical analyses by Jessen and Bugge that proved that word forms in the runic language before c.800 would violate the new metrical laws.[9] As an example of Bugge's panache at its best, we can glance at a short paper on syllable length and the rules for line endings in *málaháttr* and in the full line of *ljóðaháttr*, a paper read to a learned conference in 1879. At about page six of a six-and-a-half-page article, Bugge drops a literary-historical bomb: no *ljóðaháttr* poem can have existed before the eighth century because its language forms would breach 'the law I have just demonstrated . . . It is, then, hereby proven that all the poems composed in *ljóðaháttr*, without exception, are younger than the Middle Iron Age. They cannot have existed earlier – at all events, not unless in a form so different that, considering it, one would have to speak of different poems' (1879: 145).[10]

The present-day scholar, aware of the multiforms of oral poetry and the ubiquity of performance could, ironically, agree with Bugge's hedging phrase: 'different poems' might be considered a concept essential to our understanding of poetry in a pre-literate society where every performance to some extent revises the material of its input, though not necessarily in the oral-formulaic sense. Communication models conceived in terms of writing and mechanical reproduction come naturally to us but can be anachronistic or simply incongruous with an oral culture. The dating consensus of Bugge's day was based on taking the final form of poems (*c.*1270 for the Codex Regius) as the objects of study. Today many of us would instead consider these final forms reifications of their poetic history. Some scholars of Bugge's day had this insight too (Fidjestøl 1999: 96–7 on Anton Edzardi), but Bugge's immediate audience in the 1879 paper, which included Grundtvig himself, seems to have been flabbergasted at the logical QED that relegated their ancient verse to the (to them, recent and decadent) Viking Period.

One favoured device for establishing relative chronology has long been (at least since Jessen) to interpret similar passages in different poems as borrowings. A good example is Jan de Vries's article on dating (1934a); the author lists and critiques most of the well-known criteria (for example, style, language, metre and poetics, etc., ending with his own kenning study). Concerning verbal echoes and the relative chronology they yield, de Vries exposes the fallacious logic employed by scholars to support their own decisions about which was the 'original' and which the borrower ('der Plagiator' [!], 258); de Vries is right in saying that the real decisions were based on preformed ideas of chronology (257). De Vries is, however, still wedded to the idea that in the examples cited either A borrowed from B or vice versa ('zwei Möglichkeiten', 257). However, not only do the varying schemes of the different scholars contradict each other, but all such arguments should be relativised by recognition of the common poetic language and especially of 'formulas'. (A recent persuasive study of such 'borrowings' is Thorvaldsen 2008b.) I would not wish to be understood as asserting that the 'two possibilities' are *never* possibilities, but the whole question deserves a discussion in terms of the third possibility presented by the oral basis of such poetry. Such a discussion, essentially a coming to grips with what it is we should be trying to date under the cover term 'the poems', exceeds the limits of this essay, but a good beginning can be found in Fidjestøl's conclusion to the first part of his book (187–203, including his account of Meulengracht Sørensen 1977 and 1991) and in Thorvaldsen's chapter in this Handbook (Chapter 4).

Once Bugge's generation had settled the date question as Viking Age or later, some of the nationalistic steam went out of the sister question: *provenance*. 'The poems' (whatever that exactly meant) could have originated in Iceland or in Norway or elsewhere in the West Norse area settled from Norway and still have shared a common language: *norrœn* or West Scandinavian. More importantly, each poem could have its own history before the period of collection and arrangement; among the clues were place names, scenery, details of language (especially vocabulary), and echoes of other poems, whether or not interpreted as a key to relative chronology. On this basis, the Icelander Finnur Jónsson (1858–1934) maintained for decades (for example, 1894: 56–78) that most of the poems came to Iceland from Norway, while his countryman Björn M. Ólsen (1850–1919) answered with a passionate but professional case for Iceland as the home of most of the collection (1894). Bugge became the chief spokesman for origins in the Norse-settled West (Britain, the Western Isles, Orkney), though he was not the first or last such spokesman. At about the same time, Guðbrandur Vígfússon was also asserting western origins (see Fidjestøl 1999: 94–6), and much earlier the German Enlightenment historian Friedrich Rühs had claimed a direct derivation of Icelandic poetry from Old English (1813) – rather a different form of the western theory and one quickly rejected in its day. Bugge's own western arguments are complicated by his internationalist beliefs (discussed below).

Of course, the provenance of one poem, *Atlamál*, seems to be made clear by the descriptor 'Greenlandic' in Codex Regius; Greenland, as point of origin or as immediate source, has been generally accepted (though usually rejected for the companion *Atlakviða*, equally 'Greenlandic' in the manuscript).[11] One of the best candidates for the localisable provenance of an individual poem is *Vǫlundarkviða*, and here we can in all brevity get a sense of the provenance debate then and now by matching Bugge's article in the *Saga-Book* for 1901 with John McKinnell's in the same journal in 1990. Bugge's fiendishly complicated discussion requires a Norwegian poet who receives a long poem in Anglo-Saxon, the common source of *Vǫlundarkviða* and the Old English poem *Deor*. One of Bugge's blind spots can be illustrated by his treatment of the Codex Regius reading *frā* with macron at *Vǫlundarkviða* st. 18/7. He rejects the standard expansion *fránn (mækir)* in favour of the Old English preposition *fram* read as postpositioned with *mér*, explaining '*fram* is here most likely preserved from the English model, with the meaning of *frá*, in spite of the fact that *fram* used as *frá* does not occur in Old Icelandic' (1901/1992: 295). This shows what Walter Ong might have called the 'chirographic imagination': Bugge's conception of what would have to have been a phase of *oral* literary history is entirely in terms of a manuscript culture. Bugge's long article makes fascinating reading today, but its reception at its reading (in his absence) before the Viking Society in 1899 was, as the minutes show, quite negative but very insightful. Mr Alfred Nutt began with: 'As usual with Prof. Sophus Bugge we find a curious instance of circular reasoning'; and the discussion went downhill from there (see Bugge 1901/1992: 'Proceedings,' 370).

By contrast, the modern version by McKinnell is one of the best articles of its kind I have read: impeccably scholarly, logical, and concise; another difference from Bugge is that part II of McKinnell's article deals insightfully with the legend and the poem as literature – the modern turn. But McKinnell's neat summary of his historical results – 'it is in the Yorkshire of the 10th or early 11th century that I would tentatively place the poem' (1990: 13) – partakes of the old chirographic concept, projecting 'the poem' back into the past. If I could revise this summary, I would substitute for 'the poem' a phrase such as 'the probable origin of the oral tradition leading to our preserved *Vǫlundarkviða*'.[12] In any case, we should not assume that this Norse-English 'origin' accounts for the legend as a whole. Bugge was at pains to reject the significance of German traces that had already been suggested in his day, while McKinnell recognises and integrates them into the development of the legend. And in fact, a Continental Weland tradition should not be discounted: a recent archaeological find in southern Sweden shows this strand of tradition, attested by the German–Norwegian *Þiðreks saga*, to be separate from the Norse-English strand and probably a little older, *c*.950 (Helmbrecht 2012). The relatively thin lines of communication in writing, even allowing for huge losses, are not comparable to the ubiquity of communications in the original human medium, of which only sparse accidentally recorded and accidentally preserved traces remain.

If we imagine provenance in concentric circles widening out from Iceland, the further out we go – Norway, Britain, the Western Isles – the more important it becomes to free our minds of the strictures of writing. The outermost circle that has been seriously claimed is Continental – in other words, older German. The Grimms and practically all later students have assumed that the heroic poems or the material out of which the main heroic poems grew – which was, after all, comprised of story material of Burgundian, Gothic, or Frankish origin with names of places such as the Rhine, individuals such as Attila, and ethnic groups such as the Huns – came to the North from Central Europe. Analogues in West Germanic medieval languages – and plain reason – make this broad generalisation impossible to deny, but there unity ends and both dating and the concepts of 'oral traditions' and 'the poems' become crucial again. And national feelings again become relevant. The topic of poetic traditions from the

Continent is, as a whole, too big and baggy for our chapter (for an earlier attempt see Harris 1985: 101–6; and Larrington's chapter in this Handbook [Chapter 8]), but a brief summary is essential here. The idea is simple: if the story material (the legend) came to the North from the Germanic-speaking Continent and at least some of the time came in poetic form, then verbal, phonological, or metrical traces of those vectors may still be traceable. A good deal depends on the assumption of verse forms and of the durability of those forms.

Hans Kuhn (1899–1988), one of the central figures of all times in eddic studies, published a series of studies in the 1930s that established certain laws of syntax and word order in the Old Germanic languages (1933) and further descriptive rules of Old Norse poetry, skaldic and eddic (1936; 1939). These three articles are exceptionally difficult, but Fidjestøl orders the material intelligibly and tests Kuhn's procedures in an impeccably scientific manner. Kuhn divided eddic poetry, that dealing with human heroes rather than gods, into three main categories: (1) 'foreign matter' poems (*Fremdstofflieder*, the heroic poems with Germanic background), subdivided into older and younger subgroups; (2) a 'domestic' group (heroic but with no South Germanic analogues) – both these groups are in *fornyrðislag*, the northern heir of Common Germanic metre – and (3) all *ljóðaháttr* poems (also 'domestic', but in the uniquely Scandinavian metre). Against these groups he tested his laws. One of Kuhn's main interests was in testing for Continental Germanic influence; but for dating (Fidjestøl's concern), the results are murky and difficult to interpret, and relatively little survives Fidjestøl's critique. The third article, however, tried to make plausible metrical (and some dictional) influence from West Germanic verse with, in my opinion, more success; in 1985 I felt that this third article was something every student of eddic poetry should take seriously. This still seems appropriate to me, but Kuhn's arguments should be reconciled more fully with the more comprehensive oralist approach so widespread beginning about 1960; the reconciliation might not be easy.[13]

We have been considering 'provenance' dispassionately as meaning simply *either* where were 'the poems' (one or more of them) incubated *or* from where did they come to Iceland? During the most nationalistic period, however, when the talk was of 'our forefathers' and 'national honour' and when eddic poetry was frequently qualified by 'our', 'provenance' tended to mean ownership of a heritage (the title of a Danish review article from as late as 1965 was 'Edda og saga: vores åndelige ejendom?' [Edda and saga: our spiritual property?]). During the 1960s and '70s a good deal of world attention was focused on the slow but peaceful way Denmark and Iceland settled the disputed ownership of the material heritage – the manuscripts – with a clear conclusion: most Icelandic manuscripts – including, crucially, the most important eddic manuscripts – were repatriated. Actually, the process was much longer, beginning in 1907 and ending only in 1986 (for a historical outline, see Gísli Sigurðsson 2004a). In the newly independent republic (from 1944) the Icelandic people felt a 'passionate and irrational love ... for this unique phenomenon'; 'To many people, the return of the manuscripts represented the final phase in Iceland's campaign for independence, insofar as such a campaign can ever end' (Vésteinn Ólason 2004: vi, v). Now the mass of Icelandic manuscripts has been declared a world heritage under UNESCO: Iceland, of course, owns and maintains the eddic manuscripts, which also belong to mankind.[14] The case of the contents – the intellectual heritage – should be similar, but a little more complex: it belongs to the centre, Iceland, and variously to the concentric rings of provenance, but as a whole to the global community, humanity generally. In fact, the German Enlightenment scholar August Ludwig Schlözer (1735–1809) had already claimed Icelandic literature, including especially 'die Edda', for 'world literature' in 1773 – using the term *Weltlitteratur* over fifty years before Goethe first popularised the idea.[15] In the twenty-first century, world literature – but also intellectual property – is again on the humanist agenda, and surely 'our' eddic poetry deserves a position there.[16]

International connections

Once students of eddic poetry had discovered (or imagined) non-native *sources* or *influences*, a search for provenance became something else. Such discoveries are based on perceived similarities, but *analogues* had and still have a different meaning and use. When, for example, Sanskrit or Avestan writings or Ossetic myth turn up analogues, scholars do not typically interpret these as sources but may be willing to entertain the idea of a hypothetical common source in the dim Indo-European past. Frequently, though, we recognise analogues without taking this reconstructive step and remain content without explanation or take explanatory refuge in similar framing conditions, such as social structures. The reconstructive procedure has most frequently taken place within a heritage framework, the Indo-European framework, and at the level of myth rather than that of poetic form.[17] Much closer to home than the far-flung analogues of anthropology and Indo-European studies, similarities from classical and early medieval Christian cultures have been more readily taken as hard sources or more softly as influences. We can clearly discern a 'stream of tradition' built on such source-hunting and again, perhaps, a chirographic thought pattern intruding into essentially oral territory (as argued below).

Faith in specifically Christian sources of eddic poetry goes back to well before the generation of 1870 (cf. above on Schimmelmann), but we can take up this story again in Bugge's Christiania (Oslo), and first with Anton Christian Bang (1840–1913), the learned (Lutheran) bishop of Oslo, whose discovery of the relationship – which he took to be one of source and derivative – of *Vǫluspá* to the Greek–Latin–Christian tradition of Sibylline Oracles.[18] Bang's booklet of 1879 may be the Prime Mover of the Christian turn in modern times; it was quickly translated into German (1880), and Bugge came out in support and early became the head of this 'tradition'. Bang's theory received some early support in the German-speaking countries, but also very strong resistance in Scandinavia, especially in the form of a rebuttal by the famous Swedish author Viktor Rydberg (1881), which received its own replique by Bugge (1881). In the introduction to his edition of *Vǫluspá*, Müllenhoff polemicised from a conservative German position against Bang's theory and Bugge's various interpretations (Müllenhoff [1883] 1908: 3–71 sporadically). In this contentious atmosphere Bugge made the shrewd prediction that in the future Bang's comparison of *Vǫluspá* with the Sibylline Oracles would be considered a major step forward (1881: 172). This came true late in the twentieth century, and in our time, when a Bangian revival has drawn in many excellent scholars, and this source claim or consequences drawn from it have become major factors in edda criticism.[19]

Strong influences from Bugge are evident toward the end of Bang's booklet (explicitly in the etymological derivation of *vǫlva* from *sibylla*; probably in Ireland as the likely nexus between the Old Norse poet and the Oracles; perhaps also in the contemptuous tone and disallowance of *Vǫluspá* as a source for Old Norse religion; cf. Müllenhoff [1883] 1908: 41–2). In any case, already by 1881 Bugge was committed to the argument that most of Old Norse mythology was based on Christian/classical sources, learned through English and Irish contacts during the Viking Age. He may have absorbed the western theory of origin from Guðbrandur Vígfússon, who had a little earlier made it a settled part of his writings (1878: clxxxiii–cxciv); Müllenhoff ([1883–91] 1908) traces Bugge's conversion to the Christian theory to 1876 (43). Bugge's theories of the 1880s acquired some important disciples, especially Kaarle Krohn, an influential founder of Finnish folkloristics.[20] By 1899, however, Bugge's fluent insistence was getting a bit old: in the already quoted minutes of the Viking Society, Dr Karl Blind protested 'against [Bugge's] always trying to prove the Scandinavian mythology to be a mixture of classical myths and Christian lore. … [Dr Blind] thought Professor Bugge's attack on the origin of the noble Scandinavian mythology had failed' (Bugge 1901/1992: 'Proceedings' 372). Bugge's restless effort to 'ruin the sacred truths' is not, as a whole, taken very seriously today: on the one hand, details such as his blunt derivation of *Loki* from *Lucifer* and of Loki's brother *Býleistr* from *Beelzebub* (Bugge [1881] 1889: II, 73–83), and, on the other, the enormous complication of his myth derivations, are likely to cool the enthusiasm of the rare contemporary reader. Bugge's strengths and weaknesses were tightly intertwined: he was learned in the whole western tradition and in languages, but an unmoderated gift for combinations and perhaps a desire to startle undercut the value of his cultural criticism. And despite extensive work with oral folklore, chirographic models dominated his sensibilities. The brilliance of the overall structure of Bugge's eddic work should, however, not be slighted: he bequeathed to us his great edition of 1867; he contributed to the development of metrical science and proved (though not alone) that 'the poems' were not older than the Viking Age; it followed that the myths and some heroic stories could be from that same period; in the Viking Age, Norwegians settled and traded in the West and so potentially came into connection with Christians who had elements of classical culture too in their keeping; ergo, similarities with those cultures could be interpreted as sources, or at least as influences.

Some principal instances of other source studies – i.e. sources outside the eddic/Germanic circle – were discussed in various places in Harris 1985 (for example, the derivation of *Lokasenna* from the Greek satirical symposium [98–100]), and I concluded that of this kind of 'source', none had been proven (106). Since that survey, the field has perhaps moved toward a vaguer concept, *influence*, such as the mooted influence of courtly love on *Skírnismál* (Heinrichs 1997). The eddic subfield of gnomic poetry is the area where, in my opinion, the source hunters have come closest to success. I surveyed this subfield down to about 1983 (1985: 107–11) with scepticism. Since then, the important publications that touch on the literary-historical or specifically source-dependency aspect of gnomic poetry include Hermann Pálsson 1985 and 1999. Larrington gives comprehensive references (up to 1993) to this aspect of *Hávamál*-studies and has

what I consider the right sceptical viewpoint (see also Larrington 1992b).
Most recently John McKinnell has patiently demolished almost all the
claims of gnomic dependency on the *Disticha Catonis* (2007a). We are
dealing with common ideas that spread orally, often in proverbs or in verse
that is part of a world of oral verse. It is true that the *Disticha Catonis* was
a school text, and some oral continuity between the schoolroom and the
oral everyday is perfectly possible. But proving a source in this arena still
seems no better than 'promising'.

A 'source', at least as I am using the word, is very closely bound up with
the written word; it is precise and unvarying in ways foreign to oral culture.
In this sense 'original, imitation, and allusion' belong to the stable (or more
stable) written language of a chirographic culture such as that of classical
Rome. True, an essentially oral genre such as the ballad sometimes takes up
fixed language from print, and in the rigid forms of oral skaldic poetry
there appear to be cases of borrowings and imitations. But insofar as eddic
poetry is oral in essence, its attested language part of a great oral sea of
poetic language never systematically attested in writing, I think that
'influence' and 'analogue' are the proper terms for its relationships outside
the circle of eddic verse itself. So I like the way Karl G. Johansson closes his
Bangian study: it is not so much a matter of a *source* as of 'the European
apocalyptic tradition ... [providing] models' (2013: 180). For one point
I would like to make about the early versions of this stream of tradition is
that Bugge saw his arguments not as an attack but as a *projection* against an
international background, perhaps a *normalisation* in terms of the Indo-
European and European contexts; for this reason he starts his 1881 series by
embedding Nordic myth within Germanic and Indo-European. Plausible
source and influence studies can be produced by this Christianising
tradition, but I would emphasise that anti-nativist approaches are most
charitably viewed as internationalising efforts that allot to eddic poetry
space in larger worlds of literature. The Chadwicks' *Growth of Literature*
and Bowra's *Heroic Poetry* are big canvases of this kind, and they leave
room for chronologically deeper contextualisations such as those of Calvert
Watkins (e.g., 1970).

Philology old and new

Philology is a tricky concept, praised and damned, and through the
centuries too variously defined for comfort. It encompassed all language
study before the birth of linguistics, later continuing alongside linguistics
as the study of language in texts or of texts themselves with special concern

for language. In the Old Norse realm it attends lovingly (*philo-*) to words (*-logy*) actually used in cultural objects – for example, manuscripts or runic inscriptions. For the medieval period in general, philology depends on writing, and any 'philology' of the spoken word (which is, strictly, only possible after recording devices – i.e. 'contemporary') goes by different names (e.g. pragmatics). This leaves a large gap between the philology of the elite literate culture and the mass orality of the early Middle Ages in Scandinavia. Since all students of eddic poetry must attend lovingly to the eddic poetic language, we are all to that extent philologists. It follows that when 'philology' is used *within* eddic studies, it connotes an extra level of attention, extra precision, and often a willingness to take on cultural objects that those of us who specialise in the 'loving' part of philology (e.g. literary types) may be less keen on. Within eddic philology, several recognisable 'streams' are treated elsewhere in this Handbook, including dating, paleography and codicology, metrics, and onomastics; but, again, there is no aspect of the study of eddic poetry as represented in this book that does not depend on 'philology'. There is no way to practise editing or to write on diction and style, for example, in the absence of 'philology'. The story of traditional philology within eddic studies is told chapter by chapter in this Handbook. In this section I wish to add only a brief consideration of the most recent branch of the discipline: the so-called New (or Material) Philology.[21]

New Philology may be part of a movement generally to emphasise the material basis of culture; more certainly, it is a revitalisation movement within medieval philology, a fundamentalism harking back to the basics of manuscript culture as those basics are redefined in postmodern ways. A rich literature has grown up on the subject since the end of the 1980s, a literature which includes first-rate theoretical contributions from Old Norse scholars.[22] New Philology largely rejects the stemma and its mind-set, with its heroicisation of the 'author' (over the scribe) and its drive to 'origins' and to the hypothetical 'archetype'. Unity and the *Stammbaum* (a genealogical or family tree) are replaced by distribution and the network. The scholar should attend to variation, for every manuscript is validated as a unique cultural expression. Bernard Cerquiglini's seminal book bears the poetic title *Éloge de la variante*, and one of his maxims is widely quoted: 'L'écriture medieval ne produit pas des variants, elle est variance' [medieval writing does not produce variants, it *is* variance] (1989: 111). This is a living, creative chirographic culture, and this abundant life is reflected also within individual manuscripts, where nothing is accidental and juxtapositioning can be art or political statement. Attention to audience is not focused on

the 'original' work so much as on 'audiences' for each manuscript, thus
involving the market and sociopolitical factors. The value of variation
applies too, though somewhat differently, at the level of content, especially
story, and includes, in contrast to modern times, regular and respected
reuse, recycling, and revision of inherited story material. Less central are
certain attitudes in conflict with (some) older philology, such as a reverence
for the preserved text over metrical laws and reluctance to emend (sometimes under any circumstances) or to reconstruct diachronically (see Fulk,
Chapter 13 in this Handbook).

Many of these views were anticipated here and there within the old
philology, but New Philology has packaged them as a doctrine.
In Old Norse, most thought directly on the doctrine has taken place
in connection with prose, especially the saga literature. Eddic poetry
poses different problems if its oral essence is to be taken seriously.
New Philology is emphatically material based, while orality is just the
opposite, located in the voice: what lasts (if it lasts) is only the written
word: *verba volant, scripta manent* [words flee, script remains] (Brink
2005). And yet, oral studies share some basic beliefs with New Philology:
for both, origin and author have less meaning than version and variant,
the *Stammbaum*, less than the network; a living oral culture is generative,
creative, in a similar way, and of course it is traditional, recycling cultural
'material' in a similar way. The decentring of postmodermism seems to
apply equally well to both.

The only essay I have come across that attempts directly to bridge the
gap between pervasive medieval orality and the new doctrine for the study
of its manuscript culture restricts its reference to Old French and does
not seem to have much immediately to offer *our*, eddic, subject.[23] (But
compare O'Brien O'Keeffe 1990, cited above.) If, however, we look to
individual elements of the package, a number of recent studies present
something like New Philology *avant la lettre*. Chief among them is
Gunnell 1995, which carefully examines eddic manuscripts for performance clues on the poetry's oral existence as drama (and see Gunnell,
Chapter 5 in this Handbook). The absence of reconstructed diachronic
dimensions (just where traditional eddic scholarship has preferred them)
perhaps qualifies Edgar Haimerl's Young Sigurd article (1993; translated
into English in 2013): he closely follows the manuscript and asks only what
a thirteenth-century audience would make of the story. By this criterion –
one or a few traits but no ideological declarations – other studies would
surely qualify.[24] One scholar of eddic poetry in its manuscript contexts,
Karl G. Johansson, has worked consistently and consciously from New

Philological premises. In his study of *Rígsþula* and its place in its manuscript, Johansson rules out extensive consideration of a previous life of the
poem (1998). But in two of his articles on *Vǫluspá*, he explicitly attempts to
combine cognisance of the poem's prior orality with methods of the New
Philology (2000; 2005), and one passage well juxtaposes the reciprocal
values of these two approaches:

> ... the interest in literacy – that is in the significance of writing and
> manuscript culture for cultural and ideological development in social
> perspective – has pointed out important new questions. For research on
> oral tradition in a preliterate society, when such research is, despite all, based
> on written documents, it is of course vitally important to study the processes
> which are at work in the transition from a society built on oral tradition to
> an increasingly writing-based society. (2000, 80)[25]

Elsewhere, Johansson has written more programmatically on New
Philology and editing (2010; 2014).[26] A younger generation of scholars
seems already to be bridging or combining the two perspectives – the
material and the vocal – in the eddic field: Bernt Øyvind Thorvaldsen
(2007; 2008a) brings performance perspectives, derivable from written
contexts, to bear on eddic verse and its use in several prose contexts;
Thorvaldsen's 2013 article on *Vǫluspá* in the Codex Regius, along with
Mats Malm's study of AM 748 I a 4° (2007), scour the manuscript contexts
for performance indicators. Both scholars and all who follow this line of
thought are much indebted to Gunnell's drama theory in his 1995 book and
elsewhere.

To close this section, no publication could be more appropriate than
Maja Bäckvall's (2013) study of the representation of eddic poetry (all 137
variant quotations) in the Uppsala version of Snorri's *Edda*. Bäckvall's
premises are those of New Philology: for example, validating this less-than-
mainstream manuscript and its variants as objects of study. She introduces
a refined set of concepts for the 'text' in different aspects and, after a deft
survey of New Philology (44–52), points out that her own approach is too
abstract to qualify fully as 'material philology'. Bäckvall does not draw
conclusions for the oral life of the verses, but in place of that she has
developed a convincing reader-response model that speaks directly to the
question of meaning and function of such a manuscript. As a reader of
O'Brien O'Keeffe (1990), I wonder if the meaning and function illustrated
would not best be understood within the concept of textualisation, the
written realisation of oral verse: assuming a reader of the Uppsala Edda was
still conscious of verse as an oral manifestation, what did he/she make of

these variants? Surely some such genre frame or set of assumptions are necessary to keep the (implied) reader from being a modern, a Stanley Fish, or, finally, ourselves.

Conclusion: the art of eddic poetry

The most difficult stream of tradition to capture in this chapter would be that of *literary criticism* – hence the short (or 'shorter') shrift given it here. It will be useful to recognise two ideal varieties I will call classic and situated criticism. The former is pure literary criticism and hardly exists in the realm of eddic poetry,[27] but some conception of it is necessary to give meaning to the latter, which could be called 'historical criticism' if that term had not been previously claimed.

The *classic* ideal would depend not on outside factors – literacy or orality, philology of any type, literary or cultural history – but simply on the basic questions one asks of any poem: how does this poem work, what work does it do, what is its form, its structure, how does it mean? The poems themselves, though only thirty-odd, depending on how one counts, are so varied that their art must be assumed to be varied as well, and yet a single manuscript tradition and, for the most part, a single collector are responsible for all the centrally 'eddic' poems. In the body of eddic criticism, representatives could probably be found that have roughly kept pace, over time, with the larger literary world in which many of us have been trained: ordinary 'literary appreciation', close reading, New Criticism, formalisms (often flavoured by Freud, Marx, Lacan, etc.), various structuralisms, and post ... Currently gender is a favoured lever for lifting less obvious structure and meaning from these poems (see Chapter 17 by Clark and Jóhanna Friðriksdóttir in this Handbook). For, despite all the importance of the science or *Wissenschaft* that dominates in the 'traditions' of eddic scholarship, it is good to remember that these objects of study *are poems* and worthy of any effort (including any *ism*) that an expounder can marshal. Even a bare trajectory of critical approaches to eddic poetry would, however, be difficult to track, in part because so many articles and books mix literary with other aims. McKinnell 1990 (discussed above) neatly separates its historical-philological component from its literary-critical one (each part representing 50 per cent of the total), but in most cases the relationship of literary to other analysis is not so easily determined. My impression is that the proportion of literary analysis has grown steadily since World War II, probably following the institutional sponsorship of criticism in universities. True, the Swiss scholar Andreas

Heusler (1865–1940) was one of the greatest connoisseurs of all time, but literary- and culture-historical theses usually accompanied his criticism despite the art-for-art's-sake ideology of his time. One would be wading into highly subjective waters in trying to classify, quantify, and assess literary criticism as a 'stream of tradition'. For Old English there was a clear turning point in the 1936 British Academy lecture of J. R. R. Tolkien, so that *Beowulf* criticism falls into 'BT' and 'AT' eras. The criticism of eddic poetry and the poetry itself seem to me too varied to offer a similar shape, or any shape at all, even that suggested by the schools I have mentioned.

A *situated* criticism of eddic poems would attempt to bring contextual factors to bear without sacrificing its essence as criticism, its admixture of the classic ideal, and in practice this is the mode of actual eddic criticism. Dates, verbal dependencies, cultural periods, and regions all influence critical judgements, and in turn scholars assume that critical judgements may contribute to the elucidation of these issues external to the poem. With a body of poetry so removed in time and space it seems impossible to avoid the reciprocal relevance of historical contexts. Does our poem reflect the late pagan revival of the tenth century, or is it to be interpreted out of what we know and believe of the Icelandic renaissance, of Christian or Irish or skaldic influence, and so on? With some of these contexts there is an obvious circularity involved, and of course their applicability varies among the poems. The two most important contexts, relevant to every poem, are its oral descent and its written (or inscribed) preservation. Manuscript context can contribute to a literary reading of the poem as it was interpreted by a thirteenth- or fourteenth-century compiler/scribe and his contemporary audience, but this is not the whole story even if we were to suppose the poem to have been composed for its manuscript context, which is unlikely in almost every case. Some scholars have been convinced of the plausibility of a chirographic origin for one eddic poem, *Grípisspá* (for example, Gutenbrunner 1955), but in my opinion even this poem, generally pronounced late and 'derivative', must necessarily be considered oral-derived: the language of eddic poetry must have been created long before any extant poem, and 'language' here includes not only metre, vocabulary, morphology, syntax, and diction, but also commonplaces, 'themes', type-scenes, and especially genres. *Grípisspá* is, in any case, an outlier, even if the question remains whether it had any life in oral tradition independent of the manuscript in which it is preserved. Criticism situated in the manuscript context is essentially synchronic to the period of the manuscript and may seem mechanically functional to the modern reader (e.g. the narrow didacticism of Haimerl 1993/2013; the simple pedagogical purpose of *Rígsþula*, according to Johansson 1998). Situating a reading in the oral, on the other hand, automatically becomes diachronic and comparative, and also potentially deeper. Of course, situated criticism need not rely on a single context, but good eddic criticism would respect at least the oral and the manuscript contexts. A best-practice example is Judy Quinn's sequence of articles on *Oddrúnargrátr* (2005; 2009): the scribe's earnest efforts speak against reorganisation of the stanzas; appropriate comparisons within the Old Norse corpus normalise *Oddrúnargrátr* as an eddic poem; and Quinn's ingenious close reading yields a meaningful and, indeed, quite a new understanding of the poem. This understanding is fully unfolded in the second study, which unravels the complex dynastic thought of the poem: one is reminded of Lévi-Strauss's myth, which seemingly infinitely generates new realisations of an original binary, here triangular, problem. (Do not Borgný's twins, a boy and a girl, two angles of an as yet unrealised triangle, paradigmatically project the dynastic problem into the future beyond the poem?) In any case, this usually neglected poem is revealed as a serious poem of ideas, and Quinn (2009) closes with an admirable statement on eddic art and criticism.

All eddic scholars are to some extent philologists, but not all have imbibed literature in the crib. Eddic literary study thus has some obligation to account for criticism itself, this largely anglophone, culturally shaped intellectual creation of a definable historical period. For me, criticism comprises two components: an aesthetic and a hermeneutic element. The former analyses mainly formal and structural features of poetry that give pleasure. The latter deals of course with interpretation, the semantics, meaning (including political meaning), affect, and effect on the reader – features of poetry that move or instruct audiences. A cogent objection to criticism might be that we do not know enough of the historical audiences and their sensibility to go beyond descriptive analysis even to aesthetics, let alone to interpretation. This objection would carry more weight if the only audiences for criticism were those of the times of the poetry's oral and manuscript circulation – a worthy goal, never satisfactorily to be attained – but the logical end of that line of thought has been memorably (if unintentionally) sent up in the amusing last chapter of Steblin-Kaminskij's *The Saga Mind*: there, the scholar meets a revenant from medieval Iceland whose language-determined understanding ends with literary scholarship being merely a 'lying saga about a saga' (1973: 151). The audiences of our own time are the audiences we actually have. How much do we have to know to interpret for them? New Criticism intentionally limited the input to the poem itself, but that doctrine silently assumed quite a lot of cultural continuity between poem and interpreter. In eddic poetry, our knowledge is severely limited, but that is no reason to disallow interpretation, which, right or wrong, builds knowledge. And there is still so much to be known about eddic poems as poems.

Notes

1. Examples of some relatively recent eddic surveys limited by period are: Hollander 1963; Mari-Catani 1979; Harris 1985; Andersson and Gade 1991; those limited to dating: Sävborg 1997 and 2004; Andersson 2003; Vésteinn Ólason 2005; those focused on a subgroup: Beck 1990. Among older surveys of dating, de Vries 1934a and Genzmer 1951–3 are particularly good; Noreen 1941 is interesting for its tone in historical context. In addition, most general histories of literature contain surveys of scholarship.

2. Another valuable source is the *Reallexikon der Germanischen Altertumskunde* (1968–2008); no single article exactly coincides with our subject here, but under 'Edda, Ältere,' 'Edda, Jüngere', and 'Eddische Dichtung' (vol. 6 [1985]: 355–94, 394–412, 413–25), together with articles on individual scholars, such as 'Bugge, Elseus Sophus' (4: 108–9), very full coverage may be pieced together. A magisterial introduction to the Poetic Edda with complete *Forschungsbericht*, but only until 1906, is Sijmons 1906: especially c–cxlii.

3. DFG-Projekt Edda-Rezeption (www.eddarezeption.de/index.html). A valuable survey mainly of reception is Clunies Ross and Lönnroth 1999. Two recent studies of reception are Malm 1996 and Böldl 2000.

4. Postwar German scholarship has struggled to come to terms with its past, and the literature on this topic is very extensive. As one example, there is the case of Otto Höfler, a creative and productive scholar whose politics during the Nazi period have (whether justly or not) compromised his work for some contemporaries.

5. Robert Kellogg (diss. 1958), a direct student of Lord and Magoun, remained an Oral-Theory fundamentalist though his articles of 1990 and 1991 have forward-looking observations on textualisation and the Codex Regius; these articles are also interesting for their big-picture generalisations on Germanic 'epic' culture.

6. *The Growth of Literature* (Chadwick and Chadwick 1932–40), a vast socio-logically oriented comparative picture of oral literature contemporary with Parry, should not be omitted here, though its influence in eddic studies has been slight.

7. Actually even this truth has been debated; see the brief treatment in Harris 1985: 78–9.

8. A nuanced appreciation of Keyser, Grundtvig, and this whole debate can be found in Fidjestøl 1999: 70–96.

9. The dating of the period of syncope varies somewhat according to the authority cited (even without Bugge's use of archaeological periods as here); its current

dating is more complex: see Bandle et al. 2002: 33, 694–6. In his paper Bugge specifies the eighth century as the earliest boundary for poems in *ljóðaháttr*.

10. '. . . den af mig påviste regel . . . Det er da dermed bevist, at alle de i *ljóðaháttr* forfattede digte uden undtagelse er yngre en mellemjærnalderen. De kan tidligere ikke have eksisteret, i al fald ikke uden i en form så forskellig, at man ved den måtte tale om andre digte.'

11. Summary of views and references in von See et al. 2012: 387–90.

12. McKinnell 2001 adds *Þrymskviða* as another poem possibly composed in northern England, and Itó 2009 builds on that article with an experimental approach to possible reciprocal eddic influences in Cumbria. For a different (Norwegian) hypothesis about *Þrymskviða*, see Harris 2012; Jónas Kristjánsson and Vésteinn Ólason 2014: I, 244–5.

13. Before Kuhn, influence ('Ausstrahlung') from the Continent was studied by, among others, Neckel 1908, but usually in terms of story and motif (e.g. 218–20 on *Guðrúnarhvǫt*). After Kuhn, Siegfried Gutenbrunner attempted several studies of Continental influence (for references and critique, see Harris 1985: 105–6); Wolfgang Mohr was a more successful proponent of similar ideas (references in Harris 1985: 102–6).

14. "Memory of the World Registry" (www.unesco.org/new/en/communication-and-information/flagship-project-activities/memory-of-the-world/register/).

15. Schlözer 1773: 2 (§ 2). The title of Schlözer's book and the sentences immediately preceding this earliest deployment of the concept of 'world literature' privilege 'the Edda' within Icelandic literature.

16. For a good introduction, D'haen 2012; for some inspired essays, Damrosch 2003.

17. There are exceptions, e.g. Schröder 1954 (and cf. Lindow 1988).

18. Bang followed up his 1879 book with one on the sibylline oracles more generally (1882). A discovery in the 1950s is said to have begun a new era for this question (see Dronke 1992b).

19. The following is a sample only: Dronke 1992b; 1997; Samplonius 2001; 2013; Steinsland 2013; Johansson 2013; Schulte 2005. A good bibliography on *Vǫluspá* generally could be derived from Gunnell and Lassen 2013.

20. De Vries (1961: 256) says of Bugge's Christian/classical obsession that it 'hat ihn nicht losgelassen' ('it did not let go of him'); see de Vries's stringent criticism of Bugge and Krohn (256–7).

21. Two recent essays on philology also make the transition to New Philology: Nichols 1990 and Wenzel 1990.

22. Quinn and Lethbridge 2010, containing an Introduction and eleven contributions, several of which are closely relevant to our current theme. The *Speculum* issue (65.1 [1990]) mentioned in Quinn's introduction remains, as a whole, the central source on New Philology. An extensive working model is provided by Rowe 2005.

23. Fleischman 1990 shows interestingly how pragmatics, the text linguistics derived from contemporary speech, can be applied to Old French prose, but the author's references to challenging philology comprise a programme alongside, not part of, the New Philological doctrine as I understand it.

24. Two of my own articles were written in innocence of New Philology, yet made use of the Codex Regius in a fashion that might have been dictated by it: Harris 1983; 1996/2008.

25. 'Även intresset för litteracitet, d.v.s. för skriftens och handskriftskulturens betydelse för den kulterell och ideologiska utvecklingen i ett social perspektiv har visat på nya viktiga problemställningar. För forskningen kring muntlig tradering i ett skriftlöst samhälle som trots allt bygger på skrivna document är det givetvis livsviktigt att studera de processer som är verksamma vid övergången från ett samhälle byggt på muntlig tradering till ett alltmer skriftbaserat samhälle.'

26. Johansson 1998, a close study of Codex Wormianus, demonstrates some features of New Philology, including the study of a manuscript within certain scribal groupings, attention to audience/patron, and perhaps applications of linguistics-inspired analysis (graphemics).

27. Only two studies come to mind as conforming to the New Critical ideal: Scher 1963 (on *Rígspula*) and, less directly, R. Harris 1971 (on *Grípisspá*).

CHAPTER 3

The editing of eddic poetry

Judy Quinn

In this chapter I offer a short survey of the way eddic poetry has been edited, noting the challenges faced by editors and considering some of the ways in which interventions by editors have the potential to distort the interpretation of the poetry. I am taking my primary examples from the edition of eddic poetry that is most often used by scholars and students throughout the world: the German edition commonly referred to as Neckel Kuhn, first produced in 1914 by Gustav Neckel, revised by him in 1927 and 1936 and then revised again by Hans Kuhn in a fourth edition in 1962 and a fifth in 1983, the last primarily an orthographic revision of the fourth. The recent Icelandic edition by Jónas Kristjánsson and Vésteinn Ólason in the Íslenzk fornrit series (2014) will also be taken into account, as will the work of earlier editors whose emendations have been adopted and have to some degree become mainstream. For reasons of space I am leaving aside here consideration of eddic poetry quoted in a piecemeal fashion (such as verse quoted in the *fornaldarsögur* and in other prosimetric contexts) to focus on editorial practice in regard to whole poems – works written conscientiously from beginning to end, as clearly marked entities in most cases – in compilation manuscripts such as the Codex Regius, GKS 2365 4° (see the first chapter in this Handbook for a full account of preservation). The editing of poetry quoted in prosimetrum presents particular challenges, especially where there is a proliferation of manuscript witnesses and stemmatic relations are difficult to chart; these are addressed by the editors of *Skaldic Poetry of the Scandinavian Middle Ages* in forthcoming volumes treating poetry composed in eddic metres.

A small collection of mythological poems is preserved in another manuscript, AM 748 I a 4°, the texts being close enough to those of the Codex Regius poems to suggest a common written source, with variations between the texts generally not very significant, although the naming of poems, their sequence, and other aspects of preservation are of independent value (Quinn 1990a). In general, eddic poems preserved as whole poems present a reasonably straightforward editorial proposition since most of the poems are preserved in just one version. There are only a handful of cases where more than one version has been recorded: two versions of *Vǫluspá* are preserved, one in the Codex Regius anthology of poems and another in Hauksbók (AM 544 4°); a version of *Helreið Brynhildar* is quoted within *Norna-Gests þáttr* (*The Tale of Norna-Gestr*), preserved in Flateyjarbók (GKS 1005 fol.); a version of *Sigrdrífumál* is quoted within *Vǫlsunga saga* (*The Saga of the Vǫlsungs*) in GKS 1824 b 4°; and many stanzas are quoted within *Snorra Edda*, either singly or in short sequences.

The Hauksbók text of *Vǫluspá* is significantly different from the Codex Regius text of the poem, with an intriguingly different organisation of the substance of the *vǫlva*'s vision as well as lines, half-stanzas, and stanzas that do not occur in the Regius text (for a detailed analysis, see Quinn 1990b). One nineteenth-century editor of the poem, Sophus Bugge, acknowledged the value of the two versions and presented them separately in his edition (1867), alongside a synthetic text derived principally from the Codex Regius text but supplemented here and there by material from the Hauksbók version of the poem. In the recent Íslenzk fornrit edition of the poem, the editors present the three texts of the poem separately – the Codex Regius version, the Hauksbók version, and the texts of the quotations used in *Snorra Edda* – a commendable editorial approach since it allows us to understand the medieval witnesses better and to appreciate the variability inherent in the eddic tradition as an oral mode (of both composition and transmission) as the transition was made into writing during the thirteenth and fourteenth centuries (Quinn 2001). In between Bugge's three-part edition of 1867 and the Íslenzk fornrit edition of 2014, however, history preserves a number of synthetic editions of the poem, each editor emending and rearranging differently from the next.

Approaches to editing medieval texts have changed significantly in recent decades, with a trend away from ingenious editorial conjecture and towards engagement with the manuscript text – even when its meaning seems confounding – in order to present readers with the actuality of the medieval record.[1] In addition, more attention is paid nowadays to the implications of oral transmission for the editing of Old Norse texts, particularly eddic poetry (see Quinn 2016). A poem preserved in a single recension, with a fairly clearly written text, should present a more or less straightforward task for the editor: to present the medieval text as faithfully as possible to readers and scholars. I am not assuming here that every line of every poem makes immediate and complete sense to the editor: a great many eddic

lines are elusively allusive, contain otherwise unknown words, or present
syntactic formulations that are challenging to construe, as well as stanzaic
shifts where speakers are not specified. What I am assuming is that it is
desirable for significant ambiguities in an eddic text to be brought to the
surface of a scholarly edition rather than interpreted away. For works
whose target audience is the general public, such as popular editions and
many translations, the aims are necessarily different, with priority given to
smoothing the text to mask disconcerting uncertainties. Nonetheless, an
edition such as Gísli Sigurðsson's popular edition of 1998, with modern
Icelandic spelling, stands out as being more in tune with developments in
textual criticism and more responsive to the particularity of editing texts
derived from oral tradition than other editions of eddic poetry produced
around the same time, or indeed since.

Before exploring some instances of editorial interpretation, it may be
helpful to distinguish between levels of editorial practice – distinctions that
to a certain extent remain notional since textual cruces may arise at any of
the levels. At the first level, the manuscript text needs to be presented in
a way that is legible for today's readers: abbreviations expanded and the text
(usually) normalised, punctuated, and formatted into verse lines and
stanzas. This task is not without its challenges, especially in cases where
stanza length is not uniform, or within dialogues where shifts in speaker are
uncertain, or within lines where the syntax is ambiguous. The second level
involves the interpretation of illegible or apparently nonsensical words or
phrases according to the known poetic and prose lexicons and patterns of
verse lines elsewhere in the corpus, while the third level, with which I am
mainly concerned in this chapter, involves the over-interpretation of the
text, through radical emendation of the manuscript witness according to
an interpretative hypothesis of the editor. At this level, new words are
introduced, the syntax reconfigured, and the order of lines and even stanzas
rearranged.

The complex semantics of poetry can also be at issue in small-scale
emendations at the first level, such as the alteration of a case ending to align
the referent of a kenning to accord with an editor's perception of
a predictable and stable kenning system. In *Hymiskviða* (the kennings of
which are treated in detail in my chapter on poetic diction later in the
Handbook; see Chapter 15), Þórr is repeatedly designated by the *heiti*
('poetic name') Véurr, which means 'guardian' (*Hym* 11/10, 17/1, 21/7).
In that poem the god is portrayed as prevailing over giant-kind both on
land and sea: he acquires an ale-brewing kettle for the gods from

a mountain-dwelling giant, having previously induced the giant to row him far out to sea, where he lands a mighty blow on the head of the ocean-dwelling *miðgarðsormr* ('world-serpent'). Þórr and the *miðgarðsormr* meet again in the closing scenes of *Vǫluspá* in a decisive encounter that sees the god mortally wounding the serpent before stumbling away.[2] In the Codex Regius version of the poem, the (normalised) text reads as follows:[3]

> Þá kømr inn mæri mǫgr Hlóðynjar,
> gengr Óðins sonr við úlf vega,
> drepr hann af móði miðgarðs véur
> – munu halir allir heimstǫð ryðja –
> gengr fet níu Fjǫrgynjar burr
> neppr frá naðri níðs ókvíðnum.

[Then the famous son of Hlóðyn [a *heiti* for Jǫrð; her son > Þórr] comes, Óðinn's son [Þórr] goes to fight the wolf; out of rage he strikes the world's guardian – all people will abandon their homes – the son of Fjǫrgyn [another *heiti* for Jǫrð; her son > Þórr], ?exhausted, steps nine paces from the serpent, unconcerned about dishonour.]

The text of the manuscript, which is very clear at this point, may be viewed on the handrit.is website.[4] Editing and translating the stanza nonetheless presents a number of challenges. To begin with, the meaning of the word *neppr* is uncertain.[5] More problematic is the identification of Þórr's opponent as a wolf in line 2 since, in line 6, his nemesis is specified as a serpent and it is a serpent that is elsewhere described as the god's opponent at *ragnarǫk* – when Fenrir will be otherwise engaged fighting Óðinn. The phrase *við úlf vega* in fact occurs a few lines earlier in the description of Óðinn's encounter with the wolf: *Óðinn ferr við úlf vega* (*Vsp* 52 R; GKS 2365 4°, 2 v/l. 13). Perhaps this is a case of dittography, with the scribe of the Codex Regius mistakenly copying an earlier phrase twice from his exemplar; or perhaps the scribe has confused the phrasing of the stanza in his recollection for transcription, momentarily distracted by the description of Þórr as *Óðins sonr*.[6] Another possible explanation could be the poetic merging of the identities of the Æsir's opponents, Loki's two belligerent children treated as one as they are confronted by the doomed gods: death the inevitable outcome of striding up to either wolf or serpent. How, then, ought an editor to treat the word *úlf*? Neckel and Kuhn (1983: 13) and Gísli Sigurðsson (1998: 15) present the manuscript text as it is – rightly, in my view – whereas Ursula Dronke (1997: 22) and Jónas Kristjánsson and Vésteinn Ólason (2014: I, 305) replace the word *úlf* with the word *orm* in their editions, indicating the emendation by italicisation.

The treatment of another editorial intervention in the text is less clearly signalled across the three editions. The word *véur* in line 3 (2 v/l. 18 in the manuscript) is spelt with a single letter 'r', indicating the accusative case. (Where the word occurs in the nominative, it ends with a capital ʀ to indicate a double consonant, i.e. *véurr*; clear examples can be seen in the text of *Hymiskviða* when Þórr is referred to as Véuʀ, at lines 15, 24, and 33 of leaf 14 r.) The 'world's guardian' in line 3 of the stanza from *Vǫluspá* quoted above must therefore be the object of the god's furious assault, with the *miðgarðsormr* – often described as encircling all lands – conceived of in the role of custodian of the territory in which people dwell. The calamitous consequences of this violent attack are quickly evident, the inhabitants of *miðgarðr* forced to abandon their homes (lines 7–8), with worse to come. The next stanza of the poem describes the sun turning black, the earth sinking into the sea and bright stars disappearing (*Vsp* R55). Because of the assumption by some editors that Véurr is a *heiti* for Þórr and cannot be used to refer to another mythological figure, the text has often been emended accordingly, *véur* changed to *véurr* so that the description 'the world's guardian' is brought into apposition with *Óðins sonr*. Neckel and Kuhn make the change silently (without acknowledging the manuscript reading *véurr* in the textual apparatus); Dronke acknowledges the changed inflection within square brackets but exaggerates the identification with Þórr by translating the phrase 'shrine-guarder of Miðgarðr' (1997: 22) and by suggesting the *heiti* in *Hymiskviða* has 'possibly been taken from *Vsp*' (1997: 150). Jónas Kristjánsson and Vésteinn Ólason silently change the word to *véurr* without mentioning the original text in the footnotes; instead their note directly identifies Þórr as 'Miðgarðs véurr' (2014: I, 305).

A rather differently configured stanza is quoted within *Gylfaginning* (52), in which the kenning *miðgarðs véurr* is the subject, rather than the object, of the verb *drepa*, which is syntactically independent of the clause identifying the actor as Jǫrð's son:

> Gengr inn mæri mǫgr Hlǫðynjar
> nepr at naðri níðs ókvíðnum.
> Munu halir allir heimstǫð ryðja
> er af móði drepr Miðgarðs véorr.

> [Then the famous son of Hlóðyn, ?dying, goes up to the serpent, unconcerned about dishonour. All people will abandon their homes when the world's guardian, out of rage, strikes.]

As Anthony Faulkes observes in his Glossary to *Gylfaginning* (152), the word *véurr* could mean 'protector' here (pointing to Þórr as the referent), but it may also mean 'encircler', pointing to the *miðgarðsormr*.[7] Lines of poetry that are difficult to construe – and which entail mythological complexity – are intrinsic to the eddic record and need to be treated as a valuable facet of the medieval source, however tempting it may be to simplify the text and harmonise mythological details. There will often necessarily be a tension between the apparent meaning of a *heiti* or kenning in the context of a particular stanza and the patterns apparent across the wider poetic corpus (which in its extent is to some degree the consequence of haphazard preservation). The collocation 'surf-pig', which is discussed in my chapter on kennings (see Chapter 15), is a case in point: the patterns evident across the corpus would suggest the kenning's referent is 'ship', yet the context of the kenning in stanza 27 of *Hymiskviða* could also plausibly lead to the identification 'whale'. In editing and interpreting stanza 54 of the Codex Regius text of *Vǫluspá*, the possibility that the mythological figure identified as *miðgarðs véurr* might be the *miðgarðsormr* needs to be borne in mind despite the description of Þórr as Véurr in another poetic context.

Two further examples from *Vǫluspá* will illustrate the kinds of interventions by editors that overstep the mark into over-interpretation and have the potential to lead readers of the text astray. In the last stanza of the poem (in both the Codex Regius and Hauksbók versions), the last vision of the *vǫlva* is followed by a narrative shift, moving out of the *spá* ('prophecy') to the situation of the recitation itself. The text below is normalised from the Codex Regius version:

> Þar kømr inn dimmi dreki fljúgandi,
> naðr fránn, neðan frá Niðafjǫllum;
> berr sér í fjǫðrum – flýgr vǫll yfir –
> Níðhǫggr, nái – nú mun hon søkkvask.

> [There comes the dark dragon flying, gleaming snake, from beneath the Niða-mountains;[8] Níðhǫggr carries corpses on its wings – it flies over the plain – now she will sink down.]

The last clause constitutes the end of the frame narrative of the *vǫlva*'s prophecy, which in the Regius version was elaborated earlier in the poem in a dialogue between the reluctant speaker and the insistent god, Óðinn, who challenges her to provide him with detailed information about the future of the world and the gods (R28–30). The last stages of her vision include descriptions of the death of Óðinn and the re-emergence of the earth, newly populated by resurrected gods. Unlike the *vǫlva* of *Baldrs draumar*, who is described as being raised from her grave by Óðinn's incantations, the speaker of *Vǫluspá* is not identified as dead, although the last clause of the poem suggests she may be sinking back down into the ground. Wherever she has come from to respond to Óðinn's challenge, she appears to return there at the close of the poem, according to the texts of both Codex Regius and Hauksbók.

In synthetic editions combining readings from both versions of the poem, most editors have generally left well alone when the two manuscript versions are identical. Not Müllenhoff, however. He emended the pronoun – quite clearly *hon* ('she') in both manuscript texts – to *hann* ('he'), sinking the dragon in a defiant act of eschatological redrafting and leaving the *vǫlva* up in the air (Müllenhoff [1883] 1908: 86). Like Finnur Jónsson after him (1932: 20), Müllenhoff favoured a mythology in which the destructive force represented by Níðhǫggr was overcome, his justification for the emendation being one that, he felt, 'surely no-one can deny' ('doch wohl niemand bestreiten?'; Müllenhoff 1908: 36).

In his 1914 edition of *Vǫluspá*, Gustav Neckel adopted the emendation to the last line of the poem:

> Þar kømr inn dimmi dreki fliúgandi,
> naðr fránn, neðan frá Niðafiǫllom;
> berr sér í fiǫðrom – flýgr vǫll yfir –
> Níðhǫggr, nái – nú mun h*ann* søkkvaz.

The gender realignment was carried over into Neckel's second and third editions, the medieval text only being restored in Kuhn's revision of 1963. Müllenhoff's editorial intervention had the potential to alter a fundamental facet of Scandinavian mythology, since the appearance of Níðhǫggr in the reborn world suggests a cyclical return to trouble and the continuing penetration of the world of the living by forces from the world of the dead. This extraordinary emendation was accepted by Finnur Jónsson, more than once (1888: 9; 1905: 19; and 1932: 20). Sijmons and Gering also adopted it, although they omitted the pronoun altogether from the text, and in the commentary remarked that the subject of the last clause can only be Níðhǫggr (1906: 78).

While Müllenhoff's improvement to the text has now been relegated to the apparatus of the Neckel Kuhn edition, other old emendations to the text of *Vǫluspá* have been left to stand, and some even appear in the recent Íslenzk fornrit edition. One such example comes within the sequence of stanzas – only in the Codex Regius text – elaborating the frame narrative of the poem (sts R28–R33), mid-prophecy, with a description of the encounter between the *vǫlva* and Óðinn. She is said to have been sitting outside when the god confronted her, causing her to turn on him, reminding him that she knows everything (*alt veit ek Óðinn*) and that she should not be tested. Apparently in order both to mollify her and to induce her to move deeper into her prophetic knowledge – in a vision which will reveal the uncomfortable details of Baldr's death – a transaction takes place between Óðinn and the *vǫlva* (the text is normalised from the Codex Regius, st. 29):

> Valði henni Herfǫðr hringa ok men,
> fé, spjǫll spaklig ok spáganda,
> sá hon vítt ok um vítt of verǫld hverja.

> [War-father [a *heiti* for Óðinn] chose for her rings and necklaces, treasure, wise words and prophecy-wands; she saw ever wider into every world.]

As a consequence of this extravagant bribe, the *vǫlva* envisions first valkyries gathering before a killing (*Vsp* R30) and then the bloodied god, Baldr (*Vsp* R31). This is, in many ways, a mysterious transaction, but we must assume from it that jewellery and valuables were coveted from the world of the dead, or from whatever world the *vǫlva* hails. The alliterative pattern of lines 3–4 is unusual; as Jón Helgason (1964: I, 7) has noted, a noun in the initial position in the line might be expected to carry alliteration. The attitudes of editors to emendation *metri causa* are discussed in Fulk's chapter in this Handbook, most editors in most cases treading cautiously when it comes to reconstructing lines of poetry deduced to have been the forerunners of those preserved in manuscript texts. Moreover, across the eddic corpus, a significant number of lines do not fit with the versification 'rules' derived by Eduard Sievers for early Germanic poetry, a situation which should at least give us pause before semantic interventions are made.

In 1861, Ludwig Ettmüller proposed an emendation that involves a radical syntactic change: the noun *fé* being altered to *fekk*, the past tense of the verb *fá*. The emendation was adopted by Neckel (the text below is from his first edition of 1914):

> Valði henni Herfǫðr hringa ok men,
> fekk spiǫll spaklig ok spáganda;
> sá hon vítt ok um vítt of verǫld hveria.

> [War-father chose for her rings and necklaces, got wise words and prophecy-wands; she saw ever wider into every world.]

The emendation continues to appear throughout the revisions by Kuhn of Neckel's edition right up to the current, fifth edition of the Poetic Edda (where the added letters are italicised); it is also reproduced by Jónas Kristjánsson and Vésteinn Ólason (2014: I, 298), although, curiously, the whole word is italicised (*fekk*). Once again, the intervention has consequences for our understanding both of the underlying situation of the poem and the mythological dynamics it describes. This is a ritual moment of some importance, the emended text treated as a source in studies of religion and mythology. For some editors, the desire to emend goes deeper than metrical tidying, as Sigurður Nordal commented (in John McKinnell's translation): '*fé, spjǫll spaklig* . . . could pass metrically . . . but [it] would be unseemly and ugly; . . . *fé* would be colourless and feeble after the choice of rings and brooches has been described' (1978: 61). Maybe so, but that is what the manuscript text preserves: a series of five nominal groups forming the direct object of the verb *valði*. Jónas Kristjánsson and Vésteinn Ólason suggest that the emendation improves not just the metre but also the content of the verse (2014: I, 298).

After the *vǫlva*'s violent outburst, Óðinn needed to choose his words carefully to make her compliant, and he needed to choose just the right jewellery for her. The emendation of *fé* to *fekk* falsifies the witness, changes the nature of the transaction between Óðinn and the *vǫlva*, and alters our understanding of the mythological dynamic between them. In fact, Óðinn gives, and gives more, and keeps on giving, the inducement working, we may infer, since the *vǫlva* sees more widely than before. Just a few editors have allowed the manuscript text to stand, among them Jón Helgason (1964: I, 7) and Gísli Sigurðsson in both his early, velvet-bound 'confirmation' edition of *Vǫluspá* and *Hávamál* (1987: 29) and in his later edition of eddic poems (1998: 10).[9]

Turning now from the editorial emendation of particular words, I want to look briefly at the editorial reallocation of speakers within poems. Towards the end of the eddic poem *Hyndluljóð*, which is only preserved in Flateyjarbók (GKS 1005 fol.), the dialogue between the giantess Hyndla and the goddess Freyja intensifies into a kind of *senna* ('insult exchange'), with Freyja's request that a memory beer be brought to her favourite, Óttarr (st. 45), unleashing a torrent of insults from the giantess (sts 46–9). The insults are tied together by a repeated refrain, which likens Freyja to a she-goat on heat:

> . . . hleypr þú, eðlvina, úti á náttum
> sem með hǫfrum Heiðrún fari.
>
> [. . . you run about, noble friend, out into the night, just like Heiðrún among the goats.]

The four-line refrain is written out in full in stanza 46, shortened to two lines in stanza 47, one line in stanza 48, and to just the openings words (*hleypr þú*) in stanza 49 (GKS 1005 fol. 3 ra ll. 48–54). While the speakers of the stanzas are not indicated in the manuscript, the sense of the stanzas and the repeated refrain makes attribution fairly straightforward (a fuller analysis can be found in Quinn 2002). In his edition of 1859, Hermann Lüning, however, attributed stanza 48 to Freyja – throwing the same insult of nymphomania back at Hyndla – and he therefore emended the preposition in the second line from *af* to *of* (1859: 262). Curiously, Gustav Neckel kept the emendation but excised the refrain from the stanza, leaving it as a half-stanza in his 1914 edition:[10]

GKS 1005 fol.	Neckel 1914
48 [Hyndla] Ek slæ eldi af iviðju	48 [Freyja] Ek slæ eldi *of* iviðio
svá at þú ei kemz á burt heðan;	svá at þú ei*gi* kømz á b*rau*t heðan.
hleypr þú, eðlvina, *úti á náttum*	
sem með hofrum Heiðrún fari.	

[*Flateyjarbók text*: I will cast fire from the forest-dweller [a *heiti* for giantess > Hyndla], so that you may never get away from here; you run about, noble friend, out into the night, just like Heiðrún among the goats.]

According to Lüning's emended text, the stanza reads 'I [Freyja] cast fire around the giantess, so that you can never get away from here' – which makes little sense deictically or mythologically, since Hyndla is at home and longing to be left alone to go back to sleep (*Hdl* 46). In order to make the re-attribution of speaker work, the flames which the speaker throws surround Hyndla in her own cave rather than being cast by the irate giantess around the visiting goddess, Freyja. This example of over-interpretation has prevailed right up to the fifth revision by Kuhn of Neckel's edition and it is reproduced by the editors of the *Edda Kommentar* (III, 827–31). Happily, neither Gísli Sigurðsson's edition of the poem (1998: 405) nor the Íslenzk fornrit edition excises the refrain from stanza 48 (though in the latter case the preposition is silently changed to 'of'), with Jónas Kristjánsson and Vésteinn Ólason noting that the omission of the refrain in earlier editions and the identification of the speaker as Freyja is without justification ('ástæðulaust') (2014: I, 469).

Eddic dialogue is very often oblique – and all the more fascinating for it – a feature that editors have sometimes tried to iron out by rearranging stanzas. In *Oddrúnargrátr*, for instance, a radical reordering of half-stanzas has often been made to make the content of Oddrún's account of her life proceed as linear chronology. In the poem, Oddrún recalls the words of her dying father when he expressed his will that she be married to Gunnarr (*Od* 13), even if events conspired to have Gunnarr marry her sister Brynhildr instead (*Od* 17).[11] As I have explained in a literary reading of the poem which respects the integrity of the extant text (Quinn 2009), Oddrún's reminiscences are discursively complex: as well as responding to an outburst by her interlocutor Borgný (sts 11–12), Oddrún also recounts Brynhildr's suicide following Sigurðr's death (st. 19). She then says (in the manuscript text of the poem, GKS 2365 4°, 39 r/ll. 14–15):

> En ek Gunnari gatk at unna,
> bauga deili, sem Brynhildr skyldi.
> Enn hann Brynhildi bað hjálm geta,
> hana kvað hann óskmey verða skyldu.

> [Yet I got the chance to love Gunnarr, the sharer of rings, as Brynhildr should have. And he said that the helmet should be given to Brynhildr, he said that she should become a wish-maid [> valkyrie].]

In the context of her condensed and interrupted account, the antecedent of 'hann' must be the father of Oddrún and Brynhildr, who had earlier been reported as setting out the destinies of both his daughters (*Od* 13). Editors unhappy with such poetic complexity have split the stanza in two, Neckel (and, after him, Kuhn) moving the second half-stanza back four stanzas to bring it closer to the earlier reported speech of the father. (The order of stanzas in their edition, which entails other rearrangements as well, is: 10, 13, 14, 15, 16, 11, 12, 16/5–8, 17, 18, 19, 16/1–4 [counted as st. 20], 21). Based on the assumption that Oddrún's harkings back to her father's words must be contiguous, the emendations made by editors muffle the original voice of the monologue to make Oddrún's lament more straightforward and linear – and less poetic. The editors of the *Edda Kommentar* present the stanzas in manuscript order but number them according to a rearranged schema – the half-stanza 16/1–4 inserted between their stanzas 20 and 21 (VI, 897–902) – maintaining that such an approach does not prejudice the interpretation of the poem despite the fact that one half-stanza is declared to be in the wrong place ('steht eindeutig an falscher Stelle', 2009: 878). Both recent Icelandic editions of the poem, by Gísli Sigurðsson (1998: 368–9) and Jónas Kristjánsson and Vésteinn Ólason (2014: I, 368–69), retain the order of stanzas in the manuscript.

Finally, an example of a different kind of editorial problem: a marginal emendation in the manuscript itself, by a younger hand than the manuscript text of the last stanza of *Hávamál* (GKS 2365 4°, 7 v/l. 8). This is editorial emendation as part of the earlier reception history of the manuscript, albeit by an unidentifiable editor. The manuscript text is set out in the left-hand column below, with Neckel's edited text of 1914, which incorporates the marginal emendation, on the right:

GKS 2365 4°	Neckel 1914
Nú eru Háva mál kveðin, Háva hǫllu í,	Nú eru Háva mál kveðin, Háva hǫllo í,
allþǫrf ýta sonum,	allþǫrf ýta sonum,
óþǫrf ýta sonum;	óþǫrf iǫtna sonum;
heill, sá er kvað, heill, sá er kann!	heill, sá er kvað, heill, sá er kann!
njóti, sá er nam,	njóti, sá er nam,
heilir, þeirs hlyddu!	heilir, þeirs hlyddu!

[*Codex Regius text*: Now Hávi's recitation has been spoken, in Hávi's hall, very useful to the sons of men, completely useless to the sons of men; Good luck to the one who recited, good luck to the one who knows! May he benefit, the one who learnt, good luck to those who listened!]

As I have argued in a study of the representation of the transfer of knowledge in *Hávamál* (Quinn 2010: 213–24), the manuscript text makes clear the paradox of Óðinn's position with regard to passing on the arcane lore he has acquired: it is very useful to men, but perfectly useless because they will never acquire some of it. In the manuscript, a younger hand has 'corrected' the reading *allþǫrf ýta sonum, óþǫrf ýta sonum* by writing *jǫtna* ('of giants') in the margin to replace *ýta* ('of men'), and this emendation has been carried over by editors and translators of the poem more or less without question (and, very frequently, silently). Emending the text to read 'very useful to the sons of men, completely useless to the sons of giants' changes the dynamic of the exchange to render Óðinn a reasonable and kindly teacher. Even less mythologically cogent is the supposition of the emended text that giants need the knowledge Óðinn has to a large extent learnt from them in the first place. In this instance, the recent Íslenzk fornrit edition simply replicates the treatment by Neckel and Kuhn, which remains the same up to the fifth edition.[12]

When interpreting eddic poems, we need to be mindful of changes that have occurred in textual criticism in Old Norse over the last half century, particularly the move towards material philology and, with it, higher regard for manuscript versions of works and greater wariness of synthetic editions and the editorial over-interpretation of texts. The interpretation of eddic poetry, especially phases of dialogue, does present challenges, but those challenges are best faced by addressing the manuscript text of the dialogue rather than an emended text which has already been filtered through editorial interpretation. The oblique and often elusive dialogic moves of eddic speakers are an important aspect of its aesthetic, as is the temporal range of their reference, which frequently departs from linear chronology. The full meaning of the utterances of mythological and heroic figures – as well as deductions that can be made about their motivation – can only be explored by acknowledging the inherent complexity of the eddic record.

Notes

1. The broader literature on textual criticism is extensive; for a recent discussion of the editing of Old Norse texts, see Driscoll 2010.
2. The god's death from the serpent's poison is made explicit in *Gylfaginning* (50).
3. The stanza number in Neckel and Kuhn's composite edition of the poem is 56 although it is the 54th stanza of the Regius text (Jónas Kristjánsson and Vésteinn Ólason 2014: I, 305). The text of the Hauksbók version of the poem is badly damaged at this point in the text; Jón Helgason's attempted reconstruction (1964: I, 44–6) draws heavily on the Regius text, with the result that it is not of independent value.
4. See http://handrit.is/en/manuscript/view/is/GKS04-2365. The text of the stanza is on lines 17–20 of leaf 2 v.
5. See the entries in *Lexicon poeticum antiquae linguae septentrionalis* (Sveinbjörn Egilsson and Finnur Jónsson 1931); La Farge and Tucker 1992; and Faulkes's glossary to *Gylfaginning* (2005).
6. In a note to his first edition, Gustav Neckel cites a suggestion by Björn Magnússon Ólsen that faulty recollection from oral tradition may have been responsible for the appearance of the wolf in this line (1914: 13)
7. For a survey of scholarly opinions about the meaning of the word in *Hymiskviða* and *Vǫluspá*, see *Edda Kommentar* II, 301–2.
8. On the possible meaning of the place-name, see Chapter 9 by Brink and Lindow, in this Handbook.
9. The manuscript text is also faithfully rendered in the second edition of Carolyne Larrington's translation of *Vǫluspá*, which presents translations of both the Regius version and the Hauksbók version of the poem (2014: 4–12 and 274–81).
10. Neckel also cut the refrain from the following stanza, though there seems to be little doubt that stanza 49 is also spoken by Hyndla. Finnur Jónsson had gone even further, omitting stanzas 46, 47, and 48, and the first half of 49, reducing Hyndla's part in the exchange to a mere four lines (1905: 396–7).
11. The numbering of stanzas given here follows the Neckel Kuhn edition; an edition and translation based on the manuscript text is presented in Quinn 2009.

12. Neckel and Kuhn (1962: 44): 'iǫtna *von. jüng. hand am rande verbessert für* ýta'; Jónas Kristjánsson and Vésteinn Ólason (2014: I, 355): '*jǫtna*: leiðr. með yngri hendi, *ýta* K'. The same emended text appears in the editions of Gísli Sigurðsson (1998: 54) and Ursula Dronke (2011: 35). The second edition of Larrington's translation renders the unemended manuscript text (2014: 35).

CHAPTER 4

The dating of eddic poetry

Bernt Ø. Thorvaldsen

Origins and delivery

This chapter discusses how eddic poetry is dated, and deals mainly with the poems preserved in the Icelandic manuscript Codex Regius, GKS 2365 4° (R), from around 1275, and similar poems in a few other medieval manuscripts from Iceland (see the Introduction for a discussion of how the corpus of eddic poetry is defined). The poems that are peripheral to the main corpus are nonetheless important to the question of dating. Runic inscriptions bearing similar characteristics to the poems of the Poetic Edda are preserved throughout much of Scandinavia and date from centuries before the Icelandic manuscripts were written as well as long after manuscript culture was introduced into Scandinavia. Formal similarities to Old English and Old High German poems, such as *Beowulf* and the *Hildebrandslied*, are also relevant to the history of eddic poetry. The basic verse couplet of the Old Norse metre *fornyrðislag* is paralleled in the metrical form of these poems, which present comparable content in their tales of past heroes. Thus the use of *fornyrðislag* in a certain poem indicates a considerable range of possibilities: the poem could be as old as the manuscript, or it could be much older; it may originate in Iceland or elsewhere in Scandinavia, or perhaps in a Scandinavian colony abroad.[1] For different views on the age and origin of eddic poetry in the history of eddic research, see Harris, Chapter 2 in this Handbook.

Since the aim in dating eddic poetry is usually to determine the age of the original composition, the transmission of the poems presents a major complication. Eddic poems are rarely associated with named poets or historic events that refer to the moment of composition. It is possible to approach the stages of written transmission in an empirical way when a poem exists in two or more versions thought to derive from a common written exemplar, such as the poems preserved in both R and AM 748 I a 4° (A). In general, however, the oral transmission of eddic poetry presents fundamental methodological challenges for the reconstruction of past versions. Different extant versions of some eddic poems are regarded by many to be independent oral variants: the most famous examples are *Vǫluspá* (see Quinn 1990b and 2016) and the sequence of stanzas known as *Hjálmarr's Death-Song* (Lönnroth 2011a [1971: 191–218]). In both cases, considerable differences exist between the manuscript texts, but the kind of variation does not suggest that eddic poets behaved like the South Slavic singers of tales studied by Milman Parry and Albert Lord, as these performers did not conceive of the song as a fixed text, but rather as a story related in a particular formulaic language (Lord 2000 [1960]). There are passages in the different versions of *Vǫluspá* that are identical, and this is clearly not due to the use of similar formulas. Hence, we can say that eddic poetry was certainly both memorised and revised, if the two complete versions of *Vǫluspá* have arisen as variants through oral transmission. The Old Norse terminological distinction between *yrkja* ('to create') and *flytja, fœra fram* ('to recite') also reflects this contrast with the South Slavic case (Lönnroth 2011a [1971]: 193–4). The verbs document what Harris (2008 [1983]: 191) terms 'deliberative composition' – that is, composition before performance instead of in performance. For a discussion of the general terms 'literacy' and 'orality', and the influence of Parry and Lord on eddic studies, see Harris, Chapter 2 in this Handbook.

Even if the variation between the different versions of *Vǫluspá* may be a consequence of written transmission (Dronke 1997: 61–92; Johansson 2000; 2005), that would show how eddic poetry could change substantially as the result of conscious revision (Mundal 2008). Harris's study of the poems about Helgi Hundingsbani and Helgi Hjǫrvarðsson, discussed below, suggests extensive revision in both oral and written transmission (Harris 2008 [1983]: 189–225). It is, however, possible only in exceptional cases to detect the kind of variation that may have arisen during oral transmission. When a poem or story survives in only a single version, or in more or less identical copies, few methods exist to uncover the prehistory of the text. In early philological studies in the nineteenth and early twentieth century, attempts to discern different revisions, authors, and chronological layers of eddic poems turned out to be mostly unconvincing, since the conclusions differed significantly from scholar to scholar despite their detailed studies. Thus, if the aim of dating an eddic poem is to date its original composition on the basis of the extant text, a high degree of uncertainty is an inescapable part of the exercise.[2]

This situation is clearly expressed in two methodological principles proposed by Bjarne Fidjestøl (1999) in *The Dating of Eddic Poetry: A Historical Survey and Methodological Investigation*. The first principle is that the extant version of a poem considered to have an oral prehistory represents the original composition. The original oral composition and the extant form 'are taken to be the same text, in a rather vague interpretation of "same" and "text"' (Fidjestøl 1999: 199). The second principle deals with a related problem: 'If there are not particularly strong arguments against it, the text is considered as a unified whole' (Fidjestøl 1999: 199). In early philological scholarship, it was sometimes argued that extant poems combined different older poems. This would complicate the dating process, since dating a certain stanza, or any other element, may be relevant only for the source poem and not the extant text. In some cases, there are 'particularly strong arguments' (Fidjestøl 1999: 199) for considering an extant text to have combined older sources; *Hávamál* is a prime example of this. These two methodological principles assume what Fidjestøl terms 'reasonable identity' (Fidjestøl 1999: 197) between an original composition and an extant version; this kind of textual identity implies a high degree of stability in oral transmission.

The dating of eddic poetry is usually based on dating specific elements of the text, such as loan words, syntactic constructions, verse-forms, motifs, textual loans, and possible references to archaeological objects. Some scholars have even attempted to reconstruct the poet's intention: for example, by arguing that a mythological poem served a certain religious purpose in pre-Christian contexts, or was composed in Christian times to falsify or ridicule the old beliefs or by suggesting that the author had an antiquarian motive.[3] The specific nature of oral traditions is rarely emphasised in discussions of the dating of eddic poetry: for example, in the coverage of the age and origin of poems in the *Edda Kommentar*, published in seven volumes from 1997 onwards, oral transmission receives little attention. Preben Meulengracht Sørensen (1991) in fact argued (with reference to oral-formulaic theory) that dating oral texts is impossible from the extant forms; Harris (1985: 93–126) and Gunnell (2005: 93–5) have also addressed the challenges involved. The following sections will suggest how the understanding of some common dating criteria – linguistic features and textual loans – may need to be modified when oral transmission is taken into consideration.

Register and linguistic criteria

A linguistic feature that has played an important role in dating eddic poems is the expletive particle *of* / *um*, a word apparently devoid of meaning and occurring before verbs, nouns, and adjectives (Kuhn 1929). Hans Kuhn argued convincingly that the use of *of / um* in skaldic compositions decreased over the centuries. Hence, the frequency of the particle in an eddic poem might indicate its age when compared to the distribution in the skaldic corpus.

In addition to testing and improving Kuhn's older statistical method, Fidjestøl (1999: 207–30) provided valuable guidelines for the possible interpretation and use of such statistics. He confirmed that the occurrence of expletive particles did decrease significantly throughout the centuries, but that the correlation between frequency and age was imprecise: "Although highly positive, the correlation is not perfect, and as far as I can see, this inevitably means that *the frequency of the particle cannot be used as a criterion of dating in connection with any one particular poem*" (Fidjestøl 1999: 217). As evidence, Fidjestøl pointed to the skaldic poetry of the ninth-century poet Þórbjǫrn hornklofi ('horn-cleaver'), who used the particle only twice. If the correlation between age and frequency were perfect, Þórbjǫrn's poetry would have to be considered at least one hundred and fifty years younger than normally assumed on the grounds of other dating criteria, such as references to historical context. Hence, a naïve application of these statistics to eddic poetry could lead to similar errors. According to Fidjestøl, the main purpose of studying the particle is not to date individual poems, but to suggest more general trends in the corpus or parts of the corpus.

In the case of *Þrymskviða*, a notable discordance occurs between the usual dating of the poem and the high number of expletive particles present in it (Fidjestøl 1999: 224). This requires an explanation since the poem is often dated to the twelfth or even thirteenth century (see, for example, *Edda Kommentar* II, 526). While the skaldic poetry of Þórbjǫrn hornklofi presents an unexpectedly low frequency of the particle, we face the opposite situation in *Þrymskviða*: the frequency is higher than expected. Thus, if one argues for a twelfth or thirteenth century origin, the particle cannot be explained as contemporary linguistic usage. Fidjestøl suggested two other reasons why poets might have used the particle: either as a stylistic device or as 'a deliberate means of archaizing the style' (Fidjestøl 1999: 228). How one might distinguish between these two purposes in practice is difficult to determine; the rationale can perhaps be detected in Fidjestøl's description of the second: "If archaization is intended, there ought to be other signs of archaization as well. The question would also have to be raised whether a medieval writer is likely to have possessed the necessary knowledge of language history to be able to use this means of archaization consistently" (Fidjestøl 1999: 228). According to Fidjestøl, archaisms may be intentional or unintentional; an intentional archaism is a reconstruction by 'a medieval

writer' who would have needed some knowledge of language history to
produce a convincing archaic form. Fidjestøl argued that the archaisation
hypothesis is weakened by the fact that the particle violates Kuhn's rules in
only one skaldic stanza and yet such violations are not seen in eddic
poetry.[4]

Fidjestøl did not follow up on the other possibility, the idea that *of* /
um may be a stylistic device with an emphatic function, as argued by
Ingerid Dal (1930: 9–34). Dal's suggestion is worth investigating,
although in doing so I prefer to use the term 'register' instead of the
more general term 'style'. The former term was used by John Miles Foley
with reference to a certain language variety used in traditional oral art
as 'an idiomatic version of the language that qualifies as a more or less
self-contained system of signification' (1995: 15).[5] Archaic linguistic forms
are known to linger in the registers of oral poetry, as Foley discussed in
relation to the Homeric case:

> As diachronically based studies have shown, the Homeric epic register consists
> of a kind of linguistic equilibrium that records the ever-modulating outcome
> of the competition between archaism and contemporary usage. Over time
> some battles are won and some are lost, according to the rules of contest in the
> medium, with the result that the register attains a special character as a way
> of speaking, constituting a marked species of language that no one used as
> an idiom for everyday communication (as would be expected because of its
> dedicated function). Some have thus viewed the diachronic mixture typical
> of Homeric diction as 'artificial', but from the perspective of register we can
> see that it is no more unreal or deviant than any other speech variety. (Foley
> 1995: 83)

Foley also referred to archaisms in Old English and South Slavic poetry.
Perhaps the expletive particle, as it is used in *Þrymskviða*, should not be
explained as the kind of 'reconstructive archaism' described by Fidjestøl
above, nor as a remnant from the time in which the poem was composed.
Rather, what may be termed a 'traditional archaism' could be part of the
poetic register even after it has become obsolete in other registers. This may
explain why all occurrences of the expletive particle in eddic poetry abide
by the rules described by Kuhn. If the particle were used as a reconstructive
archaism, the chances of errors would be greater. The expletive particle
may be seen as a recognisable and meaningful expression to those familiar
with the register and it may have served emphatic purposes, as Dal argued.
The possibility that the particle is an archaism of either sort renders it less
useful as a dating criterion, for how are we to determine if an occurrence is
an archaism or not? This is probably impossible in most cases, although

guesswork may be supported by studying other aspects of the poem in question, including other dating criteria.

Another linguistic phenomenon often used in dating eddic poems is the loss of initial *v-* in words originally beginning with *vr-*, such as *reiðr, reiði, reini, reka, rengja,* and *Rindr* (Fidjestøl 1999: 231–245). This change occurred in pre-literary Old West Norse, while *v-* was preserved in East Norse. In several cases, manuscripts preserve lines in which the absence of the initial *v-* causes inconsistent alliteration, as in the following case from *Vafþrúðnismál,* in which the initial *v-* in *vreka* is added by Neckel and Kuhn:

> Úlfr gleypa mun Aldafǫðr,
>   þess mun Víðarr *v*reka. (*Vm* 53/1–3)

[The wolf will swallow The Father of Men, Víðarr will avenge this.]

Here, the full line is without alliteration unless we assume *vreka* instead of the manuscript form *reka* (found in both R and A). This may indicate that the line was either composed before the transition from *vr-* to *r-,* or that it is influenced by East Norse. If the latter is the case, the requirement for an initial *vr-* would not reveal anything about the time of composition.

Since eddic poems were revised in transmission, as noted in the previous section, one might perhaps expect that the texts were changed to satisfy the demands of alliteration, either by preserving the initial *v-* or by revising the text to avoid the required initial *v-* in cases such as the one quoted from *Vafþrúðnismál* above. Such cases reflect both linguistic updating (the manuscripts omit initial *v-*) and alliterative dependence on the older form. Here one may detect a conservative attitude towards the poems during transmission, with alliterative inconsistency preferred to revision.

There is another, admittedly more complex, explanation. Since the old form *vreka* conflicts with the newer form *reka,* which is used in the very same manuscripts, some sense of consequence may have kept the scribes from writing out the initial *v-,* although it may have been preserved as a traditional archaism in oral performance (including recitations from manuscripts). As Fidjestøl noted, Óláfr hvítaskáld Þórðarson ('white-poet') (AD 1210–59) was aware that forms with *vr-* were old, but sometimes required in poetry, and, in his *Third Grammatical Treatise,* he gave a comparative explanation with references to initial *vr-* in other Germanic languages (Fidjestøl 1999: 232–3). The hypothesis that initial *vr-* was preserved in the register of eddic poets is perhaps supported by the fact that several cases in which *vr-* is required for the sake of alliteration occur in the phrase *vreiðr vega* ('to fight in anger'), which can be seen as a traditional expression, an oral formula within the poetic register.[6] Hence, the formula may have contributed to preserving knowledge of initial *vr-* among eddic poets and their audiences.

In other cases, alliteration rules require the shift *vr->r-*, as in this line from *Atlamál in grœnlenzku*:

> Rúnar nam at rísta, rengði þær Vingi (*Am* 4/1–2)
>
> [She carved some runes, Vingi defaced them . . .]

The form *vrengði* cannot be assumed here, since only *rengði* satisfies the alliterative demands and, unlike the previous example, there is only one probable explanation for the form: the line was composed in West Norse after the shift *vr->r-*. This is not very helpful for dating an eddic poem either, since forms with *r-* are present even in the early phase of skaldic poetry: for example, in the poetry of ninth-century skalds Bragi Boddason and Þjóðolfr ór Hvini ('from Hvinr'). Thus, forms with initial *r-* are expected across the entire period in which eddic poems are normally dated.

Some poems appear to have alliteration with *vr-* as an established principle, such as in *Vafþrúðnismál* and *Sigrdrífumál*. In a second group of poems, including *Atlakviða* and *Hávamál*, the forms are mixed, according to Fidjestøl. In a third group of poems, including *Grípisspá* and *Atlamál*, the forms with *r-* predominate. Fidjestøl suggested that the first group is, relatively speaking, older than the second and third groups (1999: 244–5). When it comes to absolute dating, Fidjestøl proposed that the first group may have been composed before the year 1000, and the second and third group after 900. From the perspective of register, we may note what Foley described above in the Homeric case as a 'competition between archaism and contemporary usage'. The presence of forms assuming both initial *vr-* and *r-* indicates that this feature lost ground when eddic poetry was composed and transmitted. If initial *vr-* was preserved as a traditional archaism, however, it may be easier to accept the relative chronology between the three groups of poems than any postulations about absolute age. As argued in the case of the expletive particle, one would expect disagreement between forms to be preserved in the poetic register and the language in general.

Loan words are another important criterion for dating some eddic poems, not least in the *Edda Kommentar*, where loan words are often taken to indicate that the text as a whole is no older than the loan words it includes. For example, the word *skillingr* in *Þrymskviða* is otherwise documented only in prose from the twelfth century. Hence, this and other young forms in *Þrymskviða* are held to support a dating of the poem to the twelfth century (II, 522–3, 526). Loan words and young words are clearly significant for questions of age and origin, but we must also consider the possibility of change during both oral and written transmission. The poems or stories that are preserved in several versions reveal that lexical revision was part of eddic transmission.[7] Thus, the age of specific words may possibly affect our view only of particular lines, a stanza, or a group of stanzas; this points to the importance of carefully considering the relationship between the element that it is possible to date and the text as a whole (see also Schier 1986: 378–9).

In some cases, the meaning of an already existing Old Norse word appears to be influenced by a West Germanic cognate (see Harris 1985: 103). In *Vǫlundarkviða*, the verb *draga* is used in the sense 'to bear, wear' (cf. modern German *tragen*) while it is normally used to mean 'to drag, draw' in Old Norse. This lends support to the idea that the poem has a West Germanic antecedent. Another case is the verb *svelta* ('to be hungry'; 'die from hunger'), the West Germanic cognate of which has the wider meaning 'to die'. In the heroic poems relating West Germanic material, the meaning is consequently 'die' (twelve occurrences), in accordance with the meaning of the verb in West Germanic languages. In this case, however, the meaning 'to die' is attested twice in Old Norse poems about Scandinavian heroes and once in *Merlínússpá*. The examples of *draga* and *svelta* exemplify the importance not only of loan words, but also of semantic influence on already existing Old Norse words.

Linguistic features occurring in eddic poems and in West Germanic languages may, however, be explained differently. Haukur Þorgeirsson (2012) has investigated a rare feature of *fornyrðislag* poetry which is often taken to indicate West Germanic influence: the late placement of the verb in conflict with Kuhn's rule V2. This 'rule' requires the finite verb to be located in the second syntactic position of the clause and is generally upheld in Old Norse prose, while eddic poetry, at times, has lines such as these (examples are taken from Haukur Þorgeirsson [2012: 239], with the finite verb italicised):

1) Þórr einn þar *vá* (*Vsp* 26/1)   [Þórr alone struck a blow there]
2) Karl orð um *kvað* (*Hym* 32/5)   [the old man spoke these words]
3) hrafn at meiði hátt *kallaði* (*Br* 5/3–4)   [a raven called out loudly from a tree]

Haukur Þorgeirsson has argued that the late placement of the verb need not be explained by influence from West Germanic, but may represent archaic syntactic structures also preserved in West Germanic, rendering the language of *fornyrðislag* even more archaic than that of the *dróttkvætt* metre, where the V2 rule is always followed in unbound clauses (see also Einar Ól. Sveinsson 1962: 239–40). Could a similar explanation account for the case of the verbs *draga* and *svelta*? Are the meanings occurring in eddic poetry which deviate from those found in Old Norse prose archaic rather than foreign? With regard to *svelta*, this may be the case, since the meaning 'to die' is arguably the older (Bjorvand and Lindeman 2007: 1084–5); the semantic development of *draga* is more uncertain (see Ásgeir Blöndal Magnússon 1995: 123; Bjorvand and Lindeman 2007: 180).[8]

I am in full agreement with Haukur Þorgeirsson (2012: 267) that the late placement of the verb in *fornyrðislag* and the frequency of the expletive particle indicate that the language in some *fornyrðislag* poetry is archaic, the more so when it correlates with other early traits, such as the use of *svelta* with the meaning 'die' and the dependence of alliteration on initial *vr-*. Yet even if we accept that these phenomena belong to an early stage of language development, it is far from obvious that the poems themselves do. These features may be preserved within a register that is distinct from everyday language. This clearly renders conclusions drawn from the statistics of occurrences (for example, of the expletive particle) more uncertain. But the presence of traditional archaisms may be significant for the consideration of the age of the register itself, a subject worth pursuing on its own. After all, eddic poems have numerous parallels throughout Scandinavia and even in other Germanic sources, and the history of this kind of poetry may be as important as the history of the extant poems.

Tradition and textual influences

In eddic studies, it has frequently been argued that similarities between different texts are caused by textual influence – that is to say, by a poet borrowing from an older text. If such arguments are accepted, they are significant for the process of dating the poems, since the borrowing obviously postdates the source text. Fidjestøl commented briefly on textual borrowing as a criterion for dating, but the chapter he planned on the subject was not finished before his untimely death. According to his brief notes on the subject, supplied in the postscript to *The Dating of Eddic Poetry*, Fidjestøl intended to address several problematic aspects of theories of textual influence. For example, he believed that the direction of influence 'can in only a very few cases be established with any certainty' (Fidjestøl 1999: 334). This is a serious problem for those who wish to use textual influence to establish relative chronology and it will be addressed below. However, the main purpose of this section is to investigate how ideas about oral transmission may moderate claims about textual influence.

There are cases in which textual influence is certain, as in, for example, the Helgi poems. In the presentation of *Helgakviða Hundingsbana II*, there are direct quotations from other poems which are referred to by title in the prose before stanzas 14 and 25: *Vǫlsungakviða in forna (The Ancient Poem about the Vǫlsungar)* and *Helgakviða* (that is *Helgakviða Hundingsbana I)*. The presentation of *Helgakviða Hundingsbana II* in R is clearly the result of extensive written revision; this is also seen in the way the poem is edited to complement *Helgakviða Hundingsbana I* (Harris 2008 [1983]). Yet, the Helgi poems do not only illustrate how texts were revised in manuscript transmission; the stories of Helgi Hundingsbani and Helgi Hjǫrvarðsson are so similar that they arguably derive from the same story pattern, in a manner 'characteristic of oral literature' (Harris 2008 [1983]: 196). A quarrel presented in both poems is set within the frame of a *senna*, a formalised flyting with a recognisable pattern, a 'semi-independent unit' (Harris 2008 [1983]: 202) that is evidently present in other texts (Harris 1979; Swenson 1991). The similarity between texts containing the *senna* may have little to do with borrowing poets and more to do with shared knowledge of an oral form.

Although the term 'register' is flexible enough to cover linguistic features as well as, for example, formulas and stock motifs, a wider concept that includes such things as the *senna* and the story pattern in the Helgi poems is still needed. The term 'tradition' may be elusive and problematic in several ways, but it does serve the purpose here as a term that includes register and inherited knowledge about, for instance, mythological and heroic material, and different kinds of performances that are echoed in extant written sources.[9] The term 'tradition' is therefore used here since it is a useful corrective which challenges textual influence as the only explanation for similarities between different texts. The *Edda Kommentar*, for example, suggests a variety of influences on the Helgi poems other than those mentioned above. One suggestion is that *Vǫluspá* influenced *Helgakviða Hundingsbana I* (IV, 156–7). In this case, it is not a matter of direct quotation, but rather of similarities in formulations and motifs, mainly at the beginning of *Helgakviða Hundingsbana I* (1–16) and in the *senna* part of the poem (32–46). The most convincing verbal correspondences, exclusive to the two poems, are *ár var alda* ('it was a long time ago', *HH I* 1/1, *Vsp* 3/1) and *forn spjǫll* ('ancient lore', *HH I* 36 and *Vsp* 1). Other similarities emphasised in *Edda Kommentar* IV are the motifs 'norns', 'war', and the 'appearance of valkyries' occurring in that exact order (*HH I* 2–16; *Vsp* 20–26, 30). Another example cited by the *Edda Kommentar* is the association of fratricide with 'wolfishness' (*HH I* 36, *Vsp* 45). According to the *Edda Kommentar*, the poet of *Helgakviða Hundingsbana I* has, by means of the phrases and motifs from *Vǫluspá*, attempted to place Helgi in the mythic light of a distant heroic prehistory. The direction of the influence is determined in the *Edda Kommentar* by arguing that it is unlikely for the *Vǫluspá* poet to model Old Norse cosmogony and eschatology on the biography of a human hero or the grotesque allegations in the *senna*. Tradition is not considered as a possible background for the similarities, although this possibility may well be worth investigating.

The precise wording *ár var alda, þat er* ... ('it was a long time ago that ...') is unique to the two poems, but it is functionally related to expressions found elsewhere in eddic poetry and serves to locate the story in the distant past. Phrases such as *ár var þat er* ('it was early that') and other variants and even *í árdaga* ('in the early days') occur in a number of eddic poems serving a similar purpose (Kellogg 1988: 22). These are expressions with a meaning and function comparable to the English phrase 'once upon a time', and certainly bear the mark, as pointed out by Lönnroth (2011 [1981]: 222), of oral tradition. They should probably be seen as belonging to the register of eddic poetry, which may also be the case with *forn spjǫll* ('ancient lore'). The three motifs 'norns', 'war', and the 'appearance of valkyries' certainly do not suggest textual influence as separate motifs; at least the latter two are too common for that. The valkyries are often present in battle and escort dead warriors from the battlefield; hence, the order of the motifs 'war' and the 'appearance of valkyries' reflects a common way of thinking about these beings, rather than representing a specific association with *Vǫluspá*. After all, the function and logic of the motifs are quite different in the two texts. The wolfishness associated with fratricide is an even less convincing example of a textual loan, for dishonourable acts are generally associated with the wolf in Old Norse culture, and fratricide also belongs to this category (see Thorvaldsen 2011).

Thus, one can easily accept the idea that the poet of *Helgakviða Hundingsbana I* alludes effectively to mythology without assuming direct textual influence from *Vǫluspá* on the poem. Similarity in formulation should be expected, since formulas and other elements in a register will be associated with certain themes or functions. This is an important aspect of the register, according to Foley, since a traditional expression carries an immanent meaning. For example, the wording *ár var alda* may stimulate wider associations with the creation myths that are not directly described in the two texts. Another example is present in *Helgakviða Hundingsbana I* and describes the sound of a fleet approaching the battlefield: *sem bjǫrg eða brim brotna myndi* ('as if mountains or surf might break asunder', *HH I* 28/5–6). This is comparable to *Grímnismál* 38, which refers to Svǫl, who shields humans from the sun and whose destruction would ignite *bjǫrg ok brim*. The formulaic pair *bjǫrg ok brim* ('mountains and sea') is associated with destructive events, even those of cosmological proportions.[10] There are a number of other parallels in Old Norse poetry presenting critical and violent situations in terms of nature burning, shaking, breaking, etc., and not surprisingly such expressions and motifs also occur in descriptions of world destruction (Thorvaldsen 2012: 256–7). In this case, tradition can be considered as an alternative and even more probable explanation for the similarities between *Vǫluspá* and *Helgakviða Hundingsbana I* than the postulated influence of one text on another.

It is possible to delimit a number of other expressions, motifs, and themes, which, due to their use and distribution across the eddic corpus, do not indicate textual influence, but rather poets' knowledge of the eddic tradition. The examples below are noted in the *Edda Kommentar*, but why these similarities should occur across many eddic poems remains mostly unexplained in the commentary. Textual influence is not suggested in these cases:

1. *unz rjúfask regin*   [until the gods are torn asunder]
2. *við himin sjálfan*   [against heaven itself]
3. *láta hjǫr standa til hjarta*   [let the sword stab the heart]

These expressions may be regarded as part of a poetic register, albeit one not limited to eddic poetry (*láta hjǫr standa til hjarta* is also documented in skaldic poetry). The first example is a specific reference to *ragnarǫk* as the time when the gods will be destroyed, and the whole phrase is used to refer to something which will prevail until *ragnarǫk* such as the wolf remaining chained (*Ls* 41), Þórr residing in Þrúðheimr (*Grm* 4), and the use of powerful runes (*Sd* 19); in *Vafþrúðnismál* 52, Óðinn asks what will happen to him *þá er rjúfask regin* ('when the gods are torn asunder'). The poet of *Fjölsvinnsmál*, a poem preserved only in post-medieval manuscripts, also knew the expression (st. 14; see Bugge 1867: 345). Of course, the expression is intimately linked to the motif of the fall of the gods, described in even more sources and in comparable terms. The second prepositional phrase *við himin sjálfan* ('against heaven itself') occurs in two descriptions of the end of the world, describing the flames (*Vsp* 57) and the sea (*Hdl* 42). In *Helgakviða Hundingsbana II* 38, Helgi is compared to a glorious calf, whose horns glow *við himin sjálfan*. The third example is not limited to eddic poems, but also appears in skaldic poetry, and many similar constructions exist with other words for 'sword' and other weapons (Sveinbjörn Egilsson and Finnur Jónsson 1931: 533). This kind of verbal patterning is very probably traditional.

The problem with the *Edda Kommentar* is that the role of oral tradition is hardly discussed, and claims about textual influence are seldom balanced against the possibility of traditional expression. Since textual influence plays such an important role in the *Edda Kommentar*, there is a reason to suspect that greater awareness of tradition might have affected its dating of the poems. This would seem to be the case for *Þrymskviða*, as I have argued in earlier publications (Thorvaldsen 2008b; 2012). Most of the similarities between *Þrymskviða* and other poems, which are taken to be textual influences in the *Edda Kommentar* and in earlier scholarship, are simply what we might expect from an oral tradition.

There are also examples of passages that are perhaps too long to be considered formulas, as Kurt Schier (1986: 382) has pointed out. His first example is from *Baldrs draumar*:

> Senn vóru æsir allir á þingi
> ok ásynjur allar á máli,
> ok um þat réðu, ríkir tívar,
> hví væri Baldri ballir draumar. (*Bdr* 1)

> [All together the Æsir came in council and all the Asynior in consultation, and what they debated, those dauntless gods, was why Baldr was having baleful dreams.]

In *Þrymskviða* exactly the same formulation appears with a different concluding long line: *hvé þeir Hlórriða hamar um sœtti* ('how he [Loki] and Þórr [Hlórriði] should get back the hammer', *Prk* 14/7–8). Schier argued that the wording is applicable to a variety of contexts and that it is formulaic (*formelhaft*). The motif of the 'assembly of the gods' occurs in a number of eddic poems and in skaldic poetry as well. In the quoted stanza, we may note that it also contains the formula *æsir ok ásynjur* (Thorvaldsen 2008b: 152–3, 158–9). Although it is possible that the stanza is borrowed from one poem into the other, it is important to recognise that both the motif conveyed in the stanza and the formula *æsir ok ásynjur* could also be regarded as traditional.

Schier's second example presents the myth of how Váli avenges the killing of Baldr:

> Baldrs bróðir var of borinn snemma,
> sá nam Óðins sonr einnættr vega.
> Þó hann æva hendr né hǫfuð kembði,
> áðr á bál um bar Baldrs andskota. (*Vsp* 32/5–33/4)

> Rindr berr *Vála* í vestrsǫlum,
> sá man Óðins sonr einnættr vega;
> hǫnd um þvær né hǫfuð kembir,
> áðr á bál um berr Baldrs andskota. (*Bdr* 11)

> [Baldr's brother was born quickly; Óðinn's son started killing at one night old. He never washed his hands nor combed his hair until he brought Baldr's adversary to the funeral pyre. (*Vsp* 32/5–33/4)]

> [Rindr will give birth to Váli in western halls, Óðinn's son will fight when one night old; he won't wash his hands nor comb his hair until he's brought to the pyre Baldr's enemy. (*Bdr* 11)]

Here the variation is greater than in the previous example and the whole passage is less transferable to other contexts. Schier considers it to be a clear example of direct textual influence. It could be added that parts of this passage bear close resemblance to other poems and texts. The remarkable child, ready for battle one day old, is also present in *Helgakviða Hundingsbana I*:

> Stendr í brynju burr Sigmundar,
> dœgrs eins gamall. (6/1–3)

> [The son of Sigmundr, one day old, stands in his mail-coat.]

Whether this should be seen as a traditional motif or not depends on whether we accept the claim that *Helgakviða Hundingsbana I* is influenced by *Vǫluspá* (see above). The lines about washing hands and combing hair are also paralleled in a description of how a corpse should be prepared for the coffin by washing the hands and the head, and by combing and drying: *þvá hendr ok hǫfuð, kemba ok þerra* (*Sd* 34/3–4). In *Reginsmál* (st. 25/1), the still highly relevant advice is given that every warrior should be *kemðr ok þveginn* ('combed and washed'). Considering the close association of the two activities referred to by the verbs (even today), it is not surprising that they are also associated in prose (Fritzner 1886–96, 2: 272); this expression is clearly not limited to a poetic register.

There are other examples of long parallel passages, such as the descriptions of Ymir in *Vafþrúðnismál* 21 and *Grímnismál* 40. In that case, there is a rearrangement of verse lines that excludes direct copying as an explanation and makes it more likely that the lines have been recovered from memory or that the stanza has been consciously revised by the borrowing poet, whether during oral or written transmission. We can keep open the option that borrowing may occur in oral and written transmission as long as the South Slavic analogy is not taken for granted. If it is argued, however, that the eddic poems were in the same state of flux as the ones described by Parry and Lord in the South Slavic case, it leads inevitably to the conclusion that cases of verbal similarity, which are seemingly not the results of oral formulas, must *only* be the product of written transmission.

The relevance of textual influence in establishing the relative chronology of eddic poems should not be completely dismissed, but its importance is limited. In each case of conspicuous similarity, it needs to be considered whether the coincidence depends on tradition or textual influence. The cases in which several and significantly different versions of a story or poem exist are exceptional, and the study of these cases is important in identifying the possibility of changes during transmission. The Helgi poems and the versions of *Vǫluspá* are prime examples of this. The concept of tradition should not simply replace that of textual influence as an explanation for similarities between different eddic poems, but it may challenge many of the numerous existing claims about textual influence in eddic poetry, such as those set out in the *Edda Kommentar*.

Another of the major problems with older theories of textual influence is the question of the direction of influence, as Fidjestøl noted (1999: 334). For example, in many cases it was argued that an expression or motif that occurs in several texts was original to the source in which it was used in the most successful way. This idea relies on subjective considerations of quality and also fails to recognise the possibility of a poet improving on what he or she found in older texts (Thorvaldsen 2008b: 144–50; 2012: 251–2). Even if we were to accept the idea that *Vǫluspá* influenced *Helgakviða Hundingsbana I*, as argued in the *Edda Kommentar*, it is difficult indeed to present a cogent argument that the *Vǫluspá*-poet could not have drawn inspiration from a poem about a human hero, even from the grotesque *senna*; as a consequence, *Helgakviða Hundingsbana I* could be considered to be the source of *Vǫluspá*. Why should the mythological subject matter be seen as too exalted to allow for such borrowing? Overall, it is rarely possible to find compelling arguments for the direction of textual influence.

We know that some eddic poems which are no longer extant did once exist, such as the heroic poem *Vǫlsungarkviða in forna*, mentioned above. *Heimdalargaldr* (*The Chant of Heimdallr*) may stand as an example of a lost mythological poem, since only a single long line and the title are preserved in *Snorra Edda* (*Gylfaginning*: 26). It is, of course, impossible to determine the nature of eddic poems that are known to have existed, but are no longer preserved, and more poetry probably existed without leaving any recognisable trace in written sources. This poses a problem for employing textual borrowing as a criterion for dating, since it depends on a certain passage or motif occurring in a small number of sources, preferably two, if the direction of borrowing is to be explained in a reasonable way. The number of possible directions of influence increases with the number of occurrences of a certain conspicuous similarity, and thus the problematic nature of such assumptions tends to become apparent in cases where a similarity between three or more sources is explained as the result of textual influence. Since any expression or motif may also have occurred in now-lost poems, hypotheses of textual influence would most likely be weakened if we knew what had been lost (see also Fidjestøl 1999: 335).

Logically, each and every conspicuous similarity could be explained as effects of either or both textual influence and tradition. Although the *Edda Kommentar* is an excellent tool for eddic scholars, it serves as an example of how the power of tradition is often forgotten, even in cases where textual influence is not suggested, as in the three examples given above. In these cases, understanding eddic poetry as orally derived poetry would clearly be helpful, since these expressions are easily explained as formulaic elements drawn from the poetic register. However, such considerations come at a price, for even in cases where the *Edda Kommentar* and earlier scholarship claim textual influence, explanations based on tradition may often be preferable. Thus, the concepts of register and tradition pose serious challenges to some of the most common criteria used to determine when the first version of a poem came into existence, such as the linguistic criteria studied in the previous section and the textual influence studied in this section. At the same time, these concepts bring something to the table which may perhaps compensate for the loss.

Tradition and dating

A common reason to undertake the dating of eddic poetry is to determine the source value of the poems: for example, in the study of religion or literary history. Edwin Jessen (1871) argued that the extant eddic poems were considerably younger than was commonly thought at the time, but he also argued that the poems are mostly trustworthy sources for mythology.

This view is developed by Preben Meulengracht Sørensen (1991), who defends the use of eddic mythological poems as sources for pre-Christian religion, though he does not see the poems themselves as pre-Christian (see also Schjødt, Chapter 7 in this Handbook). The methods for dating the poems can hardly be trusted, Meulengracht Sørensen argued, and eddic poems may have been more prone to change than skaldic ones. Meulengracht Sørensen more or less dismissed the possibility that the texts themselves could be considered pre-Christian, but still considered them to be relevant sources for the study of pre-Christian religion: a text may be young, but its subject matter may be old. Fidjestøl notes that although the poems are redeemed as sources for pre-Christian religion, 'they are lost as sources to the history of Old Norse poetry anterior to the period when they were written down' (1999: 194).

My investigation confirms Meulengracht Sørensen's doubts about the methods used to determine the age of eddic poetry. The examples from *Vǫluspá* and the Helgi poems may indicate that eddic poetry was generally revisable, and the shift *vr->r-* is only one example of linguistic updating. Even if memorisation and recitation were prominent forms of oral transmission, we may expect that changes occurred that are no longer detectable, unless we intend to resurrect the half-forgotten practices of early philological scholarship. In addition, tradition may explain both linguistic archaisms and conspicuous similarities between different poems. This reduces the importance of both these criteria for the dating of eddic poetry. Fidjestøl's 'reasonable identity' between the original composition and the extant form of the text is a highly problematic assumption that begs the question of whether such identity may reasonably be expected; for example, why should we assume the linguistic forms of the extant text will reflect the period of composition? This chapter suggests (as have other scholars before me) that such an assumption is misguided.

The likely role of tradition in the composition and transmission of eddic poetry does not, however, support the separation of form and content that is central to Meulengracht Sørensen's argument. For instance, archaic linguistic forms standing in contrast to a scribe's contemporary language require a diachronic interpretation: they may be remnants of the first version of a poem, but they may also, as comparative perspectives suggest, be traditional archaisms preserved in the register that poets employed. Formulas that are more-or-less specific to mythology also show that linguistic form and mythological content cannot be completely separated, such as in the cases noted above (*unz rjúfask regin* and *við himin sjálfan*),

and in the formula *jǫrð ok upphiminn* ('earth and heaven above') studied by
Lars Lönnroth (2011 [1981]: 219–41). These expressions are likely to have
been elements of the poets' register, and are dependent on mythological
ideas and imagery. The border between form and content is consequently
utterly blurred.

Meulengracht Sørensen argued that the subject matter of a poem may be
regarded as pre-Christian if the content was based on a trustworthy
mythological tradition.[11] Fidjestøl (1999: 194) observed, however, that the
trustworthiness of a myth or mythological motif has often been hotly
contested, and that the prehistory of a poem's content may be as difficult
to determine as the prehistory of the poem itself. In fact, the concept of
tradition clearly renders the separation of the content from its expression
problematic. When a mythological idea is associated with a formula, it
certainly strengthens the trustworthiness of the source, since it is less likely
to express a particular idea which is not in accord with mythological
tradition. The use of all kinds of traditional expressions in a text, not just
those directly associated with mythology, would indicate that the poet
possessed general familiarity with tradition, thus increasing the value of the
text as a source for myths and mythological knowledge. In addition, the
concept of register assumes that its components carry meaning which may
be more-or-less specific to it, and these would be missed if register and
tradition are not taken into consideration by historians of religion (see, for
example, the case in Lönnroth, 2011 [1981]). Hence, even if the age of an
eddic poem is seen as more or less indeterminable, historians of religion can
hardly confine themselves to the study of subject matter as something
completely separate from the form of expression.

If we return to the perspective of the historian of literature, the concept
of tradition means that the poems are not lost as 'sources to the history of
Old Norse poetry anterior to the period when they were written down'
(Fidjestøl 1999: 194). Unless we explain every linguistic archaism as
a reconstruction, and every formula and stock motif as the result of textual
influence, the extant forms do reveal something about the prehistory of
eddic poems. Formulas and stock motifs may cause various problems for
dating the first version of an eddic poem, but they allow the literary
historian to develop theories about the tradition and register it expresses.
Lönnroth's article (2011 [1981]) is worth mentioning again since it docu-
ments a geographically widespread formula and indicates that parts of the
eddic tradition are indeed archaic. For the literary historian, it could be
argued that the age and nature of tradition may be a more important and
more accessible object of study than the prehistory of the extant poems

themselves. But do the arguments presented here render the dating of specific eddic poems an impossible task?

Although the concept of 'reasonable identity' is perhaps more useful than it is trustworthy, I tend to agree with Fidjestøl (1999: 195) when he argues that 'the question of their dating is accessible to rational deliberation'. Although the date of the first oral performance of an eddic poem is probably out of reach in most cases, the failure of our methods does not necessarily indicate that the poems are young, or that the oral delivery of eddic poetry is comparable to that of the South Slavic songs. After all, many eddic poems are explicitly presented as old in *Snorra Edda* and in the *fornaldarsögur* (sagas of ancient times), and the eddic mode is associated with heroes of the distant past (see Clunies Ross 2005: 6–13). One may gain more by asking in what ways the poems may or may not be considered old, and from whose perspective they were regarded as old, than by searching for the lost moment when a poet performed something which eventually became the extant text.[12]

Notes

1. Both Terry Gunnell (2005: 93–5) and Preben Meulengracht Sørensen (1991: 219–20) address the comparative material in their discussions of the dating of eddic poetry.
2. This is apparent, for example, in the case of *Rígspula*, preserved in Codex Wormianus (AM 242 fol.). The poem has been dated to both the pre-Christian period and to the twelfth and thirteenth centuries (see the discussions in Dronke 1997: 174–208 and *Edda Kommentar* III, 488–513).
3. The poem *Grímnismál* has been interpreted as presenting a pre-Christian initiation ritual of a king (Fleck 1970), and the same goes for *Hyndluljóð* (see the analysis by Schjødt, Chapter 7 in this Handbook). *Skírnismál* was seen by Anne Heinrichs as a 'travesty of pagan religious belief' (1997: 36) in which the love-sick god Freyr is ridiculed. Deliberate archaisation has been extensively argued in the case of *Þrymskviða*; see *Edda Kommentar* II, 509–75 and references there.
4. The expletive particle may occur before nouns, adjectives and verbs that had a prefix in Proto-Germanic (see Fidjestøl 1999: 207–8).
5. Peter H. Matthews gives the following description of *register* in more general terms: 'A set of features of speech or writing characteristic of a particular type of linguistic activity or a particular group when engaging in it' (Matthews 2007: 339).
6. Several scholars have commented on this formula (see Fidjestøl 1999: 235; Schier 1986: 379; Sveinbjörn Egilsson and Finnur Jónsson 1931: 461–462).
7. There are many examples of possible eddic rephrasing identified by Harris in his article on the Helgi poems (2008 [1983]); and the variants of *Vǫluspá* also

reflect interesting differences in wording. One of the most famous examples is: *Ár var alda, / þat er Ymir byggði* ('Young were the years when Ymir made his settlement', *Vsp* 3/1–2). In *Snorra Edda* the line is quoted as *Ár var alda / þat er ekki var* ('Young were the years when nothing existed', *Gylfaginning*: 9).

8. There are several other reasons to question the theory of 'Fremdstofflieder' (see Fidjestøl 1999: 294–323, and Harris, Chapter 2 in this Handbook).

9. See especially Gunnell 1995. Foley makes a necessary distinction between register and performance throughout *The Singer of Tales in Performance* (1995), with the use of a register determined by the specifics of performance.

10. On these kinds of formulaic pairs, see Gurevič 1986.

11. 'Det er tilstrækkeligt at tage stilling til, om det i henseende til de dele, der benyttes, bygger på en troværdig tradition' ('It is sufficient to consider whether it builds on a reliable tradition with regard to the parts of the poem that are used') (Meulengracht Sørensen 1991: 218).

12. I wish to express my thanks to Terry Gunnell, Else Mundal, and Haukur Þorgeirsson for offering valuable advice on previous drafts of this chapter.

CHAPTER 5

Eddic performance and eddic audiences

Terry Gunnell

What exactly was an eddic poem? The first thing that can be stated with
any certainty is that it was not what it has become – in other words, a poem
written in ink on parchment or paper, gathered together in a book with
other poems in a format designed essentially for silent, private reading, in
which all the stanzas can be quickly viewed side by side and reread at will.
Prior to the early thirteenth century (when *Grímnismál, Vafþrúðnismál,*
and *Vǫluspá* were transcribed in the small collection probably used by
Snorri Sturluson for the *Prose Edda*), there is little doubt that most of the
eddic poems lived in the oral tradition. Indeed, this would seem to be
underlined by Snorri's statements with regard to eddic quotations that
words were said (*sagt*) and figures named (*nefndar*) in *Vǫluspá* and
Grímnismál; and that stanzas could be heard (*máttu heyra*) in
Grímnismál, or were uttered by Vafþrúðnir (*hér segir Vafþrúðnir jǫtunn*).[1]
That the poems lived in this form for some time before they came to be
recorded would also appear to be stressed by the fact that, unlike with
many of the skaldic poems, Snorri does not appear to know the identities of
the authors of these works, referring to *Vǫluspá* simply as – or alongside –
what he calls *forn vísindi* ('ancient wisdom') (*Gylfaginning*: 12). The poems'
potentially 'ancient' nature and origin are supported still further by the use
of the expression *fornyrðislag* (literally 'old story metre') for one of the main
eddic metres, and the regular mention in the poems of trees, animals,
objects, societies, attitudes, and beliefs that seem to have been unknown in
Iceland (where the poems were transcribed). All this suggests that many of
the poems must have originated in one form or another in a different
environment (see below with regard to *Grímnismál*, for example; see also
Einar Ólafur Sveinsson 1962: 202–66).

This chapter will not be concerned with suggesting any precise 'original'
date for any of the eddic poems. The environmental features of the poems
and the suggestions of 'age' are mentioned above first and foremost to
remind us of the fact that (not least in Snorri's mind) these were works that

originated, travelled, and had lived for some time in the medium of *sound* rather than in writing.[2] The wide-ranging implications and ramifications of this feature need careful consideration. Among other things, they mean that whoever created and decided the format of the first versions of these poems, and whoever passed them on to the eventual thirteenth-century transcriber(s) would have conceived of his or her 'work' as something that was not read, but performed. In other words, rather than being encountered in the form of silent written symbols, the poem would have been passed on by a human speaker to a human listener, as part of what can be termed a 'performance interaction'. The interaction in question would also have taken place in a particular space and time (a living context which the 'composer' would have been well aware of at the time of composition, just like all subsequent performers who later passed on the work). In addition to the fact that the interaction would have involved at least two senses (sight and hearing, rather than merely sight, as in reading), it should also be remembered that personal memory, association, and expectation would have also played key roles in the ways in which each member of the audience would have received and (particularly important) *experienced* the piece in question. Among other things, they would also have affected the group dynamic that would have been established between the performer and audience as part of the performance.

As anyone who knows anything about the nature of the oral tradition will be aware (merely on the basis of the stories that they, their friends, family, and colleagues regularly pass on in a range of situations in daily life), all of the aforementioned features would have meant that the poem that was performed and received would have subtly changed with each performance. Here, I am not only referring to the text itself, which would probably always have undergone some degree of variation, especially if one considers the sensible arguments of earlier eddic scholars such as Joseph Harris (1983, 1985, 2000a, b; 2003), Robert Kellogg (1988), and Gísli Sigurðsson (1986, 1992, 1998, 2013), inspired in part by the groundbreaking work of pioneering scholars such as Albert Lord and John Miles Foley (see Lord 1960; Foley 1988, 1991, 1995, 2002). As regular performers are well aware, a different time, a different audience, and a different place will mean an essentially different performance, even when the same performer is presenting essentially the same text. They will not only have affected the way the work was understood, but also how it was experienced. In a sense, we must always consider some degree of restoration (Schechner 2013: 28–9), recreation, or rebuilding in space and time, rather than repetition.

The degree of changeability noted above means, among other things, that attempting to date oral poetry prior to its earliest recording will always be extremely difficult. It is clear that focusing on the presence of one or two apparently thirteenth-century lines (also encountered elsewhere) in a transcribed text of an oral poem as a means of dating the work *as a whole* is going to be a very untrustworthy process. It certainly does not mean that we are necessarily dealing with a work that was created as a whole in the thirteenth century, simply because the words in question could well be a recent (even temporary) addition to a work that was constantly 'under construction' (as one can see by comparing the Codex Regius and Hauksbók editions of *Vǫluspá*, neither of which can be considered more 'correct' or 'original' than the other) (see further Einar Ólafur Sveinsson 1962: 322; Jón Helgason 1964: viii; and Quinn 1990b). The fact that the words are also found in other works could indicate a borrowing. However, it could also have a background in the common use of older formulas.

The essential nature of an oral text as something that existed in the form of sound rather than writing also means that any written transcription of the text is bound to be a 'translation' of some kind (from one medium to another) rather than a direct recording (in the sense of an audio recording of music). The extent to which the eventual transcription is going to be different from the 'original' work is effectively summed up by John Miles Foley:

> Any oral poem, like any utterance, is profoundly contingent on its context. To assume that it is detachable – that we can comfortably speak of 'an oral poem' as a freestanding item – is necessarily to take it out of context. And what is the lost context? It is the performance, the audience, the poet, the music, the specialized way of speaking, the gestures, the costuming, the visual aids, the occasion, the ritual, and myriad other aspects of the given poem's reality. ... And when we pry an oral poem out of one language and insert it into another, things will inevitably change. We'll pay a price. (Foley 2002: 60)

Foley's words need to be borne in mind by anyone working with texts that lived in the oral tradition. If nothing else, they stress that the static printed versions of the eddic poems are about as close to the nature of the 'living' works as they were conceived by the 'original' poets and performers as sheet music is to a performed symphony at the Last Night of the Proms in London's Royal Albert Hall. Admittedly, there is no question that the 'original' performance on which the transcription is based is going to be irrecoverable (as with any performance). Nonetheless, totally ignoring the nature of the missing original form and contextual background when analysing an eddic work is going to mean that one is going to be analysing something quite different from the 'original' work as it was originally conceived, received, and passed on prior to its eventual transcription. In short, as Foley points out (see above), if one wishes to examine the 'original' oral work and how it functioned, it is essential to try to assemble as much of the original context as possible, engaging in a process that I have termed 'performance archaeology' (see, for example, Gunnell 2013b: 189).

Considering merely the key element of sound, we can be sure that we are dealing with entities that would have been conceived as being closer to music than writing. Like the work of the beat poets, or slam poetry today, as Foley notes, the poems would have been conceived not only in terms of story, direct meaning, and implication, but also in terms of chosen sounds, rhythms, timing, tones, and volume, which would naturally have varied by performer and venue (as Foley stresses; see also Millward 2015).

Over and above the element of sound, we can also be certain that those present at the time of the performance would have *observed* the performer standing or sitting in front of them. This means that while listening and reacting instinctively to the sounds of the work, they would have been simultaneously watching and interpreting his or her gestures and movements and facial expressions, looking him or her in the eye, and thereby bonding for a moment amidst particular surroundings and a particular society, often inside a hall, in the evening, among males, in firelight, smoke, and shadows, and after a fair amount of drinking. Both the words and the experience of the performance as a whole within the setting would have also played off personal memories and associations within each listener. It might be said that all of the above features would have played essential parts in the poetic work as it was received (and originally conceived).

As the American theatre and performance studies scholar Richard Schechner usefully reminds us, like any human performance, the oral performance of an eddic poem would have found itself somewhere on the variable dyad between 'ritual' and 'play' (Schechner 2013: 49, 79–80).[3] This placement would also have varied over time, with the ritualistic elements gradually reducing in importance as Christianity gained a hold over society. This feature reminds us also that all poetic works are seen by their creators and performers as having a function. The same applies to the eddic poems which were naturally originally 'created' with a purpose in mind which would have been closely connected to the society which would have been expected to receive them in performance.[4] It should also be borne in mind, though, that this 'original' purpose might have been quite different from the functions the poem might have later attained when people decided it should be passed on orally, performed again, preserved in writing, or even placed on show in a museum. Each of these functions will have had a key role to play in the overall 'meaning' of the poem at different times, and it is natural that each should be borne in mind when analysing the eddic poems. In this chapter, emphasis is naturally being placed on the functions that lay behind the creation of the 'original' work and the ensuing performances that came about as the work was passed on in the oral tradition, much of which can be assessed by reading the poems closely and analysing exactly how the poems might have 'worked' in performance.

As part of this analysis, as Schechner stresses (2013: 225–49), one must realise that all performances, when it comes down to it, involve more than just the performance itself, and often have more than one function. Few, if any, performances are totally impromptu or limited to the time and place of the performance. Almost all performances will involve a wider framework, which might begin with a period of preparation (possibly involving elements of long-term training and learning, as well as the creation and/or rehearsal of the piece that is to be performed). Even the day of performance itself will usually include immediate preparations and a warm-up of some kind before the performance itself commences (both for the performer and the audience). The performance is then followed by the immediate reactions to what has been witnessed, heard, and experienced; the 'cool down' for performer and audience; and what Schechner terms the longer-term 'aftermath' as people consider exactly what took place during the performance and how effective it was. This will, among other things, raise the question of whether the performance actually changed anything in people's lives, and if so what? Considering this wider temporal framework, one realises that the performance will have had personal and social functions, immediate functions, and long-term functions; these last will have been more closely associated with the critical aspects involved in the aftermath. It is essential, then, that we consider a poem's creation, recreation, and later preservation as potentially separate entities.

Types of eddic performance

With regard to function, performance, and reasons for preservation, as I have noted elsewhere (Gunnell 1995: 185–94; 2006b, 2008, 2011), it seems apparent that eddic poetry cannot be considered as a unified genre. It should never be forgotten that the poems were not grouped together as 'eddic poems' because of their essential shared nature or form, but because many of them came to be gathered together in a couple of manuscripts which contained material that had similar themes. The Codex Regius and AM 748 I 4° (see further Clunies Ross, Chapter 1 in this Handbook) can thus be viewed as being comparable to other hybrid collections such as Hauksbók or the *Carmina Burana* manuscript. From the viewpoint of genre, form, and, not least, oral performance, the works contained in these two main eddic collections can be divided into at least two distinct groups on the basis not only of metre but also of the genres associated with the various metres, which seem to demand very different forms of performance. Those poems composed in *fornyrðislag* (see Fulk, Chapter 13 in this Handbook) would have involved a performer relating a poetic narrative set in the past (or the mythical world) to an audience in the present. While the performer would often quote the words of speakers from the past (or the mythical world) to those in the present, sometimes at length, he or she would have essentially remained in the role of storyteller standing in the present with the audience, in their time.

Those eddic works composed in *ljóðaháttr*, and the closely associated *galdralag* (see Fulk, Chapter 13 in this Handbook), are very different in nature. Over and above the fact that these metres are primarily used for mythological subjects, the names given to them imply that they were at some point seen as having had associations with *ljóð* (with the meaning of 'charm' or 'spell'; cf. *Hávamál* st. 146) and *galdr* (literally 'magic'). Both words were directly associated with sound, as can be seen in the close association *ljóð* has to the word *hljóð* ('sound'), and the modern Icelandic expression *að ljóða á* ('to direct a poetic spell at [someone]': see further Gunnell 1995: 343–6); while *galdr* is related to the verb *að gala* ('to crow'). It might also be remembered that magic and charms always involve both words and action, implying that at some point an accepted association must have existed between the *ljóðaháttr* and *galdralag* metres and 'magical' (or at least efficacious) ritual of some kind. This idea is strengthened by the fact that any performance of works involving these metres will have involved a form of 'uppvakning' – in other words, a summoning up of figures from the past or another world in front of a living audience in the performance space (see below). In short, unlike the performance of most poems in *fornyrðislag*, living performance of the *ljóðaháttr* poems would have opened the gates to an active state of between-world or dual-world liminality (especially in a time when people believed in the

Old Norse gods). This is because, with only one exception (*Vafþrúðnismál*
st. 5: see further Gunnell 1995: 277), poems in the eddic *ljóðaháttr* metre
always take the form of direct first-person speech, with no intermediary
(suggesting that this format was directly associated with the metre). This
use of direct speech means that in a performance of a *ljóðaháttr* poem,
characters from the past or the mythological world speak 'directly' to the
audience (as happens in a theatrical performance) rather than through
a storytelling intermediary. The characters (speaking through the performer's mouth, and now directly associated with his or her actions) thus
seem to be present in the room with the audience, creating what Lars
Lönnroth has referred to as a 'double scene' (Lönnroth 1971, 1979; see also
Harris 2000c), a situation in which two worlds exist at once (that of the
characters and that of the audience), causing those of the audience who
momentarily 'believe' or sympathise with the speaking characters to question the borders between the worlds. In short, in performance, these
mythically associated monologic or dialogic works usher in a momentary
'sacred time' (Eliade 1958: 388–408), in which the gods manifest themselves
among, or in front of, the audience (who, it would seem, would probably
have stood or sat on the same level as the performer in or outside the hall,
which would have allowed even more interaction and blurring of
borderlines).

Some might sneer at this idea and argue that audiences are always aware
of the difference between the worlds they inhabit and the world of
performance. Such an argument, however, ignores the degree to which
modern audiences can get involved in a theatrical play, and the descriptions of both ancient drama and of the Middle Ages, or even many kinds
of African drama in the present, which underline how uncertain many
audiences are about the 'unreality' of a theatre performance.[5] That a similar
blending of imaginary and real worlds existed in Old Norse perception can
perhaps be sensed in the way that Gunnarr Hámundarson 'becomes'
(rather than 'acts') Kaupa-Heðinn in *Njáls saga* (*The Saga of Njáll*); Qrvar-
Oddr 'becomes' the *næframaðr* ('bark-man') in *Qrvar-Odds saga* (*The Saga
of Arrow-Oddr*); Gunnarr helmingr 'becomes' Freyr in *Ögmundar þáttr
dytts ok Gunnars helmings* (*The Tale of Ögmundr Dint and Half-Gunnar*);
and Þorleifr jarlsskáld 'becomes' a *stafkarl* ('beggar') in *Þorleifs þáttr
jarlsskálds* (*The Tale of Þorleifr Earl's Poet*) (see Gunnell 1995: 84–5). It is
clear that when the line between the performed world and that of the
audience starts blurring in this fashion, 'stuff happens', not least in the
sense that everything and everyone in and around the performance space
starts to change and/or become potentially charged.

Almost all the research work I have carried out into the eddic poems up until now (Gunnell 1995, 2004, 2006b, 2008, 2011, 2013a, 2013b) has focused on examining the mythological and heroic poems in *ljóðaháttr* from the above performance viewpoint, examining them in the same way as scholars of drama examine the texts of medieval dramas or Shakespeare plays, or modern scholars of oral tradition examine the works of the Serbian *guslars*.[6] I have underlined that when considering the nature and content of the 'original' oral versions of the eddic poems that were passed on to the transcribers, it is necessary to be wary of including the extant prose introductions to the eddic poems, many of which seem to derive from, or be influenced by, Snorri's scholarly *Prose Edda* (see Gunnell 1995: 223–35). I have stressed, furthermore, that the marginal speaker notation found in both eddic anthology manuscripts (alongside *ljóðaháttr* poems) should be viewed as having also been added at the time of transcription, following the contemporary foreign examples of manuscripts of dramas in northern France and southern England (Gunnell 1995: 206–18, 282–329). In the case of the *ljóðaháttr* poems, the above considerations mean that if we wish to consider how the 'original' oral versions worked and functioned in performance, we need to limit ourselves solely to the stanzas of direct speech, considering them as one considers a play – from the viewpoint of sound, performance, space, and movement.

I have argued earlier (Gunnell 2006a), on the basis of such a consideration of *Skírnismál* and *Fáfnismál / Sigrdrífumál*, that these two bodies of poetry appear to have essentially the same performance structure, which, among other things, seems to indicate that both would have been expected to be performed outdoors.[7] They involve the same movement in space from inside buildings to outside spaces, from lower down to up in the mountains, from night to day, and from male-dominated environments to those belonging to females. They also involve a similar use of so-called 'mansions' (static settings for characters, often used in medieval drama: see Tydeman 1978: 57–61) in the landscape between which a main performer moves as part of a form of narrative that seems to indicate the attainment of a new status. Over and above these features, the two works make use of similar lighting effects: the fire (*vafrlogi* or *eikinn fúr*) burning around the heroine (*Skírnismál* sts 8–9, 17–18; *Sigrdrífumál*, prose introduction, cf. *Vǫlsunga saga*, chs. 27–28); the same generally nocturnal time setting (*Sigrdrífumál* st. 3; *Skírnismál* sts 9 and 42); and even the same kinds of properties (swords, horses, and circles of fire, along with cups or horns of alcohol which are ritually handed to men by women at the end of the works). Both works also make reference to active use of runic magic. I have suggested that the form of these works also seems to demand the participation of more than one performer, or, at the very least, a highly adept actor capable of playing several parts at once, and have underlined that this feature would take any performance of these two works beyond 'mere' poetic storytelling into the realms of *dramatic* performance, with all that that entails (Gunnell 1995: 236–81; 2006a, 2011).

All performed narratives subtly change the perception of the space in which they are performed, and those within it, in a range of different ways (see Gunnell 2006b). This would have been particularly relevant in the case of those other eddic poems in *ljóðaháttr* that imply expectations of an indoor performance. This applies in particular to works such as *Vafþrúðnismál, Lokasenna, Grímnismál*, and the closely related *Eiríksmál* in which, during the first-person monologic and dialogic performances, the halls in which the performances took place would have been temporarily 'transformed' into the halls of Vafþrúðnir, Ægir, Geirrøðr, and even Valhǫll. This, in turn, would have resulted in those others present being instinctively forced to participate in the roles of *jǫtnar, goð*, or even *einherjar* for the duration of the said performances, with all the later memories that this would have entailed for them (see Gunnell 1995: 236–47, 275–80; 2011; forthcoming a).

As I have noted elsewhere (Gunnell 2004, 2011), it seems apparent that all Iron-Age Nordic halls and longhouses, like churches, mosques, or even the Navajo hogan, would have had the potential occasionally to take on the role of a mythical microcosmos, if they were not always seen as having this symbolic role in some way or other (cf. Heorot in *Beowulf*): The main beam (*ás*) in all Nordic houses was held up by small pieces of wood which rested on the beams, which were called *dvergar* (literally 'dwarfs'), at least as far back as the twelfth century.[8] At that time, it is clear that the word was adopted in its pagan cosmological sense – the dwarfs, according to Snorri, having had the role of holding up the sky (cf. *Skáldskaparmál*: 33).[9] This in turn suggests that the roof of the hall was viewed as being like the sky (cf. many Nordic church ceilings, which are decorated with stars to underline the symbolic role of the buildings). If one follows this train of thought, it is hard to ignore the potentially symbolic role of the pillars shaped from tree trunks (cf. Yggdrasill?) that ran down from this 'sky' inside the hall (cf. *Vǫlsunga saga*, chs. 2–3); and the *ǫndvegi* (high seat; cf. *Hlíðskjálf*) that was set beneath the key so-called *ǫndvegissúlur* ('high seat pillars'). According to *Eyrbyggja saga* (*The Saga of the People of Eyrr*) and *Landnámabók* (*The Book of Settlements*), the pillars in question were sometimes carved with images of the gods, and occasionally had special earth beneath them which had been carried between countries (*Landnámabók* 1968: 307; and *Eyrbyggja saga* 1935: 7). Archaeological evidence demonstrates that before the *ǫndvegi* would have been a long fire, and the likelihood is that a cauldron of some kind would always have hung over this (cf. *Urðabrunnr* / *Mímisbrunnr*?) Any mythical poem performed in such a space (*Háva hǫllu at, Háva hǫllu í* ['At the hall of the High One; in the hall of the High One', *Háv* III/10–11]) would have been able to play effectively on all of these features, creating a temporary state of between-world liminality. This would have been a natural occurrence if the performers entered into a first-person monologue in which they took on the role of one of the gods, and not least if they were wearing a helmet-mask such as that found at Sutton Hoo. This object seems to have had one eyebrow (the right) marked out by garnets over gold foil which would have lit up in firelight, giving the impression that only one eye was alive (see further Price and Mortimer 2014; and Gunnell 2013b on masks). One can expect that such a temporary transformation of space would have taken place in the case of the performances of all of the 'indoor' eddic poems in *ljóðaháttr* noted above, to a greater or lesser extent.

Case study 1: Grímnismál

The following two sections will contain two case studies designed to demonstrate the essential differences between the performance demands of eddic poems in *ljóðaháttr* and *fornyrðislag*. I will first examine *Grímnismál* (composed in *ljóðaháttr*) from the performance viewpoint in order to demonstrate a little better how a form of 'transformation of space' might have taken place when the poem was performed, and also how this poem, like the other works in question, seems to contain various 'signposts' which (as in a Shakespearean play) make both direct and indirect reference to the performance situation in question. It should be stressed immediately that I feel there is good reason to question whether the prose introduction of *Grímnismál* should be considered an intrinsic part of the 'original' transcribed work. For that reason, neither the introduction nor the information it provides will be included in the following discussion, which will keep to the extant poetic text. (For further discussion of the prose and the 'meaning' of the poem, see in particular de Vries 1934b; Fleck 1971; Ralph 1972; Einar Ólafur Sveinsson 1962: 270–3.)

That *Grímnismál* was originally an oral work that was passed on within the oral tradition and performed orally and visually in a performance space would seem unquestionable. The title of the poem (which, as noted above, was known by Snorri) underlines that it involved both living speech (*mál*) and masked appearance (or double identity); Óðinn stresses his use of the names 'Grímnir', 'Grímr', and 'Grímni' not once, but three times, in the *nafnaþulur* at the end of the poem (sts 46–7 and 49). The poem also immediately establishes a setting (Grímnir sitting or standing *milli elda* ('between fires') *hér* ('here') apparently *in* a hall (sts 1–2; see also: *skal inn koma Ægis bekki á* ['shall come in to Ægir's benches', *Grm* 45/6–7]), and an audience, first of all in the shape of Agnarr, the son of Geirrøðr (st. 3), and then (at least later) his father, but one can never forget the continuous presence of the living audience in the real hall, without whom the performance could not have taken place.[10]

The form of the poem itself also seems to imply expectations that it would be heard and experienced rather than read in silence. I have earlier noted the way in which *Vǫluspá* seems to deliberately play with sound to add a further dimension to the performance (Gunnell 2013a).[11] The same seems to occur in *Grímnismál*, where a number of stanzas appear to suggest the deliberate use of sound to echo visual image, as in the drumming sounds in stanza 23 which describe Valhǫll: *fimm hundruð dura* ('five hundred doors', *Grm* 23/1); in stanza 7, which seems to bring the gulping of water to life: *Óðinn ok Sága drekka . . . glǫð ór gullnum kerum* ('Óðinn and Sága drink . . . happily from golden goblets', *Grm* 7/4–6); and in stanza 19, in which the growling of wolves runs behind the words: *Gera ok Freka seðr gunntamiðr, hróðigr Herjafǫðr* ('The proud Father of Hosts, battle-tamed, satiates Geri and Freki', *Grm* 19/1–2).

With regard to action, there can be equally little question that if the performance of *Grímnismál* is placed on Schechner's ritual-play dyad noted above, it would have been closer to a ritual (see further Schjødt 2008). It involves a man-god bound between fires in an indoor environment (st. 45), who has received neither food nor drink for eight nights, and, at the start of the poem, is in danger of being burnt alive:

> Heitr ertu, hripuðr, ok heldr til mikill;
>   gǫngumk firr, funi!
> Loði sviðnar, þótt ek á lopt berak,
>   brennumk feldr fyrir. (*Grm* 1)

[You're hot, fire, and rather too great; get back, flames! Fur is singed, even though I raise it in the air, the skin cloak burns before me.]

Everything implies *this* must be the all-important ninth night, and that during the course of the poem that follows, somewhat like a shaman or a participant in a Native American Sun Dance initiation ritual (which also involved thirst, hunger, and pain as a means of gaining access to the next world), the central speaker is experiencing visions within the present environment of the hall, seeing things that the audience does not – something that would be bound to disturb the audience's concept of reality. The visions follow an initial state in stanza 1 where the apparently masked man, head down (cf. st. 45, where his head is later deliberately raised), surrounded in bright firelight, smoke, and shadows, apparently raises his hands, lifting his skin cloak away from the encroaching fires in what seems to be a double means of attracting the attention of the audience (along with the breaking of silence with the first words). The speaker's monologic vision in *ljóðaháttr* follows directly on from the formal acceptance of a drink from Agnarr, who, in stanza 3, is given a form of formal blessing often associated with other granting of alcoholic drinks in other eddic poems (cf. *Skírnismál* st. 37; and *Sigrdrífumál* sts 3–5).

Especially interesting is that way in which throughout the course of the vision, the audience is constantly reminded both directly and indirectly of the performer's situation and, not least, his thirst: drinks of various kinds are mentioned in stanzas 3, 7, 13, 19, 25, 36, 45, and 51; and rivers, lakes, surf, and sunken settings appear in stanzas 7, 21, 26–9, 38, and 50. Fire, burning, and boiling are not only mentioned at the start and in stanza 42, but also in stanza 18. They are also alluded to in Óðinn's names, Sviðr and Sviðrir (st. 50); in the mention of Eldhrimnir in stanza 18; in the idea of Þórr burning bridges in stanza 29; in the description of the heat of the sun which needs a shield in stanzas 37–8; and in the way in which both Yggdrasill and the sun are under threat of being gnawed to death by animals in stanzas 35 and 39. Perhaps most effective of all is the way in which the image of the anguished Yggdrasill would seem to be effectively paralleled by that of the standing speaker with his raised arms and hanging, singed cloak, something that would seem to involve the performer in momentarily representing the tree (see sts 30–5; and st. 35 in particular, bearing in mind the cosmological symbolism of the hall noted above). The poem ends with the masked figure, who has been increasingly talking about death (cf. sts 8, 14, and 22, which deal with the 'chosen'; sts 18, 23, 36, and 51, which deal with the *einherjar*; and sts 22, 28, and 31, which mention Hel and its entrance), first of all calling on the *valkyrjur* for assistance (st. 36), and then requesting all of the gods to enter what he now refers to as Ægis hall as witnesses to what is occurring (st. 45), in what seems to be a deliberate progression. (While none of these figures is seen by the audience, the speaker clearly views them as now being present.) The speaker then makes the second deliberately marked movement of the poem, raising his head to those bothphysically and supernaturally present: *Svipum hefi ek nú ypt* ('I have now raised my face', *Grm* 45/1), before uttering a long *þula* ('list') of the names by which he has been called (sts 46–50). He ends by announcing:

> nú knáttu Óðin sjá,
>   nálgastu mik, ef þú megir!
> Óðinn ek nú heiti (*Grm* 53/5–6; 54/1)

> [now you can see Óðinn; approach me if you can. My name now is Óðinn]

There is now little question that whoever the audience (like Agnarr and Geirrøðr) may have thought the masked figure between the fires was, dying amidst the flames, a god has now 'entered the building'.

As noted above, by this point in the performance Óðinn is not the only figure present to have come from another world. Even though the audience still cannot see them in physical terms, the hall now seems to be full of supernatural observers who, by the end, not only include the *goð*, *valkyrjur*, and possibly also the *dísir* (cf. st. 53), but also the *einherjar*, who have been mentioned four times. Within the physical hall, during the course of the poem, the audience has been taken on a guided tour across the worlds of the gods, which eventually comes to focus first of all on Óðinn's own hall, then Valhǫll and its inhabitants, and then, finally, at the centre of everything, the threatened tree/god. In a sense, this present performance space (that is, the physical hall) has been transformed into Geirrøðr's hall, and then Valhǫll, the audience (as in *Eiríksmál*) temporarily finding themselves placed in the roles of the *einherjar* (something that would be particularly applicable if they were warriors: see further Gunnell forthcoming a).[12] The poem ends with a blend of all three worlds as Óðinn speaks directly to the fated Geirrøðr in his own hall, and simultaneously to the audience in the performance space.

In recent years, Gísli Sigurðsson (echoing Björn Jónsson (1989) before him) has argued that in *Grímnismál* Óðinn is describing the constellations of the night sky (see, for example, Gísli Sigurðsson 1998: 82–3; and 2009). Considering what has been said above about the potential of the hall building to represent the cosmos symbolically, such an idea could certainly be brought to life in a performance. Indeed, it would help transform the roof into the heavens (held up by the *dvergar*), towards which the performer himself would be apparently reaching with his arms, possibly eventually taking on the role of Yggdrasill itself, standing amidst a grove of wooden pillars, beside a probable pool in the shape of the likely cauldron noted above. Another faint possibility is that in the performance, the various 'halls' of the gods might have been represented by those present in the hall at the time of the performance: outside *Snorra Edda*, for which it is a key source, *Grímnismál* is one of the few works that implies that all of the gods lived together in a form of a pantheon – an idea that I have recently questioned, partly on the basis that Óðinn seems to have had little role in Iceland or the rural parts of western Norway in pre-Christian times (see Gunnell 2015 and forthcoming b). I have suggested in these articles that the idea of the family of gods under the leadership of an *alfǫðr* ('all-father') would seem to have a background in the idea of the warrior comitatus or the courts or army-camps of the new national or semi-national Nordic kings, in which those involved would often have come from a range of areas in which different gods might have played leading roles in their lives. A single gesture by the performer to different members of the audience when referring to different gods and their homes would have had a similar effect to reference to the roof in terms of altering the surroundings and those within it, now underlining their role as representatives of their unseen gods within the performance space.

As noted at the start of this chapter, I have no intention here of suggesting a definitive 'date' for *Grímnismál*. Indeed, considering the fact that the work in question would probably have changed over the years, one would have to be very clear about which version is being referred to in this context: the poem which was first 'created', that which has been preserved, or one associated with one of the many interim performances. All the same, it does seem to be evident that, compared with *Vǫluspá*, *Grímnismál* contains few if any signs of Christian influence. Indeed, its deliberately chosen monologic first-person format involves bringing a pagan god to life in front of an audience and (as noted above) filling the performance space with invisible pagan supernatural beings. At heart, *Grímnismál* would thus seem to be a pre-Christian work. It is also highly un-Icelandic, if one considers its talk of ash, oak, and yew trees (sts 5, 26, 29–32, and 34), the apparently underwater *gull ker* ('golden cups', *Grm* 7/6), and *vé* and *hǫrgar* (sts 13 and 16) ('shrines' and 'altars'), none of which are applicable to what we know of pre-Christian Iceland.[13] The fact that the poem says nothing about farming, mentions the drinking of wine (st. 19), and stresses the all-male society of Valhǫll would also seem to suggest a mainland Nordic contextual environment, and most likely one related to an essentially aristocratic warrior society.[14] Also of interest with regard to general age and provenance are the names of the gods that are mentioned – or not mentioned, which is equally important – in the poem. Indeed, Týr is notably absent in *Grímnismál*, as is Loki. When the other gods are mentioned, one notes that Þórr is first in line (st. 4), followed in stanza 5 by Ullr, a god that Snorri Sturluson evidently knew little about in spite of the number of place names bearing the god's name in southern Sweden and Norway (see further Brink 2007b; Vikstrand 2001). Freyr and Freyja are, interestingly enough, given the key third and ninth positions in the order of gods (sts 5 and 14). The Vanir are also represented by Njǫrðr, who, along with Heimdallr (also sometimes seen as being associated with the Vanir: cf. *Þrymskviða* st. 15), is placed in direct association with the religious practices of the *vé* (sanctuary) and the strangely *hátimbraðr hǫrgr* ('high-timbered altar', *Grm* 13/3; 16/6).[15] The Vanir maintain their central presence in the poem with Skiðblaðnir being described as best of ships in stanzas 43 and 44, and in the mention of Skaði, whose inherited *jǫtunn* ('giant') homestead Þrymheimr is here found amongst those of the gods (st. 11). This latter point seems to suggest that in the world-view of this poem, some *jǫtnar* live amongst the gods. Also of interest is that, in *Grímnismál*, the battlefield dead are said to be shared between Óðinn and Freyja (sts 8 and 14), and that the only god to be called on specifically by name at the end of the poem is the earlier-noted and near unknown Ullr (st. 42). Considering the place-name evidence noted above, the absence of Frigg (here seemingly replaced by Sága in st. 7), the lack of Týr (mostly known in Danish and English place names: see Brink 2007b), and the importance of Ullr, Þórr, and especially the Vanir would seem to point to a southern Norwegian or Swedish provenance. Furthermore, the mention of Ullr, the *vé, hǫrgar,* and the golden cups found in 'Sǫkkvabekkr' (which would seem to reflect the earlier bog offerings that were beginning to come to an end in around 500 AD: see Fabech and Näsman 2013) would also seem to lend support to the poem having roots in a pre-Christian mainland Scandinavian environment.

This brings us back to considerations of the likely performance space of *Grímnismál* in its earliest stages (indeed, the environment that gave shape to the poem). As suggested above, everything seems to point to the poem having been designed to be performed in a pre-Christian Norwegian (or southern Swedish) royal and/or military hall in which many of those present would probably originally have been adherents of other gods than the ruling *alfǫðr*, Óðinn, such as Þórr, Ullr, Freyr, Freyja, Njǫrðr, Skaði, and Heimdallr (see above). If performances of the poem did take place in such a warrior environment (which one can expect to have known initiation ceremonies of figures such as Agnarr: see Schjødt 2008), then it might be argued that, as with *Eiríksmál* (see Gunnell forthcoming a), the experience of watching and partaking in a performance of the poem would have reminded the military audience that the Valhǫll which awaited them was essentially a grand mirror image of their own present living space. Even more than that, the performance would have not only have temporarily turned the performance space in which the audience was sitting into that of Valhǫll, it would have also simultaneously placed those watching in the role of the *einherjar*. All that would be needed in bring about this transformation, in addition to the words of the poem, are a few gestures, a few facial expressions, and a little emotional identification on the part of the performer standing amidst the smoke and the firelight.

The performance analysis of an eddic work such as *Grímnismál* would thus seem to have a great deal to say not only about the intrinsic nature of the work, but also about its background, provenance, and ever-changing functions (and especially those associated with its 'creation'). To my mind, there is little question that any performance of the work in pre-Christian times would have temporarily introduced a state of liminality and ritualistic 'sacred time' into the performance space, invoking a powerful situation in which roles could be potentially changed for the long term, the initiation of warriors, kings, and even poets being just one form of such a change. Naturally, in later times, the poem almost certainly went on to live a very different life in the oral tradition of the Icelandic poets who had been at court, taking on another role as a source of necessary mythological knowledge that would have been important for any poet. While one can expect the poets' own performances of *Grímnismál* after the time of the conversion to have been rather different from those in pre-Christian times, it might be argued that they would have been no less effective in bringing Óðinn into their lives as a living force.

Case study 2: Þrymskviða

The monologic and dialogic eddic poems in *ljóðaháttr* on which the previous section has focused were quite different in form to those in *fornyrðislag*, in which a mythological or heroic story of the past was 'told' to the living audience (rather than enacted) in the present. In spite of this, one can expect that even with these poems, performers would have regularly made use of tone, rhythm, emotion, gesture, facial expression, and even momentary dramatic involvement as a means of drawing in their audiences and maintaining their interest. Here, too, it would appear to be essential for the poems to be considered as works that functioned in sound, time, and space rather than as symbols on a page, if one really wishes to understand them as they were originally conceived.

In terms of performance dynamics, *Þrymskviða*, which in its extant form comprises thirty-two stanzas of varying length in *fornyrðislag* dealing with Þórr's temporary loss of his hammer to the *jǫtunn* Þrymr, and the resulting need for him to dress up as Freyja in order to retrieve it, is very different in form to *Grímnismál* and the other eddic poems in *ljóðaháttr*. While it uses direct speech, the speech in question is firmly framed by narrative stanzas which either tell the events of the story in past tense, or introduce speakers and speech, with many stanzas (sts 2–3, 12–13, 17–18, 20, 22, 25–30) taking the form of a blend of direct speech and introductory narrative or character description. The stanzas in question regularly start with short formulaic introductions to direct speech which prepare the audience for what is to come: *Þá kvað þat Heimdallr, hvítastr ása* ('Then said Heimdallr, the whitest of the *æsir*', *Þrk* 15/1–2); *Þá kvað þat Þórr, þrúðugr áss* ('Then said Þórr, the powerful *áss*', *Þrk* 17/1–2); *Þá kvað þat Loki, Laufeyjar sonr* ('Then said Loki, son of Laufey', *Þrk* 18/1–2; 20/1–2); and *Þá kvað þat Þrymr, þursa dróttinn* ('Then said Þrymr, lord of the ogres', *Þrk* 22/1–2; 25/1–2; 30/1–2). Each of these introductions not only underlines the fact that the speech that follows is being quoted by the storyteller-poet, but also (once again) stresses that the events and words in question are not actively taking place in the present known by the performer and the audience, but, rather, occurred in a safely distant mythological past.

The time setting is immediately evident at the start of the poem from the use of the past-tense verb *var* ('was') in the introductory stanza, which tells of Þórr's reaction on waking up to find his hammer absent: *Reiðr var þá Vingþórr, er hann vaknaði* ('Þórr was furious when he awoke', *Þrk* 1/1–2). After this, the audience is regularly reminded of the setting throughout the poem in numerous other stanzas which begin with a past-tense verb describing action: *gengu* ('walked'); *fló* ('flew'); *bundu* ('bound'); *laut* ('bent down'); *hló* ('laughed'); and *drap* ('killed') (sts 3, 5, 9, 19, 27, 31, and 32).[16] Alongside these stanzas are others describing situations or reactions (sts 6, 13, 14, 21, 24, 26, 28) in which the past-tense verbs *sat, varð, váru*, and *var* occur either in the first or second place in the introductory line of the stanza. In short, for those listening, there is rarely any question that the account (including the speech) is essentially a past-tense narrative which is being passed on to them by a performer-poet who is 'here' in the present, standing in front of the audience, and personally uninvolved with events in question even if he or she adds some personality to the direct speech. Even if some sense of liminality momentarily begins to arise for the audience during those few stanzas of uninterrupted dialogue that occur in the poem (sts 7–8; and 10–11), the quick return of the poem's third-person past-tense narrative rapidly re-establishes a safe sense of alienation, and disruption in belief (see Brecht 1964). No attempt is ever made to suggest that the action described is taking place 'here' in the hall (or some other place of performance). This (among other things) means that the performance is bound to be more in the field of entertainment (play) than ritual, if one considers Schechner's play-ritual dyad noted above.

As the name of the poem suggests, even if it deals with mythological events (such as those recounted in *Grímnismál, Skírnismál, Vafþrúðnismál, Hárbarðsljóð*, and *Lokasenna*), *Þrymskviða* was viewed by the poet (or scribe) as belonging to the same narrative genre as other poems in *fornyrðislag* (and *málaháttr*), such as *Helgakviður, Sigurðarkviður, Guðrúnarkviður, Atlakviða in grænlenska*, and *Vǫlundarkviða*, all of which use a similar blend of speech and narrative, and take place in the past. Nonetheless, I am in full agreement with Bernt Øyvind Thorvaldsen (2008b) that, like *Grímnismál* and most other eddic poems, *Þrymskviða* contains all the signs of having been composed for oral performance, and of having actively lived within the oral tradition for some time (see also Einar Ólafur Sveinsson 1962: 280–4).[17] As Thorvaldsen underlines, this is evident from the poem's simplicity and clear structure, its use of recognised formulas (see, for example, sts 1 and 13; sts 3, 9, and 12; and st. 7, in addition to the speech introductions noted above); listings (sts 23–24); and repetitions and variation (especially with regard to the simple movement between Þórr's hall (and those of the Æsir), Freyja's *tún* ('home field'), and Jǫtunheimar in sts 3 and 12, and sts 5 and 9. (For other examples of deliberate variation, see also sts 10 and 11; 15 and 19; 26 and 28; and 29 and 32.) Indeed, as in *Grímnismál* and *Vǫluspá*, it seems clear that the poem deliberately makes use of sounds (especially alliterated consonants), not least to reflect moods and action, as in the first stanza where Þórr's anger is echoed in a row of growling *r* trills allied with spluttering *sk* consonant clusters:

> Reiðr var þá Vingþórr, er hann vaknaði
> ok síns hamars um saknaði,
> skegg nam at hrista, skǫr nam at dýja,
> réð Jarðar burr um at þreifask. (*Þrk* 1)

> [Þórr was furious when he awoke and missed his hammer; his beard began to quiver, his hair began to shake, the son of Earth was groping about.]

Similar effects occur in the deliberately parallel stanza 13 describing Freyja's wrath at the suggestion that she should be given to Þrymr in exchange for the hammer, although the sound here is now dominated by hissing *s*, *z*, and *f* fricatives, along with trills and *k* plosives, ending with a highly effective stuttering sound (*ek ek*) towards the end:

> Reið varð þá Freyja ok fnásaði,
> allr ása salr undir bifðisk,
> stǫkk þat it mikla men Brísinga:
> 'Mik veiztu verða vergjarnasta,
> ef ek ek með þér í jǫtunheima.' (*Þrk* 13)

[Freyja was furious then and snorted, the hall of the *æsir* all shook, the great necklace of the Brisings shattered: 'You know I'd have to be really desperate for a man if I were to drive to Jǫtunheimar with you.']

As with the first stanza, the deliberate choice of the sounds encourages some degree of deliberate emphasis and role-play by any performer. The same applies to the rhythmic sound of the wings of Freyja's bird-costume, which echoes across stanzas 5 and 9: *Fló þá Loki, fjaðrhamr dunði* ('Then Loki flew, the bird-costume thundered', *Þrk* 5/1–2; 9/1–2); the deliberately chosen use of stiff formulaic question and answer that occurs at the start of Loki's first meeting with Þrymr in stanza 7: *Hvat er með ásom? Hvat er með álfom? Hví ertu einn kominn í jǫtunheima?* ('What goes with the æsir? What goes with the álfar? Why have you come alone to Jǫtunheimar', *Þrk* 7/1–3), which is closely reminiscent of the giant's speech in 'Jack and the Beanstalk'; and in the thundering sound of Þórr's wagon running across the landscape in stanza 21: *bjǫrg brotnuðu, brann jǫrð loga* ('rocks broke, the earth burnt in flames', *Þrk* 21/5–6), where the *br* consonant cluster deliberately occurs not twice but three times to give added emphasis. It is especially apparent in the violence and sounds of laughter that echo throughout Þórr's final slaughter of the *jǫtnar* at his planned wedding:

> Hló Hlórriða hugr í brjósti,
> er harðhugaðr hamar um þekði;
> Þrym drap hann fyrstan, þursa dróttin,
> ok ætt jǫtuns alla lamði.

> Drap hann ina ǫldnu jǫtna systur,
> hin er brúðfjár um beðit hafði;
> hún skell um hlaut fyr skillinga,
> en hǫgg hamars fyr hringa fjǫld. (*Þrk* 31–2)

[Hlórríði's courage laughed in his breast, as he hard-heartedly recognised his hammer; he killed Þrymr first, lord of the ogres and walloped all of the giant's family. He killed the aged sister of the giants, the one who had asked for the dowry; she got a whack for the shillings, and a hammer blow for the collection of rings.]

On the basis of the quick review of tonal qualities given above, there is little question in my mind that the extant version of *Þrymskviða*, like *Grímnismál*, was designed to be heard in space rather than merely read, and that it also plays on sound effects and varying rhythms, as well as expectations of accompanying gesture.

In terms of provenance, context, and potential performance space, the poem would nonetheless appear to come from a different background to *Grímnismál* (suggesting that we should be wary of placing them alongside each other as part of a unified body of mythology). While the poem says little about landscape, it does seem to focus on halls (st. 27) and take place in a world in which herding (st. 6) and women (and objects associated with women: see especially sts 12–13, 15–16, and 19) play a key role. Interestingly enough, while Þórr, Loki, Freyja, and Heimdallr play central roles, nothing is said about Óðinn (or Sif), which, considering what has been said above about the apparent lack of interest in Óðinn in Iceland and many parts of Norway, would seem to point to a western Scandinavian environment (and one that is less militaristic). It would also seem to fit comfortably alongside other archetypal Þórr myths that were probably well known in this area (such as Þórr's trips to Geirrøðr and Útgarða-Loki) in that it takes the shape of an *ur*-fairy tale of Proppian structure (Propp 1968) involving the god making a trip to and from the world of the *jǫtnar* to retrieve something that has been lost or damaged and thereby put the dislocated world back into joint. This is somewhat different from the kind of semi-ritualistic narratives found in the *ljóðaháttr* poems.

Conclusion

As this chapter has underlined, analysing the eddic poems as objects that were designed to be received in the form of sound accompanied by observed action in a particular performance space, rather than as ink on paper, has numerous advantages, especially if researchers are interested in considering the works in the form they were originally designed to take by their 'creators' or those who passed them on to the scribes. Naturally, academia depends primarily upon writing, and most of the formal knowledge that scholars have has been drawn from the book and the library, but it is important to remember that the book and the original eddic poem are worlds apart. It might be said that attempting to consider how oral narratives work in space (even in our own time) should be a prerequisite for gaining a deeper understanding of how these poems might have worked and functioned during the centuries before they came to be recorded. Such an approach can be not only rewarding, but also highly revealing.

Notes

1. These expressions are used by Snorri when referring to the origin of stanzas he is quoting: *Vǫluspá* is referred to as a recognised entity in *Gylfaginning* (never in *Skáldskaparmál*) eleven times: see *Gylfaginning*: 9, 10, 12, 14, 15, 17, 20, 35, 49, and 51). *Grímnismál* is mentioned by name in this way three times in *Gylfaginning* (23, 30, and 33). *Vafþrúðnismál* is never mentioned by name. For the expression *hér segir Vafþrúðnir jǫtunn*, see *Gylfaginning*: 10. Similar expressions are used with regard to *Vǫluspá* six times in the *Uppsala Edda* (14, 24, 28, 34, 62).

2. As stressed below, when I use the expressions 'origin' and 'originate' I am not talking of the poems as stable entities that have passed through time and space without change; rather, I am referring to the earliest versions of the poems which may well have been quite different, although one can expect that their form and storyline would have been similar.

3. For Schechner (who worked closely with the anthropologist Victor Turner), the key difference between the ritual and play is that while pure 'ritual' (in the sense of religious or social ritual) will be seen as having long-term effects on those present, pure play exists in the moment, and, as a form of entertainment, induces no such long-term change. A strong element in deciding the positioning is going to be that of 'belief' in what is going on and its importance. See further Schechner 2013: 52, 72–4.

4. As with the use of 'original' above, when I use the word 'created' here, I am referring to the first versions of the work, not the eventual work that came to be transcribed.

5. See also Schechner (2013: 93, 120) on Augusto Boal's 'invisible theatre' in which actors deliberately take on roles in the street to provoke passers-by ('audiences'?) into real action. See also Boal (2002: 277–288). In such cases, the 'audience' is totally unaware that a performance is taking place, meaning that their roles as audience and participant are blurred.

6. In many ways, this work can be regarded as a follow-up to Bertha Phillpotts' earlier *The Elder Edda and Ancient Scandinavian Drama* (1920), which made a similar argument from a slightly different perspective.

7. Following directly on from *Reginsmál*, without interruption, *Fáfnismál* and *Sigrdrífumál* are not distinguished as separate poems in the Codex Regius. I should stress that when referring to these two works are a single entity, I am referring solely to the *ljóðaháttr* stanzas of *Fáfnismál* and *Sigrdrífumál*, which seem to form a logical, single body of material: see further Gunnell 1995: 256–69 (and the other works cited there). See also Quinn 1992 for a slightly

different approach to *Fáfnismál*, which also considers the element of sound and performance.

8. As noted in Gunnell 2004, this word seems to have been used for the same items in all the Nordic countries at least into the nineteenth century.

9. The earliest reference to the use of *dvergar* in this sense is in *Íslensk hómilíubók* (*The Icelandic Homily Book*), in a sermon explaining the symbolic message that the church building as a whole offers to the congregation: see *Íslensk hómilíubók* 1993: 150.

10. Unless otherwise stated, all translations in this article are those of the author.

11. Whether the eddic poems were sung, chanted, or spoken remains open to question. See further Harris 2003; Opland 1980; Heimir Pálsson 1999 and 2001; Bagby 1999 and 2006; and the experiments conducted with eddic performance over the years by Benjamin Bagby and Sequentia (Sequentia 1999 and 2001); and recently by the Norwegian performer Einar Selvik (various performances of parts of *Vǫluspá* on YouTube). Nonetheless, one cannot ignore the fact that, however it was presented, the poetic metre would have 'sounded' different (not least more rhythmic) from normal speech, and thus created a special atmosphere of its own, with its own special associations.

12. Indeed, the mention of wine in stanza 19 suggests a cosmopolitan setting where trade makes foreign products available.

13. The sagas make no reference to either *hǫrgar* or *vé*, and, to date, no firm archaeological evidence of such structures has been found in Iceland.

14. Even when Freyja is mentioned (in st. 14), her name occurs in the context of the choosing of the dead (in short, the 'other world'). The same applies to the references to the *valkyrjur* and *dísir* in the poem.

15. It is interesting that the word *Vanir* seems to be replaced by *álfar* (literally, 'elves') in stanza 4, and that Freyr is said to be the owner or ruler of *álfheimr* in stanza 5.

16. Sts 12 and 23 are exceptions, in which the verb *ganga* ('walk') is given in the present, although such switches in tense in the middle of a previously established past-tense account are a natural feature of oral narrative even today. In st. 29, the verb *kom* ('came') occurs in the second position in the introductory line, in a similar place to the verb *kvað* ('said') in the speech introductions noted above.

17. For a review of recent scholarly material which has attempted to suggest that *Þrymskviða* is one of the more recent eddic poems, and possibly composed with pen in hand, see the references given in Thorvaldsen 2008b.

CHAPTER 6

Eddic poetry and mythology

John Lindow

Introduction

When the Germanic peoples – the ancestors of the English, Germans, and Scandinavians – met the Romans during the first centuries CE, they translated the Roman weekday names bearing the names of Roman deities. Thus, we know that Týr (Tuesday), Óðinn (Wednesday), Þórr (Thursday), and Frigg (Friday), to use the names in their Old Norse forms, must have been worshipped or at least known in pre-Christian times across the Germanic speech area, and many other sources support this conclusion. Also, in the *Interpretatio romana* (ch. 43) of the Roman historian Tacitus' *Germania* (Benario 1999), we can easily recognise traits of Óðinn, Þórr, and Týr in descriptions of Mercury, Hercules, and Mars among the Germani, and in doing so we postulate the existence of narratives (myths) about these deities. Such narratives were almost certainly in verse.[1] Since we can reconstruct the existence of alliterative poetry in early Germanic times on the basis of the verse that has survived in Old English, Old High German, Old Saxon, and Old Norse (and on runic inscriptions, many of which technically precede what we call Old Norse), we may infer that mythological alliterative poetry existed among the ancestors of the Anglo-Saxons, Germans, and Scandinavians. For the most part, however, such poetry has survived only in Old Norse. The exception is some charm poetry in Old English and Old High German, where names of mythological beings seem to figure. These include the Old English *Charm Against a Sudden Stitch* (Elves) and *Charm Against Unfruitful Land* (Erce, mother of earth) and, especially, the Old English *Nine Herbs Charm*, which shows Woden (~ Óðinn) in a healing role.

> Wyrm com snican,   toslat he man;
> ða genam Woden   VIIII wuldortanas,
> sloh ða þa næddran,   þæt heo on VIIII tofleah.

þær geændade   æppel and attor,
þæt heo næfre ne wolde   on hus bugan.

[A snake came crawling, it bit a man. Then Woden took nine glory-twigs, struck then the serpent so that it flew into nine parts. There apple caused this against poison, that she nevermore would enter her house.]

The very late date of the manuscript containing the charm is of course problematic, and any manuscript from Anglo-Saxon England is by definition post-Conversion, but what is at stake here is the potential existence of alliterative poetry bearing the name of a deity and acting in a way that ultimately affects the lives of humans.

The Old High German *Second Merseburg charm* also includes Woden, alongside other mythological figures, again in a healing context.

Phol ende uuodan uuorun zi holza.
du uuart demo balderes uolon sin uuoz birenkit.
thu biguol en sinthgunt, sunna era suister;
thu biguol en friia, uolla era suister;
thu biguol en uuodan, so he uuola conda.

[Phol and Wodan were in the forest; then Balder's horse wrenched its foot; then Sinthgut sang charms, Sunna her sister; then Friia sang charms, as she well could.]

Thus, the burden of the evidence is that alliterative pre-Christian mythological poetry existed in the Germanic languages, and it therefore follows that the extant eddic poetry about the gods, as we see it in the first poems of the Codex Regius, in AM 748 I a 4°, and in a few other manuscripts, descends from that tradition and probably contains lines, stanzas, or perhaps even poems that have Viking Age or earlier antecedents directly. The issue of oral tradition and transmission is taken up elsewhere in this Handbook (see Clunies Ross [Chapter 1], Harris [Chapter 2], and Thorvaldsen [Chapter 4]), but even the strictest adherence to a theory of recomposition at every performance – something few scholars would take seriously for eddic poetry – would not negate the likelihood that mythological poetry existed for many centuries before the eddic poems came to be recorded.

Pre-Christian mythology in Christian contexts

There was Christian missionary activity in Scandinavia from the eighth century onwards, primarily directed towards the rulers of the nascent kingdoms and/or carried out in trade centres. While the missionaries achieved limited success, it was not lasting, and the conversion of the Nordic kingdoms was to occur only in the tenth and eleventh centuries. In Iceland it occurred famously in a dramatic scene at the *alþingi* ('general assembly') in 1000 AD (999 by modern time reckoning). In this scene, for which the best source is the *Íslendingabók* (*c.*1120) of the priest Ari Þorgilsson inn fróði ('the learned'), the adherents of the two sides have nearly come to blows, when the decision is left to the pagan law-speaker (the highest office in the assembly), Þorgeirr. After spending a night under a cloak, he announces his decision: the country will be torn apart if there are two laws, he says, and all shall take baptism, while a few pre-Christian rituals will continue to be permitted.

In framing the issue as having to do with laws and ritual behaviour, Þorgeirr shows that religion was regarded more as praxis than as a belief system, and this attitude was also expressed in the word for religion: *siðr* ('custom', 'way of doing things'). This view of religion would seem to leave open the possibility of transmission of mythology, so long as it took place outside of ritual contexts. Probably, however, the view of pre-Christian religion was similar in the other Scandinavian and Germanic conversions, where the mythology was not retained. What this must mean is that there was something special about the attitude towards the old gods in Iceland, since that is where the mythological eddic poetry was retained.

We can seek this willingness to retain the old myths in their importance in poetry,[2] especially in the kind of poetry that developed only in the North and that we now call skaldic poetry, after the noun *skáld* ('poet'). Like eddic poetry (and unlike West Germanic alliterative poetry), this alliterative poetry is divided into stanzas, but unlike eddic poetry, it requires the counting of syllables and complex schemes of rhyme, half-rhyme, and cadence. In addition, skalds used quite complicated kennings (see Quinn, Chapter 15 in this Handbook) – complicated not only because the modifier could be replaced by another kenning,[3] but also because many kennings cannot be understood without knowledge of mythology. Thus, the famous tenth-century Icelandic skald Egill Skallagrímsson referred to poetry, a common topic in the self-conscious verse of the skalds, as 'Óðinn's mead', calling on the complex myth in which Óðinn acquired the gift of poetry, in the form of mead, by stealing it from the giants. The tenth-century Norwegian skald Eyvindr Finnsson's kenning *Hárs lið* ('Hár's ale') and the eleventh-century Icelandic skald Arnórr Þórðarson jarlsskáld's *Alfǫður brim* ('All-father's malt-surf') require the audience to know two of Óðinn's many names,[4] and the eleventh-century Icelandic skald Hofgarða-Refr's *heilagt full hrafn-Ásar* ('the raven god's holy drink') that Óðinn possess two ravens. Understanding the tenth-century Icelandic skald Glúmr Geirason's *gildi beiðis hapta* ('feast of the gods' ruler') requires knowledge that Óðinn was the head of the pantheon and that he subsisted on wine alone. The myth of the acquisition of poetry itself has many players other than Óðinn. The mead is first made by two dwarfs out of the body of the god Kvasir, whom they kill. They then give it to a giant, Suttungr, in compensation for killing his parents. Suttungr in turn has his daughter Gunnlǫð look after the mead in a mountain, and Óðinn acquires it by boring into the mountain, entering it as a snake, and seducing or raping Gunnlǫð. In the form of an eagle, he flies away with it. In a single *helmingr* ('half-verse'), the tenth-century Icelandic skald Einarr Skálaglamm kenned poetry through reference to two motifs in this myth: *Kvasis dreyra* ('Kvasir's blood') and *brim dreggjar fjarðleggjar fyrða* ('yeast-surf of the men of the fjord-bone'), in which the fjord-bone is a stone and its men dwarfs. Drawing on the later part of the story, the little-known poet Steinþórr kenned Óðinn as the 'cargo of the arms of Gunnlǫð'.

Skaldic poetry dates back to the ninth century, and the first skalds were Norwegian. It seems to have been an elite art, given that the very first skald, Bragi Boddason, left behind a poem describing the carvings on an elaborate shield he had received as a gift, and, further, that skalds practised in the retinues of chieftains and kings. Indeed, the name of the main metre, *dróttkvæðr háttr* or *dróttkvætt*, contains in it the word for a chieftain's retinue: *drótt*. As time passed, the art was increasingly taken up by Icelanders, and by the eleventh century it seems that nearly all skalds were Icelandic. There were skalds in the retinues of the Norwegian missionary king Ólafr Tryggvason, of the Anglo-Danish king Knútr the Great, and of Óláfr Haraldsson, who was to achieve sanctity soon after his demise in the battle of Stiklastaðir (Norwegian Stiklestad) in 1030; Óláfr's miracles appear for the very first time in a skaldic poem from a few years after his death, Þorarinn loftunga's *Glælognskviða* (*Sea-calm Poem*), and, at the promotion of Niðarós, where Óláfr's remains lay, to an archdiocese in 1152–53, the Icelandic poet Einarr Skúlason recited a long skaldic poem in praise of the saint, *Geisli* (Lindow 2008, Chase 2005).

To lose skaldic poetry would therefore have been to lose an elite part of the Icelanders' cultural heritage, not least because their national history had them settling the island from Norway. But to keep skaldic poetry was to keep the mythology. Thus, while the strategy of the Church was to demonise the old gods, skalds and their audiences needed to keep the narratives about them, and these narratives were almost certainly the ancestors of eddic poetry.

A project to keep narratives of the old gods alive, to deprive them of the religious danger they might have posed, could have been aided by euhemerism: the theory that the gods were once men. That is the strategy adopted by Snorri Sturluson (c.1179–1241), the greatest author of the Icelandic Middle Ages. Snorri's fame rests on two works: his *Edda* (c.1220–30), a handbook of poetics and the only medieval text to bear witness to the title *Edda*; and the compilation of sagas of Norwegian kings now usually called *Heimskringla* (*The Circle of the World*) (c.1230). In the opening chapters of the first saga of *Heimskringla, Ynglinga saga* (*The Saga of the Ynglings*), Snorri writes about a king in Troy named Óðinn, who is so charismatic that his followers call on him for success. Óðinn foresees that his future lies in the North, and he leads a migration to what is now Sweden, specifically to the areas around Lake Mälar now known as Old Sigtuna and Old Uppsala. He places his followers, such as Þórr, in charge of various places, and he establishes funerary customs and teaches magic. After his death, Njǫrðr succeeds him, then Freyr, then the Yngling line. Snorri describes Óðinn as a master of magic, rather like a Sámi shaman that his audience might recognise (Lindow 2002). This Óðinn may have been an outsider and a magician, but he was not a demon.

Writing a generation or two before Snorri, the Danish historian Saxo Grammaticus also explained in his *Gesta Danorum*, a history of the Danish *patria*, the existence of pre-Christian mythology by means of euhemerism.

> Olim enim quidam magice artis imbuti, Thor uidelicet et Othinus aliique complures miranda prestigiorum machinatione callentes, obtentis simplicium animis diuinitatis sibi fastigium arrogare coeperunt. [Book VI]

> [At one time certain individuals, initiated into the arts of sorcery, namely Thor, Odin, and a number of others who were skilled at conjuring up marvellous illusions, clouded the minds of simple men and began to appropriate the exalted rank of godhead.]

The pre-Christian gods do in fact act in *Gesta Danorum*, in ways that are wholly consistent with their actions in eddic poetry and other vernacular sources, even if details differ. Saxo may have acquired these narratives from Icelanders, whom he praises in his Preface as excellent sources of ancient history, but even so his learned Danish audience presumably found the narratives credible. Here, again, the ancient gods are no longer dangerous.

In his *Edda*, Snorri told many of the myths that underlie skaldic kennings. One section of his *Edda*, and the most popular in the Icelandic Middle Ages, was *Skáldskaparmál*. Besides a systematic treatment of kennings, in the beginnings of most versions of the text he recounts at some length the myths of the alienation of Iðunn to the giants, the subsequent murder of her captor, Þjazi, and the compensation awarded to Þjazi's daughter, Skaði; the origin and theft of the mead of poetry; and Þórr's battles with the giants Hrungnir and Geirrøðr. But it is in the preceding section, *Gylfaginning*, that we find most of the myths. Gylfi is a prehistoric Swedish king deluded by three wizards who tell him stories about the Æsir (gods, but construed by Snorri explicitly in *Ynglinga saga* and probably so here as 'men of Asia'). Gylfi subsequently retells these stories, and, Snorri writes, they were passed down; thus, Snorri presents Gylfi's delusion as the origin of the mythology. In *Gylfaginning*, Snorri's wizards quote (versions of) the eddic poems *Vǫluspá*, *Vafþrúðnismál*, and *Grímnismál*, and so Snorri implies that the original mythology was in the form of eddic poetry. Euhemerisation is also present throughout the work in the idea that the stories originally took place in and around Troy, but in time the names were updated to Nordic ones: thus, Hec-tor became Þórr, and so forth.

Some form of euhemerisation probably took place in Iceland a century before Snorri wrote, indeed in the foundational work of Icelandic history. This is the *Íslendingabók* (*c.*1020–30) of Ari fróði, the best source for the conversion story mentioned above. In the much later manuscripts that contain it, it is termed *Libellus Islandorum* (*Little Book of Icelanders*), and *Libellus* is an apt title, for the work as we have it is quite short. After ten chapters on Iceland's foundational history, with an emphasis on ecclesiastical matters, Ari ends with the genealogies first of Icelandic bishops and then of the Ynglings and the people of Breiðafjörður in Iceland (leading ultimately to himself). He derives the Ynglings from Yngvi, king of the Turks, through Njǫrðr, and then Freyr. Probably another name for Freyr, Yngvi is in any case the name of a god.

We cannot know whether such euhemerisation occurred earlier than in Ari, but it was found in Anglo-Saxon royal lines as well (Faulkes 1978–9), and some of the traditions concerning the aftermath of the death of Freyr in *Ynglinga saga*, and the analogous Frotho III in Saxo, might well have circulated before the conversion. Some kind of euhemeristic view would certainly have eased the maintenance of mythological traditions. But in any case, the myths may have offered interesting exegetic possibilities (McKinnell 2007b) and have been good to think with in the Icelandic Middle Ages (Clunies Ross 1998a).

Mythological poetry in the Codex Regius

Scholars have long noted the careful arrangement of the main manuscript of eddic poetry, the so-called Codex Regius (GKS 2365 4°). The mythological poems are followed by the heroic poems, and a paleographic break certifies the conceptual break. Heinz Klingenberg (1971) called the overall organisation of the codex 'Endzeitprogrammiert', referring to the fact that Last Things loom large, that the eschatology of the first poem, *Vǫluspá*, finds an echo in the fall of Hamðir and Sǫrli in the last poem, *Hamðismál*.

The Codex Regius contains eleven mythological poems. The first is *Vǫluspá*, a synopsis of the mythology – or, to put it more accurately, a synopsis of the mythology focusing on the beginning and end of time. The next three poems have Óðinn as their focus: *Hávamál*, *Vafþrúðnismál*, and *Grímnismál*. The compiler (or his predecessor) presumably placed the Óðinn poems here because of Óðinn's role as head of the pantheon. The next poem, *Fǫr Skírnis* or *Skírnismál*, has Freyr as its divine focus, even though the god only appears in the beginning and end of the poem. A number of Þórr poems follow. Scholars have noted that *Vǫluspá* 53 (51 R, 46 H)[5] presents the deaths of Óðinn and then Freyr at *ragnarǫk* in that order, with Þórr's death following later in stanza 55 (48 H; the stanza is lacking in R). It may well also be that learned thirteenth-century Icelanders knew that euhemerised versions of both Óðinn and Freyr had been kings, whereas no such claim could be made for Þórr, and this too might account for the placement of *Skírnismál* directly after the Óðinn poems and before the Þórr poems. The conventional wisdom has it that four Þórr poems follow *Skírnismál*: *Hárbarðsljóð*, *Hymiskviða*, *Lokasenna*, and *Þrymskviða*. The final two poems, according to this wisdom, deal with non-divine mythological beings: an elf in *Vǫlundarkviða*,[6] and a dwarf in *Alvíssmál*.

The conceit of *Vǫluspá* is that a seeress (*vǫlva*) is speaking to Óðinn, addressed here by his name Valfǫðr ('Carrion-father'). The scene is something of a literary commonplace (McKinnell 2003, 2005b), but such seeresses probably really practised the art of prophecy in medieval Iceland (Sundqvist 2007). Here the prophecy looks both backwards, to the origins of the cosmos, and forwards, to its demise. The gods create the world, establish time reckoning, and enjoy a golden age, which is broken by the arrival of three giant maidens. Here we have the overall structure of the mythology, namely conflict between the gods and giants (the term is conventional, but it is the embodiment of an ongoing threat to the order of the gods, rather than size, that is the central feature of the 'giants' of the mythology). The seeress alludes obliquely to a few other cosmogonic and cosmological myths: the creation of human beings, the war between two groups of gods, the norns who give fate, the building of a stronghold for the gods. At stanza 30 (R31; this myth does not appear in the Hauksbók version of the poem) the seeress begins to recount the myth of the death of Baldr, killed by one brother, avenged by another, while additional vengeance is meted out to Loki. Now the seeress sees the beginning of the end, the dissolving of bonds, the breaking of oaths, the return of the dead, culminating in the cataclysm of the final battle between gods and giants and the sinking of the earth into the sea. Thrice in the poem the seeress refers to these coming events as *ragna rǫk / rǫmm, sigtíva* ('the terrible fate of the powers, of the victory gods'), and in fact the terms *ragna rǫk* and *tíva rǫk*, and presentations of eschatology in general, are characteristic of eddic rather than skaldic vocabulary. Although it is conventionally translated as 'fate' in this context, *rǫk* really means 'history, development', and this meaning could take in also what follows the demise of the gods and the cosmos in *Vǫluspá*: the earth rising green and new again, with Baldr and the brother who murdered him surviving, alone tokens of the previous generation.

Vǫluspá is a poem of great power and significant interpretive challenges; see Gunnell and Lassen (2013) for a series of essays showing the enormous range of interpretive possibilities. The version in the Codex Regius presents the death of Baldr as the linchpin to the entire mythological 'plot', the progression from beginning to end to new beginning. Gods may kill giants, but they themselves cannot be killed. But when Baldr dies at the hand of his brother Hǫðr (blind, according to Snorri), the first death of a god leads to the death of them all. It also unmasks the problem of a slaying within a family, and the return of the two brothers may offer a mythological solution to this intractable problem (Lindow 1997).

The three Óðinn poems that follow *Vǫluspá* in the Codex Regius also focus on cosmogony, cosmology, and eschatology, although the first of them, *Hávamál*, also contains numerous stanzas of a gnomic nature, attributed to Óðinn; these fill roughly the first half of the poem (sts 1–80) and a section usually called *Loddfáfnismál* (*Words of Loddfáfnir*) because the gnomes are addressed to Loddfáfnir, who is otherwise unknown (Larrington 1993). Besides these gnomic stanzas, *Hávamál* clearly combines disparate material that may well have circulated separately at some previous stage of transmission (von See 1972). The great cosmogonic myth in the poem is Óðinn's self-sacrifice and subsequent acquisition of runes and magic charms (sts 138–63), but the poet had earlier also included stanzas musing on faithfulness and fickleness before recounting the stories of Óðinn's failed attempt to seduce the daughter of Billingr and his successful seduction of Gunnlǫð, leading to the acquisition of the mead of poetry. The first of these offers a tantalising perspective on the second, for Óðinn's amorous activities usually have cosmic consequences: not just the acquisition of the mead of poetry, but also the siring of an avenger for Baldr.

Whoever arranged the order of the poems in the Codex Regius may have put *Hávamál* first among the Óðinn poems because in it Óðinn speaks in his own hall. In the next two, Óðinn travels: he visits a giant (*Vafþrúðnismál*) and a human king (*Grímnismál*). In the first of these, Óðinn and the giant Vafþrúðnir wager their heads on their knowledge of mythic wisdom, cosmogony, and especially eschatology. Much mythic information comes forth before Óðinn triumphs, but only by asking the giant a question to which only he knows the answer: what did Óðinn say into the ear of Baldr before he mounted the funeral pyre? As is consistent within the mythology, a god triumphs over a giant and the giant loses his life. In the next poem, Óðinn visits the human king Geirrøðr under the assumed name Grímnir ('Masking'). Although the prose introduction motivates the visit to Geirrøðr as involving a dispute between Óðinn and his wife Frigg and tells us that Geirrøðr has placed Óðinn between two fires for eight nights, the poem itself is a monologue: first of Óðinn's visions of the abodes of the gods and of the sacred places of the cosmos, then of cosmogony, these visions leading to a powerful epiphany in which the god catalogues his many names before revealing to Geirrøðr that the king is looking on Óðinn himself. The prose footer has Geirrøðr, in his haste to free the god, fall fatally upon his sword, and we may infer that Óðinn has involved himself in dynastic succession, since Geirrøðr's son Agnarr, who according to the prose introduction gave Grímnir/Óðinn a drink that set off the ecstatic wisdom performance, will succeed his father. Besides this plot, the motifs of the vision and of the epiphany offer or confirm valuable information on the mythology.

Fǫr Skírnis ('Skírnir's Journey'; called *Skírnismál* in AM 748 I a 4°, treated below) takes its name from its main character, Freyr's servant, Skírnir. It falls to him to travel to giantland to woo the giantess Gerðr, with whom Freyr has fallen in love, by seeing her from afar. The poem is a series of dialogues, of which the most important is Skírnir's wooing of Gerðr. He tries precious gifts and physical threats, which do no good, but succeeds by means of a series of curses. In the end Freyr gets not the bride, but the information that he is to get her in nine nights, a delay which he laments in the final stanza:

Lǫng er nótt, langar ro tvær,
  hvé um þreyjak þrjár?
opt mér mánaðr minni þótti,
  enn sjá hálf hýnótt. (*Skm* 42)

[A night is long, two nights are long, how will I endure three? often a month seemed less to me than this half night before the wedding.]

Freyr belongs to the Vanir gods, who are associated with fertility, so it is appropriate that he concerns himself with marriage. More generally, it is appropriate that the gods should take women from among the giants, for the flow of goods is all in one direction.

The order of the Þórr poems may take into consideration that Óðinn is a key player in the first, *Hárbarðsljóð*. From our perspective it would appear to be an Óðinn poem, since in it Þórr engages in a verbal duel with a disguised Óðinn, seeking transit across a sound, which is refused to him. In their dialogue, the gods boast of their deeds, and while Þórr's are mostly the giant-slaying for which he is known, Óðinn's are murky, sexually charged, and ethically questionable. From that perspective, perhaps Þórr emerges the winner, even if he must walk around the sound. As he says:

mikil myndi ætt jǫtna, ef allir lifði,
vætr myndi manna undir miðgarði. (*Hrbl* 23/5–8)

[great would be the family of giants, if all (of them) lived; hardly a human would be in the shelter of Miðgarðr.][7]

Óðinn has a ready answer:

Óðinn á jarla, þá er í val falla,
enn Þórr á þræla kyn. (*Hrbl* 24/5–8)

[Óðinn has the jarls who fall in battle, and Þórr the race of slaves.]

While the second half of this claim is unsupported elsewhere, it does seem that this poem establishes a hierarchy within the mythology between the two deities.

Hymiskviða represents the high-water mark for Þórr in the Codex Regius. The poem is framed as an acquisition story: acquiring a kettle for the gods to brew beer. However, in the course of his visit to the giant Hymir in quest of the kettle, Þórr enacts the myth of his fishing up the *miðgarðsormr* ('Midgard serpent'), a monster that lies in the sea encircling the earth. This myth is known from Bragi Boddason (the first skald), from other poets, and from images carved on stone during the Viking Age in

Altuna, Uppland, Sweden, and Gosforth, Cumbria, England (see Lilla Kopár, Chapter 10 in this Handbook). One of the interpretive questions concerning this myth is whether Þórr kills the serpent. Bragi has Þórr's companion cut the fishing line, but a late tenth-century Icelandic poem describes Þórr's blow to the serpent's head as a terrible hurt. In my opinion, *Hymiskviða* has Þórr kill the beast:

> Dró djarfliga dáðrakkr Þórr
> orm eitrfán upp at borði;
> hamri kníði háfjall skarar,
> ofljótt, ofan úlfs hnitbróður.
>
> Hreingálkn hlumðu, enn hǫlkn þutu,
> fór in forna fold ǫll saman.
> Søkkðisk síðan sá fiskr í mar. (*Hym* 24–5)

[Ready to act, Þórr boldly pulled the snake, glistening with poison, along-side. From above he struck with his hammer the hideous high mountain of the hair [head] of the wolf's (Fenrir's) brother. Reindeer-enemies (wolves) howled, stony grounds resounded, all the ancient earth shuddered. That fish sank into the sea.]

Some editors imagine an omission between the blow and the sinking of the 'fish', in which Hymir might cut Þórr's line. There is no evidence for such an omission in the manuscript, and if the stanza seems to be short a long line, so are the next two, and so are others. The evidence of *Hymiskviða* is that Þórr obtains the kettle, kills the *miðgarðsormr*, and, before leaving, kills Hymir and an army of other giants.

In all these myths Þórr is out travelling, and the same is true of *Lokasenna*, in which Þórr is absent until the end of the poem. Up until the end, the poem consists of a series of dialogues between Loki and the other gods, in which Loki insults them, often with matters that we know elsewhere from the mythology, sometimes clearly, sometimes dimly. Probably the most important piece of information in the poem is the fact that Loki and Óðinn swore an oath of blood-brotherhood (*Ls* 9). This oath can account for the presence of Loki, the offspring and father of giants and monsters, among the gods. Beyond that, the gods as Loki describes them are a flawed society indeed, apparently ripe for the fall that will come at *ragnarǫk*. Þórr himself is not immune from such criticism from Loki's wicked tongue, but his threat with the hammer silences Loki, who says:

> Kvað ek fyr ásum, kvað ek fyr ása sonum,
> þats mik hvatti hugr;

enn fyr þér einum mun ek út ganga,
  þvíat ek veit, at þú vegr. (*Ls* 64)

[I said before the Æsir, I said before the sons of the Æsir, what my mind urged me to; but for you alone I will go out, for I know that you will attack.]

In *Þrymskviða*, Þórr is required to retrieve his hammer from a giant. The retrieval of the hammer requires Þórr to dress up as a woman in order to impersonate Freyja, the price the giant Þrymr demands for restoring the hammer. The poem feels broadly satiric in style, but the loss of the hammer, and the loss of one's honour by cross-dressing, were serious matters. At the end, Þórr restores order by retrieving the hammer and killing Þrymr and the rest of the giants at his hall. *Þrymskviða* can thus be read alongside *Hymiskviða* as myths of acquisition. It may be worth noting that Þórr acquires or reacquires objects, whereas Óðinn's efforts at acquisition focus on knowledge and wisdom.

Vǫlundarkviða, the poem following *Þrymskviða* in the Codex Regius, tells a version of the legend of Wayland the smith, here called a prince of the *álfar* ('elves'). With its focus on terrible vengeance, the poem's plot accords better with the heroic poems that are to follow. Nevertheless, the maiming of Vǫlundr finds parallels in the mythological motifs of Óðinn's missing eye and Týr's missing hand, as does Vǫlundr's ability to fly.

The final poem in the mythological section of the Codex Regius is *Alvíssmál*. In it Þórr engages in an unlikely dialogue with a dwarf who sues for the hand of Þórr's daughter. Þórr requests the vocabulary for thirteen items among various groups: gods, giants, humans, the dead, and so forth. The dwarf, indeed all-wise, knows all the terminology, but he is undone when the sun rises and bursts him or turns him to stone. Þórr thus protects his daughter, just as he protected Freyja in *Þrymskviða*, and just as he protects order by slaying giants. The focus on vocabulary and the idea of different worlds of various beings is also certainly a concept that attaches to the mythological rather than to the heroic realm (Lindow 2007).

Mythological poetry in other manuscripts

The other major manuscript of eddic poetry is AM 748 I a 4° (*c*.1300). The compiler (or a predecessor) had a notion of the mythological poems as belonging together, for its contents are seven whole or partial poems, all of them mythological: *Hárbarðsljóð* (sts 19–60), *Baldrs draumar*, *Skírnismál* (sts 1–27), *Vafþrúðnismál* (sts 20–55), *Frá Hrauðungi kóngi* (prose introduction to *Grímnismál*), *Hymiskviða*, and the opening of the prose introduction to *Vǫlundarkviða*. Unlike the Codex Regius, this manuscript does not appear to have followed any discernible organising principle, although it is difficult to make a final judgement since we do not know what preceded the first extant leaf, which begins with st. 19 of *Hárbarðsljóð*. It does not seem unjustified to presume that there were additional eddic poems. AM 748 I a 4° and 748 I b 4°, a manuscript of *Skáldskaparmál*, were once a single entity, and it is therefore possible that the mythological eddic poems served the function that *Gylfaginning* plays in other manuscripts of Snorri's *Edda* (Guðrún Nordal 2001: 58).

Of the seven poems and fragments, six are also preserved in the Codex Regius. The exception is *Baldrs draumar*, a short poem that recalls *Vǫluspá* in that Óðinn calls up a dead seeress for cosmic information. In this case the subject is exclusively Baldr's death, and the poem helps us understand that myth by asking not only who will die (Baldr) and who will kill him (Hǫðr), but also who will avenge him (a son of Rindr, as in other sources; the imperfect alliteration suggests that the name Váli has been omitted). There is a fourth question, rather like the final question in *Vafþrúðnismál* in function, in that it reveals the identity of the questioner and is difficult to answer.

Hauksbók is the name given to an early fourteenth-century manuscript partially written by Haukr Erlendsson, a *lǫgmaðr* ('lawman') who died in 1334. The manuscript is a miscellany of learned and other material, and it includes a version of *Vǫluspá*, as mentioned above. This version differs in significant ways from that of the Codex Regius, most importantly in the omission of the Baldr story and the addition, before the last stanza, of two long lines (Quinn 1990b). This version of mythic history, without the Baldr story, does not depend on the death of a god or a killing within the family to precipitate the end. This direct move from the creation of the cosmos and its structure to the disorder and final battle of *ragnarǫk* may imply greater inevitability within the basic mythic structure. Such inevitability might accord with the two lines that occur before the last stanza:

Þá kømr inn ríki at regindómi,
ǫflugr, ofan, sá er ǫllu ræðr. (H58)

[Then the mighty one will come to power, powerful, from above, he who rules all.]

These lines would certainly seem to embed the mythology into the linear narrative of Christian history. With the new world, after the inevitable end of the old one, comes a new ruler from on high, presumably to be understood as Christ.

AM 242 fol. (*c.*1350), usually called Codex Wormianus because it was once in the possession of the Danish antiquarian Ole Worm, is one of the main manuscripts of Snorri's *Edda* and also contains the four so-called grammatical treatises from medieval Iceland, placed between two sections of *Skáldskaparmál*. After *Háttatal*, the final section of Snorri's *Edda*, the compiler has included a narrative poem, in *fornyrðislag*, which has come to be known as *Rígsþula*. It explains the origins of the social orders. According to the prose introduction, the otherwise enigmatic god Heimdallr took the name Rígr and travelled the earth, visiting three couples with widely differing habits and appearances, and siring a social class in each case. From Ái and Edda ('Great-grandfather' and 'Great-grandmother') come the slaves, from Afi and Amma ('Grandfather' and 'Grandmother') come the free-born farmers, and from Faðir and Móðir ('Father' and 'Mother') come the jarls or nobles. Rígr coaches one of them, especially in runes. He is called *Konr ungr* ('young son' or 'young warrior'), and it seems evident that the poet meant his listeners or readers to assume that he was the proto *konungr* ('king'). This view of the origin of kingship – as coming from the gods – would accord well with the euhemerism of the high Middle Ages and probably also with pre-Christian notions of kingship. The tripartite division of the social classes, with an opposition between free men and the nobility, suggests a high medieval context, but dating the poem is an impossible task, and of course it could have been adapted in oral transmission (see Thorvaldsen, Chapter 4 in this Handbook).

The important fourteenth-century Icelandic manuscript GKS 1005 fol., usually called Flateyjarbók, is Iceland's most impressive medieval manuscript. Primarily devoted to sagas of the Norwegian kings, near its beginning it contains a poem in *fornyrðislag* called *Hyndluljóð*. It too seems ultimately to have to do with matters of inheritance and kingship, although the frame is a dialogue between the goddess Freyja and the giantess Hyndla that brings out the ancestry of Freyja's protégé Ottarr heimski ('the foolish'). Stanzas 29–44 comprise what Snorri refers to in *Gylfaginning* as the 'Shorter Vǫluspá', a catalogue of mythological information with no strong organising principle, except that two powerful beings receive mention in the final two stanzas. The stanzas are quite elusive. For example, sts 35–9 tell of a powerful one born in days of yore from nine giantesses, whose names are listed.

Other sources indicate that Heimdallr had nine mothers, but we cannot be certain that he is the powerful one alluded to here.

Lost mythological poems?

As was mentioned above, Snorri's *Gylfaginning* is based primarily upon mythological eddic poetry: *Vǫluspá, Vafþrúðnismál*, and *Grímnismál*. He also quoted a few other lines and stanzas. One is the stanza from *Skírnismál* quoted above: Freyr's lament that he must wait for his bride. This is the only stanza Snorri cites about this myth. On that basis, one may infer that when he quotes other lines and stanzas, there may be whole poems, now lost, behind them. For example, Snorri ends his rehearsal of the Baldr myth with lines spoken by Þǫkk, an orgress in a cave. It is her refusal to weep for Baldr that keeps the god in the world of the dead. Was there an eddic poem about the Baldr myth? Another example is offered by verses spoken by Njǫrðr and Skaði, whose marriage fails because neither can tolerate living in the other's abode (Njǫrðr's by the sea, Skaði's in the mountains).[8] A *ljóðaháttr* exchange between 'some Vanir' and the mysterious figure Gná might be the most memorable point of a now lost poem about her.[9]

In addition to these lines in *Gylfaginning*, there are others in *Skáldskaparmál*. In Snorri's prose recounting of Þórr's visit to the giant Geirrøðr, one finds a *ljóðaháttr* stanza spoken by Þórr when the raging river Vimur is at its height and a line that may be *fornyrðislag* (or a proverb): *At ósi skal á stemma* (*Skáldskaparmál*: 25) ('a river must be dammed at the source'). After Þórr has arrived at Geirrøðr's abode, he kills two giantesses, Gjálp and Greip, and the Codex Upsaliensis version of the Edda contains a verse in *ljóðaháttr* at this point (*Uppsala Edda*: 97–8).

In at least one case we have a title. In *Gylfaginning*, Snorri says that Heimdallr himself speaks these lines in *Heimdalargaldr* (*The Chant of Heimdallr*):[10]

> Níu em ek mœðra mǫgr,
> níu em ek systra sonr.[11]

[I am the offspring of nine mothers, I am the son of nine sisters.]

Snorri refers to this poem again in *Skáldskaparmál*:

> Hvernig skal Heimdall kenna? Svá at kalla hann son níu mœðra, vǫrð guða, svá sem fyrr er ritat, eða hvíta Ás, Loka dólg, mensœkir Freyju. Heimdalar hǫfuð heitir sverð; svá er sagt at hann var lostinn manns hǫfði í gǫgnum.

Um hann er kveðit í Heimdalargaldri, ok er síðan kallat hǫfuð mjǫtuðr Heimdalar; sverð heitir manns mjǫtuðr. (19)

[How shall Heimdall be referred to? By calling him son of nine mothers, guardian of the gods, as was written above, or the white Ás, Loki's enemy, recoverer of Freyja's necklace. A sword is called Heimdall's head; it is said he was struck through with a man's head. He is the subject of the poem *Heimdalargaldr*, and ever since the head has been called Heimdall's doom; man's doom is an expression for sword.] (Faulkes 1995: 76)

Based on the one stanza of it that we still have, and the above statement, the poem *Heimdalargaldr* may have contained biographical information about Heimdallr, some of it spoken by the god himself.

Taken together, these verses surely offer evidence of a considerably larger body of mythological eddic poetry now lost to us. To put this another way, among the conclusions we must draw from the evidence of eddic poetry regarding mythology is that there must have been more mythology than we now have. If we compare the eddic situation with more recent oral traditions that have been extensively recorded, such as Balto-Finnic, we can appreciate how much we may not have (Lindow forthcoming).

Mythological eddic poetry and mythological skaldic poetry

Some myths were also recounted at length in skaldic metres by pre-Christian skalds. Snorri has two longish sequences in *Skáldskaparmál*: Þórr's journey to the giant Geirrøðr, which he assigns to Eilífr Goðrúnarson's *Þórsdrápa* (*Drápa of Þórr*), and Þórr's duel with Hrungnir, which he assigns to the *Haustlǫng* (*Autumn-long*) of Þjóðólfr of Hvinir. Although one can make a stronger case for the pre-Christian provenance of these poems than one can for eddic poetry, the diction varies greatly from that of eddic poetry, and we are grateful for Snorri's paraphrases. In addition, Snorri cites a number of verses from Bragi Boddason about Þórr's fishing up the *miðgarðsormr*, and these can be edited into a coherent whole. Skaldic mythological poetry constitutes an invaluable source of mythology and pre-Christian religion, but, as a glance at the above survey shows, it focuses on Þórr, whereas eddic poetry has a far wider range.

Concluding remarks: An inclusive understanding of mythology?

Given the palaeographic break between the mythological and heroic poems, it is clear that the thirteenth-century scribal culture that produced the Codex Regius had the same view that we have today about clear separation between gods and humans. Still, a discussion of eddic poetry and mythology should point out two reasons to be wary of this distinction.

The first has to do with the definition of mythology – of which there are many (see, for example, Segal 2004). My own definition is that a mythology is not just a corpus of narratives, but a system of related narratives with implicit cross-referencing. This system is therefore inter-textual: all or most of it is latent in each part of it. Furthermore, the narratives within the system must be set away from the here and now, in the distant past – that is, a past that is recognisably not today, and in a place that is not recognisably here. The characters in them cannot be from today's world, and they may not play by the same rules as we do. For this reason gods often feature in them, but they are not a requirement (see, for example, Doty 1986: 33–4). The narratives in a mythology frequently are foundational, in that some aspects of today's world may be traced back to them, including the origins of objects, behaviours, and structures. And, finally, they should be good to think with.

By this definition, narratives about the heroes of the North make up a part of mythology, just as do those about the gods. Indeed, the line between gods and humans was probably nowhere near as sharp in pre-Christian times as it is now (Schjødt and Lindow forthcoming), and this is the second reason to be wary of the rigid distinction between the groups. The *einherjar* – fallen warriors who have joined Óðinn in Valhǫll – comprise a category that is no longer human but probably not divine in the way the gods are. Similarly, the concept of euhemerism is broad enough to take in not only historical figures who might become gods, such as Bragi the poet, whom most would take to have been a living being, and who almost certainly became Bragi, god of poetry in the mythology, but also the obverse:[12] gods such as Óðinn and Freyr, who from our perspective surely never existed, being taken as historical figures who founded royal genealogies. From this perspective, all eddic poetry, including the so-called Eddica minora, is mythological.

Notes

1. In chapter 2 of his *Germania* (*c*.98 AD), Tacitus wrote: *Celebrant carmini-bus antiquis, quod unum apud illos memoriae et annalium genus est, Tuistonem deum terra editum* ('They celebrate in ancient songs, their only way of remembering or recording the past, the god Tuisto who emerged from the earth').

2. To supplement the following paragraphs, see McKinnell 2007b.
3. If a warrior is a 'tree of battle', and battle is a 'din of spears', then a warrior may be kenned as 'tree of the din of spears'.
4. For these and the following kennings, I follow the language in Anthony Faulkes's translation of Snorri's *Edda*, sometimes adapted for additional clarity (Faulkes 1995: 67–72).
5. I cite *Vǫluspá* by stanza numbers in the composite editions that have become common, with the stanza numbers in Codex Regius (R) and Hauksbók (H) following in parentheses. The most recent edition of eddic poetry, that of Jónas Kristjánsson and Vésteinn Ólason (2014), like one of the first (that of Sophus Bugge in 1867), edits the versions separately.
6. *Elf* is somewhat misleading here, since the Old Norse *álfar*, though cognate with English elves (Old English *ælfe*), are hardly identical to them. See Gunnell 2007 and Hall 2007.
7. *Miðgarðr* ('Central enclosure') is where humans live. According to *Vǫluspá* st. 4, it was created by the sons of Bur who created the cosmos.
8. However, these verses may be all there ever was about this myth. Saxo tells it too, replacing Njǫrðr and Skaði with Hadingus and Regnilda, and each recites only one verse, identical except for the Latin diction with the verses Snorri cites (*Gesta Danorum* i.8.18–19: 68–71).
9. On Gná, see Mitchell 2014.
10. *Heimdallargaldr* in Codex Upsaliensis (Heimir Pálsson and Faulkes 2012: 44, 146).
11. Instead of *mœðra mǫgr*, Codex Upsaliensis has *meyja mǫgr* ('offspring of nine maidens') (Heimir Pálsson and Faulkes 2012: 44–45), thus providing another example of the value of variant readings when we have them.
12. On the figure of Bragi, see Lindow 2006.

CHAPTER 7

Eddic poetry and the religion of pre-Christian Scandinavia

Jens Peter Schjødt

The eddic poems have traditionally played a significant role as sources for historians of religion concerned with the pre-Christian religion of Scandinavia. Most of the Nordic sources can be divided into 'contemporary' (archaeological evidence, a few skaldic poems, runic inscriptions, and a few other categories) and 'medieval' (sagas, the works of Snorri, and much more). Whereas the first category, in a sense, can be said to be reliable, it usually requires a great deal of interpretation in order to be used in our reconstructions of the pre-Christian world-view, and the information it offers constitutes only bits and pieces of this world-view. In general, it can be said that without taking the later medieval material into consideration, our reconstructions of pre-Christian religion would be very limited. The medieval material, on the other hand, can usually be dated to at least a couple of centuries after the official conversion of the Nordic countries, and most of the medieval sources were written down by Christians, which naturally affects their reliability with regard to earlier beliefs. In contrast, the eddic poems (at least in most cases) are believed to have originated in the pagan period, although they are preserved in medieval manuscripts. They thus offer a good deal of information, although there is far from as much as could be wished for (see below). For this reason they have occupied a unique position within the history of scholarship, and they have been used, for instance, to evaluate the sources from the second category and to suggest interpretations of the first. This summary of the source situation is of course very simplified in relation to the actual 'state of the art' within Old Norse studies, including the history of religions, but it encapsulates the important problems that we face in our investigations of the pre-Christian religion of Scandinavia. Consequently, this chapter will examine some of the problems associated with the use of the eddic poems in our attempts to reconstruct the pre-Christian religion of the North. I shall begin by identifying these problems, then go on to point to some possible strategies that may help us to address them, and, finally, as an example of what can be done, briefly analyse the poem *Hyndluljóð*, in order to argue that it is possible to use an eddic poem to illuminate our knowledge of the pre-Christian religion.

It is common knowledge that the value of the eddic poems as sources for the pre-Christian religion in the North has been a matter of great controversy. This is due to several factors, of which I shall only mention a few here. First and foremost is the problem of dating the poems (see Thorvaldsen, Chapter 4 in this Handbook). Gabriel Turville-Petre famously maintained – and I think we all have to agree – that 'in general, it must be admitted that critics fall back on subjective arguments in dating the mythological lays' (1964: 13). In an article published in 1991, Preben Meulengracht Sørensen stated that 'den kildemæssige benyttelse forudsætter ... ikke nødvendigvis, at digtet i den form, der er bevaret, kan henføres til førkristen tid. Det er tilstrækkeligt at tage stilling til, om det i henseende til de dele, der benyttes, bygger på en troværdig tradition' (1991: 218) ('The use of the sources ... does not necessarily mean that the poem, in the form that is preserved, can be traced back to pre-Christian times. It is sufficient to take a position on whether it builds on a reliable tradition with regard to the parts of the poem that are used'). He continued: 'når det gælder indholdet, er digtene i den bevarede form af denne forms datering ... kun af sekundær interesse, nemlig som et hjælpemiddel til at forstå indholdet' (1991: 222) ('with regard to content, the poems in their preserved form and the dating of this form ... are only of secondary importance, namely as an aid to understanding the content'), and he concluded that if we wish to relate the poems in their preserved form to people's thoughts and history, we have to interpret them, and, indeed, 'opgive objektiviteten i traditional forstand' (1991: 226) ('give up objectivity in the traditional sense').

Most scholars nowadays would probably find it hard to disagree, but at the same time the implications have seldom been taken into account. The implication is that, in order to use the poems as sources for the history of religions, we should turn our focus away from the poems themselves and towards the individual pieces of information related in them. And even if we might succeed in dating a certain poem, we still cannot be certain how to estimate the value of this information: if the poem is pre-Christian, the information might be expected to be pre-Christian as well, but we cannot be sure since Christian ideas were of course already known by many during the pagan period. If, on the other hand, the poem can be dated to Christian times, it might still very well contain some genuine pagan notions since folklore – but also common sense – teaches us that religious notions do not change overnight. Thus, when the dating of the poem in itself has no great impact on our view of the reliability of the information about certain phenomena, we must ask, as a consequence, what methodological tools do we have for using this or that individual piece of information?

And it is not only the dating of the poems which is problematic. We also face the fact that in many of the eddic poems we do not have full mythological narratives, but only allusions to myths or parts of myths. For instance, it would only be possible to reconstruct the Baldr myth at a certain general level from the few relevant stanzas in *Vǫluspá*, even if we included information from *Baldrs draumar* and other allusions to the myth in various poems. In the case of this myth we are fortunate to have Snorri's account in *Gylfaginning* (45–9). It may or may not tell the story as it was conceived in pagan times, but at least it makes sense to view the allusions in the poems within the framework of the myth as related by Snorri, although with some variations in detail. If we take the Baldr myth, therefore, as an example we may learn a good deal about the ways myths are related in the poems and the problems that these retellings entail for our reconstructions. Comparing the information about Baldr in the poems to Snorri's version, we find the following:

1) Unlike Snorri's text, no one poem presents a comprehensive narrative, something which must have existed either across poems or in some other form.

2) In order for the audience to have made sense of the mythological allusions in the poems, they (or at least some of them) must have had some culturally shared mythological knowledge, i.e. they must have known a story about Baldr to which they could relate the various references.

3) We must therefore assume that such a story – or, rather, several versions of such a story – did once exist (even if it was not recorded in written form).[1] In the case of the Baldr myth we have prose versions preserved from the Middle Ages by Snorri as well as by Saxo Grammaticus (*Gesta Danorum* 3. 2–3), whereas for many mythological references in the eddic poems we do not have such extended narratives.[2] We must nevertheless assume that in pagan culture there were many other myths beyond those that have been preserved in writing. Some are preserved as allusions, whereas others are not mentioned at all in the written corpus.

4) It follows that some myths may very well have existed only in oral form.[3]

5) Consequently, *argumenta ex silentio*, which take into consideration only the written corpus, are not persuasive in relation to the eddic poems, since the written corpus constitutes only a very limited part of the pagan mythological corpus.

Although I believe there are reasons for accepting that Snorri's version was at least partly rooted in the pagan era, it must also be acknowledged that the usefulness of Snorri for our reconstructions has been as much debated as the usefulness of the eddic poems has, and many scholars are very critical of most of the mythological information that we get from *Snorra Edda* (e.g. Kure 2010). Nevertheless, it seems inevitable that comparisons should be made between the mythological information given in the poems and that related in *Snorra Edda*. This has mostly been done in one of two ways: either we use Snorri's narratives in order to put the often scattered pieces of information in the poems 'in order', as is the case with the Baldr myth (although this method requires that we accept that Snorri had access to sources, oral or written, that we do not know today); or we focus on the differences between the content of the poems and that of Snorri's *Edda*, often leading to the conclusion that Snorri 'misunderstood' the poetic sources that are available to us today, with the implicit assumption that Snorri was in the same position as the modern scholar, with no greater access to the pagan mythology than we have. The 'truth' should probably be sought somewhere in between these two positions. Like the saga authors of the thirteenth century, Snorri would definitely have had access to a large amount of orally transmitted material, but this would not have passed down through the Christian centuries unaltered and the possibility of 'misunderstandings' and idiosyncratic interpretations certainly cannot be ruled out.

The problem addressed here, however, is how and to what extent we are able to reconstruct the narrative units lying behind the mythological allusions in the poems – and perhaps even to postulate the existence of myths which are not alluded to at all (that is, where we do not have versions in any extant sources at all, whether contemporary or medieval). It seems obvious that this endeavour cannot be carried out solely with source-critical techniques. Such a critique will inevitably yield negative results because of the late date of most of the sources: the result will be that we cannot know anything about this or that myth because it stems from sources that, for a variety of reasons (particularly the late date of extant texts), cannot be seen as reliable. For almost the same reasons, traditional philology seems unlikely to be the most efficient approach, since philology must of necessity focus on the texts that have survived. The examination of manuscript versions may indicate the existence of other, now lost, versions and encourage the reconstruction of some passages, but only if the surviving versions are so similar that they can be proven to derive from a common written source and we can rule out multiple oral precursors (Gísli Sigurðsson 2013: 56–8). This is rarely the case when we consider the mythological information in the eddic poems, where the similarities may be better explained with reference to oral formulaic theory in some cases (see Harris, Chapter 2 in this Handbook), and in others simply by accepting that stories and narratives existed in variant forms throughout society as a kind of shared cultural knowledge.[4]

The philological method naturally depends on extant texts, but would anybody nowadays seriously contend that the skaldic corpus and the twelve or so mythological eddic poems which have been preserved were all the mythological works that ever existed? Probably not, and the consequence of that recognition is that all of the poets and most of their audiences would have known many poems and myths referenced in them which do not exist in any manuscript extant today (cf. Dronke 1992a: 656). Therefore, when we use the poems as sources for the religious world-view of pagan times, it does not really make sense to treat the extant mythological poems as a closed corpus, as was often the case in earlier scholarship. Rather, the texts should be seen as more or less 'coincidental' written examples of what once existed as an extensive oral tradition in Iceland as well as in mainland Scandinavia.[5] The idea that similar formulations in two or more poems point to a sort of interdependence between them is thus, at most, a possibility. It definitely cannot be used for any sort of relative dating, since there were doubtless many more poems (and probably also many myths not contained within poems, but which nevertheless existed in the minds of a certain group of people). We should not, of course, attempt to reconstruct such lost poems, but to reject the supposition that they existed and that they may have had a significant effect on the form and content of what actually has been transmitted would be a serious mistake.

For these reasons, using philological or source-critical means alone to reconstruct the Baldr myth from the poems would not get us very far. What perhaps could be done would be to reconstruct the main lines of the myth: a god, Baldr, dreams about his own death (*Bdr* st. 1),[6] and his father, Óðinn, eventually learns that Baldr will be killed by his brother, Hǫðr (*Bdr* sts 8–9, *Vsp* st. 32), and another god, Loki, would probably also play a role (*Vsp* st. 35, *Ls* st. 28). A splendid funeral takes place after the killing

(*Húsdrápa* 7–11), and Baldr goes to Hel (*Bdr* sts 6–7), but his brother, Váli, son of Óðinn and Rindr (*Vsp* sts 32–4, *Bdr* sts 10–11), takes revenge and kills Hǫðr. Loki is afterwards put in chains (*Vsp* st. 35). We could add further details, but the point here is that a 'Baldr myth' can be reconstructed at a certain level, even without the help of Snorri. It may lack many of the details that are related in his *Edda*, but it includes others which are absent from his account.[7] This would probably be the situation with many other mythological references in the eddic poems, although we are better provided for in relation to some myths than others. But even such a reconstruction is, from a source-critical perspective, dependent upon the dating of the sources, and since *Vǫluspá* as well as *Baldrs draumar* and other sources used for this simple outline have (correctly or incorrectly) been dated to the post-pagan era by some, they should not be accepted.[8] The bottom line is that if we insist on purely philological methods, we would discover next to nothing about the myths of pre-Christian Scandinavia from eddic sources. Is this a realistic position?

I have dealt with the question of reconstruction elsewhere (Schjødt 2012a, 2013, forthcoming a, forthcoming b), and shall therefore only briefly repeat a couple of my arguments here. One main problem is that of diversity. Even if we imagine that we could meaningfully draw some connecting lines between the scattered elements hinted at in the poems – which I believe we can, in some cases, with the help of comparative evidence (of which more below) – we cannot be certain that they all contribute to the same version of the myth. In all oral cultures it is the nature of myth to be transformational in the sense outlined by Claude Lévi-Strauss (1971: 603). A group of individual myths may constitute a transformational group, i.e. they become different in a systematic way: if one element in one myth is substituted by another element in another myth, other elements will also have to change. There is then no prototype which is 'older' than the variants in a chronological sense; the 'myth' consists of all its variants. Thus, we cannot posit that a single, 'original' version ever existed.

Therefore, all the Old Norse myths that we know of from the various sources should be regarded as conglomerates of influences of all kinds, from different ages and from different cultures. Some of them are, no doubt, heavily dependent on Christian views, not least in their medieval prose renderings into narrative form, whereas the way in which the poetic sources often only hint at mythological themes in itself suggests pre-Christian roots.[9] That said, it should also be noted that versions of myths similar to those which we can reconstruct from eddic poems are likely to have been meaningful, to some at least. Therefore, it is pertinent to search for the significance and the function of a certain myth both externally (that is, in relation to other social and psychological aspects including ritual) and internally (in relation to other myths). As Lévi-Strauss proposed many years ago (1971: 576), the explanatory value of a myth is not only related to something 'out there' in 'the real world', but also to other myths. As a consequence, myths should not be read and interpreted in isolation, but as part of a mythological corpus, and thus of a world-view. In the case of the myths featuring in eddic poems, recon-struction should focus on the function and significance of their structure and content within the pagan discourse or discourses, to the extent that these can be constructed by scholars in the twenty-first century by means of the available tools and models. These involve comparisons with material from various cultures and necessitate informed knowledge of myth and religion in general, an issue I shall return to below (see, in particular, Schjødt 2013). What we cannot hope for is the reconstruction of indivi-dual, coherent narratives free from contradictions. Such narratives hardly exist in oral societies.

A discourse, therefore, should be understood as the framework sur-rounding a semantic centre, within which there are certain limitations regarding what can be said (for further details, see Schjødt 2013 and 2012b). An example could be a certain god, for instance Þórr, who cannot be said to be a weakling, because an important part of his semantic centre is precisely his strength, or, perhaps expressed in a more abstract way, his 'physicality' as opposed to that of other gods in the pantheon. In *Hárbarðsljóð*, for instance, it is Þórr who is bragging of his success in battles, whereas Óðinn here (as in other poems) relates how he gains wisdom (e.g. *Hávamál* sts 138–41), because his semantic centre is exactly knowledge and its acquisition.

Hyndluljóð: *A case study*

Bearing all this in mind, I shall now turn to *Hyndluljóð* to illustrate some of these considerations. The questions for the historian of religion are whether this poem can be used to reconstruct parts of pagan discourse, and, if so, how? Two issues which occupied earlier generations of scholars do not seem to matter as much, namely the dating of the poem,[10] and whether we can find influences from the Christian world-view in it. In many sources there are no doubt influences from a Christian world-view, but that does not necessarily influence the evaluation of an individual piece of information. Even if it could be proven that the 'composer' saw himself as Christian (which is highly unlikely), the content of the poem is decidedly pagan. There are many pagan figures and none that are Christian and, as I shall demonstrate in a moment, even the structure and at least part of the content falls fully within a pagan context. Therefore, no matter when the poem is dated to or what the poet's religious conviction, it needs to be seen as a pagan poem in the sense that the discourse is pagan, whether or not it is possible to parallel some of the notions with Christian ideas. It is therefore possible to use the poem as a source for a pagan world-view, as will be illustrated by the analysis below. As mentioned above, it is not necessary to determine whether a poem in its *entirety* mediates pagan notions; it is only relevant to determine this for each individual piece of information to be used in a world-view reconstruction. Further, in speaking about influences from Christianity, we have to be aware of the very meaning of the notion of 'influences'. The way the term has been used in many works on pre-Christian Scandinavian religion presupposes that at a certain time, before there were any 'influences', there existed a 'pure' Germanic or Scandinavian religion.[11] The problem here is twofold. First, we must ask when this state of affairs is supposed to have existed, and, second, what kind of 'influences' are meant. The two questions are interrelated and constitute different aspects of the basic, albeit tacit, hypothesis that this 'pure' religion was exclusively Scandinavian, and that at a certain time it became 'influenced' by other cultures. Here it is important to observe that interaction with other cultures will inevitably create influences of one kind or another; in that sense, religion is no different from language, warfare, art, and all kinds of technology or other aspects of culture. Such interaction seems to have been part of Scandinavian culture since the Stone Age. That would mean that long before the Bronze Age, Scandinavian religion must have been 'mixed up' with religious features from other cultures, i.e. cultures that were not Scandinavian. And in that case it would not make sense to talk about a pure Scandinavian religion, as distinct from all other religions. A much more realistic characterisation of 'Scandinavian' religion would be that it consisted of a world-view which included Indo-European elements, elements 'borrowed' from neighbouring peoples (including, from a certain date, Christians), and all kinds of 'folk religious' patterns, all of them more or less transformed during the long history from the Stone Age up to the conversion to Christianity. We would expect to find remnants of all these different influences in the eddic poems or, for that matter, in source material more generally that is concerned with pre-Christian Scandinavian religion.

One of the issues that has been an important strand in the scholarship on *Hyndluljóð* is whether the poem, as we have it in Flateyjarbók, was 'originally' one poem or two, since Snorri cites a stanza from *Hyndluljóð* but identifies the source as *Vǫluspá in skamma* (*The Short Prophecy of the Seeress*).[12] We can of course never know for sure, but in the context of an oral culture it is probably not the right question to ask. It would seem quite probable that stanzas of the poem (as preserved in Flateyjarbók) may have been used in an oral performance together with stanzas from other poems, known and unknown to us. This can never be proven, of course, but it should not surprise us if it was the case, and at the very least we cannot rule such a possibility out. So, the question might constructively be answered by acknowledging that sometimes it may have been one poem, and sometimes two, and sometimes some of the stanzas may have belonged to other contexts as well. What matters is whether the run of stanzas that editors have identified as constituting *Vǫluspá in skamma* should be regarded as part of *Hyndluljóð*; to my mind they definitely should be. Gro Steinsland (1991) has shown that this run of stanzas exhibits the same concern with the ideology of rulership as the rest of the poem, as has Jere Fleck (1970), using different arguments; and, from the perspective of the structure of the dialogue between Freyja and Hyndla, Judy Quinn has argued the same case (2002: 262–4). So, without postulating any 'original' unity (about which we cannot know anything), it seems quite plausible to argue that the poem, as it is presented in Flateyjarbók, was a meaningful entity to some (cf. *Edda Kommentar* III, 679; Gurevich 1973: 83). I propose, furthermore, that the basic structure of the poem and many of the details contained in it would also have been meaningful to pagans long before Christianity became the dominant ideology in Scandinavia.

The frame situation of the poem is that Freyja wakes up a giantess, Hyndla, who lives in a cave (*í helli býr*, *Hdl* 1/4) in order to persuade her to ride with her to Valhǫll and to the holy place (probably two designations for the same location). While Freyja is riding a boar, which turns out to be her protégé Óttarr, Hyndla is asked to ride her wolf. During the ride it is Freyja's intention that Hyndla should tell her what she knows about Óttarr's genealogy so that he can win his bet with his opponent Angantýr.

Þeir hafa veðjat valamálmi,
Óttarr ungi ok Angantýr;
skylt er at veita, svá at skati inn ungi
fǫðurleifð haf eptir frœndr sína. (*Hdl* 9)

[They have wagered foreign gold, young Óttarr and Angantýr; it's vital to help, so that the young warrior should get his father's inheritance after his kinsmen's death.]

Regarding the information that is required, it is said in st. 8 that they will talk about the noble families that descend from the gods, and in st. 11 Freyja says explicitly that she wants to know about the members of some of the most famous families in Scandinavia, so that Óttarr can learn it. And in the end (st. 45) she asks for a memory drink (*minnisǫl*) for her boar, so that he will remember everything Hyndla has related for use in the competition with Angantýr:

Ber þú minnisǫl mínum gelti,
svát hann ǫll muni orð at tína
þessar rœðu á þriðja morni,
þá er þeir Angantýr ættir rekja. (*Hdl* 45)

[Give some memory-ale to my boar, so that he can recount all these words, this conversation, on the third morning, when he and Angantýr reckon up their lineages.]

But Hyndla sees through Freyja's plan, and refuses to go to Valhǫll, so the whole scene of the transmission of knowledge takes place in the cave, which must be seen as an underworld locality. Hyndla's attitude towards Freyja and Óttarr is very hostile, and the drink she is going to offer, she says, will be filled with poison.[13]

So what we have here is a poem in which there could well be some Christian elements, especially in the stanzas which have traditionally been seen as belonging to *Vǫluspá in skamma*, such as st. 44, which refers to the coming of another still more powerful figure (*annarr enn mátkari*). Therefore, when we attempt to use the eddic poems as sources for the history of religions, the question is not whether the poems or part of the poems were influenced by Christian notions, but whether there are *also* elements that can be used for reconstructions of the pagan past. In order to decide that we must return to what might be termed the 'pagan discourse', i.e. the semantic space that can be attributed to the pagan past. Methodologically this involves consideration of comparative material from other religions of the 'same kind', and of course the other sources for Old Norse religions, which also constitutes a kind of comparative enterprise because of the diversity with which we must reckon, even within the Old Norse area.[14]

Leaving aside comparative considerations here, it seems clear that, whether or not we are dealing with one or two original poems, the sequence and the essential idea lying behind the stanzas is connected to an initiation theme (Schjødt 2008: 253–7). Óttarr should be viewed as a king-to-be, who is to be initiated into kingship, a hypothesis proposed by Gro Steinsland (1991) and Jere Fleck (1970), and central to this initiation is the acquisition of the knowledge he receives from Hyndla.[15] The frame story implies that he and the goddess who protects him come from the upper world to the underworld, which is how we should understand the cave (*hellir*) in which Hyndla lives. Whether she is thought of as dead is not so important here; the parallel scenarios in *Baldrs draumar* and in *Gróugaldr* might indicate that she is, although Quinn has argued against such an assumption (2002: 255). In this liminal scenario, knowledge is transferred to Óttarr and the poem seems to imply, at the end, that he and Freyja will return to the upper world where he will become a king. Thus, all the ingredients that we might expect of an initiation are present: the initiand moves into a liminal space where he acquires numinous knowledge so that he can go back transformed into his new position. We even see, as in many initiation rituals all over the world, that he has a helper, a so-called initiator, who prepares the way for him, namely Freyja. The structure of the poem, therefore, seems to be fully within the discourse which we know from initiations in many cultures and from other examples in the Nordic sources. There is certainly nothing to suggest that it has been influenced by Christian ideas in any way, although Christianity, of course, also has initiation rituals. Beyond the structure of initiation, we might probe whether there are any further elements in the narrative scenario which clearly connect it to a pagan discourse.

Indeed, some elements of this sort do seem to be involved, elements which are specifically part of the pagan discourse as we can reconstruct it from other Nordic sources. Starting with the knowledge that is transferred to Óttarr, we can see that it is acquired from the underworld with a female otherworldly being (who can be aligned with the dead) acting as medium, exactly as in other knowledge-acquisition situations. The content is mainly about descent (although mythological lore of other sorts is also present), and lines of descent, as we know from several genealogies both in the North but certainly also in other parts of the Germanic speaking world, were extremely important for the legitimisation of royal power. And, although both Óðinn and Freyr are regarded as ancestors of royal families, it seems, for reasons which cannot be elaborated here (cf. North 1997 and Schjødt 2012b), as if it was essentially Freyr from whom royal ancestry was derived. This is evident for the Ynglinga dynasty (cf. Sundqvist 2002), with both *Ynglinga saga* and *Ynglingatal* portraying Freyr as the forefather of kings. Therefore, it seems possible that this idea was implicitly present in *Hyndluljóð* even if it was not consciously formulated by the poet(s).

In addition, the incestuous marriage patterns of the Vanir gods (as ascribed to them by Snorri (*Ynglinga saga*, ch. 4)) are in play here. We notice that Freyja is riding a boar which is identical to Óttarr, the future king. A boar called Gullinbursti is an attribute of Freyr, according to Snorri (*Skáldskaparmál*: 18). The fact that Freyja also has the byname *Sýr* ('sow', *Gylfaginning*: 29), thus connecting both of the siblings to pigs, suggests that this animal, which in large parts of the world is associated with fertility, is being foregrounded here, confirming the fertility aspect of the Vanir. The sow's riding of a boar – which is described in the poem as *gullinbursti* ('golden-bristle', *Hdl* 7/6) – seems to refer to the incestuous relations among the Vanir. Therefore, since Óttarr is in the form of a boar and, from a ritual point of view, is a descendant of Freyr, the mythological point of reference is most likely a sexual relationship between Freyja and Óttarr – the sow and the boar, the sister and the brother. This seems to be confirmed by the designation *verr* ('husband' or, here, perhaps 'lover', *Hdl* 6/5), just as we know that Freyr was also Freyja's lover (*Lokasenna* st. 32). Without probing further into this relationship here, what is at stake is a discourse which circles around the Vanir gods and their connection to kingship, including their peculiar sexuality. Without being able to prove it, of course, we may see a relationship between the king, identified with the eponymous forefather, and his sister and lover, most likely representing the fertility of the land. This would certainly be an interpretation that would accord well with both comparative material and other sources dealing with pre-Christian Scandinavian religion. Many details remain enigmatic, perhaps not only for modern scholarship, but probably also for the audience that listened to the poem a thousand years ago. Nevertheless, the ideology lying behind it seems to be strongly influenced by pagan notions concerning the king and his relations with the other world and the gods who belong to it. We may even speculate that some stanzas of the poem were perhaps part of ritual performances, most likely having to do with the initiation of kings.[16]

This is not to deny that Christian ideas might well have played a role in some of the stanzas of the poem. Rather, since the entire period which we usually call the Viking Age was a period of transition and hybridisation, this is what we should expect. Whether or not people saw themselves as pagans or Christians, the two ways of 'being religious' were both part of the religious world-view of most people. For these reasons, it does not really make sense to ask whether the eddic poems can be used as sources for pre-Christian Scandinavian religion. On the one hand, the answer is obviously 'yes', because the discourse within which the mythological poems and most of the heroic poems are set is clearly pagan: the beings of the other world who are featured are exclusively pagan and the way they are presented seems to be in accordance with the knowledge we have from all the other sources, and in accordance with the models we would propose for a religion like that of pre-Christian Scandinavia. On the other hand, however, to argue that the versions we have in the extant manuscripts bear no traces at all of a Christian world-view would no doubt be very naïve. The poems were transmitted orally by pagans as well as by Christians for centuries, although the performative contexts may have changed drastically over time; and they were written down by Christian scribes, so of course we would expect that parts or whole stanzas of the poems might be expressive of Christian ways of viewing the world. Some may consider this attitude towards the poems as vague and hanker after the black-and-white categorisation of an older generation of scholars: are the poems Christian or are they pagan? The view presented here may be less spectacular, but I would certainly argue that it is a more realistic one for interpreting these poems.

Notes

1. As has been pointed out by folklorists, historians of religion, and many others, in dealing with narratives in oral cultures, it is necessary to accept that there is no such thing as an 'original narrative', as different versions would have existed from the moment that two or more people shared a narrative. I return to this briefly below.
2. A famous example is the statement in *Vm* sts 38–9 that Njǫrðr will return to the Vanir at Ragnarǫk; others that might be mentioned include the coming of the giant maidens in *Vsp* st. 8 and the forming of blood-brotherhood in *Ls* st. 9 (see also note 7, this chapter).
3. A splendid and very recent discussion of the orality of the eddic poems (although here confined to *Vǫluspá*, but certainly with implications for all of these poems) is Gísli Sigurðsson (2013). The publication in which this article appeared, *The Nordic Apocalypse: Approaches to* Vǫluspá *and Nordic Days of Judgment*, reveals the differences in opinion between scholars: one group speaking about 'the author' of the poem, apparently without reflecting on

whether such a person ever existed, and tending to regard the poem along the same lines as modern artistic creations, and another group who argue for an oral tradition behind this famous poem. I am strongly in favour of the latter perspective, and Gísli's article seems to me to have shown the naïvety of the older view that eddic poems were composed almost like modern ones. That is, in an oral society, they were part of an oral tradition that makes the search for 'the poet', 'the origin', and 'the original form' both impossible and irrelevant.

4. Thus, in my opinion, it is clearly erronenous to deduce, as is done in the *Edda Kommentar* (III, 687): 'Die Häufung von Formulierungen in Hdl. 1 f., die ein Gegenstück in den Hákonarmál (um 960) des Eyvindr skáldaspillir haben, und zwar dort ebenfalls im Kontext einer Fahrt zu Odin nach Valhǫll, beruht sicherlich auf Kenntnis und Benutzung des Skaldendichtes' ('The number of expressions in *Hdl* 1 f. which have a parallel in *Hákonarmál* (around 960) by Eyvindr skáldaspillir, in the context of a journey to Óðinn in Valhǫll, is certainly due to knowledge and use of the skaldic poem'). It is not that the poet of *Hyndluljóð* cannot have known the poem of Eyvindr (or the other way round, depending of the dating of the eddic poem). It is the lack of logic in the argument: because there are parallels, then one of the poets must have known the other. The idea, however, that it is possible to visit Óðinn in Valhǫll can hardly be ascribed to a single author: transportation between worlds, and the dead going to visit Óðinn, cannot be unique. Would anybody postulate that Eyvindr must have read Ibn Fadlan, because in his description the chieftain is also going to 'his master' (probably Óðinn)? The argument is, of course, absurd: dead persons (and gods) may well go to Valhǫll, and that idea may well have generated a lot of poems, using different or similar formulations, with some being preserved whereas others are lost.

5. The term 'coincidental' in this connection should not be taken too literally: there may well have been particular reasons behind which texts were written down, such as the agenda (sometimes tacit) of the individual authors for relating precisely this or that myth, but that does not tell us much about their importance in pagan times.

6. This stanza speaks only about Baldr, having bad dreams, but the following stanzas confirm that these are about his death.

7. For instance we do not hear anything about the revenge against Hǫðr from Snorri. For an overview of the sources as well as the research history of the Baldr myth, see Lindow (1997).

8. See, for instance, Samplonius 2013, regarding *Vǫluspá*; and for *Baldrs draumar*, Holtsmark 1956–78, V, col. 533.

9. The examples of such hints in the eddic poems where the medieval sources do not help us are very numerous: consider, for instance, the arrival of the giant maidens in *Vsp* 8, or the mingling of blood between Óðinn and Loki in *Ls* 9. In order for such hints to work they certainly must have created associations in the minds of the audience, associations about which we have no information today because the mythic narratives (whether they were ever written down or not) have been lost.

10. See, for instance, Steinsland 1991 and Näsström 2003. Dating cannot be said to be completely irrelevant, however. If it could be shown that the poem was composed in pagan times, the likelihood that the content was part of pagan discourse would be increased. But the evaluation of whether the information is Christian or pagan cannot depend solely on dating: Christian elements could easily be imagined to be part of late pagan discourse, and pagan elements likewise were no doubt part of the early Christian discourse.

11. See for instance de Vries (1956–57: 1, 29), where it is said that in the first century AD the religion of the south Germanic tribes was 'rein von fremden Elementen' ('unpolluted by foreign elements').

12. For a discussion of this issue, see *Edda Kommentar* III, 671–3.

13. For a discussion of these lines, see *Edda Kommentar* III, 833–4. Interesting points of comparison with this drink are the memory drink offered in *Sigrdrífumál* (st. 5) and the wisdom drink in the Gunnlǫð myth (*Hávamál* st. 105).

14. It is worth noting here that the same point was made by Ursula Dronke more than twenty years ago in another article on the value of eddic poems for the history of religions. She writes: 'Any attempt to interpret the text of the eddic mythological poems forces us to confront non-Christian traditions' (1992a: 683). Dronke was mainly focusing on Indo-European comparisons, which are certainly relevant (cf. Schjødt forthcoming a), but more wide-ranging comparisons may also be of importance.

15. Britt-Mari Näsström accepts the initiation pattern, but argues that it is initiation into warrior status rather than kingship (2003: 123–44).

16. It has been argued convincingly by Gunnell (1995) that several of the eddic poems were performed in connection with ritual celebrations. Gunnell does not include *Hynduljóð*, but it is not hard to imagine a ritual scenario in which the poem could be meaningfully recited: the three figures, Freyja, Hyndla, and Óttarr (who might be impersonated by the king-to-be, perhaps disguised as a boar), situated in a cave-like setting with the two females doing the talking, and thus functioning as initiators, so that afterwards the male protagonist would be supposed to know the secret lore of the *ljóð*.

CHAPTER 8

Eddic poetry and heroic legend

Carolyne Larrington

Introduction

In his preface to a recent collection of essays on eddic heroic poetry and heroic legend, Tom Shippey remarks on the nineteenth-century realisation that 'there was something recognisable in the heroic poems of what came to be called "the Elder Edda"' (Shippey 2013: xiv). The compendium's heroes – Sigurðr, Atli, Jǫrmunrekkr, Þjóðrekr, even Brynhildr – were identifiable from historical sources such as Ammianus Marcellinus, Jordanes, and Gregory of Tours, and, in some cases, from their appearances in Old English or Old High German poetry – poems which predated the manuscripts in which the Old Norse verse was preserved by hundreds of years (see Shippey 2013, 1982; C. Tolkien 1953–57). The names – also sometimes the place names – remained the same, but the details of their stories, from dragon-slaying to unwitting cannibalism, from being rendered limbless to falling foul of Óðinn, were very different. A good number of eddic heroic poems, primarily the verse preserved in the Codex Regius, relate to a pan-Germanic legendary; they recall the Migration Age heroes whose names and deeds survived almost a millennium in the oral tales of the Anglo-Saxons, the Germans, and the Scandinavians. Tales of Vǫlundr the smith, of Hildibrandr, and the probably ancient sequence of verses sometimes known as *Hlǫðskviða* (*Poem of Hlǫðr*) or *The Battle of the Goths and Huns* also belong in this category. The poems associated with these legends span a remarkable range of genres, for, as Shippey notes, though eddic 'heroes may choose not to speak . . . heroines have different speech privileges' (2013: xviii). Thus, heroic narrative expands to encompass both male and female perspectives and heroic behaviour is both celebrated and critiqued in the poems preserved in the second half of the Codex Regius (see Clark 2012: 17–45; 67–88).

These ancient Germanic figures were not, of course, the only heroes commemorated in eddic poetry; by heroes, I mean humans who take up arms against human or supernatural foes, who are brave and fearless, but not necessarily morally admirable. The *fornaldarsǫgur* preserve poems about certain exclusively Scandinavian figures: Starkaðr, Angantýr, Hjálmarr, and Qrvar-Oddr (see Clunies Ross 2013). The famous battle on Sámsey (modern Samsø) between Angantýr and his eleven brothers on one side and their opponents Hjálmarr and Oddr appears in more than one saga; the ramifications of Angantýr's demand that he be buried with his sword Tyrfingr give the narrative impetus for the striking poem known as *The Waking of Angantýr* (Burrows forthcoming b). The poem has no title in the saga in which it is preserved. These intertextual heroes move freely between narratives, accompanied by the verse associated with them, and they probably generate new stanzas in their new saga contexts. Other heroes associated with the legendary ancestors of Icelandic families begin to appear in subsequent *fornaldarsǫgur* (sagas of ancient times) (though the relative dating of these prose texts is highly problematic: see Rowe 2013; 2012). Thus, Qrvar-Oddr acquires a lineage originating in the island of Hrafnista (modern-day Ramsta in Norway), and although Oddr's own descendants make their careers largely in Garðarríki (Kievan Rus'), membership of this lineage is also attributed to important Icelandic *landnámsmenn* (original settlers). The poems that are preserved in the *fornaldarsǫgur* no doubt represent a small fraction of the eddic heroic poems which must once have existed, but which have not survived.

Heroic poetry is not purely a phenomenon of the Codex Regius and the *fornaldarsaga* contexts. The great elegies for the Norwegian rulers Hákon jarl and Eiríkr blóðqx ('bloodaxe'), preserved in the *konunga-sǫgur* (kings' sagas), show a heroicisation process at work. Although these kings fell defeated in battle, their glorious reputation qualifies them for entry to Valhǫll, and thither they are conducted by the valkyries who are imagined as overseeing their final moments. Whether they like it or not, the kings become assimilated into this heroic imaginary: the benches are strewn, the ale is brewed, and heroes such as Sigmundr and Hermóðr rise to welcome them. Finally, the heroic eddic mode crosses over into the *Íslendingasǫgur* (sagas of Icelanders) in very specific, probably late, contexts, and it is reframed once again in later *fornaldarsaga* texts. In these sagas the focus shifts from the ancestors of the Icelanders and the Germanic Ur-past to newly emerging types of hero. The late *Friðþjófs saga* (*Friðþjófr's Saga*), with its marked romance-like features, appealed enormously to later Scandinavian readers, and generated the revived version of the Scandinavian heroic for the nineteenth century.

These different heroic modes fired the imaginations of Old Norse eddic poets, stimulating a kind of poetry which is recognisably heroic in its tropes. Stanzas in which heroes proudly name themselves, robustly challenge their enemies and provoke troll-women and berserks to battle combine with other types of speech act. Laments, praise-poems, riddle- and other wisdom-contests, flytings, curses, and even love poetry all vividly incorporate heroic topoi. The poems are predominantly struc- tured as dialogue rather than as third person narrative, but the speakers are by no means restricted to the hero, the antagonist, and the hero's best friend. Giantesses and royal counsellors, princesses and foster-parents all find voice in heroic poetry, and genre-switching is frequent. Only some of the poems associated with heroic legend are given names, whether in manuscript or by subsequent editors; elsewhere, sequences of verses occur within discrete episodes. How far the prose accounts of the sagas (or the prosimetrum of the Codex Regius) are generated from pre-existing verses and how far individual stanzas, in relatively easy-to-compose eddic metrical form, are newly created by saga authors is a moot question (see Quinn et al. 2006). Eddic poetry is, nevertheless, pre-eminently the medium for the transmission of both older and more recent heroic legends in Old Norse.

Pan-Germanic heroic poetry and the Codex Regius

The poems preserved in the second half of the Codex Regius manuscript have been highly instrumental in shaping our general understanding of heroic legend and eddic verse.[1] The first heroic figure (apart from Agnarr in *Grímnismál*) to be encountered in the codex, Vǫlundr, the hero of *Vǫlundarkviða*, is known also in Old English poetry and Anglo-Saxon material culture: elements from his story are alluded to in the Exeter Book poem known as *Deor* and they are illustrated on the eighth-century whalebone Franks Casket (on the possible British provenance of *Vǫlundarkviða*, see McKinnell 1990). The legendary smith, hamstrung and brutalised by King Niðúðr, takes savage revenge on his persecutor. Vǫlundr murders the king's two young sons, shaping their skulls, eyes, and teeth into jewellery, and then rapes (or seduces) Bǫðvildr, the king's daughter. Before he flies away, the smith communicates the nature of his vengeance to the traumatised king:

> Enn þær skálar, er und skǫrum vóru,
> sveip ek utan silfri, senda ek Níðaði;

enn ór augum jarknasteina
senda ek kunnigri kván Níðaðar.

Enn ór tǫnnum tveggja þeira
sló ek brjóstkringlur, senda ek Bǫðvildi;
nú gengr Bǫðvildr barni aukin,
eingadóttir ykkur beggja. (*Vkv* 35–6)

[And their skulls[2] which were under their hair, I chased with silver, sent them to Níðuðr; and the precious stones from the eyes, I sent to Níðuðr's cunning wife. And from the teeth of the two of them I struck round brooches; sent them to Bǫðvildr; now Bǫðvildr is with child, the only daughter of you both!]

The poems which follow *Vǫlundarkviða* in the second half of the Codex Regius are linked together, most likely by the collection's compiler, as the adventures of the sons and daughter-in-law of Sigmundr. Very little is related of the patriarch, though poems about him seem likely to have existed, and a half-verse (*helmingr*) about Sigmundr and his incestuously conceived son Sinfjǫtli is preserved in *Vǫlsunga saga* (13). The Codex Regius compiler (or one of his immediate predecessors) incorporates as Sigmundr's son the recurring figure of Helgi, the hero loved by a valkyrie who chooses him as her husband. *Helgakviða Hundingsbana I* is unusual in that it consists at least partly of narrative verse rather than dialogue. Perhaps the most stirringly heroic verses in the manuscript, if not the corpus, describe the sea-voyage of Helgi and his men to challenge Hǫðbroddr for the hand of Sigrún the valkyrie:

Varð ára ymr ok járna glymr,
brast rǫnd við rǫnd, reru víkingar;
eisandi gekk und ǫðlingum
lofðungs floti lǫndum fjarri. (*HH I* 27)

[There was the splash of oars and the clash of iron, shield smashed against shield, the vikings rowed on; hurtling beneath the heroes surged the leader's ship far from the land.]

Draga bað Helgi há segl ofarr,
varðat hrǫnnum hǫfn þingloga,
þá er ógurlig Ægis dóttir
stagstjórnmǫrum steypa vildi. (*HH I* 29)

[Helgi ordered the high sail to be set, his crew did not cringe at the meeting of the waves, when Ægir's terrible daughter (> wave) wanted to capsize the stay-bridled wave-horse (> ship).]

The sonic patterning, the rhymes and half-rhymes (*ymr* / *glymr; Helgi* / *segl*), and the vivid *heiti* and kennings (*stagstjórnmarar*) show affinity with skaldic techniques, and they intensify the surging drama of this sequence, celebrating the hero's vigour, resolve, and skilled seamanship.

Helgi is fated to die at the hands of his wife's oath-breaking brother; in the related *Helgakviða Hjǫrvarðssonar* the hero is slain by the son of his mother's thwarted suitor, who is thus a kind of brother *manqué* (Larrington 2011b). With their focus on sibling and affinal loyalties and estrangements, the Helgi poems signal the importance of lateral relationships in the heroic poems which follow. Parents are virtually absent as brothers, sisters, brothers-in-law, and wives zealously promote ideals of individual honour, prosecute vengeance for offences against their kingroup, or lament the damage which honour culture inflicts on both men and women. The subject positions of women, unwillingly exchanged in marriage, denied their autonomy, and surviving as sole witnesses to male violence, are particularly highlighted in the Codex Regius poems. In *Hamðismál*, Guðrún Gjúkadóttir gives striking expression to her isolation, brought about by her own single-minded adherence to the vengeance ethic:

> Einstœð em ek orðin sem ǫsp í holti,
> fallin at frændum sem fura at kvisti
> vaðin at vilja sem viðr at laufi,
> þá er in kvistskœða kømr um dag varman. (*Hm* 5)

> [I have come to stand alone like an aspen in the forest, my kinsmen cut away as a fir's branches, bereft of happiness, as a tree of its leaves, when the branch-breaker (a girl collecting leaves, or possibly fire) comes on a warm day.]

Preceding the poems in which catastrophic ruptures between Sigurðr, his brothers-in-law Gunnarr and Hǫgni, and the implacable valkyrie Brynhildr play out in the court of the Gjúkungs comes a sequence of poems not paralleled in other versions of the Sigurd legend. Following a proleptic overview of his history, delivered by his prophetic uncle in *Grípisspá*, that leaves him profoundly shaken, Sigurðr encounters a series of 'remarkable beings' (Quinn 1992, 120). In a prosimetric sequence – traditionally divided by editors into *Reginsmál, Fáfnismál,* and the incomplete *Sigrdrífumál* – switching between various eddic metres as well as prose, Sigurðr learns the wisdom that is crucial for a hero and a king (Haimerl 2013). His education, and elucidation of his relationship with the valkyrie Sigrdrífa, is truncated by the manuscript's missing leaves. The next gathering contains the fragmentary poem *Brot af Sigurðarkviðu* and a second poem about Sigurðr (*Sigurðarkviða in skamma*) which recounts his murder, Brynhildr's conflicted reaction, and her spectacularly staged suicide. There ends the story of Sigurðr, Sigmundr's posthumously born son; as in the versions of the legend recorded in the Middle High German *Das Nibelungenlied* (*The Poem of the Nibelungs*) and in the probably thirteenth-century Old Norse *Þiðreks saga* (*Þiðrekr's Saga*), the compilation next traces the fates of Sigurðr's brothers-in-law and of his wife, Guðrún Gjúkadóttir.

In contrast to the versions dependent on the south German tradition, where the interest is on Kriemhilt / Grimhildr's execution of vengeance for her murdered husband, the eddic legend turns to Atli, leader of the Huns and brother of Brynhildr, for its next villain (Larrington 2015a, 184–9; 204–5). *Guðrúnarkviða I* narrates the young widow's traumatised refusal (or incapacity) to lament for her husband until her sister finds a way to release her pent-up grief, while the second *Guðrúnarkviða* poem, narrated by Guðrún herself, explains how she returned from exile in Denmark to marry Brynhildr's brother Atli at her mother's insistence. Principles of exchange – Atli gave Gunnarr his sister with disastrous consequences, now the Gjúkungar owe him a woman – underlie the marriage, while Guðrún's prophetic misgivings are discounted (Quinn 2009). How Atli betrays his in-laws is related twice in the eddic corpus: in the tense and allusive *Atlakviða*, and the more expansive *Atlamál in grœnlenzka*. *Atlakviða*'s language is highly wrought and often metaphorical: the wolf is described as a *heiðingi* ('heath-wanderer', *Akv* 8/3), bears have *preftannar* ('tenacious teeth', *Akv* 11/6), and Hǫgni, who laughs as his heart is cut out of his chest, is a *kvikvan kumblsmiðr* ('living smith of scars', *Akv* 24/3). The allusiveness almost cloaks the horror of Guðrún's vengeance: her murdered children are *gnadda niflfarna* ('little creatures gone into darkness', *Akv* 33/8), but when she reveals what Atli and his Huns are eating along with their ale, all obfuscation is over:

> Sona hefir þinna, sverða deilir,
> hjǫrtu hrædreyrug við hunang of tuggin;
> melta knáttu, móðugr, manna valbráðir,
> eta at ǫlkrásum, ok í ǫndugi at senda. (*Akv* 36)

> [Your own sons'–sharer-out of swords–hearts, corpse-bloody, you are chewing up with honey; you are filling your stomach, proud lord, with dead human flesh, eating it as ale-appetisers and sending it to the high seat.]

Atlamál, composed in the more leisurely metre *málaháttr* (see Fulk, Chapter 13 in this Handbook), retells these earth-shattering events on an intimate, domestic scale; Atli and his wife live in a farmhouse across the fjord from Gunnar and Hǫgni, the murder of the brothers follows a tough battle in which Guðrún fights alongside her brothers, and, even after Atli's inadvertent cannibalism, husband and wife snipe at one another across the hall until Atli is finally killed (Larrington 2013). The final two poems of the cycle, *Guðrúnarhvǫt* and *Hamðismál*, depict Guðrún's final act of vengeance, sending her last sons on a futile mission to avenge their murdered sister Svanhildr, Guðrún's daughter with Sigurðr. The two poems share the scene in which Guðrún urges the reluctant Hamðir and Sǫrli to attack Jǫrmunrekkr, their half-sister's husband and killer, but while the second poem follows the young men on their journey, witnessing how they violently strike down their own half-brother before realising that his support would have guaranteed success in their vengeance, the first poem remains with Guðrún. After lamenting the many losses she has sustained through her male kinfolk's adherence to heroic codes of vengeance (and ignoring her own murders) she comes to the end of her journey, hoping, like Brynhildr before her, to be reunited in death with Sigurðr:

> Hlaðit ér, jarlar, eikikǫstinn,
> látið þann und hilmi hæstan verða!
> megi brenna brjóst bǫlvafult eldr,
> ... um hjarta þiðni sorgir! (*Ghv* 20)

[Nobles, build high the oak-wood pyre! Let it be the highest among the princes. May fire burn up the breast so full of wrongs, ... may sorrows melt about my heart.]

The heroic poems of the Codex Regius then link together legends of different ages and from different sources in a chain of dynastic episodes, unified largely by the figures of Sigurðr and Guðrún. The poems celebrate the grandeur of the heroic will, the capacity to laugh as one's heart is excised, or to play the harp as serpents strike at one's limbs. Heroic self-control shades into mulish determination; the dying Sigurðr comforts his wife by reminding her that her brothers live still; those same brothers accept Atli's invitation despite warnings of treachery; Brynhildr insists on her right, when she is united with Sigurðr in the next world, to claim him as her own: *okkrum aldri slíta ... saman* ('to live fully all our time together', *Hlr* 14/5–7). Within the Codex Regius, the cumulative effect of so many deaths, so much horror, so many oaths broken and women left to weep, has been seen by some scholars as offering a critique of the heroic ethos (Jóhanna Katrín Friðriksdóttir 2013a and b; Clark 2005). The penultimate poem of the Codex Regius ends with a woman's last words, offering consolation to other women: *at þetta tregróf um talið væri* ('that this chain of griefs has been recounted', *Ghv* 21/5–6), while the final poem concludes with the self-congratulation of the heroic brothers: *Vel hǫfum við vegit, stǫndum á val Gotna* ('We have fought well, we stand on Goth corpses', *Hm* 30/1–2). However transgressive Guðrún's actions, however resentful her sons at the final duty imposed on them, heroic utterances in the Codex Regius remain polarised by gender. *Feminis lugere honestum est, viris meminisse* ('It is fitting for women to lament and for men to remember'), as Tacitus long ago observed in his *Germania* (Benario 1999: ch. 27).

These thematic preoccupations – honour, vengeance, kin-group bonds versus exogamic loyalties – are intrinsic to heroic legend. But the poems also explore the boundaries between the living and the dead, the nature of heroic and royal wisdom (in which the mythological plays a substantial role), and they also interrogate gender models in the flytings of the Helgi poems (Clark 2013) and the murders committed by Guðrún (as argued by Clark and Jóhanna Katrín Friðriksdóttir, Chapter 17 in this Handbook). The formal qualities of the poems vary considerably, showing how the flexibility of eddic metres permits stirring narrative, quick-fire dialogue, moving lament, and furious self-assertion. Metrical variation expedites the expressive possibilities of these best-known of eddic poems: relaxed *málaháttr*, the deliberativeness and balance of *ljóðaháttr*'s alternating line lengths, and the brisk concision of *fornyrðislag*.

Eddic poems generated by other Germanic heroic legends are preserved outside the Codex Regius. *The Battle of the Goths and Huns*, also known as *Hlǫðskviða* (Christopher Tolkien 1953–57), and the probably later *Death-Song* of Hildibrandr are both to be found in *fornaldarsǫgur* contexts. *The Battle of the Goths and Huns*, along with two other major poetic sequences – *The Waking of Angantýr* and the riddle-contest of King Heiðrekr and Óðinn, known as *Gestumblinda gátur* – is incorporated into *Hervarar saga ok Heiðreks* (*The Saga of Hervǫr and Heiðrekr*). *The Waking of Angantýr* is discussed below. The saga author(s) effectively anthologised these three sequences, most likely earlier preserved in quite unrelated contexts, within the new prosimetric narrative, integrating them as discrete episodes associated with successive generations of the same dynasty (Love 2013). *The Battle of the Goths and Huns* (Burrows forthcoming a) relates how, after the death of King Heiðrekr, his son Angantýr (the third hero of that name in the saga) refuses the demands of his half-brother Hlǫðr for half the kingdom. Although Angantýr makes a generous counter-offer to his illegitimate brother, battle becomes certain when Gizurr Grýtingaliði, an Odinic figure who had fostered both Angantýr and his father, insults Hlǫðr:

Þetta er þiggjanda þýjar barni,
barni þýjar, þótt sé borinn konung*i*;
þá hornungr á haugi sat,
er ǫðlingr arfi skipti. (*SkP*, GizGrý Lvı^{VIII})[3]

[That's acceptable for a bondsmaid's child, a bondsmaid's child, though he may be born to a king, then the bastard sat on the mound, where the prince divided the inheritance.]

Shippey (2013: xvii–xviii) shows how concisely the insult works here, in particular the sneer of *sé*, with its suggestions of disbelief. *Konungi* and *hornungr* jangle together, enacting the mismatch in status, while the illegitimate child perhaps positions himself to make his claim by seating himself on the mound that plays a role in kingly initiation rites – or, conceivably, sitting on the mound implies the bastard's continuing exclusion, consigned to a marginal position while the *ǫðlingar* make the decisions. The details of character and place names in this poem seem likely to date from earlier than the Viking Age; parallels are found in the Old English *Widsith* (*Far-journeyer*) and in the sixth-century Gothic historian Jordanes. Although the attempts to identify the poem's plot with historical events have been unconvincing, these ancient names and the verses' less strict metrical form suggest that it may be one of the oldest poems preserved in Old Norse. Perennially popular in Germanic heroic legend, the theme of conflict between half-brothers frames the events of the poem, though it may not belong to the earliest stratum of material.

Hildibrandr's legend takes differing forms in Old High German (where a father unwittingly kills his son) and in Old Norse, where the tragedy is fratricidal. Although Hildibrandr's death-song is recorded in Old Norse only in the late *fornaldarsaga Ásmundar saga kappabana* (*The Saga of Ásmundr, Slayer of Champions*), the same tale, featuring a hero called Hildigerus and his half-brother Haldanus, is related in Saxo Grammaticus's *Gesta Danorum* (*History of the Danes*) (Book VII), where another version of the hero's *Death-Song* is preserved in Latin (Matyushina 2012; Ciklamini 1966). In the saga (ch. 9), the dying Hildibrandr acknowledges the history of which his half-brother Ásmundr is ignorant.

In six terse verses Hildibrandr recalls their mother Drótt, the dwarf-forged accursed swords with which her father's grandsons were fated to kill one another, and the son whom Hildibrandr had killed in fury on the way to his final battle, and he requests that he be given honourable burial in his brother's garments (*SkP*, Hildibrandr Lv 1–6[VIII]). The poem summarises neatly the events of this quite short saga and ends on a note of real pathos. Meanwhile, Ásmundr produces a short sequence of four unrepentant, triumphant verses about his exploits when he returns home (ch. 10); he is surprisingly little moved by his half-brother's dying revelation (Larrington 2015a, 71–3). Hildibrandr's *Death-Song* corresponds closely to the events of the saga prose, and seems likely to have been their source. Ásmundr's tasteless boasts, in contrast, suggest that they have been composed to fit the saga's new emphasis on the hero's victory rather than the guilt and horror of fratricide.

Scandinavian heroes in eddic verse

Heroic figures imagined as having lived before the settlement of Iceland are celebrated in many poems preserved in the *fornaldarsǫgur*. Among them are Starkaðr (a major character also in the *Gesta Danorum*); the berserk warrior Angantýr and his eleven brothers who fell in the great battle on Sámsey; and their valiant opponents, the sworn-brothers Hjálmarr and Qrvar-Oddr. Ragnarr loðbrók (hairy breeches) might also be included among these heroes, though, unusually, the verses in his saga are almost all composed in skaldic metres. Exceptions are the metrically indeterminate *Krákumál* (*The Speech of Kráka*) (McTurk 1991; forthcoming a) and three *fornyrðislag* stanzas (McTurk forthcoming b) spoken by a wooden man, some kind of idol who laments that no one sacrifices to him any longer. He contrasts his neglect with the old days:

> Þá var ek blótinn til bana mönnum
> í Sámseyju sunnanverðri. (*SkP*, *Ragn* 9[VIII])

> [Then I was sacrificed to ... so that men were slain in Sámsey down in the south.]

The sagas concerning these Scandinavian heroes often contain long, apparently complete poems, such as *The Waking of Angantýr*, *Víkarsbálkr* in *Gautreks saga* (*The Saga of Gautrekr*), and the various death-songs, or the *ævidrápur*, which chronicle the heroes' autobiographies as their lives draw to a close. Other kinds of eddic verse associated with these heroes or their descendants include occasional stanzas such as those preserved in *Gautreks saga*, exchanges with giantesses and troll-women, or challenges to other heroes. The opening episode of *Gautreks saga* (chs. 1–2), which relates how Gautrekr came to be born into a maternal family prone to committing suicide when they sense a dimunition of their material wealth, contains a comic sequence of verses: 'The Misers' Verses', as Ranisch and Heusler (1903) call them (Clunies Ross forthcoming b, *SkP*, Gill Lv 1^{VIII}, Fjǫl Lv 1–2 ^{VIII}, Íms Lv 1^{VIII}). These are uttered by Gautrekr's uncles, who bewail their very minor losses when a guest billets himself upon them:

Þat var spell er spörr of vann
    á akri Ímsiguls.
Axi var skatt, ór var korn numit;
    þat mun æ Tötru ætt trega. (Íms Lv 1^{VIII})

[That was ruin, when a sparrow conquered Ímsigull's field; a corn-ear was damaged, the grain seized from it; this will ever grieve Tötra's lineage.]

However, most of the saga's verses constitute the poem *Víkarsbálkr* (Clunies Ross forthcoming b), which relates the life-story of Starkaðr (Saxo's Starcatherus) (Ciklamini 1971; Grimstad 1976; 1988; Meulengracht Sørensen 2006). Starkaðr's parents were burnt in their hall when he was very small; fostered by the Odinic figure Hrosshársgrani, he wastes his life as a *kólbítr* ('a coal-biter, good-for-nothing'), who was *fás forvitinn í fleti niðri* ('curious about little, down in the hall', *SkP*, StarkSt Vík 5^{VIII}/7–8). Then Starkaðr is recruited by King Víkarr. Starkaðr celebrates the fierce conflicts in which Víkarr's retainers fight, in a poundingly rhythmic series of verbs:

Svá **kómu** vér til konungs garða
hristum grindr, **hjuggum** gætti,
brutum borglokur, **brugðum** sverðum (*SkP*, StarkSt Vík 10^{VIII}/1–6)

[So we came to the king's courts, we shook the gates, hacked at the door-frames, broke the fortress-locks, swung swords]

And, with a clattering assonance (*kjálka . . . jaxla*), he calmly catalogues his own horrifying injuries. His opponent had hewn (*lét höggva*):

hjálm af höfði, en haus skorat
ok kinnkjálka klofinn í jaxla,
en it vinstra viðbein látit. (*SkP*, StarkSt Vík 14^{VIII} /6–11)

[my helmet from my head, my skull sliced into, and my jawbone cloven to the back-teeth, and the left collar-bone ruined.]

Starkaðr's foster-father manifests his Odinic identity to his fosterling at an assembly of the gods. Here Óðinn blesses Starkaðr with many attributes, including a lifetime that is three times as long as other humans. Þórr, however, resents the fact that the hero's grandmother had preferred a giant to Þórr himself and lays counter-curses on the warrior. Thus, Starkaðr comes to commit the crime of sacrificing his beloved king to Óðinn; Víkarr's fate was prophesied for him before birth, according to a verse preserved in *Hálfs saga ok Hálfsrekka* (*The Saga of Hálfr and his champions*) (ch. 1) (Seelow forthcoming):

> Ek sé hanga á háum gálga
> son þinn, kona, seldan Óðni (*SkP*, Alrekr Lv 1[VIII]/5–8)
>
> [I see hanging on high gallows your son, woman, given to Óðinn]

Starkaðr's poem, and his history in the saga, ends when he finds a new home in Uppsala, sitting among serving-men and being mocked for his ugliness by the other warriors:

> Hlæja rekkar er mik sjá,
> ljótan skolt, langa trjónu,
> hangar tjálgur, hár úlfgrátt,
> hrjúfan háls, húð jótraða. (*SkP*, StarkSt *Vík* 33[VIII])
>
> [Warriors laugh who they see me; my ugly chops and long muzzle, hanging branches (arms), wolf-grey hair, rough neck and scarred skin.]

Starkaðr's later history and the circumstances of his death are related in *Norna-Gests þáttr* (*The Tale of Norna-Gestr*) and *Gesta Danorum*. *Gesta Danorum* also preserves a series of Latin verses, uttered by the hero in rebuke to Ingellus, *Beowulf*'s Heathobard prince Ingeld; these very likely translate a lost series of verses, which were probably also composed in eddic metre.

The legend of Angantýr and his eleven brothers, their death on Sámsey at the hands of Ǫrvar-Oddr and his sworn-brother Hjálmarr, Hjálmarr's demise when victory has been won, and the expedition of Angantýr's daughter Hervǫr to retrieve her father's sword Tyrfingr give rise to a series of poems and stanza sequences, preserved in two sagas (*Hervarar saga* and *Ǫrvar-Odds saga* [*The Saga of Arrow-Oddr*]) and across different recensions of those texts (see Lönnroth 1971; Leslie 2012, 304–24; 367–91; Leslie 2014; Love 2013). Oddr and Hjálmarr exchange stanzas before the battle (Burrows forthcoming a and b), noting how the berserk brothers *grenjandi gengu af öskum / tírarlausir váru tólf saman* ('howling advance from their ships, twelve inglorious ones together', *SkP*, *QrvOdd* Lv2[VIII]/1–4).

Hjálmarr gloomily surmises that the two sworn-brothers are doomed: *vit skulum í aptan Óðin gista* ('we will be lodging with Óðinn this evening', *SkP*, Hjálm Lv3^{VIII}/5–16) – that is, in Valhǫll. Only once victory is assured, and the twelve brothers are themselves Óðinn's guests, does Oddr notice his friend's pallor and many wounds. Hjálmarr's *Death-song* (*SkP*, Hjálm Lv4–19^{VIII}) is both moving and tightly structured, contrasting the splendid *fimm tún* ('five farms', *SkP*, Hjálm Lv5^{VIII}/2) that he owns with the bleak island where he finds death, and the mead supped by the retainers at his father's court with the sword-wounds on his body. Above all, he contrasts his love for the beautiful Ingibjǫrg, who had prophesied his death on this adventure, with his failure to return to her at Uppsala or Sigtuna. Rather than enjoying the pleasures of his father's hall once more – or, even, like Angantýr and his brothers, those of Valhǫll – the despairing Hjálmarr finds no consolation and recognises that he is now destined to become carrion:

Hrafn flýgr austan af hám meiði,
flýgr honum eptir ǫrn í sinni;
þeim gef ek erni efstum bráðir,
sá mun á blóði bergja mínu. (*SkP*, Hjálm Lv10^{VIII})

[A raven flies from the east, from the tall tree, the eagle flies behind him as companion; I provide food for that last eagle, he will sup on my blood.]

As Lars Lönnroth (1971: 18) suggests, the *Death-Song* was 'evidently meant to be recited with a good deal of gusto and pathos, possibly emphasised by means of gestures'; it ranks among the most dramatic of the eddic poems preserved outside the Codex Regius. Hjálmarr's chief concern, like most traditional heroes, is with his posthumous reputation for courage; although the trope 'women will hear of my bravery' is familiar from skaldic verse (Frank 1990), the poem embeds that boast within a lament for the suffering that the beloved Ingibjǫrg will face when she hears of his death. Of the nineteen verses Hjálmarr utters in his final hours, five refer directly to Ingibjǫrg, while two evoke the collective women back in the hall – those who tried to dissuade him from his heroic journey and who sang so beautifully: a significant re-orientation of heroic regret. The poem ends, however, with a roll-call of Hjálmarr's bench-mates at the feast, comrades whom he will never see again. Romantic attachment is foregrounded, a poetic move perhaps influenced by the thirteenth-century translations of French romances; a profound regard for the beloved lady tempers the older model of heroism in the poem, yet the homosocial bond to Hjálmarr's male companions carries considerable – and final – weight.

In *The Waking of Angantýr*, Hervǫr, Angantýr's fearless daughter, braves the *draugar* (undead) of Sámsey, who stand at the doors of their burial-mounds as an eerie flame burns around them, for she intends to retrieve her father's sword, Tyrfingr. Angantýr is astonished by his daughter's boldness:

> Kveðkat ek þik, mær ung, mönnum líka,
> er þú um hauga hvarfar á nóttum,
> gröfnum geiri ok með Gota málmi
> hjálmi ok með brynju fyr hallar dyrr. (*SkP*, Angantýr Lv 6^{VIII})

[Young girl, I declare you are not like most men, hanging around mounds by night, with an engraved spear and in metal of the Goths, a helmet and corslet before the hall-doors.]

Although Angantýr tries to retain the sword, claiming first that he does not have it, and then revealing (truthfully) that the sword bears a curse, he relinquishes it at last in the face of Hervǫr's counter-curses:

> svá sé yðr öllum innan rifja,
> sem þér í maura mor
nið haugi! (*SkP*, Herv Lv 11^{VIII}/3–6)

[May you all within your ribs be as if you were shrivelling up in an ant-heap!]

The girl returns triumphantly to her ships, dismissing the curse with its threat to the lineage's future. Nevertheless, Heiðrekr, Hervǫr's intemperate son, will lose his riddle-contest with Óðinn, and, because he tries to strike at the god with Tyrfingr, he is doomed to die at the hands of his thralls; later, the saga's third Angantýr, Hervǫr's grandson, mentioned above, will kill his half-brother with the same sword.

Hervarar saga ok Heiðreks, like *Hálfs saga* (see below), unites three doubtless originally distinct legends: the berserk brothers and the reclaiming of the sword, the riddle-contest, and the half-brother conflict, each generating or transmitting an extended poetic sequence with very different generic affiliations. Hjálmarr's death-song belongs with other death-songs and autobiographical poems, such as *Víkarsbálkr*, Ǫrvar-Oddr's very long *ævidrápa*, or *Hrókskviða* in *Hálfs saga ok Hálfsrekkar*. The riddle-contest known as *Gestumblinda gátur*, pitting human and god in a confrontation modelled on the wisdom-performances of *Vafþrúðnismál* and *Grímnismál*, foregrounds a riddle-tradition otherwise unrecorded in Old Norse sources, while *The Battle of the Goths and Huns* reduces the clash of two of the Migration Age's most important tribes to an intimate family drama: a dispossessed half-brother, a sister who dies defending her brother's fortress, a trouble-making foster-father, and a shrewd grandfather who knows how to prepare for battle.

Heroic legend, genealogy, and eddic poetry

Later *fornaldarsǫgur* – or at least sagas which are thought to have been composed in the fourteenth century – are frequently driven by genealogical imperatives. The great families of Iceland, both before and after the take-over by the Norwegian crown, were exceptionally interested in their genealogies, tracing their history back to the first *landnámsmaðr* ('settler') in the lineage and thence venturing beyond Icelandic oral tradition back into the legendary Norwegian past. Thus, as Elizabeth Ashman Rowe has noted (2012), the genealogy of Ragnarr loðbrók and his sons is not only engineered to connect Sigurðr fáfnisbani to the kings of Norway, but also to provide important Icelandic families, among them the Sturlungar and the Haukdœlingar descended from *landnámsmenn* such as Hǫfða-Þórðr and Auðunn skǫkull, with heroic ancestors. Qrvar-Oddr too is assimilated to a line of ancestors and lateral family branches, originating in the island of Hrafnista, whose descendants are active in Iceland. Án of *Áns saga bogsveigis* (*The Saga of Án Bow-Bender*) is an ancestor of Ingimundr, patriarch of the Vatnsdœlinga clan; Ketill hængr (salmon), *landnámsmaðr* in southern Iceland, shares his name with his grandfather, hero of *Ketil hœngs saga* (*The Saga of Ketill Salmon*), and Grímr loðinkinni ('hairy-cheek'), Ketill's uncle, sires a different line of Icelandic descendants. The four sagas of the Hrafnistumenn contain an impressive quantity of eddic poetry; even the short saga of Grímr has a five-stanza exchange (la Farge forthcoming a) between the hero and two young troll-girls bent on breaking up his ship.

> Skal ek ykkr báðum skjótliga heita
> oddi ok eggju í upphafi;
> munu þá reyna Hrungnis mellur,
> hvárt betr dugir broddr eða krumma. (*SkP*, Gríml Lv 3[VIII])
>
> [I shall quickly promise point and edge to you two at the start; then Hrungnir's lovers (the giantesses) can test out whether weapon-point or claw avails better.]

Grímr's father Ketill also exchanges verses with supernatural creatures: with a friendly troll Bruni, with whom he spends the winter; with the Sámi wizard Gusi, from whom he acquires the arrows which become a family attribute; and with a troll-woman who has caused a dearth of fish around the island. The saga's long final episode includes a sequence recording the verse-exchanges between the hero and Bǫðmóðr, the amiable son of Framarr, a thoroughly nasty Viking king (*SkP*, Bǫðmóðr Lv 2–3[VIII], Keth Lv 18[VIII]). Ketill wins Bǫðmóðr's friendship, for the son thoroughly disapproves of his father's *fjǫlkynngi* ('magic') (Mitchell 2009). Finally Ketill and Framarr himself fight. Framarr's adherence to Óðinn-worship gives him confidence, but an eagle, perhaps Framarr's *fylgja* ('fetch'), attacks the Viking before the battle and Framarr remonstrates with it in *heiti*-laden *málaháttr*, calling it a *valgagl* ('slaughter-goose', *SkP*, Framarr Lv 1[VIII] /8) and a *vígstari* ('battle-starling', *SkP*, Framarr Lv 2[VIII] /5). The ungrateful bird should remember how often Framarr has fed him and his kind, protests the outraged warrior. And then it is Ketill hœngr's turn to provide the *krás arnar* ('eagle's delicacies' [a warrior's corpse], *SkP*, Keth Lv 20[VIII]/2). Tension mounts as Ketill's sword Dragvendill seems to fail him, blunted by Framarr's Odinic spells, but on the third attack, Dragvendill proves its superior mettle and Framarr falls, acknowledging that the god's favour is unreliable in terms which recall both *Hávamál* and *Vafþrúðnismál*:

> Hugr er í Hængi, hvass er Dragvendill,
> beit hann orð Óðins sem ekki væri;
> brásk nú Baldrs faðir, brigt er at trúa hánum;
> njóttú heill handa, hér munum skiljask. (*SkP*, Framarr Lv 4[VIII])

> [There's spirit in Hængr, Dragvendill is keen, he (the sword) bit (against) Óðinn's sword as if it did not exist; but Baldr's father is fickle, tricky it is to trust him; enjoy your hands' luck; here we must part.]

The traditional and often formulaic nature of the lexis makes it difficult to establish valid dating criteria for eddic verse, however (see Thorvaldsen, Chapter 4 in this Handbook), and it is not impossible that the sequence of verses embedded in Ketill's fight with Framarr could date from an earlier century. The verses share the eddic topoi familiar from the poetry generated by earlier heroic legend. Heroes declare their names, threaten their enemies, and invoke the beasts (in particular the birds) of battle. Eddic styles remain accessible, adaptable to all sorts of circumstances encountered in the *fornaldarsǫgur*, and they are highly expressive within these later contexts, recounting and celebrating here the heroic deeds of the Hrafnistumenn lineage.

Heroicising moves: assimilating kings to heroic legend

The kings' sagas (*konungasǫgur*), relating the histories of the kings of Norway and mostly composed in the thirteenth century, depend very largely on skaldic verse as source-material and authority for the events related. Snorri Sturluson's famous dictum that poets must be truth-tellers if they are not to embarrass the patrons for whom they compose (*Heimskringla* I: 5) does not necessarily apply to anonymous eddic poets. Heroic fantasy is deployed to celebrate the first three kings of a united Norway; eddic styles and imagery are harnessed to reconfigure the monarchs as recognisably heroic. The preservation of these poems is complicated; outside the anthology manuscripts (the Codex Regius, AM 748 I a 4°) verses are preserved as fragmented quotation and the reconstruction of such poems (see Clunies Ross, Chapter 1 in this Handbook) is very often a matter of conjecture. The earliest of these three poems for kings, reconstituted by modern editors, Þorbjǫrn hornklofi ('horn-cleaver')'s *Haraldskvæði* (also known as *Hrafnsmál*)(*SkP*, Þhorn *Harvk*[I]), was composed around 900 in a mixture of *málaháttr* and *ljóðaháttr*. A eulogy rather than a memorial poem, it begins with a valkyrie addressing a raven, enquiring where he has come by the carrion that he clutches in his claws and whose stink issues from his beak. The raven attributes his booty to Haraldr hárfagri ('fair-hair'), whom he has followed since he hatched from the egg, and he celebrates Haraldr's determination to abandon the cosy kitchen, the comfortable women's quarters, and the downy softness of mittens for the hard life of men, blood, and battle (st. 6). Enemies are humiliated by Haraldr, they tumble dramatically from their rowing-benches with their arses in the air, grovelling in the bilge-water (st. 10). The poem concludes with a series of questions, mostly in *ljóðaháttr*, in which the valkyrie asks the raven about Haraldr's generosity to his warriors, his poets, and to his court-entertainers: the final verse ends with a strange, hard-to-explain comic vision of jesters performing tricks with an earless dog and with fire.

Two important poems, *Eiríksmál* (*c*.954), commissioned in memory of Eiríkr bloodaxe by his widow Gunnhildr, and the *Hákonarmál* of Eyvindr skáldaspillir ('poet-despoiler') Finnsson (probably composed somewhat after 961, in response to *Eiríksmál*) strike a more dignified tone (*SkP*, Eyv *Hák*[I] and *Eirm*[I]). They depict how the two tenth-century Norwegian rulers Eiríkr and his half-brother Hákon Haraldsson are welcomed into Valhǫll after death, and are incorporated into the number of the *einherjar*, the very finest warriors chosen to fight on the side of the gods at *ragnarǫk*.

Eiríksmál, which may be incomplete (though its most recent editor thinks that little if anything has been lost), is, like many other eddic poems, a dialogue (Fulk *SkP* I, 1004). It opens in Valhǫll where Óðinn dreams that his hall must be made ready for the multitude of dead men who are approaching, *svá es mér glatt hjarta* ('so that my heart is glad', *SkP, Eirm* 2^1/4). The benches must be strewn with fresh straw, the goblets rinsed out and ready so that the valkyries may bring wine to the new guests. Bragi, the god of poetry, notes that the thundering of the new arrivals causes the bench-supports to tremble as if Baldr were returning, but Óðinn sets him right. Eiríkr is the cause of the noise, and Sigmundr and Sinfjǫtli, the heroes of the first part of *Vǫlsunga saga*, are dispatched to invite Eiríkr inside. His reputation for warfare is well known to Óðinn, who explains why he has awarded defeat to the heroic king:

> því óvíst es at vita nær ulfr inn hǫsvi
> sœkir á sjǫt goða. (*SkP, Eirm* 7^1/3–6)

> [for it is not known for certain when the grey wolf will launch his attack on the gods' dwellings.]

The poem ends somewhat abruptly as Eiríkr observes that another five kings follow him from the battlefield, but their identities are not revealed.

Eiríkr is thus successfully assimilated into Valhǫll, the ultimate heroic milieu, despite his defeat in battle. Óðinn knows him by name and has engineered his defeat, just as he broke Sigmundr's sword before his final battle, and took Sinfjǫtli's corpse out of the arms of his grieving father, as related in *Vǫlsunga saga* (18–19), and the Codex Regius's prose fragment *Frá dauði Sinfjǫtla*. Such men are worthy of dwelling where *valkyrjur vín bera* ('valkyries bring wine', *SkP, Eirm* 1^1/9). The initial heroic mode shades into the eschatological; Óðinn corrects Bragi's error in thinking that Baldr might be returning this side of *ragnarǫk*, yet the wolf's predatory gaze is directed towards the gods' palaces and there will be great need of Eiríkr and his five royal companions to battle the forces of cosmic evil when the doom of the gods comes.

While Eiríkr seems to feel that his invitation to join the heroes of the past in Óðinn's hall is no more than his due, Hákon inn góði ('the good') is decidedly put out to find that the god has awarded him defeat against Eiríkr's sons at the battle of Fitjar in 961 (Fulk 2012b). At the beginning of the poem Óðinn sends two valkyries to choose which of the line of Yngvi will come to Valhǫll; by implication these could be either Eiríkr's sons (Hákon's half-nephews) or the king himself. Several verses of stirring battle-poetry follow before Gǫndul the valkyrie reveals that the gods have invited Hákon and his followers home. Hákon challenges the decision that he should die:

'Hví þú svá gunni skiptir, Geir-Skǫgul
   órum þó verðir gagns frá goðum?'
'Vér því vǫldum, es þú velli helt,
   en þínir fíandr flugu.' (*SkP*, Eyv *Hák* 12[I])

['Why have you decided the battle so, Spear-Skǫgul, though we deserve favour from the gods?' 'We brought about that you have won the field and your enemies have taken to flight.']

Skǫgul tries to mitigate the unfairness of Óðinn's decision by inviting Hákon to ride through *grœna heima goða* ('the gods' green dwellings', *SkP*, Eyv *Hák* 13[I]/3) to come to Valhǫll and she titles him *allvaldr* ('supremely powerful ruler', *SkP*, Eyv *Hák* 13[I]/5), raising him to at least equal status with Óðinn. But Hákon is scarcely mollified by the valkyrie's flattery, nor by the dispatch of two gods, Hermóðr and Bragi, surely more senior figures than Sigmundr and Sinfjǫtli, to perform the welcoming ritual. The defeated king accuses Óðinn of bad faith, of being *illúðigr* ('ill-disposed', *SkP*, Eyv *Hák* 15[I]/4), and he refuses to set down his armour and weapons despite the god's offer of *griðr* ('truce', *SkP*, Eyv *Hák* 16[I]/1) from himself and all the *einherjar*. The warmth of Hákon's welcome into the gods' abode is ascribed to his restoration of their worship and rebuilding of their sanctuaries, in the face of pressure from the Danish King Harald bluetooth, and his own Christian upbringing at the court of King Athelstan of England. As in *Eiríksmál*, the tropes of *ragnarǫk* are invoked, but rather than suggesting that the *einherjar* are in need of the king's skills in the final confrontation, Eyvindr notes, in a striking *adynaton* or impossibility-trope, that Fenrir will have launched his assault on the homes of gods and men before another such ruler is born. The poem's final stanza shares the proverbial wisdom formulation about the enduring nature of heroic reputation that is also reflected in *Hávamál* sts 76–7 (Larrington 1993: 181–4).

Deyr fé, deyja frændr,
   eyðisk land ok láð,
síz Hákon fór með heiðin goð;
   mǫrg es þjóð of þéuð. (*SkP*, Eyv *Hák* 21[I])

[Cattle die, kinsmen die, the land and folk are laid waste, since Hákon journeyed away with the heathen gods; many a nation is enslaved.]

The difference in emphasis between the two poems testifies to the later poet's desire to make use of eddic metre and eddic tropes for new purposes. Eyvindr seems to sense that the new Christian ideology will henceforth offer a marked challenge to the models of heroism and the poetic styles associated with the Norwegian monarchy. Eyvindr's other poems include

Háleygjatal (Enumeration of the People of Hálogaland), composed in *kviðuháttr* and enumerating the ancestors of Hákon jarl Sigurðsson, another Norwegian ruler who identified strongly with the old gods. Eyvindr has been justly identified as the last of the important Norwegian skalds (Fulk *SkP* I, 171; see also Boyer 1990a, 201); from the end of the tenth century onwards named poets would compose almost exclusively in skaldic styles, and mastery of the art would pass to Icelandic poets. Haraldr and his two sons are, however, successfully assimilated into different kinds of heroic milieu: the rambunctious, swaggering triumphalism of *Haraldskvæði* modulates into the dignified conversation between equals in *Eiríksmál*, and subsequently appears as the resentful *Realpolitik* of Hákon, unpersuaded by the valkyrie's claim that victory has been achieved. Despite the king's entry into Valhǫll, his doubts are underlined by the poet's own nostalgic invocation of all that has been lost and of the apocalypse to come.

Creating a new legendary

Later medieval Icelandic texts, particularly those ascribed to the *riddara-sǫgur* (knights' saga) genre, or the *meykonungasaga* (maiden-kings' saga) subgenre (Kalinke 1990), largely eschewed poetry, whether eddic or skaldic, for declarations of intention, the performance of various kinds of speech act, or the mediation of the characters' inner life. Many *fornaldar-sǫgur* contain no verse at all (see Harris 1997 for the variable quantities of verse quotation across different saga genres). Nevertheless, some apparently later-composed (or rewritten) sagas, such as the *Íslendingasaga Svarfdæla saga* (*The Saga of the inhabitants of Svarfardalr*) or the *fornaldar-saga Friðþjófs saga*, contain significant quantities of eddic verse in a more or less heroic mode. In *Svarfdæla saga* a series of *lausavísur* in *fornyrðislag* are assigned to Klaufi, the violent and difficult nephew of Þorsteinn, one of the saga's main protagonists. While he is still alive, Klaufi's verses are usually insulting, but when he walks after death, his rhymes become insistently repetitive and threatening:

> Suðr er ok suðr er, svá skulum stefna (*Skjald*, AI 206, BI 220)
>
> [Southwards and southwards, so we shall steer]

declaims Klaufi. He has been riding on the farmhouse roof, and now stalks away, carrying his head in his hand. When he reaches his destination, Steindyrar, he hurls his head at the hall doors and pronounces:

> Hér er ok hér er, hví skulum lengra? (*Skjald*, AII 206, BII 220)

[Here we are and here we are, why should we go further?]

His subsequent verses, though fuller, indicate his undead status through the use of *galdralag* ('spell-metre'), and they elaborate his malevolence further. Although in his final verse he vanishes into dark skies, *svimmk nú við ský, grimmum* (*Skjald*, AII 208, BII, 222) ('I swim up now into a grim cloud'), he also foretells the imminent death of Karl, one of the saga's heroes.

The case of Klaufi illustrates the different role that eddic verse plays in the *Íslendingasǫgur*. There is no room in these realist and often anti-heroic narratives for *ævidrápur*, death-songs, or heroic posturing of the kind found in the very different genre of the *fornaldarsǫgur*. Where eddic verse is preserved in the *Íslendingasǫgur*, it is usually the province of the outcast, the anti-social being (like Klaufi), or the supernatural. So *Njáls saga* preserves the unusual *fornyrðislag* poem *Darraðarljóð* (Fulk forthcoming), a weaving-song sung by a group of valkyries who use a spear as a shuttle, and whose loom, weighted with the heads of slain men, is warped with warriors' guts. Whether or not the poem originates in the saga context, where it is associated with the historically important Battle of Clontarf, fought in Ireland in 1014, the verses offer a traditional perspective on the business of battle, one that is reminiscent both of skaldic and eddic poetry: the presence of valkyries, the good battle-luck of the man whom they protect, and the swift diffusion of news about the battle's outcome.

> Ok munu Írar angr of bíða,
> þats aldri mun ýtum fyrnask.
> Nús vefr ofinn en vǫllr roðinn;
> mun of lǫnd fara læspjǫll gota. (*Darr* 8^V)

> [And the Irish must expect a grief which men will never forget. Now the web is woven and the field is reddened; over the land must pass terrible news of men.]

Elsewhere in the sagas of Icelanders, eddic verse is assigned to giantesses, unipeds, or berserks. So too in the shorter *þættir* (tales), verse in eddic metre is marked as strange. In *Vǫlsa þáttr* (*The Tale of Vǫlsi*), a long sequence of stanzas is uttered as the eponymous cultic horse-penis is passed from hand to hand, while in *Þorsteins þáttr tjaldstœðings* (*The Tale of Þorsteinn tent-pitcher*) (Perkins forthcoming), preserved in the fourteenth-century Flateyjarbók, a new-born baby whose father intends to have him exposed speaks up in order to save his life:

> Láti mǫg til móður, mér es kalt á golfi;

hvar myni sveinn in sœmri an at síns fǫður ǫrnum?
Þarfat járn at eggja, né jarðar men skerða;
léttið ljótu verki, lifa vilk enn með mǫnnum. (*SkP*, Þtjald Lvɪ[IV])

[Put the boy to his mother, I'm cold on the floor; where is more fitting for a boy to be than beside his father's hearths? There's no need to put an edge on iron, nor to cut a necklace of earth (prepare a grave); don't do this dreadful deed, I want still to live among men.]

Unsurprisingly, baby Þorsteinn, whose story is fully narrated in *Landnámabók* (*The Book of Settlements*), grows up to be a considerable fighter. When his father is murdered by an agent of Haraldr hárfagri in a quarrel over tax, Þorsteinn decides to emigrate to Iceland, to live 'free'. But on the night before his departure he recalls that his father did not grant him his life in order that he should neglect vengeance for his father, and he duly burns his enemy's farm before he sails away.

Very different from these strange portents and utterances of the dispossessed are the verses in the relatively late saga *Friðþjófs saga* (Mundal 2012; Quinn 2014: 86–7). In this saga the hero's stanzas encompass both romance and adventure, themes that are subordinated to the saga's bridal-quest structure. Sent on a perilous voyage to Orkney by the hostile sons of the king of Sogn, the brothers of his beloved Ingibjǫrg, Friðþjófr contrasts the magically induced storm raging around his ship with his calm sorties across the Sognefjord to visit the princess (Clunies Ross forthcoming a):

Þat var forðum á Framnesi,
rera ek opt á tal við Ingibjǫrgu.
Nú skal ek sigla í svǫlu veðri,
láta létt und mér lǫgdýr bruna. (*SkP*, FriðÞ Lv4[VIII])

[Long ago by Framness, I would often row to talk with Ingibjǫrg. Now I must sail in a chilly storm and make the sea-beast glide smoothly beneath me.]

Friðþjófr fears that the ship will founder in the tempest; again, he contrasts the dangers on board the ship with a sunlit domestic scene back at home:

Mjǫk drekkr á mik; mær mun klǫkkva,
ef ek skal søkkva í svana brekku,
– austr er orðinn í Elliða –,
þó lá blæja á bliki nǫkkut. (*SkP*, FriðÞ Lv8[VIII])

[The ship takes on much water; the girl will sob, if I sink into the swans' slope (sea), bailing had to be done on Elliða (Friðþjófr's ship) though bed-linen lay out for bleaching.]

This sequence continues with Friðþjófr and his companion Bjǫrn noting wistfully past comfort and present perils, until Friðþjófr recognises that marine troll-women, sent by his enemies, are the main threat to the ship, and the verse reverts to the threats against the supernatural enemies familiar from hero–troll-woman encounters in other *fornaldarsǫgur*. Elliða crushes the sea-troll-women and the crew survive to make landfall on Orkney. Buoyed by this success, Friðþjófr concludes that he will live to wed Ingibjǫrg. *Friðþjófs saga* has forty-one verses, all in *fornyrðislag* with the exception of st. 36 (in an unclassifiable metre), in which Friðþjófr lists the names by which he has been known when he reveals his identity at the court of king Hringr. The poetry of this saga picks up traditional eddic themes – sea-faring, battle with troll-women, challenge, vows of vengeance – but it also expresses romantic love and the hero's warm gratitude to King Hringr for his magnanimity in ceding his wife to the man who loves her. *Friðþjófs saga*, together with *Þorsteins saga Víkingssonar* (*The Saga of Þorsteinn, son of Víkingr*), the tale of Friðþjófr's father, brought into existence a new and extraordinarily popular heroic tradition. The saga continued to be copied innumerable times into the nineteenth century and was the source for the Swedish bishop Esaias Tegnér's wildly popular poem *Frithiofs saga* (1825). *Frithiofs saga* did much to establish the nineteenth-century vogue for stories of Viking adventure, and its setting, the stunningly beautiful Norwegian Sognefjord, became a much-visited tourist destination for English and German travellers. Thus, the last-born heroic legend of the medieval Icelandic imagination gave birth to the new Viking legendary of the modern period.

Conclusions

Christian poets who wished to mediate different kinds of new wisdom – namely the two translations *Hugsvinnsmál* and *Merlínússpá*, and the hybrid wisdom-vision poem *Sólarljóð* – made use of eddic metre, perhaps sensing a continuity with the wisdom poems preserved in the Codex Regius. There is also the little *málaháttr kredda* ('creed') of Þrǫndr í Gǫtu, found in *Færeyinga saga* (*The Saga of the Faroe-Islanders*). As a mode for the composition of Christian heroic narrative, eddic metre does not seem to have found favour. Unlike Old English, where four-stressed alliterative verse offered a flexible and effective medium for the tales of saintly perseverance, hagiography in Old Norse was mediated in prose, or, in the case of the very early *Plácitusdrápa* (*The Drápa of Plácitus*), in *dróttkvætt*, as perhaps befitted its noble subject matter.

Eddic verse that dramatised key scenes from ancient and newer heroic legend was preserved in a good number of contexts in medieval Icelandic manuscripts. The division of the Codex Regius compilation into two clear halves (though see Clunies Ross, Chapter 1 in this Handbook) has served to define our understanding of eddic heroic verse: indeed, the poems relating the adventures of Sigmundr's sons, Guðrún Gjúkadóttir and their siblings and affines, and the poems conventionally included in the Poetic Edda corpus offer in microcosm almost the full range of themes and kinds of speakers of eddic verse. From heroic celebration to female lament, from defiance to misery, men, women, giantesses, and animals speak in eddic forms to express their emotions and intentions.

Eddic heroic verse is formally various; its subgenres include narrative, lament, whetting, autobiographical *ævidrápur*, death-songs, challenges, riddles, and self-identifying naming stanzas. Heroic ethics are celebrated in the retrospective summations of the hero's life: he boasts of the number and nature of his foes, his many victories, his faithful service to a generous lord, and his thirst for new adventures. Romantic attachments tend not to feature in these accounts; eddic heroines are enabled to speak on their own account, giving voice to their love for the heroic male. So Sigrún the valkyrie, of *Helgakviða Hundingsbana II*, figures a passion which lasts beyond death itself. Lament for the dead hero, that inevitable concomitant of the heroic life, and the whetting to vengeance for him, invites the poetic exploration of the female subject position (Sävborg 2013). In the thirteenth-century context in which such poems are preserved in the Codex Regius, these genres offer a searching critique of heroic honour culture, tracing in their 'chain of grief' (*tregróf*, Ghv 21/3) the cycle of death, vengeance, and fresh killings, until only the mourning woman is left alive.

The heroic figures that gave rise to the poems of the Codex Regius, with their distant roots in Migration Age Europe, were no doubt known to the compiler of the collection as shadowy Germanic figures whose deeds were recalled from a different kind of past, one which must nevertheless have remained culturally significant. Place names such as the reference to the Carpathians or the possible reference to Worms in *Atlakviða: rosmufjǫll* ('mountains of Worms'?, Akv 17/5) flag up the likely age of these traditions. The relative simplicity of eddic metre allowed for the composition of new heroic verse; poems accreted around Scandinavian heroes whose histories might often be no less conflicted or problematic than those of their Germanic forerunners. Questions of loyalty, of tensions between kinship and obligations to a lord, the challenges of subjugating the supernatural and of outfacing fate persisted as key heroic themes, even if the poems which explored these feelings may be of relatively recent composition. The dating of heroic eddic poetry, whether that of the Codex Regius or the poetic sequences which perhaps generate the *fornaldarsaga* prose narratives in which they are preserved, is highly problematic and almost impossible to resolve (Quinn 2006; and Harris [Chapter 2] and Thorvaldsen's [Chapter 4] in this Handbook). The likelihood that some poems, such as *Atlakviða* or *Hamðismál*, with their allusive styles, their occasional use of kennings, and concentration of hapax legomena, are ancient, is strong, yet the Helgi poems, in the distinct versions in which the Codex Regius preserves them, also make frequent use of kennings for ships and the sea, for example (Harris 1983). The poetry of *Friðþjófs saga*, at the other extreme, incorporates themes, if not the lexis, of European romance, recast within a familiar heroic framework.

What becomes clear from investigating the relationship between eddic poetry and old and new heroic legend is the degree to which eddic metrical forms and genres overlap with types of poetry conventionally considered to be skaldic. What is the status of *kviðuháttr*, the simple alliterating metre in which Egill Skallagrímsson composes his testament to his friend Arinbjǫrn and *Sonatorrek* (*Loss of Sons*), his lament for his two dead sons? Egill's lexis is more complex than the usual eddic registers, but his *heiti* are at times matched in the heroic verse. To praise and to lament are his aims in these two poems, and, although Arinbjǫrn and the dead sons are not legendary figures in the same way that Helgi, Ǫrvar-Oddr, or Friðþjófr are, Egill's poetic consciousness directs him to heroic styles in order to celebrate these men who were so dear to him. Heroic tropes, heroic comparisons become important tools for the Icelandic poets who work mainly in skaldic metres; Gísli Súrsson in *Gísla saga súrssonar* (*The Saga of Gísli, Son of súrr*) (ch. 19) summons up the heroic resolution and sibling loyalty of Guðrún Gjúkadóttir when he realises that his sister Þórdís has betrayed him to her new husband. Heroic lexis, the valkyrie, raven and eagle, the sea-king, and the wolf stalk through skaldic poetic modes as much as they haunt the eddic imagination.

Notes

1. For bibliography on heroic eddic poetry up to 2012, particularly in the Codex Regius, see the bibliographies in Acker and Larrington 2013.
2. Vǫlundr puns on the word for 'bowl' (*skál*).

3. Verses in the *fornaldarsǫgur* are cited from the online draft of *SkP* VIII, forth-coming in 2016. My grateful thanks to the volume's editor, Margaret Clunies Ross, for permission to make use of these texts; these are of course drafts and may not reflect the final published text. The translations are my own, but are in some case informed by the *SkP* editors' own translations.

CHAPTER 9

Place names in eddic poetry

Stefan Brink and John Lindow

There have been few analyses of place-name usage in Old Norse poetry. We have the odd article discussing names in poems such as *Ynglingatal* (e.g. Noreen 1925; Åkerlund 1939; Vikstrand 2004) and, of course, the related Old English *Beowulf* and *Widsið*. There are many cases where single names found in eddic poetry have been commented on and etymologised, but no one has, to our knowledge, taken a holistic approach to this material. The personal names of gods, goddesses, giants, *dvergar* ('dwarfs'), etc. in the poems have attracted more interest (for an overview, see Mundal 1990). Our aims in this chapter are: first, to outline some of the material; second, to probe the meaning of the names (hence their etymology); and third, to see if there are any noticeable tendencies indicative of toponymic 'genres', especially between the mythological and the heroic poems. It is impossible to cover all the place names mentioned in the Codex Regius here; therefore, we concentrate on three of the most important poems for mythological place names – *Vǫluspá*, *Vafþrúðnismál*, and *Grímnismál* – taking them as samples which may enable us to draw some conclusions. One would expect the mythological poems to contain descriptive, fictional names, enhancing the mythic story, while in the heroic poems more 'real-world' place names might be expected, employed to situate the heroes within a European heroic past. The skaldic poems, in particular *Ynglingatal*, have many more place names; these add plausibility to the historical claims made in the poems, although the geographical designations may or may not be historically valid.

Names comprise an important element of *frœði*, or mythological knowledge. Take *Vafþrúðnismál*, a contest of *frœði*, for instance. The wisest of all giants asks his unknown interlocutor for four names: two personal names and two place names, and when he answers all four correctly, Vafþrúðnir admits: *fróðr ertu nú, gestr* (*Vm* 19/1) ('wise you are now, guest'). Óðinn, on the other hand, asks for narratives instead: the origin of the cosmos, of earth, day, the seasons, and so forth, and then finally the details of *ragnarǫk*.

In some cases the answers are little more than personal names, such as *Vindsvalr, Svásuðr*, or *Hræsvelgr*, but some of the narratives require toponyms. *Vanaheimr* is an essential part of Njǫrðr's list of attributes and the survival of Líf and Lífþrasir depends upon the forest (*holt, Vm* 45/3) of *Hoddmímir*, although whether we should take that as a toponym is unclear. It is worth pointing out that the *ragnarǫk* sequence in the poem, leading up to the unanswerable final question, contains numerous personal names, but no place names; whether this suggests a hierarchy within the category of *frœði* is unclear.

Certainly the *frœði* that Óðinn chooses to impart to the doomed Geirrøðr and his soon-to-be successor Agnarr in *Grímnismál* emphasises toponyms – at least for the first twenty-nine stanzas. Stanza 29 mentions the rivers *Kǫrmt* and *Ǫrmt* and two bodies of water: *Kerlaugar*, which Þórr must cross, and *askr Yggdrasills* ('the ash of Yggdrasill'). From that point on only personal names are listed, with the apparent exception of *Bilrǫst* (see discussion below) in stanza 44: *Bilrǫst* is said to be the best of bridges, just as *askr Yggdrasills* is best of trees, *Skíðblaðnir* of ships, *Óðinn* of the Æsir, *Sleipnir* of steeds, *Bragi* of poets, *Hábrók* of hawks, and *Garmr* of hounds. Should we really regard *Bilrǫst* as a toponym in this context? From stanza 44 on, Óðinn is only interested in personal names, namely his own. More important to his mythological identity is how to name him, rather than the places which might be associated with him. The relative absence of Óðinn in the landscape in which humans lived – especially in Iceland – is striking; given Óðinn's importance in mythology, there is a comparative lack of theophoric place names incorporating the element 'Óðinn-'. In the verbal duel between Óðinn and Þórr in *Hárbarðsljóð*, Óðinn uses many more names than Þórr, including toponyms. Óðinn mentions *Ráðseyjarsund, Algrœn, Valland*, and *Verland*; Þórr only mentions *Hlésey*. This distinction reinforces our impression that Óðinn wins this verbal duel, displaying more *frœði* than Þórr.

In the following sections, we discuss the proposed etymologies of some of the significant place names in *Vǫluspá, Vafþrúðnismál*, and *Grímnismál*. Often the etymology can illuminate the interpretation of the stanza in question, but we also find that poets often play with the semantics for poetic ends.

Vǫluspá

In *Vǫluspá* stanza 2, the *vǫlva* recalls nine worlds (*níu man ek heima*). The first is *Miðgarðr* (sts 4, 56), the world of human beings. From a toponymic point of view the word *garðr* for 'world' is odd, if frequently attested. *Garðr*'s original meaning is 'fence', but must soon have developed into 'fenced-in area' (= ON *tún*), and thence 'farm, home', as in the Gothic *gards* 'house, family' (de Vries 1962: 156; Feist 1939: 137). Larrington (1996: 4; also Neckel 1936: 1) translates *miðgarðr* as an appellative: 'the world between'. This is possible, but we prefer to understand it as a name: *Miðgarðr*. Recently, Steinsland and Meulengracht Sørensen (1999: 10), Larrington (2014: 4), and Jónas Kristjánsson and Vésteinn Ólason (2014: 292) have taken this interpretation.

The next name we meet is *Iðavǫllr* (sts 7, 60), the deities' recreational space. The first element of this name is hotly debated. Lindow (2002: 198) summarises the differing views: 'Idavǫll means either "eternal field" or perhaps "shimmering field" or even "field of pursuits [of the gods]." The first makes the most sense.' Thus, Lindow prefers the meaning '[eternal] time' for *ið* (f.), which is possible, but etymologically problematic. A totally different interpretation has been proposed by Krogmann (see de Vries 1962: 283; and noted by Lindow), who links *ið* with ON *eisa* 'fire, glowing ash'; hence, *Iðavǫll* means 'das glänzende gefilde' ('the resplendent realm'). Müllenhoff (1883: 92) explains *ið* or *iða* as 'to move', an explanation accepted by Clunies Ross (1994: 161 n. 7), as referring to 'the assiduous (Swedish *idoga*) work the æsir did during the Golden Era'. Finally, Scheungraber and Grünzweig (2014: 193) argue that the first element *ið* goes back to **iði* 'Glanz' ('shine').

It has also been suggested that the first element in *Iðavǫll* could be identified with the *idisi*, a group of supernatural women mentioned in the ninth/tenth-century First Merseburg Charm (Helm 1950: 10; see also Simek 2006: 216; refuted by Scheungraber and Grünzweig 2014: 193). Many scholars have proposed that the *idisi* could be related to the *dísir*. In his *Annales* (Damon 2012, II, 16: 406–7), Tacitus mentions a *campus* ('field') called *Idistaviso* where in AD 16 a Germanic army fought a bloody battle against Roman legions. Jakob Grimm corrected this to *Idisiaviso*; Müllenhoff proposed *Idisiovisa* ('the plain of the *Idisi*') (see de Vries 1970, I: 322; Simek 2007: 171). The *ides Scyldinga* ('*ides* of the Scyldings') in *Beowulf* l. 1168 has been linked to this complex. However, Shaw (2011: 62) is reluctant to see a link between these female (supernatural) beings; the etymological connection between *idisi* (OE *ides*, OSax *idis*, OHG *itis* 'frau'), and ON *dís* has been refuted (see e.g. de Vries 1962: 77). As the etymology of *dís* is obscure, the etymology of the first element of *Iðavǫllr* has often been linked to the ON verb *ið* ('to work, to be busy') and the noun *ið* ('work, pursuit'; f.) (de Vries 1962: 282–3), congruent with the proposal by Müllenhoff and Clunies Ross. While the interpretation of the first element of *Iðavǫllr* remains uncertain, Mark-Kevin Deavin has proposed an interesting new interpretation of *Iðavǫll* (2014: 9; 2015: 86). He understands *vǫllr* as a poetic metaphor for 'sea'. The first element *iða* occurs as a *heiti* for sea in a *þula* recorded by Snorri, and connects with the English word *eddy* 'swirling water'; Deavin thus translates the name as 'swirling plain', the sea.

In stanza 8 three giantesses arrive from *jǫtunheimum*. Is this a word or a name? Larrington (1996; 2014) takes it as a name, Neckel (1936) as a word. *Jǫtunheimar* is transparent as a name, containing *jǫtunn* ('giant') and the plural of *heimr* ('home'). The second element has a dual function, expressing both 'home, farm', as in *Sáheim/Sæheim* ('the farm by the lake'), and 'district', as in *Trondheim* and *Böhmen* (see Brink 1991). *Jǫtunheimar* ('homes of the giants') fits into the second category.

Next comes the so-called *Dvergatal* (*Tally of Dwarfs*), several *þulur* which contain odd and not so odd names. Interestingly, some look like proper place names, with direct equivalents or homonyms in the Nordic onomasticon, such as *Hornbori* (cf. *Hornborga* in Västergötland in Sweden, OSw *Hornbori*; Hellquist 1948: 363), and also *Aurvangr* and *Hlévangr*. *Dvergar* from the halls of stone seek sand or gravel fields at *Jǫruvellir* (st. 14). The name *Jǫruvellir*, unsurprisingly, is a synonym for *Aurvangar* (< *aurr* 'sand, gravel' and *vangr* 'field'); hence, 'sandy fields or plains'. It probably contains the stem found in ON *jǫrfi* ('sand'; m.) (< *erwan*; related to *jǫrð* f. 'earth', found in Scandinavian place names such as *Järva* in Stockholm (Ståhle 1945: 277)).

The World Tree *Yggdrasill* is presented as an evergreen ash tree (st. 19). The tree can be interpreted as an Óðinn-*heiti*: 'Yggr's horse', as first proposed by Sophus Bugge (1881: 394), alluding to *Hávamál* stanzas 138–9 in which Óðinn hanged himself for nine nights on this tree to gain knowledge of the runes. The name is heavily debated and no consensus has been reached, but, in our opinion, Lennart Elmevik (2007) has solved the problem. He correctly identifies the first element with the word underlying the Óðinn-*heiti*, *Yggr* 'the terrible one': namely, the adjective *yggr* ('terrible'). The second element, *drasill*, m., undoubtedly denotes a horse in poetic language. Elmevik is able to show that the word is found in the archaic East Swedish dialects in Österbotten and Åland: *drassel*, m. 'stor otymplig karl, som är oskicklig el. vårdslös i rörelser o. beteende', 'åbäkligt ting', 'lymmel, lurk' ('a big ungainly man, who is unskilled or reckless in movements or behaviour', 'hulking thing', 'rascal, lout'). The word must go back to an OSw *drasil*; we also find the stem in words such as Swedish dialect *drase* ('a huge man'; m.), and Norwegian dialect *drasse* ('a huge, thick thing'). Elmevik's plausible interpretation of *Yggdrasill* is thus 'the fearsome colossus/hulk'; hence, 'the huge, awesome tree trunk'. It is an apt name for a World Tree; the first element must have been ambivalent, evoking Óðinn and the adjective *yggr*.

Under this tree is a well, *Urðarbrunnr*. The first element is identical with the name of one of the *nornir, Urðr* ('the one who is in possession of people's fate, destiny'), past participle of the verb *verða* ('to become'), related to OE *wyrd* ('fate, destiny') (see Simek 2007: 342–3; Lindow 2002: 301; de Vries 1962: 635). Mímir's well appears in stanza 28. Whether *Mímir* is a god or a giant (see Simek 2007: 216), he is probably associated with 'memory'; compare Latin *memoria* ('memory'), *memor* ('mindful') (de Vries 1962: 387; Lindow 2002: 230–2).

Stanza 30 offers another problematic case: *goðþjóðar* ('to the Goths / the gods'). Some editors, such as Neckel (1936), see this as a name, *Goðþjóðar*; some an appellative *goðþjóðar*; some translate it as 'the Goths' (such as Bugge 1867: 40) or 'the Gothic nation' (Larrington 1996: 8, but 'gods' realm' in 2014: 8); and some as the gods (*gudefolket*: Meulengracht Sørensen and Steinsland 1999, *ad loc.*) However, it seems unlikely that this should be interpreted as referring to the Goths. First, this would involve an emendation of the Codex Regius text to *Gotþjóðar* (as Müllenhoff assumed, see Neckel 1936: 7). Second, there are very few instances in *Vǫluspá* where an allusion is made to a 'real-world' name, beyond the mythological. Our interpretation – in line with that of Jónas Kristjánsson and Vésteinn Ólasson (2014: 298) – would be to see here a compound *goðþjóð*, a word for the collective gods and goddesses.

The halls *Fensalir* and *Valhǫll* are named in stanza 33. *Fensalir* is the abode or hall(s) identified with Frigg, and the first element seems to be the *fen* ('wetland, marsh'; f.) (< **fanja*); why poor Frigg should be endowed with a dwelling in a wetland is unknown and rather strange (de Vries 1962: 117; Lindow 2002: 114). The second element is the word for a feasting-hall in the Old Scandinavian languages, *salr* (pl. *salir*). It occurs in poetry and in some prestigious place names in Norway and Sweden, e.g. *Uppsala* (< *Upsalir*), *Skíringssalr, Odensala* (< *Óðinssalr*) (see Brink 1996: 255–8). *Valhǫll* is Óðinn's hall (Clunies Ross 1994: 252–7; Simek 2007: 346–8; Lindow 2002: 308–9). It seems clear that in eddic poetry *salr* and *hǫll* are used as synonyms for 'feasting-hall'. The first word has found its way into Nordic toponymy, as noted above, whereas *hǫll* is never found in Old Scandinavian old place names (see Brink 1996).

The first element of *Valhǫll* is identified by most scholars with *valr* m. 'the slain in battle', a crucial concept in Old Norse mythology. Yet its etymology remains obscure (de Vries 1962: 642). Magnus Olsen (1931: 164 and *passim*) has given a different and – as always – ingenious interpretation. He considers the possibility that it derives from **Walha-hallō* ('den "vælske" hall', 'foreign hall'). This is the word *val*, OE *wealh*, found in *valskr* ('foreign, exotic'), *valhnot* ('walnut'; f.), the name *Wealhþeow* in *Beowulf,* and modern English 'Welsh'. For Olsen this represents the Roman Colosseum imaginatively transferred to a Nordic context!

The river *Slíðr* (st. 36) is probably also named as *Slíð* in the river-*þulur* in *Grímnismál* (sts 27–8); so too in *Gylfaginning* (9). The name seems to be a nominalisation of the adjective *slíðr* 'grim, dangerous'; it could be translated as 'the dangerous one' (cf. Steinsland and Meulengracht Sørensen 1999: 106).

Another hall is said to stand at *Niðavellir*, a hall of gold belonging to the *dvergar* of the Sindri *ætt*:

> Stóð fyr norðan, á Niðavǫllum
> salr ór gulli, Sindra ættar; (*Vsp* 37/1–4)

> [In the north, at *Niðavellir* stood a hall of gold, (belonging to) Sindri's lineage;]

This is the hall of the *dvergar* ('dwarfs'), found in the north. The *dvergar*-hall might have been expected to be located in the underworld, and not made of gold. *Niðavellir* is normally translated as 'dark plains' (see e.g. Simek 2007: 231), but the etymology is not easily established (see below). Who or what is *Sindri*? He seems to be understood to be a member (perhaps the progenitor) of a lineage. Snorri, in contrast (*Gylfaginning*: 53), gives *Sindri* as the name of the actual hall, standing on the mountain *Niðafjǫll*. Lindow (2002: 267) is uncertain whether *Sindri* is a being or the hall-name; Larrington (2014: 284, 342) and Simek (2007: 285) think *Sindri* is a *dvergr*; Steinsland and Meulengracht Sørensen (1999: 106) think he is a giant. Consistency within mythology cannot be expected (see e.g. Brink 2004a).

Sindri should doubtless be connected with ON *sindr* ('cinder, slag'; n.). Given the role of the *dvergar* as master-smiths, this would be a logical semantic implication, whether Sindri is a being or a building. *Niðavellir* is much more difficult to explain. There are several interpretative possibilities for the first element in this name. 'Darkness' (due to the waning moon?) is the one preferred by scholars, linked to *nið* f. ('new moon, waning moon'; f. (n.?)) (de Vries 1962: 408). Both Lindow (2002: 239) and de Vries

(1962:409) assume a name of a *dvergr, Niði*. De Vries links this to ON *nið* ('new moon'), meaning 'dark like the new moon'; less probably, writes de Vries, it could be connected to *niðr* ('relative, descendant'; m). The *Vǫluspá* context makes more probable the link between the first element in *Niðavellir* and de Vries's lesser probability *niðr* ('relative, descendant'). If so, *Niða-* would not necessarily allude to an individual *dvergr*, but could refer to the collective of (different kinds of) *dvergar*, all descendants of the *dverg*-lineage.

In the same stanza we are told of another hall, *Ókólnir*, a beer-hall belonging to the giant Brimir. To have his own beer-hall, Brimir must have been an important giant; *Vǫluspá* stanza 9 appears to identify him with Ymir. The actual hall-name *Ókólnir*, with the negative prefix *ó-*, is the opposite of *kólnir* m. ('that which has a cooling effect'), from *kólna* ('to cool', cf. *kaldr* adj. ('cold')). *Ókólnir* should thus be translated as 'Uncold'.

In the next stanza we encounter an uncanny hall at *Nástrǫnd* (st. 38). Its uncanniness is indicated by the surrounding serpents and the poison dripping through the roof, and it is situated on *Nástrǫnd*, the beach of the dead (Simek 2007: 228). The first element is the word *nár* ('corpse'; m.) (< *nawir*) (de Vries 1962: 405), a word often found in compounds in eddic poetry.

The forest *Járnviðr* ('Iron wood') (*járn* n. 'iron'; n. and *viðr* 'forest, wood'; m.) cannot have been a particularly pleasant one, since the 'Old One' sat here, rearing the kin of the wolf Fenrir, the enemy of the gods. One of them will eventually swallow the sun. The second element, *viðr*, occurs fairly frequently in Scandinavian place names, such as those ending in *-ved*, as in *Tiveden*, and a related *-vi*, difficult to distinguish from *vi*/*vé*/ *vœ* ('cult site') (< *wiha-*) which is also attested.

In stanza 43 (also 47, 56) we are told of the baying of the hound Garmr, guarding the rock cave *Gnipahellir*. *Gnipahellir* (sometimes *Gnípahellir*), the cave which is the entrance to Hel, the world of the dead, occurs only here (cf. Meulengracht Sørensen and Steinsland 1999: 107). The name-elements are *hellir* ('rock cave'; m.) (< *halliar*: an *ia*-derivation to *hallr* < probably *halluz* 'stone') (de Vries 1962: 205, 221) and probably *gnípa* ('overhanging crag'; f., if so here gen. pl.). The etymology of the first element is problematic. It obviously has a counterpart in Scottish *gniopa* ('rocky coastline'), but also in Norwegian and Swedish *nipa* ('steep sand escarpment, drop-off'), often occurring in conjunction with rivers in Norrland with high and steep sandy banks. Brink (1990: 245–6) has discussed the possibility of semantically related words beginning in *gn-*, *kn-* or *n-* in Scandinavian languages in trying to explain the parish name *Gnarp* in Norrland. Although the etymology of *gnípa* (f.) is problematic, the meaning of the name *Gnipahellir* seems unproblematic: it probably means a 'rock cave with overhangs'.

Another hall, covered with gold and more beautiful than the sun, stands at *Gimlé*, according to *Vǫluspá* stanza 62. People will live here after *ragnarǫk*, and thus the place has positive connotations which are reflected in the name. *Gimlé* is considered to be a compound of *hlé* ('shelter, lee'; n.) (< **hlewa*) and a word found only in poetic language: *gim* ('fire'; m.), probably evidenced in Norwegian dialect *gim* ('damp, moisture, smell, esp. fragrance'; m.) (Torp 1963: 153). Other cognates are most likely Faroese *gima* ('to have a strong smell') and Shetland *gimp* ('reddish dust on the horizon') (Torp 1963: 153). Meulengracht Sørensen and Steinsland (1999: 10) translate it as 'the place which gives shelter against fire', a place not destroyed by fire at *ragnarǫk*. They also suggest (based on an idea of Bugge's) that the name could be translated as 'the gemstone's lee'. Bugge regarded *Gimlé* as a counterpart to Jerusalem, alluding to the Revelation of St John. The semantics seem clear here: *Gimlé* gives the impression of a hazy, gleaming mirage in the far distance, a pleasant shelter for people after *ragnarǫk*.

Finally, in *Vǫluspá* (st 63) the dark dragon comes flying in from *Niðafjǫll* carrying corpses and then the speaker, 'she', sinks apocalyptically down. *Niðafjǫll* seems to contain the same *nið* (f. (n.?)), found in names such as *Niðavellir*, assumed to mean 'darkness' (due to the waning moon?). As an alternative possibility, since the dragon is said to come from below (*neðan frá*), it could be thought to come from the dark underworld. *Niðafjǫll* could therefore be translated as 'dark mountains' (Simek 2007: 231; Lindow 2002: 238).

Vafþrúðnismál

Compared to *Vǫluspá*, many fewer place names are deployed in *Vafþrúðnismál*. The first name encountered is a much-discussed tribal name, the *Hreið*-Goths (st. 12). Why the poem refers here to some Gothic tribe, the *Hreið*-Goths, is unknown. This name is (probably) also found in the famous Rök runic inscription:

> Þat sagum annart, hvar fur níu aldum an urði fiaru meðr Hraiðgutum, suk do meðr hann umb sakar.
>
> Reð Þioðrikr
> hinn þurmoði,

stillir flutna,
strandu Hraiðmarar.

[This I tell second who nine generations ago lost his life with the Reidgoths; and he died with them, because of his offences. Theodric the bold, king of sea-warriors, ruled over Reid-sea shores.][1]

The tribe are also alluded to in the OE poem *Widsið* (ll. 7, 57), and the name *Reiðgotaland* is also found in *Hervarar saga ok Heiðreks* (H-version) and *Skáldskaparmál* (105–6). Since the word occurs in *Vafþrúðnismál*, *Snorra Edda*, and *Hervarar saga*, we think there is an argument that it also occurs in the Rök runic inscription. The place name must have been important in Old Norse mythology and widely used. Snorri locates the land in Scandinavia, but we believe it is more plausible to regard it as a mythic name, linked to the famous (at this time, mythical) Goths, perhaps Goths located in the east or south-east (Ostro-Goths?). The first element, *Hreið-*, remains utterly obscure (cf. e.g. Schütte 1933; de Vries 1962: 253 with refs; Lönnroth 1995: 128).

In *Vafþrúðnismál* stanza 16 a river, *Ifing*, is mentioned. The name has an obscure etymon. Lindow (2002: 200) suggests that a river which is never ice-covered must run swiftly, and this accords with de Vries's suggestion that the river name should be translated as 'the impetuous, intense one'. He compares the name with Icelandic *ýfing* ('ripple, incitement; quarrel, hostility') (1962: 283). Whether this link is valid is uncertain.

The battlefield *Vígríðr* is where the gods will fight with the mighty giant Surtr (*Vm* 18). The name *Vígríðr* is well chosen by the poet, since it is a compound of *víg* ('fight, battle, manslaughter'; n.) and *-ríðr* (m.), which de Vries (1962: 445, 661) interprets as 'field', without further explanation beyond a reference to the strong verb *ríða* ('ride, swing, defeat'). This seems unlikely, but alternative explanations are not forthcoming.

Élivágar (*Vm* 31; *Hym* 5) is perhaps a river or a well; it is clearly a body of water. Larrington (2014: 288) translates the name as 'mighty waves', and glosses it as 'some sort of icy primeval matter'. In *Gylfaginning* (9), Snorri asserts that the *Élivágar* are a number of rivers: *Ár þær er kallaðar eru Élivágar.* Lindow (2002: 108–9) writes that *Élivágar* are mythic rivers, associated with the proto-giant Ymir or Aurgelmir. In *Hymiskviða* stanza 5 *Élivágar* seems to be located on the periphery of the mythological world, *at himins enda* ('at the edge of heaven'). The name *Élivágar* thus seems to designate waters or rivers, very far away both in time and space. They lie on the edge of the world and seem to be associated with the beginning or the end of time (cf. Lindow 2002: 109).

Etymologically, the name *Élivágar* is a compound of *vágr* ('sea, lake, bay'; m.) and *él* ('rain-/snowfall, storm, fight'; n.) (Fritzner *s.v. él*; de Vries 1962: 99). *Él* is an obscure word, with an uncertain (or, rather, unknown) etymon. Perhaps it is to be linked to Lat *eō, īre*, etc., to a root **i* ('to walk, to move'). The word *vágr* (m.) is interesting in this usage, since it cannot usually be translated as 'river', as the poems perhaps imply, but, rather, 'sea, lake or bay'. In Scandinavian place names, *vágr* is primarily used for 'bay' or 'inlet', rarely 'lake'. It often denotes a large bay of the sea, but equally often a small sea- or lake-inlet. Hence, from a toponymic perspective the most probable translation of this name would be 'stormy bays'.

Finally, nine worlds are recalled, one of which is *Niflhel*.

> Frá jǫtna rúnum ok allra goða
>   ek kann segja satt,
>   því at hvern hefi ek heim um komit;
> níu kom ek heima fyr Niflhel neðan,
>   hinig deyja ór helju halir. (*Vm* 43)

> [Of the secrets of the giants and all the gods, I can truly tell, for I have been into every world; nine worlds have I travelled through down into Niflhel, there men die out of Hel.]

In *Gylfaginning* (27), we are told: *Hel kastaði hann í Niflheim ok gaf henni vald yfir níu heimum* ('[Óðinn] threw Hel into Niflheimr and gave her authority over the nine worlds'). As Lindow (2002: 240) has noted, *Niflheimr* is never found in eddic poetry; the form here is rather *Niflhel* (also *Bdr* 2/6: *Niflheljar til*). In *Vafþrúðnismál*, *Niflhel* is described as a kind of lower or 'underground' Hel, where, apparently, certain people (already in Hel?) go when they are dead. Snorri expands on this, stating that *vándr menn fara til Heljar ok þaðan í Niflhel, þat er niðr í inn níunda heim* (*Gylfaginning*: 9) ('wicked men will go to Hel and thence to Niflhel; that is down in the ninth world'). As might be expected, *Niflhel* and *Niflheimr* often alternate in Old Norse manuscripts. *Nifl-* has, so some etymologists claim, an uncertain etymology (de Vries 1962: 409). The obvious connection seems to be with OE *nifol* 'dark, dim', OHG *nebul* 'fog' (modern German *nebel*), and Latin *nebula* 'cloud'. Thus, a plausible meaning is 'dark, dim, and obscure part of Hel'.

Grímnismál

In *Grímnismál*, Óðinn enumerates the names of the places where the gods and goddesses dwell. There are also *þulur* (lists) of river names; some of these seem to be mythological inventions, some correspond to existing river names (for discussion of some of these names, see Olsen 1925).

The names of the deities' homes or halls are as follows. In the Prologue to *Grímnismál, Óðinn ok Frigg sátu í Hliðskjálf ok sá um heima alla* ('Óðinn and Frigg sat in *Hliðskjálf* and saw into all the worlds'). Obviously this place was a watchtower in the mythological world, from where Óðinn could view everything, across space but also across time. Snorri corroborates this in *Gylfaginning* (13): he says that from here Óðinn *sá . . . of alla heima* ('saw over all the worlds'). In *Skírnismál*, Freyr sits in *Hliðskjalf* in order to see into all the worlds, and in the land of the giants he saw a beautiful girl, confirming the implication that *Hliðskjalf* is the ultimate watchtower in the mythological world.

Hliðskjalf is a compound where the first element is a word *hlið* ('door, limb, lock', cf. Eng *lid* in *eyelid*), from a PIE root **kel* 'wattle, fence'. This does not fit particularly well, however, with *Hliðskjalf* in eddic poetry. Instead we must reckon on a secondary meaning of 'opening, narrow inlet', and this meaning is also found in Old Norse, especially in poetic contexts (Sveinbjörn Egilsson and Finnur Jónsson 1931: 262). Magnus Olsen (1926: 276) calls it the *borgporten* ('fortress-gate') to Ásgarðr. The second element *skjalf, skjǫlf* (f.) is found in some Scandinavian place names, as *-skälv* in Sweden, where the exact meaning is rather obscure (cf. Olsen 1926: 274–84; Elgqvist 1944; Vikstrand 1996). The word is obviously related to English *shelf*; normally the place-name element *skjalf* is translated as 'shelf, elevation in the landscape, hillock'. This is semantically close to 'seat', to which the name must allude in the poems. The name *Hliðskjalf* thus suggests a high seat from where Óðinn could look over all the worlds, the watchtower on top of the world (Elgqvist 1944: 61–2).

In *Grímnismál* stanza 3, Óðinn can see the hall of Þórr, which he names as *Þrúðheimr*. The name seems to contain ON *þrúðr* ('power'; m., cf. the adjective *þrúðugr* ('strong, powerful'); *þrúðhamarr* ('Þórr's hammer'); and Þórr's daughter (according to *Skaldskaparmál*: 14), also named Þrúðr). Þórr's hall thus might, logically, have the meaning 'powerful world'. Again, the texts are inconsistent. In both *Gylfaginning* (22, 43) and *Ynglinga saga* (16) Snorri says that Þórr lives not in *Þrúðheimr* but in *Þrúðvang(a)r*. But even Snorri is inconsistent. In the *Prologue* to his Edda (5) he says that *Trór, er vér kǫllum Þór* ('Trór, who we call Þórr') conquered Thrace (*Trákiá*), *þat kǫllum vér Þrúðheim* ('which we call Þrúðheimr'). Þórr is consistently linked to a hall, world, or kingdom containing the word *Þrúð-* 'power', which has a certain logic (cf. Olsen 1935: 264). If *Þrúðheimr* is the land of Þórr, his hall is *Bilskírnir*, as in *Grímnismál* stanza 24. Snorri identifies Þórr's hall as *Bilskírnir*, both in *Gylfaginning* (22) and *Skáldskaparmál* (14), where he adds that 'Bilskírnir's owner' is a valid kenning for Þórr (Lindow 2002: 83–4). Etymologically, it is somewhat unclear. The second element, *skírnir* (also a mythological personal name, *Skírnir* as in *Skírnismál*), must be derived from the adjective *skírr* ('clear, pure, innocent', also 'shining, radiant'). The first element *Bil-* is more uncertain. Etymologists, such as de Vries (1962: 36), identify the first element with *bil* ('time, moment, instant, place of residence'; n.), which makes meaningful interpretation of the name problematic. De Vries's suggestions are 'the only temporarily cheerful' (following Mogk), or 'the place from where beams of light shine forth' (following Malone). Lindow translates the name as '(the hall) suddenly illuminated (by lightning)' or 'the everlasting'.

It is perhaps worth noting that the name of this hall has a close relative in another hall's name, an obviously 'real' hall, namely *Skíringssalr*, the old name for the royal estate/farm *Huseby*, at Tjølling, Vestfold, Norway. *Skíring-* is not known, either as a word or a name, and there have been many proposals for interpreting the name (see Brink 2007a: 60–3). These range from an old name for the bay down at Kaupang, or a by-name for Freyr. An interesting suggestion was put forward by Andreas Nordberg (2003), that the name of the hall may have meant 'the shining, radiant *salr*'.

As is well known, Ullr is a very shadowy figure in Old Norse mythology as preserved in the written sources; place names, however, present a different picture (see Brink 2007b: 116–18). He is said to live in *Ýdalir* (*Grm* st. 5). Finnur Jónsson (1931: 64) comments on this stanza: '*Ýdalir*: Yew-dale; bows are made of yew, cf. *ýbogi* ("yew-bow") and Ullr was a remarkable archer according to Snorri'. This seems a plausible explanation for the association of Ullr with the yew tree, especially given Snorri's confirmation that *hann er bogmaðr svá góðr* (*Gylfaginning*: 26) ('he is so good an archer'). The yew tree, *ýr* (m.) (< *iur* < *iwaz*), is sometimes a *heiti* for a bow (see Sveinbjörn Egilsson and Finnur Jónsson 1931: 634).

Accounting for Freyr's abode, *Álfheim*, is more complicated. It is normally translated as 'home of the *álfar*' (*Grm* 5; de Vries 1962: 5; Lindow 2002: 113). The name is also used for a district in south-east Norway (noted by e.g. Lindow 2002: 54); it occurs in various places in Old Norse literature, and has been intensively discussed by many historians and philologists. One of the more fascinating arguments has been made by Erland Hjärne (1980) (cf. also Wadstein 1892: 162 for other etymologies; see also Gunnell 2007: 127).

The hall or abode of the gods, *Válaskjalf* (*Grm* 6), contains the element *-skjalf* (discussed above) and either the name of one of Óðinn's sons, *Váli*, or the genitive plural of *valr* m. 'the fallen warriors' (cf. Lindow 2002: 307).

Søkkvabekkr is the fourth abode of the gods (*Grm* 7). Normally the first element in this name is identified with a word *søkk* ('gold, treasure'; n.) (proposed by Axel Kock; see de Vries 1962: 576 with refs). This is an obscure word, only employed in mythological names. A different approach has been taken by Ulf Drobin (1991: 124) who sees in the first element the word *søkkr* m. ('hollow, depression') (< **sankwir*); from a linguistic point of view, this is more easily explicable. It appears that Kock's only evidence for assuming the meaning 'gold, treasure' for *søkkr* is the mention of *gullnum kerum* ('golden cups') in the stanza's last line – rather meagre and far-fetched support for his hypothesis. The second element in the name is also ambiguous. It may contain the word *bekkr* ('bank'; m.) (< **bankiz*) or the homonym *bekkr* ('stream, brook, burn'; m.) (< **bakjaz*). It is impossible from the context of the stanza to decide what is meant; perhaps it is more logical to see a stream in a hollow, depression, or valley, than a bank in a hollow. If Kock's suggestion is valid, the name *Søkkvabekkr* should be translated as 'stream of treasures' or 'the stream with gold' or something similar. Drobin translates the name as 'the low-lying stream' or 'the stream down there', and Lindow (2002: 264–5) is of a similar opinion, cautiously translating the name as 'sunken-bank (?)'.

Glaðsheimr is the next Æsir abode mentioned (*Grm* 8). The name contains the adjective *glaðr* ('happy, joyful'), or Swedish dialect *glad*, Norwegian dialect *glada* ('open place in a forest') (Hellquist 1948: 285; Torp 1963: 161; cf. Eng. *glade*, probably from the adjective *glad* in the sense of 'clear, bright, shining'). The name of this 'world' would hence be something like 'the shining, joyful world' (cf. Lindow 2002: 144–5).

The farmyard (*tún*) belonging to Njǫrðr, *Nóatún* (*Grm* 16), was probably not intended by the poet to evoke a *tún* as such. It has been proposed that the compound should be translated as 'shipyard', where the first element is (the plural of) *nór* ('ship'; m.) < **nōwa*, where the *-w-* has disappeared in the compound form (de Vries 1962: 411, building on a proposal by Adolf Noreen). This explanation fits better with Njǫrðr's connection with the sea and naval activities, as reported by Snorri (*Gylfaginning*: 23–4).

Þund is a roaring river with violent currents, according to stanza 21 of *Grímnismál*. This river element *þund* is also found in Scandinavia. We think the meaning here is 'swell, overflow', for rivers which habitually burst their banks during the spring floods (Brink 2004b: 19). *Valgrind* is the name of a gate which few know how to pass (*Grm* 22). The name is a compound of *grind* ('gate, wicket'; f.), and perhaps *valr* ('fallen warriors'; m.).

One of the more important geographical features in this mythological world is *Bilrǫst* (which may or may not be considered a place name, as discussed above), the bridge that connects earth and heaven (*Grm* 44), the world of the humans with the world of the gods, which Snorri identifies with the rainbow (*Gylfaginning*: 15). Snorri, however, names the bridge *Bifrǫst*. The bridge has a counterpart in the *Gjallarbrú*, which connects the earth with the underworld, the human world with that of dead ancestors (see Lindow 1997: 118).

The first element in the name *Bilrǫst* is obviously the same as in *Bilskírnir*, while the second element is more obscure. There seem to be two possibilities: 1) *rǫst* ('rast, mile'; f.), a word found in Scandinavian dialects as *rast* ('road distance', or perhaps even 'road', cf. Goth *rasta* 'mile'). The old meaning of the word must be 'pause' (cf. English *rest*); the meaning 'road distance' must be a secondary: 'the distance you can walk between two rests'; 2) *rǫst* ('whirlpool, maelstrom'; f.) (< *vrǫst*), a word found in Scandinavian dialects as Norw *røst* ('currents'; f.) (Torp 1963: 561); the word has been linked to Lat *vortex* ('whirlpool'). Of these two possibilities, perhaps the latter fits best semantically, although the meaning 'pause, rest' might be expected in older eddic poetry. Lindow (2002: 80) suggests a compound of the aforementioned *bil* ('stopping place, time, instant, weak spot') and *rǫst* '"league", "current", but here apparently with the meaning "road"', which seems plausible. Recently Deavin (2012: 108) has proposed the name *Bilrǫst* / *Bifrǫst* as a poetic metaphor for the sea, and hence the name denoting a bridge that connects the sea and the world; he also links the name *Iðavǫllr* (see above) to a similar connotation.

Is the eddic mythological landscape mapped onto the real world?

Since we believe that the pagan Scandinavians imagined their gods and goddesses as surrounding them in their own world, are there any signs that this mythological world is transposed onto a particular Nordic landscape?

A first contender would be *Gudme* on Fyn in Denmark. Scholars have long observed that encircling this settlement, with its extraordinary archaeology, there are some interesting place names: *Gudbjerg, Galdbjerg,* and

Albjerg, grouped around the central settlement of *Gudme* < *Guðheimr* (see e.g. Simek 2003: 68). The Danish archaeologist Lotte Hedeager (2001 and 2002) has developed the argument that these names found in the landscape have been 'created' to reflect the mythological world of pre-Christian religion. Admittedly the constellation of names around Gudme is unique and probably requires a detailed interpretation. Hedeager, however, presses the interpretations of the names too far in order to fit her model. In our opinion these few, not particularly informative names offer insufficient evidence to argue for the reflection of a pagan mythological world.

Magnus Olsen discussed a similar possibility for the West Norwegian island of Tysnesøya. During the Middle Ages this could be referred to as *Njarðarlǫg*, which Olsen explained as the judicial district dedicated to the god *Njǫrðr*. On this island there are some cultic place names, such as *Vévatn* ('Sanctuary Lake'), but again there are too few names to consider that this island had a transferred mythological landscape. A third and more illustrative case is the island of Selaö, which does seem to be a 'microcosmos' of a large part of the pagan pantheon. Brink (e.g. 2004a: 302–3) has discussed this at length elsewhere.

Mythological cosmography: some conclusions

As noted above on several occasions, and as discussed earlier (e.g. Brink 2004a), the mythological world we encounter in eddic poetry is inconsistent, kaleidoscopic, and contradictory (and even more confusing when Snorri expands on the topic in his *Edda*). It is not a logically coherent entity. This fact has been understated by – especially – scholars working within a structuralist theoretical framework, following Saussure and Levi-Strauss during recent decades (e.g. Hastrup 1985). For most phenomena arecapable of being squeezed into a dual, contrastive model (in–out, secure–dangerous, female–male, etc.). In contrast, earlier scholars, such as Magnus Olsen (1935: 265 and *passim*) could write, after analysing *Grímnismál*: 'Det er, som vi ser, et høist eiendommelig og broket innhold, vel egnet til å forvirre forskeren' ('It is, as we can see, a most strange and motley content, well suited to confuse the scholar').

If we look at the actual poems, the poem that may be richest in toponyms is *Vǫluspá*. It is perhaps telling that so many of the names are mysterious even when we apply the well-established tools of etymology and language history. The difficulty of the etymologies reflects in a satisfying way the opacity of the names for, we would assume, the average listener in Viking and medieval times and of course for later readers – even those who, like us, know quite well what textual traditions have survived. The range and depth of opaque toponyms sits nicely with a poem setting forth a vision of an entire mythological master-narrative. And note that the conceit of the poem is that the seeress is reciting for Óðinn.

Look what happens when gods other than Óðinn take centre stage: there are only three place names each in *Skírnismál*, *Lokasenna*, and *Þrymskviða*. The dwarf Alvíss can do better than this and does, citing the names of six worlds. It is therefore all the more striking, given Óðinn's propensity to deploy toponymic *frœði*, that he names so few toponyms in the narrative portions of *Hávamál*: none in the episode of *Billings mær*, none in the episode of Gunnlǫð, with the possible exception of the arrival of the *hrímþursar Háva hǫllu í* (*Háv* 109) ('the frost-giants in Hávi's hall'). *Loddfáfnismál* (sts 111/112–137) is set *Urðar brunni at* ('at Urðr's well'), but the counsels in it contain no toponyms, nor does the self-sacrifice episode (sts 138–45), nor *Ljóðatal* (sts 146–63). This commonality is striking, and it certainly serves to bind the narratives in *Hávamál*.

One factor that should be considered, at least when the gods are involved, is whether the poem is dialogue or narrative. The evidence seems to indicate that dialogue poems employ far more toponyms. It is obvious when reading eddic poems that there is a difference between the so-called mythological poems and the heroic ones regarding the usage of place names. In the heroic section of the Codex Regius, the Helgi poems have far more toponyms than the following cycles. That is interesting, since the Helgi poems do not connect very closely with the heroic alliterative poetry from outside Scandinavia. In the mythological poems the names are very much descriptive, probably carefully created and chosen by the poet (or performer) to enhance the myth: names such as *Valhǫll*, *Nástrǫnd*, *Urðarbrunnr*, *Slíðr*, *Ókólnir*, *Glaðsheimr*, *Glitnir*, and *Nóatún*, as discussed above. Often one finds in the poems words and place-name elements which have been given a different meaning than we find in the 'normal' place-name corpus, such as *vágr* for a river, and *hǫll*, *salr*, and *garðr*, which must be assumed to denote something spatial, a 'world' perhaps. This is probably to be accounted for in terms of the 'poetic freedom' exercised by the creator. It is obvious that these names are not there in the poems to locate the myth in a place or land, but rather to spice up and explain, to add poetic effect to the story.

Place names are rather frequent in the mythological poems, except for *Skírnismál*, *Hymiskviða*, *Lokasenna*, *Þrymskviða*, and *Alvíssmál*, which have few names, but in some poems, such as *Grímnismál* and the first of the Codex Regius's heroic poems, *Helgakviða Hundingsbana* I, there are many place names. They predominate in the narrative of *Grímnismál*, where stanza after stanza presents the name of a hall or abode belonging to a supernatural figure: god, goddess, or giant (cf. Olsen 1935: 263–49; Lindow 1997: 17). Three stanzas follow, containing a *þula* of forty river names; some flow through the world of the gods, some run among men, and others plunge down into Hel.

In the heroic poems, place names play a different role. First, it is notable that there are fewer place names in these poems. Second, they are normally not descriptive (although some mythological place names also occur, such as *Gnitaheiðr, Myrkviðr, Valhǫll,* and *Hel*). Instead, they are used to *locate* the story among the Goths, the Huns, or in Valland, Denmark, etc. The heroic poems thus deploy 'real' place names: *Frakk(a)land* (Frankia), *Valland* (Gaul?), *Danmǫrk* (Denmark), *Rín* (the Rhine), *Fjón* (Fyn), *Borgund, Limafjǫrð* (Limfjord), *Svíþjóð* (Sweden), and *Hleiðrar* (Lejre).

Note

1. For a standard runic text and translation of the Rök inscription, see Brink 2005: 82–5 and Ralph 2007: 136–9. The transliteration and especially the interpretation of the inscription varies, according to each individual runologist. A new radical reading and interpretation has recently been presented by Bo Ralph (for example, 2007). This eliminates the *Hreið*-Goths from the runic inscription. Ralph here follows Ottar Grønvik (1985: 89–90), who has claimed that the plural *gotar* (or *gotnar*) often denotes 'men' in the Old Norse texts; however, in the heroic poems, almost without exception, the term obviously refers to the Goths.

CHAPTER 10

Eddic poetry and the imagery of stone monuments

Lilla Kopár

Many myths and legends preserved in eddic poetry had likely circulated in various artistic media long before they were shaped into the poetic forms that have come down to us in the Codex Regius collection of eddic poems (GKS 2365 4°; *c*.1270) and other manuscripts. It is unclear, however, how widely disseminated these stories were, geographically and chronologically, and their earlier narrative forms are equally beyond our reach. The date and place of composition of the surviving eddic poems themselves are often contested (see Thorvaldsen, Chapter 4 in this Handbook). In most cases the poems can only point to late attestations of the pagan myths and heroic legends, some of them influenced by Christianity.

Figural representations in the art of the pre-Viking and Viking periods and the corpus of skaldic poetry provide us with evidence for the early development, transformation, and dissemination of the narratives that found their way into the eddic corpus. These sources usually predate the eddic poems, and the early attestations of stories are sometimes at variance with the eddic poems as well as with Snorri Sturluson's *Edda* (*c*.1220), which offers the most detailed and coherent versions of many of these stories (see Schjødt, Chapter 7 in this Handbook). The situation is further complicated by the fact that neither skaldic poetry nor the visual art of early medieval Northern Europe are narrative art forms. They do contain references, of varying degrees of transparency, to myths, deities, and heroic figures, but in most cases without much narrative detail. Nonetheless, the evidence they provide is invaluable for understanding where and when particular mythological or heroic figures were known, in what artistic and cultural (and, by implication, social) contexts, and which elements of their stories were considered most significant and worthy of recording.

It is the varied corpus of carved stone monuments that provides the richest surviving evidence for visual representations of mythological and heroic narratives in the art of the Viking Age. There are three groups of stone monuments that are of special relevance in this context: picture stones from the island of Gotland in the Baltic Sea, runestones with pictorial representations from Scandinavia, and early medieval sculpture from the British Isles. Even though they share the artistic medium of stone, these groups of monuments are rather different in nature. The picture stones of Gotland represent a unique tradition of decorated stone monuments of commemorative and funerary function that flourished between *c.* 400–1100 at the crossroads of cultures in the Baltic Sea. The shape and size of the over 560 surviving monuments vary according to a chronological sequence, and the later ones often carry runic inscriptions as well. They bear witness to a rich visual language of pre-Christian religion and myth, and often provide us with the earliest narrative representations related to eddic poems. The runestones of Sweden, Denmark, and Norway comprise the largest corpus of stone monuments in Scandinavia (*c.*3000), but only a relatively small percentage (under 6 per cent) display figural representations that can possibly be related to myth and legend. The majority of decorated runestones carry depictions of stylised animals and occasional crosses accompanied by commemorative inscriptions laid out in decorative rune-bands. The corpus of insular sculpture is the most varied group of monuments in this context, and it shows the strongest influence of continental traditions and Christian culture. The monuments relevant for the discussion of Old Norse myth and legend are all products of the Viking Age in the British Isles and come overwhelmingly from northern England and the Isle of Man. They represent the development of a local (Christian) sculptural tradition adopted by the Scandinavian settlers, and bear witness to social and cultural interactions between the locals and the newcomers. They provide us with evidence for the survival of pagan myths and legends in the Viking diaspora and their adaptation in the context of conversion and acculturation.

Comparative material to the carvings in stone is found in occasional figural images in textile and wood. The growing number of metalwork finds further supplement the picture with representations of deities and cult figures, but they rarely present any information on narratives other than indirect references to stories that serve as explanations for the attributes of gods, e.g. Óðinn's one eye deposited in Mímir's well (cf. bronze figurine from Lindby, Sweden), as noted in *Vǫluspá* st. 29 and *Gylfaginning* (17).

Visual representations of myths and legends have long been interpreted with the help of textual sources, from the eddic poetry and Snorri's *Edda* to skaldic poetry and sagas. Nevertheless, scholars are keenly aware of the methodological pitfalls and treacherous friendships of images and texts separated by many miles and centuries. As has often been noted, myths vary across space and change over time as they participate in various networks of belief and cross cultural divides. As we shall see below, some of the pictorial representations of Old Norse myths come from a Christian context, and thus it is hard to determine their relation to earlier versions of pagan myths or to later textual sources. Nonetheless, a certain level of unity and uniformity can safely be assumed across the diverse manifestations of myths and legends, which allows us to focus on shared features and core elements, or, if so inclined, on the evidence and reasons for regional and temporal differences.

Gods and heroes in images and in texts

The art of the Viking Age is characterised by the prominence of ornament over narrative representations (Graham-Campbell 2013: 184). Naturalistic figural representations and narrative scenes do occur, however, and they were likely associated with religion and heroic legend. These images were readily interpreted by contemporary onlookers who were familiar with a network of culturally significant narratives. Skaldic and eddic poetry drew on the same cultural knowledge. Interestingly, the poems of the Codex Regius and the surviving visual evidence do not paint a balanced picture of the pantheon of gods and heroes and their myths and legends. Individuals and events that appear to be central to the world of eddic poetry are under-represented (or, to us, are unrecognisable) in visual sources. Likewise, iconographical subjects that loom large in the visual corpus (e.g. Þórr's fishing trip, see below) are only mentioned briefly in a single eddic poem. Further, apparent narrative scenes in art lack parallels in eddic poetry or elsewhere in the surviving textual corpus, and thus remain indecipherable for modern scholars.

Judging by the surviving body of evidence, the most popular subjects depicted in the art of the Viking Age and the post-conversion period were Sigurðr the dragon-slayer (and select scenes of the legend of the Vǫlsungs), Þórr's fishing expedition to catch the *miðgarðsormr* (the Midgard serpent), events related to *ragnarǫk* (e.g. the fettering of Fenrir; the binding of Loki; Heimdallr sounding his Gjallarhorn; Fenrir swallowing Óðinn), Vǫlundr the smith, Hildr and the everlasting battle, and references to the reception of heroes in Valhǫll. This selection likely reflects the popularity of these myths and legends as much as the impact of imperfect survival of a once abundant material and visual culture. Skaldic poetry bears witness to the existence of narrative shield paintings with mythological scenes (cf. *Ragnarsdrápa* [*Drápa about Ragnarr*] by Bragi Boddason or *Haustlǫng* [*Autumn-Long*] by Þjóðólfr ór Hvini), yet none has survived. The remains of damaged textiles (e.g. the Oseberg, Skog, and Øverhogdal tapestries) and occasional examples of woodcarving (e.g. the ceremonial wagon of Oseberg, or the later Sigurðr portals of Norwegian stave churches) only allow us glimpses of a rich artistic tradition in perishable media. The surviving stone monuments and metalwork reflect specific functions and cultural contexts that had an impact on the selection of iconographic subjects, but may not have been characteristic of the artistic production at large. The Gotlandic picture stones, for example, are considered commemorative or funerary monuments, and thus images of the reception of heroes in Valhǫll or ships that are assumed to carry souls to the otherworld are not surprising. Similarly, the Manx cross slabs were the products of a transitional culture, and thus their selection of subjects was influenced by perceived compatibility with Christianity (see, for example, elements of the Sigurðr story on cross slabs at Jurby, Malew, Andreas, and on a cross shaft fragment from Ramsey [now in Maughold]) or an agenda of conversion through juxtaposition (e.g. the death of Óðinn at *ragnarǫk* on the Þorvald's Cross from Andreas). Among wood carvings, a series of Norwegian stave church portals (at Hylestad, Vegusdal, Lardal, Nesdal, and Mael) depict events of the life of Sigurðr, which further illustrates the adaptation of this heroic legend in a Christian cultural context.

A comparison of textual and visual sources sometimes allows us to detect changes of emphasis in certain narratives over time and under changing cultural circumstances. In Anglo-Saxon England, for example, the emphasis of the Vǫlundr story shifted from the suffering and vengeance of the craftsman-smith (cf. the Old English poem *Deor* and the Franks Casket, front panel) to his flight from captivity with a flying contrivance (Kopár 2012: 20–2). The shift occurred in the Viking Age, under the influence of Scandinavian settlers who found new ways of interpreting the story in the local cultural context, and likely introduced new iconographic representations of the myth as well. It is not that surprising, therefore, that the closest parallel to the images of Vǫlundr in his flying contrivance on the Viking-Age monuments of Leeds 1 (Parish Church) [Figure 1], Leeds 2 (City Museum), Sherburn 2 and 3 [Figure 2], and Bedale 6 [Figure 3] are found on a picture stone from Gotland, Ardre VIII [Figure 4]. There the winged Vǫlundr is shown (in the middle of the lower panel, under the large sailing ship) fleeing his smithy with a female figure, after his revenge on the king's young sons and daughter (cf. *Vǫlundarkviða*). This iconographic parallel demonstrates not only the Scandinavian influence on Viking Age

Figure 1 Cross shaft in fragments, Leeds Parish Church, Yorkshire, England
(no. 1ghj Ciii, detail). Photo: Ken Jukes and Derek Craig.
Copyright: Corpus of Anglo-Saxon Stone Sculpture, Durham University.

sculpture in northern England, but also the permanence or longevity of
standard iconographic patterns that were transmitted via perishable media
over long distances.

The best example of the wide-ranging transmission of narratives and
their visual representations is perhaps the legend of Sigurðr the dragon-
slayer, the single most popular character of the eddic tradition (and of
the Germanic heroic tradition) in the visual arts. The iconography of

Figure 2 Fragment of cross shaft, Sherburn, Yorkshire, England (no. 3A).
Photo: Tom Middlemas.
Copyright: Corpus of Anglo-Saxon Stone Sculpture, Durham University.

Sigurðr and the Vǫlsung legend has received a great deal of scholarly attention (see, among others, Ploss 1966; Blindheim 1973; Lang 1976; Bailey 1980: 116–125; Margeson 1980; Düwel 1986; Byock 1990; Kopár 2012: 23–56), and a comprehensive discussion of all relevant depictions would exceed the limits of this chapter. Suffice it to point out here that visual retellings of, or references to, the story of Sigurðr are found on a variety of different monuments in distinct geographical and cultural contexts. These include (but are not limited to) the famous rock carving of Ramsundsberget and the runestone of Gök in Sweden [Figure 5]; a carved stone fragment from Tanberg in Norway; several cross slabs on the Isle of Man (see above); cross shafts from Halton [Figure 6] and Kirby Hill, and a grave slab from York in England; several wooden stave church portals in Norway (see above); and even on a small ceremonial axe from the Volga region in Russia. These objects span the geographical expanse of much of the Viking world and a period of three or more centuries, providing a glimpse at a breadth of transmission far greater than discernable from the later narrative sources.

Figure 3 Hogback fragment, Bedale, Yorkshire, England (no. 6A).
Photo: A. Wiper. Copyright: Corpus of Anglo-Saxon Stone Sculpture, Durham University.

Figure 4 Picture stone of Ardre VIII, Gotland, Sweden. Photo: Bengt A. Lundberg.
Copyright: Statens historiska museum. Licensed under CC-BY 2.5 <http://kultur
arvsdata.se/shm/media/html/22369>.

Figure 5 The Gök runestone, Södermanland, Sweden (Sö 327).
Photo: Lilla Kopár.

Figure 6 Cross shaft, Halton, Lancashire, England (no. 1C, detail).
Photo: John Miller.

Þórr's fishing adventure: a case study

The story of Þórr's fishing adventure to catch the *miðgarðsormr* is unusually well documented in the art and literature of the Viking Age in a variety of sources of a wide geographical scope (cf. Brøndsted 1955; Gschwantler 1968; Meulengracht Sørensen 1986; Heizmann 1999; Abram 2011: 31–50; Kopár 2012: 61–8). Therefore, it provides a representative case study to illustrate the dynamism of visual and textual sources, to map changes in a mythological narrative across space and time, and to demonstrate why images are indispensable for understanding the contemporary function and reception of myths.

The popularity of the myth of Þórr's fishing trip is not surprising. It is not merely a gripping adventure story, but an archetypal mythological narrative that captures both the ongoing struggle between the 'victory gods' (*sigtívar*) and the forces of destruction, and the delicate equilibrium of the mythical world. Most importantly, it foreshadows the events of *ragnarǫk* and the final and fatal encounter of god and monster. Þórr's fishing trip is recorded in eddic poetry as part of *Hymiskviða*, which tells of an expedition of Þórr and his companion Týr to the land of giants to acquire an ale-cauldron from the giant Hymir for the feast of the Æsir. The quest for the cauldron provides the frame narrative into which a sequence of confrontations and trials of strength between Þórr and Hymir are integrated.[1] The fishing adventure follows a scene of feasting at the giant's hall, and it is presented as an attempt to acquire food as much as demonstrating the strength and skills of the protagonists. It is followed by further trials of strength (beaching the boat and carrying home the whales; smashing the crystal goblet; and moving the cauldron), in which Þórr ultimately earns the right to take the desired ale-cauldron. The sequencing of the events foregrounds Hymir, Þórr's companion at sea, and diminishes the significance of the encounter of monster and god as a foreshadowing of an apocalyptic event. While Þórr is referred to as *orms einbani* ('the serpent's sole slayer [at *ragnarǫk*]', *Hym* 22/3), the outcome of the present encounter remains unclear, in part due to a possible lacuna in the text. We learn that Þórr strikes the monster's head with his hammer, and, amidst the dramatic collapse of 'the ancient earth', it sinks back into the sea (*Hym* 23–4): defeated, for now, but not necessarily dead.

Snorri Sturluson also records this story in his *Edda* – twice, in fact – but his retelling is different. In *Gylfaginning*, the fishing adventure follows another, earlier encounter between Þórr and the *miðgarðsormr* at a trial of strength at the hall of the giant Útgarðaloki (*Gylfaginning*: 39–43).

The connection between the two events is the repeated encounter of god and monster, embedded in the larger context of Þórr's ongoing strife with powerful and capable giants who play important supporting roles in his encounters with the *miðgarðsormr*. The connection to apocalyptic events is implied by the immediately following story of the killing of Baldr. Significantly, Snorri's narrator, Hár, expresses doubts about the outcome of the fishing adventure, as an acknowledgement of Snorri's conflicting sources:

> Ok í því bili er Þórr greip hamarinn ok fœrði á lopt þá fálmaði jǫtunninn til agnsaxinu ok hjó vað Þórs af borði, en ormrinn søktisk í sæinn. En Þórr kastaði hamrinum eptir honum, ok segja menn at hann lysti af honum hǫfuðit við grunninum. En ek hygg hitt vera þér satt at segja at Miðgarðsormr lifir enn ok liggr í umsjá. (*Gylfaginning*: 45)
>
> [And just at the moment when Þórr was grasping his hammer and lifting it in the air, the giant fumbled at his bait-knife and cut Þórr's line from the gunwale, and the serpent sank into the sea. But Þórr threw his hammer after it, and they say that he struck off its head by the sea-bed. But I think in fact the contrary is correct to report to you that the Midgard serpent lives still and lies in the encircling sea.] (Faulkes 1995: 47)

Subsequently, Hymir is thrown overboard by an outraged Þórr and he perishes, unlike in *Hymiskviða*. Snorri revisits the fishing expedition again in *Skáldskaparmál*, and associates fishing with an ox-head bait with Qkuþórr. In this version the *miðgarðsormr* clearly survives by sinking back into the sea in order to return at *ragnarǫk* to kill his divine adversary, and Hymir is killed by Þórr. In an attempt of euhemerisation, Snorri associates the story with the Trojan heroes Hector (Hec-tor) and Achilles, carefully aligning every detail of the myth with an element of the Trojan narrative. In *Skáldskaparmál* (14–17), Snorri preserves further references to the myth of Þórr's fishing trip by quoting disjointed stanzas of skaldic poetry as an explanation for Þórr-kennings.

The comparison of *Hymiskviða* and the *Snorra Edda*, both products of the post-conversion period, suggests that Þórr's fishing trip was a central narrative that likely circulated in different forms. Skaldic poetry provides evidence not only for the fact that the myth was indeed known well before the Codex Regius collection and Snorri's *Edda* were recorded, but also for the key role of visual art in the dissemination of the myth. The earliest surviving reference to Þórr's fishing trip is found in a poem by Bragi Boddason the Old (Bragi inn gamli) of the ninth century. A sequence of six stanzas, *Ragnarsdrápa* 14–19, describes a figural scene on a decorated shield, with each stanza focusing on a different element of the image: Þórr lifting his hammer in his right hand; the tight fishing line; the intense gaze of the serpent on the hook; and, finally, the scared giant cutting the line. The poem captures a central moment, the essence of the story, rather than providing a narrative sequence. The myth invoked by the shield painting is anchored in a network of mythological stories by the use of numerous kennings describing Þórr, the serpent, and the giant.[2] In order to under-stand these references, the audience must have had detailed knowledge of the myth and related narratives.

Úlfr Uggason's late-tenth-century *Húsdrápa* (*Drápa about a house*) is another ekphrastic poem that describes mythological images decorating a new hall. Similarly to Bragi, Úlfr provides us with powerful but static images: a scared giant (unnamed) and the intense gaze of the two adversaries (sts 3–5). *Húsdrápa* st. 6 does offer a significant narrative detail: the god strikes the serpent on the head. This statement clearly puzzled Snorri, who preserved this stanza in *Skáldskaparmál* (17), but noted the possible death of the monster with a hint of doubt in *Gylfaginning* (see above).

Further references to Þórr's fishing trip are found in a single stanza from an originally longer poem about Þórr by the tenth-century Icelandic skald Gamli gnævaðarskáld (quoted in *Skáldskaparmál* 16). Similarly to *Húsdrápa*, it records the destruction of the serpent by Þórr's hammer. Further, three powerful stanzas by Eysteinn Valdason (*c*.1000, Iceland) depict the preparation of the fishing line and the dynamic encounter of god and monster: the sea-serpent drags on the line so forcefully that Þórr's fists bang the gunwale. The poem breaks off at this point but further stanzas may have been known to Snorri, who preserved the text in *Skáldskaparmál* (15) and mentioned the banging of the fists in *Gylfaginning* (44). A fragmentary stanza of two lines by the ninth-century Norwegian skald Ǫlvir hnúfa also records a hostile encounter between Þórr and the 'encircler of all lands' (*allra landa umgjǫrð*; *Skáldskaparmál* 15), but it provides no further details and cannot be linked to this fishing episode with any certainty.

The evidence of skaldic poetry of the ninth to eleventh centuries confirms the dissemination of the myth of Þórr's fishing trip in Norway and Iceland. While the climax of the narrative univocally seems to be the moment of visual encounter of god and monster – their intense gaze – there is some discrepancy in narrative details, especially regarding the outcome of the adventure. The stone monuments discussed below supplement the evidence of textual accounts and provide further informa-tion about the scope of dissemination and some early narrative details not captured in skaldic poetry but known from the later sources. Last but not least, these visual sources also inform us about the use of the myth in cultural and social contexts beyond those of court poetry and the art of shield decorations and domestic ornamentation. An important thing to keep in mind about stone monuments is that they were public monuments and displayed statements intended for a wider audience and likely for generations to come. Most of the monuments were commemorative in nature, and were meant to display, confirm, or establish local power relations in the form of public art. The depiction of Þórr's fishing on stone monuments is therefore an affirmation of the applicability of this story in these varying contexts of commemoration and assertion of influence.

That the images captured in the ekphrastic poems were indeed part of an existing visual vocabulary is confirmed by the survival of four stone carvings from Scandinavia and the British Isles: the Hørdum stone in Denmark; the Altuna runestone in Sweden; the Ardre VIII picture stone from Gotland; and the Gosforth 'Fishing Stone' in England.[3] It is interesting to note that these visual representations come from geographical areas outside the home of the extant textual sources. Given the possibility that *Hymiskviða* is a late composition (Gschwantler 1993: 308), all visual representations of the myth may possibly predate the eddic poem.

The fragmentary stone monument from Hørdum in Jutland, Denmark, depicts two men in a boat, fishing for a large coiling creature below (now largely broken away) [Figure 7]. A long fishing line extends from the gunwale and is firmly held in two hands by the central figure in the boat. His foot penetrates the bottom of the boat, and the figure convincingly conveys intense physical labour in pulling on the line. His companion on the left is holding an axe-like tool in his hand, ready to strike and cut the fishing line. The carving is a product of the Viking Age, and the lack of Christian influence likely suggests a tenth-century date. The stone is damaged, with parts broken away, and the carved lines are faint. The main outlines are highlighted by modern painting, but some details remain uncertain. The combination of the iconographic elements show a remarkable resemblance to the narrative of Þórr's fishing as we know it from contemporary skaldic poetry and later written sources: two men in a boat fishing for a large serpentine creature, one of them about to cut of the fishing line while the other, in a moment of intense struggle, steadies himself by pushing a foot through the bottom of the boat. The latter detail is first mentioned by Snorri in the early thirteenth century, but evidently it

Figure 7 The Hørdum stone, Jutland, Denmark.
Photo: J.C. Schou. Copyright: Biopix.

had been part of the myth much earlier, albeit unrecorded in the surviving corpus of skaldic poetry.

A similar carving on a decorated runestone from Altuna in Uppland, Sweden (U 1161), provides further evidence for the foot motif and other elements of a standard iconography of Þórr's fishing in the Viking Age [Figure 8]. Based on style, the monument is dated to the second half of the eleventh century, and, according to its two-part runic inscription, it was erected in memory of a father and son. The figural carving on the lower half of the narrow shaft shows (only) one man in a boat, holding a hammer or axe in his right hand and grasping a fishing line in his left. His foot penetrates the bottom of the boat, similarly to the Hørdum carving, but his companion is absent, conceivably due to the lack of space. Below the boat we find the coiling body of a serpentine monster biting on an ox-head bait. Above the fishing scene there is another figural carving with a horseman and a second figure climbing a 'ladder'; its interpretation and relation to the lower image is unclear.[4] Comparing the Altuna fishing scene to the Hørdum carving raises the question of whether the figure with the hammer/axe, the fishing line, and the foot is Þórr (alone), thus omitting

Figure 8 The Altuna runestone, Uppland, Sweden (U 1161).
Photo: Bengt A. Lundberg. Copyright: RAÄ. Licensed under CC-BY 2.5
<http://kulturarvsdata.se/raa/kmb/html/16000300012708>.

the giant from the picture and the story, or indeed a combined representation of the two main characters, Þórr (with fishing line and foot) and
Hymir (with axe) – a creative solution forced upon the artist by the narrow
shaft, and allowing for a representation of the climactic moment of
encounter with a reference to the cutting of the line.

That the two-figure representation was likely the standard iconography
of Þórr's fishing trip (suggesting that Hymir was indeed part of the story) is
supported by two further carvings, although each is lacking some of the
iconographic elements noted above. A tenth-century carved slab from
Gosforth, Cumbria, in northern England, known as the 'Fishing Stone'
(or Gosforth 6 in Bailey and Cramp 1988: 108–9), depicts two figures in
a boat: one holding a fishing line, with a large bait in his left hand and
possibly a hammer in his right, the other raising an axe [Figure 9]. Between
the two men is a topped mast. Below the boat are large fish and the remains
of what appears to be a coiling creature ready to bite the bait. A second
(knotted) serpentine pattern is placed above the fishing scene, still in the
same panel. In its iconographic elements, the Gosforth carving resembles
both Hørdum and Altuna, but the penetrating foot is missing. Was that
narrative detail unknown among the Scandinavian settlers of England, or
was it considered too insignificant to record? Alternatively, perhaps
a selection of the standard elements of the iconography of Þórr's fishing
was sufficient to reference the well-known myth, which in turn gave the
artist some room for creativity, as in the case of the Altuna runestone.

Unlike Hørdum and Altuna, the Gosforth 'Fishing Stone' is a Christian
monument, which adds an interesting perspective to the reception of the
myth of Þórr's fishing. Anglo-Scandinavian sculpture in England was
a development of the local sculptural tradition that originated as an
ecclesiastical art form. Although some sculptures show the obvious influence of Scandinavian art and iconography, and thus the patronage of the
Anglo-Scandinavian secular elite, sculpture as an art form maintained its
strong ties with the Christian cultural context and ecclesiastical organisation even in the Scandinavian settlement areas of England. A small subset
of Viking Age monuments that combine pagan and Christian iconography
bear witness to a process of cultural and social integration in the
Scandinavian settlement areas (see Kopár 2012). The Gosforth 'Fishing
Stone' is one of these monuments. It was the work of the so-called
Gosforth Master (Bailey and Lang 1975), who also created the famous
Gosforth Cross, a monument that combines Christian iconography with
images of ragnarǫk. Unlike in the case of the cross, the original shape and
function of the 'Fishing Stone' is unknown (it is now broken and built into

Figure 9 The Gosforth 'Fishing Stone', Cumbria, England (no. 6).
Photo: Tom Middlemas / Corpus of Anglo-Saxon Stone Sculpture, Durham
University.

the chancel wall of St Mary's Church), but the accompanying carving
points towards a Christian cultural context. Above the fishing panel, there
is a hart struggling with two serpents – a reference to Christ's battle with
evil that also appears on baptismal fonts (cf. Melbury Bubb 1, Dorset).
The relation of the two panels has been much debated. Richard Bailey
emphasised the complementary nature of the two images and interpreted it
as a 'commentary from one theological system on another' in the context of
Viking conversions (1981: 87; see also Bailey 1980: 132; Bailey and Cramp

1988: 109). The relation of the two images depends in part on the outcome of Þórr's fishing. If he succeeds in killing the serpent, his action parallels Christ's victory over death and evil, providing a point of comparison between the two religious systems. If he does not, the two scenes may be seen as a juxtaposition of the old and new religions (in favour of Christianity). The carving itself, however, provides no clue as to the outcome of the encounter. Similarly to Hørdum and Altuna, it captures the intense moment of encounter and emphasises the cosmic struggle – just like the hart and snakes depicted above. Thus, the two images are seen as analogues, bridging cultures through the narratives of two religions in a context of socio-political and cultural integration and religious accommodation in the Viking settlement areas of northern England (Kopár 2012: 68).

On the three monuments discussed so far, Þórr's fishing was given great prominence – as if given its own text, in literary terms. By contrast, the carver of the next monument integrated the story into a larger network of narratives – similarly to the poet of *Hymiskviða*. This fourth visual representation commonly associated with the myth of Þórr's fishing is found on the picture stone Ardre VIII of Gotland, dated to the late eighth to tenth century (mentioned above in connection with the iconography of Vǫlundr; see Figure 4). The upper panel of the stone depicts a Valhǫll scene with Óðinn on his horse, Sleipnir, while the lower panel displays an array of narrative figural scenes with no internal division or panelling (unlike on other picture stones, e.g. Lärbro St Hammars I). Ardre VIII serves as an anthology, not unlike the Codex Regius (or, on a smaller scale, Bragi's decorated shield): a collection of mythological and heroic narratives told in pictures. But instead of being sequential in order, the relations between the stories are manifested in their spatial arrangement. The fishing scene appears in the mid section of the lower panel, below a large sailing ship. There are two figures in a small boat, one of them holding a fishing line with a large bait, the other steering the rudder. The faint lines under the bait might indicate the lurking serpent ready to bite (Buisson 1976: 57), but in the current state of the carving no further details are recognisable. Based on the iconographic parallels discussed above, the carving is commonly interpreted as a depiction of Þórr and Hymir fishing for the *miðgarðsormr* (Lindqvist 1941–2: I, 95–6; Buisson 1976: 57; Meulengracht Sørensen 1986; Oehrl 2006: 129).[5]

The lack of the threatening axe or hammer and the penetrating foot seems to suggest that this carving captures a different moment in the narrative, the baiting of the monster, as opposed to the moment of encounter and intense gaze that is the focus of the skaldic poems and of the images at Hørdum, Altuna, and Gosforth. It is a subtle difference that may have been shaped by the role of the myth in the context of other narratives depicted on the monument. The overall iconographic programme of Ardre VIII remains a mystery, however, given the uncertain interpretation of many of the figural scenes. It seems likely that the context for Þórr's fishing here is not that of a cosmic battle, but, rather, a tableaux of heroic feats of extraordinary individuals of the mythic past, all recorded and invoked in a commemorative context.

Images and texts: putting together the pieces of a puzzle

The evidence of visual representations and skaldic poetry suggests that the myth of Þórr's fishing was widely known in the Viking world from the late eighth century onwards in Denmark, Gotland, Sweden, Norway, and Iceland, and even in the Scandinavian settlement areas of the British Isles, long before it was recorded in the thirteenth century as part of *Hymiskviða* and *Snorra Edda*. There may have been regional differences in narrative details, and the myth was likely adapted and skillfully 'repurposed' on various occasions when recited or recorded. The carver of the Altuna runestone, for example, used it on a commemorative monument; the Gosforth Master saw it fitting into a Christian cultural context at a moment of transition. On Bragi's decorated shield the myth was employed in a heroic context, possibly with an apotropaic touch. Later, the author of *Hymiskviða* placed the story in the context of Þórr's trials of strength against giants, and Snorri attempted to integrate the myth into Trojan history through euhemerisation. For the study of eddic poetry, the evidence suggests that the recontextualisation of the myth of Þórr's fishing in *Hymiskviða* may have been a later development in the transmission of the myth. While most key elements of the narrative were retained, the emphasis shifted from the moment of intense encounter and struggle between god and monster to the trial of strength between god and giant.

Conclusion

As we have seen above, literary sources with narrative details are essential for the identification of visual representations of myths and legends. In the process of interpretation, however, we are constantly reminded of regional variants, contradictory narrative details, the conventions and constraints of literary sub-genres, possible textual lacunae, and the impact of transmission and of changing cultural and political landscapes. This leaves us with important methodological questions to consider:

How much difference between text and image should be interpreted as evidence for a different version of the narrative? What are the essential visual markers, or iconographic attributes, without which the image is no longer a representation of the myth in question but of a different narrative altogether? Do these markers shift across space and time? To what extent are they shaped by preferences of individual artists and/or patrons, or even by the availability of space on decorated objects (cf. the absence of Hymir at Altuna)? Is the lack of the detail of Þórr's foot pushed through the hull at Ardre and Gosforth a warning against interpreting those carving as Þórr's fishing, even if we have Hymir and (likely) the ox-head present? Similarly, should the absence of Hymir at Altuna undermine our interpretation even if the element of the foot is present? Narrative images are distillations of stories in pictures. They capture the most important and characteristic moments of a narrative while omitting others. They thereby offer us clues to the contemporaneous interpretation of myths and heroic legends. Images of Þórr's fishing trip suggest that the key moment of the story was the struggle between god and monster. The outcome is not revealed, and maybe it is not important at all, since an archetypal encounter of this kind, out in a liminal space, will be repeated again at the end of time.

As the above examples have demonstrated, visual representations of myths and legends complement the textual corpus in many different ways. They bear witness to the popularity of stories in areas where few or no texts survive, and bridge the gap between the ninth- and tenth-century proliferation of skaldic verse with mythological imagery and the 'mythological renaissance' of the thirteenth century (Abram 2011: 175, 194–5). Some of the surviving visual representations are contemporaneous with the beginnings of eddic poetry, and the geographical overlap of insular carvings and the proposed insular connections of the earliest pieces (Vǫlundarkviða according to McKinnell 1990; Vǫluspá in Butt 1969) certainly raise interesting questions. Eddic mythological poems emerged from the same narrative tradition that had provided visual artists with stories to retell in pictures. The richness of the visual material suggests that this network of narratives was a vast sea in which the surviving eddic poems likely only represent the tip of the iceberg, both in content and in the mode of artistic expression.

Notes

1. Although the frame narrative is the quest for the cauldron, the scribe of the Codex Regius noted the centrality of the fishing adventure by adding the 'title' *Þórr dró miðgarðz orm* ('Þórr pulled up the Midgard serpent') at the beginning of the text. The modern title *Hymiskviða* is first recorded in the later manuscript AM 748 I a 4° (*c*.1300–50) (Neckel and Kuhn 1962: 88; Dronke 2011: 67).

2. *Hymiskviða* exhibits an unusually high number of kennings as well (see Quinn, Chapter 15 in this Handbook), perhaps suggesting a link with the skaldic tradition and an affinity for depicting a narrative in verbal images or vignettes.

3. Suggestions have been made to associate three other artefacts with the iconography of Þórr's fishing trip: a bronze mount from Solberga, Sweden; the Överjärna runestone (Sö 352), Sweden; and a D-bracteate of uncertain provenance. These associations are, however, highly uncertain (cf. Oehrl 2006: 130–1).

4. For an overview of possible interpretations proposed, see Oehrl 2006: 124–8.

5. A second carving in the lower section of the panel had been suggested to depict the prequel to the fishing adventure: the acquisition of the ox head, as known from *Hym* sts 17–19, and in fact visually alluded to at Altuna and Gosforth, where the ox-head bait is visible. In a combination of two scenes (literally) under one roof, we see a male figure on the left entering a house with an ox in it. On the right, two figures are leaving the same house, one with a large object on his shoulder, possibly the ox-head bait, which somewhat resembles the bait of the fishing scene above. The spatial separation of the house scene and the boat above is problematic, and the two scenes may be unrelated.

CHAPTER 11

Eddic poetry and archaeology

John Hines

Recent years have seen a welcome growth in scholarship discussing and exploring the scope for combining expertise in archaeology with expertise in the study of literature. In the case of Old Norse literature, in particular eddic poetry, renewed interest in the archaeology of ritual and religion has directed attention to mythological sources, both in the eddic corpus and *Snorra Edda*.[1] A corollary of that topic-directed approach is that consideration of how informed literary criticism and a knowledge and understanding of material culture can be integrated has not been as thoroughly reflexive as it could have been. Less has been done to define the interdisciplinary relationship at a primary, theoretical level (cf. Andrén 1998; Moreland 2001; Hines 2004). To make this observation is not to suggest that principles and tenets which are clear and straightforward have naïvely been overlooked. Nor should there be any objection to the proposition that a more general theory of 'Archaeology and Literature' may best be derived, gradually, from pioneering empirical studies.

In respect of the extant texts and the archaeological evidence alike, the analysis and reading of the primary material is often a complex challenge – as well as being stimulating and rewarding. Ideally, we might hope that information from one field will clarify or even resolve problems in the other. Unfortunately, where any interpretations, however expert, must be inferential and usually counted as probabilities at best, if not openly speculative, the comparison and combination of two or more such perspectives is likely to lead to a compounding of the level of uncertainty. This makes it all the more vital to think carefully about what might be achieved by a cross-disciplinary endeavour; what the most practical and useful objectives are; and, methodologically, what is required to achieve those. That is much more than can be fully covered in one short chapter, but it is nonetheless hoped that the following discussion will help us along an informative and productive path.

212

One of the more obvious and familiar approaches to the correlation of archaeology and literature is to consult the archaeological record to assess to what extent (if any) literary texts portray materially realistic contexts. If they do so, in the case of ancient literature of historically unrecorded origin such as eddic poetry, such archaeological evidence may locate the literature not only in date and place, but also in terms of specific social contexts. One cannot, however, simply equate dateable archaeological details within a text with the date of that text, although of course any such archaeological – or historical – reference point must provide a *terminus post quem* for that version of the text. Both the historical and the archaeological contexts of a work of literature are usually multiple and, in theory, indefinitely extendable. While a certain reference may reflect a physically different past, there may be other textual features that reveal something of the different context in which that historical perspective was evoked; and then, even more interestingly, those features may provide clues to *why* that was done and *how* the detail was used as a literary motif.

Archaeology is not concerned only with describing the materiality of the past and with reconstructing dated contexts. As a discipline it is profoundly concerned with understanding human material culture as a phenomenon – in a nutshell, how people interact with their material circumstances. In this respect an integrated, truly interdisciplinary study of archaeology and literature can be productive. There was a time when a rather limited conception of what archaeology is, and an even more limited acknowledgement of how it could productively be related to literature, could content itself with picking out references to material items in the texts and commenting on details of current interest to the archaeological specialist. Birger Nerman's *The Poetic Edda in the Light of Archaeology* illustrates this, perhaps most graphically where the author was able simply to say things such as 'in this case there is nothing to be said' (e.g. Nerman 1931: 20, 28, 31, 55).[2] If archaeology is to be placed alongside literature, as now read by critical scholars, it is important to stress that archaeology itself has grown every bit as complex, and indeed as contested within itself, as literary studies are.

Increasingly during the past three decades, literary scholarship and archaeology have embraced theories and approaches which positively encourage interpretations of their specific subject matter in terms of how it represents, depends upon, and even interacts with, the comprehensive cultural context(s) with which each can be associated (e.g. Hodder 1987; Poplawski 2008). That, it must be stressed, cannot only mean the circumstances in which texts and objects were produced, but includes all subsequent contexts through which they have passed, down to the present. One way, then, of answering the question 'what do we do with archaeology *and* literature?' is to combine both within the writing of cultural history: a cultural history that can be very effective in identifying processes and relationships which generate the modally different expressions and outputs we can analyse with our acquired specialist knowledge (Hines 2004: 26–36). However, largely because we ourselves live within a culture that is adapted to express itself through similar categories as were operative in the past, it proves very difficult in practice to describe 'culture' in anything but extremely abstract or subjective terms.

The history and status of research

A review of how eddic poetry and archaeology have been combined hitherto helps to illustrate how both disciplines have developed: in this context the appropriate goal is to outline developments within the subject of archaeology. We may start with Birger Nerman's rather short discussion (Nerman 1931): sixty-three pages of text, sixty-one illustrations. What Nerman attempted, straightforwardly, was to look for archaeological references in the texts which could be interpreted as dating evidence – hence his negative judgement 'nothing to say' on a number of poems, such as *Vafþrúðnismál*. He was, in effect, applying a thoroughly familiar, practical, archaeological approach. In fieldwork, archaeologists use finds to characterise and date archaeological contexts or layers, or use diagnostic attributes such as a style of ornamentation to date objects. Nerman's handling of the Poetic Edda was much influenced (although this remains unacknowledged) by the emergence of a Homeric archaeology which used material references in *The Iliad* and *The Odyssey* to associate the texts with contexts from the late Bronze Age Mycenaean civilisation through to the Iron Age of around the eighth century BC (Helbig 1887; Wace and Stubbings 1962: 325–429, 489–544; McDonald 1968). Even more stimulating had been Schliemann's successful search for Troy itself. Those examples illustrate how archaeological work has been motivated and exploited in a 'modern' world to historicise literature: in other words, material remains can serve to move parts of the textual heritage from the category of 'fiction' to (or at least towards) the category of 'fact', where authoritative textual 'historical sources' would *not* place them. Such was also the inspiration for the search for and excavation of the Norse settlement site at L'Anse aux Meadows, Newfoundland (H. Ingstad 1959; and in A. S. Ingstad 1977: 11–13).

Nerman's archaeological focus was almost exclusively on treasure and very high-status, precious-metal artefacts, and he read the poems in this light. He confidently concluded that much eddic poetry was of a distinctly early date, even before the Viking Period (1931: 59–63). Nerman appears to have been incapable of conceiving of archaeology itself as a pre-modern practice. His study quite unreflectively asserts a radically primitivist view that the 'original' poets could only refer to what they themselves might immediately experience as features of their own material worlds. This badly missed the point of how archaeology is at heart a structured and meaningful relationship with any past that is still present in material form: not only a common phenomenon, but also a powerful one. The modern era – i.e. from the Renaissance to the present – has seen this relationship transform in specialised forms from connoisseurship and collecting to antiquarianism and on into an academic profession and scientific discipline. All are culturally and historically specific variants of the underlying, constant engagement between people and material culture; none of them is its essential, 'true' form. Reflecting this point in quite direct terms, the sixth- or seventh-century ring-sword referred to in *Helgakviða Hjǫrvarðssonar* sts 8–9 – *sverð veit ek liggja ... hringr er í hjalti* ('I know there is a sword lying ... a ring is on the hilt', *HHv* 8/1, 9/1) – should be understood as an antiquarian detail, from a culture that was conscious of a past and familiar with some of its material peculiarities, so that this functions as archaeological dating evidence only as a *terminus post quem* (Stjerna 1903; Nerman 1931: 40–5. Fig. 1).

For much of the twentieth century, literary scholars were hostile to archaeology (and to history). Interestingly, many early professional archaeologists nonetheless had a background in textual studies – either the classics, or, in the case of Scandinavia, often in early Germanic philology.[3] However, archaeologists also turned increasingly not only away from, but positively against ancient literature. In the twentieth century many disciplines besides these two sought to validate themselves by asserting and embracing an autonomy that was antagonistic to blurred margins, cross-pollination, and multiple or even new agendas. Modern literary-critical theory became unashamedly a Theory of Everything. Archaeology also went through a phase of 'New Archaeology', dominated by an exclusively materialist positivism, which referred to 'text-hindered' approaches to a past that was, it believed, only to be scientifically understood through anthropological modelling. In this spirit, in fact, the archaeology of the insistently historical Middle Ages (i.e. the post-Roman centuries) was frequently held up as an object of ridicule (Hodges 1989: esp. 287–91; Austin 1991: 9–14; Gerrard 2003: 172–80, 217–29).

Figure 1 The typological development of the ring-sword pommel illustrated by Nerman (1931). a: free-swivelling ring on a pommel from Bifrons House, Kent; b: a pommel with an enlarged pseudo-ring from Endregårda, Endre parish, Gotland; c: skeuomorphic ring on a sword hilt from Vallstenarum, Vallstena parish, Gotland. Illustrations from Nerman 1931: figs. 45–7.

The 1980s saw archaeology taking a new turn. More, it would appear, as an opportunistic swing of the theoretical pendulum than as a shift governed by the weight and quality of textual evidence, 'post-processualism' and 'symbolic archaeology' appeared and rapidly became all the rage. It was in this turn of the tide that, by the 1990s, a group of Scandinavian archaeologists – primarily based in Sweden – returned to Old Norse literary sources. Anders Andrén, co-director of the *Vägar till midgård* project, wrote primarily on art history and iconography to start with, with particular reference to bracteates and Gotlandic picture stones (Andrén 1989, 1991). At this juncture, it was possible to draw upon Karl Hauck's ideas concerning the 'iconology' of fifth- and sixth-century gold bracteates. Since 1970, Hauck had developed an elaborate systematisation of design elements and interpretation of the figural scenes on these distinctive gold pendants in terms of a Germanic/Old Norse mythology – in a state of splendid isolation not only from contemporary archaeological theory, but also from severe empirical and historical scepticism (see Hauck 1970; and, contra, Hines 2013).

Colleagues working in proximate fields in Sweden included Frands Herschend, who in *Livet i Hallen* (*Life in the Hall*) of 1997 and the broader

The Idea of the Good of 1998 combined literature with the archaeology of major buildings to explore the more ritual aspects of secular society in its relationships and practices rather than mythology and religion (see Andrén, Jennbert, and Raudvere 2006 and Andrén 2014; Herschend 1997 and 1998).[4] Herschend, however, drew primarily on Old English poetry – *Beowulf* and supporting fragments – not the eddic corpus. Another Danish scholar working outside Denmark at this time was Lotte Hedeager, who herself had proceeded from strongly positivist early works to explore *Skygger af en anden virkelighed* (*Shadows of Another Reality*) (1997). Hedeager interpreted the exciting discoveries of great halls and concentrations of apparently ritually deposited wealth at Gudme on Fyn as 'Åsgard reconstructed' – rather than the literary Ásgarðr being a projection of real power centres into the divine sphere of the cosmos (Hedeager 2001, 2004, and 2011).

The general position of the recent Scandinavian symbolic archaeological school of thought on (in Scandinavian terms) later Iron Age ritual and religion, ideology and mythology, is in effect that the relationship between the literature and the archaeological material runs largely one way. The archaeologists wish to understand the material life of the period better, and literature does offer such understanding, not least when it is accepted that ideological and symbolic belief systems which may be articulated through literature actually were significant, generative features of the past human culture being studied (cf. Gräslund 2007). Such deeper insight cannot depend upon us finding direct literary commentaries upon or explications of phenomena which leave archaeological traces; rather, the literary corpus (dominated, in these studies, by *Snorra Edda*) contains analogous and usable sources in light of which archaeological remains may be interpreted. To a large degree the literature provides a basis for proposing significant uses associated with sites, structures, and objects, and so gives them a potential instrumentality and more specific meaning.

That is the case, not least because the Late Iron Age and (post-Conversion) medieval archaeology of Scandinavia is very rich. The range of settlement forms goes well beyond a simple scale of variation according to the wealth and social rank of the occupants or the utilitarian function of the spaces (cf. Byock 2001: 25–42; Munch et al. 2003; Clarke and Ambrosiani 1995: 141–9). Human burials, a major field of archaeological study, are rightly understood not just as the products of blind custom, but rather as tableaux in themselves and the products of performances that may well have been dramatic (such as the funeral on the Volga so graphically described by Ibn Fadlan) (Price 2008; Schjødt 2007). In life, the human body was clothed in material attributes, and in death, in turn, became an object – indeed, in effect an artefact in the various ways it might be treated. The designs and decoration of artefacts are themselves far from either merely utilitarian or purely ornamental; rather, they express a range of values and concepts – even if, at best, we can only measure the importance of the latter in terms of impact and distribution rather than genuinely being able to interpret them.

Beyond Scandinavian Late Iron Age cultural history, the last ten years have seen a wider démarche of archaeology and literature. Scholars coming from a literary background have been drawn towards archaeology as a literary topic. Philip Schwyzer's discussion of the Middle English *Saint Erkenwald* as an account of the excavation, interpretation, and curation of an ancient grave can be cited as a particularly stimulating analysis (Schwyzer 2007: 36–59). Schwyzer nonetheless focuses primarily on the object, or on material, and its effective agency in literary texts. His work offers a sort of early history of archaeology in the broader historical terms of a persistent human, social engagement with the material context noted above.

Not long after Nerman's study was published, what was to become a far more famous study appeared that tellingly illustrates the perception of archaeology amongst textual scholars at that time. In the Gollancz Memorial Lecture of 1934, J. R. R. Tolkien introduced his arguments for an appreciation of the unity of the Old English heroic epic *Beowulf* with a critique of what he called 'historical approaches', using what he called an allegorical simile: the demolition of a tower, which offered a far-reaching perspective to a distant horizon, by people who wished to inspect its re-used stones, 'to look for hidden carvings or inscriptions', while others, 'suspecting a deposit of coal under the soil began to dig for it, and forgot even the stones' (Tolkien 1936: 248–9). Archaeologists, in other words: blinkered in focus and method and conceptually unable to perceive the importance of the whole. Tolkien also referred directly to Nerman, as 'an historian of Swedish origins' in his lecture, for in 1913 Nerman had discussed the great burial mounds of Gamla Uppsala in terms of analogous textual information (Nerman 1913; cf. also Lindqvist 1936 and 1948).

Tolkien's reductive caricature was no more justified in the 1930s than it is now. Nonetheless, the positive critical point he was seeking to make – namely, that we should strive to understand the whole and not just the parts – calls for constant reiteration. Nerman's approach to the Poetic Edda indeed focused only on certain details and possible relationships between material culture and textual records, and excluded a great deal besides. At the most ambitious level, we may argue that literary output and material culture together can make up a *tractable* cultural history of peoples and places; an informative relationship between literature and archaeology should be both bi-directional and interactive. The essential realities of what people thought, felt, did, and said in the past are not exclusively mediated by literature; neither can material determinism claim to take us to an inner reality of which literature offers only a partial reflection.

Shields

Nerman's focus on the twin topics of weaponry and treasure unquestionably reflects key elements of the value-systems of the culture of the long ages which the eddic poems represent – from when the western Roman Empire collapsed during the fourth to sixth centuries AD, up to the thirteenth century when the poems were written down. Nowadays we are more likely to express a critical consciousness of the male-focused, militarised society this value-system foregrounds; a context in which violence was endemic and prowess in warfare all but essential to male status. Using a range of sources of evidence, we would now emphasise how much we think Scandinavian society changed over this long period (e.g. Hedeager 1992; Poulsen and Sindbæk 2011); yet its core values apparently continued with little visible variation. We would emphasise even more how crucial treasure was for gift-giving and thus for economic circulation, paying for social support and power. Cloaking the struggle for Fáfnir's gold – the Rhine gold of the Nibelungs/Vǫlsungar – in motives of honour and avoidance of shame shows how literary tradition can play an important role (in this case, a politically charged one) in the real, material, social, and economic world.

Nerman passed no comment on the motif of a shield that appears in *Grímnismál*:

> Svǫl heitir, hann stendr sólu fyrir,
>   skjǫldr, skínanda goði;
> bjǫrg ok brim ek veit at brenna skulu,
>   ef hann fellr í frá. (*Grm* 38)

> [Svǫl is the name of a shield; it stands before the sun, the shining god; I know that the land and the sea must burn if it falls away.][5]

In many respects, the image used here is straightforward. The shield is protective; the sun is a good, indeed a life-giving source of energy, but also potentially a destructive power. The name of the shield, given here as Svǫl (see below), is related to a root which gives us an adjective, *svalr* ('cool'), a verb *svala* ('to screen, to shade'), and a plural feminine noun *svalar* meaning a form of veranda. The power of the sun needs to be controlled; the mythology conceives of this as achieved through an artefact, leaving it a mystery by what power this artefact was made. The shield is held (somehow) in front of the 'shining god', the sun. Should we think of this object as purposefully, even considerately, deployed by the shining god himself to control his own power? The shield before the shining god is also alluded to in *Sigrdrífumál* (st.15/1–2), but without clarifying any of these questions.

Reflection upon what we know of shields themselves deepens the image's connotations. The consistently round shape of Scandinavian shields across the first millennium AD, from the Roman Iron Age to the Viking Period, would encourage an analogy with the sun, but this is far from the full story. Throughout this period we also have abundant evidence of shields serving as major media of display. The highest-ranking officers in the defeated army whose equipment was sacrificed in the third century AD in Illerup Mose, Jutland, had elaborate silver-decorated shields (Ilkjær 2000: 98–101). The gilt and garnet-inlaid settings on the shield from the Sutton Hoo mound 1 ship-burial in Suffolk are, along with the helmet, the most emphatically Scandinavian elements of the grave-assemblage (Bruce-Mitford 1978: 91–9). At a less exclusive level, we know that the sixty-four shields in the Gokstad ship-burial of the beginning of the tenth century were displayed along the gunwale as painted, alternately, yellow or black (Nicolaysen 1882: 33, 62–3). The shield may be a piece of protective equipment, but it can nonetheless assert power. The perception of the shield-board as a display field and information source is elaborated in the imaginative (not necessarily imaginary) references to shield-boards bearing representational, even narrative art, in the skaldic shield lays *Ragnarsdrápa* (*Drápa about Ragnarr*) and *Haustlǫng* (*Autumn-Long*) (Clunies Ross et al. 2007).[6]

The actual name of this shield is something of an editorial problem. The feminine forms *Svǫl* (Codex Regius) and *Svalin* (AM 748 I a 4°) could be the otherwise unrecorded nominative singulars to the plural *svalar*; one solution has been to emend the name to a masculine *Svalinn*, the appropriate gender for *skjǫldr* ('shield'). This word appears in a list of names for a shield in the *Þulur* (poetic lists) of Snorri's *Skáldskaparmál* (123). Textually and linguistically, this is a minefield; it is, however, significant that Scandinavian and other early Germanic cultures gave women a distinct, important role in the warfare that otherwise seems such a definitively male sphere. As early as the first century AD, Tacitus had reported a Germanic custom of taking women to witness battles, encouraging the fighting men, not least by baring their breasts to symbolise the threat of slavery – and the rape that would accompany that (*Germania*: chs 7–8; Wyatt 2009: esp. 173–242). A millennium later, a remarkably similar story is told of Freydís in Vinland, rallying the Greenlandic colonists and driving off the Skrælings (*Eiríks saga rauða* (*The Saga of Eiríkr the Red*): ch. 11). Eddic poetry knows both valkyrie figures and female inciters, demanding warrior feats and sacrifices from lovers, husbands, brothers, and sons. Comparable to the cloaking of the functional economic role of treasure noted above, those literary models serve to sublimate the equally basic sexual motivations for men to achieve renown, as well as masking the crude acquisitiveness that was the primary cause of warfare.

Valkyrie figures such as Brynhildr and Sigrdrífa are transgressive females in a way, but everything about them reinforces an essentialist sexual dichotomy rather than breaking it down (see Clark and Jóhanna Katrín Friðriksdóttir, Chapter 17 in this Handbook). They are highly sexualised women who behave exceptionally and equip themselves just as prominent men, in order to excite and support just such men, reinforcing heterosexuality and clearly defined gender roles. It is a significant but very regular archaeological observation, in relation to Germanic and Scandinavian cultures of this period, that in special circumstances male attributes may cross over to be incorporated into the female range, but not vice versa.

The shield was a prominent feature of armed female valkyrie figures known from the Viking Period (Fig. 2a). There is also evidence of model shield miniatures being worn by generally richly dressed women, as laid in their graves, in Scandinavia of the Migration Period (mostly the fifth century) and the Viking Period; and in Anglo-Saxon England from the fifth century to the seventh (Fig. 2b-d). Designs found on the faces of these model shields, formed by punchmarks, embossed marks, or incised lines, are often radial, and thus sun- or star-like. The Migration and Viking period series would appear to be separate, although a fascinating hint, at least of an intermediary series, comes with a single example of such a pendant from the intervening Vendel Period from Jämtland, now part of Sweden, at the western end of the religiously important island Frösön ('Freyr's island') (Magnus 1975: 47–78; Hines 1984: 221–35; Welinder 2003: 518; Magnus 2015). A specific case would have to be made for interpreting these phenomena, inter-related or not, as no more than minor reflexes in the female sphere of something that really mattered in the male sphere, or merely as symbols of 'protection'. It is naturally tempting to consider the association with the sun god and his fertility, and to suggest an imaginative association with female fertility. We may recall here that *Sigrdrífumál* (sts 9

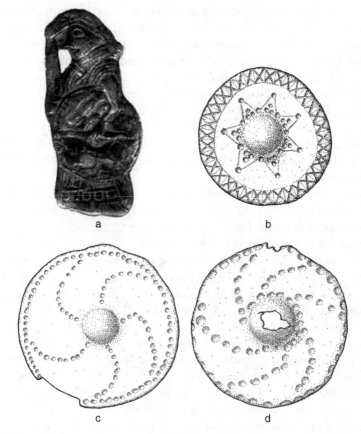

a   b

c   d

Figure 2 Miniature representations of shields. a: Valkyrie in copper alloy, Campsey
Ash, Suffolk; b–d: 'scutiform pendants'; b: Linderup Mark, Tolstrup, Børglum,
Hjørring, Jutland (Denmark): 5th century AD, gold. National Museum,
Copenhagen, 15352; c–d: Tarup, Sønder Næraa, Åsum, Odense, Fyn (Denmark):
10th century AD, silver. National Museum, Copenhagen, 20102. Scale 1:1.

and 19) includes a reference to *bjargrúnar* ('protective runes'), which will
help *leysa kind frá konum* ('to release children from women').

It may be proposed as an intrinsically positive position that there is no
single correct answer to a question of what that relationship may be; no
end-of-story interpretation of the inter-reflection of the archaeological and
literary worlds such as the shields represent. There are many possible and
equally probable explanations, governed by access to both the material
experiences and the literary motifs that embody the meaningfulness of the
objects. Meaning is constantly dynamic and negotiable. Direct and

illustrative identifications of textual references with particular finds can indeed be interesting, but secure connexions of this kind are not constraining factors on making meaningful associations between the archaeological and literary records.

Literature and the living space

Many material images in eddic poetry are used as similes or illustrations, generally reflecting a practical if often elite world of objects: weapons, tools, clothing, materials themselves (especially treasure), and ships, and a natural world of landscapes, trees, animals, birds, and fish. As an illustrative example, *Hávamál* is very precise:

> Bú er betra, þótt lítit sé,
> halr er heima hverr;
> þótt tvær geitr eigi ok taugreptan sal:
> þat er þó betra en bœnn.

> Bú er betra, þótt lítit sé,
> halr er heima hverr;
> blóðugt er hjarta, þeim er biðja skal
> sér í mál hvert matar. (*Háv* 36–7)

> [A farmhouse is better, even if it's small, every man's a real man in his home. Even if he has only two goats and a ropey roof: it's still better than begging.

> A farmhouse is better, even if it's small, every man's a real man in his home. A man's heart bleeds if he has to plead for food at every meal.]

Those are not imagined states or contrived perils; this is literary realism. Yet this is not exclusively materialistic; the effect of these verses depends utterly upon an interaction between the cognitive state evoked and the specific material conditions for that state. Both are equally essential. A householder may be poor and struggling, with limited livestock as a source of dairy food.[7] The homestead may be poorly built and flimsy. We cannot tell exactly what the term *taugreptan* conveys: it might be a specific, contemporary idiomatic term for, perhaps, a withy-panel roof (Herschend [unsigned] 2013); it could figuratively suggest a material that bends but holds rather than being rigid. Certainly it is a pejorative term in this context. In these stanzas a material and social state is described that is neither desirable nor enviable; yet it can be compared with something worse. Proprietorship is a relationship between the human subject and the material world, a relationship that really does make a difference to the former.

One of the most exciting prospects that an archaeologically informed reading of literature offers is to bring the literature into a material world: one that, as noted, can be that of the context of composition *and* of all contexts of transmission and reception through to the here and now. A more specific implication of the relationship between 'material semantics' (Hines 2004: 70) and strict structural linguistic semantics is that the former can rescue literature from the effects of a limited intertextuality that treats *only* literature as the contextual reference zone within which any piece of literature should be read and understood. In that regard, and perhaps especially in relation to eddic poetry, the wider conception of material semantics can be especially productive when the material context is appropriately appreciated as a setting for the performance of the poetry. This was an issue explored in my discussion of *Hamðismál* a few years ago, combining a close analysis of the poem in relation to practical speech-act theory along with the implicit *mise-en-scène*, identifying how evocatively the text could draw upon features of a likely context of presentation and reception in an Icelandic farmhouse, not only to make the experience of the poem imaginatively more powerful but also to sharpen the moral values and criticisms promulgated by the poem (Hines 2007; cf. Gunnell, Chapter 5 in this Handbook).

The archaeological evidence for the potential of Icelandic Viking Period and medieval farmhouses as sites and settings for performance has been considerably enhanced by the recent reassessment of the long-famous site of Hofstaðir in Mývatnssveit (Lucas 2009). The site represents a particular facet of both the constructive and the contested relationship between Old Norse/Icelandic literature and archaeology, going back to the late nineteenth century, when an enthusiasm for identifying sites and structures referred to in the sagas or *Landnámabók* with visible ruins emerged. In particular, the association of the place name Hofstaðir – of which several examples are known[8] – with 'pagan temples' elicited a critical response from Finnur Jónsson (1898), cautioning that saga literature should not be treated credulously as a source. Nevertheless, archaeological excavations conducted by Finnur and Daniel Bruun in 1908 did indeed suggest that this Hofstaðir had been an unusual ritual site in the Viking Period (Bruun and Finnur Jónsson 1911). The principal peculiarities they focused upon were the exceptional length of the bow-sided hall (more than 45 m), a possible annexed shrine with suggested bases for idols, and apparent evidence of feasting on a great scale (Lucas 2009: fig. 4.48).

Hofstaðir has been reviewed and re-excavated on several occasions since; an excavation programme on a church and churchyard site just south-west of the hall is still underway. The interpretation of many of the features identified by Bruun and Finnur Jónsson has become a good deal more mundane (Roussell 1943: 215–23; Adolf Friðriksson and Orri Vésteinsson 1997), but a core of evidence for unusual ritual remains. Olaf Olsen (1965) effectively articulated the case that the traditional religious practices of pre-Conversion Iceland were so thoroughly embedded in the social and practical material culture of the time that separate, distinctive 'temple' structures should not be expected – although he accepted that a few special 'temple farms' were evidenced, both archaeologically at Hofstaðir and through literary references. The results of the thorough recent archaeological investigations and analysis show that the hall was first raised around the year 940, at, or just after, the end of the initial settlement period. There is, frustratingly, still uncertainty over whether it was built to its full length from the start or extended in a second phase, from c. AD 980, when the farmstead complex was developed with new annexes to the main hall and outbuildings, including a small secondary 'hall', a detached latrine block, and a smithy. Certainly during this phase, although not necessarily entirely within this second phase, the hall was associated with what can be inferred to have been the regular, ritual, and spectacular slaughter of cattle – often bulls – the skulls of whose severed heads were then displayed somewhere around the site (Lucas 2009: esp. 236–54, 404–7). These skulls were found in the demolition deposits of the main hall building, dating to some time from about AD 1030, most of them collected in two major groups. Their final distribution may reflect where the skulls had been displayed. A sheep was similarly slaughtered and deposited whole as a form of closure deposit for the annex where the largest collection of cattle skulls was found. It is as yet unclear how closely this ritual sequence may relate chronologically to the establishment of the Christian church and burial area now under excavation. All in all, though, the evidence from Hofstaðir provides us with a thoroughly concrete view of the kind of fundamental reality the extremely antagonistic portrayal of feasts and probable rituals in, par excellence, *Grímnismál* and *Lokasenna* distorts in a supernaturally dramatic fashion (as argued by Haugen 1983: esp. 9–12; Gunnell 1995).

The bed as artefact and poetic motif

Shifting focus to within the living space, one particular case-study will now be offered which deepens not only an appreciation of how eddic poetry illuminatingly embodies the particular relationship between people and material culture in Viking and medieval Scandinavia (especially Iceland), but also how intimately that may be correlated with the context of the Icelandic (and indeed Scandinavian or Greenlandic) farmhouses already introduced. The basic farmhouses of Viking Period and earlier medieval Scandinavia, Iceland, and Greenland tend to be very simple, organised around one principal chamber; the fewer Scandinavian townhouses are smaller and lighter, but not much different on that point. In these situations, human relationships necessarily required creative use of the available space for special transactions: functional diversity of living space, such as we are familiar with, was not a material design feature.

Most people slept in what were variously working, sitting, and sleeping spaces. The provision of more or less private sleeping space – in box-beds, sleeping-lofts, or on open benches – and the facilities available for comfortable sleep, are matters that vary greatly and were culturally specific. Archaeologically, this does not just pertain to the study and interpretation of domestic space and architecture, but also to funerary archaeology. Both the Oseberg and the Gokstad ship burials, for instance, contained the remains of several movable beds (Fig. 3). These were more than the one (or two) required by the principal deceased individuals – although that bed was a particularly fine example in the Oseberg burial – but also far too few for a crew of either ship (Christensen 1992: 127–8). Bed-burials are a recurrent although not frequent phenomenon in early-medieval Germanic Europe. About fifteen such burials from seventh-century England, all but one of them in women's graves, have recently been suggested to be a transitional phenomenon of the Conversion Period, consistent with a new Christian concept of worldly death as a transitory state (Speake 1989; Hines and Bayliss 2013: 552).

The bed (*sæing, rekkja, beðr, hvíla*) is a common motif in eddic poetry. Inevitably, the bed appears there as anything but a mundane sleeping place: not because it was not such a thing, but simply because that function is not interesting enough to achieve notice in the poetry. Equally inevitably, the bed appears as a charged setting for sexual adventures and meetings: phrases such as 'sleeping in another's arms' or references to sleeping together appear as euphemisms for sexual intercourse (e.g. *Helreið Brynhildar*, st. 13). *Rígsþula*, of course, is a prime example in the eddic corpus, with Rígr/Heimdallr lying down in the middle of the bed to beget the three children, progenitors of Old Norse social hierarchies: *þræll* ('thrall'), *karl* ('farmer'), and *jarl* ('lord'). In *Hávamál*, sts 97–101, Óðinn introduces the episode of his adventure with *Billings mey: Billings mey ek fann beðjum á* ('I found Billing's girl on the bed', *Háv* 97/1–2).

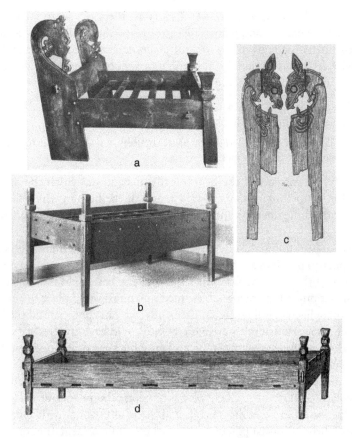

Figure 3 a–b: Two beds from the Oseberg ship-burial (drawn by the author); c–d: probable bed-posts (cf. the Oseberg find) and a bed from Gokstad ship-burial (engravings published by Nicolaysen 1882: pls. VI–VII).

A particularly memorable set of instances is the encounters, on beds or in bed-chambers, of Brynhildr, Sigurðr, and Gunnarr in the poems of the Vǫlsung cycle (especially *Grípisspá, Brot af Sigurðarkviðu, Sigurðarkviða in skamma, Guðrúnarkviður I* and *II*, and *Helreið Brynhildar*). The image of the bed with the sword laid between the sleeping couple (*Brot* st. 19) consequently cannot solely represent a practical precaution to enforce sexual abstinence, but must also reflect a more general awareness of the bed and sleep as a place of vulnerability and weakness – as well, indeed, as echoing and being echoed in the placement of weapons alongside some men and even a few women in the grave. This aspect of the bed is depicted in material detail in the first two

Guðrúnarkviður: in *Guðrúnarkviða I*, sts 13–15, there is a sharp focus on the blood-soaked blanket and pillow still surrounding the dead body of Sigurðr – echoed further perhaps in the *ársal* of *Guðrúnarkviða II*, st. 25, if that does indeed refer to a bed-curtain rather than a wall-hanging. Concluding that poem, Guðrún emphasises the changed use of the bed for her:

> Læga ek síðan – né ek sofa vildak –
> þrágjarn í kǫr; þat man ek gǫrva. (*Gðr II* 44)
>
> [I lay down then – I did not want to sleep – stubborn in the sick-bed; I remember that as a fact.]

Similarly, we may recall the bench ready at hand on which the drunken Bǫðvildr is raped in *Vǫlundarkviða* (st. 28), or the beds in which Gunnarr and Brynhildr lie sleepless and troubled by dreams in *Brot af Sigurðarkviðu* (sts 12–19).

It is not just stating the obvious to emphasise that the literature (especially eddic poetry) provides a substantial, variegated body of material that demonstrates how the utilitarian, familiar space of the bed could nonetheless, by human action and interaction, be turned into a privileged place to enter and lie in. In archaeological terms, consequently, we can appreciate all the better how the association of the grave with the bed could have involved a great deal more than a simple recognition of similarity between death, rest, and sleep. This is a vital perspective to bring to bear on variations in burial rite, grave form, and grave furnishing; and is no less significant – perhaps even particularly significant – when we try to gauge the impact of the gradual introduction of more homogeneous and materially less individual or ostentatious Christian burial practices. The richest eddic presentation of the bed in the grave, almost a 'type scene' when we allow the archaeological parallels their relevance, is in *Helgakviða Hundingsbana II*, sts 40–9. Helgi is the restless undead hero in the barrow, riding noisily around: the dramatic process – although not a ritual, it must be stressed – by which Sigrún pacifies him is to enter the mound, almost consuming Helgi with her desire (see Quinn 2006):

> Nú em ek svá fegin fundi okkrum
> sem átfrekir Óðins haukar,
> er val vitu varmar bráðir . . . (*HH II* 43/1–6)
>
> [Now I am so desirous of our meeting as the ravenous hawks of Óðinn when they see the slain, the hot food . . .]

She does this through kisses, launching a sequence of three stanzas where the flowing, multiple liquidity of the corpse is shockingly explored – Helgi's body is bloody, wrapped in 'death-dew' (*valdǫgg*), his hands also damp and cold (*úrsvalar*); her tears mix with the 'wound-' and/or 'grief-dew' (*harmdǫgg*) (for a discussion of these kennings see Quinn, Chapter 3 in this Handbook):

> ... hvert fellr blóðugt á brjóst grami,
> úrsvalt, innfjálgt, ekka þrungit. (*HH II* 45/9–12)

> [... each falls bloody on the breast of the prince, dew-damp, passionately hot, pressed from grief.]

The two end by pledging a drink of fellowship: *Vel skulum drekka dýrar veigar* ('We must indeed drink the precious brew', *HH II* 46/1–2). Then Sigrún makes a bed for Helgi: *Hér hefi ek þér, Helgi, hvílu gǫrva* ('Here I have a bed prepared for you, Helgi', *HH II* 47/1–2), where she will lie with him: *vil ek þér í faðmi, fylkir, sofna* ('I wish to sleep, prince, in your embrace', *HH II* 47/5–6). This satisfies Helgi, and he can leave the world of the living: *Mál er mér at ríða roðnar brautir* ('It is time for me to ride the reddened roads', *HH II* 49/1–2). Sigrún must accept the *harmr* and *tregi* ('sorrow', 'grief') of Helgi's loss; the unfinished story of his restless death is settled by the consummation of making the bed in the grave.

Altogether, it then becomes much easier to appreciate the cultural logic of the reference to oaths sworn by Atli to Gunnar in *Atlakviða*:

> ... at sól inni suðrhǫllu ok at Sigtýs bergi,
> hǫlkvi hvílbeðjar ok at hringi Ullar. (*Akv* 30/5–8)

> [... on the sun in its southern circuit and on Sigtýr's mountain, the hulk of the bed and the ring of Ullr.][9]

The furnishing of the living space did not merely serve as a store of props for fictional tales; references such as these are not simply the opportunistic employment of domestic realism as a setting for dramatic human exchanges. Simple and familiar though they are, these were constructed contexts which people could engage with in an intensely imaginative way. Even the mundane material context could be imbued with significance and value. The productive relationship between archaeology and literary studies as outlined here is very much more than a purely illustrative role – in which at best archaeology might serve to identify items and contexts that one might not notice or understand in the literature. A study of the use of the motifs of the bed and sleep in eddic poetry could be undertaken as a purely literary exercise – and as far as the comparative reading of ancient poems goes, that could produce all of the readings suggested above. But this would be a one-dimensional approach to the phenomenon if it were not to include the available information on beds and sleeping arrangements in the various buildings of the Viking Age and early Middle Ages in Scandinavia, Iceland, and Greenland, and the much more complex bed-in-the-grave evidence from material practice. Brought together, the two disciplines provide mutually informative and eye-opening support, representing both the potential and the impact of this particular form of cross-disciplinary initiative.

Notes

1. Particular attention may be drawn to the determinedly interdisciplinary *Vägar till Midgård* ('Roads to Midgard – Old Norse Religion in Long-term Perspectives') project supported by the Bank of Sweden Tercentenary Foundation, which ran through the first decade of the present century, leading to the publication of sixteen books to date.
2. Nerman's study was written by September 1924 and finally translated, edited, and published by the Viking Society for Northern Research in 1931.
3. Thus, for instance, Oscar Almgren, Knut Stjerna, and Birger Nerman in Sweden, and Håkon Shetelig in Norway.
4. I refer here only to those core publications of the *Vägar till Midgård* project that appeared in English.
5. Translations throughout are the author's.
6. Compare Achilles's shield manufactured by Hephaestus in *The Iliad* (18.478–608) and its equivalent, given by Venus to her beloved Aeneas, in *The Aeneid* (8.617–731).
7. Cf. Dubois 2012: esp. 75–9; despite referring to 'diet' in his title, Dubois does not discuss the food value of goats as livestock.
8. The local spelling of the name of the farm in question close to Mývatn is in fact *Hofsstaðir*.
9. I shall not discuss the problematic word *hǫlkvir* in detail here. It is otherwise recorded in Old Norse literature as the name of a horse; in the compounds *borðhǫlkvir* and *golfhǫlkvir* it is interpreted as 'ship' and 'house' respectively. In the latter case, in Bragi's *Ragnarsdrápa* st. 5, the phrase *golfhǫlkvis sá[r]* may again refer to a bed. *Pace* Ásgeir Blöndal Magnússon (1989 *s.v.* HÖLKVIR), I find it extremely difficult to exclude a link to the word that gives us English 'hulk' and various Germanic cognates. Together these imply that the term was used for some form of substantial constructed frame to start with; in the case of Old Norse poetic diction and the topic under discussion here, the association with transportation, and perhaps thus rites of passage, is also suggestive.

CHAPTER 12

Eddic modes and genres

Brittany Schorn

Part of the attraction of eddic poetry for modern readers lies in its particularly compelling blend of the familiar and the remote. It presents a strange world, distanced physically and chronologically from that of its audience; a world populated by larger-than-life characters drawn from myth and legend who experience a correspondingly heightened form of reality. The anxieties of the real-world societies of medieval Scandinavia are played out in the grandest possible terms on the eddic stage. There is much in this poetry that appeals to universal human experience, but it is inextricably framed within its own particular cultural setting. The interpretation of eddic poetry begins with investigation of this context. Approaching genre in Old Norse poetry is deeply problematic – as it is in any literary tradition – and made more so by the nature of the preservation of eddic poetry across a variety of manuscripts and by its relationship to associated prose texts (see Clunies Ross on preservation, Chapter I in this Handbook). Some of these difficulties are ultimately insurmountable if the aim is to construct a rigid and universal taxonomy. Rather than shoe-horn eddic verse into such a mould, we should therefore seek to construct a refined and nuanced – even if sometimes apparently contradictory – series of overlapping generic criteria, best conceived of as literary modes, and a similarly flexible perspective on these modes' relationship to Old Norse poetics and literature more broadly.

Genre is itself a highly malleable literary tool; one which aids composers or performers as well as audiences. It provides the former, in the terminology of Hans Robert Jauss (1982), with a 'mode of writing' (or 'mode of composing', as we might extrapolate back to the oral period) to shape new works within comprehensible frames of reference, and the latter with a 'horizon of expectations' according to which they can judge and interpret new material. Thus, genre can be interpreted loosely as any set of conventions used to contextualise a composition: it is a useful device for describing mediation between composer and audience, and can be based on a near infinite array of features finding expression in form, style, and content. This mediation does not always take the form of straightforward conformity to a generic norm. Authors or performers might introduce limited innovative elements or choose to exploit the expectations of a genre by opposing or manipulating them. A work which conformed to one genre in formal terms – for instance, a poem in eddic metre, or in one of the dialogue forms well-attested in the eddic corpus – might be malleable in other respects, calling on the conventions and characteristics of other recognisable categories of text. Questions of genre must therefore always be approached with an open mind, and rarely more so than in the case of eddic poetry.

Eddic poetry and skaldic poetry

The definition of eddic poetry itself as a distinctive branch of Old Norse poetics is an artificial one that sits increasingly uneasily with modern scholars. It describes a group of poems, to a large extent defined by the Codex Regius anthology, that share a range of formal and thematic characteristics.[1] Speaking of 'eddic poetry' is misleading in two ways: it suggests that the poems' defining features are unique to 'eddic' material, and that there was a medieval concept of 'eddic poetry' (understood by that or any other name). Old Norse has an extraordinary range of native terminology for its poetics, none of which indicates a simple binary opposition. Any attempted reconstruction of poetic categories depends on the limited and potentially far from representative body of verse which happens to have survived. Had the Codex Regius not been found in 1643, modern understanding of Old Norse poetics would be completely different. The boundaries of the eddic corpus must therefore remain fluid, and we must resist the tendency to view some verses as marginal to the corpus because they display less apparently characteristic features.

Even the formal distinctions between eddic and skaldic poetry are not entirely straightforward. The inherited traditional Germanic alliterative verse type continued to develop in Old Norse as *fornyrðislag*, and gave rise to innovative forms, skaldic and eddic, which were composed and transmitted alongside each other from the ninth century onwards.[2] The eddic forms are distinguished above all by the rules they do not observe, especially strict syllable counting, prescribed patterns of rhyme, and the syntactic completeness of the *helmingr* (half stanza).[3] Yet the extent to which these features, associated above all with the prestigious *dróttkvætt* (court poetry) form, are employed in skaldic metres varies too. First identifiable on the Rök stone alongside verses in eddic metres (Wessén 1958), *kviðuháttr* ('poem metre', usually categorised as a skaldic metre) mixes features conventionally associated with skaldic and eddic poetry as well as displaying its own peculiar characteristics. *Kviðuháttr* is characterised by syllable counting, rhyme occurs in an irregular, stylised way, and not all *helmingar* are syntactically complete (see further Gade 1995: 234–6, 2002, 2005; Clunies Ross 2005: 26–7).

Diction is an even less precise criterion. There is no doubt that kennings tend to be more complex and frequent in skaldic poetry, and different patterns can be observed in their deployment in skaldic and eddic stanzas (see further Quinn, Chapter 3 in this Handbook). These tendencies arose in response to the form, subject matter, and social context of well-attested skaldic modes, such as courtly praise poetry. Among other uses, kennings provide an additional method of lexical variation, aiding composition of strict and demanding metrical forms; they conceive of the immediate, human present in grand mythological terms using memorable imagery; and they demonstrate the skill of poets in encoding them as well as that of the audience in deciphering them. For similar reasons syntax is sometimes more variable and fragmented in skaldic verse than in eddic, but it also varies considerably between the poems and stanzas of individual skalds and between different skaldic modes.

The nature of the poetic voice differs between typical skaldic and eddic style too. Many skaldic poems contain self-referential language calling attention to the poet's skill, his function in shaping and perpetuating the memory and reputation of his human subjects, and in some cases his divine inspiration (whether pagan or Christian). These compositions represented public performances and some sort of audience – the king and court, a distant woman, or the public at large – is often specified by the verse or its prose context. For reasons discussed in my chapter on style elsewhere in this Handbook (Chapter 14), eddic poets normally sought to channel the voices of the ancient past, and the effectiveness of their poems rested in part on how successfully they distanced themselves from their immediate audiences, about which we know very little. There are again exceptions. The *erfikvæði* ('memorial poems')[4] *Haraldskvæði* and *Hákonarmál* are composed in eddic metres, although they are attributed to named skalds, Þórbjǫrn hornklofi ('raven')[5] and Eyvindr skáldaspillir ('poet-despoiler') Finnsson, and specific historical contexts. Their choice of verse type befits the nature of their content: a dialogue between a valkyrie and a raven about the deeds of King Haraldr hárfagri ('fairhair'), and the reception of King Hákon Aðalsteinsfóstri into Valhǫll, and thus the integration of the human into the mythological sphere (see Larrington, Chapter 8 in this Handbook). Equally, not all verse in skaldic metres is attributed to known human poets. Of the five verses in *Styrbjarnar þáttr Svíakappa* (*The Tale of Styrbjörn, Swedish Champion*) (all in *dróttkvætt*), three are attributed to a *finngálkn mikit* ('great monster'), the *Danir* ('Danes' [at Jómsborg]) collectively, and a *maðr rauðskeggjaðr* ('red-bearded man') identified in context as Þórr (Townend 2012). This is similar to the large body of *lausavísur* and short poetic sequences in the legendary sagas (*fornaldarsögur*), which are universally attributed to characters within the narrative. It is often the nature of the speaker or the type of speech-act that triggers the choice of an eddic or skaldic mode. Judy Quinn's observation in connection with the failure of verses in the contemporary sagas to conform to a strict eddic/skaldic dichotomy applies to the categorisation of eddic verse in the sagas more broadly: functional definitions are more useful than formal ones and should be based on 'the voice of the verse: its identity, the conventions surrounding it, the authority it lends the content of the verse, as well as the function of the verse in the text' (Quinn 1987: 54–5).

Approaches to the categorisation of eddic poetry

Though not as large as the skaldic corpus,[6] the eddic corpus is notable for its variety in subject, style, form, and tone. It defies straightforward classification, binary or otherwise, and any attempt to delineate genres serves to highlight the versatility of the tradition. We cannot pigeonhole individual poems into completely discrete categories, and most critics have long since given up on the idea that we should. Yet equally futile would be to try to read poems in isolation without taking into account their place within Old Norse literary tradition, however imperfectly we may understand it. What we can do is use multiple approaches to describe a complex and evolving range of overlapping conventions and associations that express some of the relationships between the surviving texts. Ultimately this may help us to improve our understanding of the lost corpus of which extant poems surely represent only scattered remnants. We can also gain some insight into the thirteenth- and fourteenth-century recontextualisation of eddic poetry that is responsible for the preservation of most of the eddic corpus as we have it. There is a great deal to be learned from considering the Codex Regius poems within the wider corpus of eddic poetry preserved in the *fornaldarsögur* as well as younger compositions and poetic translations.

Part of the difficulty we face is definition. Genre can be considered in terms of different types of categories, and while I will make no attempt to be exhaustive here, I briefly mention a few approaches which seem especially pertinent to eddic material. Joseph Harris, Else Mundal, and Bernt Øyvind Thorvaldsen have very lucidly demonstrated how Dan Ben-Amos's remarks about 'the incongruity between ethnic genres of oral literature and the analytical categories constructed for their classification' (1976: 215) are applicable to the study of genre in Old Norse literature (Harris 1975; Mundal 2006; Thorvaldsen 2006 and 2010). Analytic categories are not necessarily connected to medieval understandings of the tradition at all, and risk introducing concepts from other cultures (not least our own) that may not have been part of them. Yet although we are aware that they are artificial, these categories may nonetheless yield valuable insights and approaches. The term 'wisdom poetry', for example, describes a phenomenon spanning many cultures from the Bronze Age Near East to Maori New Zealand and the modern United States that cannot possibly be directly related, but serves as a general label for a common human tendency to order and transmit valued cultural knowledge. Hence, the subject matter of wisdom poetry (even just within Old Norse) is extremely diverse: magic, mythological lore, and observations about the natural world and human society sit side by side, yet find unity and relevance of a sort in the very act of assemblage. Poetry serving this function in Old Norse is marked by a number of conventional features, and although it was probably not thought of in generically specific terms (and there are many differences between poems), it is nonetheless helpful to modern scholars to read these texts as wisdom poetry. Wisdom poems also typify a problem with many analytical categories: their grouping is based ultimately on analogy with a genre originating in another cultural context (in this case biblical wisdom, itself subject to the same process of literary rationalisation). However helpful such a comparison may be, it tends to privilege shared features between traditions as generic criteria and downplay other types of connections between texts in their specific cultural context.

Ethnic genres are undoubtedly the more important, and our primary sources for them are, as Mundal observes, 'the semantic meaning of ethnic terms and the meaning of other words that are used in description of a certain phenomenon' (2006: 288). The evidence, however, is somewhat limited. We do have a number of titles and apparent generic labels attested in the medieval manuscript copies of poems and in poetic and grammatical treatises, but what exactly they were intended to signify may be a matter of debate and the problem remains that they postdate – in some cases by a margin of several centuries – the postulated date of composition of the poems they describe. Even more complex and evasive, yet in many ways more interesting, is the question of how late-medieval taxonomy might relate to the generic understandings and intentions of all those who composed and transmitted eddic material outside of the manuscripts in which we have it. This includes any life these poems, or parts of them, had in oral circulation before or alongside their surviving manuscript witnesses as they emerged into script in the thirteenth century. No certainty is possible, but we would do well to keep an open mind. Titles and generic definitions could in some respects have been subordinate to content, as discussed below. In the Old English poem *Beowulf*, for example, an imagined scene of oral recitation concerning the story of the fighting between Danes and Frisians is given no title as such, but is referred to by a summary of its subject matter as the poet is described as being obliged 'to recite about the heirs of Finn' (*mænan scolde be Finnes eaferum, Beowulf* 1067b–68a).

As they survive, eddic titles all relate in some way to speech-acts, but some are more specific than others. The majority of the poems are simply titled as the speech of a particular character (Clunies Ross 2005: 29–30).[7] Terms such as *senna, hvǫt*, and *spá* relate more directly to categories of primary utterance (though the literary and sometimes comparative evidence used to characterise the social contexts of these speech-acts is not unproblematic). In these instances, we can perhaps get a glimpse of the extra-textual cultural context that these poems developed within and which continued to be crucial to their interpretation. Challenging questions remain, though, even with these ethnic genres. How distanced were literary genres from the social behaviours they referred to? How did they relate to other potentially unnamed categories? We also see these speech types used as compositional units within poems we would otherwise assign to other genres. What does this say about the nature of eddic composition?

Similar structures are used to varying effect in different poems, and this above all complicates their identification with functional genres. We must also take account of the fact that a number of the poems – *Hávamál, Grímnismál*, and the Helgi poems, to give just a few examples – show evidence of possible reworking, perhaps multiple times, at either a written or oral stage of their transmission (or both).[8] There are intertextual connections between eddic poems as well as influences from other Old Norse literary genres (skaldic diction or saga prose, for example), and individual poems may contain learned material imported from other traditions.

Perhaps less obviously, there may be influence from foreign models in the way that native material is presented which somewhat realigns its generic affiliations. Sticking with the example of wisdom poetry, the thirteenth-century poem *Sólarljóð* provides a particularly striking instance of how this might occur in the interaction of eddic verse with otherworldly vision literature. Composed in *ljóðaháttr*, *Sólarljóð* initially relates gnomic wisdom in a style rather like *Hávamál* or *Sigrdrífumál*, its contents being linked by thematic associations and hints of narrative. Traditional maxims are given a new Christian moral dimension, however, and the gnomic mode is subordinated in the last two-thirds of the poem to a dead man's vision of heaven and (a very Nordic) hell (see further Larrington 2002; Larrington and Robinson 2007; Fidjestøl 1979; and Schorn 2011). This new generic context gives a traditional eddic mode a new function, inspiring spiritual improvement in a Christian audience.

Mythological poetry and heroic poetry

Before examining the internal evidence of the poems themselves for potential generic divisions, it is essential to note that the single most influential factor guiding scholarly readings of eddic poetry has been the arrangement of the Codex Regius manuscript (see further Clunies Ross, Chapter 1 in this Handbook). A thematic division into two main genres, 'mythological' and 'heroic', is usually inferred from it. As has often been noted, the compiler of the Codex Regius seems to have had some sort of scheme for the organisation of his material, based primarily on the seemingly fundamental distinction between poems with primarily mytho-logical subject matter and protagonists, and those centred around the more human subjects of pseudo-historical legend.[9] In the manuscript there is a general division – emphasised by a very large initial – between the mythological and the heroic poems (20 r).[10] The former account for about a third of the collection and appear to be broadly arranged by divine protagonist, while the latter are organised into narrative cycles loosely revolving around legendary heroes. The effect is a sort of *fornaldarsaga* of the half-brothers Helgi and Sigurðr, although the narratives of the poems after the manuscript lacuna (from *Brot af Sigurðarkviðu* to *Hamðismál*) overlap and contain numerous contradictions (Vésteinn Ólason 2010: 236–51). Thus, the manuscript opens with eleven poems that deal primar-ily, though not exclusively, with supernatural characters, and these are followed by, roughly speaking, two heroic cycles (though it may be more accurate to say one cycle and a prelude). Perhaps, as Quinn has suggested, the mythological poems are not integrated into a narrative in the same way because the nature of mythological time would not allow them to be linked together into a single narrative sequence (1990a: 101).

Neither division into mythological and heroic poems or by protagonist is seamless, and exceptions may immediately be noted. These include, for instance, the interference of Óðinn and the prominence of the quasi-divine valkyries in both of the heroic cycles, and the appearance of human characters in the poems *Grímnismál* and *Vǫlundarkviða*. In addition, the organisation of the mythological poems by protagonist only seems to work to a limited degree. The most unified sequence comes at the beginning of the codex with the classic Odinic wisdom poems – *Hávamál, Grímnismál,* and *Vafþrúðnismál* – which occur in sequence after *Vǫluspá.* The connection here is obvious, as *Vǫluspá* too is presented as an Óðinn-instigated revelation of mythological lore. There are other important connections to be made, however, as the sometimes baffling organisation of the remaining mythological poems demonstrates.

The basic split between mythological and heroic is reinforced by the fragmentary anthology AM 748 I a 4°, dated to the early fourteenth century. It contains six complete texts: *Hárbarðsljóð, Baldrs draumar, Skírnismál, Vafþrúðnismál, Grímnismál, Hymiskviða,* and a fragment of the prose introduction to *Vǫlundarkviða.* All of these poems belong to the mythological type and the manuscript arrangement shares some similarities with the Codex Regius. *Grímnismál* and *Vafþrúðnismál,* for example, are also copied side by side in AM 748 I a 4°, albeit in reverse order. The identity of the protagonist is not a guiding criterion, however. Form appears to be privileged above it, as the three *ljóðaháttr* dialogue poems with *mál* titles are clustered together. The collection also associates *Vǫlundarkviða* with mythological poetry, despite formal and stylistic as well as thematic affiliations with the heroic poems.[11]

The mythological/heroic division has been followed by modern surveys, such as the major German *Edda Kommentar* series, which is broken down into volumes on *Götterlieder* and *Heldenlieder;* Ursula Dronke's edition and commentary volumes (Dronke 1969, 1997, 2011), which are likewise split along heroic and mythological lines; and, most recently, the arrangement of the *Íslenzk fornrit* edition of the *Eddukvæði* into two volumes (Jónas Kristjánsson and Vésteinn Ólason 2014). In general, the subject matter of these poems supports a cleavage into (more or less chronological) narrative sequences tracing the downfall of famous Migration Age heroic dynasties, as well as a looser grouping of poems on supernatural beings within which smaller clusters are apparent, and it would be unhelpful to imply that this is flawed or invalid. What should be noted, however, is that it is not the only way one can consider the eddic poems. If one looks beyond the immediate subject matter and (to some extent) the manuscript titles of these poems, there are features which align them into different groups, often spanning the divide between mythological and heroic.

Alternative categories

To some extent, the mythological/heroic divide is reinforced by the preponderance of titles in -*mál* and -*kviða* respectively in the two sections of the Codex Regius. There is a rough correspondence between the poems with titles in -*mál* and dialogues in *ljóðaháttr*, and those in -*kviða* and heroic narratives composed in *fornyrðislag*. Still, there are notable exceptions to even this general rule. *Bjarkamál in fornu*, as it survives, is composed in *málaháttr*. *Hamðismál* is composed almost completely in *fornyrðislag* and is heroic and narrative in character. This is unlikely to be a mistake as the prose conclusion to the poem offers a second version of the title, also using *mál*: *Hamðismál in fornu*. For the most part, however, the range of poems described as *mál* includes a variety of content cast as either monologue or dialogue. *Hávamál* is a catalogue of advice and numinous lore; *Eiríksmál* is a memorial poem for King Eiríkr blóðøx ('bloodaxe'), part of the larger genre of *erfikvæði*, relating the welcome he receives into Valhǫll; and *Vafþrúðnismál* is a wisdom contest revealing valuable mythological information. Yet, for all that the speech-act takes centre-stage in these poems, the dialogue is also used quite effectively to convey narrative. *Fáfnismál* and *Reginsmál* link episodes within the Sigurðr narrative by bringing together groups of related short dialogues of varying types and metres joined together by short passages in prose. A less disjointed narrative is related by *Skírnismál* (titled *Fǫr Skírnis* (*Skírnir's Journey*) in the Codex Regius). Conversely, the poems with titles in *kviða* do not necessarily contain much more extended narratives, and direct speech is often also the main vehicle for carrying them forward or relating events by reflecting on them retrospectively (see further Schorn on style, Chapter 14 in this Handbook). Some of them are as focused on a central speech-act as the *mál*: three separate poems revolve around the speech of Guðrún as she expresses grief and defends herself against a false accusation. The two most common title elements, *mál* and *kviða*, thus correspond more closely with form than content.

As mentioned above, some of the less frequently attested title elements seem to indicate more specific types of speech-act. Some of the most straightforward are the poems of prophecy called *spá* ('prophecy') and the *senna* ('insult exchange'). The content of the *spá* poems is not unlike that of *Grímnismál* and *Vafþrúðnismál*. *Vǫluspá*, for instance, has some parallels with the theme and content of the poems that follow it in Codex Regius, which have probably led the compiler of the manuscript to order the poems as he has. The poem deals with Óðinn's quest for knowledge, which provides the narrative impetus as well as a context for the revelation of important mythological information. Yet the form of the poem, along with the identity of the speaker, suggests the distinctiveness of the *spá* genre from wisdom poetry and aligns it more strongly with other narrative poems, as the information is presented in chains of narrative and the poem is consequently composed in *fornyrðislag* (Quinn 2002: 255–6). The poem *Grípisspá* similarly serves as a narrative summary of the various events of Sigurðr's life, providing a framework within which to read the poems that follow. The relative antiquity of the poem has often been called into question, and it has even been argued that *Grípisspá* was composed for the manuscript (see further Harris, Chapter 2 in this Handbook).

The *sennur*, in contrast, find their closest parallels among the other mythological poems of the Codex Regius, though they do not always take place between mythological characters. The term *senna* essentially denotes a specific manifestation of flyting or verbal contest particular to Old Norse, though the defining generic criteria are debated: while there is little doubt that it does refer to some sort of formalised adversarial exchange, it is less clear how rigid and well defined the conventions of the *senna* actually are and whether it should be considered distinct from the related *mannjafnaðr* (see further Harris 1979; Clover 1980; and Bax and Padmos 1993). More than any other type of speech-act in eddic poetry, this form of verbal contest appears to have its roots in actual social practice. There are several uncontested poetic examples, yet it is striking that the genre is only explicitly identified by the title *Lokasenna*. In the case of the Helgi poems, it is likely to be because the *sennur* occur as episodes within a larger narrative. This does not mean that they all originated in the poetic context in which they have been preserved. The exchange between Atli and Hrímgerðr in *Helgakviða Hjǫrvarðssonar*, for instance, is set off by relatively lengthy prose summaries, which are necessary to tie it into the rest of the poem in lieu of a direct plot connection. In other cases, such as *Hyndluljóð*, the *senna* may not have a separate origin, but may simply be subjugated to the dominant mode of the poem (see Quinn 2002: 262–9). *Hárbarðsljóð* is the most difficult poem to account for, as it contains some features that are otherwise unparalleled. The poem has been alternatively considered a *senna*, a *mannjafnaðr*, or a combination of the two forms (Clover 1979; Bax and Padmos 1983). The metre vacillates wildly. The basic elements that link it to the other *sennur*, though perhaps used to varying effect in *Hárbarðsljóð*, also have parallels among the exchanges in the *mál* poems. The exchange of names, for instance, is very common and occurs in *Vafþrúðnismál* (sts 7–8), *Baldrs draumar* (sts 5–6), and at the start of *Fáfnismál* (sts 1–4). The flyting form could thus be deployed for various purposes and in this instance it seems to be content rather than form that titles privilege in distinguishing certain eddic poems from others most closely related to them in style and structure.

There is, however, an important caveat. All of this relies on the assumption that the titles as assigned in the Codex Regius and elsewhere reflect something of the poems' earlier tradition. The titles are, after all, only preserved in thirteenth- and fourteenth-century manuscripts – although the use of similar titles in multiple manuscripts suggests that the tradition goes back at least a little beyond the surviving generations of manuscripts (for full discussion, see Quinn 1990a). There are also other signs of links between speech-acts and eddic verse. The sheer quantity of direct speech in eddic poetry almost certainly bears witness to its ultimately oral origins. The context of the poems' oral performance – which above all surely dictated their earliest form and purpose – must of course remain a matter of speculation, based on the internal evidence of individual poems and comparative material.

Eddic modes beyond the Codex Regius

The body of eddic verse preserved as *lausavísur* (individually or in short poetic sequences) deployed within other prose genres, or as whole or partial verses in runic inscriptions, demonstrates even more effectively than the material in the Codex Regius and AM 748 I a 4° how the generic boundaries of eddic poetics are better conceived of as flexible modes encompassing a wide variety of functions. Specific medieval titles are rarely appended to these verses, but the context (frequently prosimetrical) is often instructive.

In *Ketils saga hœngs* (*The Saga of Ketill Salmon*), stanzas of eddic verse are attributed not only to the eponymous hero, but also to his trollish supporter Böðmóðr, a magical Finnish king and his brother, an ogress, and a heathen king in several short sequences of dialogue. In each case, the motivation for the shift into verse and between verse types reflects the rhetorical positioning of the speakers as they negotiate encounters with strange interlocutors. In one of these scenes, Ketill encounters the Finnish king Gusi. Ketill opens the dialogue, commanding an unusual *seggr* ('man') to identify himself in a half stanza of *fornyrðislag*:

> Skríð þú af kjálka, kyrr þú hreina,
> seggr síðförull, seg, hvat þú heitir. (*FS* II, 160)

> [Slide down from the sledge, calm the reindeer, late-travelling man, say, what you are called.][12]

His description of the other man serves as a warning that he has a pretty good idea of who he might be dealing with, but is not openly confrontational, much like his initial meeting with Brúni earlier in the saga. Gusi then displays the rhetorical skill required in poetic dialogues to answer in kind:

> Gusi kalla mik göfgir Finnar.
> Em ek oddviti allrar þjóðar. (*FS* II, 160)

> [Noble Finns call me Gusi. I am the leader of the whole people.]

He then raises the stakes with a shift into *ljóðaháttr*, casting his reciprocal questioning as an open challenge:

> Hvat er þat manna, er mér í móti ferr,
>   ok skríðr sem vargr af viði?
> Æðru skaltu mæla, ef þú undan kemsk,
>   þrysvar í Þrumfirði.
>
> Því tel ek þik ósnjallan. (*FS* II, 161)

> [What sort of man is that, who comes towards me and glides like a wolf from the woods? You will express fear, if you escape, three times into Þrumfjǫrðr. Thus I count you cowardly.]

The last three lines have been taken by most editors (including Heusler and Ranisch 1903: 104 and Guðni Jónsson) as a regular half stanza of *ljóðaháttr*, and the sentence following (still in direct speech) as part of the prose. In her forthcoming edition of these verses, Beatrice la Farge (forthcoming b) argues for including the final sentence as a line of verse, and reading the stanza as a half stanza of *ljóðaháttr* followed by two long lines of *fornyrðislag*:

> Æðru skaltu mæla, ef þú undan kemsk,
>   þrysvar fyr Þrumu;[13] því tel ek þik ósnjallan. (*SkP*, Gusi Lv 2[VIII])

This reading is preferable to requiring a shift into prose at this point and a rather unnatural break in the syntax, and there are precedents for this type of construction (see Schorn on style, Chapter 14 in this Handbook). It would also be in keeping with the characterisation of Gusi throughout the scene, as he tries out various rhetorical postures only to abandon them for base threats when Ketill does not engage with him. Ketill again changes the register – or perhaps picks up Gusi's change in register – refusing to take part in the sort of battle of words he is trying to initiate. Gusi is no more of a match for him intellectually than he is physically, and Ketill readily supplies his nickname along with plenty of clues to his identity, unlike (for example) Sigurðr's mysterious equivocation when questioned by the dying Fáfnir (*Fm* sts 1–4).

> Hængr ek heiti, kominn ór Hrafnistu,
> hefnir Hallbjarnar. Hví skríðr þú svá, inn armi?
> Friðmálum mæla munk-at ek við Finn ragan,
> heldr mun ek benda boga, þann mér Brúni gaf. (*FS* II, 161)

> [I am called Hængr, come from Hrafnista, avenger of Hallbjörn. Why do you glide so, wretched one? I will not speak peaceful words to a cowardly Finn, rather I will bend my bow, the one Brúni gave me.]

Gusi tries again to change register, with a stanza of solemn *fornyrðislag*, in order to avert his demise (now that the prose confirms he has recognised who he is facing) and to present the two as heroes on equal terms.

> Hverr er á öndrum öndverðan dag,
> gjarn til gunnar í grimmum hug?
> Vit skulum freista flein at rjóða
> hvárr at öðrum, nema hugr bili. (*FS* II, 161)

> [Who is that on snowshoes early in the day, eager for battle in a wrathful mood? We two should try to redden the arrow, each on the other, unless courage should fail.]

Ketill parries easily, once again using a clever reference to his nickname (received from another man who underestimated him) to mock Gusi for presuming to face him in combat and to cast himself into a heroic role.

> Hæng kalla mik hálfu nafni.
> Mun ek veita þér viðnám héðan.
> Skaltu víst vita, áðr vit skiljum,
> at búkörlum bíta örvar. (*FS* II, 162)

> [They call me Hængr as half of my name. I will give you resistance here. You shall certainly know, before we two part, that arrows bite farmers.]

At this point Gusi has run out of rhetorical ammunition and in his desperation flings open threats at Ketill, which of course prove as ineffectual as his arrows. The action of the battle plays out in a brief prose passage, but Ketill is allowed one further verse at the climax to express his triumph over the now silent Gusi, whose inferiority is now borne out:

> Feigr er nú, Finnr inn ragi,
> at hann fóttrøðr flein sinn rangan. (*FS* II, 164)

> [He is doomed now, the cowardly Finn, that he treads underfoot his own crooked arrow.]

For the plot of the saga, the significance of this episode lies in Ketill's acquisition of the sword and magic arrowheads, and the establishment of his heroic credentials. Gusi's ill-fated challenge contrasts with his more perceptive brother Brúni's immediate recognition of Ketill's superiority and pragmatic decision to subjugate himself to him – a pattern repeated later in the saga with Böðmóðr and Framarr. The poet exploits the scene for full dramatic effect by replacing narrative with dialogue. The outcome of the confrontation is determined less by what the characters do than by who they are, revealed through their deployment of various eddic modes, and through this episode the character of Ketill is further revealed to the audience. In broad terms, the strategy is a familiar one from the poems of the two principal eddic anthology manuscripts. *Vafþrúðnismál*, for instance, contains similar rhetorical shifts and is resolved with the giant's realisation of the identity of his interlocutor and the futility of a wisdom contest with Óðinn (*Vm* 55). This is not a poem, however, but a sequence of verses embedded in saga prosimetrum, and it is a matter of speculation whether they were composed for the saga or quoted from a pre-existing composition.[14] Ketill's final half stanza perhaps indicates that the battle action could have been entirely conveyed through the dialogue. If the saga author is excerpting stanzas from a longer poetic sequence, the focus of his quotation is on the formulaic challenging of an unknown newcomer. Such exchanges occur frequently in eddic poetry (with a number of innovative variations), but in the prosimetrum of the *fornaldarsögur* they play a more prominent role, concisely and effectively illuminating characters and their relationships.

Verses quoted in the *fornaldarsögur* also provide important evidence of and insight into less well-attested modes in eddic verse, such as riddles, curses, and love poetry. A particularly curious example of the latter occurs in *Áns saga bogsveigis* (*The Saga of Án Bowbender*). Early in the saga, an unusual eddic stanza is quoted, attributed to Án at the beginning of an expedition with the king. It appears to be an instance of repurposing existing material to fit the needs of the saga, as the verse is rather jarring in context – perhaps deliberately so. Án is accompanying his brother Þórir and the verse is a warning to him, based on his mistrust of King Ingjaldr, although in this instance his prescience borders on the prophetic.

Vel þér, selja,
stendr þú sævi nær
laufguð harðla vel;
maðr skekr af þér
morgindöggvar,
en ek at Þegni
þrey nátt sem dag. (*FS* II, 378)

[It is well for you, willow, you stand near the sea rather well leafed; a man shakes morning dew from you, but I yearn for (the) Þegn/þegn night and day.]

It has long been recognised by scholars that this verse is unlikely to have been composed for the scene in which the saga presents it. Heusler and Ranisch declared it certainly could not be the words of 'der bäuerliche Held Án' ('the peasant hero Án', 1903: lxxxvii). The *selja* ('willow') to which it is addressed is not mentioned in the prose; in context we are presumably meant to identify it with the harbour mark which has just been raised, the occasion on which the verse is pronounced. The actual subject seems to be a woman's love for a man: an ideal natural image is contrasted with the speaker's own longing for a *þegn*, day and night. The verb is *þreyja*, a word used most often in Old Norse poetry to refer to longing in this sense by male and female characters alike. It occurs elsewhere in eddic poetry in similar formulations. Hyndla mocks Freyja for her pursuit of her husband, *ey þreyjandi* ('always desiring', *Hdl* 47/1–2). Freyr complains impatiently about the wait for Gerðr with the words: 'long is one night, long are two, how shall I suffer (*þreyjak*) through three?' (*Skm* 42/1–3). *Vǫlundarkviða* plays on this expected use to convey the strangeness of the swan maidens.

Ein nam þeira Egil at verja,
fǫgr mær fira, faðmi ljósum;
ǫnnur var Svanhvít, svanfjaðrar dró;
enn in þriðja, þeira systir,
varði hvítan háls Vǫlundar.

Sátu síðan sjau vetr at þat
enn inn átta allan þráðu,
enn inn níunda nauð um skilði;

meyjar fýstusk á myrkvan við
alvitr unga, ørlǫg drýgja. (*Vkv* 2–3)

> [One of them began to enclose Egill in her arms, the fair living girl in bright embrace; another was Swanwhite, she wore swan feathers; and the third, their sister, wound her arms around Vǫlundr's white neck. They stayed thus for seven winters, but all the eighth they suffered anguish, and in the ninth necessity parted them; the girls yearned for the dark wood, the strange, young creatures, to fulfil fate.]

Already in consummated relationships, they are compelled to leave their lovers and return to the forest by the same force of desire that drives others to seek absent ones. Similar uses are evident in skaldic verse.[15]

Mansǫngskvæði,[16] like other verse genres with the potential to be socially or spiritually disruptive, do not survive in great number, and the eddic reflex of this tradition is particularly obscure. Most of what we might consider love verses in surviving eddic poetry is subordinated to another dominant mode. *Skírnismál* includes a sort of love complaint in the opening dialogue between Freyr and Skírnir (sts 4–7), but Freyr's words are addressed to his servant rather than the object of his desire – or to the natural world – and it is Skírnir's negotiation with Gerðr that makes up the bulk of the poem. The potential to manipulate the affections of a woman with poetry is also attested, as Carolyne Larrington has noted,[17] by *Hrókskviða*. The poem is in *fornyrðislag*, as befits the predominant mode of the speech: a narrative account of the hero's achievements, which culminates ultimately in his hopes for his beloved. When the speaker is female, expressions of romantic longing in eddic poetry tend to take the form of elegiac reflection on lost or thwarted love, after the fact. Some of these women manage to avenge the loss of love, but not to gain it as a remedy for present suffering, as Freyr's expression of present tense suffering prompts Skírnir to do on his behalf. The suffering in the stanza quoted above from *Áns saga* is also current, but we cannot tell any more about the situation than that.

For the saga author, the central point appears to be that this is evidently a woman's verse. The men who hear it mistake it as an expression of homosexual longing, prompting more mockery and missing the real warning. Þórir misses the wordplay on *þegn*: a reference both to him and to the name of the sword that will kill him, interpreting the verse as an expression of longing for possession of the weapon. Editors have proposed significant emendations because of the stanza's apparent metrical deficiencies and failure to conform with their expectations of the genre (see, for example, *Skjald* BII, 339 (c.f. AII, 319); Läffler 1912; and Heusler and Ranisch 1903:

104), but this sort of imaginative hypercorrection should be avoided (see Quinn on editing, Chapter 3 in this Handbook). Instead of viewing the stanza as a corruption or misunderstanding by the saga author – who otherwise deploys varying poetic modes so capably – we should question our preconceived notions of the stringent norms that verses should conform to, particularly for a genre we understand so incompletely. The corpus of Norwegian inscriptions in younger runes pertaining to love and sexuality assembled by James Knirk reinforces the impression of the vitality and variety of expressions of love and eroticism in eddic verse and its connections with real-life practice which are more difficult to discern in the manuscript record. The runic inscriptions run the gamut from partially to completely metrical, and in one case mix *ljóðaháttr* and *fornyrðislag*.[18] By displaying the particular cunning of its hero through his skilful deployment of varying poetic modes, *Áns saga* offers us glimpses of unusual verse types and suggests more variety and flexibility in eddic poetics than we might infer from the anthology poems alone.

Concluding case study: *Sigrdrífumál*

Naturally, it is beyond the scope of one chapter to explore all the possible generic permutations within the eddic corpus. Instead, I will take *Sigrdrífumál* as a final example of how looking at an individual poem in detail can stretch a simplistic generic classification of eddic poems to breaking point. By exploring how a few different possible criteria for defining eddic genres, both thematic and formal, play out in a practical case study, we can see how interconnections work on multiple levels, and make provision for many different ways of intellectually situating the same body of texts; we also recognise how the Codex Regius compiler's scheme may continue to limit our appreciation of the full range of eddic modes.

Starting with thematic criteria, we may note that the action in *Sigrdrífumál* takes place, according to the prose introduction, in *Frakkland*, a real (if somewhat vague) geographical setting in the human world (see Brink and Lindow, Chapter 9 in this Handbook). The speaking characters are a *valkyrja*, Sigrdrífa, and the legendary hero Sigurðr Fáfnisbani, fresh from earning his nickname. The cast of characters is somewhat expanded by references to events outside the chronology of the immediate narrative: two kings, Hjálm-Gunnarr and Agnarr, are mentioned, along with Óðinn. For all that his voice is heard only briefly, Sigurðr is the focus of the episode. *Sigrdrífumál* follows *Reginsmál* and *Fáfnismál* in the manuscript, and together they relate the mythological background of the treasure and Sigurðr's instruction by other supernatural characters.[19] The focus of these poems is the human world, but most of the agency rests with non-human characters. In this respect, it is similar to *Grímnismál* – a tale of earthly royal succession determined by successful interaction with the divine – and there are affinities with *Vǫlundarkviða* as well. The difference is one of emphasis: here the protagonist is human. *Grímnismál* is positioned in the Codex Regius (and AM 748 I a 4°) with other Odinic instruction and wisdom contests, although the prose frame makes more of the legendary narrative context than the poem itself and *Vǫlundarkviða* too ends with an image of human suffering rather than divine (or elvish) triumph. By first characterising poems as 'mythological' or 'heroic', we also risk overstating the distance between the human and the divine in Old Norse mythology (Schorn 2013).

Formal and stylistic criteria lead to similarly equivocal conclusions. *Sigrdrífumál*, like *Reginsmál* and *Fáfnismál*, is composed in a mix of verse forms with *ljóðaháttr* being the most common. *Galdralag* and *fornyrðislag* are also used and prose is intercalated into the verse several times. For the most part the use of verse-forms parallels closely what we find elsewhere. The wisdom monologue is in more or less regular *ljóðaháttr*, with occasional use of *galdralag* when the content becomes especially esoteric during the account of the origin of the runic wisdom (sts 13–19). *Galdralag* is also used for emphasis in stanza 25 of the gnomic sequence; this breaks the very regular pattern of six-line *ljóðaháttr* stanzas, opening with a refrain that dwells on the ultimate importance of reputation. In stanza 35 the shift into *galdralag* similarly underlines the frequently recurring Old Norse truism that there can be no trust with the kin of those one has slain.[20] Lines of *fornyrðislag* occur a few times in the first part of the poem along with a list in stanzas 15–17 (not unlike the one in *Hávamál* sts 85–7). The brief opening dialogue (st. 1) is cast in *fornyrðislag*, before Sigrdrífa quickly changes the tone at the start of her monologue in the second stanza. She is interrupted twice more by prose (after sts 3 and 4) and the second of these passages serves to relate an earlier narrative, including four lines of *fornyrðislag* quoted within the prose.

The structure of the poem thus presents numerous interpretive difficulties, though it is more tightly structured than the sequence of dialogues preceding it in *Reginsmál* and *Fáfnismál*. Ostensibly, *Sigrdrífumál* is a dialogue too, yet all but a stanza and a half is spoken by Sigrdrífa. Sigurðr's role is to prompt her speech, first by revealing his identity (since wisdom is not imparted to just anyone in eddic poetry: see Quinn

2010) and then to affirm that he does in fact want her advice, even if he cannot profit from it (sts 1 and 21). He ignores the warning in *Hávamál* (sts 54–6), as does Óðinn himself, that too much wisdom and knowledge of one's fate only leads to unhappiness. In context, this instruction scene is part of the story of Sigurðr's education, begun by *Grípisspá*, and establishes his heroic credentials. The speech itself, which makes up the content of the poem, is more important in thematic than narrative terms and so the poem functions on two levels: the valkyrie instructs both Sigurðr within the poem and the real human audience outside it, who also may profit from her common-sense social advice and arcane runic lore. In this respect it is very like *Hávamál*. There are hints of another narrative context, though, from which her monologue may have been extracted and repurposed. Whatever the story of Sigrdrífa, Hjálm-Gunnarr, and Agnarr might originally have been, the information that the compiler gives us (between sts 4 and 5) is enough to reconstruct a familiar basic story type and to give Sigurðr's valkyrie the pedigree if not the name we might expect.

All of the eddic wisdom poems have more or less developed narrative frames which, like the *sennur*, play out almost entirely through direct speech, occasionally supplemented by (often redundant) prose narrative and, in a couple of problematic cases, by third-person narrative verse. The avoidance of the latter in a number of poems suggests, as Terry Gunnell (1995) has demonstrated, a difference in performance. Heinz Klingenberg (1983) noted the subordinate role of narrative in mythological poetry and suggested that it could be subdivided into a dominant, enumerative type and a continuous-narrative type which has greater affinities with the heroic poems, although still showing the influence of the enumerative type. In practice, however, it is difficult to maintain hard and fast distinctions between narrative and enumerative poetry. The prose frame of *Lokasenna*, for example, suggests that it relates a crucial narrative episode within the larger story of the destruction of the gods, but the verse itself presents a catalogue. It is only in the context of the prose and in the sequence of poems in the Codex Regius that the role of the poem as a narrative in its own right is stressed. The situational nature of eddic dialogues lends itself to narrative expansion.

Sigrdrífumál does not strictly conform to any single ethnic or analytic genre as we commonly define them. Its location in the Codex Regius reflects some but not all possible narrative and thematic associations. Despite its placement within the heroic portion of the codex, in theme and style it relates most closely to mythological wisdom poetry. It does not sit entirely comfortably in the Sigurðr/Brynhildr/Guðrún love triangle and may have been stitched somewhat awkwardly into a portmanteau epic narrative. Whether such extended narratives were ever expressed in eddic verse is debatable (Lönnroth 1971). The use of largely dialogic eddic poetry in saga narrative seems to have further exacerbated a tendency already present for narrative verse to be converted to prose or employed for the dialogue of legendary characters wherever possible. In the Codex Regius, where verse is still primary, the opposite seems to happen. Prose is used to expand and link the minimal narrative frames of potentially unconnected poems to create extended narratives. The propensity of the *fornaldursögur* to preserve dialogic verse may lead to a differential preservation of dialogue as opposed to narrative verses and thus distort our view of what eddic verse is used to express. Saga authors quote verses in sequences perhaps reconstructed to fit very particular prose narrative contexts, which may or may not have been sections of complete poems of the types found in the anthologies. It is the flexibility inherent in eddic poetics itself that allows them to do so. The possibility of mixing forms and recontextualising compositional units to achieve varying aims at both oral and written stages of transmission appears to have been not only acceptable, but an integral element of the tradition. The elusiveness of eddic genres is thus much more of a strength than a weakness. It lies at the heart of what has made eddic compositions both attractive and challenging to audiences since the Viking Age. Poets could exploit the varied associations of form, content, and setting in a seemingly endless range of ways. A significant part of their artistry lay in the subtle manipulation of loose generic expectations: bending the rules (such as they were) was the eddic poet's stock in trade.

Notes

1. Helpful discussions of the scholarly delineation of eddic and skaldic poetry can be found in *SkP* I, xiii–xviii; Clunies Ross 2005: 21–8; Fidjestøl 1997b; and Jónas Kristjánsson and Vésteinn Ólason 2014: I, 5–16.
2. For a full discussion of eddic metres, see Fulk, Chapter 13 in this Handbook.
3. There are other criteria as well. For a full discussion of skaldic verse types, see Gade 2012.
4. This particularly productive and long-lived genre is attested in a range of metrical forms. For discussion and further references see Harris 2006 and Thorvaldsen 2006.
5. Literally 'Horn-cleaver'? See Marold 2012 on the difficulties of translating this nickname.

6. There are over two thousand stanzas or fragments of eddic verse preserved in more than fifty sagas, learned treatises, and anthology manuscripts, and the number rises if poetry in *kviðuháttr* is included. Stanzas in skaldic metres number perhaps twice as many, and are preserved in as wide a range of prosimetric contexts.

7. Such titles that appear in medieval manuscripts include *Hávamál, Vafþrúðnismál, Grímnismál, Hárbarðsljóð, Lokasenna, Þrymskviða, Alvíssmál, Vǫlsungakviða, Guðrúnarkviða, Kviða Guðrúnar, Guðrúnarhvǫt, Hamðismál, Skírnis mál, Hymiskviða, Vǫluspá, Helgakviða, Guðrúnarrœða, Káruljóð, Grottasǫngr, Heimdalargaldr, Alsvinnzmál,* and *Sigurðarkviða* (Quinn 1990a: 112–15).

8. On the composition of these poems, see further Ralph 1972; Harris 1983; and the note on *Hávamál* in my chapter on style in this Handbook (Chapter 14).

9. For the most complete analysis of the aims and methods of the Codex Regius compiler, see Vésteinn Ólason 2010 and Jónas Kristjánsson and Vésteinn Ólason 2014.

10. High-quality digital images of the manuscript are available at http://handrit.is /en/.

11. Scholarly views on the origins of *Vǫlundarkviða* are examined by Harris in Chapter 2 of this Handbook.

12. Translation of verses from *Ketils saga hœngs* and *Áns saga bogsveigis* are my own.

13. On manuscript variants and the interpretation of this place name, see La Farge forthcoming b.

14. On the difficulties involved with reconstruction of original poems from *lausavísur* and exerpted stanzas, see Poole 1991.

15. See Sveinbjörn Egilsson and Finnur Jónsson (1931: *s.v.*).

16. For full discussion of the genre and the meaning of the term 'mansǫngr', see Marold 2007.

17. In a paper entitled 'Eddic emotion and eddic audiences', delivered at the Sixteenth International Saga Conference in Zürich in August 2015.

18. Knirk presented this corpus in his paper 'Expressions of love and eroticism in Norwegian inscriptions with the younger runes' at the Sixteenth International Saga Conference in Zürich in August 2015. See further Liestøl 1965, Naumann 1998, and Marold 1998 (on skaldic).

19. All three titles are modern; large initials mark the beginning of *Reginsmál* after *Grípisspá* and the beginning of the verse of *Fáfnismál* in the Codex Regius, but no titles are given (28v and 30r).

20. Because the lacuna in the Codex Regius begins after the second line of stanza 29, the remainder of the poem is reconstructed from paper manuscripts.

CHAPTER 13

Eddic metres

R. D. Fulk

Definitions and metrical properties

The corpus of eddic poetry is most readily defined on the basis of poetic metre: poems composed in the metres employed in the Codex Regius may be classified as eddic, setting them apart from poems in skaldic metres and *rímur*. This means that in addition to the poems in the Codex Regius, a number of other compositions must be regarded as eddic, including *Rígsþula, Grottasǫngr*, and fragments of other poems preserved in *Snorra Edda*, as well as *Baldrs draumar, Hyndluljóð*, and poetic material contained in various *fornaldarsǫgur*. The three poems *Haraldskvæði, Eiríksmál*, and *Hákonarmál* are quasi-exceptions: although they are composed in eddic metres, they are panegyrics (and thus, in that respect, skaldic), and, unlike all other eddic poems, two of them are attributed to known poets (another skaldic trait). Accordingly, they are usually classified with the skaldic corpus, though in acknowledgement of their liminal status they are commonly referred to as 'the eddic praise-poems'.

Three metres are employed in eddic poetry, termed (on the basis of sometimes conflicting medieval sources) *fornyrðislag* ('old story metre'), *ljóðaháttr* ('song metre'), and *málaháttr* ('speech metre').[1] Whereas metres in the modern Germanic languages are isochronous – that is, their patterns are of stressed syllables at regular intervals, producing a rhythmic beat – eddic metres, like all early Germanic alliterative metres, depend upon alliteration and deploy stresses in a fashion that sounds irregular to modern ears, but which is nonetheless highly structured on the basis of a variety of linguistic properties besides stress, as analysed by Eduard Sievers (1893).[2] The most important of these other properties is syllable weight, as counted in morae. A mora is a phonological unit of length equivalent to a short vowel or a simple consonant; diphthongs and long vowels thus comprise two morae. A syllable includes an onset (zero or more consonants preceding the vowel or diphthong contained in the syllable), a peak (the vowel or diphthong at the heart of the syllable), and a coda (zero or more consonants following the peak). For the purpose of metre (and metre alone), it may be said that a syllable is heavy if three or more morae appear between the onset and the beginning of the next peak. Thus, for example, the first syllable of *hlít.a* (where the point marks the syllable boundary), *hleyp.a*, and *send.a* is heavy, whereas that of *haf.a* and *bú.a* is light.[3] The sound *x* after a vowel makes for a heavy syllable, since it stands for two consonants, but inflectional -*r* and -*s* (as in *selr, sels*) do not count as morae. A monosyllabic word such as *søk* may form a full lift (see below) even though, by the account given here, it is light: it is as if the final word boundary acts as another consonant.

Words fall into three categories with respect to lexical stress. (1) Stress-words always bear stress on the initial syllable. These are words of high semantic content, including nouns, adjectives, non-finite verbs (i.e. infinitives and participles), and most adverbs, especially if they are of more than one syllable. (2) Clitics are always unstressed. These are words of low semantic content, generally expressing grammatical and conceptual relations among stress-words. Clitics include prepositions placed before their object, conjunctions, and articles. (3) Between the two categories stand particles: these are words that may or may not be stressed depending on their position in the clause, the way, for instance, the stress on English *is* varies in the sentences *What is this?* (which may even be reduced to *What's this?*) and *Do you know what it is?* Particles include finite verbs, pronouns, and demonstrative adverbs such as *þar* ('there') and *nú* ('now'). Particles may be unstressed if they appear in the first unstressed position in the clause, either alone or with one or more other unstressed words or syllables. Particles of relatively low stress may thus appear either at the beginning of the clause, as with *Þá* and *kømr* in *Þá kømr Hlínar* (xx⏑x; 'Then comes [another sorrow] of Hlín', *Vsp* 53/1),[4] or after a stress-word that begins the clause, as with *ferr* in *Kjóll ferr austan* (⏑x⏑x; 'A ship will come from the east', *Vsp* 51/1). If a particle appears anywhere else in the clause (i.e. if it is 'displaced'), it must be stressed, as with *ferr* in *er Óðinn ferr* (x⏑x⏑; 'when Óðinn will come', *Vsp* 53/3). This principle of stress on particles by position is known as Kuhn's first law (though the formulation given here does not match Kuhn's precisely). A related discovery of Kuhn's is that, aside from auxiliaries, finite verbs in bound clauses (i.e. clauses introduced by a conjunction or an adverb) must be stressed. It will be seen below that among eddic metres Kuhn's findings apply to *fornyrðislag* only.

Different degrees of stress may be distinguished on different syllables within words. The strong stress that falls on the initial syllable of stress-words and displaced particles may be called primary stress (⏑). In true compounds (i.e. compounds in which both constituents might stand alone as stress-words) the stress on the second constituent is subordinated and may be called secondary stress (⊥), as in *gjaf-mildr* (⊥⊥) and *hús-bóndi*. If, however, the first constituent ends in an unstressed syllable following a heavy syllable, there is in most instances no reduction, and the word contains two primary stresses, as in *sendi-maðr* (⊥×⊥, where × represents an unstressed position) and *húsa-bær*. There may be reduction to secondary stress likewise in non-compounds when two primary stresses are contiguous in a verse, as in *sígr fold í mar* (⊥⊥×⊥; 'the earth sinks into the sea', *Vsp* 57/2). The second constituents of quasi-compounds (i.e. compounds in which one or both constituents might not stand alone as a stress-word) do not receive metrical stress if they are uninflected, but they gain a stress if an inflectional syllable is added; hence, *buðlungr* (⊥×) as opposed to *buðlungi* (⊥⊥×). As in Old English, compound personal names usually behave like quasi-compounds, but not consistently.[5] All inflectional syllables are unstressed.

The metrical elements that constitute a verse are lifts (⊥, with primary stress), half-lifts (⊥, with secondary stress), and drops (×, also called dips). So far, every lift and half-lift examined has been a heavy syllable, but light syllables may appear under certain conditions. Under the principle of resolution, a light syllable followed by another syllable may serve as the equivalent of a lift, as in *halir* (⌣⌣) and *megindóma* (⌣⌣⊥×). In *fornyrðislag* resolution is usually confined to the first lift of the verse (there are several exceptions in, e.g., *Vǫlundarkviða*); elsewhere an unresolved light syllable may serve as a half-lift, as in *Hornbori* (⊥⌣×); in some verse types it may serve as a lift if it immediately follows an unresolved lift, as in the verse *við aldrnara* (×⊥⌣×; 'in fire', *Vsp* 57/6); and there may be a light lift even after a half-lift, as in *hórdómr mikill* (⊥⊥⌣×; 'great adultery', *Vsp* 45/6). The first drop in a verse may contain more than one syllable, but rarely more than two, as in *fjǫlð veit hon fræða* (⊥××⊥×; 'she knows a great deal of lore', *Vsp* 44/5; 49/5; 58/5) and *munu halir allir* (××⌣⊥×; 'all men will', *Vsp* 56/7); drops of more than one syllable elsewhere in the verse are exceedingly rare. Sievers would reduce many two-syllable drops to one by means of elision when two unstressed vowels are adjacent, as in *meiri ok minni* ('more and less', *Vsp* 1/3; ⊥××|⊥× reduced to ⊥×|⊥× by elision of the vowel of the third syllable; Sievers 1893: 62). Some such reductions are in fact indicated in the manuscripts, e.g. *ro* for *ero* (which appears in some manuscripts) in *æsir ro á þingi* ('the Æsir are in council', *Vsp* 48/4).

Sievers's classification of fornyrðislag verse

In modern editions, verses in *fornyrðislag*, the commonest eddic metre and the one that most closely resembles alliterative metres in Old English, Old Saxon, and Old High German, are arranged in pairs, each pair forming a line. Lines, moreover, are arranged in stanzas, usually of four, with a major syntactic division at the end of the second line, so that each stanza comprises two half-stanzas. Although four is the normal number of lines, there is some variability: for example, of the sixty-six stanzas of *Vǫluspá* in Neckel's edition, fifty are of four lines, the remainder varying in length from two to seven. Each pair of verses is linked by alliteration, which falls on the most heavily stressed elements. The alliterating sound is called a stave. A typical pattern of alliteration is the following, where the alliterating staves are underscored:

> Þá frá ek sennu   slíðrfengligsta,
> trauð mál, talið   af trega stórum,
> er harðhuguð   hvatti at vígi
> grimmum orðum   Guðrún sonu. (*Ghv* 1)

[Then I heard the most fearsome mockery, averse talk, spoken out of immense grief, when with fierce words hard-hearted Guðrún egged on her sons to killing.]

In odd verses (also called on-verses) there may be either one or two alliterating staves, but if there is just one it must not be preceded in the verse by a non-alliterating syllable bearing primary stress. In even verses (off-verses) the first syllable bearing primary stress must alliterate, and no other alliteration is allowed in the verse. A consonant alliterates only with an identical consonant, and the clusters *sk*, *sp*, and *st* alliterate only with an identical cluster. A vowel alliterates with any other vowel, and certain words beginning with *j* alliterate with vowels because they originally began with vowels, e.g. *jǫtunn* ('giant'), which derives from **etunaz*.

Most students of eddic metres accept some version of the analysis of *fornyrðislag* devised by Eduard Sievers. The fundamental principle is that each verse comprises four metrical positions, each position filled by a lift, a half-lift, or a drop. Sievers divided each verse into two feet, and although there is scholarly disagreement about whether the foot is a necessary concept, those learning to scan generally find it useful. A foot may comprise two positions and thus be either trochaic ($\acute{}x$) or iambic ($x\acute{}$), or a foot may comprise either one position ($\acute{}$) or three ($\acute{}\acute{}x$). When these feet are combined to form verses, the requirement of four positions per verse produces just five possible stress patterns, labelled A through E in order of descending frequency in Old English verse:

A: ´×|´×, e.g. *gullnar tǫflur* ('golden game-pieces'), *festr mun slitna* ('his rope will break')

B: ×´|×´, e.g. *mun Óðins sonr* ('Óðinn's son will'), *ok um ragnarǫk* ('and about the end of the world')

C: ×´|´×, e.g. *á rǫkstóla* ('to seats of judgement'), *á Ókólni* ('at Ókólnir')

D: ´|´`×, e.g. *kván frjá sína* ('to love his wife'), *grund, valkyrjur* ('the earth', 'valkyries')

E: ´`×|´, e.g. *ginnheilǫg goð* ('most holy gods'), *Þórr einn þar vá* ('Þórr alone fought there')

These are the most abstract representations of the patterns, since there may be substitutions like those mentioned above, such as expanded drops (´××|´×, type A, e.g. *bǫls mun alls batna* ('will remedy every ill')), resolution (×⌣⌣|×´, type B, e.g. *nú hefi ek hefnt* ('now I have avenged')), or a light lift or half-lift (×´|◡×, type C, e.g. *sleit vargr vera* ('the wolf tore apart men'), or ´|´◡×, type D, e.g. *snót svinnhuguð* ('wise woman')).

Some further variants of these five types occur, and it is useful to be able to distinguish them and to assign them to subcategories:

Type A. The basic type is ´×|´×. The subtypes are these:

A1. All the verses of type A examined so far are of this type. The first lift may be resolved, and the first drop may be expanded. Examples: *ár um borna* (´×|´×; 'born long ago'), *níu man ek heima* (⌣⌣××|´×; 'I know of nine worlds').

A2. One or both of the drops is filled by a half-lift. If it is the first, the type is A2a, the second, A2b; if both drops are thus filled, A2ab. Examples: *mjǫtvið mæran* (´`|´×, A2a; 'splendid tree of fate'), *mjór ok mjǫk fagr* (´×|´`, A2b; 'slender and very pretty'), *skeggǫld, skálmǫld* (´`|´`, A2ab; 'age of axes', 'age of swords'). These types are generally confined to odd verses. A further subtype resembles A2a but has a light second lift, a deviation that appears to be licensed by the stress or weight of the preceding syllable, as in *einnættr vega* (´`|◡×; 'at one night old to avenge'). This type is called A2k (k = *kurz* ('short')) and is confined to even verses. Types A2a, A2b, and A2ab are collectively called A2l (l = *lang*).

A3. There is no alliterating lift in the first foot, e.g. *ek sá Baldri* (××|´×; 'I saw for Baldr'), *þaðan koma dǫggvar* (××××|´×; 'from there come dews'), and *er þú kveðr ver minn* (×××|´`; 'when you say my husband'). The type is infrequent in even verses. Sievers, followed by some others, was of the opinion that stress should be assigned to one of the syllables of the first foot even if it does not alliterate. There is no consensus about the issue: see footnote 4.

Type B. The basic type is x⌐|x⌐. Subtypes:

B1. The second drop contains one syllable, as in *hann sjaldan sitr* (x⌐|x⌐; 'he seldom sits') and *þeir er hǫrg ok hof* (xx⌐|x⌐; 'they who altar and temple').

B2. The second drop contains two syllables, as in *sá hon vítt ok um vítt* (xx⌐|xx⌐; 'she saw far and wide'). The type is uncommon.

B3. The first foot contains no alliterating lift, as in *Þó hann æva hendr* (xxxx⌐; 'he never washed his hands') and probably *Þá kvað þat Loki* ('Then Loki said this'; xxx◡◡, if not xxx◡x; cf. *Þá kvað þat Þórr*). The few examples of the type, all confined to odd verses, are thought by many to be due to textual corruption or to some other cause (see, e.g., Suzuki 2014: 82–3).

Type C. The basic type is x⌐|⌐x. Subtypes:

C1. The first lift is not a resolved lift. Examples are *en gras hvergi* (x⌐|⌐x; 'but vegetation nowhere') and *þar var Mótsognir* (xx⌐|⌐x; 'Móðsognir was there').

C2. The first lift is resolved. Examples are *né svalar unnir* (x◡◡|⌐x; 'nor cool waves') and *þat er Ymir byggði* (xx◡◡|⌐x; 'when Ymir lived').

C3. The second lift is light. Examples are *fyr mold neðan* (x⌐|◡x; 'beneath the ground') and *þá var grund gróin* (xx⌐|◡x; 'when the ground was overgrown'). A light lift or half-lift is not permissible after a resolved lift (i.e. no *x◡◡|◡x).

Type D. The basic type is ⌐|⌐⌐x. Subtypes:

D1. The half-lift is long and stands in third position, as in *grund, valkyrjur* (⌐|⌐⌐x; 'earth', 'valkyries') and *vá Valhallar* (⌐|⌐⌐x; 'the calamity of Valhǫll').

D2. The half-lift is in third position and is light, as in *Baldrs andskota* (⌐|⌐◡x; 'Baldr's adversary') and *mǫgu Heimdalar* (◡◡|⌐◡x; 'Heimdallr's sons').

D3. The second lift is light and the half-lift heavy, as in *lítt megandi* (⌐|◡⌐x; 'feeble') and *margs vitandi* (⌐|◡⌐x; 'knowing much'). The type is rare: see Kuhn (1939).

D4. There is inversion in the third and fourth positions, so that a half-lift ends the verse, as in *Baldrs bróðir var* (⌐|⌐x⌐; 'Baldr's brother was'), *rýðr ragna sjǫt* (⌐|⌐x⌐; 'reddens the abode of the gods'), and *Haraldr hilditǫnn* (◡◡|⌐x⌐; 'Haraldr War-Tooth'). In odd verses the type is usually distinguishable from type E on the basis of alliteration.

In type D an extra drop may appear at the end of the first foot, creating what appears to be a five-position verse. The type is called expanded D (D*). The expansion is not possible in type D3, since the first lift of the second foot must follow a heavy lift to be light, but the other three types are represented:

D*1. Examples: *gap var ginnunga* (⌐x|⌐⌐x; 'there was a gaping void'), *áss er stolinn hamri* (⌐x|◡◡⌐x; 'the god has been robbed of his hammer').

D*2. Examples: *Snemma kallaði* (⌣×|⌣⌣×; 'soon called'), *lifðu heill, konungr!* (⌣×|⌣⌣×; 'be well, king!'), *Þrymr hefir þinn hamar* (⌣××|⌣⌣×; 'Þrymr has your hammer'; cf. *ef ek minn hamar* (××⌣|⌣×; 'if I [find] my hammer')).

D*4. Examples: *søkkstu, gýgjar kyn!* (⌣×|⌣×⌣; 'sink, ogress's kin!'), *segðu, Grípir, þat!* (⌣×|⌣×⌣; 'tell, Grípir!').

Type E. The basic type is ⌣⌣×|⌣. There are no numbered subtypes. Resolution is permissible on the first lift, though the type is rare. Examples are *langniðja tal* (⌣⌣×|⌣; 'series of male descendants'), *norðr horfa dyrr* (⌣⌣×|⌣; 'its doors face north'), *Mælt hafða ek þat* (⌣⌣××|⌣; 'I had said it'), *sneru upp við tré* (⌣⌣⌣×|⌣; 'hoisted up on the mast'), *gørask slíkt, ef skal* (⌣⌣⌣×|⌣; 'such happen if it must'), and *kominn væri nú* (⌣⌣⌣×|⌣; 'would have come by now'). Although the type with a light half-lift might be expected to occur – it is found, e.g., in Old English, though rarely – it does not occur in *fornyrðislag* (cf. *Geirrøðar sonr* (⌣⌣×|⌣; 'Geirrøðr's son'), in *ljóðaháttr*). Perhaps the reason is that the pattern already occurs, but with an extra syllable, in type A, e.g. *Gunnari til handa* ('into the possession of Gunnarr'), where the second syllable must belong to the drop (⌣×××|⌣×).

In West Germanic verse it is not uncommon to encounter anacrusis, i.e. one or more unstressed syllables prefixed to a verse type that begins with a lift (A, D, E). Anacrusis is uncommon in *fornyrðislag* and can usually be attributed to imperfect transmission of the text, since the older poets are sparing of unnecessary function words in skaldic and Old English verse, and eddic poets would presumably have composed in a similar fashion. It is plain from the evidence of skaldic verse, for instance, that many unstressed words that were never intended by the poets have been introduced to texts, as discussed below. Eddic examples of anacrusis are confined to type A: *né brúði minni* (×||⌣×|⌣×; 'nor my bride'), *enn ókátr Níðuðr* (×||⌣×|⌣×; 'but gloomy Níðuðr'), *er máls kveðr Grípi* (×||⌣×|⌣×; 'who asks to speak with Grípir').

A fair number of verses comprising just three positions are to be found interspersed among normal verses. In many instances these can be explained as the result of language change, as with *vǫlu velspá* ('a seeress good at prophecy'), for earlier *-spáa*, and *á Gimlé* ('in Gimlé'), for earlier *-léi*. But in others no such explanation is apparent, as with *mistilteinn* ('mistletoe'), *dáðrakkr Þórr* ('valiant Þórr'), and *þrúðugr áss* ('mighty god'). Since these usually end in a stressed syllable, Sievers (1893: 68) regards them as catalectic, i.e. patterned on normal verses but lacking a final, unstressed syllable, these three cited verses, for example, resembling type A without the final drop. Possibly they are formed by analogy to verses such as *vǫlu velspá* and *á Gimlé* in which a final syllable has actually been lost. In favour of this view is the consideration that such verses are particularly common in poems generally thought to be relatively late compositions, such as *Hymiskviða* and *Helgakviða Hundingsbana I.*

Unstressed *um* and *of*, which are interchangeable, standing in front of verbs and sometimes nouns or adjectives, often appear to have no meaning, though they are essential to the metre, as in *yðr um líkr* ('like you') and *of borinn snemma* ('born soon after'). The explanation is that *um/of* replaces prefixes, usually **ga-*, which were lost before c.900, when all pretonic vowels (i.e. those in syllables preceding the stressed syllable) disappeared. On this see Fidjestøl (1999: 207–30), in a most enlightening book that explains the bases for dating eddic poems.

Alternative analyses of fornyrðislag

Sievers's analysis of *fornyrðislag* is not the only one that has been proposed, though most approaches adopt some version of his principles. The most prominent challenge to Sievers's views is the approach of Heusler (1891, 1894, 1925–29), whereby each verse is to be analysed as equivalent to a pair of musical measures in 4/4 time, with each full lift equivalent to a half-note. Each measure begins with a stressed syllable and may include rests; all unstressed syllables at the start of a verse are anacrustic and may be scanned with the preceding measure, if possible. For example, applying Heusler's principles and notation one might scan the opening verses of *Helgakviða Hundingsbana I* thus (where ∧ is a rest and ᴗ a syllable in anacrusis):

Ár var alda, þat er arar gullu,	ǀ˵×∧ǀ˴×ᴗᴗǀǀᵡ×∧∧ǀ˴×∧ǀ
hnigu heilug vǫtn af Himinfjǫllum;	ǀᵡ×∧∧ǀ˴××ᴗǀǀᵡ×∧∧ǀ˴×∧ǀ
þá hafði Helga, inn hugumstóra,	ǀᵡ×∧∧ǀ˵×ᴗǀǀᵡ×∧∧ǀ˵×∧ǀ
Borghildr borit í Brálundi. (*HH I* 1)	ǀ˵ᵡ∧ǀᵡ×∧ᴗǀǀ˵∧∧ǀ˴×∧ǀ

[It was in the early ages, when eagles shrieked, holy waters dropped from the Celestial Mountains; then Borghildr had given birth to Helgi the Great-Minded in Brálundr.]

Although Heusler found many adherents at one time, his method of scansion currently enjoys little favour.[6] It appealed to some scholars no doubt because it is far simpler than Sievers's and is easily comprehended by speakers of modern Germanic languages with traditions of isochronous verse, in which syllable quantity plays no fundamental role. It has been shown, however, that Sievers's approach must be right at least in its basic premises because the principle of resolution is demonstrably real, having survived in some of the earliest isochronous poetry in Icelandic and Middle

English, and if resolution is real, the four-position principle must be correct, since resolution can be explained only on the basis of that principle (see Fulk 2002). Moreover, including anacrustic syllables in the preceding measure renders the concept of a verse beginning with one or more unstressed syllables incomprehensible, and yet it is plain from the discussion in Snorri's *Háttatal* that many skaldic verses (and therefore verses in *fornyrðislag* to which they are structurally similar) must begin with an unstressed syllable.[7]

Unlike Heusler's approach, that of Russom (1998) is compatible in most essentials with Sievers's findings, though not all. Russom's central insight is that the stress pattern of a foot is like that of a word, and the greater the mismatch between the two, the more disfavoured the verse type. This results in different patterns of footing: for example, the verse *né upphiminn* ('nor heaven above'), scanned ×⊥|◡× (type C3) in Sievers's system, must be scanned ×|⊥◡× in Russom's (x/Ssx in his notation) because there are no stressed words in Old Icelandic with an unstressed initial syllable. See further Russom (2009), with many valuable insights not afforded by Sievers's approach.

Eddic poems composed in *fornyrðislag* include *Vǫluspá, Hymiskviða, Þrymskviða, Vǫlundarkviða,* the Helgi poems (excluding *Helgakviða Hjǫrvarðssonar* sts 12–30), *Grípisspá, Brot af Sigurðarkviðu, Guðrúnarkviða I-III, Sigurðarkviða in skamma, Helreið Brynhildar, Oddrúnargrátr, Guðrúnarhvǫt, Baldrs draumar, Rígsþula, Hyndluljóð, Grottasǫngr,* and *Hlǫðskviða,* along with portions of *Reginsmál, Fáfnismál,* and eddic verse found in *Snorra Edda* and the *fornaldarsögur,* as well as brief passages in poems in other metres. The commonest name for a poem in this metre is thus *kviða,* and the metre is most frequently employed in heroic rather than mythological poems. *Fornyrðislag* is also employed in *lausavísur* preserved in various places, and in *Darraðarljóð* in *Njáls saga (The Saga of Njáll),* as well as in some twelfth-century praise-poems.

Ljóðaháttr

A stanza of *ljóðaháttr* most commonly comprises six verses arranged in modern editions in four lines with a major syntactic break after the second line. Odd lines contain a pair of verses linked by alliteration, whereas even lines are lone, somewhat longer verses (so-called full verses), with internal alliteration usually unlinked to any other verse. A typical stanza is the following, in which the alliterating staves are underscored:

E̱lds er þǫrf,   þeims i̱nn er kominn,
    ok á kné̱ ka̱linn;

matar ok váða   er manni þǫrf,
þeim er hefir um fjall farið. (*Háv* 3)

[There is need of a fire for the one who has come in and is chilled to the knee. There is need of food and clothing for a person who has travelled the mountains.]

In the subtype that Snorri calls *galdralag* ('spell metre') (*Háttatal* st. 101), one or the other full verse (or both) is given a mate, often with a degree of parallelism, as in *Hávamál* 1/3–4, where the full verse *um skoðask skyli* ('must be examined') is immediately followed by another, similar full verse, *um skygnask skyli* ('must be looked into').

Alliteration in the odd lines of *ljóðaháttr* is like that found in *fornyrðislag*, but stress patterns are considerably more flexible. Hypometric verses of three positions (e.g. *Ósviðr maðr* ('unwise person')), occasionally even two (*deyr fé* ('livestock die')), are to be found in the on-verse, whereas hypermetric verses of five positions (*nema haldendr eigi*, ××⌣×⌣×; 'unless someone who can hold it owns it') or even six (*kømr heimisgarða til*, ×⌣×⌣×⌣; 'comes to his homestead'), appear often in the off-verse, though there is a general tendency such that one of every pair of verses will scan as a four-position verse. Resolution is freer than in *fornyrðislag*, probably being suspended in an on-verse such as *Vesall maðr* ('wretched person'), and probably occurring after the first lift in a verse such as *sá er æva þegir* ('he who never stops talking'), given how frequently this would produce a four-position verse paired with a three-position one, and given restrictions on the coda of the full verse (see below). Kuhn's first law fails, so that, for example, there is no stress on the verb *deyr* in the verse pair *en orðstírr deyr aldregi* ('but renown never dies'). Neither are finite verbs in bound clauses obliged to bear stress, as this example illustrates.

About 75 per cent of full verses contain three lifts, all of which may alliterate, though it is much commoner for two of them to do so, most frequently the second and third. This pattern is intelligible if, as argued by Russom (2009), the full verse comprises a normal short verse of *ljóðaháttr* plus an extra foot, in much the way that a skaldic verse in *dróttkvætt* may be analysed as a normal verse of *fornyrðislag* plus an extra, trochaic foot. Alternatively, Bliss (1972) analyses the sequence of odd plus even line as the reflex of a prehistoric tripartite structure which developed in Old English into the hypermetric long line, a metrical type roughly half again as long as a normal verse pair. When there is no internal alliteration in the full verse, the verse commonly alliterates with the preceding verse pair. The full verse usually ends in a monosyllable (⌣, e.g. *annars brjóstum í*,

⌣x⌣x⌣; 'in the breast of another') or, about twice as often, a word to be scanned ⌣x, the equivalence suggesting that the latter is to be resolved (e.g. *lof ok vit, meðan lifir,* ⌣x⌣xx⌣⌣; 'praise and intelligence, while he lives'). Trochaic endings are thus plainly avoided in both full verses and off-verses.

Poems in *ljóðaháttr* include *Hávamál, Vafþrúðnismál, Grímnismál, Skírnismál, Lokasenna, Alvíssmál, Reginsmál, Fáfnismál, Sigrdrífumál, Svipdagsmál, Sólarljóð,* and *Helgakviða Hjǫrvarðssonar* sts 12–30. The commonest name for a poem in this metre is thus *mál*, and it is employed in mythological and sententious poems, only rarely in heroic ones. *Ljóðaháttr* is also the metre of most of *Heiðreks gátur* in *Hervarar saga*, and it is used in isolated stanzas preserved in various places, especially in the *fornaldarsögur*, in a few runic inscriptions, and in portions of the three skaldic poems known as the eddic praise-poems, i.e. Þorbjǫrn hornklofi's *Haraldskvæði*, the anonymous *Eiríksmál*, and Eyvindr skáldaspillir's *Hákonarmál*; in the last two *ljóðaháttr* is employed in mythological passages. These praise-poems are not unusual in the way they shift from one metre to another, sometimes even in the middle of a stanza, as this is a characteristic of other eddic poems, for example *Helgakviða Hjǫrvarðssonar*, which shifts from *fornyrðislag* to *ljóðaháttr* in the middle of stanza 12 and returns to *fornyrðislag* at the start of stanza 31. *Reginsmál* and *Fáfnismál* alternate between *fornyrðislag* and *ljóðaháttr* even more frequently.

Málaháttr

Alliterative patterns and stanza structure in *málaháttr* are like those in *fornyrðislag*, the most notable difference between the two metres being that a normal verse in the former comprises five positions, as may be illustrated by *Atlamál* 5/1–4:

> Ǫlværir urðu   ok elda kyndu,   ⌣⌣x⌣x‖x⌣x⌣x
> hugðu vætr véla,   er þeir vóru komnir.   ⌣x⌣⌣x‖xx⌣x⌣x

[They grew friendly and kindled fires, contemplated no fraud, when they had arrived.]

Resolution is suspended at many places where it would be required in *fornyrðislag*, as in *kona kapps gálig* (⌣x⌣⌣x; 'a woman mindful of eagerness') and *hryti hár logi* (⌣x⌣⌣x; 'a high flame sprang') (if these are not in fact *fornyrðislag* verses of type D interspersed among *málaháttr* verses). Also unlike in *fornyrðislag*, anacrusis is not uncommon, as in *af bragði boð sendi*

(×‖⏑×⏑⏑×; 'sent a message at once') and *at endlǫngu húsi* (×‖⏑⏑×⏑×; 'from end to end of the building'). Kuhn's observations about word order and stress in *fornyrðislag* do not apply to *málaháttr*.

The only poem that conforms to this metre with any consistency is *Atlamál*, though even there the metre is sometimes mixed with verses of greater or fewer than five positions. Mixture of metrical types is in fact a trait of not a few eddic poems: the metre of *Hamðismál* and *Atlakviða*, for example, mixes *fornyrðislag* with *málaháttr*, seemingly randomly within stanzas, and *Hávamál* shifts from *ljóðaháttr* to a mixture of *fornyrðislag* and *málaháttr* in a number of stanzas.[8] Among skaldic poems, portions of the three eddic praise-poems mentioned above are in *málaháttr*, and in one of these, *Hákonarmál*, the metre is limited to battle scenes.

Comparison to other alliterative metres

Of these three metres, *fornyrðislag* most closely resembles what must have been the oldest form of Germanic versecraft, since the principles governing the construction of most West Germanic alliterative verse, and particularly Old English verse, are very similar. West Germanic verse similarly conforms to Sievers's five types, the chief differences being that drops early in the verse may be much longer than in eddic poetry, anacrusis is common, and resolution on lifts other than the first is normal. Hypermetric verses occur, but usually in recognisably hypermetric passages (given that West Germanic verse is non-stanzaic), so that comparison may be drawn to the way *fornyrðislag* often alternates with short passages of verse in different metres.

The primacy of *fornyrðislag* is underscored by the observation that *dróttkvætt* and related skaldic metres appear to have been devised as expanded forms of *fornyrðislag*, since the stress patterns, at least, of *dróttkvætt* resemble Sievers's five types with the addition of an extra, final foot of the form ⏑×. This structural similarity is of considerable importance, since Snorri has a great deal to say about the construction of *dróttkvætt* and similar metres in *Háttatal*, whereas nearly all that is known about the structure of *fornyrðislag* must be divined from examination of the verse form itself. Important corroboration for crucial aspects of Sievers's findings about *fornyrðislag* is thus to be derived, by extrapolation, from *Háttatal*. For instance, Snorri's discussion of *dróttkvætt* verses of more than six syllables, though admittedly vague, is hard to interpret except as alluding to resolution – and, as pointed out above, the existence of resolution, if it can be confirmed, furnishes solid evidence for the correctness of the five-type analysis. Both *ljóðaháttr* and *málaháttr* are generally assumed to be derived also from *fornyrðislag*, either by the addition of material to types of that metre (as with *málaháttr*), the way material is apparently added in *dróttkvætt*, or by the reduction of *fornyrðislag* types through the loss of unstressed syllables (as with the three-position verses of *ljóðaháttr*): for extensive discussion, see Suzuki (2014).

Metre and textual criticism

An understanding of eddic metres is essential to the process of editing eddic poems. Since, in the Codex Regius, these texts are written continuously, as if they were prose, there is no indication of how the poems are to be divided into lines, and metre is the primary basis for such divisions in modern editions. In addition, irregularities of metre frequently indicate ways in which the language of the extant manuscripts differs from the language in which poems were originally composed, due both to language change and to alterations made in the course of the poems' transmission. Such information gleaned from the metre may result in textual emendation. While there is no consensus among editors about the circumstances under which formal defects licence emendation of the text, some broad patterns may be observed.

Easiest to recognise as an indicator of textual change is imperfect alliteration. Some apparent defects of alliteration are attributable to linguistic change that occurred after a poem's composition. For example, the words *reiðr* ('angry'), cognate with Old English *wrāð*, and *reka* ('avenge'), cognate with Old English *wrecan*, often occur in lines that lack alliteration, and the explanation is that the initial *w (> v)* was lost from these words after the tenth century. Even very conservative editors generally emend these words to *vreiðr* and *vreka* when the alliteration so demands.

Editorial practices in regard to other alliterative imperfections vary considerably, and the practices of individual editors often seem inconsistent. Even conservative editors usually admit readings from paper manuscripts when the text in the Codex Regius (hereafter R) and other parchments seems defective. An example is the insertion of *vinna* into the verse pair *Ek vætr hánum / vinna kunnak* ('I did not know how to withstand him', *Vkv* 41/7–8) in Neckel's edition (followed by Kuhn), where *vinna* is missing from R. Here, of course, the alliterative problem is matched by a metrical one (the off-verse would scan as $\angle\times$ without *vinna*) as well as the problem of defective sense, and the emendation is supported by the following verse pair, *ek vætr hánum / vinna máttak*, a near repetition. Only less conservative editors follow the paper manuscripts when alliteration alone is defective, as with the verse pair *Fram setti hon / skutla fulla* ('She set out full trenchers', *Rþ* 32/1–2), in which many editors transpose the final two words on the authority of one paper manuscript.

Conjectural emendation, without any manuscript support, is avoided, to the extent possible, in some editions, but occasionally it is practised for the sake of alliteration and sense even by conservative editors. An example is the half-stanza

> en in þriðja,   þeira systir,
> varði hvítan   háls *Vǫl*undar (*Vkv* 2/7–10)

[but the third, their sister, embraced Vǫlundr's white neck]

For *Vǫlundar*, the manuscript instead indicates *Qnundar*, a man's name not otherwise encountered in the Poetic Edda, here used in a poem about Vǫlundr. Even Neckel (and after him Kuhn) accepts this emendation, though they accept few that are motivated primarily by alliterative misfits. They also accept the change of *ǫðlings* to *lofðungs*, both meaning 'prince's', in the verse pair *á landi ok á vatni / borgit er* lofðungs *flota* ('on land and on water the prince's fleet is protected', *HHv* 29/4–5), without manuscript witness. They decline, however, to emend the verse pair *nam hon svá bert / um at mælask* ('so she began to narrate openly', *Sg* 6/3–4), whereas some editors alter *bert* ('openly') to one or another word beginning with a vowel, such as *ǫrt* (readily), e.g. Finnur Jónsson (1926: 270), or the verse pair *né in mætri / mægð á moldu* ('nor [is there] the more excellent marriage-match on earth', *Sg* 18/7–8), in which *moldu* ('earth'), with abnormal alliteration on the final lift, is regularly changed to *foldu*, with the same meaning, in other editions, e.g. Guðni Jónsson (1954).

Conservative editors are even more reluctant to emend on the basis of metre than of alliteration. As in the case of *(v)reiðr* and *(v)reka*, discussed above, language change sometimes affects poetic form. It may alter the number of syllables in a verse, as with words such as *fá* ('get') and *sjá* ('see'), which derive from disyllabic *fáa* and *sea* and when contracted often cause a verse to contain fewer than four metrical positions. Although such words are decontracted in many editions for the sake of the metre, they are allowed to stand by conservative editors such as Dronke (1969, 1997, 2011). Likewise, the verse *sina magni* ('power of sinews', *Vkv* 17/8) appears to be metrically defective, with a light initial lift, the reason being that *sina* derives from **sinva*, to which the word is altered in some editions, though not in Neckel and Kuhn's (1962). They do emend the verse *oft í jǫlstrum* ('often in laurels', *Gðr I* 19/7), since *í* is not in the manuscript, but without *í* not just the metre but also the grammar is deficient; and in *um borin Buðla* ('born to Buðli', *Sg* 15/3) they have deleted *bróðir minn*, which follows in R, apparently because the triple alliteration is defective, in addition to the metre. On the other hand, they do not emend *sínar hendr* ('her hands', *Sg* 25/2), which is short a syllable, even though in an otherwise identical verse pair in a later stanza R reads *sinni hendi* (29/4; dative).

Less conservative editors sometimes make conjectural emendations on the basis of metre alone. An example is *ok iðgnógan* ('and over-abundant', *HH I* 21/5), found in some editions (e.g. Finnur Jónsson 1888–90: 2.3), though *ok* is not in R. Most emend the verse *Frýra maðr þér engi, Gunnarr* ('no person will reproach you, Gunnarr', *Sg* 33/1), with alliteration on *f*, which has too many lifts. Some eliminate *engi* ('no') (since *-ra* already provides negation), others *Gunnarr*, and *maðr* is sometimes also deleted, as an unnecessary impersonal pronoun. In the verse *Hví sitið kyrrir* ('Why do you sit quiet', *Ghv* 2/1), *kyrrir* is supplied by Hugo Gering (Hildebrand, Gering, and Möbius 1922: 443) and others, whereas Finnur Jónsson (1932: 332) supplies *ér* ('you'), though this makes for inferior metre ($\times \cup | \times \_$). Even the most interventionist editors, however, generally decline to supply an entire missing verse (as at, e.g., *Am* 101/8).

It is evident that the older poets tended to be sparing in their use of function words such as pronouns and determiners, so that the drops in their poetry are short. Because syllable count is important in skaldic verse, it is particularly evident that many function words have been added to skaldic poems in the course of transmission, and so it is only natural to assume that the same has happened to eddic poems. Syllables have also been added in many other ways. For example, older *svát* ('so that'), *þót* ('although'), and *þvít* ('because') may often be assumed for younger *svá at*, *þó at*, and *því at*; the older adverb suffix *-la* has been expanded to *-liga*; constructions such as *veit ek eigi* ('I do not know') and *skyldu eigi* ('should not') may stand for earlier *veitkak* and *skyldut*; for the relative particle *er* must be assumed the earlier form *es*, which may be contracted in forms such as *sás* ('he who') and *pats* ('that which') (instead of *sá er* and *þat er*); the initial vowel in forms of 'to be' may similarly be elided, as in *nú'mk* (i.e. *nú em ek*) ('now I am'), *hann's* ('he is'), and *þǫ'ro* (i.e. *þau eru*) ('they are'), and so forth (Sievers 1893: 56–8). Some editors actually make these changes in the text. For example, in the edition of Finnur Jónsson (1932), *vask* is substituted for the first two words, and the last word is bracketed, in *ek var einn faðir þeira* ('I alone was their father', *HH I* 39/4); *fljótla* appears for *fljótliga* in *heitr þú fljótliga fǫr* ('you will readily commit yourself to a journey', *Grp* 35/7); and *hon þá* ('she them') is missing from *Eldi gaf hon þá alla* ('She gave them all to the fire', *Akv* 42/1). Sievers (1893) is a strong advocate of introducing such changes for the sake of the metre wherever they can be introduced, so that the drops in eddic verse become nearly as spare as those in skaldic, though heavy drops cannot be eliminated entirely by this means, as in *stjǫrnur þat né vissu* ('nor did the stars know it', *Vsp* 5/7) and *æsir'ro á þingi* ('the gods are in council', *Vsp* 48/4).

Considerations such as these mean that editions may differ widely, as may be illustrated by a stanza of *Vǫlundarkviða* (34) in the conservative edition of Neckel and Kuhn (1962, on the left) and the normalising edition of Finnur Jónsson (1926, stanza 35, on the right):

Gacc þú til smiðio, þeirar er þú gorðir,	Gakk til smiðju, es gerðir þú,
þar fiðr þú belgi blóði stocna;	þar fiðr þú belgi blóði stokna,
sneið ec af haufuð húna þinna,	sneiðk af hǫfuð húna þinna
oc undir fen fioturs fœtr um lagðac.	ok und fen fjǫturs fœtr of lagðak.

[Go to the smithy which you constructed; there you will find the bellows spattered with blood. I cut off the heads of your cubs and buried the corpses underneath the forge (?).]

Because the structure of *fornyrðislag* is more rigid – or, at least, is better understood – than that of *ljóðaháttr* and *málaháttr*, it is poems in this metre that are most commonly emended *metri causa*. Editors' reasons for emending or not emending may be influenced by personal attitudes toward the treatment of received texts, but they are also tied closely to the purpose of the edition and the audience for which it is intended (see, e.g., Fix 1997). The conservative edition of Neckel and Kuhn (1962), for example, is plainly intended for advanced scholars, since the apparatus of variants is detailed and there is no interpretive commentary. In the preface to the first edition, Neckel explains that it was his intention to establish linguistic norms based on the language of R itself, but he also is somewhat dismissive of the implications of metrics for the form of the text. Dronke (1997) generally declines to emend on the basis of metre alone, though she emends *reiðr* to *vreiðr* for the sake of the alliteration. In her extensive commentary she identifies irregularities of metre and alliteration and commonly offers reasons not to regard them as defects (e.g. in the comments on *Akv* 33/1, 42/8; cf. 43/3), thus implying a distrust of the findings of metrists. Hers is not an uncommon attitude among students of Old English, a readership for which her edition is (at least partly) intended (vii).

Editors who freely emend usually justify the practice on metrical grounds. For example, Gering (Hildebrand, Gering, and Möbius 1922) and Finnur Jónsson (1926) both expressly refer to Sievers in their introductions. The former also speaks of normalised orthography as having a didactic aim: plainly, he envisages a readership different from Neckel and Kuhn's. Emendation on the basis of metre is undeniably an act of reconstruction. Machan (1992: 226) objects that such reconstruction is a futile endeavour: an eddic poem's 'original' form can never be fully recovered, and, at all events, to attempt to establish a poem's original form is to lend it a 'static' quality, whereas to grant authority to its form as recorded in the thirteenth century is to recognise its dynamism. Similar arguments have been offered in the more contentious and better-documented debates about editing in Old English. In response to them it has been pointed out that: (1) it has almost never been a conjectural editor's aim to reconstruct the 'original' text but only, in most cases, to reverse such changes to the text over time as can be identified with some confidence; and (2) the terms 'static' and 'dynamic' are regrettably confused in this debate, since an emended text that is constructed to make it plain that its thirteenth-century form differs from earlier forms – for instance, by indicating emendations through brackets and italics (as in Gering's edition) – is more dynamic. It reveals layers of textual history at a glance, whereas a text that hews close to its earliest recorded form is more static, privileging a single layer in the text's history (see, e.g., Fulk 1996).

Yet these considerations alone do not justify emendation on the basis solely of metre, and valid objections may still be raised. Sound changes such as the contraction of *fáa* to *fá* cannot be dated with any precision on grounds other than poetic metre itself. It therefore cannot be known for certain that when *fáa* is required by the metre, the word was not yet contracted in the poet's language, or whether among the poetic conventions known to the poet was the licence to use certain monosyllabic words as if they were disyllables. An analogous situation is plainly demonstrable in regard to Old English poetry, though there it is in evidence because poets could choose either value, randomly, for words that had undergone contraction. Thus, rather than decontracting words, some editors of Old English poetry use diacritics to indicate metrical values – a circumflex accent, in the case of forms to be metrically decontracted – a practice which has the virtue of retaining manuscript readings while indicating the historically layered nature of the text. It should be noted that the rationale for emending eddic poems *metri causa* by analogy to skaldic poetry has been weakened in some ways in recent years, since editors of skaldic poetry are more sparing in the application of metrical remedies than formerly (see, e.g., Marold 2002: 43–6).

Regardless of how discrepancies between a poem's recorded form and its metrical structure are addressed, it should be apparent that no single solution will suffice for all editions of eddic poetry. The extent to which metre and alliteration influence an editor's textual choices will continue to be determined in large part by the intended audience of an edition and the uses to which it is intended to be put.[9]

Notes

1. For a succinct account of how the three metres are distributed in the Old Norse poetic corpus, see Gade (2012: liv–lvii). For a bibliography of scholarship on eddic metres, see Fulk and Gade (2002). The metre called *kviðuháttr* (narrative metre) may be mentioned here: it is a skaldic metre, but it is apparently derived from *fornyrðislag* by the loss of final syllables, and, like *fornyrðislag*, it conforms to the findings of Hans Kuhn about the metrical treatment of sentence elements of variable stress (as explained below). For an enlightening account of *kviðuháttr*, see Gade (2002: 863).

2. Sievers (1878) represents his first exposition of his views as regards Old Norse poetry; Sievers (1893) is a synthesis of his views on the North and West Germanic traditions. Sievers was, however, deeply indebted to earlier work, particularly that of Konráð Gíslason (Konráð Gíslason and Eiríkur Jónsson 1875–89) and Max Rieger (1876). For a concise account in English of eddic metres as analysed in the Sieversian tradition, see Gade (2002). The most compendious work on the topic is Suzuki (2014).

3. It should be stressed that this analysis of syllable structure is applicable only for metrical purposes. For other purposes, the syllabifications *hlí.ta, hley.pa, sen.da,* and *ha.fa* must have applied: this is the syllabification required in West Germanic alliterative verse, and it is the syllabification required to explain the development of vowels in Modern Icelandic. For an explanation of why a different syllabification is required in skaldic verse (and hence, almost certainly, in eddic verse), see Gade (1995: 29–34).

4. Particles in verses of this type (A3, as explained below) must not be unstressed altogether, as in skaldic verse the first unstressed word in type A3 may bear the rhyme even though it does not alliterate. That the stress is relatively low, however, may be judged from the observation that stress-words always alliterate at the beginning of the verse (see Kuhn 1983: 151–6).

5. For example, *-hildr* must be unstressed in verses such as *Brynhildr í búri* and *Svanhildr um heitin*, as otherwise the verse would comprise five metrical positions (as explained below: incorrect ⌣́⌣̀x|⌣́x, as opposed to correct ⌣́xx|⌣́x), whereas it must receive some degree of stress in a verse such as *Svanhildr vera* (⌣́⌣̀|⌣̆x, according to Sievers).

6. Although Sievers's approach to alliterative metrics lost ground to Heusler's and others' over time, and was eventually repudiated by Sievers himself (see, e.g., the references in Fulk 2007: 138 n. 17), the past thirty years have seen a thoroughgoing rehabilitation of Sievers's initial views, which now dominate metrical scholarship, with rare exceptions. On these developments, see Fulk (2007: 135–42).

7. For weighty objections to some of the ways in which Heusler's and similar isochronous analyses contradict observable facts, see Pope (1966: 29–37), Stockwell (1996), and Fulk (2002).

8. Suzuki (2014: 972–3) identifies these mixed stanzas as 73, 81–3, 85–7, 89–90, and 144. For an index to the scansion of poems in Neckel's edition, distinguishing the three eddic meters and thus identifying such shifts, see Suzuki (2014: 831–1057).

9. Warm thanks are due Kari Ellen Gade, Megan E. Hartman, and Rafael J. Pascual, who read this chapter in draft and offered most helpful advice. I remain, of course, responsible for any errors.

CHAPTER 14

Eddic style

Brittany Schorn

The style of eddic poetry is as distinct as its subject matter, with character-istics that go hand in hand with its unique form. This Scandinavian reflex of traditional Germanic alliterative verse was highly innovative and productive for half a millennium,[1] spanning and responding to profound cultural change whilst maintaining the essence of the ancient character that con-stituted a large part of its allure for medieval redactors. The voices of ancient heroes and supernatural beings had a particular style that lent them authen-ticity and commanded the rapt attention that the seeress calls for at the opening of *Vǫluspá* (1/1–3), which begins the Codex Regius eddic collection. The ways in which eddic poets exercised their skill and originality in this tradition distanced them from courtly skaldic compositions (see Schorn on genre, Chapter 12 in this Handbook). Masters of traditional aspects of form, structure, diction, and rhetoric, individual eddic poets manipulated the poetic idioms in which they worked with varied and sophisticated effect and were thus able to draw out ever new meaning from ancient lore. The tools they used to do so are the primary focus of this chapter:[2] diction, verse-form, and, above all, dramatic dialogues used mimetically to recreate crucial moments and encounters, allowing the characters themselves to debate their choices and motivations, their wisdom and world-views, and to argue for the meaning of their lives and legacies.

Diction

Eddic style shows the development of tendencies already present in Old English, Old Saxon, and Old High German poetry, such as the extensive use of dialogue and an aesthetic that favours allusion and economy of phrase. Old Norse likewise possesses an expansive poetic lexicon, employ-ing a range of vocabulary that is rarely or never attested in prose, and which is in some cases likely quite archaic. Using a variety of terminology with subtle variations in meaning to reference the same object – sometimes in quick succession – allowed poets to explore aspects of its identity or role in context. Thus, the mysterious and contradictory nature of Vǫlundr's elusive wife in *Vǫlundarkviða* emerges as she is named *mær* ('girl'), *alvitr* ('strange creature'), *drós* ('woman'), *ljóss* ('shining [one]'), and *brúðr* ('bride') (*Vkv* 1, 2 3, 5, and 19).[3] She is defined by family relationships as the *systir* and *dóttir* (*Vkv* 2, 10, 15) of her extraordinary kin, which indicate that she is both human and otherworldly, belonging to the domestic sphere and yet unable to remain in it. Varied terminology for frequently recurring concepts (i.e. words for warriors, gods, treasure, and weapons) facilitated alliteration and allowed conventional scenes to be imaginatively recast. *Alvíssmál*, for instance, includes a catalogue of such poetic synonyms for aspects of the natural world, attributing them to the various languages of supernatural beings (a suggestion paralleled in other traditions, but for which there is limited evidence in Old Norse; see Moberg 1973).

Compounds and kennings (see Quinn, Chapter 15 in this Handbook) created further scope for variation along similar lines. The eddic lexicon includes a significant number of hapax legomena (see La Farge and Tucker 1992), and a high proportion of these are innovative compounds. Most are formed from varying combinations of frequently recurring nouns or adjectives and have readily apparent meanings. *Valr* ('corpse') is a predictably ubiquitous element, and the recurring terms *valkyrja* ('valkyrie, chooser of the slain'), *Valhǫll* ('hall of the slain'), and *Valfǫðr* ('father of the slain') all refer to the myth in which Óðinn populates his army in the afterlife with dead *einherjar* ('champions'). Such well-established compounds inspire new variations, and so the giantesses in *Grottasǫngr* (sts 18 and 20) speak of *valdreyri* ('corpse-blood') and weapons being *valdreyrugr* ('corpse-bloody') in their violent song. Through the compound *valdýri* ('corpse-beast'), the wolf Fenrir is conceived of as a carrion animal in stanza 55 of the Codex Regius text of *Vǫluspá*, evoking the widespread beasts-of-battle motif. Similarly, in *Helgakviða Hundingsbana I* (13/6–7) the violent rage of Helgi and the sons of Hundingr when they meet in battle is expressed in terms of the wolf's hunger: *fara Viðris grey valgjǫrn* ('corpse-eager ... ran Óðinn's hounds'); and Sigrún coins the apt term *valrúnar* ('slaughter-runes', *HH II* 12/7) to describe Helgi's attempts at evasive answers to her questions about the battle he has just come from (this episode is discussed in detail by Quinn; see Chapter 15 in this Handbook).

Beyond such compounds, many of the apparent neologisms in eddic poetry involve recasting familiar terms as different parts of speech. Thus, in *Skírnismál* Gerðr is cursed with the utterance *þik morn morni* ('may pining waste you away', *Skm* 31/5). *Morna* ('to mourn, waste away') is a verb used in curses in eddic poetry (Kellogg 1988: 311) (it occurs only in a formulaic phrase in prose: see *ONP*: s.v.), but this is the only attestation of the feminine noun *morn* from the same root, meaning 'the resultant state'. A smaller number of uniquely occurring words in eddic poetry are genuinely obscure. The reason may be that many words, such as *morna*, are usually confined to poetry, and even to particular poetic registers, that are not well attested in the surviving corpus. Other obscure words may have once been part of the prose lexicon, but appear to have fallen out of use by the time the bulk of surviving material was preserved. Interpreting these words can be problematic. In *Sigurðarkviða in skamma*, Brynhildr foresees the death of Atli at his wife's hand:

> Þvíat honum Guðrún grýmir á beð,
> snǫrpum eggjum, af sárum hug. (*Sg* 60/7–10)

> [For Guðrún will smear their bed [with blood], by means of sharp sword-edges, from her wounded heart.]

Grýma is not otherwise attested and commentators do not agree on its etymology.[4] The general sense of the action can be deduced from the immediate context and from what we know about the episode alluded to from other poems, in particular a pair of verses from *Atlakviða*: *hon beð broddi gaf blóð at drekka* ('with a sword-point she gave the bed blood to drink', *Akv* 41/1–2). Yet the evident wordplay in *Sigurðarkviða* indicates that there is more to it here; the semantic connection between the alliterating *sárr* ('wounded'; that is to say, in pain) and *snarpr* ('sharp') suggests a complex portrayal of Guðrún as both the agent and the victim of her own violent action. We can only speculate on exactly what the poet is getting at, however, without a full understanding of *grýma*. These more recondite elements of eddic diction may have already been a challenge for readers of surviving manuscripts written in the thirteenth century and later. Like the unusual meanings of familiar terms and occasional forgotten archaisms which wrong-foot speakers of Modern English in a Shakespearean text, the specialised diction of eddic verse may well have become part of its literary aesthetic.

Form

It is in form more than in lexicon that eddic verse most obviously departs from its literary cognates in other Germanic languages. Eddic poetry is stanzaic and represented by several well-attested metres: primarily, *fornyrðislag* and *ljóðaháttr*, and, to a lesser extent, *málaháttr* and *galdralag* (a subtype of *ljóðaháttr*, see Fulk, Chapter 13 in this Handbook, for a full description of each metre). The stylistic consequences of these verse forms are considerable. Perhaps the most immediately noticeable effect is in the terse quality of eddic stanzas, which are relatively short and syntactically self-contained. Word order is rarely fragmented to the extent that we find it in some skaldic poetry, necessitated by more demanding metres and displays of poetic prowess. Yet eddic syntax too is markedly poetic: it is rhythmic and clipped in progression, complimenting a lexicon that is highly allusive and idiomatically distinct from literary prose. This is owed in part to the conventions of stanza division as well as the metre as such.[5] There are eight lines on average in a stanza of *fornyrðislag* and six in a stanza of *ljóðaháttr*, but the length is by no means fixed or regular. Stanzas as short as two lines or as long as twelve are not uncommon. Poets could manipulate stanza length for a variety of reasons, and extremes of both long and short stanzas and their effects are vividly exemplified by *Atlakviða* and *Sigurðarkviða in skamma*.

Poems in fornyrðislag

Often in poems composed in *fornyrðislag*,[6] stanzas are extended by a few lines to increase dramatic tension and suspense at significant moments in the narrative. Terse and quick-moving, with alternating stanzas of dialogue and narrative, *Atlakviða* slows at stanza fourteen to dwell for sixteen lines on a description of the fateful approach of Gunnarr and Hǫgni to the imposing *borg* ('stronghold') where Atli treacherously lies in wait to end their lives. The poet draws out this moment before the violent conflict erupts, at which point the suspicions voiced earlier (sts 2 and 8) in the poem are unequivocally confirmed. The brothers know exactly what they are charging into and Guðrún pronounces their fate bitterly – even tortuously – in a second extended stanza (*Akv* 16). The story of the brothers' deaths was in all likelihood well known to the poem's audience; the terror in this retelling comes from dwelling on the moments within the narrative when the characters themselves become aware of the scale of the tragedy.

The technique is almost cinematic, allowing the unfolding events to slow down and the audience's attention to be drawn deeply into moments of pathos or complexity. In *Sigurðarkviða in skamma*, an extended stanza of fourteen lines (or seven long lines) effectively expresses Gunnarr's mental state, plagued by contradictory desires and paralysed by indecision as he contemplates murdering his brother-in-law Sigurðr.

Reiðr varð Gunnarr ok hnipnaði,
sveip sínum hug, sat um allan dag;
hann vissi þat vilgi gǫrla,
hvat honum væri vinna sœmst,
eða honum væri vinna bezt,
alls sik Vǫlsung vissi firðan
ok at Sigurð sǫknuð mikinn. (*Sg* 13)

[Gunnarr was angry and cast down, he wavered in mind, and he sat all day;
he did not know at all clearly what would be most honourable for him to do,
or what would be best for him to do, he knew he would have to get rid of the
Vǫlsungr and he knew Sigurðr would be a great loss.]

There is never any doubt about the outcome: the Gjúkingar will kill
Sigurðr. What the poet is interested in exploring is why the story must
play out as it does, through a combination of social mores, human nature,
and individual choice. All are interwoven in one stanza. From this quasi-
psychological perspective, the moment is crucial and very much worth
dwelling on. The most complex character, and the one around whom the
poem centres, however, is Brynhildr, who engineers the deaths of herself
and the man she loves. Juxtaposed with Gunnarr's indecision, her decisive
action comes across as almost manic. Some of the most revealing moments
for her character, in contrast to Gunnarr's, come in short, almost abrupt
stanzas. These brief insights are shockingly plain and direct. When Sigurðr
and Guðrún go to bed together at the beginning of the poem, she speaks
alone outside:

Vǫn geng ek vilja, vers ok beggja,
verð ek mik gœla af grimmum hug. (*Sg* 9)

[I go without both happiness and husband, I'll pleasure myself with my
savage thoughts.]

The truth, plainly spoken, is no less dangerous for lack of audience.
Gunnarr's ineffectiveness is never more apparent than in the failure of
his own words. Dialogue proves futile later in the poem, as the brothers
debate Brynhildr's planned suicide. Full stanzas of their direct speech are
punctuated by short staccato stanzas reporting Brynhildr's actions, as she
resolutely presses on with her chosen course:

Hratt af hálsi hveim þar sér,
léta mann sik letja langrar gǫngu. (*Sg* 43)

[Quickly she pushed away each one from embrace, she'd have no man
hinder her from the long journey.]

From this point on neither of the brothers are heard, and Brynhildr's
speech expands to fill the silence; she ends the poem triumphantly with
an operatic nineteen-stanza monologue (sts 53–71) pronounced with her
dying breaths. This interplay between narrative and dialogue serves to
create immediacy, control narrative pacing, vary perspective, and nuance
characterisation, and is typical of several other poems on both heroic
and mythological subjects (see, for instance, *Hymiskviða*, *Þrymskviða*,
Hamðismál, and *Atlamál*).

Although stanzas and poems vary somewhat in length, the organisation
of eddic poetry into stanzas always entails frequent breaks and pauses in
syntax and in thought. Poets exploited this characteristic to the full. Rather
than unfolding through continuous narrative as such, stories are told as
a series of impressions, reflections, or short bursts of dialogue. In *Helreið
Brynhildar*, for example, Brynhildr offers her own perspective on her life in
response to a giantess who accosts her on the road to Hel (and Sigurðr),
accusing her of ruining the Gjúkingar. The conflict between the two, in
Judy Quinn's analysis, moves the debate to the mythological level; the
giantess represents the Gjúkingar, and Brynhildr is aligned in contrast with
the united forces of mankind and the Æsir. Thus, the poet sets the stage for
the audience to side with the valkyrie, and Brynhildr's triumphant presentation of her own biography constitutes the bulk of the poem (Quinn
2015b: especially 93–9). As Heather O'Donoghue (2011) has noted, her
narrative is structured as a direct response to the giantess's charges and
organised thematically as much as chronologically. Dialogue and thought,
rather than forensic recreation of the past, drive the poem and lend it
a powerfully introspective quality. In a ten-stanza speech (sts 5–14) that
takes up most of the short poem, Brynhildr begins by setting out her
counterclaim, that

> gørðu mik Gjúka arfar
> ástalausa ok eiðrofa. (*Hlr* 5/5–8)

> [the heirs of Giúki made me love-bereft, and made me an oath-breaker.]

Her life is then presented as a series of key moments and events leading up
to this conclusion. The links between them are for the most part implicit,
and the chronology of events is only made explicit three times. The sole
reference to an absolute chronology is the detail that she was twelve years
old at the time of her first life-changing event, an allusive reference to her
early life as a valkyrie.[7] A four-line stanza is then sufficient to convey the
substance of Brynhildr's career:

Hétu mik allir í Hlymdǫlum
Hildi undir hjálmi, hverr er kunni. (*Hlr* 7)

[They all called me in Hlymdale, anyone who knew me, War-lady in the helmet]

The kenning is enough to evoke the conventional role of the valkyrie in battle (see Quinn on kennings, Chapter 15 in this Handbook), and the detail of the location suffices to connect it with Brynhildr's particular experiences. For knowing members of the audience, such allusions may reference an immanent narrative linking back to stories associated with her early life; but such knowledge is not necessary to grasp the immediate point in context, which is that Brynhildr lived as a valkyrie. As well as allowing poets to avoid excursus and to call on a complex web of references, such allusions could also serve to draw attention to the varying levels of knowledge which probably existed among the medieval audience. The value of much Old Norse poetry was underlined by the fact that its meaning was not equally available to everyone who heard it. For many hearers or readers, arriving at the point may have required careful thought, or consultation with those more learned in mythology. Both eddic and skaldic poets flattered the proficient and enticed the novice by encoding meaning in ways that required specific cultural and technical poetic knowledge (and raw intellectual ability) to access.

The brevity of stanza 7 of *Helreið Brynhildar* helps build the impact of the full eight-line stanza that follows. It opens with the second reference to the chronology of events, the relative adverb *þá* ('then'), which marks out what follows as a similarly significant change of course, in that it consists of a single sequence of events that leads to an inevitable conclusion: her relationship with the human hero Sigurðr. Asserting her own will against Óðinn's, Brynhildr offers him the elder warrior in order to spare the life of the younger and so earns his wrath. We are given just enough information to understand why, through the characterisation of Hjálm-Gunnarr as *gamall* ('old') and his opponent as *ungr* ('young', *Hlr* 8/1 and 5). Brynhildr's version of events takes the form of a quick succession of short declarative sentences stressing her own agency in the constructions *let ek* and *gaf ek* ('I let'; 'I gave', *Hlr* 8/1 and 5) before conveying her powerlessness as Óðinn takes over the nominative position to become angry with *mér* ('me', *Hlr* 8/7). Stressing this loss of power and consequent responsibility for her fate is the basis of Brynhildr's defence for what follows. Brynhildr's impotence is reiterated by Óðinn's continued role as subject of each active verb over the next two stanzas, before finally assigning Sigurðr to the same position at the end of stanza 10 so that the next line takes up the story with *reið góðr* ('the good man rode', *Hlr* 11/1).

The course of her life at this point is presented as a series of decisions made by Óðinn and (at his behest) Sigurðr to bring the lovers together. Both the choice of events related in the poem and the perspective offered on them have the clear aim of exculpating Sigurðr from blame and establishing his unique suitability for Brynhildr. Stanzas 9 and 10 are similarly structured in two halves: the first contains a dramatic image of her captivity (overlapping shields and a hall encircled by flames, respectively) and the second considers the necessary qualities to breach it. The man *er hvergi lands hræðask kynni* ('who in the land knew no fear', *Hlr* 9/7–8) can only be Sigurðr, who slew Fáfnir. Her account skips over the actual rescue, and so presents it as a *fait accompli*. Sigurðr's pursuit of her is the natural and necessary consequence of his own heroic nature. Agency is restored to both characters in stanza 12 as *sváfu við* ('we [two] slept', *Hlr* 12/1). Again, an image is offered in place of a depiction of action, this time of what did *not* occur: limbs entwined. The detail that they slept in *sæing einni* ('one bed') for *átta nóttum* ('eight nights') suggests the opportunity and desire to consummate the relationship, and so the virtue of their inaction.

This then sets the stage for Brynhildr's outrage in stanza 13, when abruptly *brá mér Guðrún ... at ek Sigurdi svæfak á armi* ('Guðrún accused me ... that I slept in Sigurðr's arms', *Hlr* 13/1–4). A second use of the *þá* ('then') indicates a final reversal in the second half of the penultimate stanza and forces the audience (and the giantess) to read the treachery of the Gjúkingar in the context of the moment of Brynhildr's discovery of it.

þá varð ek þess vís, er ek vildigak,
at þau véltu mik í verfangi. (*Hlr* 13/5–8)

[then I discovered what I wish I'd never known, that they'd betrayed me in my taking a husband.]

Rather than narrating any part of the story of Sigurðr's death or her own suicide, Brynhildr presents the outcome of her discovery as a gnomic revelation about the suffering that men and women must endure while they are living (*kvikkvir*), and so proclaims her decision to end her life (*aldri slíta*) to be with Sigurðr in death. Her choice of verb, *slíta*, evokes its primary meaning ('to tear, break, or end') as well as its common metaphorical extension 'to wear out one's life' (La Farge and Tucker 1992), and so she owns up to the destruction she was initially accused of wreaking (*glata* and *bregða*) (*Hlr* 4/6 and 8). For it is her own life, in her view, that she has destroyed, and her experiences have justified that destruction; the Gjúkungar are simply collateral damage and have merited their fate. The natural syntactic breaks between, and within, stanzas are capitalised on in this poem to represent Brynhildr's story as she experiences it in the context of a particular argument. Each stanza presents a tableau, briefly encapsulating a self-contained narrative. Consequential links are expressed occasionally within stanzas but rarely between them as, for example, in stanzas 12 and 13, which are linked by *því* ('and yet', *Hlr* 13/1). The poet skilfully exploited the features of *fornyrðislag* to create a dialogue poem as disjointed, illogical, and subjective as the experience of human memory, and all the more effective for it.

Similar strategies can be found in several poems in the Codex Regius that revolve around the laments and whetting of two other eddic heroines, Brynhildr's rival Guðrún and her sister Oddrún (*Guðrúnarhvǫt, Guðrúnarkviða I, Guðrúnarkviða II, Guðrúnarkviða II,* and *Oddrúnargrátr*) (for more on the style of these poems, see Quinn 2009; McKinnell 2014; Sävborg 2013; Jóhanna Katrín Friðriksdóttir 2013a). Autobiographical monologues in *fornyrðislag* are even more characteristic of the male heroes of the *fornaldarsǫgur* (sagas of ancient times), who reflect on the victories and tragedies that will ensure their lasting fame in death-songs (*ævikviður*, or in German *Sterbelieder*) (see Clunies Ross 2013: 195 and Larrington on heroic legend, Chapter 8 in this Handbook).

Poems in ljóðaháttr

The structure of poems primarily composed in *ljóðaháttr* tends to be more regimented, as the length and structure of the stanzas is more regular. Individual stanzas are made up of three-line units (one long line followed by one full line); most consist of two such units, running to six lines, and the most common variations in length are stanzas of three and nine lines. It is the preferred form for a number of non-narrative speech genres, such as wisdom poetry, curses, and *sennur* (see Schorn on genre, Chapter 12 in this Handbook). Syntactic units are shorter, with breaks occurring after each full line, resulting in a natural division of each stanza into two halves. The content of the individual stanzas in these poems is even more self-contained than in *fornyrðislag*; these poems are catalogues of wisdom, threats, and insults. *Ljóðaháttr* allows very little scope for complex syntax and necessitates extreme brevity. It thus forces speakers to encapsulate arguments and narrative allusions in short, pithy statements. As an illustration, *Hávamál* st. 31 reads:

Fróðr þykkisk, sá er flótta tekr,
   gestr at gest hæðinn;
veita gǫrla, sá er um verði glissir,
   þótt hann með grǫmum glami.

[Wise that man seems who retreats when one guest is insulting another; the man who mocks at a feast doesn't know for sure whether he shoots off his mouth amid enemies.]

Each half of the stanza contains a gnomic statement that could stand on its own, grammatically and logically. At first glance, their content verges on tautology. But when taken together, the two halves make the same point from opposite perspectives (the meaning of each gnome on its own is somewhat different), and so the positive advice of the first half of the stanza is reinforced by imagining the negative consequences of the contrary action in the second. The relationship between the two halves is often under-scored by aural strategies as well, such as verbal echoes and parallel sentence structure. Here the alliteration of the first full line links the hypothetical *gestr* ('guest') of the first half of the stanza to the foolish speech of the second amid *gramir* ('enemies').

Rather than relating a chronological series of events, individual stanzas are linked together in patterns of alternating speech in dialogues or by thematic association in monologues. *Vafþrúðnismál* is perhaps the most sophisticated example. The pattern of alternating speakers is never broken, aside from a single narrative stanza (5) providing a transition between the prefatory dialogue between Óðinn and Frigg to the wisdom contest in the giant Vafþrúðnir's hall. In the contest itself, the speakers take turns asking a series of thematically and chronologically linked questions (see Ruggerini 1994 for a full analysis of the contest format). In dialogues, speakers must not only answer to the substance of the questions or insults (on the stylistic similarities of wisdom contests and *sennur*, see Schorn on genre, Chapter 12 in this Handbook) thrown at them, but also prove their rhetorical skill by mirroring and surpassing the language and form of the initial volley (Anderson 1981 on *Lokasenna* is a good example; cf. *Hárbarðsljóð, Alvíssmál, Helgakviða Hundingsbana I, Helgakviða Hjǫrvarðssonar, Helgakviða Hundingsbana II*).

The lengthy *Hávamál* is much more loosely structured in what appears to be a monologue,[8] but nevertheless exhibits a number of the strategies used to order other poems in *ljóðaháttr* (particularly *Grímnismál* and the curse poems *Skírnismál* and *Buslubœn*). A minimal narrative frame provides the subject matter: the occasion of a visit, prompting a series of observations about the social behaviour of hosts and guests. Within this context, the poem follows a logical series of considerations, as one point suggests another in a continuous train of thought. Thus, the stanza quoted above is preceded by an admonition against mockery (*Hávamál* st. 30) and followed by an observation that *aldar róg þat mun æ vera* ('amongst men there will always be strife', *Háv* 32/4–5). This is typical of the way that *Hávamál* constructs its distinctly cynical world-view out of seemingly straightforward proverbs.

Another technique for linking stanzas is through the use of refrains. In this respect Old Norse poetic style differs markedly from West Germanic verse, where refrains are comparatively rare. The most striking exception is the Old English poem *Deor*, which consists of a series of brief references to famous legendary characters and stories punctuated by the repeated reflection *þæs ofereode; þisses swa mæg* ('that passed, so will this'). The breaks this creates in the poem are recognised by the scribe of the Exeter Book, who begins each word following the refrain with a capital letter which functions quite like a stanza division, an effect recognised by the way many editions have chosen to present the poem (Klink 1992: 22–3 and 90–1). In Old Norse skaldic poetry, it is a structural requirement of the prestigious *drápa* form to include a refrain called a *stef* (see further Clunies Ross 2005: 36–9; Clunies Ross et al. 2012: lxviii–lxix).

In eddic verse, refrains are particularly common in *ljóðaháttr*, which easily accommodates them as a substitution for a regular half-stanza, which is to say one long line and one full line (e.g. *Hávamál* st. 10), or an addition to a regular six-line stanza (cf. *Hávamál* sts 116 and 177). They serve to draw individual stanzas together by explicitly relating them to the frame narrative. Thus, Óðinn reminds his addressee, the silent Loddfáfnir (and by extension the audience of the poem), of the value of his advice and the precarious nature of knowledge transfer with the refrain:

> Ráðomk þér, Loddfáfnir, at þú ráð nemir,
>   njóta mundu, ef þú nemr,
>   þér munu góð, ef þú getr. (*Háv* 112/1–4)
>
> [I advise you Loddfáfnir, to take his advice, it will be useful if you learn it, do you good, if you have it.]

Repetition is also used in enumerative phrases which are incorporated into some refrains to structure lists and mark progression through them by numbering their contents. The opening refrain of Óðinn's list of spells in *Hávamál* show the mnemonic value of this technique:

> Þat kann ek it sétta, ef mik særir þegn
>   á rótum rás viðar:

ok þann hal, er mik heipta kveðr,
　　þann eta mein heldr enn mik. (*Háv* 151)

[I know a sixth one if a man wounds me using roots of the sap-filled wood:
and that man who conjured to harm me, the evil consumes him, not me.]

The alliteration between the first pair of verses, on *sétta* and *særir*, links the
number of the spell to the difficulty for which it is a remedy. The second
half of the stanza then describes what the spell accomplishes. Through
these techniques, non-narrative poems – even composite works like
Hávamál – were carefully and deliberately structured to draw coherent
meaning from their constituent parts.

Mixing metres

Óðinn's half-stanza address to Loddfáfnir in *Hávamál* (quoted above) is
composed in *galdralag*, a variant of *ljóðaháttr* with an additional full line,
associated with the repetitive incantation of spells (see Fulk, Chapter 13 in
this Handbook). The effect on the rhythm and tone of the poem is striking.
Initials at the start of stanzas 111 and 138 in the Codex Regius graphically set
off this section of the poem from those that precede and follow it. There is
a new tension between speaker and addressee as the advice comes now in
a pointed barrage, with the threat of failure expressed in the repeated
conditional clauses of the full lines, and the change in metre indicates
the more esoteric nature of the contents of the last third of the poem. Eddic
poets could switch freely between metres, between and within stanzas.
Shifts between metres within a poem when the demands of a particular
metre did not suit the content or rhetorical mode of a stanza is one of the
most characteristic aspects of eddic style. To stick with *Hávamál*, stanzas
85–8 make a point about life's unpredictability with a list of over twenty
things that *trúi engi maðr* ('no man should trust', *Háv* 88/2). The power of
the list lies more in its cumulative force than in its individual elements, and
so the poet casts the bulk of it in *fornyrðislag*: each item comprises a single
verse without pause or elaboration.

　　This potential for metrical variation was understood and exploited right
across the period of eddic composition – from the composer of the Rök
inscription to the authors of *fornaldarsögur*. Among the anthology poems,
Hárbarðsljóð represents perhaps the most extreme example, so much so
that it is difficult to interpret, though Carol Clover (1979) has suggested
a very sophisticated poetic scheme at work rendering the poem as generic
farce. Shifts between metres in eddic poetry could occur within and between

individual stanzas and between different sections of a poem or poetic sequence. This aspect of eddic style is more pronounced in prosimetric compositions such as the sequence of poems on Sigurðr's youth (*Reginsmál, Fáfnismál,* and *Sigrdrífumál*) and *Helgakviða Hjǫrvarðssonar* in the Codex Regius, and it is an even more striking feature of poetry preserved outside of it.[9] When quoted in saga prose, eddic dialogue is deployed above all for rhetorical effect. In *Ketils saga hœngs* (*The Saga of Ketill Salmon*) and *Áns saga bogsveigis* (*The Saga of Án Bowbender*) (see *FS* II for both), the Hrafnistumenn (legendary saga heroes from Ramsta, Norway) Ketill and Án establish their heroic credentials both through their deeds and through their accompanying displays of verbal prowess, successfully deploying multiple modes and metres, that make these deeds memorable.[10]

In some cases, mixing of verse types within stanzas is likely a function of the texts' adaptation to their immediate saga contexts. The riddles of *Hervarar saga ok Heiðreks* (*The Saga of Hervör and Heiðrekr*) provide one clear example: the *fornyrðislag* refrain *Heiðrekr konungr, hyggðu at gátu* ('King Heiðrekr, consider the riddle', *SkP*, Gestumbl *Heiðr* 1[VIII]; Turville-Petre 1956: 37–50) is added on to otherwise complete stanzas (most in *ljóðaháttr*) most probably in order to give unity to the collection and anchor the individual riddles to the saga episode. Other examples, however, suggest more complex poetic purpose.

Take, for instance, stanzas 6 and 7 of *Eiríksmál*, preserved in the kings' saga compilation *Fagrskinna*.

> Hví es þér Eiríks vǫn
> heldr an annarra konunga?
> Þvít mǫrgu landi
> hann hefr mæki roðit
>   ok blóðugt sverð borit.
>
> Hví namt þú hann sigri þá,
> es þér þótti hann snjallr vesa?
> Þvíat óvíst es at vita,
> nær ulfr inn hǫsvi
>   sœkir á sjǫt goða. (*SkP*, Eirm 6–7[I])

[Why do you expect Eiríkr rather than other kings? Because he has reddened his blade in many a land and borne a bloody sword. Why do you deprive him of victory then, when he seemed to you to be valiant? Because it cannot be known for certain when the grey wolf will attack the home of the gods.]

These stanzas also depart from the usual practice of poetry in *ljóðaháttr* of avoiding changes of speaker within a stanza. Sigmundr poses his questions

in *málaháttr* and Óðinn answers in *ljóðaháttr*. The change certainly helps
to distinguish the voices of the characters within the stanzas, but they are
not consistent across the poem (Óðinn speaks *málaháttr* in st.1 and
Sigmundr speaks *ljóðaháttr* in st. 8). It has more to do with immediate
rhetorical purpose: Sigmundr's questions are about the action of the
moment, being specific and immediate. In *Lokasenna* the same great
mythological paradox is expressed (in *ljóðaháttr*) as an insulting definition
of Óðinn's character.

> opt þú gaft, þeim er þú gefa skyldira,
> inum slævurum, sigr. (*Ls* 22/4–6)

> [often you've given what you shouldn't have given, victory, to the faint
> hearted.]

In *Eiríksmál* Sigmundr is asking about *this* king, but Óðinn answers in
terms of more universal truths and so casts his reply in a gnomic mode,
using the most appropriate verse-form. This particular death – and the
death of every similarly deserving warrior – possesses cosmic significance.

Dialogue and poetic voice

The preponderance of direct speech in eddic poetry is the most immediate
source of its rhetorical complexity. Narratorial interference is consistently
minimised and many poems are cast entirely, or nearly entirely, as dialogue
(see Gunnell 1995 on the implications for performance). Eddic poets
consistently avoid calling attention to their role in mediating their content
in order to preserve its authority (and their own distance from it) and its
dramatic effect. Almost all poems are anonymous,[11] and mentions of the
poet him or herself are exceptional.[12] The penultimate stanza of
Hymiskviða contains an unusual reference to the eddic poet's craft:

> Enn ér heyrt hafið – hverr kann um þat
> goðmálugra gørr at skilja – (*Hym* 38/1–4)

> [But you have heard this already – everyone knowledgeable about mytho-
> logy can tell it more clearly –]

Successful poetic composition is presented by this stanza as a matter of
accuracy; a good eddic poet would know *goðmál*, an unusual poetic
compound and otherwise unattested expression for mythology in terms
of the manner of its transmission (for full discussion, see *Edda Kommentar*
II, 359). Anonymous Old High German and Old English poets represented
their role similarly, in conventional formulaic phrases such as *ik gihorta ðat*

seggen ('I heard that said', *Hildebrandslied* (*The Song of Hildebrand*) l.1) and *mīne gefrǣge* ('as I have heard say', *Beowulf* l. 776). Skaldic verse in Old Norse, on the other hand, tends to reflect a much more current and situational setting, in which the identity of poet and subject were normally made clear.

In contrast, most eddic poets sought to establish their distance from the audience's present, which is never directly referenced, and seldom alluded to even indirectly. As Judy Quinn has put it, 'the self-effacing poet assumes the role of a hidden microphone, relaying the conversations most interesting to hear because they have occurred in places that are accessible only through a feat of imagination'.[13] To this end their setting, in time and space, is sketched broadly and briefly, and details are for the most part confined to the strict requirements of the plot. The events of *Hamðismál*, for example, occur

> nú né í gær,
> þat hefir langt liðit síðan,
> er fát fornara, fremr var þat hálfu (*Hm* 2/1–6).

> [not today nor yesterday, a long time has passed since then, – few things are so long ago that this is not twice as long –]

and *Helgakviða Hundingsbana I* opens simply by observing: *ár var alda* ('it was long ago', *HH I*, 1/1).

Rather than relating action through third-person narration, eddic poets were much more interested in recreating the interactions of the most important players at pivotal moments. They homed in on individuals and their discourse. Dialogue was used to explore multiple perspectives on well-known stories, letting the characters defend their own actions and interrogate each other's motivations. The violent confrontations of *Fáfnismál* and *Helgakviða Hundingsbana I* are transferred into combative speech acts, wherein the participants themselves explore their significance. The actual dragon slaying and battle are very minimally narrated in a short passage of prose and two stanzas of verse (53–4) respectively. By this means eddic poets – themselves always behind the scenes, speaking through familiar stories of the ancient, legendary past – breathed new life and relevance into tales retold again and again.

If eddic poetry was compelling because it effectively evoked the voices of the ancient past, it could be dangerous for the same reason. Eddic poets and redactors may also have had cause, particularly after the conversion of Scandinavia to Christianity, to distance their own voices from the lore they were propagating. It is telling that the Old Norse translator of the *Disticha Catonis* (*Dicts of Cato*), a popular Latin didactic text of the Christian

Middle Ages with Classical pagan origins, composed his *Hugsvinnsmál* in *ljóðaháttr*, on the model of *Hávamál*, and described its advice as that *er heiðinn maðr kendi sínum syni* ('which a heathen man taught his son', *SkP, Hsv* 1^VIII/5–6). Pre-Christian wisdom remained valuable, but potentially suspect and limited in its usefulness (see further Schorn 2011). Nor indeed were eddic modes always treated with reverence. In *Gautreks saga* (*The Saga of Gautrekr*), a ridiculous, backwards pagan family living in isolation destroy themselves through greed, all the while quoting pithy verses of *ljóðaháttr* to justify their absurd outlook and outrageous materialism (see Larrington, Chapter 8 in this Handbook). To this saga author, *ljóðaháttr* does not encode the utterance of gods, supernatural beings, and the greatest of heroes, but foolish pagans in this comedic exemplary tale of people who see the world in stark universal terms and so fail to live in it.

It was the unique blend of conservatism and flexibility characteristic of eddic style that allowed poets to accommodate material so widely varying in subject matter and tone, and to keep older poetry meaningful and accessible to many generations of Scandinavian audiences. Its formal innovations complemented its unprecedented development of complex rhetorical modes to convey subtleties of speech acts and characterisation. The skill of eddic poets is most evident in their consistent anonymity, to us and to their medieval audiences. Letting the voices of the ancient past speak for themselves, they provided a window onto a timeless world of great heroes and all kinds of supernatural beings, where fundamental human concerns could be explored again and again through narratives pared down to their essential core.

Notes

1. For general discussion of constitutive features, see the General Introduction to *SkP* (I, li–liv).
2. A brief discussion of the style and vocabulary of many eddic poems can be found in the introduction to each individual poem in the *Edda Kommentar*.
3. Translations are quoted from Carolyne Larrington (2014) with occasional modifications by the author.
4. Sveinbjörn Egilsson and Finnur Jónsson (1931: 206) conclude that the text is corrupt, while de Vries favours the interpretation popular with most recent commentators, tentatively linking it to modern Icelandic *gróm* ('dirt') as well as various Swedish dialect forms (1957–61: 124; see also *Edda Kommentar* VI, 454–6 for further discussion and alternatives).
5. In some cases, the content of stanzas and divisions between them varies between manuscripts, and the stanzas as they are presented in editions,

therefore, are to some extent editorial constructions. Compare, for example, the division of stanzas in *Vǫluspá* in Hauksbók (AM 544 4°) and the Codex Regius in the facsimile editions at www.menota.org.

6. The discussion of *fornyrðislag* here applies equally to the closely related *málaháttr*, which appears alongside it in some poems.

7. The episode is otherwise obscure. On various proposed interpretations, see Larrington 2014: 307; *Edda Kommentar* VI, 532–6; and O'Donoghue 2011.

8. In its extant form, the poem is likely a composite of pre-existing poems, associated by Óðinn's probable role as speaker. The number and nature of the constituent parts is debated. See further Evans 1996: 4–38; Larrington 1993: 15–19; and McKinnell 2005a and 2007a.

9. The original poetic context of stanzas quoted individually or together in a single sequence in saga prose must remain a matter for speculation.

10. These examples are discussed in Schorn (Chapter 12) on genre in this Handbook.

11. An exception is Gunnlaugr Leifsson's 'neo-eddic' poem *Merlínússpá*; see further Poole 2014.

12. As John McKinnell observed in a roundtable discussion at the Sixteenth International Saga Conference in Zürich in August 2015, eddic poetry 'was not accidentally anonymous, but functionally so'.

13. In a paper delivered at the Sixteenth International Saga Conference in Zürich in August 2015.

CHAPTER 15

Kennings and other forms of figurative language in eddic poetry[1]

Judy Quinn

The kenning, a poetic circumlocution comprised of two or more nouns, is usually associated with skaldic praise poetry in *dróttkvætt* metre, where the kenning's lexical complexity and its allusive power – invoking the grand narratives of myths – could enhance a poet's tribute to his aristocratic patron. Thus, the death-toll arising from Hákon jarl Sigurðarson's military campaigns is celebrated in Tindr Hallkelsson's *Hákonardrápa* (*Drápa of Hákon*) by means of the description of the jarl generously providing food – the corpses of his enemy – to the geese of Yggr (a poetic name, or *heiti*, for the god Óðinn, his 'geese' being his carrion-loving ravens): *Yggs ... gnótt ... veitti gǫglum* (*SkP* I, 8/2–3). The usual terminology for describing kennings is by head-word (here 'geese'), determinant ('Yggr'), and consequent referent ('ravens').[2] The jarl's fame, the poet proclaims, will last as long as people inhabit the earth, which is itself denoted by the kenning *Þriðja man*, 'Þriði's girl' (Þriði is another *heiti* for Óðinn), whose referent is the god's quondam lover, the giantess Jǫrð, a figure whose name also serves as the common noun for 'earth'. Through this densely woven verse, something of the grandeur of the god Óðinn rubs off on Hákon: the god's enthusiasm for battle and for subjugating those who threaten him resonates through the choice of determinant in each case, Hákon's territory standing synecdochally for the natural world seen through the lens of Old Norse mythology. At the same time, Tindr's construction of kennings meets the complex requirements of assonance (*hendingar*) and alliteration in the metre he composed in, a feat which redounded well on his reputation as well as conferring prestige on his patron. Not infrequently, poets also deployed kennings to effect their own self-aggrandisement: the poet Kormákr Ǫgmundarson, for instance, referred to his shield as the 'foot-platform of the giant Hrungnir' (*Hrungnis fóta stalli*), thereby rhetorically wielding in his defence a giant's shield.[3]

The extant corpus of Old Norse poetry creates the impression of a correlation between the use of kennings and verse-forms involving assonance such that it is often deduced that instances of kenning use in eddic metres were the result of skaldic influence.[4] The partial preservation in writing of both traditions, however, makes the evolution of the figure difficult to chart. A runic inscription dated *c.* 700 from Eggja in western Norway, for example, seems to preserve the kenning 'corpse-sea' for 'blood' in a text that appears to be metrical in phases, yet its verse-form is no more conclusively skaldic than eddic.[5] Most probably the idea of allusive, some-times metaphoric expression by means of a pairing of nouns was inherent in the earliest stages of the Scandinavian poetic tradition (and indeed of the poetic traditions that surfaced in manuscript texts of Old English and other Germanic verse), with what became the skaldic mode developing a taste for the form beyond the pair (to create kennings where the determinant was itself a kenning), as a substitute for a noun. Poets in the skaldic mode tended to avoid naming the referent directly elsewhere within their verse – maintaining the intrigue of lexical play – whereas poets in the eddic mode often (though not invariably) deployed kennings in apposition to a noun rather than as a substitute for one. For example, two kennings are used in apposition with the referent in the lines *vaknaði Brynhildr, Buðla dóttir, dís skjǫldunga* ('Brynhildr – daughter of Buðli, goddess of princes – woke up', *Br* 14/3),[6] the first a straightforward display of kinship relations and the second invoking the other-worldly power of Brynhildr through the head-word *dís* ('supernatural female being'), and the determinant *skjǫld-unga*, the descendants of ancient royal houses whose marriages and conquests eddic poets were preoccupied with.

While the figure of the kenning was clearly within the repertoire of poets composing in the eddic mode, they drew on it less systematically than poets composing in skaldic metres did, not least because in the quintessentially anonymous eddic tradition there was less incentive for the kind of flam-boyant word play through which a professional poet might build his reputation with a show of lexical dexterity.[7] The demands of eddic metres were less stringent as well, with a freer patterning of syllables in the line and words bound only by alliteration, without *hendingar* (which, in *dróttkvætt*, function as magnets for *heiti* in contexts where phonic value is crucial). Because of the relative metrical freedom of eddic rhythm, its syntax tends to be less convoluted than that of skaldic verse, which in turn makes greater demands on its audience in construing the sense of the verse. A corollary of this, as we have seen, is that kennings tend to be used as substitutes for nouns in skaldic verse, whereas when kennings occur in eddic verse they tend either to be appositive, amplifying the meaning of the noun that they accompany, or, if serving as noun substitutes, to be in close enough proximity to the named referent that identification is straightforward. Since the subject matter of much eddic verse tended to be ancient myths and legends themselves, there was also less need for the kind of compact allusion beyond the immediate situation of the poem that gives skaldic poetry a cultural depth beyond its generally sparse referential meaning. By and large, skaldic verse presents the voice of the poet as an outside observer whereas eddic verse typically presents the dialogue of the partici-pants in the action themselves.

Kennings in dialogue

Where kennings do occur in eddic verse, they often come from the mouths of the poem's speakers, rather than serving to embellish the narrative voice as they mainly do in skaldic poetry. So it is at the climax of *Oddrúnargrátr*, when, in Oddrún's eulogy for her lover Gunnarr, she refers to him using a circumlocution for a king which would not be out of place in a skaldic praise poem: *deilir sverða* ('distributor of swords' > war-leader, *Od* 33/7).[8] In the same stanza she also uses a kenning to describe her interlocutor, the dying princess Borgný, whom she calls *línvengis Bil* ('goddess of the linen pillow' > woman), and with this apostrophe she echoes the company of skalds who sent reports back to women on the home-front from the arena where heroes' reputations were forged.[9] Whereas in the skaldic record that arena was usually geographically distant, in *Oddrúnargrátr* it is separated in time from the audience, those sitting and listening to Oddrún's lament as it is related in successive performances (*Od* 34) from the crucible of eddic heroism, the courts of the Gjúkungar and Buðlungar.

Other speakers in eddic heroic poems coin unique kennings for situations which do not have ready parallels in the world depicted in skaldic encomia; the valkyrie Sigrún refers to sleep as an 'assembly of dreams' (*draumþing, HH II* 50/10), while her anxious maid warns her not to go alone at night among the grave-mounds, referring to them as 'ghost-homes' (*draughús, HH II* 51/3). In the same stanza, the unnamed maid apostrophises her mistress as *dís skjǫldunga*, the same kenning that is used to describe Brynhildr in *Brot af Sigurðarkviðu* (mentioned above). In this kenning, both the head-word and the determinant oscillate between their metonymic value (any female deity and any noble warrior) and their literal meaning (like the valkyrie, the *dís* is counted among the female agents of fate and the Skjǫldungar are descendants of an ancient Danish royal dynasty). Accordingly, the referent reflects the polyvalence of Sigrún herself since she, like Brynhildr, is both a valkyrie ('goddess of warriors') and a royal princess ('lady of princes').

Sigrún's maid is depicted as having a keen ear for kennings, as her earlier announcement of Helgi's surprise re-appearance at his grave-mound reveals:

> dólgspor dreyra, dǫglingr bað þik,
> at þú sárdrópa svefja skyldir. (*HH* II 42/7–10)

> [his battle-traces [> wounds] bleed, the prince asked for you, that you might staunch the wound-drops [> blood].]

The poet generates a variety of kennings for blood within this grave-side dialogue, each choice reflecting the perspective of the speaker: Sigrún recognises the blood seeping from Helgi's wounds as 'slaughter-dew' (*valdǫgg*, *HH II* 44/8), a refreshing sight for a valkyrie but not so for the mortally wounded Helgi, who describes his own blood as it flows from his wounds as 'sorrow-dew' (*harmdǫgg*, *HH II* 45/4). Whereas the poet of a skaldic praise poem might have drawn on the motif of bloodshed as a sign of battle ferocity bringing glory to the victor, in an extraordinary move the poet of *Helgakviða Hundingsbana II* ventures within the motif itself to let one of the mythological agents of battle-fate give voice to her own experience of the phenomenon. In her initial reaction to Helgi's reappearance, Sigrún adopts the perspective of a carrion-loving bird – with which valkyries were often associated – in order to express the joy she feels at the prospect of being with her chosen one again:

> Nú em ek svá fegin fundi okkrum
> sem átfrekir Óðins haukar,
> er val vitu, varmar bráðir (*HH II* 43/1–6)

> [I am now as delighted by our meeting as Óðinn's greedy hawks are when they know of men's slaughter, the warm flesh]

Rather than observing the conceit from afar, as her serving-woman does and skaldic poets might do, Sigrún is depicted as having internalised the sensation of relishing dead men's flesh even as she contemplates the seeping wounds of her beloved (see further Quinn 2006). A kenning, a compacted allusion to this phenomenon, would not have been nearly as effective as this dramatic enactment of what is so often but rarely so sensationally referenced.

The poet of *Helgakviða Hundingsbana II* engages with the concept of
the kenning at a deeper level in an earlier phase of the poem as well.
The noun *kenning* is derived from the verb *kenna*, 'to know or to
recognise', the expression *kenna einhvern við eitthvert* meaning 'to
name something in terms of something else'. After the valkyrie Sigrún
has singled out Helgi as her chosen warrior and protected him
in the battle in which he kills Hundingr (thereby gaining his fame
as Hundingsbani, 'the slayer of Hundingr'), she and Helgi spar in
conversation. Sigrún asks Helgi where he has been fighting – or, in her
idiom, where he has fed the goslings of Gunnr's sisters, Gunnr being the
name of a valkyrie, her sisters also valkyries and their goslings, ravens
(*hvar hefir þu ... gǫgl alin Gunnar systra?, HH II* 7/1–4). Identifying
himself only as 'descendant of the Ylfing dynasty' (*niðr Ylfinga*), Helgi
tells her the location of his recent battle – or, as he puts it, where he has
been hunting bears and feeding the race of eagles with sword-points (*er
ek bjǫrnu tók... ok ætt ara oddum saddak, HH II* 8/5–8).[10] The language
of battle kennings is rendered here as active description, with finite verbs
used rather than *nomina agentis* within nominal phrases. That is, Helgi is
not described as 'the feeder of birds of prey', as a warrior king might be
within a skaldic encomium; rather, he describes his own active role in
fighting, drawing on the conventional lexis of battle description. Like
Sigrún, he speaks from within the figure of speech rather than being
described by it.

When Sigrún correctly identifies his battle-victim as Hundingr, Helgi is
amazed at her knowledge, saying:

> Hvat vissir þú, at þeir sé,
> snót svinnhuguð, er sefa hefndu?
> margir ro hvassir hildings synir
> ok ámunir ossum niðjum. (*HH II* 11)

> [How could you know, clever-minded woman, whom we took our kin-
> vengeance out on, when many keen warriors look like us?]

Using a kenning to address him – 'spear-head of the army' > war-leader
(*folks oddviti, HH II* 12/2) – the knowing valkyrie discloses her presence at
the killing of Hundingr. She also indicates that the attempts by the son of
Sigmundr (another kenning for Helgi) to dupe her through obscure
language have failed:

> þó tel ek slœgjan Sigmundar bur
> er í valrúnum vígspjǫll segir. (*HH II* 12/5–8)

[though I declare the son of Sigmundr to be sly, when he tells news of a killing in battle-runes.]

Sigrún, in other words, has outsmarted Helgi in the play of words. She then explains that she had spied him before the battle, declaring:

nú vill dyljask dǫglingr fyr mér,
enn Hǫgna mær *Helga* kennir. (*HH II* 13/7–10)

[now the prince wants to conceal his identity from me, but Hǫgni's girl [> Sigrún] recognises Helgi.]

The valkyrie's ability to *kenna* is emphasised by the text (particularly bluntly in the manuscript text, which reads *enn Hǫgna mær kennir* – the object of the verb, *Helga*, imported by editors from a later paper manuscript). By weaving kennings into the dialogue between Helgi and Sigrún, the poet of *Helgakviða Hundingsbana II* intensifies the power-play between them as well as elaborating the conceit of recognition. When Sigrún identifies herself through her kinship relations (her father is a king by the name of Hǫgni, the prose between stanzas 4 and 5 tells us), the kenning echoes another *Hǫgna mær* familiar from the skaldic corpus: the valkyrie Hildr, whose intriguing relationship with her father and lover is the subject of *Ragnarsdrápa* by the ninth-century Norwegian poet Bragi Boddason, a legend retold by Snorri Sturluson in *Skáldskaparmál* (72).[11] Whether or not Helgi is presented as recognising such a referent at this stage of the poem is not clear: when he later describes Sigrún as 'Hildr' in stanza 29 he certainly understands the implications of tangling with a valkyrie, a point the poet has meanwhile reinforced by identifying Sigrún as *Hǫgna mær* in third-person narration as well (*HH II* 17/1). The story of Helgi and Sigrún is also the subject of the first *Helgakviða Hundingsbana*, and in this iteration the valkyrie is first introduced by the narrator as 'Hǫgni's daughter' (*Hǫgna dóttir, HH I* 17/2), the strains of the Hildr legend audible from the outset. It is not until stanza 30 that she is identified as Sigrún and, when she refers to herself, it is through the kenning *Hǫgna dóttir* (*HH I* 56/7).[12]

Kennings and characterisation

Kennings in eddic dialogue accordingly have significance for characterisation as well as for deepening the resonance of speakers' observations in relation to poetic tradition. In a recent paper, Kate Heslop has referred to this as the 'echo chamber' which eddic kennings sound in, where there is potential for intradiegetic reference to resonate beyond the immediate plot to the legendary tradition more generally.[13] So it is when Brynhildr rehearses the wrongs done to her in *Sigurðarkviða in skamma*, insisting on her own probity in the face of others' treacherous deception, and declaring that 'the mind of the necklace-valkyrie [> woman] was not for turning' (*bjóat um hverfan hug men Skǫgul, Sg* 40/3–4). Invoking the name of a valkyrie as the head-word in a kenning referring to herself reinforces that dimension of her identity as the one who chooses and abides by her choice. In many kennings, the semantic residue of the components of the kenning can be understood to contribute to their literary effect (Quinn 2012).

The assumption that the referent of a kenning will be understood is central to the riddling advice offered to Sigurðr by birds after he has killed Fáfnir. They refer to the young prince as *spillir bauga* ('destroyer of rings' > leader, *Fm* 32/6), to the dragon's heart as *fjǫrsegi* ('life-muscle', *Fm* 32/7), to Reginn as *smiðr bǫlva* ('smith of misfortune', *Fm* 33/7), to fire as *lindar váði* ('destruction of the linden', *Fm* 43/4), to Brynhildr as *hǫr-Gefn* ('goddess of flax', *Fm* 43/7), and to gold as *ógnar ljómi* ('radiance of the river', *Fm* 42/8). Here it is the character of the addressee that is being developed by the use of kennings, Sigurðr's ability to grasp the referents an aspect of his rite of passage from boyhood to kingship. (It goes without saying that birds who talk are prima facie extraordinary, their figurative diction a further mark of their sophistication.) In an earlier encounter with the disguised Óðinn in the same poem – during which Reginn answers on behalf of his companion Sigurðr – a series of kennings for 'ship' are rehearsed: *Rævils hestar* ('horses of the sea-king'), *seglvigg* ('sail-steeds'), *vágmarar* ('wave-horses'), *sætré* ('sea-trees'), and *hlunnvigg* ('steeds of the rollers') (*Rm* 16–17). While it is hardly surprising that the masterful word-smith Óðinn or the crafty Reginn might know how to turn a kenning, part of the significance of the figurative language in this exchange lies in its role as an induction for Sigurðr into the language of aristocratic warriors. Such a facility is exhibited later in the poem in the doomed soliloquy of Hǫðbroddr (Helgi Hundingsbani's rival for the love of Sigrún), as he recognises the might of his competitor before battle. Hǫðbroddr registers the impressive nature of Helgi's fleet, referring to his *rakka hirtir* ('harts of the mast-ring', *HH I* 49/3) and his *brimdýr* ('surf-beasts', *HH I* 50/7), before acknowledging *muna nú Helgi hjǫrþing dvala* (*HH I* 50/11–12) ('Helgi will not now delay the sword-meeting [> battle]'). The narrator of the first *Helgakviða Hundingsbana* had displayed an interest in ship kennings at an earlier stage of the poem as well – calling them *gjalfrdýr* ('beasts of the roaring sea') and *stagstjórnmarar* ('stay-bridled wave-horses') – in a lively sequence in which the valkyrie Sigrún wrests control of Helgi's fate out of the hands of malevolent sea-deities (*HH I* 29–30) (see also Larrington, Chapter 8 in this Handbook). The raw materials out of which sea kennings are formed (the personification of waves as the daughters of Ægir or the sisters of Kólga and the personification of the sea as the sea-deity Rán; see Quinn 2014) are deployed in the metaphorical description of the outcome of Helgi's sea journey; once again the eddic poet has chosen to play out the mythological conceit as live action rather than presenting a static image through the construction of a complex nominalisation.

Substitutive kennings

Another instance where a kenning's reach beyond the immediate context of the referent may also be observed comes from *Oddrúnargrátr*, when Oddrún recounts her sister Brynhildr's tragic life, pinpointing the moment when, as a powerful queen, she sat peacefully embroidering:

> jǫrð dúsaði ok uphiminn,
> þá er bani Fáfnis borg um þátti. (*Od* 17/5–8)

> [the earth resounded and heaven above when the slayer of Fáfnir [> Sigurðr] recognised the fortress.]

Even though Sigurðr is not named in the poem until stanza 19, his identity as dragon-slayer is so well-established that a kenning can be used here as a substitute for his name without disturbing the flow of Oddrún's lamentation. Similarly, when Oddrún describes the compensation the Gjúkungar offered her brother Atli as bride-price for her, gold is referred to with another familiar allusion, as *hliðfarmr Grana* ('the side-load of Grani', *Od* 21/7), Grani being the name of Sigurðr's horse whose saddle-packs were loaded with the gold Sigurðr retrieved from Fáfnir's lair. Presumably because of their familiarity, kennings for gold are often used substitutively in the eddic corpus: *ógnar ljómi* ('radiance of the river') occurs in *Helgakviða Hundingsbana I* (21/6) as well as by one of the birds in *Fáfnismál* (*Fm* 42/8). Gunnarr refers to gold as 'metal of the Rhine' (*Rínar málm*, *Sg* 16), while Brynhildr calls gold *góð Menju* ('Menja's goods', *Sg* 52) and *eldr ormbeðs* ('fire of the serpent's bed', *Gðr I* 26). In the version of *Helreið Brynhildar* preserved in *Norna-Gests þáttr* (*The Tale of Norna-Gestr*) in Flateyjarbók, Brynhildr is attributed with the gold kenning *Fáfnis dýna* ('Fáfnir's feather-bed') in the line *þann er fœrði mér Fáfnis dýnu*

('that one [Sigurðr] who brought me [> gold]'). In the version of the poem
in the Codex Regius, by way of contrast, the line is composed without
a kenning – *þanns mér fœrði gull, þats und Fáfni lá* (*Hlr* 10/7–8) ('that one
who brought me the gold which lay under Fáfnir') – suggesting that during
transmission the impulse towards phrasing mythological allusions as finite
clauses was in play as well as the syntactically opposite impulse towards
compact kennings as substitutes for nouns. In the same stanza, the referent
'fire' is expressed by kennings which share a determinant but have different
head-words in each version of the text: *herr alls viðar* ('destroyer of all
wood' in the Codex Regius text) and *hrotgarmr viðar* ('howling hound of
wood' in the Flateyjarbók text).[14] This too suggests that the craft of
kenning composition may have been an aspect of the creative recollection
of poems during transmission, including during the long period of
oral transmission which, as Thorvaldsen has shown in Chapter 4 in this
Handbook, makes dating the origin of most eddic poems impossible.
Changes small and large are likely to have occurred along the way, including to the figurative language of the poems.

Many of the kennings that are used as substitutes for nouns in eddic
heroic poems come from the arena of war, where the audience's familiarity with the conventions of battle poetry can be inferred. Thus, as part
of his coming-of-age wisdom contest with Fáfnir, Sigurðr refers to blood
as *hjǫrlǫgr* ('sword-liquid', *Fm* 14/5); and when Hǫðbroddr, alarmed at
the sight of Helgi's fleet, calls for reinforcements, he appeals to anyone
who can wield a *benlogi* ('wound-flame [> sword]', *HH I* 51/9).[15] Helgi's
distinction, even as a new-born baby, is conveyed by the gift to him from
his father of a *blóðormr* ('blood snake [> sword]', *HH I* 8/7), described
also by the *heiti, ítrlaukr* ('splendid leek', *HH I* 7/8). Brynhildr's elaborate description of the sword Sigurðr laid between their bodies – probably one of the best known scenes in legendary history – is anchored by
a kenning: the *benvǫndr* ('wound-wand', *Br* 19/1), she says, was chased
with gold and patterned with drops of poison. Unsurprisingly, battle
kennings tend to arise at the mention of valkyries, the poet of *Helgakviða
Hundingsbana I* alluding to *randa rymr* ('din of shields', *HH I* 17/3) at
the first appearance of Sigrún, with her final appearance in the poem
(*HH I* 54) heralded as follows:

> Komu þar ór himni hjálmvitr ofan
> – óx geira gnýr – þær er grami hlífðu
> ... sárvitr fluga,
> át hǫlða skær af Hugins barri.[16]

[Helmet-creatures [> valkyries] came down there out of the sky – the clash
of spears [> battle] increased – they who protected the prince [Helgi] ... –
wound-creatures [> valkyries] fly, the draught-horse of men [> wolf?] ate
Huginn's barley ([raven's food > corpses].]

The protection of Helgi by valkyries is also underwritten by a kenning in the
description of the journey made by his troop towards battle: *skalf Mistar mar
hvar megir fóru* (*HH I* 47/7–8) ('the sea of Mist [a valkyrie *heiti* > air]
trembled where the young men rode'). The very idea of the valkyrie attracts
expression through kennings even outside the context of the battlefield:
when Oddrún describes how their father intended her sister Brynhildr to
become a valkyrie, she uses the kenning *óskmey* ('wish-maid [> valkyrie]', *Od*
16/3),[17] while Guðrún's sense of her superiority over other women encompasses the exalted valkyries in Óðinn's retinue, expressed through a kenning:

> Ek þóttak ok þjóðans rekkum
> hverri hœrri Herjans dísi; (*Gðr I* 19/1–4)

> [I seemed higher among the prince's retinue than any of the *dísir* [super-
> natural women] of the War-Leader [a *heiti* for Óðinn] [> valkyries];]

Valkyries themselves are adept at using kennings, as was evident
from Sigrún's words quoted earlier. The valkyrie Sigrdrífa addresses
Sigurðr as an 'apple-tree of the assembly of mail-coats [> battle]' (*brynþings
apaldr, Sd* 5/2) and a 'maple of sharp weapons' (*hvassa vápna hlynr, Sd*
20/3), deploying the convention common in skaldic verse of composing
a warrior kenning using a tree-name as the head-word. The determinant in
the former case is itself a kenning ('assembly of mail-coats'), forming
a nested kenning of the sort that is very common in skaldic verse. While
much less common in eddic verse, such complex kennings are elsewhere
attested in the corpus: in his advice to Sigurðr, the disguised Óðinn refers
to warriors as 'whetters of sword-play [> battle]' (*hjǫrleiks hvatir, Rm* 23/7),
while Guðrún predicts that if Atli betrays her brothers she will take the life
of the 'instigator of the play of the sword-edge [> battle]' (*eggleiks hvǫtuðr,
Gðr II* 31/11). In all of the cases just cited the referent of the kenning is
readily apprehended from the context, even though the kennings serve as
substitutes for a named individual. As noted above, substitutive kennings
used in eddic heroic verse tend to be conventional and are used in close
proximity to the named referent. In *Guðrúnarhvǫt*, for instance, Hamðir
declares that his mother has stirred them to combat, to what he calls an
'assembly of swords' (*hjǫrþing, Ghv* 6/4) and he subsequently refers to
himself as a 'spear-god [>warrior]' (*geir-Njǫrðr, Ghv* 8/5), but just one line

earlier the narrator had identified the speaker as Hamðir. Before identifying her addressee as *Brynhildr, Buðla dóttir* (*Hlr* 4/1–2), the *gýgr* ('giantess')
who accosts Brynhildr on her journey to Hel addresses her using a kenning
for woman, 'goddess of gold' (*Vár gulls, Hlr* 2/5). As it is presented in the
manuscript (after a prose introduction identifying both speakers of the
dialogue), the referent of this kenning is clearly legible, and it would have
quickly become so in oral performance as well as through the context
elaborated by the dialogue alone.

   The most common sort of kenning in the eddic corpus is one which
identifies figures through their kinship relations, such as *Brynhildr, Buðla
dóttir*. In meeting the requirement of alliteration across stressed syllables in
a line, poets were of course well served by many of the names of eddic
figures – Helgi Hjǫrvarðsson and Guðrún Gjúkadóttir among them – and
by the alliterating relationship between individuals and their social groups,
such as *Gunnarr . . . Gotna dróttinn* ('lord of the Goths', *Grp* 35/5–6), or
Niðuðr, Njárar dróttinn ('lord of the Njárar', *Vkv* 13/1–2). Even the composition of some individuals' names betrays a taste for the kenning's
allusive effects: Sigrún ('victory-symbol') or Brynhildr ('chain-mail-battle'),
for instance.

   So far in this chapter I have focused on kennings that appear in poems
about the legendary past, which have on average a higher incidence of
kennings than poems on mythological subjects – though the gross statistics
hide the sharp contrasts between poems and between phases within
a poem.[18] Two poems among the mythological sequence in the Codex
Regius, *Vǫluspá* and *Hymiskviða*, exhibit a marked interest in kennings
(though to very different effects) and I will now briefly discuss some of the
ways in which kennings are exploited in each of them.

Kennings in *Vǫluspá*

Kinship relationships are prominent in the corpus of kennings in mythological poems, just as they are in the heroic poems – though the family
units are, of course, more extraordinary. There is also some telling variation
in the nature of the poem's kennings between the two extant versions of the
whole poem, in the Codex Regius and in Hauksbók (AM 544 4°), which
I will touch on in what follows. The *miðgarðsormr*, for instance, is
described in stanza 53/5 of the Codex Regius version of *Vǫluspá* as 'Loki's
son' (*mǫgr Hveðrungs* [a *heiti* for Loki]); and in both versions Loki is
identified as the brother of Býleiptr (*bróðir Býleipts*, R49/7–8; H43/7–8)[19]
and Freyja as *Óðs mey* (R25/8; H21/8), a kenning whose head-word in the

context of the heroic poems designated 'daughter,' as we have seen, whereas here it seems to mean 'lover' (of the mysterious deity Óðr). The referent of the kenning *Surtar sefi* ('kinsman of Surtr') only in the Hauksbók text (H39/7–8) is uncertain, and creates a significant crux in the mythology. The context is the swallowing of the ash-tree Yggdrasill in the prelude to *ragnarǫk*, the tree being consumed by someone or something related to Surtr. Since a later stanza refers to Surtr wielding fire – denoted by the kenning *sviga læ* (R51/2; H44/2) ('branch's destruction') – fire has been deduced as the possible referent of the kenning *Surtar sefi* as well, with *sefi* understood figuratively. But if weight is given to the kinship dimension suggested by the head-word, an animate relative of Surtr's could be posited as the agent of destruction. Mythological sources provide only a fragmentary portrait of the figure Surtr (Lindow 2001: 282–3), allowing some leeway in imagining who the members of his extended family might have been. The wolf Fenrir has been proposed as the referent of the kenning, the world-tree a side-order to his meal at *ragnarǫk* during which (according to *Gylfaginning*) he swallows Óðinn and the sun.[20]

Óðinn's death is prophesied by the *vǫlva* (the speaker of *Vǫluspá*) in a rather delicate fashion, as the second sorrow of Frigg (Óðinn's wife, who has already suffered the loss of their son Baldr): *þá mun Friggjar falla angan* (H45/7–8) ('then Frigg's beloved [> Óðinn] will fall'). The Codex Regius text of this line reads *þá mun Friggjar falla Angantýr* (R52/7–8) ('then Frigg's Angantýr [> Óðinn] will fall'), a reading that only makes sense if the name known from ancient legends, Angantýr, serves as the head-word for an unusual kenning for Óðinn that denotes him as Frigg's warrior-hero (Quinn 2001: 83). Here again there is evidence that the construction of kennings is an aspect of the kind of variation that could occur in the recollection of eddic poetry during transmission, oral or written.[21]

Kennings that identify figures through their relationship with others extend beyond kinship ties, with the formula 'the killer of someone' being widely attested in both heroic and mythological poems. Freyr, for instance, is called the slayer of Beli (*bani Belja*, R52/5; H45/5). In some cases it is difficult to distinguish a potential kenning from a metaphorical phrase: *vá Valhallar* (R33/7) ('the woe of Valhǫll'), for instance, which is used in connection with the death of Baldr. Metaphors more deeply embedded in the mythology, such as *ragna rǫk* in the refrain of the poem (R43/7–8ff; H31/7–8ff) ('doom of the gods') – and perhaps even *gap ginnunga* (R3/7–8; H3/7–8) ('chasm of *ginnungs*')[22] – have formal similarities to kennings and may once have signalled a referent even if it is not one that is readily identifiable in our lexicon. *Vǫluspá* is also full of metaphorical names – too many to treat in detail here – such as the tree-like figures Askr and Embla who are given life by the gods (R17/7; H17/7), or the many place-names with mythological resonance (on which see Brink and Lindow, Chapter 9 in this Handbook).

The kinship relationships that are to the fore in *Vǫluspá* are those involving Þórr and Óðinn, the gods whose tragic deaths are described in the culmination of the poem. At the point of his defeat, Þórr is twice described in relation to his mother, the giantess Jǫrð – though in both cases she is identified by a *heiti*: *Fjǫrgynjar burr* (R54/10; H48/2[23]) ('Fjǫrgyn's boy') and *mǫgr Hlóðynjar* (R54/2) ('Hlóðyn's son'). In the same stanza in the Regius text (but stanza 47 in H), Þórr is less obliquely identified as *Óðins sonr* ('Óðinn's son'). Óðinn himself is identified with reference to another of his sons, Viðarr, in the Regius text through the extended kenning, *mǫgr Sigfǫður* ('son of victory-father', a kenning for Óðinn) (R53/2), and as *Herfǫðr* ('army-father') (R29/1), also only in the Regius text. The determinant 'army' implicates the human world in the god's characterisation, as does the determinant *val* ('battle-corpses') in the Óðinn kenning *Valfǫðr* ('corpse-father') (R1/5; R27/7–8 and R28/13–14). In the latter two instances, the kenning is part of an extended kenning *veð Valfǫðrs* ('Óðinn's pledge'), whose referent is the eye the god traded for a drink from Mímir's well, although in context the kenning refers to the well itself: water pours forth from *veð Valfǫðrs* (R27) and the mysterious Mímir drinks from *veð Valfǫðrs* (R28).

Another mythological crux arises from a kenning towards the end of the poem, when the new world, inhabited by the resurrected Baldr and Hǫðr, is described (R60/5–7; H54/5–7): the gods, who settle in a place referred to as the 'victory-sites of Óðinn' (*sigtóptir Hropts* [a heiti for Óðinn]), are called *valtívar* ('corpse-gods') in the Regius text but possibly *velltívar* ('golden gods') in the damaged Hauksbók text.[24] Earlier in the poem (R51/3–4; H44/3–4), as fiery Surtr approaches from the south, the sun of the corpse-gods is said to shine from his sword (*skínn af sverði sól valtíva*). Is the phrasing *sól valtíva* simply descriptive (the sun, like everything else, being an attribute of the powerful gods), or is it a kenning, with an obscure referent?[25] In either case, the role of the gods in relation to warriors who die in battle is implicated in the expression, as it is in the opening of the poem when the *vǫlva* identifies her addressee as *Valfǫðr* and her audience as encompassing the sons of the god Heimdallr (*megir Heimdalar*), a kenning whose referent is probably 'humans'.[26] People are elsewhere referenced in *Vǫluspá* through a kenning as well: as the 'children of men' for whom the list of dwarf-names is tallied (*ljóna kindir*, R14/3; H14/3). The varied use of kennings in *Vǫluspá* illuminates not just our understanding of mythology, but also the nature of eddic poetry, not least since the poem is generally regarded as having its origin in the pre-Christian past (albeit an origin that we can neither pinpoint in time nor reconstruct as text).

Kennings in *Hymiskviða*

Kennings abound in another of the eddic mythological poems, *Hymiskviða*, which tells the story of Þórr's mission to obtain an ale-brewing kettle for the gods from the giant Hymir, whom the god joins on a fishing trip during which he opportunistically attempts to kill the *miðgarðsormr*. The kettle is referred to by the kennings 'liquid-boiler' (*lǫgvellir*, *Hym* 6/2) and 'beer-ship' (*ǫlkjóll*, *Hym* 33/4), as well as by the simplex nouns *ketill* (*Hym* 5/6) and *hverr* (*Hym* 1/8, 3/6, 5/7, 9/4, 13/3, 33/8, 34/6, 36/2, 39/3), which provide ample context for the two kennings when they are used non-appositively, the first by Þórr and the second by Hymir. The word *hverr* is also used metaphorically to refer to the basin in the landscape (*Hym* 27/8) through which Þórr drags his load back to the giant's home after their fishing trip, signalling the lexical play the poet of *Hymiskviða* clearly delighted in. Once back, the giant sets Þórr a challenge of smashing a goblet in order to win the kettle. In the staging of this episode, the simplex term *kálkr* is repeatedly used: by the narrator (*Hym* 28/8), by Hymir's helpful wife (*Hym* 30/8) – who is also the mother of Þórr's companion Týr – and by Hymir himself as he concedes defeat (*Hym* 32/3). Once again, this provides sufficient context for the kenning 'wine-vessel' (*vínferill*, *Hym* 31/7) when it is used by the narrator in the climax of the episode, as Þórr bashes the object against the giant's own skull.

The poet also enjoyed conjuring up kennings for 'head' during the different episodes narrated in the poem (Hallberg 1983: 63–4; Clunies Ross 1989: 19–20): Þórr smashes the *vínferill* down on the giant's *hjálmstofn* ('helmet-stump', *Hym* 31/6), having earlier brought his hammer down on the *háfjall skarar* ('high mountain of the hair', *Hym* 23/6) of the *miðgarðsormr*, whom he had baited with the *hátún horna tveggja* ('stronghold of the two horns', *Hym* 19/3–4) of an ox. As Þórr leaves the territory of giants with his kettle, he is pursued by a many-headed troop of warrior-giants (*fólkdrót fjǫlhǫfðaða*, *Hym* 35/7–8), an alarming spectre given that Hymir's own mother is said to boast nine hundred heads herself (*Hym* 8). The highest tally of kennings, however, is reserved for Þórr, whose importance within the kinship network of the Æsir is repeatedly stressed: he is 'child of Yggr [a heiti for Óðinn]' (*Yggs barn*, *Hym* 2/6), 'Óðinn's son' (*Óðins sonr*, *Hym* 35/3), 'husband of Sif' (*Sifjar verr*, *Hym* 3/5, 15/5 and 34/6), and 'father of Móði' (*faðir Móða*, *Hym* 34/1). Þórr's defining trait – his animosity towards giants – is repeatedly emphasised through kennings: he is the 'adversary of Hróðr [a giant]' (*Hróðrs andskoti*, *Hym* 11/8), 'the one who makes the giantess cry' (*gýgjar grœtir*, *Hym* 14/3), 'pre-meditated murderer of the giant' (*þurs ráðbani*, *Hym* 19/2), and, in an extended kenning, the 'breaker of rock-Danes [> giants]' (*brjótr berg-Dana*, *Hym* 17/7). Even as he contends with the *miðgarðs-ormr*, Þórr is celebrated as the 'single-handed killer of the serpent' (*orms einbani*, *Hym* 22/3), though whether and when he kills the world-serpent was clearly a variable aspect of this myth in its many representations (see Kopár, Chapter 10 in this Handbook). The god's status is also conveyed by the kenning 'lord of goats' (*hafra dróttinn*, *Hym* 20/2 and 31/2), and his protective relationship towards people indicated by the kenning *vinr verliða* ('friend of humans', *Hym* 11/9), a point underscored by the frequent use of the *heiti* 'Guardian' (*Véurr*) as a substitute for the name Þórr (*Hym* 11/10, 17/1, 21/7).

The bonds between the enemies of the gods are also alluded to through kennings. The 'high mountain of the hair' mentioned above belongs to the 'close brother of the wolf' (*úlfs hnitbróður*, *Hym* 23/8), a reference to Fenrir's sibling, the *miðgarðsormr*. Hymir is called 'playmate of Hrungnir [a giant]' (*Hrungnis spjalli*, *Hym* 16) and 'descendant of apes' (*áttrún apa*, *Hym* 20), kennings that work to denigrate giant-kind at the same time as registering their destructive energy. Giants are also denoted by the kennings 'rock-Dane' (mentioned above), as well as 'mountain-inhabitant' (*bergbúi*, *Hym* 2/1), 'lava-dwellers' (*hraunbúar*, *Hym* 38/5), and 'whales of the lava-field' (*hraunhvalar*, *Hym* 36/5). This last kenning depends on the same kind of incongruity between base-word and referent that lies behind the ship kennings constructed with a head-word that denotes a horse or land-based animal (which, as we saw above, appear in a number of eddic heroic poems as well as in the skaldic corpus). Much is made, through kennings, of the rowing-boat Hymir owns, which Þórr persuades him to row beyond his usual coastal fishing ground in order to get within striking distance of the *miðgarðsormr*. In comparison with the martial splendour of a war-ship – which ship kennings usually connote – the effect of Hymir referring to himself as 'master of long-ships' (*kjóla valdi*, *Hym* 19/7) is surely ironic.[27] In light of this, his subsequent reference to his boat as a 'floating goat' (*flotbrúsi*, *Hym* 26/5) invites a comic interpretation of his instruction to Þórr after they return to land with their catch of two whales:

> Mundu um vinna verk hálft við mik,
> at þú heim hvali haf til bœjar
> eða flotbrúsa festir okkarn. (*Hym* 26)

[You'll be doing half the work with me if you carry the whales home to the farm or secure our floating-goat [> boat].]

Similarly, the cartoon-like image towards the end of the poem (*Hym* 34), of the huge up-turned kettle engulfing Þórr's body as he carries it – the handles dangling around his heels – is preceded by Hymir challenging Þórr to try to manoeuvre the 'ale-ship' out of the giant's home (*ǫlkjóll, Hym* 33/4), drawing into parallel the motifs of the poem's two quests. And when in stanza 20/1–4 the narrator says:

> Bað hlunngota hafra dróttinn
> áttrunn apa útarr fœra;

[The lord of goats [> Þórr] told the descendant of apes [> Hymir] to row the stallion of the rollers [> ship] out further;]

his rhetoric is presumably channeling Þórr's derogatory opinion of the giant and his fishing boat. (It remains an irony of the mythology that Þórr does not seem able to approach the *miðgarðsormr* in its natural habitat except by this means, however.)

An interesting crux arises in the construal of one particular kenning in *Hymiskviða* 27, about which there is little scholarly consensus:

> Gekk Hlórriði, greip á stafni,
> vatt með austri up lǫgfáki;
> einn með árum ok með austskutu
> bar hann til bœjar brimsvín jtuns
> ok holtriða hver í gegnum.

[Þórr went and took hold of the prow, turned over the sea-stallion with the bilge-water; single-handed – with the oars and the bailer – he carried the giant's surf-pig home to the farm over the wooded hills and the kettle-shaped valley.]

The first kenning *lǫgfákr* clearly refers to a ship – or, in this context, the giant's rowing-boat. Elsewhere in the eddic corpus, the kenning type 'animals of the surf' also patently refers to a ship (for example, *brimdýr, HH I* 50/7, mentioned above) and there is a parallel in the skaldic corpus, in a *lausavísa* by Eyvindr skáldaspillir Finnsson, in which a ship is referred to as a 'wave-pig' (*unnsvín*, *SkP*, Lv 13^I/8). To some scholars, however, the kenning 'surf-pig' is taken to refer to a whale, even though there are very few kennings for whales in the skaldic corpus – Meissner (1921: 116) lists just two, both following the pattern 'giant's boar' – and in *Hymiskviða* whales are elsewhere referred to by the simplex *hvalr* (*Hym* 21, 26), which otherwise also appears, as we have seen, as the head-word within a giant kenning (*hraunhvalar*).[28] While the attraction of imagining a whale as a surfing pig is possibly too hard for the modern mind to resist, this example raises an interesting methodological issue: to what extent should kennings in the eddic corpus, whose subject matter is often so wildly different from that of *dróttkvætt* praise poetry, be interpreted in terms of the attestations in the skaldic corpus?

Other forms of figurative language

In many cases across the eddic corpus, poets seem to have been as likely to use a simile as a kenning in emphasising a point, the semantic fields they drew on being nonetheless similar in many instances to those which underlie kennings. So it is that Helgi is said to surpass other warriors, like a beautifully shaped ash-tree rising above a thorn-bush (*sem ítrskapaðr askr af þyrni*, *HH II* 38/3). The implied metaphor behind the equation of warriors and trees in the formation of warrior-kennings using the names of trees as head-words becomes explicit when Helgi is described earlier in the same poem simply as a splendidly-born elm (*álmr ítrborinn*, *HH I* 9/3). Botanical similes also encompass species smaller than trees, with Sigurðr likened by Guðrún to a leek rising above the grass (*sem væri geirlaukr ór grasi vaxinn*, *Gðr I* 18/3–4), her brothers just low blades of grass in the eyes of their sister. Relative height and the cultural connotations of the species give meaning to these comparisons, whereas in other similes the distinction is between the copse and the individual specimen. After the loss of husbands and sons, Guðrún imagines herself standing alone, like a single aspen in a forest, like a tree stripped of leaves (*sem ǫsp í holti. . . sem viðr at laufi*, *Hm* 5/2, 5/6). Having once regarded herself as higher in status than *Herjans dísir* (quoted above), Guðrún now admits to feeling as little as a leaf among the bay-willows (*nú em ek svá lítil sem lauf sé. . .í jǫlstrum*, *Gðr I* 19/5–6).

The distinction between a high leek and low grass through which Sigurðr is characterised in the first *Guðrúnarkviða* is extended in the second *Guðrúnarkviða* into the animal realm – with Sigurðr likened to a tall stag among beasts (*hjǫrtr hábeinn um hvǫssum dýrum*, *Gðr II* 2/5–6) – and further into the sphere of precious metals. He is likened to gold which glows red beside dull silver (*gull glóðrautt af grá silfr, Gðr II* 2/7–8). The same initial comparison in the first *Guðrúnarkviða*, by way of contrast, prompts two further lapidary comparisons instead: Sigurðr is like a bright stone threaded on a cord, or a precious gem compared with his lacklustre peers (*bjartr steinn á band dreginn, jarknasteinn yfir ǫðlingum, Gðr I* 18/7–10). Similes can trigger similes, in other words, without the field of comparators being so conventional that the sequence is necessarily repeated verbatim. Just as remembered kennings could generate variable formulations in oral transmission (as was noted in the case of *Hlr* 10), so too concatenated comparisons in the eddic tradition could engender different similes. The similes mentioned here are just a small sample: other examples include Sigrún's appraisal of Hǫðbroddr's valour as like that of a cat's kitten (*sem kattar son, HH I* 18/8); Brynhildr's description of Svanhildr, daughter of Sigurðr and Guðrún, as more radiant than a bright day or a ray of sunshine (*hvítari enn inn heiði dagr* ... *sólar geisla, Sg* 55/3–4); and Jǫrmunrekkr roaring like a bear (*sem bjǫrn hryti, Hm* 25/3) as he orders the brothers Hamðir and Sǫrli to be stoned in the last scene of the last poem in the Codex Regius, *Hamðismál*.

Hamðismál ends with a dark meditation on the similarities between warriors and the carrion-creatures they feed – those figures of speech in eddic and skaldic verse that define the triumphant combatant but whose behaviour also serves as a troubling comparator to their own. One or other of the brothers Hamðir and Sǫrli (the manuscript text does not specify which) says:

> stǫndum á val Gotna,
> ofan, eggmóðum, sem ernir á kvisti; (*Hm* 30/2–4)
>
> [we stand on the bodies of Goths, sword-weary, above them like eagles on a branch;]

It is as if in their ethical confusion – having ill-advisedly killed their own half-brother in pursuit of kin vengeance – the brothers identify with the determinant by which a warrior might be recognised (a bird of prey) rather than the conventional head-word (the feeder of the bird). With their campaign over, it is not valkyries who congregate in the brothers' minds, but the personified forces of fate who, far from protecting their subjects, drive them on to their doom: 'the *dísir* urged me on, they drove me to killing ... no man outlasts the evening after the decree of the norns' (*hvǫttumk at dísir* ... *gǫrðumsk at vígi* ... *kveld lifir maðr ekki eptir kvið norna, Hm* 28/6, 28/8, 30/7–8). In fact, at the point in the poem when they prepared to kill their brother, the narrator of *Hamðismál* described them unsheathing their weapons 'to the joy of the troll-woman' (*at mun flagði, Hm* 15/4). An eddic hero's mind-world was inhabited by personifications and anthropomorphised beasts; different kinds of figures that served to elaborate martial prowess. But for these doomed warriors, now in the unhappy company of the determinants of battle kennings rather than their conventional head-words, the heroic values their behaviour represents are hard to articulate. As his inevitable death draws nearer, the speaker even ruminates over the appropriateness of the simile:[29]

> Ekki hygg ek okkr vera úlfa dœmi,
>   at vit mynim sjálfir um sakask,
> sem grey norna, þau er gráðug eru,
>   í auðn um alin. (*Hm* 29)
>
> [I don't think it is for us to follow the example of wolves and fight among ourselves, like the dogs of the norns, reared in wilderness, greedy beasts.]

There are also many examples of metaphoric language in the eddic corpus – beyond, that is, the metaphoricity inherent in kennings and mythological personifications already described.[30] Space allows just a few examples here. The sword given to Helgi Hjǫrvarðsson by the valkyrie Sváva is described as having courage in its middle and terror in its pommel (*hugr er í miðju, ógn er í hjalti, HHv* 9/2–3); the mortally wounded Brynhildr tells her husband Gunnarr that his ship will not quite stay afloat (*muna yðvart far alt í sundi, Sg* 53/5–6) and that, to many men, Guðrún will be a destructive missile (*skeyti skœða skatna mengi, Sg* 56/3–4). In addition, many of the proverbs and gnomic aphorisms in *Hávamál* and other poems rely on metaphor for their significance to be construed (Hallberg 1983: 74–7).

In eddic poetry both mythological and heroic, the landscape itself is often portrayed as having attitude – clouds can be callous (*harðmóðgu ský, Grm* 41) and the weather hostile (*veðr válynd, Vsp* R40/7; H25/7) – while the natural world often reacts violently to the activities of gods and heroes. When Þórr attacked the *miðgarðsormr*, the creatures of the ocean responded with eerie shrieks (*Hym* 24), while when Guðrún, enraged with the norns, tried to drown herself, high waves carried her defiantly to the shore (*Ghv* 13). The road to Hel roared when Óðinn rode along it (*BD* 3), and, when Þórr and Loki flew through the air to a giant's court, mountains split apart and the earth caught fire (*Þkv* 21). In *Vǫluspá*, the world-tree groans (R46; H39), rocky cliffs collapse, and the sky splits apart (R51; H44). This is not pathetic fallacy, as such motifs might appear to be in other literatures where human emotions are projected onto the landscape. This is the expression of mythology itself, where metaphoricity is inherent – where the earth is a giant.

Notes

1. In writing this chapter I benefitted from hearing two papers presented at the 'Kenning and Context' conference at the University of Kiel in July 2014: Kate Heslop, 'Kennings and metaphors, eddic and skaldic', and Rob Fulk, 'Kennings in Old English literature'. Conversations over recent years with students at Cambridge University (particularly Katherine Olley and Charlotte White) have also proved stimulating, as have discussions with my co-editors.
2. A valuable introduction to the skaldic kenning forms part of the General Introduction by the editors to *Skaldic Poetry of the Skandinavian Middle Ages* (*SkP* I, lxx–lxxxv). For earlier scholarship on the kenning, see Meyer 1889, Meissner 1921, Mohr 1933, and Marold 1983; useful discussions in English include Lindow 1975, Amory 1988, and Fidjestøl 1997a.
3. *SkP*, KormQ Lv 14^{V}. Þórr's encounter with the giant Hrungnir is described in *Skáldskaparmál* (20–2): the giant is fooled into believing the god's approach will be subterranean and therefore misguidedly stands on his defensive weapon.
4. See, for example, *Edda Kommentar* IV, 144 and Clunies Ross 2013: 193.
5. KJ101^{VI} cited from the General Introduction to *SkP* (I, lxx); kennings such as *stillir flotna* ('controller of fleets' > leader) and *skati Mæringa* ('prince of the Mærings'), referring to Theoderic, also occur within the runic inscription on the Rök-stone in lines that resemble *fornyrðislag* (Lönnroth 1977a).
6. Translations are the author's own, informed by the definitions in the glossary of La Farge and Tucker (1992) and by Larrington's translation (2014).
7. While pointing up the distinctive traits of eddic and skaldic style is a useful way into this subject, I do not wish to suggest they were separate traditions; individual poets may well have composed and/or performed in both styles.
8. On the use of *heiti* as well as kennings in eddic heroic poetry, see Wessén 1927.
9. See Frank 1990 for a discussion of skalds' addresses to women; and Quinn 2009 for an analysis of the style of *Oddrúnargrátr*.
10. The word 'bear' is probably a metaphor for warrior in this context; see the discussion in *Edda Kommentar* IV, 673–4.
11. The determinant 'Hǫgni's girl [> Hildr]' is used in kennings for shield in *Ragnarsdrápa* 2, *Hákonarkviða* 22, and *Háttatal* 49; and for a warrior in *Háleygjatal* 7. See Quinn 2007 for a discussion of Hildr's role in kennings of this sort.
12. On the relationship between the two poems of Helgi Hundingsbani, and the idea of the first as a 'skaldic revision' of the second, see Harris 1983.
13. The term 'echo chamber', borrowed from Roland Barthes, was usefully adapted in Heslop's paper 'Kenning, system and context: how kennings

construct referential space', delivered at the Sixteenth International Saga Conference in Zürich in August 2015.

14. A similar kenning for fire is recorded in the eddic *Ævidrápa* in *Qrvar-Odds saga* (*SkP*, QrvOdd *Ævdr* 14[VIII]); see Clunies Ross 2013: 195–6 and 200.

15. The attribution of speakers in this phase of dialogue is not explicit in the text or in the manuscript; see further *Edda Kommentar* IV, 348.

16. The quotation is of the Codex Regius text: *fluga* is often emended by editors to *flugu* and *hǫlða* to *hálu* ('troll-woman'); the recent Íslensk fornrit edition of the poems makes the first emendation but not the second (Jónas Kristjánsson and Vésteinn Ólason 2014: II, 257); see further *Edda Kommentar* IV, 358–65.

17. On the semantics of this kenning see further Quinn 2009: 317 and *Edda Kommentar* VI, 901–2.

18. For an overview of the occurrence of kennings in the poems of the Codex Regius, see Hallberg 1983: 49 and 60–1.

19. The numbering of stanzas of the two complete versions of *Vǫluspá* accords with the separate editions of the poem in Jónas Kristjánsson and Vésteinn Ólason 2014: I, 291–316.

20. For speculation over the referent of the kenning, see La Farge and Tucker 1992: *s.v. sefi*, Dronke 1997: 87 and Sigurður Nordal 1978: 92–4. In the recent Íslenzk fornrit edition of the poem, the referent proposed is 'fire' (Jónas Kristjánsson and Vésteinn Ólason 2014: I, 313). Similarly unclear is the precise identity of *Míms synir* ('the sons of Mímr') who, at the commencement of *ragnarǫk*, are said to play (R45/1; H38/1).

21. A discussion of the other aspects of *Vǫluspá* that appear to have been liable to variation during transmission may be found in Quinn 1990b.

22. The meaning of *ginnunga* is unclear: John Lindow has suggested 'a gap of ginnungs . . . was probably a proto-space filled with magic powers' (2001: 141). See further Sigurður Nordal 1978: 12–13 and Dronke 1997: 112–14, who notes '*ginnunga* presents a tortuous problem'.

23. The Hauksbók text at this point in the poem is difficult to decipher with the kenning part of the reconstruction by Jón Helgason (1964: 44–6).

24. For a discussion of these two readings and emendations that have been proposed, see Quinn 2016.

25. The genitive plural noun *valtíva* ('of the slaughter-gods') could also be construed with *sverð* (Sigurður Nordal 1978: 103–4), the sword in that case argued to be the one which Freyr unwisely gave away.

26. The Hauksbók text reads *Váfǫðr* ('woe-father'?) rather than *Valfǫðr*, which introduces a further complication into the interpretation of its version of the poem.

27. The manuscript text of the poem does not make explicit who speaks these lines, nor is its syntax unambiguous. For a survey of the interpretative possibilities, see Hallberg 1983: 64, *Edda Kommentar* II, 312–17, and Jónas Kristjánsson and Vésteinn Ólason 2014: I, 403.

28. Meissner categorises *brimsvín* as a kenning for a ship (and not a whale), but observes that the referent could possibly be a whale (1921: 219–20); Hallberg concludes that the kenning 'surely refers to the whales' (1983: 65); *Edda Kommentar* (II, 333) canvasses a range of different opinions, while Jónas Kristjánsson and Vésteinn Ólason (2014: I, 404) note the kenning's referent could be a ship, but suggest it is more likely that a whale would be carried to the farmstead.

29. The wolfish potential of people is often referenced in the eddic corpus (see *HH II* 1, *Rm* 11, *Sg* 12 and *Akv* 8). See further Jesch 2002.

30. Hallberg's (1983) survey includes a discussion of metaphors involving the idea of brightness, sharpness, and coldness, as well as a survey of verbs in eddic poetry which are used metaphorically.

CHAPTER 16

Alliterative lexical collocations in eddic poetry

Maria Elena Ruggerini

Lexical collocations stem from the diction of traditional oral alliterative poetry and may be regarded as one of the stylistic features which characterise the corpus of mythological and heroic lays preserved in Codex Regius (GKS 2365, 4°). The versifiers' creation of privileged, though not necessarily semantically close, combinations of two or more words coupled at a short metrical distance served different purposes: certainly as an aid to composition and memorisation, but also – and most interestingly – to generate a dynamic interaction between words in different narrative contexts.

A collocative approach to eddic verse enables us to understand its compositional mechanisms and requirements better, and to outline its aesthetics more incisively. Moreover, a comparison of the collocations deployed by eddic versifiers with those which abound in Old English and Old Saxon alliterative poems confirms that the former should not be considered as typical only of the Old Norse milieu, but rather as a continuation of a widespread and long-standing feature of poetry in the old Germanic languages.

Collocations may derive almost naturally from pre-existing semantic and cultural links between words with the same initial sound, as in the case of the attested pairs *ráða* ('to advise') and *ríkr* ('powerful') or *níð* ('hostility') and *nótt* ('night'), but they can also be of a subtler nature, as when the words *bróðir* ('brother') and its near homophone *brúðr* ('bride') are brought into connection with the noun *bani* ('slayer'), where nouns denoting close family relationships are associated with a word that often implies the duty of heroic revenge. The received repertoire of basic collocational sets was liable to be enlarged or modified mainly on the basis of phonetic similarity; the interplay between stability, repetition, and a varying degree of adaptability must then have created audience expectations which would in turn be fulfilled or challenged or overturned.

The notion of collocation applied to Germanic
alliterative verse

A collocation, as studied by linguists and lexicographers, is a recurrent combination of words within a language, or within the same text or texts, marked by different degrees of fixedness. The combination is not as rigid as an idiom, and its characteristics vary depending on the corpus chosen for investigation and on the aim of the observer (Gledhill 2000: 7–20). The relationship between its constituent parts – lexical, syntactical, or altogether absent – can be freely established or bound. Typically, a base-term may occur together with more than one partner-word, thus generating a series of equally valid collocations (McKeown and Radev 2000: 509), such as '*diplomatic* edition', '*critical* edition', '*conservative* edition'.

Moving from the field of linguistics to the domain of early Germanic verse, the term 'collocation' can still be usefully employed, but requires a preliminary redefinition: on the one hand, the language of poetry is per se different from the technical language which offers corpora linguists their main research area for the study of collocations; on the other, the specific requirements of Germanic metre and style necessarily call for some distinctions.

The ancient Germanic peoples' poetic production – including eddic poems – stems from different areas and was copied onto parchment at various times. However, it forms a relatively homogeneous corpus since it presupposes a pattern of initial alliteration as its main cohesive characteristic and the use of common stylistic devices across corpora, of which formula and collocation are essential features. Furthermore, the fact that Germanic verse-making relied heavily on existing compounds and on the possibility of creating new ones may have produced other kinds of word combinations. Finally, the long phase of oral tradition most probably fostered collocations as a useful tool in the process of verse-making, memorisation, delivery, and performance.

For the purposes of the present investigation,[1] a poetic collocation is defined as a recurrent combination of two or more mostly alliterating lexical words within the long line, or in contiguous verses; such repeated co-occurrences may be internal to one text, or attested in different poems.[2] A collocation implies a special relationship between the partner-words, which may be innate and stable, determined by context, or established arbitrarily by the versifier. The fact that collocations are by their very nature repeated associates them with formulas, but the two processes should be kept distinct, mainly because the components of a collocation do not necessarily combine in a tight syntactic and metrical unit as formulas do; the co-occurring words may even belong to different phrases, and yet remain recognisable as a meaningful and evocative conjunction.

Some well-attested pairs or longer units of combining words must in part stem directly from the common stock of Germanic oral versification; others are likely to have been modified or perhaps even created at a given time and in a particular milieu by a poet or performer, subsequently gaining diffusion through the influence of a circle or a 'school'. In other words, the use of collocations can be explained as the result either of long-established usage or of an authorial choice which gained consensus in the course of transmission. Certainly, awareness of a pre-existing repertoire of associative sets did not preclude individual invention, as shown by the occurrence of 'internal collocations', devised on the basis of traditional units that are attested elsewhere.[3]

Such pairs of poetic words which seem from their frequent occurrence together to have 'gone together well', or to 'belong to each other', prove that within the wide range of possible combinations of words sharing the same initial sound, Germanic versifiers tended to prefer some over others. It seems as if they acknowledged a consolidated (though not binding) usage handed down by oral tradition, and, within this system, changes could be operated through phonetic similarity or subject affinity. Both trends can best be verified by searching the large corpus of Old English poetry, which comprises religious, secular, and heroic subjects. This is the reason why all previous studies of collocations have focused exclusively on this corpus (Quirk 1963/1968; Reinhard 1976; Kintgen 1977; Tyler 2006; Szőke 2014).

The poetic collocations devised by Germanic versifiers are a system exploiting a dual-track mechanism: they produce cohesion, but at the same time allow and generate combinatory variations and the inclusion of new members, associated words, most notably through paronomasia and near-homophony. Thus, a word whose *sound* – but not necessarily meaning – accords with one of the basic components of a collocational set (for example, one with the same consonantal root but a different vowel) could be annexed to the collocational series to suit the narrative context. This point is well exemplified by two passages in *Atlamál in grœnlenzku*, where the well-attested collocation *rún* + *ráð* ('secret', 'rune' + 'counsel') is extensively deployed in its basic form and also varied by substituting its members with words which have a similar sound but a cognate or altogether different meaning:

hygðu at **ráðum**! / Fár er full**rýninn** ... / **Réð** ek þér **rúnar**

[Hǫgni, listen to **advice**! / Few are very **learned in runes** ... / I **interpreted** the **runes** (which your sister cut)] (*Am* 11/2–3; 5)

skǫmm mun ró **reiði**, ef þú **reynir** gǫrva

[your **anger** will not be slaked for long, when you **find out** what results] (*Am* 78/7–8)

Such feasibility, favoured by the high degree of sound similarity which characterises the Germanic word-hoard, places collocations at the intersection between tradition and innovation.

The repeated (though not mechanical) pairing of some significant words[4] – originally in the service of memorisation and perhaps of *ex tempore* performance – must have been perceived and appreciated by audiences as a poetic ingredient that was both familiar and appropriate (Tyler 2006: 123). At the same time, word-pairing could be used in an unexpected way, to create an effect contrary to the audience's expectations, or as a signal directing attention to a theme or motif.

Since alliterative collocations are a distinctive and productive feature of Germanic poetry, a systematic analysis of their formal and semantic characteristics and of the limitations that may apply to them would be most desirable. This is particularly true of eddic poetry – as we have it handed down in the Codex Regius collection – where a new stanzaic arrangement of verse made further adaptations necessary.[5] In this case we are dealing with a small corpus (around 11,000 verses (i.e. half lines or full-lines) against about 60,000 half lines of Old English poetry) recorded at a relatively late date, which was barely, if at all, affected by the need that was felt elsewhere to re-define or augment the poetic word-hoard in order to adapt it to the new Christian discourse.[6] Research into the 'grammar' of eddic alliterative collocations – especially from a comparative perspective – can provide an extra tool for gaining a better understanding of the compositional techniques of eddic poetry.

For the time being, I shall leave aside the thorny question of the maximum metrical span within which a collocation can be considered to be an intentional device.[7] In the limited space of a single chapter in a book and without a fully searchable digital edition of the complete poetic corpus it would be hazardous to try to offer a large-scale survey of this hitherto neglected feature of eddic style. Therefore, I have deemed it wiser to select and illustrate the three best-attested large-scale examples of collocational sets found in the eddic poems, placing special emphasis on reconstructing their basic strings and possible expansions. I shall also give a few examples of how collocations could be artfully placed at the service of the narrated story, since this is the most rewarding aspect of their study in terms of textual analysis.

The collocational set generated by the sequence /m+V+r/

In eddic verse, a variety of semantically or morphologically significant words based on the phonetic chain /m+vowel+r/ are employed: the adverb *meir/meiri* ('more', 'moreover'), the personal pronoun *mér* ('to me'; dat. sg.),[8] the adjective *mærr* ('famous', 'illustrious'),[9] and the nouns *mær* ('girl'; f.), *marr* ('horse'; m.). Strangely enough, the word *marr* ('sea'; m.), which would potentially fit well into this group, has limited occurrence, and only sporadically collocates with the other words in it.[10]

The class of **m+V+r** words operates as a collocational set, since several examples occur where two or three of its members are matched together in a loose (but not random) way that suggests the exploitation of an intentional device. A few basic combinations are likely to be ancient, while others may have originated in the process of rephrasing and retelling traditional stories, possibly for different audiences, or simply as a result of the fondness for paronomastic verse, systematic syllable repetition, and homophonic sound-sequences which are common features of eddic and skaldic poetry. By adopting a comparative approach, we may obtain further evidence in this regard.

Thus, it is noteworthy that, although the Old English and Old Norse vocabularies both include a rich variety of **m+V+r** words, it is only in Old Norse that they are significantly exploited to build up homophonic collocations. This remark corroborates the observation that in the eddic corpus, alliterative combinations of this kind mainly occur in poems which are generally regarded as relatively late, as can be seen from the list below:[11]

Þrk 25/7–8	meira (mjǫð) + mey	= more (mead) + girl
HHv 28/1–4	meyja + mær + marir	= girls + girl + horses
Grp 36/5–6	mærrar + meyjar	= famous + girl
Grp 41/3	mærr + meyju	= famous (lord) + girl
Gðr I 16/7–8	mœrir + mær	= splendid (bird) + girl
Gðr II 1/1	mær + meyja	= girl + girls
Hm 14/3–4	mærr + mars	= famous (Erpr) + horse
Hdl 1/1	mær + meyja	= girl + girls

We might highlight the comic effect achieved in *Þrymskviða* by substituting the traditional coupling *mærr* 'famous' and *mjǫðr* 'mead'[12] with the unprecedented *meira mjǫð* + *mær* ('more mead' + 'girl'), and by putting this combination into the mouth of the foolish giant Þrymr, who wonders at the enormous amount of mead that the supposed woman in front of him (the mock-goddess Freyja, impersonated by Þórr in disguise) is able to drink. The opposite effect, of intensifying the tragic atmosphere which surrounds the newly widowed Guðrún, is accomplished in *Guðrúnarkviða I* 16/7–8 by connecting the high-resounding adjective *mærr* ('imposing', 'splendid') not, as was usual, to the following word *mær* (= Guðrún), but to the common word *fuglar* ('birds' (the geese in the yard)), whose cackling responds to the noblewoman's long-delayed outburst of grief at the sight of the dead body of her husband Sigurðr.

Expanding the scope of the investigation, some external (i.e., non-homophonic) collocates can be identified which combine regularly with members of the **m+V+r** set. This is true, for example, of the *m*-word *mækir* ('sword'), a potentially important element in any heroic narrative, and as such easily associable with either *marr* ('horse') or *mærr* ('famous'). Not surprisingly, it is in *Skírnismál* that we find an expansion of the collocational set to include the word *mækir*, since a *marr* (on which Skírnir rides to Gerðr's hall), an exceptional *mækir* (entrusted by Freyr to his servant to secure his safety among the giants), and a *mær* (the reluctant object of the god's desire) are all essential ingredients of the plot:

mars → *mæra* (*mjǫð*)	= horse → renowned (mead) (*Skm* 15/2 + 16/3)[13]	
mæki + *mær*	= sword + girl (*Skm* 23/1)	
mæki + *mær*	= sword + girl (*Skm* 25/1)	

A concentration of *mækir* + **m+V+r**-collocates occurs in the limited metrical space of *Hávamál* 81–4, where 'sword' is matched twice with 'girl' (*mær*) and once with 'horse' + 'girl' (*marr* + *meyjar*). This creates a startling effect, deriving from the fact that in all three instances, two subjects are included in a list and paired in a long line ('sword' + 'girl'), which do not traditionally 'belong to each other':[14]

mæki + *mey*[15]	= sword + girl (*Háv* 81/3–4)	
mæki + *mey*	= sword + girl (*Háv* 82/7–8)	
mar + *mæki* → *meyjar*	= horse + sword → girls (*Háv* 83/3–4 → 84/1)[16]	

In contrast, in the ten-line st. 4 of *Sigurðarkviða in skamma* the matching words *mæki* (l. 3) and *mey* (l. 9) are separated by two long lines. This looks like an intentional device meant to parallel, on the stylistic and syntactic level, Sigurðr's decision to place a naked sword (*mækir*) between himself and Brynhildr (*mær*) – whom he has overcome in the form of Gunnarr – to mark his intention of avoiding physical intercourse with her, thereby keeping his promise to the Gjukung brothers.

Elsewhere in the corpus, the more traditional collocate *marr* ('horse') + *mæki* ('sword') is employed to describe the apparel of a noble warrior, his finest belongings, and the most desirable of gifts:

Ls 12/1	mar + mæki	= horse + sword
Vkv 33/5–6	mars + mækis	= horse + sword
Akv 7/5–6	mar + mæki	= horse + sword
Hunn 1/6–7	mæki + mari	= sword + horse

If we search the corpus for other examples of *m*-words which appear to combine more than once with any member of the *marr* ('horse') + *mær* ('girl') + *mærr* ('famous') set, we shall find that the nearly homophonic words *myrkr* ('dark') and *mǫrk* ('borderland', 'forest') respond to this requirement (and always act as the second member of the collocation). The plural noun *meiðmar* ('treasures'; f.) should perhaps also be counted among the collocating members of this set, as it alliterates exclusively with words that belong to it:

Skm 8/1–2 (= 9/1–2)	mar + myrkvan	= horse + dark (flame)
Vkv 1/1–2	meyjar + Myrkvið	= girls + dark (forest)
Vkv 3/6–7	meyjar + myrkvan (við)	= girls + dark (forest)
Akv 3/3–4	mar + Myrkvið	= horse + dark (forest)
Akv 13/3–5	marina + Myrkvið + Húnmǫrk	= horses + dark (forest) + Hunland
Rþ 37/1–2	meirr + myrkan (við)	= moreover + dark (forest)
Hunn 1/6–8	mæki + mari + mǫrk	= sword + horse + forest
Hunn 9/1–2	mæra[17] + Myrkviðr	= famous (forest) + dark (forest)
Sg 2/1–2	mey + meiðma	= girl + treasures
Sg 15/7–8	meyjar + meiðmum	= girls + treasures
Sg 38/3–4	meirr + meiðmar	= more + treasures
Sg 46/3–4	mǫrk + meiðmum	= forest + treasures
Akv 5/5–8	meiðmar + mœra + Myrkvið	= treasures + splendid + dark (forest)
Am 95/1–2 + 6	mœrri + meiðma + meira	= splendid + treasures + more
Rþ 38/5–6[18]	meiðmar + mara	= treasures + horses

The *rún* + *ráð* ('secret'; 'rune' + 'counsel') collocation
and its extensions

An example of a particularly productive and seemingly ancient collocational series is the one which pivots on the combination of the sapiential
roots *rún-* ('secret'; 'rune'), and *ráð-* ('counsel'), which is also well attested
in Old English, Middle English, and Old Saxon verse. Often employed as
a reversible and connective binomial filling a half-line,[19] the *rún* + *ráð* pair
exhibits semantic congruity[20] to the point that its members were perceived
as being linked even when dislocated in a stanza. Each member of the
binomial (according to a mechanism already pointed out for the sequence
m+V+r) could also collocate with any word sharing its own or the
other's consonantal sequence. Therefore, in *Lokasenna* 28/4–5, pseudo-
paronomasia nicely serves Loki's cruel intentions of upsetting Frigg with
the revelation of his role in the killing of Baldr:

> ek því **réð**, er þú **ríða** sérat
>
> [I **brought** it **about** that you will never again see (Baldr) **ride** (to the halls)]
> (*Ls* 28/4–5)

Occurrences in eddic verse oscillate between combinations made up of the
two original roots and variations or extensions, fostered mainly but not
exclusively by near-homophony; the latter tendency is the reason why the
set includes words such as *ríða* ('to ride'), *reið-* ('anger', 'angry'), *rauðr*
('red'),[21] *reyna* ('to prove'), and even *reini* ('stallion'), as shown in the
following table:

Háv 80/1–2	reynt + rúnum	= to prove + runes
Háv 102/4–5	reynda + ráðspaka	= to prove + sagacious
Háv 111/7–8	rúnar + ráðum	= runes + counsels
Háv 116/1←115/7	ráðumk + ráð ← eyrarúnu	= to advise + counsel ← (close) confidant
Háv 142/1–2	rúnar + ráðna	= runes + meaningful
Hrbl 53/1	ráð + ráða	= advice + to advise
Ls 28/4–5	réð + ríða	= to bring about + to ride
HH II 49/1–2	ríða + roðnar	= to ride + to redden
HHv 21/1–2	reini + reyna	= stallion + to try
Rm 9/1–2	rauðu + ráða	= red + to own
Br 18/1–2	reyndi + riðit	= to prove + to ride
Gðr II 22/3–4	roðnir + ráða	= to redden + to interpret
Akv 9/3←8/6–8→11/1	rýnendr + ráðendr ← riðit + rauðum + ríða → ráða	= adviser + counsellor ← to twist + red + to ride → to own

Am 11/2–5←10/6←9/4–10	ráðum + fullrýninn + réð + rúnar ← réð ← rúna + ráða	= advice + learned in runes + to interpret + runes ← to manage ← runes + to interpret
Am 42/6–7←40/4→43/2	reiðir + fullráða ← reyna → ráðit	= angry + intentioned ← to prove → to decide
Am 54/1–2	ræða + reiðr	= to advise + angry
Am 60/3–4	reynask + reynt	= to prove + to prove
Am 78/7–8	reiði + reynir	= anger + to prove
Am 80/1+6	ráðumk + reynir	= to intend + to prove
Am 93/2–4	stórráða + reyndum	= counsel + to prove
Hm 19/5	ræðit + ráð	= to advise + advice
Rþ 11/5	ræddu[22] + rýndu	= to talk + to whisper
Rþ 21/5–6	rauðan + rjóðan + riðudu	= red + rosy + to move quickly (of eyes)
Rþ 36/1–4←35/9	runni + rúnar ← ríða	= thicket + runes ← to ride
Hdl 5/3–4	renna + runa	= to race + boar

In sts 6–11 of *Atlakviða*, the use of this set aptly serves the needs of the narrative, since *ráð* ('advice' (given or not given)) plays an important role in the initial part of the story. In st. 9/3, the couple *rýnendr* + *ráðendr* ('advisors' + 'counsellors') is included in the list of those who might have urged Gunnarr (to go or not to go to Atli's court), but remained silent. The centrality of this theme emerges from the poet's choice to anticipate the binomial (in 6/3) and to echo it (in 11/1) with two more occurrences of the verb *ráða*, which exploit different meanings of the verb (respectively, 'to rule over' and 'to advise'). Lastly, the subtle paronomastic triplet (in 8/6–8) *riðit* ('twisted around'), *rauðum* ('red'), and *ríða* ('to ride (on an errand)') functions as an overture, in which mention is made of Guðrún's concealed warning (the wolf's hair *twisted around* the ring), of the feared bloody outcome of the Gjukungs' expedition (the *golden-red* colour of the ring), and of the fatal *riding* which the two brothers will nonetheless undertake, partly as a result of the king's advisors failing to offer advice.

Later in *Atlakviða* (in 27/5) we find an original adaptation of the binomial *rún-* + *ráð-* which parallels the Old English usage of generating *ad hoc* collocations by playing on onomastic puns, when the name of the river Rhine (*Rín*) is substituted for the original member (*rún*).[23] The fact that this is intentional wordplay in *Akv* 27 is confirmed by a second occurrence of the matching pair *Rín* + *ráða*, in *Sigurðarkviða in skamma*:

Rín skal **ráða**

[The **Rhine** shall **rule** (over the treasure)] (*Akv* 27/5)

gott er at **ráða Rínar** málmi

[it is good to **control** the metal of the **Rhine**] (*Sg* 16/3–4)

In this case, a toponomastic pun is built upon the common knowledge of the ultimate destination of the Nibelungs' treasure, which, once the gold has been disposed of by its last human owners, becomes the legitimate property of a river. The 'treasure'-kenning *Rínar rauðmalmr* (the *Rhine*'s red metal) attested in *Bjarkamál in fornu* 6/5 (probably from the tenth century) is a valuable and early example of the same kind.

Alongside the section of *Atlakviða* just discussed, sts 9–11 of *Atlamál* – another version of the killing of Gunnarr and Hǫgni at Atli's – show a conspicuous concentration of occurrences (seven of them) of the noun *rún* and of the verb *ráða* in the initial part of the narration. They convey the basic meanings of 'advice/to advise' and 'rune', apart from one interesting case (in 10/6), where *réð* (pret. sg. from *ráða*) accompanies the infinitive *vakna* ('to awaken') with no semantic role (the phrase simply means 'she awoke'), but with the structural function of connecting *rúna* + *ráða* in 9/4+10 to the next stanza (11), which exploits four *ráð-/rún-* collocates (listed in the table above).[24]

A high density of near-homophones in a restricted metrical space is not uncommon, as proven by sts 20–26 of *Fáfnismál*, where different combinations – including the etymological figure *ráða ráð* – are employed with an intentional, resounding effect:

Fm 20/1–5:	ræð + ráð + ríð + glóðrauða	= to advise + advice + to ride + (glowing) red
Fm 21/1–2:	ráð + ráðit + ríða	= advice + to advise + to ride
Fm 22/1–2:	réð + ráða	= to betray + to betray
Fm 26/1–5:	rétt + ríða + réði	= to contrive + to ride + to possess

In a later passage in the same poem, which describes the choral monologue of the nuthatches (*Fm* 32–8), the poet once again plays with the different nuances of the verb *ráða*: in st. 33, Reginn is described as plotting to himself in anger (*ræðr um við sik ... af reiði*); in the following stanza, one of the birds advises Sigurðr to 'shorten Reginn by a head' if he wants to possess (*ráða*) the treasure. In sts 37–8, the echo lingers on: in two parallel lines (37/5 and 38/5), both meanings of the verb occur once more, one after the other: since Reginn is still plotting against Sigurðr (*er hann ráðinn hefr*) – says one nuthatch – and if the young man wants the treasure that Fáfnir owned (*þess er Fáfnir réð*), the young man had better chop his head off.

As already discussed with reference to the **m+V+r** set, we must also take into consideration a restricted number of words which seem to belong to the *rún + ráð* collocative string, even though they bear no phonetic resemblance to either of its two basic components. Caution should be exercised when such occurrences are all internal to a poem, as in the case of the adjective *rǫskr*, which in *Atlamál* (but nowhere else) is placed three times in close proximity to a *ráð-/reyn*-word (54/1–2; 60/3–4; 90/1–2). But when the combination is attested in different poems we can be fairly confident that it was perceived as a true collocate. The noun *rǫnd* ('rim', 'shield'), for example, in more than half of its total occurrences combines with two near-homophones of *ráð* chosen on the basis of semantic affinity: the adjective *rauðr* ('red') – the possible painted colour of the shield – and the verb *ríða* ('to ride'), which evokes the image of a riding warrior armed with a shield.

The nouns *ríki* ('power') plus the adjective *ríkr* ('powerful'), *rekkr* ('warrior'), and other related homophones also meet these requirements and partake in this combinatory set:[25]

Vsp 65/1–4	ríki + ræðr	= powerful + to rule over
Háv 64/1–2	ríki + ráðsnotra	= power + wise in counsel
Þkv 14/5–6	réðu + ríkir	= to debate + powerful
HH I 56/3–4	rauðir + ríkja	= red + powerful
HHv 6/2–3	ráða + ríkr	= to rule over + powerful
Grp 17/1–2	ríkjum + rúnar	= powerful + runes
Grp 26/1–3	reiði + ríks + góðráðs	= anger + powerful + (good) advice
Grp 49/1–2	reiði + rík	= anger + powerful
Akv 15/5–6	ráðinn + ríkr	= to betray + powerful
Akv 29/1–2	ríki + reið	= powerful + to ride
Am 37/1–4	ríki + reiðir	= strength + angry
Am 66/7[26]	ríkri + ráð	= powerful + fate
Fjöl 7/4–5 (+ 8/4–5)	ræðr + ríki	= to rule over + power
Bdr 1/5–6	réðu + ríkir	= to debate + powerful
Hrbl 8/3–4	rekkr + ráðsvinni + Ráðseyjarsundi	= warrior + wise in counsel + Counsel-island Sound
Alv 5/1–2	rekka + ráðum	= warriors + possessions
HHv 18/4–5	rekka + Rán	= warriors + Rán
Grp 6/3–4	ráðspakir + rekkar	= sagacious + warriors
Gðr II 15/5–6	randir + rauðar + rekka	= shields + red + warriors
Akv 17/5–6	Rínar + rekka	= the Rhine + warriors
Am 65/3–4	rekkum + rakklátum + ráð	= warriors + courageous + plan

Study of the extant eddic verse allows us to postulate the following chain of recurrently combining members:

> //*rún-* ('secret', 'rune') + *ryna/reyna* ('to try', 'to examine') + *ráð-* ('(to) counsel', 'to rule') + *ríða* ('to ride') + *rauðr* ('red' (+ *rjóða* 'to redden')) + *reið-* ('angry', 'anger') + * rík-* ('powerful', 'reign') + *rekkr* ('warrior', 'man')//

A parallel between this reconstructed string of matching words and its Old English counterpart reveals a marked similarity and a few distinctive features.[27] In both corpora, r+V+ð/d members have a density higher than r+V+n-ones, a ratio which mainly derives from the numerical predominance of the former root in the poetic vocabulary of both languages. But it is also true that in both eddic poetry and in Old English verse, there are words belonging to the r+V+n-family which tend not to be involved in the alliterative pattern of the line, and which for this reason do not collocate in a significant and recognisable way. In the Poetic Edda, this is the case of *rann* ('house'), *raun* ('trial'), *runnr* ('grove'), and the common verb *renna* ('to run').[28]

A dark collocation centred on hostility: *níð* + *nótt* ('enmity' + 'night')

The last example of an extended collocative set which I should like to present is a well-attested one, centred on the words *níð* + 'nótt' ('enmity' + 'night'). At least in its basic form, it is marked by semantic congruity, since its partner-words refer to a situation of physical or mental hardship. This 'distress' collocative system largely coincides with the one attested in Old English verse:[29] in particular, both take advantage of the seminal homophony between *níð* ('enmity'; OE *nið*) and *nið* ('man'; OE *niþþas*, pl.). The eddic set can be reconstructed as follows:

> //*níð* ('hostility', 'hostile words') + *nið* (/*niðar*, pl.) ('the waning [or the dark] of the moon') + *niðr* ('descendant', 'man') + *niðr/neðan/neðarr* ('down [below]', 'from down below') + *nauð-*[30] ('necessity') + *nótt* ('night')//

This could then be extended, as is customary with alliterative combinatory chains, by incorporating nouns and adjectives with a similar sound (such as *nýtr* ('useful')), or other *n*-words chosen on a semantic-based affinity (and also their possible homophonic doublets): *nár* ('dead body') (+ *nýr* 'new' + *ný* 'the new moon') + *ná-* ('near', 'belonging to the same family') (+ *níu* 'nine') + *nagl* ('nail') + *nifl* ('obscurity')[31] + *norð-* ('north').

The most frequent collocational patterns are made up of two or three members in a single long line, although there are instances of combinations stretching over the boundaries of the single stanza,[32] and of richer and more elaborate sequences.[33] One noticeable feature of the set under discussion is just how many near or complete homonyms it includes, starting from the two similar-sounding but etymologically unrelated phonetic sequences *níð-* and *nið-*. These yield a variety of meanings ('hostility', 'the new moon/dark of the moon, lunar phase, dark', 'relative (n.), descendant, man', 'down, below'). Other examples of this kind are the pair *nár* ('corpse') and *nýr* ('new'), as well as the combination *ná/náinn* ('to go near', 'near' (adj.)) and *ný* ('the new moon'). Grammatical variations can also produce new paronomastic pairs, as in *Vafþrúðnismál* 13/6, repeated in 14/3, which matches *nótt* ('night') with *nýt* (nt., pl. acc. of *nýtr* ('beneficent')).[34] That this latter combination was perceived as belonging to the *nið* + *nótt* series is proved by the fact that both its components are employed again in the central portion of the poem in connection with the head-word *nið*:

nótt of **nýt** regin

[**night** to the **beneficent** gods] (*Vm* 13/6 and 14/3)

nótt með **niðum**

[**night** with its **new moons**] (*Vm* 24/6)

... **Nótt** var Nǫrvi[35] borin;
ný ok **nið** skópu **nýt** regin;

[**Night** was born of **Nǫrr**; / **new moon** and **dark of the moon** the **beneficent** gods made;] (*Vm* 25/3–5)

Vǫluspá stands apart in its use of the *nið* + *nótt* series: it not only has the highest rate of occurrences, but also shows a taste for variety within the large pattern of possible combinations, a feature which accords well with the density of paronomastic wordplay in the poem. Furthermore, the distribution of the collocations in the stanzas suggests intentional choice, culminating in a special concentration of alliterating members in the last stanza of the poem.

The first *nið*-collocation in the poem occurs as early as st. 6/5–6, where the seeress recalls the dawn of time, when the gods gave names to the various partitions of time, beginning with the night, by which the Germanic people counted the passing of days. This pre-eminent act is expressed through the combination: *nótt* + *niðjum* + *nǫfn* ('night' + 'descendant' + 'name'). Further on in the poem, a series of dwarves' names are coupled in two consecutive stanzas of the R-version, all of them belonging to the *nið*-combinatory series:

Nýi ok Niði,[36] Norðri ...
Nóri ... + Nár ok Nýráðr'

[New Moon and Dark of the Moon, North ... Little Shaver? + Corpse and Clever-in-New-counsels] (*Vsp* 11/1–2+6; 12/5)

Appropriately, the 'dark' *niðr*-collocation plays a central role in the section of *Vǫluspá* dealing with the apocalyptic events, and the following pairs occur in sts 37–9 and 50, each containing an ominous place-, personal-, or object-name matched with a component of the set:

norðan + Niðavǫllum   = to the North + Dark-of-Moon Plains
Nástrǫndu + norðr   = Corpse-strand + North
Níðhǫggr + nái   = 'Malignant Striker' + corpse
nái + neffǫlr + Naglfar   = corpse + pale-beaked + Naglfar (Nail-ship).

Again, in sts 55H–6, different combinations pertaining to the same set are exploited (*niðja + níu + neppr + naðri + níðs* = 'descendant' + 'nine' + 'exhausted' + 'serpent' + 'enmity'), leading to the climax of the final st. 66, where the powerful image of the dragon persists, flying over the concepts of darkness, violence, and death which rise up from below and saturate the universe. The long coda of 'distressing' words – *naðr* + *neðan + Niðafjǫllum + Níðhǫggr + nái* ('dragon' + 'from below' + 'Dark-of-Moon Plains' + 'Malignant Striker' + 'corpse') – is brought to an abrupt end by the (unusually) alliterating adverb *nú*, which shifts the narration back to the present time of the prophetess, who *now* intends to sink and speak no more.

One of the reasons for the frequent use of the *nið* + *nótt* set, especially in the mythological poems, may be the strong evocative power of its basic set of words, which picture the negative forces opposed to the positive ones in the fragile balance within which society and the cosmos survive: enmity/strife (*nið*), darkness (*nið* and *nótt*), the north (*norðr*), corpse (*nár*), the underworld (*niðr*). As a result, this collocation produces 'linguistic and mythological harmony'.[37] But it may also prove apt in the depiction of a psychological human situation, as we can see from *Guðrúnarkviða II*, 12/1–2, where Guðrún recalls remaining next to the dead body of Sigurðr and her amplified perception of a night as dark as the moonless sky: *Nótt þótti mér niðmyrkr vera.*

Vǫluspá 50/7–8: two readings, one collocation

To give an example of the kind of textual approach which may stem from the analysis of collocations, let us return to the passage in *Vǫluspá* which describes the release of Naglfar (possibly a ship, or a giant), in the two versions which have come down to us (*Vsp* 50/7–8):

> slítr nái neffǫlr, Naglfar losnar.

> [(the eagle) tears the corpse, pale-beaked; Naglfar (a ship? a giant?) breaks loose.] (R)

> slítr nái niðfǫlr, Naglfar losnar.

> [(the eagle? Niðfǫlr?) tears the corpse, darkly pale (?); Naglfar (a ship? a giant?) breaks loose.] (H; *Gylfaginning*: 51)

The two long lines only differ as regards the first element of the compound in the a-line, whose second member (the adjective *fǫlr*; cf. OE *fealu*) conveys the idea of a subject characterised by a dull appearance (somebody or something 'pale, livid'), and non-bright, non-saturated colour. In the R-version, *nef-* ('nose', 'beak')[38] probably refers to the eagle (often described in poetry as a corpse-eater) mentioned in the preceding line, while in the H-version (also attested in the manuscript tradition of *Gylfaginning*: 51), *nið-* might be connected to *nið(ar)* ('the waning', or 'the dark of the moon'; nt. or f. pl.), thus yielding the meaning 'darkly pale' to the compound, and possibly referring to a being who lives (or has lived for a long time) underground – more appropriate than a reference to an eagle. The word (or name?) *niðfǫlr* is not attested elsewhere, but might have been perceived as a fitting fictional name for a person or animal living in an underground dwelling, or for a hellish creature; either would be well suited to the apocalyptic context of the passage.

I should like to propose an interpretation of the double-reading *neffǫlr* (R) / *niðfǫlr* (H) in *Vǫluspá* 50 as the result of the modus operandi of versifiers trained in the art of 'collocating words' while performing or reciting the poems. They were well able to exploit the wide range of possible combinations within a set, and it is also plausible that they might have introduced minor changes, while making use of an established collocation. These changes were particularly likely when a traditional collocation had to be adapted to a different narrative context, or when it was felt necessary to alter the wording that had become faded or was no longer understandable due to a prolonged transmission process or to having been exported to a new context.

Within the eddic corpus, the initial phonetic sequence *nef-* occurs six times (including the line in *Vsp* 50) in an alliterative combination, always matched with one or more words belonging to the *nið + nótt* set.[39] All possible outcomes of the phonetic sequence */nefl* are exploited:[40] *nef* ('beak'), *nefi* ('nephew'), *nefna* ('to name'), as if they were interchangeable within the set. It therefore follows that, in the logic of collocative systems, the two versions of line 50/7 are not mutually exclusive, and both epithets (*neffǫlr* and *niðfǫlr*, 'pale-beaked' and 'darkly pale') can be considered fitting in this context. Nonetheless, even though each of these is plausible, neither completely satisfies our expectations, nor is their meaning entirely clear. Precisely because the actors of the apocalyptic scene described here might no longer be well known to the contemporaries of the R and H versions of *Vǫluspá* – or to Snorri – ambiguity might have arisen as to whether an epithet should be interpreted as a name or an attribute, and changes fostered by homophony and with combinatory congruity were likely to be considered legitimate and even inevitable.

In closing, let us consider the name *Naglfar* in *Vǫluspá* st. 50/8,[41] which provides the opportunity for remarking on the different treatment sometimes attributed to the same collocation member (here: *nagl*) in different contexts. The compound literally means 'nail(/rivet)-vehicle(/ship)',[42] and is interpreted by Snorri (*Gylfaginning*: 51) with reference to the folk-motif of its being made from the uncut nails of the dead. At the same time, the audience might have perceived a wordplay involving *nagli*,[43] yielding the secondary or alternative meaning of 'riveted boat', notwithstanding the fact that in eddic poetry *nagl* always refers to an anatomical detail.[44]

Of special interest is the ability shown by some individual poetic personalities in the generation of new collocations. In the second part of *Elene*, Cynewulf recounts the laborious finding of the nails used to crucify Jesus: when they are 'freed' from their dark prison (the earth in which they had been buried), they are no longer an instrument of the Passion, but shine like the stars, signifying their new status as relics. This process of 'conversion' is reflected in the two different combinations created for the word *næglas* ('nails') in this context: the first plays with the word *nearu* ('constraint'), while the second adopts a positive, salvific perspective and introduces, by means of phonetic variation, the new Christian word *nergend* ('Saviour').[45] While the *Beowulf* poet resorts to a collocation involving *nægl* only once, he uses it with great originality, creating the sword name *Nægling* ('adorned with nails') and matching it with the standard couple *nið + nyd* ('enmity' + 'need') in l. 2680: **niþe genyded;**

Nægling forbærst ('forced with violence; Nægling broke'). This line is structured (as regards its collocation) in the same way as *Vǫluspá* 50/7–8 (*slítr nái neffǫlr* [or *niðfǫlr*], *Naglfar losnar*) and demonstrates the parallel excellence of the two poets.

The impact of collocations on eddic poetry: a preliminary evaluation

Only after a full study of this kind has been completed will it be possible to evaluate, on the basis of significant statistical data, the impact of collocations on the corpus of eddic poetry handed down to us. The same method could also be profitably applied to the much larger corpus of skaldic poetry. It is very likely that court poets and anonymous singers considered some combinations of words more significant than others, but the artificial word order which they practised in their verse and the frequency of kennings employed in them are likely to have obscured or altered the original appearance of collocations.

The restricted scope of the present survey makes it inadvisable to draw general conclusions on the incidence of collocations in eddic poetry, but even the limited number of examples discussed is enough to give an idea of the potential productivity of this combinatory mechanism, and of its versatility in the hands of skilful sound-weavers. Judging from the limited samples scrutinised here, it seems safe to say that alliterative conjunctions of words are not distributed evenly throughout the corpus of eddic poetry: a few poems (*Atlakviða, Atlamál, Vǫluspá, Guðrúnarkviða II*) exploit this device extensively, while others (notably *Hymiskviða, Guðrúnarkviða I*, and *Guðrúnarkviða III*) tend not to make use of the traditional device of combining words.

The comparative perspective adopted here, focused on Old English parallels, has granted access to a larger record of cases in the investigation of a stylistic feature which may have lost part of its appeal to versifiers at the time when the eddic poems were put down in writing. In both written traditions, alliterative collocations appear to be remnants of aural correspondences which gained a particular conventionality and status – including as theme-markers – as suggested by their peculiar mode of repetition. They appear to be recurrent but not fixed, expected but not predictable; they also function as models for the creation of new matching pairs. Studying the various degrees of density that word-pairing exhibits in the eddic corpus and the kinds of eventual remodelling they underwent can perhaps provide a useful criterion for grouping poems, thus contributing to a better understanding of the chronological and stylistic relationships between lays composed and transmitted over a long span of time.

Notes

1. In this chapter I shall leave aside the complex issue of whether collocations as a system – as opposed to the sporadic use of traditional matching words – can be considered a peculiar feature of eddic poetry in contrast to skaldic verse, and of the (eventual) total extent of single shared collocates. Where relevant, I will take into consideration some comparable examples from Old English poetry, for parallel lexical collocations are of course attested in the poetic corpora of cognate languages (Watkins 1995: 157).

2. Given the relative paucity of Old Germanic verse handed down to us – especially with regards to some poetic genres – it is not always easy to judge whether two occurrences of the same poetic combination of words may be counted as a collocational unit.

3. Szőke (2014: 64–9 and *passim*) draws attention to the peculiar rewording of traditional collocations in the signed poems by the Old English poet Cynewulf; on this, see also Orchard 2003.

4. As Szőke observes, 'Using combinations of interrelated words allowed the poet to rapidly sketch a situation and concisely recall several layers of associations' (2014: 55).

5. In the present study I shall also take into consideration, when useful, eddic poems from beyond the Codex Regius collection.

6. See the count offered in Suzuki 2014: 2.

7. As a matter of fact, this is an issue which concerns Old English verse organisation rather than eddic stanzaic verse, for which there is no need to posit strict metrical limitations, since stanzaic arrangement necessarily results in a tendency to isolate lines within each stanza, except where a collocational unit may be anticipated or echoed by the use of a partner-word in an adjoining stanza.

8. The examples of combinations involving the pronoun *mér* will not be taken into consideration as collocates, given the weak lexical content of the personal pronoun.

9. The adjective *mær* ('small', 'fragile') is a hapax (*Vsp* 32/2). In Kuhn's *Glossary* (1968: *s.v.*), *mœrr* ('big', 'powerful') is listed as a separate entry from *mærr* ('famous'), whereas in La Farge and Tucker's *Glossary* (1992: *s.v.*) and in Kellogg's *Concordance* (1988: *s.v.*), occurrences of both adjectives are listed under the latter head-word. In a collocational perspective, apart from one occurrence (*Gðr I* 16/7–8: *mœrir* + *mær*), *mœrr* does not follow the behaviour of its homophones.

10. In the eddic corpus, the noun *marr* ('sea') occurs 7 times, against the 29 instances of *marr* ('horse'), the III of *mær* ('girl'), and the 25 of *mærr* ('famous').

11. Here, as elsewhere, quotations follow the sequence in the Codex Regius (GKS 2365 4° (R)), and are normalised from the fourth edition of Neckel and Kuhn

(1962). An arrow signals the occurrence of a collocate in the previous [←] or in the following [→] stanza. Words are quoted in the grammatical form in which they appear in the context. On the criteria for dating eddic poetry, see Thorvaldsen, Chapter 4 in this Handbook.

12. Examples are *Skm* 16/3 (*inn mæra mjǫð*); *Ls* 6/5–6 (*mér* + *mæran* + *mjaðar*); *Akv* 9/7 (*mærr í mjǫðranni*); and *Am* 8/1 (*mjǫð mærar*).

13. Only one full and one long line separate the two words in the R-version, since in st. 15 the second *helmingr* appears to be missing.

14. In Einarr Skulason's *Øxarflokkr, mey* is coupled with *mækis* in 5/5, but the words belong to two distinct kennings: 'Gefn's (= Freyja's) maid [> jewel]' and 'the controller of the meeting of swords (= battle) [> warrior/king]'; cf. *Skj.* I B: 450.

15. This example shows that the internal cohesion of a collocation also persists when the case-marking (here, the inflected form *mey vs.* the nominative *mær*) obscures the original phonetic similarity between the partner-words.

16. If McKinnell's proposal to read st. 84 as the beginning of an independent poem ('The Poem of Sexual Intrigue' = *Háv* 84–110; McKinnell 2014) is accepted, then the occurrence of *meyjar* at its supposed beginning creates a clever link with the preceding stanza(s).

17. This is the reading in the text of Flateyjarbók (AM 203 fol.) (cf. *Akv* 5); AM 2845 4° has the reading *meira*; while Upsaliensis 715 8° reads *mæta* (which has been adopted in the Neckel and Kuhn edition).

18. In Old English verse, 'horse' + 'treasure' (*mearh* + *maþm*) has turned into a fairly widespread alliterative pair (Tyler 2006: 49–51).

19. The Anglo-Saxon translator of *Disticha Catonis*, faced with the oxymoron *tacito sermone* '(in) silent talk' (I, 17), resorts to the formulaic pair and translates it as *rædon oððe runion* ([Do not mind what they may] say or whisper) (Cox 1972: 6).

20. The pair occurs in the *þula* where *heiti* for the nobleman's retinue are listed: *rúni ok þópti ok ráðgjafi* (*Manna heiti*, 6/7–8; *Þula IV j* 6,7–8; *Skj.* I B, 662; *Skáldskaparmál:* 117). In Old English the two words are matched not only in poetry, but also in legal texts.

21. The combination of the adjective *rauðr* ('red') with members of the *ráð* + *rún* set may originally have been validated by the connection between the carving of runes and their painting (in red), or consecration (with blood). Cf. *Gðr II*, 22/ 3–4: *ristnir ok roðnir – ráða ek né máttak –* ('cut and **red**-coloured – I could not **interpret** them'); also *Egils saga* ch. 44 (v. 9), where a stanza opens with the line: *Ristum rún á horni, rjóðum spjǫll í dreyra* ('We write **runes** on the horn, **redden** the spell with blood') (Sigurður Nordal 1933: 109; Bjarni Einarsson 2003: 59).

22. From the verb *ræða*.

23. This is comparable with Cynewulf's *Juliana* (l. 302) and *Fates of the Apostles* (l. 13), where the name of the Roman emperor *Nero* is allusively paired with *nearu* ('distress'); these passages are analysed in Szőke 2014: 64–6.

24. The poet of *Atlamál* may have known this scene in *Atlakviða* and been directly influenced by it; on the possible relationship between the two poems, see Andersson 1983.

25. Cf. *rakkar* + *renna* + *ráðask* ('dogs' + 'to run' + 'to bark') (*Am* 25/1–2); *ríðr* + *rekr* ('to ride' + 'to drive') (*Háv* 71/1–2); *ræddu* + *rýndu* + *rekkju* ('to talk' + 'to whisper' + 'bed') (*Rgþ* 11/5–6); *rǫk* + *ráð* ('destiny' + 'to interpret') (*Am* 22/5–6); *rǫkr* + *rǫkra* + *ríða* ('darkness' + 'darkness' + 'to ride') (*Hdl* 1/5–6); *reið* + *rekkvið* ('to ride' + 'to grow dark') (*HHv* 35/1–2); *ræða* + *rakðisk* ('to advise' + 'to stretch') (*Am* 90/1–2). A further onomastic combination is found in *HHv* 18/4–5: *rekka* + *Rán* ('men' + '[the goddess] Rán').

26. Echoes of this collocation are found in sts 69/4 (*reynir*) and 70/2 (*ráð*).

27. The Old English chain includes: //*run-* ('letter'; 'secret') + *ryne* ('course') + *ræd-* ('(to) counsel', 'to rule') + *rad* ('riding') (+ *ridan* 'to ride') + *read* ('red') + *reþe* ('fierce') + *rodor* ('firmament') + *ric-* ('powerful'; 'kingdom') + *rinc* ('warrior')//.

28. Out of twenty-seven occurrences, only two exhibit a *rún-ráð*-collocation. In the Old English corpus, *rinnan* ('to run') collocates in two out of five occurrences (one of which is from the metrically unrefined *Paris Psalter*, a product of school versification).

29. The basic members of the Old English set (discussed in Szőke 2014: 58–64) are: *niþ* ('enmity') + *niþþas* ('men') + *nied* ('need') + *niht* ('night') + *nearo* ('oppression') + *nama/nemnan* ('(to) name').

30. The grammatical form most often involved is the adjective *nauðigr*, rather than the noun *nauð(r)*. Interestingly, the unusual use of *nauðir* meaning 'fetters' in *Vkv* 11/6 is not part of a collocation, whereas the corresponding OE *nede* in *Deor* 6 is; this may suggest that this sense was familiar in Old English, but exotic and not part of the traditional poetic language of Old Norse.

31. Also *nipt* ('a relative').

32. Cf. *Hdl* 10/5–6: *nýju* + *nauta* (+ *niðja*, at 11/2).

33. As in *Vm* 24–5.

34. The eddic hapax *nyt* ('enjoyment'; f.) also collocates with *ná-* + *neðan* (*Skm* 34/8 + 35/3).

35. By analysing onomastic evidence on the giant Nǫrvi, father of Nótt ('Night'), in a collocational perspective, Szőke posits the existence of a primordial couple made up of Nǫrvi (*Nǫrr) and a female entity called Njǫrun, both incorporating the concepts of narrowness and obscurity (2014: 80–1).

36. AM 544 4° (Hauksbók) has the reading *niði* ('traitor').

37. Roberta Frank speaks of 'linguistic and theological harmony' with reference to the use of paranomasia in Old English scriptural verse (1972: 218).

38. Cf. *á arnar nefi* in *Sd* 16/4 and the name *Arinnefja* in *Rþ* 13/4.

39. Cf. *HH I* 12/3–4; *Sd* 17/7–8; *Akv* 35/5–6; *HHv* 16/2–4; *Rg* 10/5–6, where the following combinations occur: *nef-* + *nefi* + *nefna* + *nið* + *niðjar* + *nagl* + *nauðugr* + *nágráðugr* + *nár* + *níu* + *neðarr* + *niðr-*.

40. The sequence /*nifl*/ also combines with members of the *nið* + *nótt* collocational set (in five out of six occurrences), while /*naf-*/ appears non-productive for word-combination: even the common term *nafn* ('name') only collocates in its plural, *u*-mutated form *nǫfn* (cf. *Vsp.* 6/5–6: *nótt ok **niðjum nǫfn** um gáfu* ('to night and her children they gave names').

41. Meli (2008: 184–6) discusses in detail the possibility that the original reading was 'Naglfari', a giant who is also mentioned in *Gylfaginning* (10) as husband of Nótt.

42. In Bragi's *Ragnarsdrapa* (st. 5), it is a kenning for 'sword', referring to the rivets fixed onto the hilt (and the word is not involved in alliteration).

43. This is possibly also an echo of the word *nár* ('corpse'), though the different vowel length might detract from this.

44. The opposite holds true for the Old English root *nægl-/negl-*, which is involved in the collocative series only with the meaning of 'a thin piece of metal with a head'. Old English poetry often refers to riveted ships using compounds whose first element is the past participle *nægled* ('nailed'), as, for example, in *Genesis* 1418 (*nægled bord*, collocating with *niht* ('night')), 1433 (*nægled bord*, collocating with *nearu* ('distress')), or in *Brunanburh* 53 (*nægled cnearrum*, collocating with *Norþmen* ('Norsemen')).

45. Other occurrences are in ll. 1157 (*nearwe* + *næglas*) and 1172 (*nerigend* + *næglas*).

CHAPTER 17

The representation of gender in eddic poetry

David Clark and Jóhanna Katrín Friðriksdóttir

Introduction

The text of the Codex Regius begins with a seeress asking for silence so that she can recite her prophecy about gods, giants, and men; a story of creation and destruction, rise, fall, and rebirth. We learn how Óðinn and his two brothers set up Miðgarðr, the realm of the gods, and bring order to chaos, ostensibly living in civilised harmony until discord arrives in the guise of Heiðr. The vǫlva (seeress) then describes how – through escalating discord – the gods bring their own universe to destruction, causing it to be ravaged by monsters. No one survives apart from a select few individuals who people a new world, but the vǫlva disappears into the ground at the end of the poem. Vǫluspá sets the thematic tone for what is to come in the rest of the eddic corpus, where characters appear in multidimensional roles, whether positive or negative, active or passive, human or monstrous, traditional or subversive, admired or stigmatised.

In this chapter, we begin with an overview of how normative versions of masculinity and femininity are represented in eddic poetry, as well as of those characters and behaviours that fall outside these categories. More importantly, perhaps, we also examine where male and female gender roles blur or overlap, or where they are rendered ambiguous. Our readings are informed by different aspects of gender theories and the tools they offer in analysing eddic texts, as well as the work of previous Old Norse scholars, which has contributed to a better understanding of gender representations. Finally, we present several case studies of gendered images, highlighting what we consider to be some of the most important aspects of gender representations and their ideological functions. The goal of this chapter, then, is to give the reader an insight into the diverse, complex, and fascinating perspectives on gender found in eddic poetry, and to offer possible ways of interpreting them.

Defining 'gender'

Arguably, the inclusion of gender perspectives has until recently been marginalised in Old Norse scholarship (and in eddic studies more narrowly). Nonetheless, gender constructions condition every subject's identity and limit the scope of available and forbidden roles, both for male and female figures. They are thus fundamental to understanding eddic texts and the society from which they emerge.

Gender constitutes a radically contested category in a number of ways. Gender studies have increasingly tended towards conceptions of masculinity and femininity as multiple and fragmented, inflected by various categories such as race, age, ableness, class, sexual role, and preferred object of desire (Sedgwick 1990). Theorists have increasingly moved away from an opposition of sex and gender, biological essence and social category, to complicate and blur the lines between the two (Moi 1999). Judith Butler's *Gender Trouble* recognised the performative character of gender: the idea that there are no essential categories of masculinity and femininity, but that we are always already imitating a performance that has no claim to originary status (Butler 1990). However, in later work Butler explored the constructed nature of the man–woman binary itself, drawing on the narratives of intersex and transgender individuals alongside the evidence of other countries and cultures which do not divide humans along the male–female binary (Butler 2004). There is thus no uncontested place from which to begin an analysis of gender in eddic poetry, and most scholars take a stance somewhere between universalist essentialism and social constructionism. Indeed, from the broader perspective of the study of gender and related categories right now, it may be that it is the contest itself that is interesting. Gender and sexuality have come to seem more like questions than concepts, and the fact that they are so fiercely debated says something about their fundamental importance for us at this point in our history.

Scholars of Old Norse have been inspired by the whole gamut of gender theories, making productive use of the work of Thomas Laqueur, Judith Butler, Eve Kosovsky Sedgwick, Julia Kristeva, and Jacques Lacan, amongst others. This chapter employs the framework advocated by Rachel Alsop, Annette Fitzsimmons, and Kathleen Lennon in *Theorizing Gender* (2002). The book provides an inspiring example of patient tolerance of different interpretive models, aiming collaboratively to follow not the Enlightenment model of debate to reach consensus, but rather a productive continuing dialogue. Engaging in dialogue with different theories produces a richer perspective on the material, enabling us to ask different questions and to arrive at different answers. At a more abstract level, however, privileging dialogue over univocality enables us to engage with our own subjectivity and fallibility in a more productive way.

> Fróðr sá þykkisk, er fregna kann
> ok segja it sama. (*Háv* 28/1–3)

> [Wise he esteems himself, who knows how to question and how to answer as well.]

Gender categories

Traditional or Second Wave femininist studies, generally speaking, tend to categorise various types of women and examine what they say about women's status, their relation to men, and the degree of freedom or autonomy they exercise. They also seek to identify or recover women's 'voices' or 'images'. The first of these approaches focuses on poems in which women are the primary subjects or speakers.[1] The second approach examines poetic representations where women are found in recurring, identifiable roles (avenger, inciter, valkyrie) that ostensibly bestow on them some degree of power (Jochens 1986, 1995, 1996; Jesch 1991; Motz 1991; Thomas 1952–53; Straubhaar 2011; Jóhanna Katrín Friðriksdóttir 2013b). Such studies tend not to focus on men and masculinity except in relation to women's oppression or autonomy, perhaps because traditional masculinity, based on virility, strength, courage, and dominance (both physical and sexual) was – and often still is – taken as a given, and considered as a norm against which women's attributes or typical interests were negatively contrasted or found lacking. In discussion of *Skírnismál*, to take one example, gender issues were long glossed over and the poem was analysed from a patriarchal hegemonic perspective, where its primary characters were seen as metaphors for phenomena such as fertility and the earth awakening in spring, or the legitimation of kingship, or social groups and strategies for mediating disputes (Olsen 1909; Steinsland 1991; Lönnroth 1977; Mitchell 1983). More recently, feminist readings have suggested that maleness is predicated upon the subjugation of women, and uncovered female subjectivities and perspectives (Larrington 1992a; Kress 2002). Moreover, scholars have recognised that masculinity is hardly a monolithic, straightforward category. Masculine gender categories came under serious scrutiny later than feminine ones, and when they did, it was often from a queer position, focusing, again, on subversive masculinities (Meulengracht Sørensen 1980/1983). More recently, the focus has shifted to analysing the mechanisms and tensions that underlie more traditional forms of normative masculinity, and their impact on the social fabric (Ármann Jakobsson 2007, 2008; Clark 2012).

'Woman', as a category, may be divided up into various functions in the eddic corpus, although of course the boundaries sometimes prove to be blurred. For instance: there are over twenty named valkyries, most notably Brynhildr and Sigrún; eight giantesses, including the object of Freyr's desire, Gerðr; a dozen goddesses; and a handful of norns, troll-women (not always easily distinguishable from giantesses), and swan maidens. These mythological women are often defined in terms of their relation to a man – as lover, wife, mother – and some of them are not developed in any greater depth. The same is true of the human women, but in their realm, private and public matters tend to be less separate, and the dynamics of complex inter- and intra-familial relationships open up possibilities for women to inhabit highly complex roles (Larrington 2011b, 2013; Quinn 2009, 2015a). Those who feature prominently sometimes transcend or even subvert their relational statuses – most notably Guðrún Gjúkadóttir. There are also individuals who are defined in terms of their function, such as the vǫlur in Vǫluspá and Baldrs Draumar, or the girls who chose the lives of men (Vǫluspá 20–1). The kinds of questions of interest here are: do poets and audiences conceive goddesses or valkyries as being governed by the same norms as human women, or does their unusual status free them from some normative constraints? Is there a hierarchy of identity categories – that is, would eddic audiences evaluate characters' behaviour according to normative human rules? Or, rather, should we view figures such as goddesses and valkyries as fulfilling particular narrative or symbolic functions which bear only an uneasy relation to other female characters?

Similarly, we could create a taxonomy of 'Man' which divides male figures into their roles as warriors (pre-eminent among them Sigurðr), figures that embody wisdom (such as Óðinn and Reginn), dwarfs, gods, and giants. However, the imaginative worlds depicted in eddic poetry are, to a great extent, men's worlds in which male power is conditional upon outstanding physical ability and military prowess, extensive knowledge, and/or sexual conquest. Take, for example, Óðinn's boasting about the women he has bedded or tried to bed in Hárbarðsljóð (sts 16, 18) and Hávamál (sts 96–102), or the Helgi poems, which might be seen as laying out a normative gender dynamic in which masculine men fight to win treasure and the women's love and/or approval, and in which it is shameful to be feminine or effeminate (e.g. Helgakviða Hundingsbani I sts 34–44). They raise the question of how far normative gender roles are straightforwardly accepted, and how far poets and audiences were actively exploring their fragility and the immense efforts required to construct and maintain normative masculinity in heroic society (Clark 2012). *Skírnismál*, for instance, might be seen as opening up the issue of antagonism between men and women and their unequal power dynamic, whether as normative or open to resistant readings which problematise male violence and validate female desire (Larrington 1992a; see also Schorn on genre, Chapter 12 in this Handbook). So, too, *Lokasenna*, where Loki accuses the gods of all kinds of sexual deviance, and *Þrymskviða*, where Þórr is forced to dress up as Freyja, have provided ample material for discussion about normative masculinities (McKinnell 2000; Jón Karl Helgason 2002). The anxieties these poems, as well as the less-discussed *Hárbarðsljóð*, lay bare suggest that eddic poems reflect fear of public accusations of deviance, and consequent loss of social status, rather than reprehending actual behaviour (Ármann Jakobsson 2008).

In such a world, femaleness could be considered a negative attribute; *Hávamál*, for instance, has been seen as a collection of gnomic wisdom read by some critics as evincing a largely misogynistic attitude to women (Kress 1993, 2002; Swenson 2002). They are discussed largely from a male per-spective and depicted as untrustworthy: a woman should be praised only when she is cremated, a girl only when she is married (st. 81); women are changeable and deceitful (st. 84); their 'pillow-talk' is not to be trusted (st. 86); and their love is slippery and uncontrollable (st. 90). The reader is warned of the dangers of sleeping in the arms of a witch (sts 113–14) and to be wary of another man's wife (sts 115 and 131). Women achieve what they want by flattery (st. 92) and are fickle and humiliate men (st. 102). The sentiment can be found in other poems: take, for example, *Vǫluspá*'s magic-wielding Heiðr, who plays with the minds of men and is given the epithet *angan illrar brúðar* ('a wicked woman's favourite', *Vsp* 22/8), and the gods' apparent golden age comes to an end when the three *þursa meyjar* ('ogre-girls', *Vsp* 8/6) enter the stage. It is easy enough to build up a picture of misogyny and contempt for women couched in the universalising language of gnomic wisdom, or when they are blamed for events that lead to the calamities described in *Vǫluspá*.

However, if we shift perspective slightly, the picture shifts accordingly. Other comments in *Hávamál* indicate that men are fickle towards women (st. 91); we are also told, on the one hand, that men need the love of a woman (sts 95–6) and, on the other, that various spells can be used to manipulate women towards love (sts 161–3). These, and other comments suggesting that men are made foolish by desire (sts 93–4), could be used to create a more balanced, if equally jaundiced, picture of all humans as fallible, manipulative, and deceitful. Alternatively, the advice that one should make and keep promises to get a female confidante (st. 130) could be taken as evidence that more trusting, positive male–female relations are possible. Indeed, women and men are not, on the whole, represented as diametrically opposed to one another, and this idea is certainly in line with the Old Norse–Icelandic corpus more generally. The role of women in sagas of various genres is important: female characters are often explicitly valued for wisdom, sound counsel, and support, in both private matters and public (Gos 2009; Jóhanna Katrín Friðriksdóttir 2013b), and *Hávamál*'s praise of female confidantes also suggests that this is the case.

Another shift of perspective would emphasise men's treacherous behaviour towards women, such as the actions of Óðinn in *Hávamál*. The poem relates the narrative of the god's encounter with Billingr's girl and what he sees as her betrayal (sts 97–102). Óðinn also admits his ill-treatment of Gunnlǫð, as he repays her badly for his open-hearted reception (sts 104–10). It may be possible to read Óðinn's sexual adventures in *Hárbarðsljóð* as exploitative (though mutual pleasure-giving seems also to be involved) while in *Vǫluspá* 39, men are punished as murderers, oath-breakers, and philanderers, seducing other men's confidantes. Narratives such as this open up the question of how far we can see individual gnomic pronouncements and other instances of negative attitudes towards women as typical of Old Norse social attitudes, and how far we should see them as a selection used to characterise Óðinn and other similarly deceitful figures.

Moreover, Óðinn is not the only character portrayed as deceitful, nor is this attribute limited to men. We might think of Herkja and her false accusations of Guðrún's adultery in *Guðrúnarkviða III*, or Grímhildr and her drink of forgetfulness in *Guðrúnarkviða II*.[2] This is not to mention Guðrún herself, who feeds her own children to her husband Atli after he has killed her brothers, disguising their flesh and blood as delicious morsels:

> krǫpp var þá Guðrún, kunni of hug mæla
> . . . lék hon tveim skjǫldum. (*Am* 74)

> [Guðrún was impenetrable, she knew how to dissemble . . . played a double game.]

Often, we see female characters behaving just as 'badly' – cunningly, deceitfully – as male ones, refusing to accept their family duty and the wishes of their male kin, or subverting the traditional, passive gender roles they are expected to fulfil (Sigrún, Borgný, Oddrún, Guðrún, Brynhildr,

Billingr's girl, Herkja). However, these women can be seen simply to be privileging their own desires above the wishes of others and pursuing the avenues of power available to them (Jóhanna Katrín Friðriksdóttir 2013a). Eddic poetry thus often represents characters, whether male or female, as motivated by their personal ends, and using (or attempting to use) whatever tactics necessary to achieve their goals. Eddic poets clearly had no qualms about showing women to be scheming and calculating, just like men, and their poetry can generally be regarded as explorations of the complexity of human nature and relationships where perspectives are relative. Thus, focusing only on perceived instances of male misogynistic attitudes towards women oversimplifies a much broader spectrum of gender relations, as we show in the following sections.

Scholars interested in analysing eddic verse in terms of theories of sex difference could find productive material in interpersonal relationships. Those interested in marriage dynamics might look at Frigg and Óðinn's relationship and balance his seeking of her advice in *Vafþrúðnismál* (although he rejects it immediately) with their competitive and mutually undermining behaviour throughout the prose prologue to *Grímnismál*. Male and female figures seem to be fundamentally opposed when one focuses on the extent of marital disharmony in eddic poetry: the implications of the mutual incompatibility of Njǫrðr and Skaði in an eddic verse preserved only in *Gylfaginning* (24);[3] the terrible bickering of husband and wife in *Atlamál in grænlenzku*; and the disturbing threats of sexual violence in *Skírnismál*. This is perhaps countered by the more balanced and supportive relationships of Helgi and Sigrún, Guðrún and Sigurðr – at least by Guðrún's own account (*Gkv I* 20) – and the female speakers in *Oddrúnargrátr* and their lovers, though the best relationships seem doomed, usually sabotaged by the woman's male kin. Interestingly, the swan maidens in *Vǫlundarkviða* (sts 3–5) appear to want freedom from marriage while the men desire the 'committed' relationship; this might open up questions of power struggle and possessiveness in marriage-type relations.

Some eddic scholars have identified a binary dynamic of male action and female lamentation (Frank 1982; Clover 1986a). Guðrún and the valkyries, however, provide strong counter-examples of female action to this pattern, and of course there are famous examples from outside the eddic world of men who lament, such as Egill Skallagrímsson's *Sonatorrek* (Sävborg 1997, 2013). It could be argued that these men are thereby feminised, along with the memorialising skaldic poets who describe themselves as the 'widows' of their kings (Harris 1993). But, alternatively, these men may provide evidence that grief is not gendered in this way, or at least that its gendering was open to question (compare Straubhaar 2002). After all, men do weep or sob in eddic poetry (*Atlakviða* sts 12 and 38, *Atlamál* st. 66), but, unlike female lament, this is referred to in passing rather than focused on. Such male weeping thus forms part of a widespread medieval Scandinavian tradition in which male tears are acceptable following the death of an exceptional ruler, rather than for kindred (Mills 2014).

Complicating gender

As we have seen, many qualities that, on the surface, might be exclusively associated with either men or women turn out to be gender neutral. The principle (associated with contemporary gender studies) that biological sex is stable, but that gender is socially constructed, has stimulated much challenging work on the sagas, and recent articles have started to disentangle and lay out the various distinctions that we need to make with Old Norse texts, both prose and verse. For instance, it is desirable to distinguish between the dominant ideologies of gender at the time of a text's composition, its writing down, and its readings, medieval and modern (Ármann Jakobsson 2007). Similarly, a text may promote, question, or subvert the dominant gender ideology, for instance in its representation of male–female inequality (Phelpstead 2003; Jóhanna Katrín Friðriksdóttir 2012, 2013a). In hermeneutic terms we also need to query the extent to which literature reflects social reality, whether it is really always only self-reflexive, and whether there is a dialogic relationship between literature and life, such that literature not only reflects, but also shapes, historical discourse (Phelpstead 2007).

Old Norse gender studies have particularly focused on issues such as how the masculine–feminine binary is constructed or changes over time (Borovsky 2002; Clover 1986b). From this perspective, Guðrún Gjúkadóttir in particular might be seen to reveal that many of the attributes we today might associate with – or exclude from – ideals of femininity and womanhood are not essential: Guðrún is not traditionally maternal or passive or soft, and she is a successful warrior and avenger in *Atlakviða* (sts 41–3). She might be seen as subverting stereotypes of femininity (or hegemonic gender roles) by adopting masculine attributes such as martial prowess and ruthlessness (Clark 2012). Other eddic military women (valkyries and shield-maidens) might also be seen as embodying what Judith Halberstam would call female masculinities (Halberstam 1998). Embodied, for example, in Hervǫr in *The Waking of Angantýr* (preserved in *Hervarar saga ok Heiðreks*), female masculinity characterises several other *fornaldarsögur* women. Often the model expands and ultimately overlaps with normative masculinity: women adopt a masculine name and successfully occupy a normative male role, albeit for a limited period (Jóhanna Katrín Friðriksdóttir 2013b, following Butler 1990; see also Layher 2007; Norrman 2000). At least some members of medieval audiences might have themselves experienced or at least responded to these subversive identities since the paradox of the female ruler also blurs the strict behavioural divide between genders.

From the more radical perspective of social constructionism theory, where not only gender but *sex itself* is unstable and constructed, military women such as the valkyries and shield-maidens might be seen not as embodying female masculinities, but as indicating the fundamental instability of categories of sex and gender. For instance, Thomas Laqueur's notion of the one-sex model has been applied to Old Norse material (Laqueur 1990; Clover 1993). The argument here is that, as ancient and medieval medical authorities suggest, some medieval people may have conceived not of two separate sexes (in the way we tend to), but rather of a single sex, where normative men represent the top and positive pole of a continuum and where normative women and non-normative men represent the bottom and negative pole.

Particularly interesting from this point of view is the figure of Loki. Loki impregnates the giantess Angrboða, but he himself is also impregnated (*Hdl* st. 41). To this pregnant man we might compare the breast-feeding viking Þorgils of *Flóamanna saga* (ch. 23), and ask how seriously we should read this type of material. It is easy enough to dismiss transvestism and sodomy in comic and satirical contexts, such as Þórr's cross-dressing in *Þrymskviða*, or the gendered or sexualised insults contained in *Lokasenna* and the flytings of the Helgi poems and *Hárbarðsljóð*. However, if they are *not* disregarded, they enable us to think about the various non-normative gendered and sexual identities to which these texts give space, and which can validate such identities through resistant readings (Jón Karl Helgason 2002).

Reflecting on such texts also opens up the complicated question of pagan and Christian material in the corpus. There is ample evidence that Christianisation has a wide-ranging impact on converted peoples' attitude to gender and sexuality, but exactly what that impact was in medieval Scandinavia and Iceland is difficult to assess. Would eddic audiences have seen Þórr's cross-dressing as a comic inversion of gender? Or does this depend on the date? That is, would later Christian audiences have a different attitude from earlier pagan ones? Does *Þrymskviða* provide evidence of pagan ritual practices, however mediated or muddled? (See Jens Peter Schjødt [Chapter 7] and Terry Gunnell [Chapter 5] in this Handbook.)

The fact that Loki and other male figures are said to have been impregnated by other men might point to a pre-Christian dynamic whereby so-called active men who take the insertive role in sex with other men are not stigmatised, but where the so-called passive man is stigmatised. The penetrable body is viewed as shameful, hence women and unmanly men are identified as *blauðr* (soft or weak; metaphorically feminine) (Meulengracht Sørensen 1983; Clark 2012). On the other hand, Loki does not seem to suffer unduly from such stigmatisation. Perhaps, therefore, we should take more seriously the evidence of *Hyndluljóð* and *Lokasenna* that biology as well as gender is unstable. We might ask how different audiences would react to accounts of male pregnancy or breast-feeding, and whether that would be as literal or metaphorical representations of male nurturance. And we might ask the wider and perhaps unanswerable question of whether the eddic poems give us access to a less Christianised view of sex and gender in the North. While eddic poems are irrecoverable in their 'original' pre-Christian form – if indeed they were composed in a heathen milieu – they have evolved and been adapted by each generation that preserved and retold them. Consequently, they cannot be regarded as affording unproblematic access to pre-Christian attitudes (McKinnell 2000; Quinn 2013b; see also Ármann Jakobsson 2007; see also Margaret Clunies Ross [Chapter 1] and Bernt Øyvind Thorvaldsen [Chapter 4] in this Handbook).

A related question here, in terms of the intertwined nature of gender and sexuality, is whether the heterosexual pair is seen as normative. As ever, the answer depends on one's emphasis. If one is thinking about dynasty and lineage in poems such as *Rígsþula*, with its lists of representative couples and their offspring, then the answer might be yes. However, the existence of valkyries shows that a career beyond the domestic sphere was conceivable. The poems involving the Gjúkung and Buðlung dynasties indicate the fundamental tensions aroused by marriage: no one in this world lives 'happily ever after' (Quinn 2015a). Representations of male homosocial pairs and groups such as those found in heroic poetry and in the *fornaldarsögur* (for instance, *Hjálmþés saga ok Ölvis*), and particularly examples of sworn-brotherhood (such as that contracted between Sigurðr and the Gjúkungs), also bring up the question of whether marriage, kinship, or friendship is perceived as the more 'intimate' and lasting relationship, if indeed we can detect a hierarchy of ties. In this connection, the vexed relationship of Óðinn and Loki becomes relevant. Their blood-brotherhood and association with *seiðr* provide just one indication that affective relations are fundamentally complex and have a complex interaction with gender and sexuality. Moreover, in Óðinn and Loki's dealings, the compromised masculinity of neither god leads to loss of status or power. One might ask what separates Óðinn and Loki from other male beings, given that masculinity is a precarious quality, riddled with anxieties, and constantly under threat (as for example in *Hárbarðsljóð, Lokasenna,* and *Helgakviða Hjǫrvarðssonar*).

Femininity: maternality and wisdom

To examine the representation of women in more detail, let us turn to some of the recurring roles in which they appear. Scholars looking for evidence of strong, autonomous women – characteristic of 1970s to '90s feminist scholarship – have focused on figures such as the valkyries, or Guðrún and Brynhildr in their more heroic moments as whetting women and female combatants (Jochens 1996; Clover 1986a; Kress 1993; Motz 1980; Mundal 1994b; Anderson 2002; Tolmie 2003). Those evaluating evidence of male oppression and female victimhood look to Bǫðvildr in *Vǫlundarkviða* or the litany of female woes in *Oddrúnargrátr* (Motz 1986; Kress 1993, 2002). *Oddrúnargrátr* has more recently been analysed from a perspective that highlights Oddrún's actions and agency (Quinn 2009). Earlier scholarship manifesting an ideological agenda includes Anne Heinrichs's speculation about the 'prepatriarchal woman', i.e. an inhabitant of a proto-feminist utopia before the arrival of Christianity, patriarchy, and female oppression (1986), and work surveying women's important role in pagan religious practices and culture (Kress 1993; Jochens 1996; Mundal 1994a).

From the perspective of sex-difference theory – wherein men and women are equal but different, and gender is not independent of biological sex – Guðrún and Brynhildr might be seen as unnatural or non-standard women because they reject traditional aspects of womanhood such as maternality and food preparation (cf. Bynum 1992). Correspondingly, Freyja's association with fertility, and her status as the object of the giant Þrymr's desire in *Þrymskviða*, might be viewed as normative, although Loki's accusations of her enjoyment of multiple sexual partners in *Lokasenna* (in fact he accuses all the goddesses of promiscuity) seem more in line with what might be expected of a fertility goddess (Larrington 1992a). Such approaches are compatible with more recent studies, such as Tarrin Wills's recent article about testosterone production and viking values (2013). Moreover, one corollary of a sex-difference standpoint is that a particular focus on, or understanding of, women in texts may be taken as evidence of female authorship in whole or in part

(Thomas 1952–3; Scott 2002; Gísli Sigurðsson 1990; Auerbach 1998). However, this approach runs the risk of ascribing universal aspects to the 'female mind' and thus needlessly isolating shared human qualities by its exclusion of men.

One element of interest in this kind of approach is to explore how eddic constructions of maleness and femaleness might differ from or overlap with our own. For instance, women might be associated with fertility and maternality (via figures such as Freyja and Frigg, respectively, and the numerous mothers who weep for their children or who, like Guðrún, are criticised for not doing so). Eddic poetry in fact presents a varied view of mothers: among those who conform to traditional (perhaps Christian-influenced) ideas about maternity, a much-cited example is Frigg, weeping for her son Baldr in *Vǫluspá* 33. Another notable case is Guðrún and the affection she expresses for her daughter Svanhildr, comparing her to a *sæmleitr sólar geisli* ('a splendidly glowing sun-ray', *Ghv* 15/7–8); unusually, she incites her sons Hamðir and Sǫrli to avenge their sister (Larrington 2015a, 99–102). From one perspective, Grímhildr could be regarded as a good mother, as she relentlessly works to advance the position of her family, doting on her children (according to Guðrún in *Atlamál* st. 72), and acting on her daughter's behalf in securing her a most excellent second husband, Atli, son of Buðli. On the other hand, Guðrún, recovering from the loss of her husband Sigurðr in self-imposed exile in Denmark, is hunted down by her mother, summoned home and a potent drink is administered to make her agree to the marriage. From this point of view, Grímhildr's actions are not beneficial, and she embodies an alarming, even terrifying image of maternality that stops at nothing for material or political gain. The two women quarrel furiously about Grímhildr's proposal (*Guðrúnarkviða II*) and Grímhildr's pleading, threats, and offers of bribes to Guðrún suggest that she is driven by ambition to try to form prestigious social ties, regardless of her daughter's wellbeing. Finally, maternity turns to an abject image of horror when Guðrún slits her own sons' throats in her pursuit of vengeance. Thus, the image of the mother becomes multi-dimensional, oscillating between a protecting, nurturing, and loving figure, and one that is ambitious, self-centred, and ruthless.

Beyond these transgressive mothers, femininity is strongly associated with wisdom, foresight, sound advice, and, consequently, protection, whether in descriptions of women or through narrative events; whether human, divine, or monstrous females. *Hávamál* (st. 91) portrays women as *horskar* ('wise') when it advises men on how to seduce them by flattery and deception:

þá vér fegrst mælum er vér flást hyggjum,
  þat tælir horska hugi. (*Háv* 91/4–6)

[when we speak most fairly, then we think most falsely, that entraps the wise mind.]

Guðrún, Glaumvǫr, and Kostbera are all called *horskar* ('wise') in *Atlamál* (sts 3, 10, and 35), and so too is Brynhildr in *Grípisspá* (st. 31). Billingr's *mær* is similarly described with epithets relating to wisdom: *iþ ráðspaka* ... *horska man* ('the sagacious ... clever woman', *Háv* 102/4,8), and is depicted as outwitting Óðinn when he intends to seduce her. Seeresses, described as *vittugar* ('magic-wise', *Bdr* 4/5), possess the knowledge of the future that Óðinn tirelessly seeks to acquire from them (Quinn 2002), although it does not enable him to prevent *ragnarǫk*. Likewise, *framvísar* ('knowledgeable about the future', *Grt* 1/2) are the two giantesses in *Grottasǫngr*, Fenja and Menja, who offer to tell Fróði *sǫgur fornar* ('ancient tales', *Grt* 18/8).

Women are also expected to impart some of their wisdom to male recipients. *Hávamál* (st. 115) refers to a woman as a man's *eyrarúna* (a woman into whose ears one tells secrets, a confidante), suggesting that they have a role of giving counsel, and we consistently find female characters performing the role of advisor. *Sigrdrífumál* is the most extended depiction of this figure: the valkyrie's gnomic advice to the young Sigurðr encompasses many aspects of ordinary and military life, much like the more frequently quoted *Hávamál*. Sigrdrífa teaches Sigurðr runes for gaining victory on the battlefield, ale-runes against being drugged through drink, runes to help with childbirth, sea journeys, healing wounds, to prevent slander, and to be pleasant to one's companions, and she prescribes how to treat the remains of the dead. Above all, *vit ok vápn* ('common sense and weapons', *Sd* 36/4) are needed, since quarrels and strife, and grief as a result, are ever-present in human society (see Schorn on genre, Chapter 12 in this Handbook). Advice dealing with social behaviour is also imparted: loyalty to one's kin and oaths, and caution, are the running themes in her speech, and this tradition reaches all the way to the romance-inflected *Hjálmþés saga ok Ölvis*, in which the princess Hervör advises the hero Hjálmþér (in two *fornyrðislag* ('old story metre') verses, ch. 14) on how to behave in front of her father, the king, in order to advance himself at court. Women are thus seen as agents of protection: in *Grógaldr*, the fearful Svipdagr asks his dead mother Gróa to chant incantations that will help him with the difficult task of finding Menglöð, set by his *lævís* ('cunning, malicious', *Gg* 3/3) stepmother:

galdra þú mér gal, þá er góðir eru,
   bjarg þú, móðir, megi. (*Gg* 5)[4]

[chant me some chants – those which are good ones; mother, save your son.]

Gróa complies, chanting nine incantations sometimes reminiscent of Sigrdrífa's runes: each of them has the potency to protect the young man against harm from potential foes, evil or hostile beings, perilous sea journeys, and inclement mountain storms, or to release him from fetters. Most importantly, Gróa casts a spell that he be his own master, *sjálfr leið þú sjálfan þik* ('you must be your own guide', *Gg* 6/6), and grants him wisdom and articulacy when he must bandy words with the *naddgöfugr jötunn* ('the spear-magnificent giant', *Gg* 14/2).

Conversely, if whetting also functions as a type of advice (rather than a request or command or a female duty), then women do have an important part to play in this aspect of heroic life. Hamðir and Sǫrli identify this clearly in their critique of their mother in *Hamðismál* (sts 6–10). The incitement speech has tended to be foregrounded by scholars in preference to women's peaceful advice, but women's advocacy of caution is both common and vital: men who do not pay heed to their advice generally fare badly (Jóhanna Katrín Friðriksdóttir 2013b). Gunnarr and Hǫgni ignore their wives Kostbera and Glaumvǫr's warnings (*Atlamál* sts 9–29), hard on the heels of Guðrún's thwarted attempt to send similar messages. Sigrdrífa's wisdom, however, does not have the intended result since Sigurðr is killed by the Giúkungs; perhaps more circumspection at their court might have saved him from the fateful sworn-brotherhood and Grímhildr's manoeuvrings. On the whole, eddic poets often explicitly describe women as wise and depict them as giving sound advice, attributes that contribute to a positive image of femininity. In these poets' minds, there are roles for women that are supportive, helpful, and highly valued by the men who depend on them.

Gender and monstrosity

Eddic poetry often resists easy binaries and groupings, and Loki is the prime example of an anthropomorphic figure that defies categorisation. He possesses giant blood and engenders monstrous offspring, yet sustains close ties to the Æsir – he and Óðinn are sworn brothers – and is therefore located on the border of what it is to be human, acting as a warning and a threat to those who would breach the boundaries of acceptable behaviour (Cohen 1996; Larrington 2006). The son of a giant, Loki is associated with the deviant magical practice of *seiðr*, he gestates and gives birth to the eight-legged horse Sleipnir, and, with the giantess Angrboða, he begets the terrifying creatures that will descend upon the world at *ragnarǫk* (*Vǫluspá* sts 47–8, 52 and *Gylfaginning* 27–9). Sex, reproduction, and offspring are intimately linked to monstrosity, connecting with anxieties about (prestigious) lineage and the mixing of blood between social and/or racial groups. Such paradigms are also discernible in the *fornaldarsögur*, particularly in the three *Hrafnistumannasögur*, where sexual and romantic relationships with giants' daughters, as with Gerðr and Skaði, are particularly prominent.[5] Many of these relationships result in offspring and even love, albeit a love which is not meant to last and is only permissible in the wilderness (Schulz 2004). Sex with male giants seems to be considered the horror of horrors: in *Skírnismál*, this awful fate appears as a threat, and the goddess Freyja is appalled and furious at the idea of having been promised to Þrymr in *Þrymskviða*. However, the gods have fewer objections to giantesses as sexual companions, and several Æsir are the products of such liaisons between races. Indeed, giantesses seem to bestow positive qualities on their children. For example, Óðinn has a sexual relationship with the giantess Jǫrð, who is the earth itself, resulting in the birth of Þórr, the mightiest of all gods (denoted as *Jarðar burr* ('son of Earth', *Ls* 58/1); *mǫgr Hlóðyniar* ('Hlóðyn's glorious boy') and *Fjǫrgynjar burr* ('Fjǫrgyn's child', *Vsp* 56/2,10)). Despite the giantesses' attractiveness, these relationships must remain short term, figuring the insurmountable obstacles surrounding marriage between different social or ethnic groups (Jóhanna Katrín Friðriksdóttir 2013b). Alternatively, giantesses provoke violence; like the Hrafnistumenn, Þórr is also the slayer of female giants (*Hárbarðsljóð* 20). Their giant blood generates no kin loyalty, and the male heroes seek to suppress and eradicate monstrous forces – unsurprisingly, since giants and the monsters will bring the world to an end at *ragnarǫk*.

Often portrayed as hostile and dangerous, monstrous characters are typically found having verbal contests or hostile exchanges with humans in which their power is threatened or defied. *Hyndluljóð, Helreið Brynhildar, Helgakviða Hjǫrvarðssonar*, and several *fornaldarsögur* all feature verse flytings between a god or heroic figure and a giantess (see e.g. *Hjálmþés saga ok Ölvis* and the *Hrafnistumannasögur*). With her verbal aggression, Hrímgerðr in *Helgakviða Hjǫrvarðssonar* is reminiscent of the loathsome giantesses, Feima and Kleima (referred to as Þjazi's daughters, probably figuratively), who in *Gríms saga loðinkinna* (ch. 1) attack Grímr's ship whilst uttering *fornyrðislag* verses threatening violence. Hrímgerðr boasts of having drowned Hlǫðvarðr's sons (*HHj* 19), while in *Helgakviða Hundingsbana I* (st. 40) giantesses are said to have castrated Sinfjǫtli. These aggressive and unruly characters represent all that men fear, and are usually dealt with through simple extermination. The *gýgr* ('giantess') in *Helreið Brynhildar* reproaches Brynhildr for seducing another woman's man, stating that it would be more fitting for her to be doing embroidery. She, perhaps surprisingly, aligns herself with traditional femininity in policing Brynhildr's behaviour, but in this case Brynhildr has trespassed so much against her fellow humans that even the giantess sides with the Gjúkungs.

At this intersection between gender and monstrosity, the feminine and the monstrous become doubly deviant. Their horror is intensified by abject physical aspects, such as in *Lokasenna* (st. 34), where giantesses treat Njǫrðr as their chamber pot, urinating in his mouth. In *Grottasǫngr*, the giantesses Fenja and Menja are linked with the fates and valkyries, on the one hand, and with nature on the other: all forces beyond Man's control. They even shape the landscape itself, moving mountains (st. 11). The sisters are situated against human, masculine greed and overuse of resources (Quinn 2013a; see also Linke 1992), and, in the end, they crush Fróði's reign with an army ground out from their millstone. *Vǫluspá* similarly links giantesses with the end of an era, with the Æsir living in bliss until the three giant maidens arrive (st. 8), heralding the end of a golden age, although we are not told why. The old woman (*in aldna*) in Járnviðr (st. 40), who raises the wolf that will swallow the moon, seems to play her part in *ragnarǫk* by nurturing destruction (see Brink and Lindow, Chapter 9 in this Handbook). The forces of nature and old age are not the only feminine qualities made monstrous: maternity is also a locus of fear when the vengeful Guðrún, referred to as *afkár dís* ('formidable woman', *Am* 71/3), kills her sons and serves them to their father. Women's rage is horrifying if not contained and channelled through the proper avenues: Freyja begins to snort (*fnása*) when Þórr and Loki suggest that she must marry Þrymr. She is so irate that the whole hall shakes and her necklace, the famous *Brísinga men*, breaks apart (*Þrymskviða* st. 13). Less comically, after Sigurðr's death, Brynhildr's eyes burn with anger, and she seems to turn into a terrifying creature reminiscent of a dragon:

> Stóð hon und stoð, strengði hon elvi;
> brann Brynhildi, Buðla dóttur,
> eldr ór augum, eitri fnæsti,
> er hon sár um leit Sigurði. (*Gðr I* 27)

> [She stood by the pillar, she summoned up all her strength; from Brynhildr, daughter of Buðli, fire burned from the eyes, she snorted out poison, when she looked at the wounds upon Sigurðr.]

These monstrous female characters, and their fury, physicality, and sub-version of maternity, all turn traditional femininity – epitomised in eddic images of compliant embroiderers and mourning mothers – on its head, and into something threatening and terrifying. Eddic poets clearly explored a wide range of ideas about femininity and motherhood; these are themes which invite further scholarly exploration.

Conclusion

As this chapter has shown, eddic poetry depicts male and female char-acters in astonishingly rich and diverse ways, showing human relations in all their complexity, in their most poignant but also most destructive forms. Female beings appear in many divine, human, and monstrous guises. They prophesy and decide the fate of men, and choose which of them will go to Óðinn and which to Hel. Women in eddic heroic poems dispatch their men to avenge grievances, or they manipulate them with magic and potions. They are cherished lovers, loyal wives, devoted mothers, grieving widows, and trusted confidantes, but they can also be fickle, deceitful, and conniving. They threaten men with words and with their monstrous bodies, but also protect them with their charms and knowledge of runes. Female figures also operate outside human society, as valkyries riding across the sky or as flying swan maidens, as giantesses living in the wilderness, and as seeresses who sit alone seeking knowledge (*Vǫluspá* st. 28; Raudvere 2012). They are also central to men's dealings with each other, as passive, subjugated brides or as unwilling wives, bullied into submission. Other female figures seize possibilities for autonomy by seeking out their lovers or escaping their family.

It is true that many eddic male figures are 'tough guys' who never show signs of pain – whether physical or emotional – who, like Hǫgni, are unflinching in the face of danger or death, who engage in macho verbal exchanges, whose world-view is 'kill or be killed', and whose honour is more important than life itself. But the poems also show the cracks and fissures in such strenuous performances of masculinity: at the divine level the Æsir cannot contain forces such as Loki or his monstrous kindred who threaten or resist gender dichotomies. The male figures of the heroic world similarly seem to be challenged in fulfilling certain aspects of maleness, such as regulating the sexuality of their female kin or in modelling success-ful fatherhood.

Notes

1. Women may even be the authors of some poems, though the anonymity of the eddic corpus makes this impossible to establish.
2. In *Vǫlsunga saga* 26, relating events which belong to the lacuna in the Codex Regius, Grímhildr also administers a drink of forgetfulness to Sigurðr.
3. Though of course, as Vanir god and giantess, that incompatibility may stem from a number of factors and not just gender.
4. Cited from the edition of Jónas Kristjánsson and Vésteinn Ólason (2014: II, 438).
5. The sagas known as *Hrafnistumannasögur* are *Ketils saga hœngs*, *Gríms saga loðinkinna*, *Qrvar-Odds saga*, and *Áns saga bogsveigis*.

CHAPTER 18

The reception of eddic poetry

Heather O'Donoghue

Introduction

Eddic poetry has been far and away the most influential genre of Old Norse literature. Its reception – not only in Western Europe and North America, but throughout the world – has been wide-ranging, far-reaching, and long-lasting. Although its influence has been most evident in literary texts, there are representations of eddic scenes in the visual arts – from Viking Age sculpture to Western European romantic art and beyond. In spite of rather little evidence for musical performance in Old Norse, eddic poetry has also inspired music of various kinds – most notably, of course, Richard Wagner's *Ring Cycle*. As a vehicle for Old Norse mythology, and the supposed vessel of ancient Germanic religious beliefs, its influence on the history of ideas, and especially on political thought, has been particularly significant, and the subject matter and ethos of eddic poetry have continued to make their mark on popular contemporary culture.

I shall use the term 'reception' to refer to three processes: the post-medieval dissemination of the texts themselves, direct critical response to them, and evidence of their influence on later works. I will discuss the influence of eddic poetry on literature (primarily in English) in three sections: the influence of the verses in *fornaldarsögur* (sagas of ancient times) (especially the sequence of verses known as *The Waking of Angantýr*), the influence of mythological verse, and the influence of the heroic poems about Sigurðr and Brynhildr. Along the way, I will consider the influence of eddic poetry on visual art and on music, and then on the history of ideas; I conclude with a brief account of its reception in popular contemporary culture. I will be as inclusive as possible about which poems may be designated 'eddic'. As we shall see, some of the most widely and popularly received eddic poetry is found outside the Codex Regius.

Before examining the post-medieval dissemination of eddic poetry, we should briefly consider its oral prehistory. Its existence is evident from Viking Age sculpture, such as representations of Sigurðr the Dragon-Slayer, many of them from Britain, and a number of Viking Age sculptures seem to represent scenes from *ragnarǫk* as alluded to in *Vǫluspá*.[1] There are also a number of depictions of the smith Vǫlundr, unmistakeable with cleverly wrought wings strapped on to his arms and legs (Bailey 1980: 105), and the Franks Casket also shows a composite scene from *Vǫlundarkviða*. Such representations imply knowledge of the fuller narrative from which they are taken, although we cannot know whether these narratives took the form of verse. Similarly, the poet of the Old English poem *Beowulf* clearly knew something of Old Norse myth and heroic legend, although as one might expect from an Anglo-Saxon Christian poet, his allusions to it are imprecise and oblique. But significantly, the poet seems to have taken his eddic allusions from a wide spread of sources; he certainly knew more than one poem, if his source was indeed in the form of poetry (O'Donoghue 2014: 16–24).

The existence of eddic poetry before the Codex Regius is of course clearly evident from Snorri Sturluson's *Edda*, which quotes or paraphrases poetry bearing a close relation to the poems which have come down to us. Texts such as Snorri's *Edda*, or the *Vǫlsunga saga*, which also quotes and paraphrases eddic poetry that has not survived elsewhere, as well as verses which have been preserved in the Codex Regius, have themselves been influential in their own later reception, and it is difficult – if not impossible – to distinguish between the secondary influence of these later texts and the direct influence of the verse itself. This dilemma of course persists throughout reception history, particularly with regard to the mythological poems of the *Edda*, as the body of Old Norse myth derived from them becomes, over time, an accretion of sources which can no longer be distinguished or disentangled.

Snorri includes many quotations from eddic poetry in *Gylfaginning*. He never contradicts the evidence of the verses, although on occasion his version of a verse differs from the version preserved in the Codex Regius, and sometimes he paraphrases the content of a verse rather than quoting it. And at the end of *Gylfaginning*, Snorri quotes a long sequence of stanzas from *Vǫluspá* without any paraphrase or comment: he simply allows the stanzas to speak for themselves without intervention. All this tells us about Snorri's reception of eddic poetry; he relied on it for information and confirmation, and did not always see the need to intervene between his readers and the verse. He evidently recognised and respected it as a valuable authority. The author of *Vǫlsunga saga* based his work on eddic heroic poems – including some now lost from the surviving manuscript of the Poetic Edda – and valued it enough to turn the sequence of Vǫlsung poems into a continuous saga narrative.

The author of *Vǫlsunga saga* sometimes uses his verse quotations to substantiate his narrative, as Snorri almost always does, or presents them as the speech of his characters. Neither he nor Snorri attributes a quotation to a poet, rather than a speaker, with the extraordinary exception of a stanza from *Grímnismál* quoted in *Gylfaginning*. Snorri introduces his verse quotation as follows: *Svá er hér sagt í orðum sjálfra Ásanna* ('As is said here in the words of the Æsir themselves', *Gylfaginning*: 34). Since the verse which follows is spoken by Óðinn, Snorri may be suggesting that eddic verse was the product of the historical Æsir, and thus very ancient indeed.[2] Eddic-style verse in *fornaldarsögur* – themselves set in an indistinct northern prehistory – is also presented as the speech of the characters. More significantly, in the *samtíðarsögur* (contemporary sagas), as Judy Quinn has shown, eddic-style verses are put into the mouths of supernatural characters, or figures who speak in dreams (Quinn 1987: 54–72). It seems that in its medieval reception, the actual origins of eddic verse lay beyond the knowledge of prose writers, and that the poetry itself was associated with the supernatural or legendary world, and was treasured as a cultural resource, preserving old wisdom and traditions which, in thirteenth-century Iceland, it might well have seemed imperative to record and preserve. These key elements in the medieval reception of eddic poetry continue to characterise the reception of eddic poetry in post-medieval times.

Knowledge of Iceland's literary heritage died out elsewhere in Europe towards the close of the Middle Ages, and it is only from around the middle of the seventeenth century that we can begin to pick up its reception history again.[3] The ownership or whereabouts of the Codex Regius itself is not known until it came into the possession of the Icelandic Bishop Brynjólfr in 1643; he presented the manuscript to the king of Denmark (hence its name) in 1662 (Larrington 2007: 21). During the seventeenth century, the several Scandinavian nations engaged in a competitive exploration of the early history of their peoples, and it soon became evident that medieval Icelandic manuscripts – made accessible to Scandinavian historians through the scholarship of Icelanders themselves – might provide just the material they needed. In this intellectual climate the first editions of eddic poems were produced, and, just as importantly, a number of treatises about the literature, culture, and religious beliefs of the supposed ancestors of the Scandinavian peoples, works which quoted eddic poetry as evidence for their information.

The first major move in the dissemination of eddic poetry was the 1665 edition of Snorri's *Edda*, together with the eddic poems *Vǫluspá* and *Hávamál* – key mythological texts – by Peder Hansen Resen (Resen

1665).[4] Resen supplied a Latin translation of the poems, making them accessible to scholars all over Europe. For English-speaking scholars, accessing Old Norse poetry through a literal Latin translation was the norm for almost the next two centuries, which meant that the distinctive poetic qualities of eddic poetry – metre, diction, and figurative language – were not always evident.

Resen's work was highly influential; a copy was presented to the Bodleian Library, for instance (Seaton 1935: 342–3), and the British antiquarian Robert Sheringham had been sent a copy (Quinn and Clunies Ross 1994: 193); in his *De Anglorum Gentis Origine Disceptatio* (*Discussion about the Origin of the English People*) he quotes from *Vǫluspá* and the whole of the runic section in *Hávamál* (Sheringham 1670). He did not understand Old Norse (Faulkes 1977b: 45), and was not at home with Resen's Danish (Fell 1996: 28–9), but relied on the Latin translation. Aylett Sammes, in his eccentric but entertaining *Britannia Antiqua Illustrata* (*Old Britain Illustrated*) (Sammes 1676; O'Donoghue 2014: 43–4), translates Sheringham's Latin quotations from the *Edda* into English. Many early scholars turned to Old Norse texts on the understanding that Scandinavians and the English shared a common Gothic heritage of which these texts were ancient products.

Eddic-style verse preserved outside the Poetic Edda

Texts which are now counted amongst the least historically reliable in the Old Norse canon – the *fornaldarsögur* – are set in an unspecified chronotope of early Scandinavia, and so scholars supposed that these sagas provided information about the early history of their nations. So it was that *Hervarar saga* (*The Saga of Hervör*) was edited by the Swedish scholar Olaus Verelius in 1672, with a Swedish rather than a Latin translation, though with Latin notes (Verelius 1672). This saga contains the eddic-style poem which came to be known in English as *The Waking of Angantýr* – the first complete Old Norse poem to be presented in an English translation, and hugely influential in its own right.

Thomas Bartholin's treatise on the death-defying bravery of the ancient Danes was also richly documented with quotations from Old Norse poetry, including very many eddic stanzas (Bartholin 1689). However, as its full name suggests, the *Antiquitatum Danicarum* (*Antiquities of the Danes*) was primarily concerned with illustrating what was believed to be evidence of the behaviour and attitudes of early Scandinavians, rather than their mythology, legends, or religious beliefs, and so eddic poetry did not take pride of place. Bartholin's work was extremely influential, however, and most notably made available a text of *Baldrs draumar* (under the name of *Vegtamsqviþa* (*The Poem of Vegtamr*)) which the poet Thomas Gray used for his celebrated *Descent of Odin* (Starr and Hendrickson 1966: 32–4). The Icelander Þormóður Torfason included the eddic-style poem *Darraðarljóð* in his collection of Orkney-related texts, *Orcades*, because the poem is associated in *Njáls saga* (*The Saga of Njáll*) with the Battle of Clontarf, at which Scandinavian Orcadians fought (Þormóður Torfason 1697).⁵ This poem was also taken up by Gray (as *The Fatal Sisters*) and these two *Norse Odes* (published in 1768, but composed several years earlier) were the most influential re-workings in English of eddic poems (Starr and Hendrickson 1966: 27–31). However, the concept of the death-defying Viking warrior dominated the reception of Old Norse verse, such that only *The Waking of Angantýr* continued as part of the canon of the most often translated, adapted, and imitated eddic poems in English. This canon was very largely determined by the publication of Bishop Percy's *Five Pieces of Runic Poetry Translated from the Islandic Language*; *The Waking of Angantýr* was included, along with perhaps the most popular death-defying poem, the so-called *Death Song* of Ragnarr loðbrók – a skaldic poem – and other poems which are neither mythological nor heroic-legendary (Percy 1763).⁶ Again, Percy translated from Latin literal translations of Old Norse poetry, and, moreover, translated into 'plain language', which disappointed some reviewers (Farley 1903: 33).

Percy's second major contribution to the dissemination of eddic poetry was his translation of Mallet's two-volume treatise on ancient Danish manners and literature, *Northern Antiquities* (Percy 1770). The material corresponding to Mallet's second volume comprises a translation of Snorri's *Gylfaginning*, an 'idea' of *Skáldskaparmál* ('It would tire our Reader's patience to insert it here intire'; Percy 1770: 184), and then 'An Idea of the More Ancient Edda' – that is, the Poetic Edda. This is described as 'a collection of very ancient poems, which had for their subject some article of the Religion and Morality of Odin'. But, unfortunately, 'this collection is at present considered as lost, excepting only three pieces': *Vǫluspá*, *Hávamál*, and the runic stanzas of *Hávamál*, presented as a separate piece (Percy 1770: 201). *Vǫluspá* is paraphrased rather than quoted, on the grounds that Snorri's *Gylfaginning* quotes plenty of stanzas from it. There follow other Old Norse poems: firstly, the opening stanzas of *Baldrs draumar*, credited to Bartholin, and then examples of the canon Percy himself had made central, including the ever-popular *Death Song*. *Northern Antiquities* was reissued six times in the course of the nineteenth century; Andrew

Wawn called it 'the natural starting point' for nineteenth-century readers interested in Old Norse themes (Wawn 2000: 184).

Percy's note on the lost Poetic Edda is fascinating: 'It were to be wished, that the possessors of such a treasure could be induced to esteem the communication of it to the world ... and they are now urged, in the name of the public, to this generous action' (Percy 1770: 201). But as Frank Farley notes, the public had not exactly been crying out for more Old Norse material: although by the middle of the eighteenth century, 'opportunities were at hand, and fairly accessible, for the scholar who wanted to make a special study of ... "Gothic matters" ... the great mass of English people knew little and cared little about them' (Farley 1903: 27). Well into the second half of the eighteenth century, there was still strong critical resistance to Old Norse myth, described by hostile reviewers of Old Norse-derived poetry as 'incomprehensibly wild and uncouth', a 'tissue of the most absurd and preposterous fictions', 'little adapted to the purposes of modern poetry' (Tucker 1962–5: 233–47). Nevertheless, the publication of the first volume of the so-called Copenhagen Edda in 1787, with facing translations in Latin, and, perhaps most importantly, as Margaret Clunies Ross has noted, a glossary, was a major step forward (Arnamagnæan Commission 1787; Clunies Ross 1998b: 183).

Within the decade, undergraduate Amos Cottle spent a Cambridge University vacation translating this volume (without Vǫluspá or Hávamál, which were not included in the first volume, and also omitting Sólarljóð, which he scorned as being 'filled with little else but the absurd superstitions of the Church of Rome'; Cottle 1797: xxix–xxx).[7] Cottle made some notorious errors in his translation (Larrington 2007: 36), but overall he does not deserve the acerbic judgement of William Herbert that had he claimed the poems as his own work, he 'could scarce have been accused of plagiarism' (Herbert 1804: 46). Cottle was as usual translating from the Latin, not knowing Old Norse. Herbert himself claimed to have been working from the original Old Norse, which was another step forward, although Margaret Clunies Ross has called this claim into question (Clunies Ross 1998b: 183–5).

The fashion for poetry ancient and sublime was fading. Cottle's translations were read by Southey, Wordsworth, and Coleridge, but did not inspire the canonical Romantic poets to compose on Old Norse themes (O'Donoghue 2014: 104–5). And eddic poetry *as poetry* was lost in the scholarly analysis of Old Norse myth as evidence of ancient thought rather than ancient poetry. William Roscoe protested in eloquent italics about this effacement: 'what we have transmitted to us in the *Edda* are *poems*, their best value is as poems' (Roscoe 1852: 475). But the poetic qualities of eddic verse had never really been on show.

One final landmark in the history of eddic dissemination is Benjamin Thorpe's 1866 translation of the Poetic Edda (Thorpe 1866). Thorpe worked from a German edition (revealingly noting of Cottle: 'this work I have never met with' (Thorpe 1866: vii), indicating the very limited circulation of Cottle's flawed but ground-breaking translation). Thorpe's collection is impressively inclusive, with a number of eddic poems outside the Codex Regius, such as *Hrafnagaldr Óðins* (*The Chant of Óðinn's Ravens*) and *Grottasǫngr*. But even more significant is the fact that Thorpe's translation was published as a popular edition, designed to be affordable, portable, and all-in-all accessible. Subsequent editions and translations of the Poetic Edda, such as that included in Gudbrand Vigfusson and York Powell's *Corpus Poeticum Boreale* (*Northern Poetic Corpus*) (1883), became the preserve of academic audiences. Notable exceptions are the translations of William Morris, who appended translations of individual eddic heroic poems to his collaborative (with Eiríkur Magnússon) translation of *Vǫlsunga saga* (*The Saga of the Vǫlsungs*) (1870), and the translations of W. H. Auden (Auden and Taylor 1969; 1981).[8]

Morris's translation technique was to preserve the 'otherness' of the text, with archaisms which have not pleased every reader. Auden too was a creative rather than literal translator, but his status as a poet lent eddic poetry an important place in the high modernist tradition of English literature. As we move to more modern editions and translations, we are looking less at reception and more at the history of scholarship, as dealt with by Harris, Chapter 2 in this Handbook. I therefore return at this point to consider the specific reception of one of the most often translated eddic-style poems: *The Waking of Angantýr*.

George Hickes, in his immensely scholarly *Thesaurus Linguarum Septentrionalium* (*Treasury of the Northern Languages*) printed a translation of the Angantýr verses in half lines, parallel with the original text from Verelius's *Hervarar saga* (Hickes 1705; Fell 1996). But although the poet John Dryden reprinted *The Waking of Angantýr* in his *Miscellany* of 1716, Hickes's scholarship did not ignite a passion for eddic-style poetry; it was not until the poem was included in Percy's *Five Pieces* with the thrilling title *The Incantation of Hervor* that its huge popularity began. Working from Hickes, with the help of Verelius's Latin notes, Percy did not attempt to convey the poetic qualities of his original text. But the subject matter of *The Waking of Angantýr* was enough to ensure its success with a public newly enamoured of sublime and ancient poetry. The saga tells the story of the hero Angantýr, who is killed in a battle in Sweden, and dramatically raised from his grave by his daughter Hervǫr who, disguised as a viking warrior, is determined to avenge his death, with his own sword, buried with him in the gravemound. But the sword is cursed, and Angantýr is unwilling to give it over to Hervǫr. Their exchange, in eddic metre, is the basis of the poem (Tolkien 1960: 14–19).

This poem was translated a number of times in the late eighteenth century – for instance, as one of Thomas Mathias's *Runic Odes* (Mathias 1781). Anna Seward called her 1796 'bold paraphrase' *Herva at the tomb of Argantyr* [sic]*: A runic dialogue* (Seward 1796: 22–36), and it was reprinted in her collected works by Sir Walter Scott in 1810. Roesdahl and Sørensen even used the title of the poem as a metaphor for the reception of Old Norse literature as a whole in post-medieval Europe (Roesdahl and Sørensen 1996). It was certainly one of the texts which both met and promoted the eighteenth-century taste for wild and romantic incident, but when that fashion passed, so too did the popularity of the poem itself. However, although they were not in the Codex Regius, the Angantýr verses were translated by W. H. Auden and Paul Taylor in their *Elder Edda* (Auden and Taylor 1969: 101–5). Perhaps the poem's popularity may yet reawaken: Auden's translation can now be found online (for example, meadhall.homestead.com/Angantyr.ht ml), subtitled 'A Warrior Woman's story', with a lurid illustration, a note explaining that the page has been created 'to bring to wider attention a very fine Norse poem which has been too much neglected', and links to both fantasy literature and neo-paganist websites.

The mythological poems

As we have seen, although *Vǫluspá* and *Hávamál* were the earliest mytho-logical poems to be made available outside Scandinavia, this early promi-nence ironically resulted in neglect of both poems, since they were not included in later eddic collections – such as the first volume of the Copenhagen Edda – precisely because they were already available. Furthermore, *Vǫluspá*, with its allusive, oblique style, is not an immediately accessible poem even in translation. *Hávamál*, with its down-to-earth wisdom, never met the taste for the sublime, and neither one became part of the small group of often translated poems. For a number of reasons, then, the influence of eddic mythological poetry was eclipsed by the conception of the heroic viking warrior, and, more especially, his proto-type: Odin the Asiatic chieftain whose Gothic warriors routed the Romans (O'Donoghue 2014: 12 *et passim*). In the closing decades of the eighteenth century, however, three poets – Thomas Mathias, Edward Jerningham, and Joseph Sterling – used the material of *Vǫluspá* to great effect in their poetry, and attracted a large number of reviews, not all of them complimentary (O'Donoghue 2014: 82–91).

Mathias worked from Percy's *Northern Antiquities*, but he appends Bartholin's Latin translation of the relevant stanzas at the end of his *Runic Odes*, since 'the books whence they are taken are rather scarce' (O'Donoghue 2014: 82). But reviewers called his material 'wild and monstrous . . . [containing] little that can be interesting' (Farley 1903: 100). This was a harsh verdict on eddic poetry. Edward Jerningham's *The Rise and Progress of Scandinavian Poetry* fared a little better with the reviewers (Farley 1903: 102). Again, the author refers his readers to Percy's work. Joseph Sterling's *Odes from the Icelandic* were much criticised on the grounds of poor poetic technique,[9] but Sterling does seem to have engaged with Old Norse myth as poetry, which he did not know in the original but praises on the grounds of its 'liberal and generous sentiments' and its 'noble and extravagant style'. However, he notes that Old Norse poetry lacks 'that justness of sentiment, or that purity of diction' characteristic of classical verse (O'Donoghue 2014: 89).

These poets, and others like them, were heavily influenced by Thomas Gray (Mathias dedicates his volume to Gray; Jerningham's verse is full of echoes of Gray's *Norse Odes*; Sterling describes himself as happy to follow in the footsteps of his 'sublime' master, Gray). Gray did not publish translations of *Vǫluspá* and *Hávamál* – although he planned to include them in his collection of 'British' poetry (Toynbee and Whibley 1935: vol. II, 517) – but his work inspired poets to engage with other eddic poems. William Blake's poetry provides an even more dramatic example of Gray's influence. Blake created the illustrations for Gray's *Poems* (1797), including the *Norse Odes*, and their influence on Blake's own work is very evident. Blake would almost certainly have also known *Northern Antiquities* with its many *Vǫluspá* quotations and substantial translation of *Hávamál* (Omberg 1976: 126), and it is possible to distinguish in Blake's poetry – especially in *Vala, or the Four Zoas* – the direct influence of eddic verse (O'Donoghue 2014: 93–103).

The Swiss artist Henry Fuseli produced a number of illustrations for Gray's *Descent of Odin* (based on *Baldrs draumar*) and the similarities between these pen, pencil, and wash pieces and Blake's illustrations are very clear. Fuseli's human figures, like Blake's, are heavily influenced by classical and renaissance sculpture, but Fuseli was evidently drawn to the perceived sublimity of Old Norse myth. His most celebrated painting is the wildly dramatic 'Thor battering the Midgard Serpent' – evidently a sublime moment when, in Fuseli's own words, 'passion and suffering become too big for utterance' (Schiff 1975: 45). Much of Fuseli's work illustrated literary works – most notably, by Shakespeare, Milton, and Dante; some pieces depict scenes from the *Nibelungenlied* (*The Poem of the Nibelungs*). It is hard to distinguish eddic sources from the influence of Germanic legend more generally. However, as Clunies Ross notes, Fuseli was the author of a very detailed and learned review of the Copenhagen Edda, which even contained his own translations of *Skírnismál* and *Hymiskviða* (Clunies Ross 1998b: 130).

Fuseli's thrilling and sometimes spine-chillingly imaginative works stand in complete contrast to Scandinavian illustrations of eddic scenes, such as Johannes Wiederwelt's curiously static depiction of Þórr in his chariot pulled by goats (Wilson 1997: 28). The following century saw a rising up of Nordic nationalism, but the resulting works, again indebted to classical art, such as Eckersberg's *The Death of Balder* or Constantin Hansen's *Aegir's Banquet* (illustrating *Lokasenna*), are even more static and lifeless; Wilson attributes their strange flatness to the fact that Viking Age archaeology had not yet provided artists with authentic models of material culture to bring their scenes to life (Wilson 1997: 47).

To return to mythological poetry: at the beginning of the nineteenth century, *Vǫluspá* was at last translated into English as a complete poem, by the Rev. James Prowett, in 1816 (Prowett 1816), by Ebenezer Henderson in 1819 (Henderson 1819: II, 522–8), and by William Herbert, who had originally intended to make it part of his long poem *Helga* but published it separately as *The Song of Vala* (Herbert 1842: vol. I, 143–8). But times had changed. Prowett, like Jerningham in the previous century, draws attention to the existence of a 'superior being' responsible for creation, and goes further in ascribing *ragnarǫk* to a distinctly Miltonic sinful universe. Herbert's *Song of Vala*, in spite of Herbert's self-proclaimed expertise in Old Norse, completely effaces the poetic qualities of the original, and concludes in the style and sentiments of a Christian hymn. And Old Norse myth – its eddic sources subsumed into a synthetic narrative – was becoming the object of interest as a precursor, and ancient parallel, to Christianity.

Throughout the nineteenth century, it is difficult to distinguish engagement with eddic poetry itself from a more generalised knowledge of Old Norse myth. In writing *Balder Dead*, for example, Matthew Arnold relied on an old (possibly even eighteenth-century) edition of *Northern Antiquities* (O'Donoghue 2014: 157). And yet, by the beginning of the twentieth century, the number of eddic texts and translations available – not only in English, but also in other European languages, especially German – meant that direct engagement with eddic poetry was increasingly possible, and this is manifest when authors make their sources explicit. Thus, for instance, David Jones cites *Hávamál* in both *In Parenthesis* (though he mistakenly attributes the passage to *Vǫluspá*; Jones 1937: 204) and *The Anathemata* (Jones 1952: 106); and C. S. Lewis, as well as describing his attempts to read eddic poetry in the original using Vigfússon and Powell's *Corpus Poeticum Boreale* (1883), prefaces his long poem *Dymer* with the words of Óðinn from *Hávamál* (O'Donoghue 2014: 187–9). Both of these poets are exploring the parallels between Óðinn's sacrifice and Christ's crucifixion, continuing the tradition of Old Norse myth re-imagined through a Christian lens. Much of the poetry of Hugh MacDiarmid – especially his celebrated long poem *A Drunk Man Looks at the Thistle* – is inflected by eddic themes, and he too engaged directly with eddic poetry (O'Donoghue 2009).

So what did eddic myth signify for modernist poets? As we have seen, eddic myth, with its accounts of creation and apocalypse, and a young god sacrificed, could shed provocative light on Christian theology. It could also be embraced as part of the cultural make-up of the British, or English, people. Finally, by contrast, the very alterity of eddic verse offered an exciting 'myth-kitty' for modernist and postmodernist poets, a range of alternative symbols to the classical material they were turning away from, ideas and motifs which were still arcane to English-speaking readers. But before turning to the reception of eddic poetry in contemporary culture, I want to consider the reception of the heroic poems of the Poetic Edda.

The heroic poems

The heroic poems of the Poetic Edda, the cycle of texts comprising the history and story of Sigurðr and his widow Guðrún, were much slower than the mythological poems to reach a wider public. As we have seen, they are described as 'lost' in *Northern Antiquities*, and they were not part of the first volume of the Copenhagen Edda, and thus not translated by Cottle. So, in spite of Sigurðr's prowess as a hero, he was not co-opted into the stereotypical image of the death-defying viking. However, the legend of the Vǫlsungs has perhaps proved to be the most enduringly influential subject of eddic poetry.

As early as 1806, Herbert had translated the heroic poem *Helreið Brynhildar* – the first heroic poem of the Codex Regius to be translated into English (Herbert 1806); *Sigurðarkviða in skamma* and *Atlamál* were included in a later volume (Herbert 1842). His long poem *Brynhilda* makes the most of the sentimental and erotic aspects of the material, and its description of how the armour of an alluring Brynhilda is penetrated by Sigurðr marks the beginning of a new response to eddic verse. Herbert's scholarly knowledge of eddic poetry was impressive, as the very many allusions to it in his works demonstrate. But in spite of his claims to direct engagement with original texts, he was more inspired by 'the poetical images which the manners and religion of the northern nations appeared to present' than by the poetry itself, and feeling constrained by his duty to translate faithfully was therefore moved to create original poetry based on Old Norse themes (Herbert 1842: 26).

William Morris translated not only *Vǫlsunga saga*, but also a number of heroic poems from the Codex Regius, which were published as an appendix to the saga translation (Morris and Eiríkur Magnússon 1870). Thus, Morris's epic poem *Sigurd the Volsung* – described by George Bernard Shaw as 'the greatest epic since Homer' – might very well be read as a response to the poetry itself (Morris 1887). Morris does not attempt to reproduce or imitate the distinctive metre of eddic poetry, or its poetic lexis (though he does echo the alliteration of eddic verse in his translations, and, to a lesser extent, in *Sigurd the Volsung*); in fact, *Sigurd the Volsung* is remarkable for its own distinctive metre of anapaestic hexameters, with a pronounced caesura splitting each long line. A response to eddic verse which does reproduce the qualities of the original poetry is J. R. R. Tolkien's posthumously published *The Legend of Sigurd and Gudrún* (Tolkien 2009). As an academic who taught Old Norse poetry, Tolkien knew eddic poetry well in its original form, and many elements in his popular works show evidence of engagement with poetic texts. But the two poems which make up *Sigurd and Gudrún* – given Old Norse names by Tolkien: *Völsungakviða en nýja* / *The New Lay of the Vǫlsungs* and *Guðrúnarkviða en nýja* / *The New Lay of Guðrún* – are neither translations nor original poems on eddic themes, but rather represent a considerable reordering and tightening up of both the individual heroic poems of the Poetic Edda and the imperfect cycle of the Codex Regius. They are written in what Tolkien describes as 'the old eight-line *fornyrðislag* stanza' of eddic verse – that is, 'modern English fitted to Old Norse metre' (Tolkien 2009: 4–6).

Tolkien regretted that William Morris's hope that the Vǫlsung story might become for his countrymen 'what the Tale of Troy was to the Greeks' was a vain one (Tolkien 2009: 13). The reception of *Sigurd and Gudrún* bears out the grim pronouncement of one of Morris's reviewers:

'To make the Eddas interesting is no easy task' (Faulkner 1973: 246). Few of Tolkien's readers were attracted by the eddic substance, which made for a no-win situation: only those who were already Tolkien fans were interested in this volume, and such readers were for this very reason disappointed that the poems were so little like Tolkien's popular works. One reviewer, with an unforgivable pun, likened the whole project to flogging a dead Norse (Sanderson 2009).

The most celebrated creative response to eddic poetry in the nineteenth century was Richard Wagner's *Ring Cycle*. Its debt to eddic poetry (rather than to the *Nibelungenlied*) has not been widely recognised, but it has perhaps been neglected because the opening of the opera is dominated by the Rhinemaidens, who are not eddic, and because of Wagner's distinctively Germanic name for the Old Norse Niflungar, the Nibelungs. However, as Árni Björnsson has demonstrated, very many episodes and *topoi* in the *Ring* are particular to the Poetic Edda (for example, the curse on the ring itself, taken from *Reginsmál*), and where eddic poetry and the prose of *Vǫlsunga saga* correspond, close verbal echoes from the poetry make the source certain (Árni Björnsson 2003). Further, as Stewart Spencer has argued, 'Wagner believed that the Poetic Edda was a spontaneous product of the *Volk* ... and that by recreating its "natural" diction, he would be instantly understood: the more insistent the *Stabreim* ... the more authentic the language of the *Ring*' – though Spencer concludes that Wagner too 'counterfeited a style which all too often proves an obstacle to our understanding' (Spencer 2000: 13).

Successful as independent creations are the many novels which use eddic themes – for example: James Joyce's *Finnegans Wake* (packed with Old Norse references of all kinds); Thomas Hardy's *Return of the Native* (based on the legend of Sigurðr and Brynhildr); Herman Melville's *Moby Dick* (referencing the story of Þórr and the World Serpent); and Günter Grass's *The Tin Drum* (with its many allusions to Old Norse myth). The old problem of distinguishing specifically poetic influence is compounded in these works by the creative transformations made by their authors, and the shift in medium from verse to prose, although Gabriel Garcia Marquez also imaginatively adapted the substance of *Vǫlundarkviða* in a short story he called 'A Very Old Man with Enormous Wings' (Garcia Marquez 1972).

Tolkien and Wagner may be compared in their re-workings of eddic heroic verse which sought to reflect – with mixed results – the features of the poetry itself. But the afterlife of their works has been entirely different. Tolkien was at pains to distance himself from Wagner: of Wagner's opera and his own most famous work, he noted tersely 'both rings were round, and there the resemblance ceases'.[10] Tolkien's popularity and influence have been huge, but Wagner raised the material of the eddic heroic poems to the status of national myth, and his music has remained a staple of high-brow adult European culture. By contrast, through the twentieth century in English-speaking countries, works based on the Poetic Edda have been increasingly concentrated on texts in different ways marginal to the literary canon: on children's or young adults' literature, such as Melvin Burgess's *Bloodsong* (2005) and *Bloodtide* (1999),[11] or on fantasy novels and films, or role-playing video games.

Ideology and popular culture

Wagner's work has been associated with the racism of Nazi ideology in the twentieth century, with anti-Semitic stereotypes used to characterise the despised Nibelungs, and the prominent dynamic of the powerful triumph-ing over the weak. Notoriously, Wagner became Hitler's favourite com-poser. It is worth noting that these elements are not especially evident in eddic poetry. Rather, Old Norse material was taken up by German nationalists in the belief that a pan-Germanic culture had preserved therein its most ancient beliefs; that the purest bearers of supposedly and so-called Aryan culture had been driven out of their Germanic homelands and into Scandinavia and Iceland, where their culture was encoded in precious written texts – primarily, the Poetic Edda. Thus, it was not so much the actual substance of the Poetic Edda which attracted racists and anti-semites, but its supposed origins (Poliakoff 1977).

But Nazi ideology also involved an occult strand, and here eddic poetry – in particular, *Hávamál*, with its runic stanzas attributed to Óðinn – played an important part (Goodrick-Clarke 1985). Óðinn – as Wotan – was adopted by German occultists and neo-pagans as the god of what they supposed was their ancestral race, and his acquisition of the runes, and their magical properties, became a central feature of Nazi occultism; runic letters are one of the most recognisable features of Nazi iconography, though Hitler himself was scornful of 'Wotanism'. But the status of runes as occult symbols in popular culture persists. Even though most surviving runic inscriptions are either secular and mundane, or straight-forwardly Christian, the association between runes and magic is taken for granted in new-age or neo-pagan circles, and is even encoded in English idiom: to 'read the runes' is to see into the (usually political or economic) future. Practices such as 'runic yodelling' or 'rune gymnastics' are perhaps less mainstream, but the instructions make diverting reading for the non-practitioner (O'Donoghue 2007: 111–18).

Nazi occultism viewed the Poetic Edda as a sacred text for Aryan peoples, and its supposed religious or philosophical wisdom is still revered by contemporary neo-pagan and white-supremacist groups – again, more because of its supposed origins than for its content, which tells us practically nothing about the practice of any pre-Christian religion. One of the most eccentric exponents of the 'true meaning' of the Poetic Edda was L. A. Waddell, whose book *The British Edda* attempted to demonstrate that the poems of the Codex Regius are not Scandinavian, but British in origin, and are actually the sad remains of a 'great Epic Poem of the Ancient Britons on the Exploits of King Thor, Arthur or Adam and his Knights in Establishing Civilization, Reforming Eden and Capturing the Holy Grail about 3380–3350 BC' (Waddell 1930). The capitals, and the swastika decorating the title page, say it all. *The British Edda* has not been very influential, though respectful reviews can be found on white-supremacist websites, and the poet Hugh MacDiarmid was briefly interested in it (O'Donoghue 2009: 20).

Supposed Germanic or Nordic paganism based – more or less – on the Poetic Edda has also taken its place alongside (or superseding) other non- or anti-Christian cultural manifestos – for example, the late twentieth-century family of musical genres based on heavy metal: Black Metal, Pagan Metal, Viking Metal, and even National Socialist Metal. Their debt to the Poetic Edda is evident in their lyrics, titles (the Swedish Viking Metal band Bathory recorded an album titled *Twilight of the Gods*, for instance), and the artwork of their record sleeves (Goodrick-Clarke 2002: 193–212). Nevertheless, this debt is less to the actual poetry of the Poetic Edda than to what has come to be understood as a pagan, Viking ethos. Very different is the much gentler work of Sequentia, whose reconstructions of medieval musical traditions include recordings of eddic poems set to music. The lyrics are actual eddic poems, in Icelandic, but the music is less authentic because though it is based on medieval musical systems, there is simply no surviving record of what kind of music might have accompanied eddic recitals, if indeed they were performed with music at all. So, at last we have original poetry in the European cultural domain (if not original music).

Performances by Viking Metal bands characteristically play up adult themes of horror, violence, and death, whilst at the same time names and lyrics reference the much less dark world of Tolkien's popular fiction. For instance, the founder of the Viking Metal band Burzum, the convicted murderer Varg Vikernes, explains on his website: 'as most Tolkien fans should know "burzum" is one of the words that are written in Black Speech on the One Ring of Sauron ... so all in all it was natural for me to use the name Burzum' (Angle 2010). A very popular contemporary American fantasy television series, *Game of Thrones*, based on the best-selling *A Song of Ice and Fire* by George R. R. Martin, also includes Old Norse material in its wildly eclectic medieval themes and settings (Larrington 2015b). *Game of Thrones* has been criticised for its graphic violence (especially sexual violence). Perhaps we may relate this – and the deliberate shock techniques of Viking Metal – to early responses to eddic poetry, provoked by the shock of the sublime and the thrill of heroic violence, evident not only in eighteenth-century literary texts, but also in the visual arts, such as the work of Henry Fuseli. It seems that eddic poetry has offered the possibility of both the cosiness of a mythology for children and far darker and more extreme re-workings. This process of re-working has tended to eclipse the original poetry, obviously and necessarily with regard to language, but often too in relation to poetic form, so that eddic substance has been more enduring and far more influential than eddic form. And eddic substance has always proved attractive to readers and authors, whether mythological or heroic (with its attendant sexual themes and violence). The appeal of an ancient literature (and eddic verse has often been supposed to be very much more ancient than contemporary scholars believe) has also proved important, and its evident links – whether actual or mystical – with English-speaking cultures (William Herbert was moved to note that Scandinavia was 'intimately allied to England in ancient blood and language'[12]) made it doubly fascinating, although its supposed 'Aryan' origin has attracted racists. It is perhaps not surprising, then, that eddic poetry has been so wide-rangingly, far-reachingly, and long-lastingly received.

Notes

1. See Kopár 2012 and Chapter 10 in this Handbook.
2. See *Skáldskaparmál*: 66, note to ll. 16–24.
3. For a full account of the early modern reception of Scandinavian literature in England, see Seaton 1935.
4. See also Faulkes 1977b.
5. See Starr and Hendrickson 1966: 29 for Gray's acknowledgement of his debt to Bartholin and Torfæus.
6. For a full account of Percy's translations, see Clunies Ross 1998b and 2001.
7. The first translation into English of *Sólarljóð* was by James Beresford, in 1805 (Clunies Ross 1998b: 183).

8. For an assessment of the influence of Old Norse myth on Auden's own work, see O'Donoghue 2010.
9. See, for instance, Anon. 1790.
10. See Carpenter and Tolkien 1981, Letter 229, dated 23 February 1961.
11. See also Larrington 2011a: 199–213.
12. See Herbert 1804, prefatory material.

Consolidated bibliography

Primary works

Arnamagnæan Commission (ed.) 1787. *Edda Sæmundar hinns Fróda*. Copenhagen: Sumptibus Legati Magnæani et Gyldendalii

Auden, W. H. and Taylor, Paul B. (trans.) 1969. *The Elder Edda: A Selection*. London: Faber and Faber

Auden, W. H. and Taylor, Paul B. (trans.) 1981. *Norse Poems*. London: Athlone Press

Bartholin, Thomas 1689. *Antiquitatum Danicarum de Causis Contemptae a Danis adhuc Gentilibus Mortis*. Copenhagen: Joh. Phil. Bockenhoffer

Benario, H. W. (ed. and trans.) 1999. *Tacitus, Germania/Germany*. Oxford: Oxford University Press

Beowulf = Fulk, Robert D. et al. (eds.) 2008. *Klaeber's Beowulf and the Fight at Finnsburh*. [4th revised edn of *Beowulf and the Fight at Finnsburh*, Fr. Klaeber (ed.)] Toronto, Buffalo, and London: Toronto University Press

Bjarni Einarsson (ed.) 2003. *Egils saga*. London: Viking Society for Northern Research

Bugge, Sophus (ed.) 1867. *Norrœn fornkvæði: Islandsk samling af folkelige oldtidsdigte om nordens guder og heroer, almindelig kaldet Sæmundar Edda hins fróða*. Christiania [Oslo]: Malling [repr. 1965. Oslo: Univesitetsforlaget]

Burgess, Melvin 1999. *Bloodtide*. London: Anderson
2005. *Bloodsong*. London: Anderson

Burrows, Hannah (ed.) forthcoming a. 'Verses of *Hervarar saga ok Heiðreks*', in *SkP* VIII
(ed.) forthcoming b. 'Verses of *Qrvar-Odds saga*', in *SkP* VIII

Carpenter, Humphrey and Tolkien, Christopher (eds.) 1981. *The Letters of J. R. R. Tolkien*. Boston: Houghton Mifflin

Chase, Martin (ed.) 2005. *Einarr Skúlason's Geisli: A Critical Edition*. Toronto: University of Toronto Press

Clunies Ross, Margaret (ed.) forthcoming a. 'Verses of *Friðþjófs saga*', in *SkP* VIII
(ed.) forthcoming b. 'Verses of *Gautreks saga*', in *SkP* VIII

Cottle, A. S. 1797. *Icelandic Poetry*. Bristol: N. Biggs

Damon, Cynthia (ed. and trans.) 2012. *Tacitus: Annals*. London: Penguin Classics

Dronke, Ursula (ed. and trans.) 1969. *The Poetic Edda. 1: Heroic Poems.* Oxford: Clarendon
(ed. and trans.) 1997. *The Poetic Edda. 2: Mythological Poems.* Oxford: Clarendon
(ed. and trans.) 2011. *The Poetic Edda. 3: Heroic Poems II.* Oxford: Oxford University Press
Egils saga = Sigurður Nordal (ed.) 1933. *Egils saga Skallagrímssonar.* Íslenzk fornrit 2. Reykjavík: Hið íslenzka fornritafélag
Einar Ólafur Sveinsson and Matthías Þorðarson (eds.) 1935. *Eyrbyggja saga.* Íslenzk fornrit 4. Reykjavík: Hið íslenzka fornritafélag
Eiríks saga rauða = Einar Ólafur Sveinsson and Matthias Þorðarson (eds.) 1935. *Eyrbyggja saga, Grænlendinga sögur.* Íslenzk fornrit 4. Reykjavík: Hið íslenzka fornritafélag
Faulkes, Anthony (ed.) 1977b. *Two Versions of the Snorra Edda from the 17th Century.* 2 vols. Reykjavík: Stofnun Árna Magnússonar
(trans.) 1995. *Snorri Sturluson, Edda.* London: Dent
Finnur Jónsson (ed.) 1888–1890. *Eddalieder: Altnordische Gedichte mythologischen und heroischen Inhalts.* 2 vols. Halle: Niemeyer
(ed.) 1905. *Eddukvæði.* Reykvavík: Sigurður Kristjánsson
(ed.) 1926. *Sæmundar-edda: Eddukvæði.* 2nd edn. Reykjavík: Sigurður Kristjánsson
(ed.) 1931. *Edda Snorra Sturlusonar.* Copenhagen: Gyldendalske boghandel
(ed.) 1932. *De gamle Eddadigte.* Copenhagen: Gad
FS = Guðni Jónsson (ed.) 1954. *Fornaldarsögur Norðurlanda.* 4 vols. Reykjavík: Íslendingasagnaútgáfan
FSN = Rafn, Carl Christian (ed.) 1829–30. *Fornaldarsögur Nordrlanda.* 3 vols. Copenhagen: Popp
Fulk, R. D. (ed.) 2012a. *Eiríksmál,* in *SkP* I, pp. 1003–15
(ed.) 2012b. *Hákonarmál,* in *SkP* I, pp. 174–96
(ed.) 2012c. *Haraldskvæði,* in *SkP* I, pp. 94–116
(ed.) forthcoming. *Darraðarljóð,* in *SkP* V
Garcia Marquez, Gabriel (trans. Gregory Rambassa) 1972. *A Very Old Man with Enormous Wings.* Available at: www.ndsu.edu/pubweb/~cinichol/Creative Writing/323/MarquezManwithWings.htm [last accessed 19 February 2016]
Gering, Hugo and Sijmons, Barend (eds.) 1927–31. *Kommentar zu den Liedern der Edda.* 2 vols. Halle: Waisenhaus
Germania = Warmington, E. H. (ed.) and Hutton, M. (transl.) 1970. *Tacitus. Agricola, Germania, Dialogus.* Loeb Classical Library 35. 2nd edn. London/Cambridge, MA: Heinemann/Harvard University Press
Gesta Danorum = Friis-Jensen, Karsten (ed.) and Fisher, Peter (trans.) 2015. *Saxo Grammaticus. Gesta Danorum. The History of the Danes.* 2 vols. Oxford: Oxford University Press
Gísli Sigurðsson (ed.) 1998. *Eddukvæði.* Reykjavík: Mál og menning
Guðni Jónsson (ed.) 1954. *Eddukvæði (Sæmundar-edda).* Reykjavík: Íslendingasagnaútgáfan
Gylfaginning = Faulkes, Anthony (ed.) 2005. *Snorri Sturluson Edda. Prologue and Gylfaginning.* 2nd edn. London: Viking Society for Northern Research

Háttatal = Faulkes, Anthony (ed.) 2007. *Snorri Sturluson Edda. Háttatal.* 2nd edn. London: Viking Society for Northern Research

Heimskringla = Bjarni Aðalbjarnarson (ed.) 1941–5. Snorri Sturluson, *Heimskringla.* 3 vols. Íslenzk fornrit 26–8. Reykjavík: Hið íslenzka fornritafélag

Henderson, Ebenezer 1819. *Iceland.* 2nd edn. 2 vols. Edinburgh: Waugh and Innes

Herbert, William 1804. *Select Icelandic Poetry.* London: T. Reynolds

1806. *Select Icelandic Poetry,* in (his) *Miscellaneous Poetry.* 4 vols. London: Longman, Hurt, Rees, and Orme

1842. *Works.* 3 vols. London: H. G. Bohn

Hickes, George 1705. *Linguarum Vett. Septentrionalium Thesaurus Grammatico-Criticus et Archæologicus.* 2 vols. London: E Theatro Sheldoniano

Hildebrand, Karl, Gering, Hugo, and Möbius, Theodor (eds.) 1922. *Die Lieder der Älteren Edda.* 4th edn. Paderborn: Schöningh

Hildebrandslied = Broszinski, Hartmut (ed.) 1985. *Das Hildebrandslied: Faksimile der Kasseler Handschrift mit einer Einführung.* Kassel: Johannes Stauda Verlag

Jón Helgason (ed.) 1964. *Eddadigte.* I: *Vǫluspá – Hávamál.* 2nd edn. Copenhagen: Munksgaard

Jónas Kristjánsson and Vésteinn Ólason (eds.) 2014, *Eddukvæði.* 2 vols. Reykjavík: Hið íslenzk fornrítafélag

Jones, David 1937 [repr. 2010]. *In Parenthesis.* London: Faber and Faber

1952 [repr. 2010]. *The Anathemata.* London: Faber and Faber

Klinck, Anne L. 1992. *The Old English Elegies: A Critical Edition and Genre Study.* Montreal and London: McGill-Queen's University Press

Konráð Gíslason and Eiríkur Jónsson (eds.) 1875–89. *Njála, udgivet efter gamle håndskrifter.* 2 vols. Copenhagen: Thiele

La Farge, Beatrice (ed.) forthcoming a. 'The Verses of *Gríms saga loðinkinna*', in *SkP* VIII

(ed.) forthcoming b. 'The Verses of *Ketils saga hœngs*', in *SkP* VIII

Landnámabók = Jakob Benediktsson (ed.) 1968. *Íslendingabók. Landnámabók.* Íslenzk fornrit 1. Reykjavík: Hið íslenzka fornritafélag

Larrington, Carolyne (trans.) 2014. *The Poetic Edda.* 2nd revised edn. Oxford: World's Classics. [First edn. 1996]

Larrington, Carolyne and Robinson, Peter (eds.) 2007. *Sólarljóð,* in *SkP* VII, pp. 287–357

Lassen, Annette (ed.) 2011. *Hrafnagaldur Óðins (Forspjallsljóð).* Viking Society for Northern Research, Text Series 20. London: Viking Society for Northern Research

Lüning, Hermann (ed.) 1859. *Die Edda: Eine sammlung altnordischer götter- und heldenlieder.* Zurich: Meyer & Zeller

Mathias, Thomas 1781. *Runic Odes.* London: T. Payne, T. Becket, J. Sewell, and T. and J. Merrill

McTurk, Rory (ed.) forthcoming a. *Krákumál,* in *SkP* VIII

(ed.) forthcoming b. 'The Verses of *Ragnars saga*', in *SkP* VIII

Meli, Marcello (ed. and trans.) 2008. *Vǫluspá: Un'apocalisse norrena.* Biblioteca medievale 117. Roma: Carocci

Morris, William 1887. *The Story of Sigurd the Volsung and the Fall of the Niblungs.* London: Reeves and Turner

Morris, William and Eiríkur Magnússon (trans.) 1870. *Völsunga saga.* London: F. E. Ellis

Neckel, Gustav (ed.) 1914. *Edda. Die Lieder des Codex Regius nebst verwandten Denkmälern.* I: *Text.* (Heidelberg: Winter) [2nd edn 1927; 3rd edn 1936; 4th edn (rev. Hans Kuhn) 1962; 5th edn (rev. Hans Kuhn) 1983]

Neckel and Kuhn = Neckel, Gustav (ed.) and Kuhn, Hans (rev. ed.) 1962. *Edda. Die Lieder des Codex Regius nebst verwandten Denkmälern. I. Text.* 4th edn. Heidelberg: Winter

Percy, Thomas 1763. *Five Pieces of Runic Poetry Translated from the Islandic Language.* London: R. and J. Dodsley

1770. *Northern Antiquities.* London: T. Carnan

Perkins, Richard (ed.) forthcoming. 'Verses from *Þorsteins þáttr tjaldstœðings*', in *SkP* IV

Prowett, James (trans.) 1816. *The Voluspa.* London: Payne and Foss

Ranisch, Wilhelm and Heusler, Andreas (eds.) 1903. *Eddica minora: Dichtungen eddischer Art aus den Fornaldarsögur und anderen Prosawerken.* Dortmund: Ruhfus

Resen, Peter Hansen (ed.) 1665. *Edda Islandorum.* Copenhagen: Henricus Gödianus

Sammes, Aylett 1676. *Britannia Antiqua Illustrata.* London: Tho. Roycroft

Seelow, Hubert (ed.) forthcoming. 'Verses from *Hálfs saga ok Hálfsrekka*', in *SkP* VIII

Seward, Anna 1796. *Llangollen Vale.* London: G. Sael

Sheringham, Robert 1670. *De Anglorum Gentis Origine Disceptatio.* Cambridge: Joann. Hayes

Sigurbjörn Einarsson, Guðrún Kvaran, and Gunnlaugur Ingólfsson (eds.) 1993. *Íslensk hómilíubók. Fornarstólræður.* Reykjavík: Hið íslenzka bókmenntafélag

Sigurður Nordal (ed.) [1923] 1978. *Vǫluspá* (trans. B. S. Benedikz and John McKinnell). Durham: Durham and St Andrews Medieval Texts [originally published 1923. Reykjavík: Gutenberg]

Sijmons, Barend and Gering, Hugo (eds.) 1906. *Die Lieder der Edda.* Germanistische Handbibliothek 7. Halle: Waisenhaus

Skáldskaparmál = Faulkes, Anthony (ed.) 1998. *Snorri Sturluson Edda. Skáldskaparmál.* I: *Introduction, Text and Notes.* London: Viking Society for Northern Research

Skjald = Finnur Jónsson (ed.) 1912–15. *Den norsk-islandske skjaldedigtning.* A: *Tekst efter håndskrifterne* I-II, B: *Rettettekst* I-II. Copenhagen: Gyldendal

SkP = Clunies Ross, Margaret et al. (eds.) 2007–. *Skaldic Poetry of the Scandinavian Middle Ages.* 9 vols [3 to date]. Turnhout: Brepols [cited by vol. number and page numbers or by poet, poem and superscript volume number (for poetic text)]

Vol. 1: Whaley, Diana (ed.) 2012. *Poetry from the Kings' Sagas.* 1: *From Mythical Times to c. 1035.* 2 vols.

Vol. 2: Gade, Kari Ellen (ed.) 2009. *Poetry from the Kings' Sagas.* 2: *From c. 1035 to c. 1300.* 2 vols.

Vol. 7: Clunies Ross (ed.) 2007. *Poetry on Christian Subjects.* 2 vols.

Starr, H. W. and Hendrickson, J. R. (eds.) 1966. *The Complete Poems of Thomas Gray.* Oxford: Clarendon Press

Tegnér, Esaias 1825. *Frithiofs saga.* Stockholm: Nordström

Thorpe, Benjamin (trans.) 1866. *Edda Sæmundar hinns Fróða.* London: Trübner

Tolkien, Christopher (ed.) 1960. *The Saga of King Heiðrek the Wise.* London: Nelson

Tolkien, J. R. R. and Tolkien, Christopher (ed.) 2009. *The Legend of Sigurd and Gudrún.* London: Harper Collins

Tolley, Clive (ed. and trans.) 2008. *Grottasǫngr.* London: Viking Society for Northern Research

Toynbee, Paget Jackson and Whibley, Leonard (eds.) 1935. *Correspondence of Thomas Gray.* 3 vols. Oxford: Clarendon Press

Turville-Petre, Gabriel (ed.) 1956. *Hervarar saga ok Heiðreks.* London: Viking Society for Northern Research

Uppsala Edda = Heimir Pálsson (ed.) and Faulkes, Anthony (trans.) 2012. *Snorri Sturluson: The Uppsala Edda: DG 11 4to.* London: Viking Society for Northern Research

Verelius, Olaus (ed.) 1672. *Hervarar saga.* Uppsala: Henricus Curio

Vigfusson, Gudbrandr and Powell, Frederick York (eds. and trans.) 1883. *Corpus Poeticum Boreale.* Oxford: Clarendon Press

Vǫlsunga saga = Finch, R. G. (ed. and trans.) 1965. *Vǫlsunga saga. The Saga of the Volsungs.* London: Nelson

Waddell, L. A. 1930. *The British Edda.* London: Chapman and Hall

Þiðreks saga = Guðni Jónsson (ed.) 1954. *Þiðreks saga af Bern.* 2 vols. Reykjavík: Íslendingasagnaútgáfan

Þormóður Torfason (Torfæus) 1697. *Orcades.* Copenhagen: Literis Justini Hög

Secondary works

Abram, Christopher 2011. *Myths of the Pagan North: The Gods of the Norsemen.* London and New York: Continuum

Acker, Paul 1998. *Revising Oral Theory: Formulaic Composition in Old English and Old Icelandic Verse.* New York and London: Garland

Acker, Paul and Larrington, Carolyne (eds.) 2002. *The Poetic Edda: Essays on Old Norse Mythology.* New York: Routledge

(eds.) 2013. *Revisiting the Poetic Edda: Essays on Old Norse Heroic Legend.* New York: Routledge

Adolf Friðriksson and Orri Vésteinsson 1997. 'Hofstaðir revisited', *Norwegian Archaeological Review* 30: 103–112

Alsop, Rachel, Fitzsimmons, Annette, and Lennon, Kathleen 2002. *Theorizing Gender.* Oxford: Polity

Amory, Frederic 1988. 'Kennings, referentiality and metaphors', *Arkiv för nordisk filologi* 103: 87–101

Anderson, Carolyn 2002. 'No fixed point: gender and blood feuds in *Njal's Saga*', *Philological Quarterly* 81: 421–40

Anderson, Phillip N. 1981. 'Form and content in *Lokasenna*: a re-evaluation', *Edda*: 215–25 [repr. 2002. Acker and Larrington (eds.), pp. 139–57]

Anderson, Sarah M. and Swenson, Karen (eds.) 2002. *Cold Counsel: Women in Old Norse Literature and Mythology*. New York: Routledge

Andersson, Theodore M. 1964. *The Problem of Icelandic Saga Origins: A Historical Survey*. Yale Germanic Studies 1. New Haven: Yale University Press

1983. 'Did the poet of *Atlamál* know *Atlaqviða?*', in Glendinning and Haraldur Bessason (eds.), pp. 243–57

2003. 'Is there a history of emotions in eddic heroic poetry? Daniel Sävborg's critique of eddic chronology', in C. Stephen Jaeger and Ingrid Kasten (eds.), *Codierungen von Emotionen im Mittelalter/ Emotions and Sensibilities in the the Middle Ages*. Trends in Medieval Philology 1. Berlin and New York: de Gruyter, pp. 193–202

Andersson, Theodore M. and Gade, Kari Ellen 1991. 'Recent Old Norse-Icelandic studies in the German-speaking countries', *Scandinavian Studies* 63: 66–102

Andrén, Anders 1989. 'Dörrar till förgångna myter – en tolkning av de gotländska bildstenar', in Anders Andrén (ed.), *Metaltidens födelse*. Nyhamnsläge: Gyllenstiernska Krapperupsstiftelsen, pp. 287–319

1991. 'Guld och makt: en tolkning av de skandinaviska gullbrakteaternas funktion', in C. Fabech and J. Ringtved (eds.), *Samfundsorganisation og Regional Variation: Norden i Romersk Jernalder og Folkevandringstid*. Aarhus: Aarhus Universitetsforlag, pp. 245–56

1998. *Between Artifacts and Texts: Historical Archaeology in Global Perspective*. New York: Plenum

2014. *Tracing Old Norse Cosmology: The World Tree, Middle Earth, and the Sun in Archaeological Perspectives*. Vägar till Midgård 16. Lund: Nordic Academic Press

Andrén, Anders, Jennbert, Kristina, and Raudvere, Catharina (eds.) 2004. *Ordning mot Kaos: Studier av nordisk förkristen kosmologi*. Vägar till Midgård 4. Lund: Nordic Academic Press

2006. *Old Norse Religion in Long-term Perspectives: Origins, Changes and Interactions*. Vägar till Midgård 8. Lund: Nordic Academic Press

Angle, Brad 2010. 'Burzum: heart of darkness', *Guitar World Magazine* [www .burzum.org/eng/library/2010_interview_guitar_world.shtml]

Anon. 1790. 'Review of Sterling, *Poems*', *The English Review* 15: 229

Ármann Jakobsson 2007. 'Masculinity and politics in *Njáls saga*', *Viator* 38: 191–215

2008. 'The trollish acts of Þorgrímr the Witch: the meaning of *troll* and *ergi* in medieval Iceland', *Saga-Book of the Viking Society* 32: 39–68

2014. *A Sense of Belonging: Morkinskinna and Icelandic Identity, c. 1220* (trans. Fredrik Heinemann). The Viking Collection 22. Odense: University Press of Southern Denmark

Árni Björnsson 2003. *Wagner and the Volsungs*. London: Viking Society for Northern Research

Ásdís Egilsdóttir 2006. 'From orality to literacy: remembering the past and the present in *Jóns saga helga*', in Else Mundal (ed.), *Reykholt som makt- og lærdomssenter i den islandske og nordiske kontekst*. Snorrastofa rit 3. Reykholt: Snorrastofa, menningar- og miðaldasetur, pp. 215–228

Ásgeir Blöndal Magnússon 1995. *Íslensk orðsifjabók*. Reykjavík: Orðabók Háskólans

Auerbach, Loren 1998. 'Female experience and authorial intention in *Laxdœla saga*', *Saga-Book of the Viking Society* 25: 30–52

Austin, David 1991. 'The proper study of medieval archaeology', in D. Austin and L. Alcock (eds.), *From the Baltic to the Black Sea: Studies in Medieval Archaeology*. London: Unwin Hyman, pp. 9–42

Austin, J. L. 1962. *How to do Things with Words*. Oxford: Clarendon Press

Bagby, Benjamin 1999. 'The reconstruction of eddic performance' [in the booklet accompanying Sequentia 1999: *Edda*, 11–14. Deutsche Harmonia Mundi: 05472 77381 2]

2006. *Beowulf* [DVD recording of an oral performance by Benjamin Bagby with an Anglo-Saxon harp, and including a discussion of medieval oral performance by Bagby with John Miles Foley, Thomas Cable, and Mark Amodio. Loch/Charles Morrow Productions LLC and Jon Aaron]

Bagge, Sverre 2000. 'From *Rígsþula* to *Konungs skuggsjá*', in Jens Eike Schnall and Rudolf Simek (eds.), *Speculum regale. Der altnorwegische Königsspiegel (Konungs skuggsjá) in der europäischen Tradition*. Vienna: Fassbaender, pp. 7–45

Bailey, Richard N. 1980. *Viking Age Stone Sculpture in Northern England*. Collins Archaeology 1. London: Collins

1981. 'The hammer and the cross,' in Else Roesdahl et al. (eds), *The Vikings in England and in their Danish Homeland*. London: Anglo-Danish Viking Project, pp. 83–94

Bailey, Richard N. and Cramp, Rosemary J. 1988. *Corpus of Anglo-Saxon Stone Sculpture. II: Cumberland, Westmorland and Lancashire North-of-the-Sands*. Oxford: Oxford University Press

Bailey, Richard N. and Lang, James 1975. 'The date of the Gosforth sculptures', *Antiquity* 49: 290–3

Bandle, Oskar et al. 2002. *The Nordic Languages: An International Handbook of the History of the North Germanic Languages*. Handbücher zur Sprach- und Kommunikationswissenschaft 22.1, Berlin: de Gruyter

Bang, A. Chr. 1879/1880. *Vøluspaa og de Sibyllinske Orakler*. Christiania Videnskabsselskabs Forhandlinger 1879, 9. Christiania [Oslo]: Videnskabs-selskabet/Dybwad [*Vǫluspá und die Sibyllinischen Orakel*, translated and expanded, Jos. Cal. Poestion. Vienna: Carl Gerold's Sohn]

1882. *Bidrag til de Sibyllinske Oraklers og den Sibyllinske Orakeldigtnings Historie i Middelalderen*. Vol. 1. Videnskabs-selskabet Forhandlinger VIII. Christiania [Oslo]: Videnskabs-selskabet/Dybwad

Bauman, Richard 1977. *Verbal Art as Performance*. Prospect Heights, NY: Waveland

1986. 'Performance and honor in 13th-century Iceland', *Journal of American Folklore* 99: 131–50

Bax, Marcel, and Padmos, Tineke 1983. 'Two types of verbal dueling in Old Icelandic: the interactional structure of the *senna* and the *mannjafnaðr* in *Hárbarðzljóð*', *Scandinavian Studies* 55: 149–74

1993. 'Senna – Mannjafnaðr', in Pulsiano (ed.), pp. 571–3

Beaty, John Owen 1934. 'The echo-word in *Beowulf* with a note on the *Finnsburg Fragment*', *Publications of the Modern Language Association of America* 49/2: 365–73

Beck, Heinrich 1990. 'Eddaliedforschung heute: Bemerkungen zur Heldenlied-Diskussion', in Hermann Reichert and Günter Zimmermann (eds.), *Helden und Heldensage. Otto Gschwantler zum 60. Geburtstag*. Vienna: Fassbaender, pp. 1–23

Beck, Heinrich, et al. (eds.) 1968–2008. *Reallexikon der Germanischen Altertumskunde*. 2nd edn. 35 vols. Berlin: de Gruyter

Ben-Amos, Dan 1976. 'Analytic categories and ethnic genres', in his (ed.) *Folklore Genres*. Austin: University of Texas Press, pp. 213–242

Bergsveinn Birgisson 2008. 'What have we lost by writing? Cognitive archaisms in skaldic poetry', in Else Mundal and Jonas Wellendorf (eds.), *Oral Art Forms and their Passage into Writing*. Copenhagen: Museum Tusculanum, pp. 163–84

Bjorvand, Harald and Lindeman, Fredrik Otto 2007. *Våre arveord: Etymologisk ordbok*. 2nd edn. Oslo: Novus

Björn Jónsson 1989. *Stjarnvísi í Eddum*. Reykjavík: Bókaútgáfan Skjaldborg

Björn Magnússon Ólsen 1894. 'Hvar eru Eddukvæðin til orðin?', *Tímarit hins íslenzka bókmenntafélags* 15: 1–133

Blindheim, Martin 1973. 'Fra hedensk sagnfigur til kristent forbillede: Sigurdsdiktingen i middelalderens billedkunst', *Den iconographiske Post* 3: 2–28

Boal, Augusto 2002. *Games for Actors and Non-Actors*. 2nd edn. London and New York: Routledge

Böldl, Klaus 2000. *Der Mythos der Edda: Nordische Mythologie zwischen europäischer Aufklärung und nationaler Romantik*. Tübingen: Francke

Borovsky, Zoe 1999. 'Never in public: women and performance in Old Norse literature', *Journal of American Folklore* 112: 6–39

2002. '"En hon er blandin mjök": women and insults in Old Norse literature', in Anderson and Swenson (eds.), pp. 1–14

Bowra, Maurice 1952. *Heroic Poetry*. London: Macmillan

Boyer, Régis 1990. *La poésie scaldique*. Paris: Editions du Porte-Glaive

Brecht, Bertolt 1964. 'The street scene', in John Willett (ed. and trans.), *Brecht on Theatre*. London: Eyre Methuen, pp. 121–9

Brink, Stefan 1990. *Sockenbildning och sockennamn. Studier i äldre territoriell indelning*. Acta Academiae Regiae Gustavi Adolphi 57. Stockholm: Almqvist and Wiksell International

1991. 'Iakttagelser rörande namnen på -hem i Sverige', in Gulbrand Alhaug et al. (eds.), *Heidersskrift til Nils Hallan på 65-årsdagen den 13. desember 1991*. Oslo: Novus, pp. 66–80

1996. 'Political and social structures in early Scandinavia: A settlement-historical pre-study of the Central Place', *Tor. Journal of Archaeology* 28: 235–81

2004a. 'Mytologiska rum och eskatologiska föreställningar i det vikingatida Norden', in Andrén, Jennbert, and Raudvere (eds.), pp. 219–52

2004b. 'Rekonstruerade ånamn', in Stefan Brink et al. (eds.), *Namenwelten. Orts- und Personennamen in historischer Sicht*. Ergänzungsbände zum Reallexikon der Germanischen Alterturmskunde 44. Berlin and New York: De Gruyter, pp. 15–21

2005. 'Verba volant, scripta manent? Aspects of early Scandinavian oral society', in Pernille Hermann (ed.), pp. 77–135

2007a. 'Skiringssal, Kaupang, Tjølling – the toponymic evidence', in Dagfinn Skre (ed.), *Kaupang in Skiringssal*. Norske Oldfunn 22. Aarhus: Aarhus University Press, pp. 53–64

2007b. 'How uniform was the Old Norse religion?', in Quinn, Heslop, and Wills (eds.), pp. 105–35

Bruce-Mitford, Rupert L. S. 1978. *The Sutton Ship-Burial*. Vol. 2: *Arms, Armour and Regalia*. London: British Museum Press

Bruun, Daníel and Finnur Jónsson 1911. 'Finds and excavations of heathen temples in Iceland', *Saga-Book of the Viking Society* 7: 25–37

Brøndsted, Johannes 1955. 'Thors fiskeri', *Nationalmuseets arbejdsmark* [n.n]: 92–104

Bugge, Sophus 1879. 'Nogle bidrag til det norröne sprogs og den norröne digtnings historie, hented fra verslæren', in Ludv. F. A. Wimmer (ed.), *Beretning om forhandlingerne på de første nordiske filologmøde i København den 18.–21. juli 1879*. Copenhagen: Gyldendal, pp. 140–46

1881. 'Nogle bemærkninger om Sibyllinerne og Völuspá', *Nordisk tidskrift för vetenskap, konst och industry* 4: 163–72

1881–89 [1889]. *Studier over de nordiske Gude- og Heltesagns Oprindelse*. First Series. Christiania [Oslo]: Cammermeyer. [1889. *Studien über die Entstehung der nordischen Götter- und Heldensage* (trans. Oscar Brenner). Munich: Christian Kaiser]

1896/1899. *Helge-digtene i den Ældre Edda, deres hjem og forbindelser*. Copenhagen: Gad [1899 (revised edn. and trans. William Henry Schofield) *The Home of the Eddic Poems with especial Reference to the Helgi-Lays*. London: Nutt]

1901/1992. 'The Norse lay of Wayland ("Vǫlundarkviða"), and its relation to English tradition' (trans. E. Warburg), *Saga-Book of the Viking Society* 2/3: 271–312 [repr. 1992. *Saga-Book* 23/4: 275–316 along with 'Proceedings', 363–73]

Buisson, Ludwig 1976. *Der Bildstein Ardre VIII auf Gotland: Göttermythen, Heldensagen und Jenseitsglaube der Germanen im 8. Jahrhundert n. Chr.* Abhandlungen der Akademie der Wissenschaften in Göttingen, 3rd ser. 102. Göttingen: Vandenhoeck & Ruprecht

Butler, Judith 1990. *Gender Trouble: Feminism and the Subversion of Identity*. New York: Routledge

2004. *Undoing Gender*. London: Routledge

Butt, Wolfgang 1969. 'Zur Herkunft der Vǫluspá', *Beiträge zur Geschichte der deutschen Sprache und Literatur* 91: 83–103

Bynum, Carolyn Walker 1992. *Fragmentation and Redemption: Essays on Gender and the Human Body in Medieval Religion.* New York: Zone Books

Byock, Jesse L. 1990. 'Sigurðr Fáfnisbani: An eddic hero carved on Norwegian stave churches', in Pàroli (ed.), pp. 619–28

2001. *Viking Age Iceland.* Harmondsworth: Penguin.

Bäckvall, Maja 2013. *Skriva fel och läsa rätt? Eddiska dikter i Uppsalaeddan ur et avsändar- och mottagarperspektiv.* Uppsala Universitet: Institutionen för nordisk språk

Cerquiglini, Bernard 1989. *Éloge de la variante: Histoire critique de la philologie.* Paris: Éditions du seuil. [1999. *In Praise of the Variant: A Critical History of Philology* (trans. Betsy Wing). Baltimore: Johns Hopkins University Press]

Chadwick, H. M. and Chadwick, Nora Kershaw 1932–40. *The Growth of Literature.* 3 vols. Cambridge: Cambridge University Press

Chase, Martin (ed.) 2014. *Eddic, Skaldic and Beyond: Poetic Variety in Medieval Iceland and Norway.* New York: Fordham University Press

Christensen, Arne Emil 1992. 'Kongsgårdens håndverkere', in A. E. Christensen, A. S. Ingstad, and B. Myhre (eds.), *Oseberg-dronningens Grav.* Oslo: Schibsted, pp. 85–137

Ciklamini, Marlene 1966. 'The combat between two half-brothers: a literary study of the motif in *Ásmundar saga kappabana* and Saxonis *Gesta Danorum*', *Neophilologus* 50: 269–79, 370–9

1971. 'The problem of Starkaðr', *Scandinavian Studies* 43: 169–88

Clanchy, M. T. 1979. *From Memory to Written Record: England 1066–1307.* [2nd edn. 1993] Oxford: Blackwell

Clark, David 2005. 'Undermining and en-gendering vengeance: distancing and anti-feminism in the *Poetic Edda*', *Scandinavian Studies* 77: 173–200

2012. *Gender, Violence and the Past in Edda and Saga.* Oxford: Oxford University Press

2013. 'Heroic homosociality and homophobia in the Helgi poems', in Acker and Larrington (eds.), pp. 11–27

Clark, David and Phelpstead, Carl (eds.) 2007. *Old Norse Made New.* London: Viking Society for Northern Research

Clarke, Helen and Ambrosiani, Björn 1995. *Towns in the Viking Age.* London: Leicester University Press

Clover, Carol J. 1979. '*Hárbarðsljóð* as generic farce', *Scandinavian Studies* 51: 124–45 [repr. 2002. Acker and Larrington (eds.), pp. 95–118]

1980. 'The Germanic context of the Unferþ episode', *Speculum* 55: 444–68

1986a. 'Hildigunnr's lament', in Lindow, Lönnroth, and Weber (eds.), pp. 141–83

1986b. 'Maiden warriors and other sons', *Journal of English and Germanic Philology* 85: 35–49

1993. 'Regardless of sex: men, women, and power in early northern Europe', *Speculum* 68: 363–87

Clover, Carol J. and Lindow, John (eds.) 1985. *Old Norse-Icelandic Literature: A Critical Guide*. Islandica 45. Ithaca: Cornell University Press [repr. 2005. Toronto: University of Toronto Press]

Clunies Ross, Margaret 1989. 'Two of Þórr's great fights according to *Hymiskviða*', *Leeds Studies in English*, n.s. 20: 7–27

1994. *Prolonged Echoes: Old Norse Myths in Medieval Northern Society.* 1: *The Myths.* The Viking Collection 7. Odense: Odense University Press

1998a. *Prolonged Echoes: Old Norse Myths in Northern Society.* 2: *The Reception of Old Norse Myths in Medieval Society.* The Viking Collection 10. Odense: Odense University Press

1998b. *The Norse Muse in Britain 1750–1820*. Trieste: Edizione Parnaso

2001. *The Old Norse Translations of Thomas Percy*. Turnhout: Brepols

2005. *A History of Old Norse Poetry and Poetics*. Cambridge: D. S. Brewer

2013. 'The Eddica Minora: a lesser Poetic Edda?', in Acker and Larrington (eds.), pp. 183–201

Clunies Ross, Margaret and Lönnroth, Lars 1999. 'The Norse muse: Report from an International Research Project', *alvíssmál* 9: 3–28

Clunies Ross, Margaret et al. 2007. 'Approaches to skaldic ekphrasis: Round-table discussion', *Viking and Medieval Scandinavia* 3: 159–264

Clunies Ross, Margaret, Gade, Kari Ellen, Guðrún Nordal, Marold, Edith, Whaley, Diana, and Wills, Tarrin 2012. 'General Introduction', in *SkP* I, pp. i–xciii

Cohen, Jeffrey Jerome 1996. 'Monster culture (seven theses),' in Jeffrey Jerome Cohen (ed.), *Monster Theory: Reading Culture*. Minneapolis: University of Minnesota Press, pp. 3–25

Cox, R. S. 1972. 'The Old English Dicts of Cato', *Anglia* 90: 1–42

Dal, Ingerid 1930. *Ursprung und Verwendung der altnordischen 'Expletivpartikel' of, um*. Avhandlinger utgitt av Det Norske Videnskaps-Akademi i Oslo, II. Historisk-filosofisk klasse, 1929, No. 5. Oslo: Jacob Dybwad

Damrosch, David 2003. *What is World Literature?* Princeton: Princeton University Press

Deavin, Mark-Kevin 2012. 'Bifrǫst Re-interpreted', in A. M. V. Nordvig and L. H. Torfing (eds.), The 15th *International Saga Conference: Sagas and the Use of the Past, Preprint of Abstracts*. Aarhus: Department of Aesthetics and Communication, Aarhus University, pp. 108–9

2014. 'The swirling sea? A new perspective on *Iðavǫllr* in Norse myth', in *2nd International St Magnus Conference 9th–12th April 2014, Abstracts*. Lerwick: [no publisher], p. 9

2015. 'The swirling sea as sacred space? A new perspective on *Iðavǫllr* in Norse myth', in Jürg Glauser et al. (eds.), *The Sixteenth International Saga Conference: Sagas and Space, Preprints of Abstracts*. Zurich: Deutsches Seminar, Universität Zürich, p. 86

Deskis, Susan E. and Hill, Thomas D. (eds.) 2008. *'Speak useful words or say nothing': Old Norse Studies by Joseph Harris*. Islandica 53. Ithaca, New York: Cornell University Library

D'haen, Theo 2012. *The Routledge Concise History of World Literature*. London: Routledge

Doty, William G. 1986. *Mythography: The Study of Myth and Rituals*. Tuscaloosa: University of Alabama Press

Driscoll, M. J. 2010. 'The words on the page: Thoughts on philology old and new', in Quinn and Lethbridge (eds.), pp. 87–104

Drobin, Ulf 1991. 'Mjödet och offersymboliken i fornnordisk religion', in Louise Bäckman et al. (eds.), *Studier i religionshistoria tillägnade Åke Hultkrantz*. Löberöd: Plus Ultra, pp. 97–141

Dronke, Ursula 1992a. 'Eddic poetry as a source for the history of Germanic religion', in Heinrich Beck, Detlev Ellmers, and Kurt Schier (eds.), *Germanische Religionsgeschichte: Quellen und Quellenprobleme*. Berlin, New York: Walter de Gruyter, pp. 656–84

1992b. '*Vǫluspá* and Sibylline traditions', in Richard North and Tette Hofstra (eds.), *Latin Culture and Medieval Germanic Europe: Proceedings of the First Germania Latina Conference held at the University of Groningen, 26 May 1989*. Germania Latina I. Groningen: Forsten. 3–23 [repr. 1996 in her *Myth and Fiction in Early Norse Lands*. Aldershot: Variorum]

Dubois, Thomas 2012. 'Diet and deities: Contrastive livelihoods and animal symbolism in Nordic pre-Christian religions', in Raudvere and Schjødt (eds.) pp. 65–96

Düwel, Klaus 1986. 'Zur Ikonographie und Ikonologie der Sigurddarstellungen', in Helmuth Roth (ed.), *Zum Problem der Deutung frühmittelalterlicher Bildinhalte*. Sigmaringen: Thorbeck, pp. 221–71

Edda Kommentar = von See, Klaus, et al. (eds.) 1997-. *Kommentar zu den Liedern der Edda*. 6 vols to date. Heidelberg: Winter

Vol. II: von See, Klaus, La Farge, Beatrice, Picard, Eve, Priebe, Ilona, and Schulz, Katja (eds.) 1997. *Götterlieder (Skírnismál, Hárbarðslióð, Hymiskviða, Lokasenna, Þrymskviða)*

Vol. III: von See, Klaus, La Farge, Beatrice, Picard, Eve, and Schulz, Katja with Dusse, Debora, Priebe, Ilona, and Walh, Betty (eds.) 2000. *Götterlieder (Vǫlundarkviða, Alvíssmál, Baldrs draumar, Rígspula, Hyndlulióð, Grottasǫngr)*

Vol. IV: von See, Klaus, La Farge, Beatrice, Gerhold, Wolfgang, Dusse, Debora, Picard, Eve, and Schulz, Katja (eds.) 2004. *Heldenlieder (Helgakviða Hundingsbana I, Helgakviða Hiǫrvarðssonar, Helgakviða Hundingsbana II)*

Vol. V: von See, Klaus, La Farge, Beatrice, Gerhold, Wolfgang, Picard, Eve, and Schulz, Katja (eds.) 2006. *Heldenlieder (Frá dauða Sinfiǫtla, Grípisspá, Reginsmál, Fáfnismál, Sigrdrífumál)*

Vol. VI: von See, Klaus, La Farge, Beatrice, Picard, Eve, Schulz, Katja, and Teichert, Matthias (eds.) 2009. *Heldenlieder (Brot af Sigurðarkviðo, Guðrúnarkviða, Sigurðarkviða in skamma, Helreið Brynhildar, Dráp Niflunga, Guðrúnarkviða II, Guðrúnarkviða III, Oddrúnargrátr, Strophenbruchstücke aus der Vǫlsunga saga)*

Vol. VII: von See, Klaus, La Farge, Beatrice, Horst, Simone, and Schulz, Katja (eds.) 2012. *Heldenlieder (Atklakviða, Atlamál, Gudrúnarhvöt, Hamðismál)*

Einar Ólafur Sveinsson 1962. *Íslenzkar bókmenntir í fornöld*. Reykjavík: Almenna bókafélagið

Elgqvist, Eric 1944. *Skälv och skilfingar, vad nordiska ortnamn vittna om svenska expansionssträvanden omkring mitten av första årtusendet e. kr.* Lund: Olins antikvariat

Eliade, Mircea 1958. *Patterns in Comparative Religion* (trans. Rosemary Sheed). London: Sheed and Ward

Elmevik, Lennart 2007. 'Yggdrasill. En etymologisk studie', *Scripta Islandica* 58: 75–83

Evans, D. A. H. 1986. 'Introduction', in D. A. H. Evans (ed.), *Hávamál*. London: Viking Society for Northern Research, pp. 1–38

Fabech, Charlotte and Näsman, Ulf 2013. 'Ritual landscapes and sacral places in the first millennium AD in south Scandinavia', in Sæbjørg Walaker Nordeide and Stefan Brink (eds.), *Sacred Sites and Holy Places: Exploring the Sacralization of Landscape through Time and Space*. Turnhout: Brepols, pp. 53–109

Farley, Frank 1903. *Scandinavian Influences in the English Romantic Movement*. Studies and Notes in Philology and Literature IX. Boston: Ginn

Faulkes, Anthony 1977a. 'Edda', *Gripla* 2: 32–9

1978–79. 'Descent from the Gods', *Mediaeval Scandinavia* 11: 92–125

Faulkner, Peter 1973. *William Morris: The Critical Heritage*. London: Routledge and Kegan Paul

Feist, Sigmund 1939. *Vergleichendes Wörterbuch der Gotischen Sprache*, 3rd edn. Leiden: Brill

Fell, Christine 1996. 'The first publication of Old Norse literature in England and its relation to its sources', in Roesdahl and Meulengracht Sørensen (eds.), pp. 27–57

Fidjestøl, Bjarne 1979. *Sólarljóð: tyding og tolkingsgrunnlag*. Universitetet i Bergen, Nordisk institutts skriftserie 4. Bergen: Universitetsforlaget

1997a. 'The kenning system: an attempt at a linguistic analysis', in Haugen and Mundal (eds.), pp. 16–67 [translation of 1974. 'Kenningsystemet: Forsøk på ein lingvistisk analyse', *Maal og minne*: 5–50]

1997b. 'Norse-Icelandic composition in the oral period', in Haugen and Mundal (eds.), pp. 303–32 [repr. from Bjarne Fidjestøl et al. (eds.) 1994. *Norsk litteratur i tusen år: Tekhistoriske linjer*. Oslo: Landslaget for Norskundervisning: J. W. Cappelens Forlag, pp. 52–80]

1999. *The Dating of Eddic Poetry: A Historical Survey and Methodological Investigation* (ed. Odd Einar Haugen). Bibliotheca Arnamagnæana 41. Copenhagen: Reitzel

Finnegan, Ruth 1977. *Oral Poetry: Its Nature, Significance and Social Context*. Cambridge: Cambridge University Press /Bloomington: Indiana University Press. [significant new introductory essay in 1992 repr.]

1988. *Literacy and Orality: Studies in the Technology of Communication*. Oxford: Blackwell

Finnur Jónsson 1894. *Den oldnorske og oldislandske litteraturs historie.* Vol. 1. Copenhagen: Gad
1898. 'Hofalýsingar í fornsögum goðalíkneski', *Árbók hins íslenzka fornleifafélags:* 28–38
Fix, Hans 1997. 'Text editing in Old Norse: a linguist's point of view', *North-Western European Language Evolution: NOWELE* 31–2: 105–17
Fleck, Jere 1970. 'Konr – Óttarr – Geirrǫðr: a knowledge criterion for succession to the Germanic sacred kingship', *Scandinavian Studies* 42: 39–49
1971. 'The knowledge criterion in the *Grímnismál*: the case against shamanism', *Arkiv för nordisk filologi* 86: 49–65
Fleischman, Suzanne 1990. 'Philology, Linguistics, and the Discourse of the Medieval Text', *Speculum* 65/1: 19–37
Foley, John Miles 1988. *The Theory of Oral Composition: History and Methodology.* Bloomington: Indiana University Press
1991. *Immanent Art: From Structure to Meaning in Traditional Oral Epic.* Bloomington: Indiana University Press
1995. *The Singer of Tales in Performance.* Bloomington: Indiana University Press
2002. *How to Read an Oral Poem.* Urbana and Chicago: University of Illinois Press
Frank, Roberta 1972. 'Some uses of paronomasia in Old English scriptural verse', *Speculum* 47: 207–26
1982 [1979]. 'Old Norse memorial eulogies and the ending of *Beowulf*', *The Early Middle Ages, Acta* 6: 1–19
1990. 'Why skalds address women', in Pàroli (ed.), pp. 67–83
Friis-Jensen, Karsten 1987. *Saxo Grammaticus as Latin Poet: Studies in the Verse Passages of the Gesta Danorum.* Analecta Romana Instituti Danici, Supplementum 1. Rome: L'Erma di Bretschneider
Fritzner, Johan 1886–96. *Ordbog over det gamle norske Sprog.* 3 vols. 2nd edn. Oslo: Den norske Forlagsforening
Fulk, R. D. 1996. 'Inductive methods in the textual criticism of Old English verse', *Medievalia et Humanistica* 23: 1–24
2002. 'Early Middle English evidence for Old English meter: resolution in *Poema Morale*', *Journal of Germanic Linguistics* 14: 331–55
2007. 'The textual criticism of Frederick Klaeber's *Beowulf*', in Andrew Wawn (ed.), *Constructing Nations, Reconstructing Myth: Essays in Honour of T. A. Shippey.* Turnhout: Brepols, pp. 131–53
Fulk, R. D. and Gade, Kari Ellen 2002. 'A bibliography of Germanic alliterative meters', *Jahrbuch für Internationale Germanistik* 34: 87–186
Gade, Kari Ellen 1995. *The Structure of Old Norse 'Dróttkvætt' Poetry.* Ithaca: Cornell University Press
2002. 'History of Old Nordic metrics', in Oskar Bandle (ed.), *The Nordic Languages: An International Handbook of the History of the North Germanic Languages*, Vol. 1. Berlin: Walter de Gruyter, pp. 856–70

2005. 'The syntax of Old Norse *kviðuháttr* meter', *Journal of Germanic Linguistics* 17.3: 155–81

2012. 'The metres of skaldic poetry', in *SkP* I, pp. li–lxix

Genzmer, Felix 1951–53. 'Das Alter einiger Eddalieder', *Zeitschrift für deutsches Altertum und deutsche Literatur* 71: 134–51

Gerrard, Christopher M. 2003. *Medieval Archaeology: Understanding Traditions and Contemporary Approaches*. London: Routledge

Gísli Pálsson (ed.) 1992. *From Sagas to Society: Comparative Approaches to Early Iceland*. Enfield Lock: Hisarlik Press

Gísli Sigurðsson 1986. 'Ástir og útsaumur: Umhverfi og kvenleg einkenni hetjukvæða Eddu', *Skírnir* 160: 126–52

1990. 'On the classification of eddic heroic poetry in view of the oral theory', in Pàroli (ed.), pp. 245–55

1992. 'Horfin hefð: Hvernig nálgumst við eddukvæði?' *Skíma* 15/3: 21–26

1998. 'Inngangur', in his *Eddukvæði*. Reykjavík: Mál og Menning, pp. x–lxiii

2004a. '"Bring the manuscripts home!"', in Gísli Sigurðsson and Vésteinn Ólason (eds.), *The Manuscripts of Iceland*. Reykjavík: Árni Magnússon Institute in Iceland, pp. 171–7

2004b. *The Medieval Icelandic Saga and Oral Tradition: A Discourse on Method* (trans. Nicholas Jones). Publications of the Milman Parry Collection of Oral Literature 2. Cambridge MA: Harvard University Press

2009. 'Goðsögur Snorra Eddu: Lýsing á raunheimi með að ferðum Sjónhverfingarinnar', in Gunnar Þór Jóhannesson and Helga Björnsdóttir (eds.), *Rannsóknir í félagsvísindum, X: Erindi flutt á ráðstefnu í október 2009*. Reykjavík: Félagsvísindastofnun Háskóla Íslands, pp. 851–61

2013. '*Vǫluspá* as the product of an oral tradition: what does that entail?', in Gunnell and Lassen (eds.), pp. 45–62

Gledhill, Christopher 2000. *Collocations in Science Writing*. Tübingen: Gunter Narr

Glendinning, Robert J. and Haraldur Bessason (eds.) 1983. *Edda: A Collection of Essays*. Winnipeg: The University of Manitoba Press

Goodrick-Clarke, Nicholas 1985. *The Occult Roots of Nazism*. Wellingborough: Aquarian Press

2002. *Black Sun*. New York: New York University Press

Goody, Jack and Watt, Ian 1968. 'The consequences of literacy', in Jack Goody (ed.), *Literacy in Traditional Societies*. Cambridge: Cambridge University Press, pp. 27–84

Gos, Giselle 2009. 'Women as a source of *heilræði*, "sound counsel": social mediation and community integration in *Fóstbrœðra saga*', *Journal of English and German Philology* 108: 281–300

Graham-Campbell, James 2013. *Viking Art*. London: Thames & Hudson

Grieg, Sigurd 1928. 'Kongsgaarden', in A. W. Brøgger and H. Shetelig (eds.), *Osebergfundet II*. Oslo: Den Norske Stat, pp. 1–286

Grimstad, Kaaren 1976. 'The giant as a heroic model: the case of Egill and Starkaðr', *Scandinavian Studies* 48: 284–98

1988. 'Starkaðr', in Joseph R. Strayer (ed.), *Dictionary of the Middle Ages*. 13 vols. New York: Scribner, II, pp. 466–7.

Gräslund, Bo 2007. 'Fimbulvintern, Ragnarök och klimatkrisen år 536–537 e. Kr.'. *Saga och Sed* 2007: 93–123

Grønvik, Ottar 1985. *Runene på Eggjasteinen. En hedensk gravinnskrift fra slutten av 600-tallet.* Oslo: Universitetsforlaget

Gschwantler, Otto 1968. 'Christus, Thor und die Midgardschlange', in Helmut Birkhan and Otto Gschwantler (eds.), *Festschrift for Otto Höfler zum 65. Geburtstag.* Vienna: Notring, pp. 145–68

1993. 'Hymiskviða', in Pulsiano et al. (eds.), pp. 308–9

Guðrún Nordal 2001. *Tools of Literacy: The Role of Skaldic Verse in Icelandic Textual Culture of the Twelfth and Thirteenth Centuries.* Toronto: University of Toronto Press

Gunnell, Terry 1995. *The Origins of Drama in Scandinavia.* Cambridge: D. S. Brewer

2004. 'Hof, halls, goð(ar) and dwarves: an examination of the ritual space in the pagan Icelandic hall', *Cosmos* 17: 3–36

2005. 'Eddic poetry', in Rory McTurk (ed.), *A Companion to Old Norse-Icelandic Literature and Culture.* Malden: Blackwell, pp. 82–100

2006a. 'Narratives, space and drama: essential spatial aspects involved in the performance and reception of oral narrative', *Folklore, An Electronic Journal* 33: 7–26

2006b. '"Til holts ek gekk": spacial and temporal aspects of the dramatic poems of the Elder Edda', in Andrén, Jennbert, and Raudvere (eds.), pp. 238–42

2007. 'How Elvish were the Álfar?', in Andrew Wawn with Graham Johnson and John Walter (eds.), *Constructing Nations, Reconstructing Myth: Essays in Honour of T. A. Shippey.* Making the Middle Ages 9. Turnhout: Brepols, pp. 111–30

2008. 'The performance of the Poetic Edda', in Stefan Brink and Neil Price (eds.), *The Viking World.* London and New York: Routledge, pp. 299–303

2011. 'The drama of the Poetic Edda: Performance as a means of transformation', in Andrzeja Dąbrówki (ed.), *Pogranicza teatralności: Poezja, poetyka, praktyka.* Warsaw: Instytut Badań Literackich Pan Wydawnictwo, pp. 13–40

2013a. '*Vǫluspá* in performance', in Gunnell and Lassen (eds.), pp. 63–77

2013b. 'Masks and performance in the early Nordic world', in Harald Meller and Regine Maraszek (eds.), *Masken der Vorzeit in Europa (II): International Tagung vom 19. bis. 21. November in Halle (Saale).* Halle (Saale): Landesamt für Denkmalpflege und Archaologie Sachsen-Anhalt, pp. 184–96

2015. 'Pantheon? What pantheon? Concepts of a family of gods in Pre-Christian Nordic religions', *Scripta Íslandica* 66: 55–76

forthcoming a. 'How high was the High One? The role of Oðinn in Pre-Christian Icelandic society', in Stefan Brink and Lisa Collinson (eds.), *Theorizing Old Norse Myth.* Acta Scandinavica 7. Turnhout: Brepols

forthcoming b. 'Performing *Eiríksmál* and *Hákonarmál*: performance studies and the study of Old Norse religion', in Mark Amodio (ed.), *A World of Oralities: Essays in Memory of John Miles Foley.* Tempe, AZ: Arizona Center for Medieval and Renaissance Studies

Gunnell, Terry and Lassen, Annette (eds.) 2013. *The Nordic Apocalypse: Approaches to Vǫluspá and Nordic Days of Judgement*. Acta Scandinavica 2. Turnhout: Brepols

Gurevič, Elena A. 1986. 'The formulaic pair in Eddic Poetry: an experimental analysis', in John Lindow, Lars Lönnroth, and Gerd Wolfgang Weber (eds.), *Structure and Meaning in Old Norse Literature: New Approaches to Textual Analysis and Literary Criticism*. The Viking Collection 3. Odense: Odense University Press, pp. 32–44

Gurevich, Aron Ya. 1973. 'Edda and law: commentary upon *Hyndluljóð*', *Arkiv för nordisk filologi* 88: 72–84

Gutenbrunner, Siegfried 1955. 'Eddalieder aus der Schreibstube', *Zeitschrift für deutsche Philologie* 74: 250–63

Haimerl, Edgar [1993] 2013. 'Sigurðr, a medieval hero', in Acker and Larrington (eds.), pp. 32–52 [Orig. publ. in German 1993. *alvíssmál* 2: 81–104]

Halberstam, Judith 1998. *Female Masculinity*. Durham: Duke University Press

Hall, Alaric 2007. *Elves in Anglo-Saxon England: Matters of Belief, Health, Gender and Identity*. Woodbridge: Boydell Press

Hallberg, Peter 1983. 'Elements of imagery in the Edda', in Glendinning and Haraldur Bessason (eds.), pp. 47–85

Harris, Joseph 1975. 'Genre in the saga literature: a squib', *Scandinavian Studies* 47: 427–36

1979. 'The *senna*: from description to literary theory', *Michigan Germanic Studies* 5/1: 65–74

1983. 'Eddic poetry as oral poetry: The evidence of parallel passages in the Helgi poems for questions of composition and performance', in Glendinning and Haraldur Bessason (eds.), pp. 210–42 [repr. 2008 in Deskis and Hill (eds.), pp. 189–225]

1985. 'Eddic poetry', in Clover and Lindow (eds.), pp. 68–156

1993. 'Love and death in the *Männerbund*: An essay with special reference to the *Bjarkamál* and *The Battle of Maldon*', in Helen Damico and John Leyerle (eds.), *Heroic Poetry in the Anglo-Saxon Period: Studies in Honor of Jess B. Bessinger, Jr.* Kalamazoo: Medieval Institute Publications, pp. 77–114

1996 [2008]. 'Romancing the rune: Aspects of literacy in early Scandinavian orality', in *Atti, Accademia Peloritana dei Pericolanti. Classe di lettere, filosofia e belle arti, LXX* [anno accademico CCLXV (1994)]. Messina: Accademia peloritana dei pericolanti, pp. 109–40 [repr. 2008 in Deskis and Hill (eds.), pp. 319–47]

1997. 'The Prosimetrum of Icelandic saga and some relatives', in Joseph Harris and Karl Reichl (eds), *Prosimetrum: Crosscultural Perspectives on Narrative in Prose and Verse*. Woodbridge and Rochester, NY: Boydell and Brewer, pp. 131–63

2000a. 'The performance of Old Norse eddic poetry: A retrospective', in Karl Reichl (ed.), *The Oral Epic: Performance and Music*. Intercultural Music Studies 12. Berlin: VWB, pp. 225–32

2000b. 'Performance, textualization, and textuality of "elegy" in Old Norse', in Lauri Honko (ed.), *The Textualization of Oral Epic*. Trends in Linguistics: Studies and Monographs 128. Berlin and New York: Mouton de Gruyter, pp. 89–99

2000c. '"Double scene" and "mis en abyme" in Beowulfian narrative', in Stina Hansson and Mats Malm (eds.), *Gudar på jorden: festskrift til Lars Lönnroth*. Stockholm and Stehag: Brutus Östlings Bokförlag Symposion, pp. 322–38

2003. '"Ethnopaleography" and recovered performance: the problematic witnesses to "Eddic Music"', in Joseph Falaky Nagy (ed.), *Models of Performance in Oral Epic, Ballad, and Song, Western Folklore* 62/1–2: 97–117

2004. 'Sänger', in Heinrich Beck et al. (eds.), *Reallexikon der Germanischen Altertumskunde*. 2nd edn. 37 vols. Berlin and New York: de Gruyter, 25: 79–86

2006. 'Erfikvæði – myth, ritual, elegy', in Andrén, Jennbert, and Raudvere (eds.), pp. 267–71

2009. 'Philology, elegy, and cultural change', *Gripla* 20: 257–79 [*Nordic Civilisation in the Medieval World*, ed. Vésteinn Ólason. Reykjavík: Stofnun Árna Magnússonar í íslenskum fræðum]

2010. 'Old Norse memorial discourse, between orality and literacy', in Rankovic et al. (eds.), pp. 119–33

2012. 'Eddic poetry and the ballad: voice, vocality, and performance, with special reference to DgF 1', in Joseph Harris and Barbara Hillers (eds.), *Child's Children: Ballad Study and its Legacies. Ballads and Songs, International Studies* 7. Trier: WVT, pp. 155–70

Harris, Joseph and Reichl, Karl (eds.) 1997. *Prosimetrum. Cross-cultural Perspectives on Narrative in Prose and Verse*. Woodbridge and Rochester, NY: Boydell and Brewer

2012. 'Performance and performers', in Karl Reichl (ed.), *Medieval Oral Literature*. Berlin: de Gruyter, pp. 141–202

Harris, Richard 1971. 'A study of *Grípisspá*', *Scandinavian Studies* 43: 344–55

Hastrup, Kirsten 1985. *Culture and History in Medieval Iceland: An Anthropological Analysis of Structure and Change*. Oxford: Clarendon Press

Hauck, Karl 1970. *Goldbrakteaten aus Sievern: Spätantike Amulett-Bilder der 'Dania-Saxonica' und die Sachsen-'Origo' bei Widukind von Corvey*. Munich: Münstersche Mittelalter-Schriften

Haugen, Einar 1983. 'The Edda as ritual: Odin and his masks', in Glendinning and Haraldur Bessason (eds.), pp. 3–24

Haugen, Odd Einar and Mundal, Else (eds.) 1997. *Bjarne Fidjestøl, Selected Papers*. The Viking Collection 9. Odense: Odense University Press

Haukur Þorgeirsson 2012. 'Late placement of the finite verb in Old Norse *fornyrðislag* meter', *Journal of Germanic Linguistics* 24/3: 233–69

Havelock, Eric A. 1963. *Preface to Plato*. Cambridge, MA: Harvard University Press

Haymes, Edward R. 2000. 'Heldenlied und Eddalied', in Robert Nedoma, Hermann Reichert, and Günter Zimmermann (eds.), *Erzählen im mittelalterlichen Skandinavien*. Vienna: Edition Presens, pp. 9–20

Hedeager, Lotte 1992. *Iron-age Societies: From Tribe to State in Northern Europe, 500 BC to AD 700*. Oxford: Blackwell

1997. *Skygger av en anden virkelighed*. Copenhagen: Samleren

2001. 'Asgard reconstructed? Gudme – a "central place" in the North', in Mayke De Jong and Frans Theuws (eds.), *Topographies of Power in the Early Middle Ages*. Leiden: Brill, pp. 467–507

2002. 'Scandinavian "central places" in a cosmological setting', in Birgitta Hårdh and Lars Larsson (eds.), *Central Places in the Migration and Merovingian Periods*. Stockholm: Almqvist & Wiksell, pp. 3–18

2004. 'Dyr og mennesker – mennesker og andre dyr: dyreornamentikkens transcendentale realitet', in Andrén, Jennbert, and Raudvere (eds.), pp. 219–52

2011. *Iron Age Myth and Materiality: An Archaeology of Scandinavia AD 400–1000*. London: Routledge

Heimir Pálsson 1999. 'The performance of the eddic poems' [in the booklet accompanying Sequentia 1999: *Edda*, 9–10. Deutsche Harmonia Mundi: 05472 77381 2]

2001. 'The eddic poems' [in the booklet accompanying Sequentia 2001: *The Rhinegold Curse*, 14–18. Deutschland Radio and Westdeutscher Rundfunk; Marc Aurel edition: MA 20016]

Heinrichs, Anne 1986. '*Annat er várt eðli*. The type of the prepatriarchal woman in Old Norse literature', in Lindow, Lönnroth, and Weber (eds.), pp. 110–40

1997. 'Der liebeskranke Freyr, euhemeristisch entmythisiert', *alvíssmál* 7: 3–36

1999. 'Midgardschlange', in Ulrich Müller and Werner Wunderlich (eds.), *Dämonen, Monster, Fabelwesen*. Mittelalter-Mythen 2. St Gallen: UVK, pp. 413–38

Helbig, Wolfgang 1887. *Das Homerische Epos aus den Denkmälern erläutert: Archäologische Untersuchungen*. Leipzig: Teubner

Hellquist, Elof 1948. *Svensk etymologisk ordbok*. 3rd edn. Lund: Gleerup

Helm, Karl 1950. 'Erfundene Götter', in Richard Kienast (ed.), *Studien zur deutschen Philologie des Mittelalters. Festschrift zum 80. Geburtstag von Friedrich Panzer*. Heidelberg: Winter, pp. 1–11

Helmbrecht, Michaela 2012. 'A winged figure from Uppåkra', *Fornvännen* 107: 171–8

Hermann Pálsson 1985. *Áhrif Hugsvinnsmála á aðrar fornbókmenntir*. Studia Islandica/Íslensk Fræði 43. Reykjavík: Bókaútgáfa menningarsjóðs

1999. *Hávamál í ljósi íslenskrar menningar*. [Reykjavík:] Háskólaútgáfan

Hermann, Pernille (ed.) 2005. *Literacy in Medieval and Early Modern Scandinavian Culture*. The Viking Collection 16. Odense: University Press of Southern Denmark

Hermann, Pernille, Schjødt, Jens Peter, and Kristensen, Rasmus Tranum (eds.) 2007. *Reflections on Old Norse Myths*. Studies in Viking and Medieval Scandinavia 1. Turnhout: Brepols

Herschend, Frands 1997. *Livet i Hallen: Tre Fallstudier i den yngre Järnålderns Aristokrati*. Uppsala: Occasional Papers in Archaeology

1998. *The Idea of the Good in Late Iron Age Society*. Uppsala: Occasional Papers in Archaeology

[unsigned] 2013. 'Down by the farmhands and their families', *On the Reading Rest* [https://floasche.wordpress.com/2013/01/21/down-by-the-farmhands-and-their-families/; last accessed 27 October 2014]

Heusler, Andreas 1891. *Zur Geschichte der altdeutschen Verskunst.* Breslau: Koebner

1894. *Über germanischen Versbau.* Berlin: Weidmann

1914. *Die Anfänge der isländischen Saga.* Abhandlungen der königlichenen preussischen Akademie der Wissenschaften, philos.-hist. Cl. Berlin: Reimer

1925–29. *Deutsche Versgeschichte mit Einschluß des altenglischen und altnordischen Stabreimverses.* 3 vols. Berlin: de Gruyter

Hill, Thomas D. 1993. 'Rígsþula', in Pulsiano et al. (eds.), pp. 535–6

Hines, John 1984. *The Scandinavian Character of Anglian England in the pre-Viking Period.* BAR British Series 124. Oxford: British Archaeological Reports

2004. *Voices in the Past: English Literature and Archaeology.* Cambridge: D. S. Brewer

2007. 'Famous last words: monologue and dialogue in *Hamðismál* and the realization of heroic tale', in Quinn, Heslop, and Wills (eds.), pp. 177–97

2013. 'Review article: the final publication of the series "On the iconology of the gold bracteates" and Karl Hauck's legacy', *Medieval Archaeology* 57: 251–61

Hines, John and Bayliss, Alex (eds.) 2013. *Anglo-Saxon Graves and Grave Goods of the 6th and 7th Centuries AD: A Chronological Framework.* Leeds: Society for Medieval Archaeology

Hjärne, Erland 1980. *Land och ledung.* Rättshistoriskt bibliotek 31. Stockholm: A. B. Nordiska

Hodder, Ian (ed.) 1987. *The Archaeology of Contextual Meanings.* Cambridge: Cambridge University Press

Hodges, Richard 1989. 'Parachutists and truffle-hunters: at the frontiers of Archaeology and History', in Michael Aston, David Austin, and Christopher Dyer (eds.), *The Rural Settlement of Medieval England.* Oxford: Blackwell, pp. 287–305

Hollander, Lee M. 1963. 'Recent work and views on the Poetic Edda', *Scandinavian Studies* 35: 101–9

Holtsmark, Anne et al. 1956–78. *Kulturhistorisk Leksikon for Nordisk Middelalder.* Copenhagen: Rosenkilde & Bagger

Hughes, Shaun F. D. 2013. '"Where are all the eddic champions gone?" The disappearance and recovery of the eddic heroes in late medieval Icelandic literature, 1400–1800', *Viking and Medieval Scandinavia* 9: 37–67

Ilkjær, Jørgen 2000. *Illerup Ådal: Et arkæologisk tryllespejl.* Høybjerg: Moesgård

Ingstad, Anne S. 1977. *The Discovery of a Norse Settlement in America: Excavations at L'Anse aux Meadows, Newfoundland, 1961–1968.* Oslo: Universitetsforlaget

Ingstad, Helge 1959. *Landet under Leidarstjernen: En Ferd til Grønlands Norrøne Bygder.* Oslo: Gyldendal

Itó, Tsukusu 2009. 'The Gosforth fishing stone and *Hymiskviða*: an example of inter-communicability between Old English and Old Norse speakers', *Scripta Islandica* 60: 137–57

Jauss, Hans Robert 1982. *Toward an Aesthetic of Reception* (trans. Timothy Bahti). Theory and history of literature 2. Minneapolis: University of Minnesota Press

Jesch, Judith 1991. *Women in the Viking Age*. Woodbridge: Boydell

2001. *Ships and Men in the Late Viking Age: The Vocabulary of Runic Inscriptions and Skaldic Verse*. Woodbridge: Boydell

2002. 'Eagles, ravens and wolves: beasts of battle, symbols of victory and death', in Judith Jesch (ed.), *The Scandinavians from the Vendel Period to the Tenth Century: An Ethnographic Perspective*. Woodbridge: Boydell, pp. 251–71

2005. 'Skaldic verse, a case of literacy avant la lettre?', in Hermann (ed.), pp. 187–210

Jessen, Edwin 1863. 'Oldnordisk og oldtysk verselag', *Tidskrift for Philologi og Pædagogik* 4: 249–92

1869. 'Bemærkninger til Hr. Docent Capitain Svend Grundtvigs Artikkel "Er Nordens gamle Literatur norsk, eller er den dels islandsk dels nordisk?"', *Tidskrift for Philologi og Pædagogik* 8: 213–45

1871. 'Über die Eddalieder. Heimat, alter, charakter', *Zeitschrift für deutsche Philologie* 3: 1–84, 251–2, 495 [repr. in the same year separately by Waisenhaus in Halle]

Jochens, Jenny 1986. 'The medieval Icelandic heroine: fact or fiction?' *Viator* 17: 35–50 [repr. 1989 in John Tucker (ed.), *Sagas of the Icelanders: A Book of Essays*. New York: Garland, pp. 99–126]

1992. 'From libel to lament: male manifestations of love in Old Norse', in Gísli Pálsson (ed.), pp. 247–64

1995. *Women in Old Norse Society*. Ithaca: Cornell University Press

1996. *Old Norse Images of Women*. Philadelphia: University of Pennsylvania Press

Jóhanna Katrín Friðriksdóttir 2012. 'From heroic legend to "medieval screwball comedy"? The development and interpretation of the *meykongr* motif', in Annette Lassen, Agneta Ney, and Ármann Jakobsson (eds.), *The Legendary Sagas: Origins and Development*. Reykjavík: University of Iceland Press, pp. 229–49

2013a. '"Gerðit hon ... sem konor aðrar": women and subversion in eddic heroic poetry', in Acker and Larrington (eds.), pp. 117–36

2013b. *Women in Old Norse Literature: Bodies, Words, Power*. New York: Palgrave Macmillan

Johansson, Karl G. 1998. '*Rígsþula* och Codex Wormianus: Textens function ur ett kompilationsperspectiv', *alvíssmál* 8: 67–84

2000. '*Vǫluspá* – muntlig och skriftlig tradition: En discussion om skärningspunkten mellan filologi och litteraturvetenskap', in Kristinn Jóhannesson, Karl G. Johansson, and Lars Lönnroth (eds.), *Den fornnordiska texten i filogisk och litteraturvetenskaplig belysning.* Gothenburg Old Norse Studies 2. Göteborg: Litteraturvetenskapliga institutionen, pp. 64–82

2005. 'Översättning och originalspråkstext i handskrifttraderingens våld: *Merlínusspá* och *Vǫluspá* i Hauksbók', in Kramarz-Bein (ed.), pp. 97–113

2010. 'In praise of manuscript culture: texts and editions in the computer age', in Quinn and Lethbridge (eds.), pp. 67–86

2013. '*Vǫluspá* and the Tiburtine Sibyl, and the apocalypse in the North', in Gunnell and Lassen (eds.), pp. 161–84

2014. 'Till variantens lov: Behovet av nya perspektiv på medeltidens texthistoria', in Maria Bylin, Cecilia Falk, and Tomas Riad (eds.), *Variation och förändring*. Studier i svensk språhistoria 12. Acta Universitatis Stockholmiensis. Stockholm: University of Stockholm, pp. 47–61

Jón Karl Helgason 2002. '"Þegi þú, Þórr!": gender, class, and discourse in *Þrymskviða*', in Anderson and Swenson (eds.), pp. 159–66

Kalinke, Marianne 1990. *Bridal-quest Romance in Medieval Iceland.* Islandica XLVI. Ithaca: Cornell University Press

Kellogg, Robert 1988. *A Concordance to Eddic Poetry.* East Lansing, MI, and Woodbridge: Colleagues Press/Boydell and Brewer

1990. 'The prehistory of eddic poetry', in Pàroli (ed.), pp. 187–99

1991. 'Literacy and orality in the Poetic Edda', in A. N. Doane and Carol Braun Pasternack (eds.), *Vox intexta. Orality and Texuality in the Middle Ages.* Madison: University of Wisconsin Press, pp. 89–101

Kick, Donata and Shafer, John D. (eds.) 2014. *John McKinnell. Essays on Eddic Poetry.* Toronto: University of Toronto Press

Kintgen, Eugene R. 1977. '*Lif, lof, leof, lufu,* and *geleafa* in Old English poetry', *Neuphilologische Mitteilungen* 78: 309–316

Klingenberg, Heinz 1971. *Edda – Sammlung und Dichtung.* Beiträge zur nordischen Philologie 3. Heidelberg: Winter

1983. 'Types of eddic mythological poetry', in Glendinning and Haraldur Bessason (eds.), pp. 134–64

Kopár, Lilla 2012. *Gods and Settlers. The Iconography of Norse Mythology in Anglo-Scandinavian Sculpture.* Studies in the Early Middle Ages 25. Turnhout: Brepols

Kramarz-Bein, Susanne (ed.) 2005. *Neue Ansätze in der Mittelalterphilologie/Nye Veier i middelalderfilologien. Akten der skandinavistischen Arbeitstagung in Münster vom 24.- 26.10.2002.* Texte und Untersuchungen zur Germanistik und Skandinavistik 55. Frankfurt am Main and Basel: Peter Lang

Kress, Helga 1993. *Máttugar meyjar. Íslensk fornbókmenntasaga.* Reykjavík: Háskólaútgáfan

2002. 'Taming the shrew: The rise of patriarchy and the subordination of the feminine in Old Norse literature', in Anderson and Swenson (eds.), pp. 81–92

Krömmelbein, Thomas 1998. 'Jacob Schimmelmann und der Beginn der Snorra Edda-Rezeption in Deutschland', in Hans Fix (ed.), *Snorri Sturluson. Beiträge zu Werk und Rezeption.* Ergänzungsbände zum Reallexikon der Germanishcn Alterturmskunde 18. Berlin: de Gruyter, pp. 109–30

Kuhn, Hans 1929. *Das Füllwort of-um im Altwestnordischen: eine Untersuchung zur Geschichte der germanischen Präfixe: ein Beitrag zur altgermanischen Metrik.* Göttingen: Vandenhoeck and Ruprecht

1933. 'Zur wortstellung und -betonung im Altgermanischen', *Beiträge zur Geschichte der deutschen Sprache und Literatur* 57: 1–109 [repr. 1969 in Hofmann, Lange, and von See (eds.), Vol. I, pp. 18–103]

1936. 'Die Negation des Verbs in der altnordischen Dichtung', *Beiträge zur Geschichte der deutschen Sprache und Literatur* 60: 431–44 [repr. 1969 in Hofmann, Lange, and von See (eds.), Vol. I, pp. 124–34]

1939. 'Westgermanisches in der altnordischen Verskunst', *Beiträge zur Geschichte der deutschen Sprache und Literatur* 63: 178–236 [repr. 1969 in Hofmann, Lange, and von See (eds.), Vol. I, pp. 485–527]

1968. *Edda. Die Lieder des Codex Regius nebst verwandten Denkmälern. II. Kurzes Wörterbuch.* 3rd edn., Heidelberg: Winter

1969. Dietrich Hoffmann, Wolfgang Lange, and Klaus von See (eds.), *Aufsätze und Rezensionen aus den Gebieten der germanischen und nordischen Sprach-, Literatur- und Kulturgeschichte.* 4 vols. Berlin: de Gruyter

1983. *Das Dróttkvætt.* Heidelberg: Winter

Kure, Henning 2010. *I begyndelsen var skriget: Vikingetidens myter om skabelsen.* Copenhagen: Gyldendal

La Farge, Beatrice, and Tucker, John (eds.) 1992. *Glossary to the Poetic Edda, Based on Hans Kuhn's Kurzes Wörterbuch.* Skandinavistiche Arbeiten 15. Heidelberg: Winter

Lang, James 1976. 'Sigurd and Weland in pre-conquest carving from Northern England', *Yorkshire Archaeological Journal* 48: 83–94

Laqueur, Thomas 1990. *Making Sex. Body and Gender from the Greeks to Freud.* Cambridge, MA: Harvard University Press

Larkin, Philip 1955. 'Statement', in D. J. Enright (ed.), *Poets of the 1950s: An Anthology of New English Verse.* Tokyo: Kenkyusha

Larrington, Carolyne 1992a. 'What does woman want? *Mær* and *munr* in *Skírnismál*', *alvíssmál* 1: 3–16

1992b. '*Hávamál* and sources outside Scandinavia', *Saga-Book of the Viking Society* 23: 141–57

1993. *A Store of Common Sense. Gnomic Theme and Style in Old Icelandic and Old English Wisdom Poetry.* Oxford: Clarendon Press

2002. 'Freyja and the Organ-Stool: Neo-Paganism in *Sólarljóð*', in Bela Broyanyi (ed.), *Germanisches Altertum und christliches Mittelalter: Festschrift für Heinz Klingenberg zum 65. Geburtstag.* Schriften zur Mediävistik 1. Hamburg: Kovac, pp. 177–96

2006. 'Loki's children', in John McKinnell et al. (eds.), *The Fantastic in Old Norse-Icelandic Literature. Sagas and the British Isles. Preprint Papers of the 13th International Saga Conference. Durham and York, 6th–12th August, 2006.* Durham: Centre for Medieval and Renaissance Studies, pp. 541–50

2007. 'Translating the Poetic Edda', in Clark and Phelpstead (eds.), pp. 21–42

2011a. 'Melvin Burgess's *Bloodtide* and *Bloodsong:* Sigmundr, Sigurðr and young adult literature', in Katja Schulz (ed.), *Eddische Götter und Helden.* Heidelberg: Winter, pp. 199–213

2011b. 'Sibling drama: Laterality in the heroic poems of the Edda', in Daniel Anlezark (ed.), *Myth, Legends, and Heroes. Studies in Old Norse and Old English Literature in Honour of John McKinnell.* Toronto: Toronto University Press, pp. 169–87

2013. '"I have long desired to cure you of old age": Sibling drama in the later heroic poems of the Edda', in Acker and Larrington (eds.), pp. 140–56

2015a. *Brothers and Sisters in Medieval European Literature.* Woodbridge: Boydell and Brewer

2015b. *Winter is Coming: the Medieval World of 'Game of Thrones'.* London: I. B. Tauris

Layher, William 2007. 'Caught between worlds: Gendering the maiden warrior in Old Norse', in Sara S. Poor and Jana K. Schulman (eds.), *Women and Medieval Epic. Gender, Genre, and the Limits of Epic Masculinity.* New York: Palgrave, pp. 183–208

Lehmann, Winfred P. 1956. *The Development of Germanic Verse Form.* Austin: University of Texas Press and the Linguistic Society of America

Leslie, Helen F. 2012. *The Prose Contexts of Eddic Poetry, primarily in the Fornaldarsǫgur.* [Unpublished PhD dissertation, University of Bergen]

2014. 'The death songs of *Örvar-Odds saga*', in Isabel Grifoll, Julián Acebrón, and Flocel Sabaté (eds.), *Cartografies de l'ànima: Identitat, memòria i escriptura.* Lleida: Pagès editors, pp. 231–44

Lévi-Strauss, Claude 1971. *L'Homme Nu.* Paris: Plon

Liestøl, Aslak 1965. 'Rúnavísur frá Björgvin', *Skírnir* 139, 27–51

1968. 'Correspondence in runes', *Mediaeval Scandinavia* 1: 17–27

1981. 'The viking runes: The transition from the older to the younger *futhark*', *Saga-Book of the Viking Society* 20: 247–66

Liestøl, Knut 1930. *The Origin of the Icelandic Sagas* (trans. A. G. Jayne). Cambridge, MA: Harvard University Press [Norwegian original 1929]

Lindblad, Gustaf 1954. *Studier i Codex Regius av äldre Eddan.* Lundastudier i nordisk språkvetenskap 10. Lund: Gleerup

1980. 'Poetiska Eddans förhistoria och skrivskicket i Codex regius', *Arkiv för nordisk filologi* 95: 142–67

Lindow, John 1975. 'Riddles, kennings and the complexity of skaldic poetry', *Scandinavian Studies* 47: 311–27

1977. 'The two skaldic stanzas in *Gylfaginning:* Notes on sources and text history', *Arkiv för nordisk filologi* 92: 106–24

1988. 'Addressing Thor', *Scandinavian Studies* 60/2: 119–36

1997. *Murder and Vengeance among the Gods: Baldr in Scandinavian Mythology.* FF Communications 262. Helsinki: Suomalainen tiedeakatemia

2001. *Norse Mythology. A Guide to the Gods, Heroes, Rituals and Beliefs.* Oxford: Oxford University Press

2002. 'Myth Read as History: Odin in Snorri Sturluson's *Ynglinga saga*', in Gregory Schrempp and William Hansen (eds.), *Myth: A New Symposium*. Bloomington: Indiana University Press, pp. 107–23.

2006. 'Poets and poetry in myth and life: The case of Bragi', in Andrén, Jennbert, and Raudvere (eds.), pp. 21–25

2007. 'Poetry, dwarfs and gods: Understanding *Alvíssmál*', in Quinn, Heslop, and Wills (eds.), pp. 285–303

2008. 'St Olaf and the skalds', in Thomas A. DuBois (ed.), *Sanctity in the North: Saints, Lives, and Cults in Medieval Scandinavia*. Toronto: University of Toronto Press, pp. 103–27

forthcoming. 'Comparing Balto-Finnic and Nordic mythologies', in Stephen Mitchell, Pernille Hermann, and Jens Peter Schjødt (eds.), *Old Norse Mythology in Comparative Perspective*. Cambridge: Harvard University Press

Lindow, John, Lönnroth, Lars, and Weber, Gerd Wolfgang (eds.) 1986. *Structure and Meaning in Old Norse Literature. New Approaches to Textual Analysis and Literary Criticism*. The Viking Collection 3. Odense: Odense University Press

Lindqvist, Sune 1936. *Uppsala högar och Ottarshögen*. Stockholm: Wahlström and Widstrand

1941–42. *Gotlands Bildsteine*. Stockholm: Wahlström & Widstrand

1948. 'Sutton Hoo and *Beowulf*', *Antiquity* 22: 131–40

Linke, Uli 1992. 'The theft of blood, the birth of men: Cultural constructions of gender in medieval Iceland', in Gísli Pálsson (ed.), pp. 265–88

Lord, Albert B. 1960. *The Singer of Tales*, Harvard Studies in Comparative Literature 24. Cambridge, MA: Harvard University Press [2nd edn. 2000 with audio and video CD; Stephen Mitchell and Gregory Nagy (eds.)]

Love, Jeffrey Scott 2013. *The Reception of Hervarar saga ok Heiðreks from the Middle Ages to the Seventeenth Century*. Munich: Herbert Utz

Lucas, Gavin 2009. *Hofstaðir: Excavations of a Viking Age Feasting Hall in North-eastern Iceland*. Reykjavík: Fornleifastofnun Íslands

Läffler, Leopold Frederik 1912. 'En kärleks visa i Áns saga bogsveigis', *Studier i nordisk filologi* 3: 1–65

Lönnroth, Lars 1971. 'Hjálmar's death-song and the delivery of eddic poetry', *Speculum* 46: 1–20 [repr. in Lönnroth 2011, pp. 191–218]

1977a. 'The riddles of the Rök-Stone: A structural approach', *Arkiv för nordisk filologi* 92: 1–57 [repr. in Lönnroth 2011, pp. 279–355]

1977b. '*Skírnismál* och den fornisländska äktenskapsnormen', in Bent Chr. Jacobsen et al. (eds.), *Opuscula septentrionalia. Festskrift til Ole Widding, 10.10.1977*. Copenhagen: Reitzel, pp. 54–78

1979. 'The double scene of Arrow-Odd's drinking contest', in Hans Bekker-Nielsen et al. (eds.), *Medieval Narrative: A Symposium. Proceedings of the Third International Symposium organized by the Centre for the Study of Vernacular Literature in the Middle Ages at Odense University on 20–21 November, 1978*. Odense: Odense University Press, pp. 94–119 [repr. in Lönnroth 2011, pp. 243–59]

1981. '*Iörð fannz æva né uphiminn*: a Formula Analysis', in Ursula Dronke et al. (eds.) *Speculum Norrænum: Norse Studies in Memory of Gabriel Turville-Petre*. Odense: Odense University Press, pp. 310–27 [repr. in Lönnroth 2011, pp. 219–41]

1995. *Isländska mytsagor*. Stockholm: Atlantis

2009. 'Old Norse text as performance', *Scripta Islandica* 60: 49–60

2011. *The Academy of Odin. Selected Papers on Old Norse Literature*. The Viking Collection 19. Odense: University Press of Southern Denmark

Machan, Tim William 1992. 'Alliteration and the editing of eddic poetry', *Scandinavian Studies* 64: 216–27

Magnus, Bente 1975. *Krosshaugfunnet*. Stavanger: Arkeologisk museum i Stavanger

2015. 'Shield-formed pendants and solar symbols of the Migration period', in L. Larson, F. Ekengren, B. Helgesson, and B. Söderberg (eds.), *Small Things Wide Horizons: Studies in Honour of Birgitta Hårdh*. Oxford: Archaeopress, pp. 115–20

Magoun, Francis Peabody 1953. 'The oral-formulaic character of Anglo-Saxon narrative poetry', *Speculum* 28: 446–67

Malm, Mats 1996. *Minervas äpple: Om diktsyn, tolkning och bildspråk inom nordisk götiscism*. Stockholm and Stehag: Symposion

2007. 'I marginalen till eddahandskrifterna', in Karl G. Johansson (ed.), *Den norröna renässansen: Reykholt, Norden och Europa 1150–1300*. Reykholt: Snorrastofa, pp. 135–55

Margeson, Sue 1980. 'The Völsung legend in medieval art', in Flemming G. Andersen et al. (eds.), *Medieval Iconography and Narrative: A Symposium*. Odense: Odense University Press, pp. 183–211

Mari-Catani, Alessandro 1979. 'Dodici anni di studi eddici', *Annali Istituto Universitario Orientale: Filologia germanica* 22 (Naples): 343–386

Marold, Edith 1983. *Kenningkunst: Ein Beitrag zu einer Poetik der Skaldendichtung*. Quellen und Forschungen zur Sprach- und Kulturgeschichte der germanischen Völker, ns 80. Berlin: de Gruyter

1998. 'Runeninschriften als Quelle zur Geschichte der Skaldendichtung' in Klaus Düwel (ed.), *Runeninschriften als Quellen interdisziplinärer Forschung*. Ergänzungsbände zum Reallexikon der germanischen Altertumskunde 15. Berlin: de Gruyter, 666–93

2002. 'Überlegungen zum Problem der Emendationen am Beispiel der Verse von Bjǫrn Hítdœlakappi', *Skandinavistik* 32: 39–56

2007. 'Mansǫngr – a phantom genre?', in Quinn, Heslop, and Wills (eds.), pp. 239–62

2012. 'Þorbjǫrn hornklofi', in *SkP* I, p. 73

Matthews, Peter H. 2007. *Concise Oxford Dictionary of Linguistics*. Oxford: Oxford University Press

Matyushina, Inna G. 2012. 'The legend of Hildebrand in German and Scandinavian literary tradition', in Tatjana N. Jackson and Elena A. Melnikova (eds.), *Skemmtiligastar Lygisögur: Studies in Honour of Galina Glazyrina*. Moscow: Dmitriy Pozharskiy University, pp. 80–110

McDonald, William A. 1968. *The Discovery of Homeric Greece*. London: Elek

McKeown, Kathleen R. and Radev, Dragomir R. 2000. 'Collocations', in Robert Dale, Hermann Moisl, and Harold Harold, (eds.), *A Handbook of Natural Language Processing*. New York: Marcel Dekker, pp. 507–23

McKinnell, John 1990. 'The context of *Völundarkviða*', *Saga-Book of the Viking Society* 23.1: 1–27 [Pt. II repr. 2002 Acker and Larrington, pp. 195–212; complete repr. 2014 in Kick and Shafer (eds.), pp. 221–48]

2000. 'Myth as therapy: The usefulness of *Þrymskviða*', *Medium Ævum* 69: 1–20

2001. 'Eddic poetry in Anglo-Scandinavian northern England', in James Graham-Campbell et al. (eds.), *Vikings and the Danelaw. Select Papers from the Proceedings of the Thirteenth Viking Congress, Nottingham and York, 21–30 August 1997*. Oxford: Oxbow, pp. 327–44

2003. 'Encounters with *Vǫlur*', in Margaret Clunies Ross (ed.), *Old Norse Myths, Literature and Society*. The Viking Collection 14. Odense: University Press of Southern Denmark, pp. 239–51

2005a. '*Hávamál B*: A reconstructed poem of sexual intrigue', *Saga-Book of the Viking Society* 29: 83–144 [repr. 2014 in Kick and Shafer (eds.), pp. 96–122]

2005b. *Meeting the Other in Old Norse Myth and Legend*. Woodbridge: D.S. Brewer

2007a. 'The making of *Hávamál*', *Viking and Medieval Scandinavia* 3: 75–116 [repr. as 'The Evolution of *Hávamál*', in Kick and Shafer (eds.), pp. 59–95]

2007b. 'Why did Christians continue to find pagan myths useful?', in Hermann, Schjødt, and Kristensen (eds), pp. 33–52

2014. 'Female reactions to the death of Sigurðr', in Kick and Shafer (eds.), pp. 249–67 [revised from 1991. 'Female reactions to the Death of Sigurðr / Sîfrit', in Danielle Buschinger and Wolfgang Spiewok (eds.), *La Chanson des Nibelungen hier et aujourd'hui*. Wodan 7. Amiens: Université de Picardie, pp. 99–111]

McTurk, Rory 1991. *Studies in Ragnars saga Loðbrókar and its Major Scandinavian Analogues*. SSMLL Monographs 15. Oxford: Society for the Study of Mediaeval Languages and Literature

Meissner, Rudolf 1921. *Die Kenningar der Skalden: Ein Beitrag zur skaldischen Poetik*. Bonn and Leipzig: Hertz

Meletinsky, Eleazar M. 1998. *The Elder Edda and Early Forms of the Epic* (trans. Kenneth H. Ober). Trieste: Parnaso

Mellor, Scott 2008. *Analyzing Ten Poems from The Poetic Edda: Oral Formula and Mythic Patterns*. Lewiston: Mellen

Meulengracht Sørensen, Preben 1977. *Saga og samfund: En indføring i oldislandsk litteratur*. Copenhagen: Berlingske Forlag. [repr. 1993. *Saga and Society: An Introduction to Old Norse Literature* (trans. John Tucker). Odense: Odense University Press]

1983. *The Unmanly Man. Concepts of Sexual Defamation in Early Northern Society* (trans. Joan Turville-Petre). The Viking Collection 1. Odense: Odense University Press

1986. 'Thor's fishing expedition', in Gro Steinsland (ed.), *Words and Objects: Towards a Dialogue between Archaeology and History of Religion*. Oslo: Universitetsforlaget, pp. 257–78 [repr. 2002 in Acker and Larrington (eds.), pp. 119–37]

1989. 'Starkaðr, Loki and Egill Skallagrímsson', in John Tucker (ed.), *Sagas of the Icelanders: A Book of Essays*. New York: Garland, pp. 146–159

1991: 'Om eddadigtenes alder', in Gro Steinsland et al. (eds.), *Nordisk hedendom. Et symposium*. Odense: Odense Universitetsforlag, pp. 217–228 [repr. 2001 in Sofie Meulengracht Sørensen (ed.), *At fortælle Historien: Telling History*. Trieste: Parnaso, pp. 143–50]

2001. 'The prosimetrum form 1: Verses as the voice of the past', in Russell Poole (ed.), *Skaldsagas. Text, Vocation, and Desire in the Icelandic Sagas of Poets*. Ergänzungsbände zum Reallexikon der germanischen Altertumskunde 27. Berlin and New York: de Gruyter, pp. 172–90

Meyer, Richard 1889. *Die altgermanische Poesie nach ihren formelhaften Elementen beschrieben*. Berlin: Hertz

Mills, Kristen 2014. 'Grief, gender, and genre: Male weeping in Snorri's account of Baldr's death, Kings' Sagas and *Gesta Danorum*', *Journal of English and Germanic Philology* 113: 472–96

Millward, Anna 2015. 'Skaldic Slam: Performance Poetry in the Norwegian Royal Court'. [Unpublished MA thesis, University of Iceland]

Mitchell, Stephen 1983. '*Fǫr Scírnis* as mythological model: *frið at kaupa*', *Arkiv för nordisk filologi* 98: 108–22

2009. 'The Supernatural and the Fornaldarsögur: the Case of Ketils saga hængs', in Agneta Ney, Ármann Jakobsson, and Annette Lassen (eds.), *Fornaldarsagaerne. Myter og virkelighed. Studier i de oldislandske fornaldarsögur Norðurlanda*. Copenhagen: Museum Tusculanum, pp. 281–98

2014. 'Gudinnan Gná', *Saga och sed:* 23–41

Moberg, Lennart 1973. 'The languages of *Alvíssmál*', *Saga-Book of the Viking Society* 18: 299–323

Mohr, Wolfgang 1933. *Kenningstudien. Beiträge zur Stilgeschichte der altgermanischen Dichtung*. Stuttgart: Kohlhammer

Moi, Toril 1999. *What Is a Woman? And Other Essays*. Oxford: Oxford University Press

Moreland, John 2001. *Archaeology and Text*. London: Duckworth

Motz, Lotte 1991. 'The poets and the goddess', in *The Audience of the Sagas. The Eighth International Saga Conference, August 11–17, 1991, Gothenburg University*. Preprints. 2 vols. Vol. 2, pp. 127–33

1986. 'New thoughts on *Völundarkviða*', *Saga-Book of the Viking Society* 22: 50–68

1980. 'Sister in the cave: The stature and the function of the female figures of the Eddas', *Arkiv för nordisk filologi* 95: 168–82

Müllenhoff, Karl V. [1883–91] 1908. 'Über die Voluspá', in his *Deutsche Altertumskunde* 5/1. Berlin: Weidmann [repr. Roediger, Max (ed.) 1908. Berlin: Weidmann, pp. 1–230]

Munch, Gerd S., Johansen, Olav S., and Roesdahl, Else 2003. *Borg in Lofoten: A Chieftain's Farm in North Norway*. Trondheim: Tapir Academic Press

Mundal, Else 1983. 'Kvinner og diktning. Overgangen frå munnleg til skriftleg kultur – ei ulukke for kvinnene?', in Silja Aðalsteinsdóttir and Helgi Þorláksson (eds.), *Förändringar i kvinnors villkor under medeltiden. Uppsatser framlagda vid ett kvinnohistoriskt symposium i Skálholt, Island, 22.–*

25. juni 1981. Rit Sagnfræðistofnunar 9. Reykjavík: Sagnfræðistofnun Háskóla Íslands. pp. 11–25. [repr. 2012 in Odd Einar Haugen, Bernt Øyvind Thorvaldsen, and Jonas Wellendorf (eds.), *Fjǫld veit hon frœða: Utvalde arbeid av Else Mundal.* Bibliotheca Nordica 4. Oslo: Novus, pp. 79–96]

1990. 'Forholdet mellom gudar og jotnar i norrøn mytologi i lys av det mytologiska namnematerialet', *Studia anthroponymica Scandinavica* 8: 5–18 [repr. 2012 in Odd Einar Haugen, Bernt Øyvind Thorvaldsen, and Jonas Wellendorf (eds.), *Fjǫld veit hon frœða: Utvalde arbeid av Else Mundal.* Bibliotheca Nordica 4. Oslo: Novus, pp. 173–207]

1994a. 'The Position of Women in Old Norse Society and the Basis for Their Power', *NORA – Nordic Journal of Feminist and Gender Research* 1: 3–11

1994b. 'Women and Old Norse narrative', in Roy Eriksen (ed.), *Contexts of Pre-Novel Narrative. The European Tradition.* Berlin: de Gruyter, pp. 135–51

2006. 'Theories, explanatory models and terminology: Problems and possibilities in research on Old Norse mythology', in Andrén, Jennbert, and Raudvere (eds.), pp. 285–8

2008. 'Oral or scribal variation in *Vǫluspá:* A case study in Old Norse poetry', in Else Mundal and Jonas Wellendorf (eds.), pp. 209–27

2010. 'How did the arrival of writing influence Old Norse oral culture?', in Rankovic, Melve, and Mundal (eds.), pp. 163–81

2012. '*Friðþjófs saga ins frœkna:* The connection between the character of the hero and heroine and their success in life', in Tatjana N. Jackson and Elena A. Melnikova (eds.), *Skemmtiligastar Lygisögur: Studies in Honour of Galina Glazyrina.* Moscow: Dmitriy Pozharskiy University, pp. 148–157

Mundal, Else and Wellendorf, Jonas (eds.) 2008. *Oral Art Forms and their Passage into Writing.* Copenhagen: Museum Tusculanum

Mundt, Marina 1997. 'A basic scheme of oral poetry as found in ancient Scandinavia', *Tijdschrift voor Skandinavistiek* 18/2: 29–38

Naumann, Hans-Peter 1998. 'Runeninschriften als Quelle der Versgeschichte', in Klaus Düwel (ed.), *Runeninschriften als Quellen interdisziplinärer Forschung.* Ergänzungsbände zum Reallexikon der germanischen Altertumskunde 15. Berlin: de Gruyter, 694–714

Neckel, Gustav 1908. *Beiträge zur Eddaforschung mit Exkursen zur Heldensage.* Dortmund: Ruhfus

1916. 'Eddaforschung', *Zeitschrift für den deutschen Unterricht* 30: 1–16; 81–98; 162–70

Nerman, Birger 1913. *Vilka konungar ligga i Uppsala högar?* Uppsala: K. W. Appelberg

1931. *The Poetic Edda and Archaeology.* London: Viking Society for Northern Research

Nichols, Stephen G. 1990. 'Introduction: Philology in a manuscript culture', *Speculum* 65: 1–10

Nicolaysen, Nicolay 1882. *Langskibet fra Gokstad: The Viking-Ship from Gokstad.* Christiania [Oslo]: Cammermeyer

Nordberg, Andreas 2003. 'Om namnet Skíringssalr', *Fornvännen* 98: 265–9

Noreen, Adolf 1925. 'Ynglingatal', *Kungl. Vitterhets Historie och Antikvitetsakademien Handlingar* 28/2: 195–253

Noreen, Erik 1941. 'Ur Eddaforskningens historia', *Nordisk tidskrift för vetenskap, konst och industri N.S.* 17: 349–59

Norrman, Lena 2000. 'Woman or warrior? The construction of gender in Old Norse myth', in Geraldine Barnes and Margaret Clunies Ross (eds.), *Old Norse Myths, Literature and Society: The Proceedings of the 11th International Saga Conference 2–7 July 2000, University of Sydney.* Sydney: Centre for Medieval Studies, University of Sydney, pp. 375–85

North, Richard 1997. *Heathen Gods in Old English Literature.* Cambridge Studies in Anglo-Saxon England 22. Cambridge: Cambridge University Press

Näsström, Britt-Mari 2003. *Freyja: The Great Goddess of the North.* Harwich Port MA: Clock and Rose Press

O'Brien O'Keeffe, Katherine 1990. *Visible Song: Transitional Literacy in Old English Verse.* Cambridge Studies in Anglo-Saxon England 4. Cambridge: Cambridge University Press

O'Donoghue, Heather 2007. 'From runic inscriptions to runic gymnastics', in Clark and Phelpstead (eds.), pp. 101–18

2009. 'Miðgarðsormr', *Archipelago* 3: 20–33

2010. 'Owed to both Sides: W. H. Auden's double debt to the literature of the north', in David Clark and Nicholas Perkins (eds.), *Anglo-Saxon Culture and the Modern Imagination.* Cambridge: D. S. Brewer, pp. 51–69

2011. '*The Wife's Lament* and *Helreið Brynhildar*: Different responses to similar lives?', in Natalja Gvorzdetskaja, et al. (eds.), *Stanzas of Friendship: Studies in Honour of Tatjana N. Jackson.* Moscow: Dmitriy Pozharskiy University, pp. 310–320

2014. *English Poetry and Old Norse Myth: A History.* Oxford: Oxford University Press

Oehrl, Sigmund 2006. *Zur Deutung anthropomorpher und theriomorpher Bilddarstellungen auf den spätwikingerzeitlichen Runensteinen Schwedens.* Wiener Studien zur Skandinavistik 16. Vienna: Praesens

Olsen, Magnus 1905. *Det gamle ønavn Njarðarlög.* Christiania Videnskabs-Selskabs Forhandlinger 1905:5. Christiania [Oslo]: Dybwad [repr. with an appendix, in Olsen 1938, pp. 63–85]

1909. 'Fra gammelnorsk myte og kultus', *Maal og minne*: 17–36

1925. 'Körmt og Örmt', in *Germanica: Eduard Sievers zum 75. Geburtstage 25. November 1925.* Halle: Max Niemeyer, pp. 246–57 [repr. in Olsen 1938, pp. 178–88]

1926. *Ættegård og helligdom: Norske stedsnavn sosialt og religionshistorisk belyst.* Oslo: Aschehoug

1931. 'Valhall med de mange dører', *Acta philologica Scandinavica* 6: 151–70 [repr. in Olsen 1938, pp. 109–29]

1935. 'Fra Edda forskningen: Grímnismál og den høiere tekstkritikk', *Arkiv för nordisk filologi* 44: 263–78 [repr. with a 'Tillegg' in Olsen 1938, pp. 130–49]

1938. *Norrøne studier.* Oslo: Aschehoug

Olsen, Olaf 1965. 'Hørg, hog og kirke: historiske og arkæologiske vikingetidsstudier', *Aarbøger for nordisk Oldkyndighed og Historie* 1965: 5–307

Olson, David R. and Torrance, Nancy (eds.) 1991. *Literacy and Orality.* Cambridge: Cambridge University Press

Omberg, Margaret 1976. *Scandinavian Themes in English Poetry, 1760–1800.* Uppsala and Stockholm: Almqvist and Wiksell

Ong, Walter J. 1982. *Orality and Literacy: The Technologizing of the Word.* London: Methuen

ONP = Degnbol, H. et al. (eds.) 1989-. *Ordbog over det norrøne prosasprog / A Dictionary of Old Norse Prose.* 3 vols. and *Registre / Indices* and *Nøgle/ Key* Supplements [online: onp.hum.ku.dk]

Opland, Jeff 1980. *Anglo-Saxon Oral Poetry. A Study of the Traditions.* New Haven: Yale University Press

Orchard, Andy 2003. 'Both style and substance: The case for Cynewulf', in Catherine E. Karkov and George H. Brown (eds.), *Anglo-Saxon Styles.* Binghamton: State University of New York Press, pp. 271–305

Pàroli, Teresa (ed.) 1990. *Atti del 12. congresso internazionale di studi sull'alto medioevo, Spoleto 4–10 settembre 1988 / Poetry in the Scandinavian Middle Ages: Proceedings of the Seventh International Saga Conference.* Spoleto: Presso la sede del Centro studi

Phelpstead, Carl 2003. 'The sexual ideology of *Hrólfs saga kraka*', *Scandinavian Studies* 75: 1–24

2007. 'Size matters: Penile problems in Sagas of Icelanders', *Exemplaria* 19: 420–37

Phillpotts, Bertha S. 1920. *The Elder Edda and Ancient Scandinavian Drama.* Cambridge: Cambridge University Press

Ploss, Emil Ernst 1966. *Siegfried-Sigurd, der Drachenkämpfer: Untersuchungen zur germanisch-deutschen Heldensage. Zugleich ein Beitrag zur Entwicklungsgeschichte des alteuropäischen Erzählgutes.* Beihefte der Bonner Jahrbücher 17. Cologne: Böhlau

Poliakoff, Leon 1977. *The Aryan Myth.* New York: New American Library

Poole, Russell 1991. *Viking Poems on War and Peace: A Study in Skaldic Narrative.* Toronto: University of Toronto Press

2014. 'The sources of *Merlínússpá*: Gunnlaugr Leifsson's use of texts additional to the *De Gestis Britonum* of Geoffrey of Monmouth', in Martin Chase (ed.), *Eddic, Skaldic and Beyond: Poetic Variety in Medieval Iceland and Norway.* New York: Fordham University Press, pp. 16–30

Pope, John C. 1966. *The Rhythm of 'Beowulf'.* Rev. edn. New Haven: Yale University Press

Poplawski, Paul (ed.) 2008. *English Literature in Context.* Cambridge: Cambridge University Press

Poulsen, Bjørn and Sindbæk, Søren (eds.) 2011. *Settlement and Lordship in Viking and Early Medieval Scandinavia.* Turnhout: Brepols

Price, Neil 2008. 'Dying and the dead: Viking Age mortuary behaviour', in Stefan Brink and Neil Price (eds.), *The Viking World.* London: Routledge, pp. 257–73

Price, Neil and Mortimer, Paul 2014. 'An eye for Odin? Divine role-playing in the Age of Sutton Hoo', *European Journal of Archaeology* 17/3: 517–38

Propp, Vladimir 1968. *Morphology of the Folk Tale* (trans. Laurence Scott). 2nd edn. Austin: University of Texas

Pulsiano, Phillip et al. (eds.) 1993. *Medieval Scandinavia: An Encyclopedia*. New York and London: Garland, pp. 308–9

Quinn, Judy 1987. 'The use of eddic poetry in Contemporary Sagas', *Frá Suðlægri Strönd* 3: 54–72

1990a. 'The naming of eddic mythological poems in medieval manuscripts', *Parergon* N. S. 8: 97–115

1990b. '*Völuspá* and the composition of eddic verse', in Pàroli (ed.), pp. 303–20

1992. 'Verseform and voice in eddic poems: The discourses of *Fáfnismál*', *Arkiv för nordisk filologi* 107: 100–30

2000. 'From orality to literacy in medieval Iceland', in Margaret Clunies Ross (ed.), *Old Icelandic Literature and Society*. Cambridge: Cambridge University Press, pp. 30–60

2001. 'Editing the Edda: the case of *Völuspá*', *Scripta Islandica* 51: 69–92

2002. 'Dialogue with a *vǫlva: Hyndluljóð, Baldrs draumar* and *Vǫluspá*', in Acker and Larrington (eds.), pp. 245–74

2005. 'Construing habitus in eddic dialogue: The order of stanzas in *Oddrúnargrátr*', in Kramarz-Bein (ed.), pp. 83–95

2006. 'The gendering of death in eddic cosmology', in Andrén, Jennbert, and Raudvere (eds.), pp. 54–57

2007. '"Hildr prepares a bed for most helmet-damagers": Snorri's treatment of a traditional poetic motif in his *Edda*', in Hermann, Schjødt, and Kristensen (eds), pp. 95–118

2009. 'The endless triangles of eddic tragedy: Reading *Oddrúnargrátr*', in Maria Elena Ruggerini (ed.), *Studi anglo-norreni in onore di John S. McKinnell*. Cagliari: CUEC, pp. 304–326

2010. 'Liquid knowledge: Traditional conceptualisations of learning in eddic poetry', in Rankovic, Melve, and Mundal (eds.), pp. 175–217

2012. 'The "wind of the giantess": Snorri Sturluson, Rudolf Meissner and the interpretation of mythological kennings along taxonomic lines', *Viking and Medieval Scandinavia* 8: 207–59

2013a. 'Mythological motivation in eddic heroic poetry: Interpreting *Grottasöngr*', in Acker and Larrington (eds.), pp. 159–182

2013b. 'Death and the king: *Grottasöngr* in its eddic context', *Scripta Islandica* 64: 39–65

2014. 'Mythologizing the sea: The nordic sea-deity Rán', in Tim Tangherlini (ed.), *Nordic Mythologies: Interpretations, Institutions, Intersections*. The Wildcat Canyon Advanced Seminars: Mythology 1. Berkeley and Los Angeles: North Pinehurst Press, pp. 71–97

2015a. 'Precarious ties: The social critique of dynastic networking in eddic heroic poetry', in Birge Hilsmann and Susanne Kramarz-Bein (eds.), *Applications of Network Theories*. Skandinavistik 10. Münster: LIT, pp. 35–70

2015b. 'Scenes of vindication: Three Icelandic heroic poems in relation to the continental traditions of *Þiðreks saga af Bern* and the *Nibelungenlied*', in Else Mundal (ed.), *Medieval Nordic Literature in its European Context*. Oslo: Dreyer, pp. 78–125

2016. 'The principles of textual criticism and the interpretation of Old Norse texts derived from oral tradition', in Judy Quinn and Adele Cipolla (eds.), *Studies in the Transmission and Reception of Old Norse Literature: The Hyperborean Muse*. Acta Scandinavica 6. Turnhout: Brepols, pp. 47–78

Quinn, Judy et al. 2006. 'Interrogating genre in the *fornaldarsögur*: Round-table discussion', *Viking and Medieval Scandinavia* 2: 275–96

Quinn, Judy and Clunies Ross, Margaret 1994. 'The image of Norse poetry and myth in seventeenth-century England', in Andrew Wawn (ed.), *Northern Antiquity*. Enfield Lock: Hisarlik Press, pp. 189–210

Quinn, Judy, and Heslop, Kate, and Wills, Tarrin (eds.) 2007. *Learning and Understanding in the Old Norse World. Essays in Honour of Margaret Clunies Ross*. Medieval Texts and Cultures of Northern Europe 18. Turnhout: Brepols

Quinn, Judy and Lethbridge, Emily (eds.) 2010. *Creating the Medieval Saga: Versions, Variability and Editorial Interpretations of Old Norse Saga Literature*. The Viking Collection 18. Odense: University Press of Southern Denmark

Quirk, Randolph [1963] 1968. 'Poetic language and Old English metre', in Arthur Brown and Peter Foote (eds.), *Essays on the English Language: Medieval and Modern*. London: Longmans, pp. 1–19 [originally published in 1963. A. Brown and P. Foote (eds.), *Early English and Norse Studies presented to Hugh Smith*, London: Methuen, pp. 150–71]

Ralph, Bo 1972. 'The composition of the *Grímnismál*', *Arkiv för nordisk filologi* 87: 97–118

2007. 'Gåtan som lösning: Ett bidrag till förståelsen av Rökstenens runinskrift', *Maal og minne* (2) 133–57

Rankovic, Slavica, Melve, Leidulf, and Mundal, Else (eds.) 2010. *Along the Oral-Written Continuum: Types of Texts, Relations and their Implications*. Utrecht Studies in Medieval Literacy 20. Turnhout: Brepols

Raudvere, Catharina 2012. 'Fictive rituals in *Völuspá*. Mythological narration between agency and structure in the representation of reality', in Raudvere, Catharina and Schjødt (eds.), pp. 97–118

Raudvere, Catharina and Schjødt, Jens Peter (eds.) 2012. *More Than Mythology: Narratives, Ritual Practices, and Regional Distribution in Pre-Christian Scandinavian Religions*. Lund: Nordic Academic Press

Reinhard, Mariann 1976. *On the Semantic Relevance of the Alliterative Collocations in "Beowulf"*. Bern: Francke

Rieger, Max 1876. 'Die alt- und angelsächsische Verskunst', *Zeitschrift für deutsche Philologie* 7: 1–64

Roesdahl, Else and Meulengracht Sørensen, Preben (eds.) 1996. *The Waking of Angantyr: The Scandinavian Past in European Culture*. Aarhus: Aarhus University Press

Roscoe, William 1852. 'The Eddas', *The Prospective Review* 32: 456–89

Roussell, Aage 1943. 'Komparativ avdelning', in M. Stenberger (ed.), *Forntida Gårdar i Island*. Copenhagen: Ejnar Munksgaard, pp. 191–223

Rowe, Elizabeth A. 2005. *The Development of Flateyjarbók: Iceland and the Norwegian Dynastic Crisis of 1389*. The Viking Collection 15. Odense: University Press of Southern Denmark

2012. *Vikings in the West: The Legend of Ragnarr Loðbrók and His Sons*. Studi Medievalia Septentrionalia 18. Vienna: Fassbaender

2013. '*Fornaldarsögur* and heroic legends of the *Edda*', in Acker and Larrington (eds.), pp. 202–18

Ruggerini, Maria Elena 1994. 'Appendix. A stylistic and typological approach to *Vafþrúðnismál*', in John McKinnell, *Both One and Many: Essay on Change and Variety in Late Norse Heathenism*. Rome: Il Calamo, pp. 139–87

Rühs, Friedrich 1813. *Ueber den Ursprung der isländischen Poesie aus der angelsächischen: nebst vermischten Bemerkungen über die nordische Dichtkunst und Mythologie; ein nothwendiger Nachtrag zu seinen neuesten Untersuchungen*. Berlin: Reimer

Russom, Geoffrey 1998. *'Beowulf and Old Germanic Metre*. Cambridge: Cambridge University Press

2009. 'Why there are three eddic meters,' in Matti Kilpiö (ed.), *Anglo-Saxons and the North: Essays Reflecting the Theme of the 10th Meeting of the International Society of Anglo-Saxonists in Helsinki, August 2001*. Tempe, AZ: Arizona Center for Medieval and Renaissance Studies, pp. 69–88

Rydberg, Viktor 1881. 'Sibyllinerna och Völuspå', *Nordisk tidskrift för vetenskap, konst och industry* 4: 1–162

Samplonius, Kees 2001. 'Sibylla borealis: Notes on the structure of *Vǫluspá*', in K. E. Olsen, Antonina Harbus, and Tette Hofstra (eds.), *Germanic Texts and Latin Models: Medieval Reconstructions*. Germania Latina IV. Leuven: Peeters, pp. 185–229

2013. 'The background and scope of *Vǫluspá*', in Gunnell and Lassen (eds.), pp. 113–46

Sanderson, Mark 2009. 'The legend of Sigurd and Gudrun by J. R. R. Tolkien: Review' [www.telegraph.co.uk/culture/books/poetryandplaybookreviews/523 7371/The-Legend-of-Sigurd-and-Gudrun-by-J.R.R.-Tolkien-review.html; last accessed 19 February 2016]

2004. 'Om eddadikternas ursprung och alder: Gamla och nya tankar', *Arkiv för nordisk filologi* 119: 55–104

2013. 'Elegy in eddic poetry: Its origin and context', in Acker and Larrington (eds.), pp. 81–106

Schaefer, Ursula 1992. *Vokalität. Altenglische Dichtung zwischen Mündlichkeit und Schriftlichkeit*. Tübingen: Narr

Schechner, Richard 2013. *Performance Studies. An Introduction*. 3rd edn. New York and London: Routledge

Scher, Steven P. 1963. '*Rígsþula* as poetry', *Modern Language Notes* 78: 397–407

Scheungraber, Corinna, and Grünzweig, Friedrich E. 2014. *Die altgermanischen Toponyme, sowie ungermanische Toponyme Germaniens: Ein Handbuch zu ihrer Etymologie*. Philologica Germanica 34. Vienna: Fassbaender

Schier, Kurt 1986. 'Edda, Ältere', in Heinrich Beck et al. (eds.), *Reallexikon der Germanischen Altertumskunde*. 2nd edn. 37 vols. Berlin and New York: de Gruyter, 6, 355–94

Schiff, Gert 1975. *Henry Fuseli 1741–1825*. London: Tate Gallery Publications

Schjødt, Jens Peter 2007. 'Ibn Fadlan's account of a Rus funeral: to what degree does it reflect Nordic myth?', in Hermann, Schjødt, and Kristensen (eds.), pp. 133–48

2008. *Initiation between Two Worlds: Structure and Symbolism in Pre-Christian Scandinavian Religion*. The Viking Collection 17. Odense: University Press of Southern Denmark

2012a. 'Reflections on aims and methods in the study of Old Norse religion', in Raudvere and Schjødt (eds.), pp. 263–87

2012b. 'Óðinn, Þórr and Freyr: Functions and relations', in Merrill Kaplan and Timothy R. Tangherlini (eds.), *News from other Worlds: Studies in Nordic Folklore, Mythology, and Culture: in Honor of John F. Lindow*. Berkeley and Los Angeles: North Pinehurst Press, pp. 61–91

2013. 'The notions of model, discourse, and semantic centre as tools for the (re) construction of Old Norse religion', *The Retrospective Methods Network Newsletter* 6: 6–15

forthcoming a. 'Pre-Christian religion of the north and the need for comparativism: Reflections on why, how, and with what we can compare', in Stephen Mitchell, Pernille Hermann, and Jens Peter Schjødt (eds.), *Old Norse Mythology: Comparative Perspective*. Cambridge MA: Harvard University Press

forthcoming b. 'Reconstructing Old Norse mythology: source criticism and comparative mythology', in Stefan Brink (ed.), *Myth and Theory in the Old Norse World*. Turnhout: Brepols

Schjødt, Jens Peter, and Lindow, John forthcoming. 'The divine, the human, and in-between', in *Pre-Christian Religions of the North: Histories and Structures*. Turnhout: Brepols

Schlözer, August Ludwig 1773. *Isländische Litteratur und Geschichte* I. Göttingen: Dieterich

Schorn, Brittany 2011. 'Eddic poetry for a new era: Tradition and innovation in *Sólarljóð* and *Hugsvinnsmál*', *Viking and Medieval Scandinavia* 7: 131–49

2013. 'Divine semantics: Terminology for the human and the divine in Old Norse poetry', *Scripta Islandica* 64: 67–98

Schröder, Franz Rolf 1954. 'Eine indogermanische Liedform. Das Aufreihlied', *Germanisch-Romanische Monatsschrift* 35 (NF 4.2): 179–85

Schulte, Michael 2005. 'The classical and Christian impact on *Volospǫ́*: Toward a comparative topomorphological approach', *Arkiv för nordisk filologi* 120: 181–219

Schulz, Katja 2004. *Riesen. Von Wissenshütern und Wildisbewohnern in Edda und Saga*. Heidelberg: Winter

Schütte, Gudmund 1933. 'The problem of the Hraid-Goths', *Acta Philologica Scandinavica* 8: 247–61

Schwyzer, Philip 2007. *Archaeologies of English Renaissance Literature*. Oxford: Oxford University Press

Scott, Forrest S. 2002. 'The woman who knows: Female characters of *Eyrbyggja saga*', in Anderson and Swenson (eds.), pp. 225–44

Seaton, Ethel 1935. *Literary Relations of England and Scandinavia in the Seventeenth Century*. Oxford: Clarendon Press

von See, Klaus 1972. *Die Gestalt der Hávamál: Eine Studie zur eddischen Spruchdichtung*. Frankfurt am Main: Athenäum

von See, Klaus, et al. (eds.) 1997–: see *Edda Kommentar*

Sedgwick, Eve Kosofsky 1990. *Epistemology of the Closet*. Berkeley: University of California Press

Segal, Robert 2004. *Myth: A Very Short Introduction*. Oxford: Oxford University Press

Sequentia 1999. *Edda*. [Deutsche Harmonia Mundi: 05472 77381 2]

2001. *The Rhinegold Curse*. [Deutschland Radio and Westdeutscher Rundfunk; Marc Aurel edition: MA 20016]

Shaw, Philip A. 2011. *Pagan Goddesses in the Early Germanic World*. Bristol: Bristol Classical Press

Shippey, Thomas A. 1982. 'Goths and Huns: The rediscovery of the northern cultures in the nineteenth century', in Andreas Haarder (ed.), *The Medieval Legacy: A Symposium*. Odense: Odense University Press, pp. 51–69

2013. 'Foreword', in Acker and Larrington (eds.), pp. xiii–xix

Sievers, Eduard 1878. 'Beiträge zur Skaldenmetrik', *Beiträge zur Geschichte der deutschen Sprache und Literatur* 5: 449–518

1893. *Altgermanische Metrik*. Halle: Niemeyer

Sijmons, Barend 1906. 'Einleitung', in Barend Sijmons and Hugo Gering (eds.), *Die Lieder der Edda*. Germanistische Handbibliothek 7. Halle: Waisenhaus, pp. i–ccclxxv

Simek, Rudolf 2003. *Religion und Mythologie der Germanen*. Darmstadt: Theiss

2006. *Lexikon der germanischen Mythologie*. 3rd edn. Kröners Taschenausgabe 368. Stuttgart: Kröner

2007. *Dictionary of Northern Mythology* (trans. Angela Hall). Woodbridge: D. S. Brewer

Speake, George 1989. *A Saxon Bed Burial on Swallowcliffe Down*. London: Historic Buildings and Monuments Commission

Spencer, Stewart 2000. *Wagner's Ring of the Nibelung*. London: Thames and Hudson

Steblin-Kamenskij, M. I. 1973. *The Saga Mind* (trans. Kenneth H. Ober). [Odense:] Odense University Press

Steinsland, Gro 1991. *Det hellige bryllup og Norrøn kongeideologi. En undersøkelse av hierogamimyten* i Skírnismál, Ynglingatal, Háleyjatal *og* Hyndluljóð. Oslo: Solum

2013. '*Vǫluspá* and the Sibylline Oracles with a Focus on the "Myth of the Future"', in Gunnell and Lassen (eds.), pp. 147–60

Steinsland, Gro and Meulengracht Sørensen, Preben 1999. *Vǫluspá*. Oslo: Pax

Stjerna, Knut 1903. 'Hjälmar och svärd i *Beowulf*', in Bernhard Salin, Oscar Almgren, and Sune Ambrosiani (eds.), *Studier tillägnade Oscar Montelius 9/9/03 av Lärjungar*. Stockholm: Norstedt, pp. 99–120

Stockwell, Robert P. 1996. 'On recent theories of metrics and rhythm in *Beowulf*, in C. B. McCully and J. J. Anderson (eds), *English Historical Metrics*. Cambridge: Cambridge University Press, pp. 73–94

Straubhaar, Sandra Ballif 2002. 'Ambiguously gendered: The skalds Jórunn, Auðr and Steinunn', in Anderson and Swenson (eds.), pp. 261–72

2011 (ed.). *Old Norse Women's Poetry. The Voices of Female Skalds*. Cambridge: D. S. Brewer

Street, Brian V. 1984. *Literacy in Theory and Practice*. Cambridge Studies in Oral and Literate Culture 9. Cambridge: Cambridge University Press

Ståhle, Carl Ivar 1945. *Studier över de svenska ortnamnen på -inge: på grundval av undersökningar i Stockholms län*. Skrifter utg. av Kungl. Gustav Adolfs akademien 16. Uppsala: Ohlsson

Sundqvist, Olof 2002. *Freyr's Offspring: Rulers and Religion in Ancient Svea Society*. Uppsala: Uppsala University

2007. *Kultledare i fornskandinavisk religion*. Occasional Papers in Archaeology, 41. Uppsala: Department of Archaeology and Ancient History, Uppsala University

Suzuki, Seiichi 2014. *The Meters of Old Norse Eddic Poetry*. Berlin: Walter de Gruyter

Sveinbjörn Egilsson and Finnur Jónsson 1931 [repr. 1966]. *Lexicon poeticum antiquae linguae septentrionalis*. 2nd edn. Copenhagen: Lynge and Søn

Swenson, Karen 1991. *Performing Definitions: Two Genres of Insult in Old Norse Literature*. Columbia: Camden House

2002. 'Women outside: Discourse of community in *Hávamál*', in Anderson and Swenson (eds.), pp. 273–80

Szőke, Veronka 2014. '*Nearu* and its collocations in Old English verse', *Studi linguistici e filologici* 34: 53–93

Sävborg, Daniel 1997. *Sorg och elegi i Eddans hjältediktning*. Stockholm: Almqvist & Wiksell

Thomas, R.G. 1952–53. 'Some exceptional women in the sagas', *Saga-Book of the Viking Society* 13: 307–27

Thorvaldsen, Bernt Øyvind 2006. 'The generic aspect of eddic style', in Andrén, Jennbert, and Raudvere (eds.), pp. 276–9

2007. *Svá er sagt í fornum vísindum: Tekstualiseringen av de mytologiske eddadikt*. [Unpublished PhD dissertation, University of Bergen]

2008a. 'The eddic form and its contexts: An oral art form performed in writing', in Mundal and Wellendorf (eds.), pp. 151–62

2008b. 'Om *Þrymskviða*, tekstlån og tradisjon', *Maal og minne*: 142–66

2010. 'The poetic curse and its relatives' in Rankovic, Melve, and Mundal (eds.), pp. 253–67

2011. 'The *níðingr* and the wolf', *Viking and Medieval Scandinavia* 7: 171–96

2012. 'The eddic author: On distributed creativity in *The Lay of Þrymr* and *Skírnir's Journey*', in Slavica Ranković et al. (eds.), *Modes of Authorship in the Middle Ages*. Papers in Medieval Studies 22. Toronto: Pontifical Institute of Medieval Studies, pp. 251–63

2013. 'Deictic traces of oral performance in the Codex Regius version of *Vǫluspá*', *Maal og minne* 2: 97–131

Tolkien, Christopher 1953–7. 'The Battle of the Goths and Huns', *Saga-Book of the Viking Society* 14: 131–63

Tolkien, John R. R. 1936. '*Beowulf* – the monsters and the critics', *Proceedings of the British Academy* 22: 245–95

Tolley, Clive 2002. 'Oral assumptions. A warning from Old Norse', in Lauri Honko (ed.), *The Kalavala and the World's Traditional Epics*. Studia Fennica Folkloristica 12. Helsinki: Finnish Literature Society, pp. 128–35

Tolmie, Jane 2003. 'Goading, ritual discord and the deflection of blame', *Journal of Historical Pragmatics* 4: 287–301

Torp, Alf 1919 [repr. 1963]. *Nynorsk etymologisk ordbok*. Kristiania [Oslo]: Aschehoug

Townend, Matthew (ed.) 2012. 'Lausavísur from *Styrbjarnar þáttr Svíakappa*', in *SkP* I, 1076–80

Tucker, Susie 1962–5. 'Scandinavica for the eighteenth-century common reader', *Saga-Book of the Viking Society* 26: 233–47

Turville-Petre, E. O. G. 1964. *Myth and Religion of the North: The Religion of Ancient Scandinavia*. New York: Holt, Rinehart, and Winston

Tydeman, William 1978. *The Theatre in the Middle Ages*. Cambridge: Cambridge University Press.

Tyler, Elizabeth M. 2006. *Old English Poetics: The Aesthetics of the Familiar in Anglo-Saxon England*. York: York Medieval Press [in association with Boydell and Brewer and the Centre for Medieval Studies]

Vail, Leroy and White, Landeg 1991. *Power and the Praise Poem: Southern African Voices in History*. Charlottesville, VA: University of Virginia Press

Vésteinn Ólason 2004. 'The manuscripts of Iceland', in Gísli Sigurðsson and Vésteinn Ólason (eds.), *The Manuscripts of Iceland*. Reykjavík: Árni Magnússon Institute in Iceland, pp. iii–vi

 2005. 'Heusler and the dating of Eddic poetry – with special reference to "isländische Nachblüte der Heldendichtung"', in Jürg Glauser and Julia Zernach (eds.), *Germanentum im fin de siècle: Wissenschaftsgeschichtlichen Studien zum Werk Andreas Heuslers*. Basel: Schwabe, pp. 165–93

 2008a. 'Benedikt Gröndal som norrøn filolog', in Auður G. Magnúsdóttir et al. (eds.), '*Vi ska alla vara välkomna!' Nordiska studier tillägnade Kristinn Jóhannesson*. Meijerbergs arkiv för svensk ordforskning 35. Göteborg: Göteborgs universitet, pp. 319–33

 2008b. *Dialogues with the Viking Age: Narration and Representation in the Sagas of the Icelanders*. Reykjavík: Heimskringla

 2010. 'The Poetic Edda: literature or folklore?', in Rankovic, Melve, and Mundal (eds.), pp. 227–52

Vigfusson, Gudbrand 1878. 'Prolegomena', in his *Sturlunga saga including the Islendinga saga of Lawman Sturla Thordsson and other works*. 2 vols. Oxford: Clarendon, I, pp. xvii–ccxiv

Vikstrand, Per 1996. 'Kan ortnamnselementet skälv, fsv. skialf, skiælf, ha haft en sakral innebörd?', in E. Brylla et al. (eds.), *Från götarna till Noreens kor: Hyllningsskrift till Lennart Elmevik på 60-årsdagen 2 februari 1996*. Skrifter utgivna genom Ortnamnsarkivet i Uppsala. Serie B, Meddelanden 11. Uppsala: Ortnamnsarkivet i Uppsala, pp. 201–8

2001. *Gudarnas platser. Förkristna sakrala ortnamn i Mälarlandskapen.* Uppsala: Kungl. Gustav Adolfs Akademien för svensk folkkultur

2004. 'Skúta and Vendil. Two Place Names in Ynglingatal, in Stefan Brink et al. (eds.), *Namenwelten: Orts- und Personennamen in historischer Sicht.* Ergänzungsbände zum Reallexikon der Germanischen Alterturmskunde 44. Berlin and New York: De Gruyter, pp. 372–87

de Vries, Jan 1934a. 'Über die Datierung der Eddalieder', *Germanisch-Romanische Monatschrift* 22: 253–63

1934b. 'Om Eddaens Visdomsdigtning', *Arkiv för nordisk filologi* 50: 1–59

1956–57. *Altgermanische Religionsgeschichte.* 2 vols. Berlin: Walter de Gruyter

1957–61. *Altnordisches etymologisches wörterbuch.* Leiden: Brill

1961. *Forschungsgeschichte der Mythologie.* Freiburg and Munich: Alber

1962. *Altnordisches etymologisches Wörterbuch.* 2nd edn. Leiden: Brill

1970. *Altgermanische Religionsgeschichte.* 3rd edn. 2 vols. Grundriss der Germanischen Philologie 12. Berlin: Walter de Gruyter

Wace, Alan J. B. and Stubbings, Frank H. (eds.) 1962. *A Companion to Homer.* London: Macmillan

Wadstein, Elias 1892. 'Alfer ock älvor. En språkligt-mytologisk undersökning', in *Uppsalastudier tillegnade Sophus Bugge på hans 60-åra födelsedag.* Uppsala: Almqvist & Wiksell, pp. 152–79

Watkins, Calvert 1970. 'Language of gods and language of men: Remarks on some Indo-European metalinguistic traditions', in Jaan Puhvel (ed.), *Myth and Law among the Indo-Europeans: Studies in Indo-European Comparative Mythology.* Berkeley: University of California Press, pp. 1–17

1995. *How to Kill a Dragon: Aspects of Indo-European Poetics.* Oxford: Oxford University Press

Wawn, Andrew 2000. *The Vikings and the Victorians.* Cambridge: D.S. Brewer

Welinder, Stig 2003. 'Christianity, politics and ethnicity in Early Medieval Jämtland, Mid Sweden', in Martin Carver (ed), *The Cross Goes North.* York: York Medieval Press, pp. 509–30

Wenzel, Siegfried 1990. 'Reflections on (new) philology', *Speculum* 65: 11–18

Wessén, Elias 1927. 'Eddadikterna om Helge Hundingsbane, I-II', *Fornvännen* 22: 1–30 and 65–95

1958. *Runstenen vid Röks kyrka.* Kungl. Vitterhets historie och antikvitets akademiens handlingar. Filologisk-filosofiska serien 5. Stockholm: Almqvist & Wiksell

Wills, Tarrin 2013. 'Testosterone, aggression and status in early northern literature', *Northern Studies* 44: 60–79

Wilson, David M. 1997. *Vikings and Gods in European Art.* Højbjerg: Moesgård Museum

Wyatt, David 2009. *Slaves and Warriors in Medieval Britain and Ireland 800–1200.* Leiden: Brill

Åkerlund, Walter 1939. *Studier över Ynglingatal.* Skrifter utg. av Vetenskaps-Societeten i Lund 23. Lund: Gleerup

Index